Becoming Historical

The historical consciousness that emerged from the revolutionary break with tradition at the turn of the nineteenth century shaped the development of new forms of personal and collective identity. This book examines the stages and conflicts in this process of "becoming historical" through the works of prominent Prussian artists and intellectuals (Karl Friedrich Schinkel, Felix Mendelssohn, Jacob Grimm, Friedrich Karl von Savigny, Leopold von Ranke) who attached their personal visions to the reformist agenda of the Prussian regime that took power in 1840. The historical account of the evolution of analogous and interrelated commitments to a cultural reformation that would create communal solidarity through subjective identification with public memory is framed by the philosophical perspectives on historical selfhood provided by both the spokesperson for Prussian cultural politics – F. W. J. Schelling – and his radical critics – Karl Marx and Soren Kierkegaard – thus drawing this story of building selves and communities in early nineteenth-century Berlin into current debates about historically determined and contingently constructed identities.

John Edward Toews is Professor of History at the University of Washington. He is the author of *Hegelianism: The Path Toward Dialectical Humanism, 1805–1841* (Cambridge: 1981) as well as numerous articles in scholarly journals. He also is the editor of *The Communist Manifesto: By Karl Marx and Frederick Engels with Related Documents* (New York: 1999).

BECOMING HISTORICAL

Cultural Reformation and Public Memory in Early Nineteenth-Century Berlin

JOHN EDWARD TOEWS

University of Washington

CAMBRIDGE UNIVERSITY PRESS
Cambridge, New York, Melbourne, Madrid, Cape Town, Singapore, São Paulo

Cambridge University Press
The Edinburgh Building, Cambridge CB2 8RU, UK

Published in the United States of America by Cambridge University Press, New York

www.cambridge.org
Information on this title: www.cambridge.org/9780521836487

First published 2004
This digitally printed version 2008

A catalogue record for this publication is available from the British Library

Library of Congress Cataloguing in Publication data

Toews, John Edward.

Becoming historical : cultural reformation and public memory in early-nineteenth-century Berlin / John Edward Toews.

p. cm.

Includes bibliographical references and index.

ISBN 0-521-83648-4

1. Historiography – Germany – Berlin – History – 19th century.
2. Historicism. 3. Berlin (Germany) – Intellectual life – 19th century. I. Title.

DD86.T64 2004
907′.2′043155 – dc22 2003065413

ISBN 978-0-521-83648-7 hardback
ISBN 978-0-521-06298-5 paperback

For Julia and Jonathan

Contents

List of Illustrations

Preface

This book originated in a vague curiosity about the cultural significance and consequences of what appeared to be a minor historical event – the death of Frederick William III of Prussia and the accession to the throne of his son Frederick William IV, in June 1840. From my earlier investigations into the various contexts that shaped the evolution of Hegelianism and especially the Prussian Hegelian School, I was aware that the Prussian dynastic change had instigated a "new course" in academic politics. The new king, who fancied himself something of an intellectual and artist, was aligned with the academic opponents of Hegelianism and quickly used his powers of appointment to give his antipathies and sympathies public visibility and public force. Friedrich Karl von Savigny, the founder of the Historical School of Law, was appointed to a cabinet post as minister of justice in charge of preparing new legislative proposals, Leopold Ranke became the official Prussian state historiographer, Jacob and Wilhelm Grimm were invited to pursue their national project of compiling an historical German dictionary at the Prussian Academy of Sciences, and Friedrich Wilhelm Joseph Schelling was lured from Munich to Berlin as the publicly anointed philosophical spokesman for the metaphysical faith that animated the cultural program of the new regime. Frederick William IV began his reign with an agenda for a cultural "reformation" that would negate the threat of political "revolution." At the core of this agenda was what he and his intellectual allies described as the "historical principle," the implications of which resonated far beyond the squabbles between members of the Hegelian School and the Historical School at the university. The new course in Prussian cultural politics represented a programmatic attempt to redefine membership in various communities – religious, ethnic, ethical, and political – as historical identifications, that is, in terms of the subjective identification of individuals with a shared past or public memory.

My curiosity intensified and focused as I tried to clarify to myself the meaning of this cultural project of creating community through historical identification. One could clearly argue that the Prussian "new course" after 1840 was a minor incident in Prussian and German history. The reform agenda turned out to be rife with internal contradictions, and most of the cultural celebrities that were called together to give it intellectual and aesthetic substance had either died or retreated in disillusionment from their public commitments by 1845–46. For many of the individuals drawn to

Berlin to participate in the cultural politics of the new regime, the dynastic change of 1840 and its aftermath was more of an episode than a turning point. Yet this brief historical moment, in which so many important proponents of the historical principle in a diversity of cultural fields and disciplines were gathered together under the aegis of the programmatic vision of Prussia's political leadership, does provide an illuminating focal point for an examination of the cultural and historical meaning of that principle itself, and especially for the complex relationship between the cultivation of historical consciousness, or historical mindedness, and the construction of personal and communal identities. What were the affinities in historical and cultural viewpoint that produced this affiliation among such a diverse group of intellectuals, scholars, and artists? What were the perspectives and motivations that led the new king and some of his advisors to seek out these particular individuals and imagine them as the appropriate spokespersons for their cultural agenda? How did the brief affiliation of the 1840s reveal and transform the apparent affinities that had promoted and encouraged its creation? Was it merely a coincidence that two path-breaking, historically resonant, and prophetic conceptions of what it meant to live human existence in the form of historical selfhood – those of Marx and Kierkegaard – emerged, at least in part, as critical responses to this wide-ranging attempt to construct a cultural politics for historicizing identity in Berlin during the early 1840s?

Questions like this quickly led me to foreground what had been background and direct my attention beyond an examination of a particular stage in the evolution of the internal structure and external relations of a narrowly defined academic historicism. The texts and contexts of Ranke and Savigny, two individuals always prominently included in discussions of German historicism, were my first objects of analysis, but they were soon connected to a broader synchronic examination of the ways in which questions of historical self-consciousness and historical identity were addressed and represented across a variety of cultural areas and "languages." I became more interested, for example, in how Ranke's conception of human existence as essentially historical was related to representations of human historicity in the architecture of Schinkel, the musical compositions of Mendelssohn, and the linguistic–ethnographic studies of Jacob Grimm, than in how his epistemological arguments and historical narratives helped produce and nurture specific forms of historical research, understanding, and representation within the disciplinary discourse and academic institutions of a peculiarly German tradition of historical scholarship. This is not to say that the latter issues do not interest me or that I completely ignore them in my analysis, but simply that I tend to subordinate them to questions about the nature and implications of conceiving human existence as historical existence, questions that Ranke shared with individuals like Schinkel, Mendelssohn, and Grimm, who were working in different disciplines, disciplinary languages, and cultural media. I do not perceive the patterns of argument and representation that developed in architecture and music as simply a reflection of arguments and representations developed in the textually oriented academic disciplines of jurisprudence, history, and philology. Instead, I assume that spatial and tonal representations of what it means, personally and collectively, to be and to become historical entered into this "conversation" among Prussian historicizers as independent interventions with their own messages to purvey. Within the framework of this study, inclusion in the conversation about "becoming historical" simply requires belief that human existence is essentially historical and that questions about personal, communal, and religious identity must be addressed within this ontological framework.[1]

The inclusion of extended sections on Schinkel and Mendelssohn within this study was a bit of a professional stretch for me and added years to the project. It became clear as I began to examine the perspectives of the major political instigators of the Prussian program for cultural reformation according to the "historical principle" that architecture and music played critical roles in their conceptions of historical identity. Frederick William IV actually preferred to think through and articulate his vision of cultural reform in architectural terms. Even though Schinkel died during the first months of his reign, the king's close personal association with Schinkel and with Schinkel's various public projects between 1815 and 1840 was an important factor in shaping the cultural politics of the regime after 1840. I selected Christian Bunsen, the king's close personal advisor and cultural consultant, for extended treatment because the development of Bunsen's own perspectives ranged across the areas of historical scholarship, archaeology, linguistics, music, and architecture and suggested some of the ways in which these various cultural dimensions might fit together in a program of cultural reformation. Both the king and Bunsen were in full agreement in pursuing a state appointment for Mendelssohn after 1840 that would place him in the charge not only of ecclesiastical music but also of musical education and public musical performance in Prussia. In many ways the shaping of historical consciousness through spatial organization and musical performance was more influential in the broader spheres of public life, in terms of both cultural representation and ethical and cultural education, than the production of scholarly texts and academic lectures. Certainly I found that devoting so much attention to Schinkel and Mendelssohn enriched my own conceptions of the meaning of historicism and the project of becoming historical.

[1] For the most influential account of historicism as the theory and method of historical knowledge and historical writing within the disciplinary matrix of the German academic tradition, see Georg G. Iggers, *The German Conception of History: The National Tradition of Historical Thought from Herder to the Present* (rev. ed.; Middletown, CT, 1983), but also Joern Ruesen, *Konfigurationen des Historismus: Studien zur deutsche Wissenschaftskultur* (Frankfurt: 1993); Annette Wittkau, *Historismus: Zur Geschichte des Begriffs und des Problems* (Goettingen: 1992); and Friedrich Jaeger and Joern Ruesen, *Geschichte des Historismus: Eine Einfuehrung* (Munich: 1992).

Although the overall structure of this study is synchronic, its chapters share a common narrative structure. My aim was to re-create the paths that led individuals operating in different areas of culture to the particular perspective they possessed in 1840 and which made their affiliation in a common project possible, even though this affiliation may have been ephemeral and in some cases grounded at least partially in misrecognition. In crude preliminary outline, this meta-story, or ideal–typical narrative that informs the particular stories of the individual chapters, proceeds as follows. The starting point for the development of the historical consciousness of this generation was a belief that human identity was defined by participation in a spontaneously evolving, unique, ethno-cultural organism whose unifying and dynamic core was a particular life principle, "genius," or "idea" that articulated its presence as an incommensurable individuality in the production of language, ritual, myth, and customary patterns of social interaction. The purposive tendency in this development was from unconscious "natural" ethnic identity to self-conscious voluntary "ethical" identification. Religious and political institutions nurtured and cultivated cultural identity as a consciously chosen, self-imposed identification, but developed, unless artificially blocked in some fashion, from the archaic unity embodied in the "idea" in its preconscious form. The constitution of this belief, or the revelation of this historical reality, occurred for many literate and educated Germans in the twenty or so years between the beginnings of the French occupation of the Rhineland in the mid 1790s and the wars of liberation against the Napoleonic hegemony in 1813–15.[2] In particular, the national enthusiasm that accompanied the campaigns of 1813 was imagined as a critical, transformative moment of self-recognition, when Germans sloughed off the blinders of ahistorical consciousness and finally recognized themselves as members of a shared and uniquely individual German culture whose

[2] During the 1980s, there was extensive scholarly debate about the continuities and discontinuities between conceptions of historical existence and historical knowledge in the German Enlightenment, or even earlier periods, and the construction of Romantic historicism around the turn of the century. Most of the major participants in this debate are represented in the conference anthology: *Aufklaerung und Geschichte: Studien zur deutschen Geschichtswissenschaft im 18. Jahrhundert*, eds., Hans Erich Boedeker, Georg G. Iggers, Jonathan B. Knudson, and Peter H. Reill (Goettingen: 1986); but see also Horst Walter Blanke and Joern Ruesen, *Von der Aufklaerung zum Historismus: zum Strukturwandel des historischen Denkens* (Paderborn: 1984). The German discussion echoed debates about the relations between the peculiarly German form of Romantic historicism that was tied to the nationalist tradition prior to 1945 and the critical, social-scientific paradigms that emerged in the 1960s. In the mid 1990s Frank Ankersmit and Iggers debated this issue in a forum of the journal *History and Theory*, in the context of discussions about the philosophical and cultural implications of the "new historicism" that had emerged in Anglo-American academe in the 1980s: "The Meaning of Historicism and Its Relevance for Contemporary Theory," *History and Theory* 34 (1995): 143–73. My own work investigates the meaning of historicism less through its origins than through its fate after 1815 and focuses on the development of a stereoscopic vision of historical identity which, I believe, speaks in more interesting ways to the concerns of the present than the Romantic historicism of the turn of the century.

history revealed and actualized its essence. The production of historical representations was meant to nurture and maintain this historical consciousness that had emerged in the German "awakening." I will refer to this model of historical identification through the shorthand of Romantic historicism at various points in the text.

It is important to recognize that the historicism of 1840 was not synonymous with the Romantic historicism I have just described. In fact, between 1815 and 1840, the original paradigm of ethno-cultural historical identity had revealed its inner tensions and begun to break apart. This process was marked first of all by experiences of disillusionment concerning the spontaneous evolution of a shared ethno-cultural essence into freely and self-consciously affirmed membership in an ethical community. The rejection of any necessary development of ethnic identity into ethical-political identity by the Congress of Vienna in 1814–15, the repression of the national movement in 1819–24, the apparent evolution of the ethnic "people" into an anarchic mass of individual egos as revealed by the social disturbances and political unrest of the early 1830s, all operated as moments, experienced with various weight in the lives of different individuals, in this fragmentation of the cultural paradigm of Romantic historicism. The result was that the transition from ethnicity to ethical life became a problem and a task that demanded specific and contingent action, rather than simply an immanent, necessary self-determination of the "idea." The spheres of politics and religion were no longer imagined as sites for the self-conscious expression of a prior, unconscious, primal identity, but as autonomous sites with transcendent foundations where acts of historical transformation through cultural reformation could find motivational support. To recognize oneself as historical, both as an individual and as a member of a group, now gained an added dimension. To recognize oneself as historical was to understand and live both personal identity and collective identity as historically constituted, as produced in and by the process of history itself. But the constituted historical self was itself a product of cultural institutions and relations that had been constructed by the acts of individuals operating in obedience to self-imposed transcendent determinations. To become historical in the sense of recognizing that personal and communal identity were historically constituted was also to take upon oneself the obligation of constituting oneself, personally and collectively, in historical action. In this sense Marx's *German Ideology* and Kierkegaard's *Unscientific Postscript* (both written in 1845–46) cut to the quick of the historicist project of the 1840s and provide an appropriate conclusion to its implicit narrative structure.

Two dimensions of this framing narrative emerged as especially striking and important and are highlighted in the synchronic stories of the individual chapters. The first is the transformation of the shape of religious belief from a predominantly "pantheistic" form of faith in the immanent workings of divine purpose within the patterns of historical evolution to a predominantly "personalistic" belief in a transcendent divinity, a belief that could function as the source of historical actions that might intervene in the immanent development of the ethno-cultural subject, or "idea," and change its historical trajectory. The complex shift from immanent to transcendent models of religious and philosophical faith, combined with concurrent changes in ways of conceiving relations between church and state, and between religious piety and national identification, play a role in my analysis that I had not expected as I began this project. Second, I became increasingly aware that this shift away from the Romantic model of becoming historical during the 1820s and 1830s was also marked by a change in interpreting sociopolitical relations that could be crudely described as a move from a fraternal to a patriarchal model. Processes of group formation were conceived less as reciprocal identification among group members themselves (a band of brothers) and more as identification with the father as the internalized historical essence of the group. It took me a long time to grasp, or perhaps accept, what now seems to me to be almost too obvious to mention: that the transition toward what we conventionally refer to as "Victorian" piety and patriarchy was not simply a conservative historical "regression" to "throne and altar" traditions, but a central element in the complex development of the consciousness of what it meant to be historical in the middle decades of the nineteenth century (and thus of great theoretical importance in the attempt to understand "historicism" and the project of becoming historical).

The chapters that follow were not written in their current order and because of the synchronic rather than diachronic organization of the book need not be read in sequence. However, there is logic to the book's organization, and an implicit conceptual narrative in its structure. The "Philosophical Prologue" opens the book with a discussion of historical ontology, examining the claim that the essential nature of human existence, and in fact all "being," is historical through a presentation of the programmatic public lectures Schelling delivered in Berlin in the fall of 1841. This introduces the main theme of the book in its most abstract philosophical form. Part I contains two chapters that follow the paths taken by Frederick William IV and his advisor Christian Bunsen toward formulation of a vision of cultural reformation according to historicist principles, a vision they would attempt to actualize in the cultural politics of the Prussian regime after 1840 and which informed their attempts to gather Germany's historicist luminaries around the court at Berlin. Part II takes up the question of historical identity as it was given public shape in architecture, urban planning, musical composition, and musical performance, and analyzes the problematic character of the relationship of Schinkel and Mendelssohn to the program of 1840. Part III focuses on three scholar–theorists who are conventionally tagged as founding members of the Historical School – Savigny, Jacob Grimm, and Ranke – and examines the ways in which their affiliation with the Prussian regime in 1840 revealed the nature of their evolution as scholars of history and proponents of historical identity. Each of these chapters examines the problematic development from ethnic (historically constituted) to ethical (historically self-constituting) models of identity and the role played by transcendent religious principles in this development. The "Antiphilosophical Epilogue" draws out some of the implications of the project of becoming historical as given classic and historically prophetic form by Marx and Kierkegaard in 1840–46.

This book does not contain a formal bibliography. The historical and critical literature on the individual figures treated is vast and often distinguished, and I have tried to indicate my debts and disagreements in the footnotes. My general perspective on the emergence of the historical principle as a dominant cultural form during the watershed period of the early nineteenth century has been shaped in part by the comments on various historical forms of conceiving time in Reinhart Koselleck's *Futures Past*,[3] but especially by the enigmatic comments of Michel Foucault about the emergence of the modern discourse of historicist humanism as an inwardly conflicted "analytic of finitude" in which human identity was figured as both constituted by the "positivities" of historical culture and constitutive of the historical worlds in which it was constituted.[4] The more recent writings of Stephen Bann, James Chandler, and Susan Crane[5] have been especially useful in helping me to think about Romantic historicism as both a form of historical consciousness differentiating past and present and a complex set of strategies for the production of historical representations that extended far beyond the confines of the narrative texts of historians. The burgeoning scholarly literature on the historical production of national identity and cultural memory has only added to my belief that historicism is more than a form of historiography, a particular type of historical representation. My own contribution to this scholarly conversation has been to emphasize the wide-ranging transformation of Romantic historicism in the late 1820s and 1830s and draw out some of its implications, especially regarding problems of historical agency, identity construction, and ethical choice, which were

[3] Reinhart Koselleck, *Futures Past: On the Semantics of Historical Time*, transl. Keith Tribe (Cambridge, Mass.: 1985).

[4] Michel Foucault, *The Order of Things: An Archaeology of the Human Sciences* (New York: 1971), pp. 217–21, 312–22, 367–73.

[5] Stephen Bann, *Romanticism and the Rise of History* (New York: 1995); James Chandler, *England in 1819: The Politics of Literary Culture and the Case of Romantic Historicism* (Chicago: 1998); Susan Crane, *Collecting and Historical Consciousness in Early Nineteenth-Century Germany* (Ithaca: 2000). The literature on the construction of cultural memory also deals extensively with the broader cultural production of historical consciousness and the attempt to deal with historical discontinuities through the self-conscious production of historical identities. For a recent intelligent survey of the literature, see Peter Fritzsche, "The Case of Modern Memory," *Journal of Modern History* 73 (March 2001): 87–117, and Peter Fritzsche, Specters of History: On Nostalgia, Exile, and Modernity," *American Historical Review* 106, no. 5 (December 2001): 1587–1618.

so decisive in producing the affiliations among proponents of the historical principle in Berlin in 1840.

Throughout the writing of this historical study, I have also found myself persistently turning to problems of historical consciousness and historical identity within the frame of current academic and cultural debates.[6] The "new" historicism of the last decades of the twentieth century seemed to share more than simply a name with the old historicisms of the early nineteenth century. However, I hope this study does not simply project contemporary concerns into its representation of the past. Like the historicists of the early nineteenth century, I have tried to conjure up a specific cultural world of the past in its historical difference – to allow my subjects to speak within the contexts of their own concerns. There are easier ways to look in a mirror or produce an echo than writing an historical study. I am convinced that it is precisely in their cultural and temporal difference, as voices from another place and time, that my subjects claim our attention as conversational partners and expand our horizons as we struggle to grasp the tensions and dilemmas of living our lives as both products and producers of history, and thus pursue our own version of the adventure of "becoming historical."

[6] My own attempts to articulate and clarify the relations between cultural identity and ethical action, between historical consciousness and narrative meaning, between constituted and constituting historical selfhood, within the frame of current academic and cultural discussions are presented in: "The Historian in the Labyrinth of Signs: Reconstructing Cultures and Reading Texts in the Practice of Intellectual History," *Semiotica* 83 (winter 1991): 352–84; "A New Philosophy of History? Reflections on Postmodern Historicizing," *History and Theory* 36 (1997): 236–48; "Historiography as Exorcism: Conjuring Up 'Foreign' Worlds and Historicizing Subjects in the Context of the Multi-Culturalism Debate," *Theory and Society* 27 (1998): 535–64; "Salvaging Truth and Ethical Obligation from the Historicist Tide: Thomas Haskell's Moderate Historicism," *History and Theory* 38 (1999): 348–64; and "Linguistic Turn and Discourse Analysis in History," *International Encyclopedia of the Social and Behavioral Sciences*, eds. Neil J. Smelser and Paul B. Baltes (26 vols.; Oxford: 2001), vol. 13, 8916–22.

Acknowledgments

The publication of this book marks the conclusion of a long, tangled, and often interrupted historical project. This project began in the mid and late 1980s with a very different focus and aim. For years it was placed on hold and almost abandoned as I pursued other interests in the history of psychoanalysis and contemporary historical and historiographical theory. In the mid 1990s my apparently irrepressible interest in the 1840s returned, but from a different angle, enriched (I hope) by my various detours and by a new interest in music and architecture. A more recent detour into the history of Marxism reinforced my conviction that the decade of the 1840s marked a significant turning point in European intellectual history and was particularly important in framing modern and postmodern conceptions of the historical subject and historical identity.

During the years I have worked on various pieces of this project and then labored to weave them together into a single story, I have been sustained by the encouragement and criticism of friends, colleagues, and students. I would like to thank the following colleagues who invited me to present parts of this project at various campuses around the country and thus also introduced me to critics I would not otherwise have encountered: Richard M. Buxbaum, Keith Baker, Michael Steinberg, David Sabean, John McCole, Robert Nye, Anthony La Vopa, William Duvall, and Mark Micale. I would like to extend a special thanks to Carl Schorske and Stephen Bann for sending me encouraging letters (regarding the Mendelssohn chapter) at a time when I was particularly frustrated about the whole project. The three anonymous reviewers from Cambridge University Press helped me make the necessary revisions in the final stages, and Elke Schwichtenberg at the Bildarchiv Preussicher Kulturbesitz was a godsend in smoothing out problems with the illustrations at the last minute. The research and original drafting for the Schinkel and Grimm chapters were completed while I was a Fellow at the Center for Advanced Study in the Behavioral Sciences in Palo Alto, California, during the academic year 1996–97. The atmosphere of the center was perfect for healing academic burnout, and I am grateful for the financial support from the Andrew W. Mellon Foundation that made that year possible. The Grimm chapter was shaped in part by my conversations with Kveta Benes, who completed her dissertation on the relationship between German academic philology and national identity under my direction during the late 1990s.

Throughout the writing of this book I have been immersed in the experimental projects of an adventure in undergraduate education (the Comparative History of Ideas program [CHID]) at the University of Washington. My colleagues and students in this program may have taken up time that I could have spent on the research and writing of this project, but I would never have survived, intellectually or morally, without them. Thank you, Jim Clowes, and all the students, staff, and teaching assistants of CHID. The personal friendship of Eleanor Toews, Todd and Judy Coryell, Uta Poiger, Kyriacos Markianos, and Dorothee Wierling kept me sane.

This book is dedicated to my children Julia and Jonathan, whose passion for music, literature, and architecture shaped this project in ways they never imagined. Earlier versions of chapter 5 and of parts of chapters 3 and 4 have been previously published: "The Immanent Genesis and Transcendent Goal of Law: Savigny, Stahl and the Ideology of the Christian State," *The American Journal of Comparative Law* 37 (winter), 1989: 139–69, republished by permission; "Musical Historicism and the Transcendental Foundations of Community: Mendelssohn's *Lobegesang* and the 'Christian-German' Politics of Frederick William IV," in Michael Roth, ed., *Rediscovering History: Culture, Politics and the Psyche* (Stanford: Stanford University Press, 1994), pp. 183–201, copyright 1994 by the board of trustees of Leland Stanford University, by permission; and "Building Historical and Cultural Identities in a Modernist Frame: Karl Friedrich Schinkel's Bauakademie in Context," in Mark S. Micale and Robert L. Dietle, eds., *Enlightenment, Passion, Modernity: Historical Essays in European Thought and Culture* (Stanford: Stanford University Press, 2000), pp. 167–206; copyright 2000 by the board of trustees of Leland Stanford University, by permission.

Philosophical Prologue: Historical Ontology and Cultural Reformation: Schelling in Berlin, 1841–1845

"I feel the full significance of this moment, I know what responsibilities I have taken upon myself. How could I deceive myself or attempt to hide from you what is made evident simply by my appearance at this place."[1] With these words, Friedrich Wilhelm Joseph Schelling began his inaugural lecture for the course Philosophy of Revelation at the University of Berlin on November 15, 1841. Schelling's conviction that his appearance in the Prussian capital as the spokesperson for philosophy and the "teacher of the age" was a moment of world historical significance was shared by many of his contemporaries. For months the major German newspapers had speculated about the cultural impact of Schelling's move from a relatively peripheral position at the University of Munich to the influential academic center in Berlin, and about the public significance of his courtship by Prussian government leaders, including the recently installed king, Frederick William IV. In Berlin itself, excitement was high as Schelling stepped to the podium. The 290 official student places in his course had been immediately snapped up, and there was a rush on the 140 places reserved for auditors. Those denied entry by legitimate means became unruly and stormed both the office of the beadle responsible for entry cards and the lecture auditorium itself. One observer noted that the press of students around Schelling was so great when he began his lecture that many could read his notes over his shoulder.[2] Government ministers, military officers, and academic dignitaries filled the front rows of the packed hall. Reporting on this event for a Hamburg newspaper, the young Friedrich Engels asserted: "If you ask any man in Berlin who has any idea at all about the power of the spirit over the world, where the battle site for control over German Public Opinion in politics and religion, thus over Germany itself, lies, he would answer that the this battle site is at the University, and specifically in Auditorium Number 6, where Schelling is lecturing on Philosophy of Revelation."[3]

[1] F. W. J. Schelling, *Philosophie der Offenbarung, 1841–42*, edited and with an introduction by Manfred Frank (Frankfurt: 1977), p. 89.

[2] The descriptions are taken from a report which a young theology student, Adolf Hilgenfeld, sent to his father, cited in Helmut Ploecher, "Schellings Auftreten in Berlin (1841) Nach Hoererberichten," *Zeitschrift fuer Religions- und Geistesgeschichte* 4 (1954): 93–94.

[3] Friedrich Engels (under the pseudonym of Friedrich Oswald), "Schelling Ueber Hegel," from *Marx-Engels Gesamtausgabe* (MEGA), eds. D. Rjazanov *et al.* (Berlin: 1930), vol. I, part 2, pp. 173–74. Hereafter cited as MEGA.

Many of Schelling's auditors in Berlin, as well as many cultural observers and pundits throughout Germany, thought they knew perfectly well what Schelling's call to Berlin in 1841 signified. The flood of articles, pamphlets, and books interpreting this event began before Schelling arrived in Berlin and continued through the next few years. Schelling's repeated refusal to publish any substantial portions of his lectures did not hinder the public debate. Schelling warned his audience that they should reserve judgment and not cast his positions in old molds. Suddenly transported to the center of public life, he was convinced that, even at the ripe age of sixty-six, his philosophical creativity had not ceased to develop. He suggested that his audience would have to shed their preconceptions of who he was and open themselves to discovering something about him, of which nothing was known.[4] Schelling thus presented himself as a living embodiment of his new philosophy of freedom, in which every historical act disclosed new meanings about the past and opened up new paths to the future.

Schelling perceived his call as a reaffirmation of the central role of the post-Kantian philosophical tradition within German national culture. He self-consciously connected his task to the philosophical and cultural project that he had helped initiate during the period of German national humiliation, inner reform, and liberation during the first decades of the century. The expression of German national identity in philosophical knowledge was connected to the general awakening of German national feeling. Philosophy elevated this feeling to systematic knowledge, establishing common values in a secure knowledge of the ontological ground of all value. Philosophy was not just a concern of "schools," but also "a concern of the nation."[5] "Because I am a German, because I have shared in feeling and bearing the pains and the joys of Germany in my heart," Schelling insisted, "that is why I am here, for the salvation of the Germans lies in systematic, philosophical knowledge."[6]

The general outlines of this philosophical project were not placed in question. Schelling himself had played a prominent role in its formulation, and many aspects of his inaugural lecture in 1841 echoed a programmatic unpublished essay "On the Essence of German Science," which he had written in 1807, in direct response to the national humiliation by Napoleon's armies. In that earlier essay, the essence of German national identity was defined as a distinctively profound metaphysical hunger and metaphysical accomplishment. What distinguished Germans as a people was their need to test the depths and explore the boundaries of individual existence, and ultimately to produce a reconciling, "redemptive" comprehension of the apparently intractable contradictions between freedom and fate, individuality and community, finite existence and absolute being. The national quest for knowledge of individual existence as grounded in the "Absolute" and

[4] *Philosophie der Offenbarung*, p. 90. [5] *Ibid.*, p. 95. [6] *Ibid.*, p. 96.

integrated into the "totality of beings" was finally articulated in the creation of German philosophical science, which was peculiarly, in Schelling's view, a science of the Absolute as "concrete" universal, as personal existence.[7]

Schelling interpreted his call to Berlin as a renewed recognition among political and religious leaders of the central role of philosophy in German national culture. By offering him an appointment as a public professor of philosophy, outside the confines of university regulations and compensation restrictions, the Prussian government had affirmed the special public role of philosophy as a guide to "life," as a means to provide a secure ground for "those convictions that hold life together."[8] As a "superior privy councilor," Schelling was responsible not to the faculty but directly to the Ministry of Public Instruction and Religious Affairs and admitted to the deliberations of the State Council, where major issues of government policy were discussed. In the role he ascribed to philosophy in his inaugural address, Schelling gave notice that he was not ready to relegate philosophical knowledge to the role of handmaiden to either religion or politics. Philosophical knowledge both framed and centered all other dimensions of culture and society. Schelling did note that his call to Berlin to resuscitate the national mission of philosophy was an indication that something had gone awry in the years since this mission had first been formulated. The historical hopes of the period of national cultural awakening had been dashed, and the consciousness of national identity that had fueled the resistance to Napoleon seemed to have dissipated.

Schelling understood the historical crisis that had brought him back to the center of the historical stage as a radical contradiction between life and thought, between the nation as an historically evolving association of existence in time and space and the conscious self-representation of that existence in the teaching of its cultural elites, particularly its philosophers. Recent representatives of the philosophical tradition had failed to satisfy the demand from "life" for a satisfactory grounding of its ethical convictions and religious beliefs, thus instigating a general repudiation of the cultural value of philosophy. "Never before has there arisen," he claimed, "such a massive reaction against philosophy from the side of life as at this moment."[9] This reaction, which had shaken the public reputation not only of a particular philosophy but also of philosophy per se, was based on a perception of contemporary philosophy as a critical, demystifying power that undermined the traditional foundations of ethical conviction and religious belief. Philosophy had become an issue of national concern because it addressed "those questions of life to which no one should or even can remain indifferent."

[7] "Ueber das Wesen deutscher Wissenschaft" (1807), in Friedrich Wilhelm Joseph von Schelling, *Ausgewaehlte Werke*, ed. Manfred Frank (6 vols; Frankfurt: 1985), vol. 4, 13–28, esp. pp. 13, 19, 28.

[8] *Philosophie der Offenbarung*, p. 93. [9] *Ibid.*, p. 92.

"Life," that is, the vast majority of individuals in the nation who were not professional thinkers, judged philosophy by its results, not by the details of its demonstrations and arguments. And in this judgment, Schelling insisted, "Life in the end is always right."[10] If philosophy undermined "life" rather than enhancing it and bringing its potentialities to full expression, then something was wrong with philosophy. The estrangement of philosophy from national life could occur only if philosophy lost its bearings. It was not intrinsic to philosophical thinking per se. In fact, Schelling insisted that in the postrevolutionary, modern world, "life" could be sustained, and religious and ethical convictions grounded, only through the self-reflective knowledge of philosophy. The era of unquestioned custom and naive faith was irrevocably past.

The crisis produced by the failure of philosophy to fulfill its cultural function was necessarily connected to its failure to reveal the foundations and purpose, or "ground" of existence. For philosophy to fulfill its calling it would have to provide systematic and positive knowledge of the totality of "beings" (*das Seiende*) because "in particularity nothing can be genuinely known." But such systematic knowledge was not possible without an answer to the question: "Why is there being at all rather than nothing?"[11] Philosophy could accomplish the redemptive mission of integrating individual existence into the totality of beings only if it could provide knowledge of the primal ground and source, the point and purpose of all existing beings. Philosophy remained for Schelling a form of rational theology, or philosophical knowledge of God and his works. Human self-knowledge, philosophical anthropology, could not answer the questions it raised concerning the ultimate significance of human life. Human existence in history only made sense from a perspective that transcended this existence and enclosed it within the context of its origins and absolute ground. Post-Kantian German philosophy had taken this task on itself, and Schelling insisted: "Nothing shall be lost which has been achieved since Kant as genuine scientific knowledge." His task was not to replace this philosophical tradition with another but to "re-establish it" on "true foundations."[12]

For Schelling, the false turn that had betrayed the promising beginnings of modern German philosophy was easy to identify: It went by the names of Hegel and Hegelianism. Everyone in Schelling's audience knew that he had been called to Berlin to oppose the power of Hegelian philosophy at the university and in the general public culture. When Schelling spoke of the opposition of "life" to philosophy, he meant the public outcry against the allegedly atheistic implications of Hegelian philosophy as drawn out by some of the younger Hegelians (like David Friedrich Strauss, Bruno Bauer, and

[10] *Ibid.*, pp. 92–93.
[11] "Einleitung in die Philosophie der Offenbarung" *Ausgewaehlte Schriften* 5, (1842–43): 607–9.
[12] *Philosophie der Offenbarung*, p. 95.

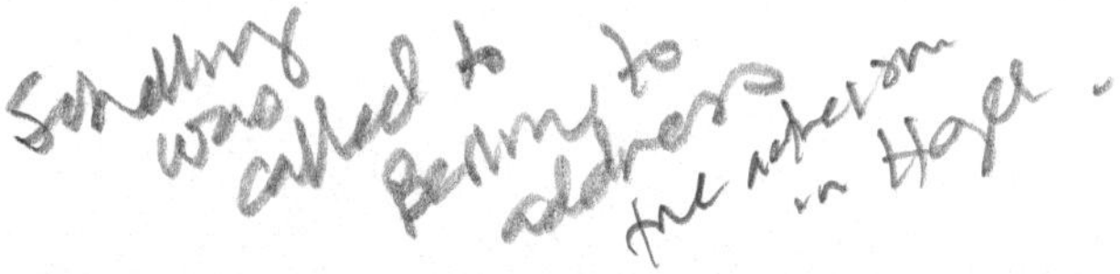

Ludwig Feuerbach), who had applied their philosophical acumen to critical analysis of the biblical narrative and Christian doctrine. But for Schelling, the current crisis was not simply a matter of partisan conflict pitting one philosophical school against the other. What was at stake was the role of philosophy in modern culture. Schelling felt that he was peculiarly qualified to address this issue because he had been present at the birth of modern German philosophy and because Hegelianism was his unruly "stepchild." "Without me," he wrote to a friend in September 1841, "there would have been no Hegel and no Hegelians as they presently exist."[13]

Schelling's critique of Hegel centered on one general claim: The Hegelian system, while purporting to be a science of the ultimate identity of reason and reality, thought and being, was in fact only a science of reason, a systematic analysis of the dynamically interconnected totality of mental categories. Hegel, according to Schelling, never broke through this closed circle of rational thought's reflection on its own operations. His science was limited to knowledge of the a priori categories that constituted the essence, or "whatness," of things, but did not encompass the sheer existence, or "thatness," of things. Hegel's writings were about the mental forms through which the mind shaped indeterminate existing being into the objects and subjects in space and time that constituted conscious experience of the world. Hegelian rationality shaped reality into a world of conceptual forms that defined experience but never penetrated beyond these forms to that prior ground of existence that made the shaping activity possible in the first place, and constantly threatened to break through the veil of concepts and reveal their contingent status. A science of thinking activity, Schelling claimed, could never reach those "things in themselves" (as Kant had called pure existence) that by definition were on the "other side" of thought's categories.[14]

In the science of reason, thinking took itself as the object of thought and developed a completely a priori knowledge of reality as a logical possibility, as "the infinite potentiality of being." This kind of rational knowledge, in Schelling's terms, was merely "negative." It might demonstrate how beings must necessarily exist if they did exist, but it could never explain why some logical possibilities actually existed and others did not. What eluded such a negative science of reason was that which was of greatest human concern – the meaning of finite human existence, the understanding of freedom as active choice, responsibility, and guilt about past actions, and hope and despair about the future.

In Schelling's view, the whole Hegelian system was actually contained within Hegel's *Science of Logic*. In this description of totality as the self-generating structure of rational reflection, the apparent otherness of real

[13] Schelling to Dorfmueller, September 10, 1841, in *Aus Schellings Leben, in Briefen*, ed. G. L. Platt (3 vols.; Leipzig: 1869–70), vol. 3, p. 166.

[14] *Philosophie der Offenbarung*, pp. 107–10.

being was sublimated into the process of thinking and reemerged as a product or manifestation of reason. But at both the beginning and the end of Hegel's *Logic*, Schelling claimed, there was a conflation of the concept of being with actually existing being. The pure undifferentiated being with which the dialectical development of categories began was actually the most abstract of concepts, and the determinate, concrete, universal "idea" at the end of the process was not the really existing highest being (God) but simply the concept of God. That Hegel implicitly recognized that his *Science of Logic* had failed to unite thought and being was displayed in the inconsistent additions of philosophies of nature and historical culture to his *Science of Logic* in order to complete the system. If the rational really encompassed the real, then natural and historical existence should have been contained within the *Logic*.

The haplessness of Hegel's panlogism in the face of reality, Schelling claimed, was especially evident in the inability of rational reflection to ground its own activity of thinking. Reason might be able to articulate its own inner structure, but it could never explain how or why it itself existed: It could not answer the question of why there was reason rather than no reason. The dialectical structure that Hegel attributed to the self-movement of concepts themselves only made sense as the real thinking activity of a living subject, the really existing being that the whole process of rational self-reflection presupposed. The existence of this thinking subject never entered into the process of rational reflection itself. However, if the process of reflection was carried a step further than Hegel was willing to pursue it, the result would be recognition that reason was ultimately dependent on something totally other to itself: It would produce an encounter with being as actual existence that made thinking possible in the first place. Thus Schelling argued that the Hegelian conception of thought as self-relating reflection could not maintain itself against the power of reflection itself. Rational reflection led to the edge of an abyss that revealed reason's own limitations, instigating a self-transforming experience that forced the rational subject to realize it was not self-sufficient but dependent on its other, on the sheer "thatness" of existence.

From Schelling's perspective, therefore, Hegel had not thought far enough. Reason was finally driven to recognize its dependence on an existing being that could never be fully, transparently appropriated in conceptual form, and thus to seek wisdom in receptivity to "revelation," in experience that was not self-generated but instigated by something beyond consciousness. Hegel's inability or unwillingness to take this extra step beyond rational thought had produced a philosophy that had to fail miserably when faced with the critical life questions of existing human individuals. The experience of unconscious powers that transcended conceptual understanding or control, the unique nature of historical events and actions, and thus the open-endedness of the historical horizon, the need for a personal god with the power and will to redeem finite human existence – none of these "realities" were addressed in Hegelian philosophy. Despite Hegel's disclaimers, his system finally dissolved concrete freedom into rational necessity, historical openness into the eternal cycle of rational reflection, real existence into abstract being, a personal god into a conceptual possibility. In its Hegelian version, philosophy had become abstract, deterministic, fatalistic, atheistic, and thus radically estranged from the needs of life as lived by real human beings.[15]

By misconstruing his merely negative philosophy of rational self-reflection as a positive comprehension of reality, Schelling believed, Hegel had vitiated his considerable achievements in logical analysis and condemned his system to the status of a mere episode in history. Hegel's detailed explication of the logic of self-reflective rationality was merely a prolegomena to the construction of a "positive" and "historical" philosophy of existence, a philosophy that would not only grasp what Hegel had omitted but would also transcend and encompass rational self-reflection within a larger perspective. Pushing self-reflection to its own boundaries opened consciousness to the abyss of prereflective, "blind" being, the pure existence that preceded language and consciousness. This primal prereflective being was the absolute starting point for any comprehension of actually existing beings, all of which achieved their specific essence on the ground of a sheer "thatness" of existence.

A philosophy that began with "the being that precedes thinking" (*unvordenkliches Sein*) could not of course take the form of a logical process pursued by negative philosophy. It demanded a method appropriate for relating consciousness to that which was not only other (as in objective worlds), but other and prior to the world of experience in which consciousness was constantly defined as a subject facing a world of objects. The production of the world of being from this *prius* could not proceed as a logical emanation, but only as "a free deed transcending being and the inert, that can only be known *a posteriori*."[16] Positive philosophy did not begin in sense experience, but with the a priori of all experience in "blind being." Positive philosophy was "empirical" in the sense that the deductions it developed through an analysis of this starting point could only be validated by experience, through documentary knowledge of the free acts that emerged from primal being. Philosophy, however, did not abstract from experience but moved "toward" experience, revealing the "what" of the "that" of existence. Such "a priori empiricism" or "metaphysical empiricism" actually consisted of two operations. First, Schelling speculatively "constructed" the nature of absolute being or God from the fact of God's ground in pure existence. Then he "proved" the validity of this construction through an interpretative analysis of the historical manifestations of absolute being in human religious consciousness.

[15] *Ibid.*, pp. 121–53. [16] *Ibid.*, p. 147.

Although the starting point of Schelling's positive philosophy was the sheer existence or blind being that preceded consciousness, he vehemently rejected the claim by his critics that his philosophy was a form of irrationalism. The path that led to the recognition of sheer existence as that which was prior to all thought and being was a path of rational reflection that proceeded inexorably to the conclusion that reason's own activity could only be grounded in a being "absolutely outside of itself." In recognizing its own radical contingency, rational reflection gained the possibility of genuine self-understanding through an open relation to its own ground. Moreover, Schelling was convinced that in this turn beyond itself, rational reflection regained the possibility of grasping the world of real beings as a rationally structured totality, but in an a posteriori, rather than a priori fashion. Although blind being was not comprehensible, could not be transparently absorbed into the conceptual structure of rational reflection, it could open itself to comprehension by revealing its implicit structure through the actions in which it made itself explicit in nature and history. As much as Hegel, Schelling claimed that the absolute totality was ultimately knowable as a systematic rational structure, but only "empirically," through an interpretive understanding of its "revelation" as a world of beings. "Positive philosophy can also be called a science of reason," he insisted.[17]

The peculiar rational irrationalism of Schelling's positive philosophy was displayed most obviously in his speculative constructions of God as the absolute ground of being and of the act that created the manifest world with which he introduced his Berlin lectures. Sheer undifferentiated existence or blind being was not in itself God, but the ground from which the Absolute generated itself as absolute spirit or self-relating, reflexive personality. The self-production of a personal divinity had a dialectical structure. Pure existence shaped itself into a spiritual being through a free confrontation and synthesis with its other – differentiated being. The principle of undifferentiated will (subjectivity) combined with the principle of differentiated form (objectivity) to create the subject–object unity of the Absolute in possession of itself, as the "Lord" of its own being. In doing so, it revealed that the deeper, absolute ground of the apparent ground of being in sheer existence was the "abyss" (*Ungrund*) of freedom. In the miraculous act through which undifferentiated chaos was shaped into differentiated form was revealed the truth of our deepest reality as absolute freedom. Schelling designated the three moments of this divine self-genesis as powers, or "potencie," which only became God when they joined together in an organized unity. God freely made his essence on the ground of his existence. This theogonic process, or "history" whereby existence was transformed into the absolute spirit, occurred prior to the creation of the actual world that had evolved in space and time. Through his speculative construction of God's dynamic self-making before creation, Schelling asserted his belief that the dynamic of

[17] *Ibid.*, pp. 159–60.

historical development, the movement from unconscious to conscious will, the formation of personality as free agency, the division of existence into a "past" of undifferentiated existence, a "present" of differentiated form and a "future" characterized by the personal identity of existence and form, was built into the very structure of being itself during the "proto-time" before existence in time. History was not just an external and thus contingent form in which being manifested itself in the created world, but the very essence of being. In this sense, Schelling believed that his philosophy was a philosophy of freedom and of history in a deeper sense than any previous philosophy. The nature of being per se was that of a narrative of free actions culminating in the creation of spiritual, personal identity.

The theogonic process of divine self-determination was not logically necessary, not a manifestation of a rational order to which God had to conform; it was a process of freely willed action. The product of this free activity, however, was the transformation of formless and speechless existence into the fully articulated trinitarian structure of the divine word, or *Logos*. Moreover, the first act, in which pure existence somehow produced the distinction between existence and potential form, must have been an unconscious act. For Schelling, self-conscious individuality, and thus personal identity – "character," or "personality" – emerged first through a "free" act that occurred within the sphere of unconscious being. Like Goethe before him and Freud after him, Schelling affirmed that "in the beginning was the deed." The "word," the realm of language, consciousness, and individuated personal identity, emerged from this "deed."[18]

Through the creation of the world, the Absolute was once again fragmented into its three modalities, the potencies were "perverted" into separate forces and thus lost their "divine" status. Only as dimensions or modalities of absolute spirit as personal identity were the potencies "divine." As separate, nonintegrated powers, they could even resist their "divinity" by opposing integration into spiritual identity. Thus pure existence could be either the ground of God or the opponent (as chaotic passion and undifferentiated desire) of divine purpose and unity. In human history, the potencies had to go through a struggle within finite human consciousness in order to reconstitute their original unity in a form freely willed by created beings. Sheer existence became the chaos or vortex of will, which needed to be disciplined by form in order to create the inner self-possession of spiritual being. Although the development of these potencies from fragmentation to ordered identity in human history was not logically determined, Schelling

[18] The connections between Schelling's conceptions of the origins of the symbolic world of historical culture from the prehistoric, silent, and never fully conceptualizable realm of things in themselves to the psychoanalytic theories (especially those of Jacques Lacan) of the origins of language, meaning, and culture have been recently discussed with great brilliance and verve in two books by Slavoj Zizek: *The Indivisible Remainder: An Essay on Schelling and Related Matters* (London and New York: 1996) and *The Abyss of Freedom/The Ages of the World: An Essay by Slavoj Zizek with the Text of Schelling's Die Weltalter* (second draft, 1813), in English translation by Judith Norman (Ann Arbor: 1997).

was convinced that the historical development of mankind's original indeterminate freedom ultimately replicated the rational totality of the divine personality. In history, the divine identity freely fragmented itself into its constituent, separate, potencies and recreated its identity within human consciousness in the progressive production of human culture. The documentary traces of mankind's historical spiritualization in mythology and revealed religion validated empirically the hypothetical construction of God's "eternal" nature prior to the act of creation. At every level of Schelling's positive philosophy, the self-relating unity of personality emerged from a sequence of freely willed acts that disciplined and spiritualized the primal indeterminacy of unconscious desire, blind-being, or sheer existence. Although Schelling's constructions, deductions, and empirical reconstructions moved from the real to the rational, from existence to essence, from indeterminate will to spiritual form, the final result appeared to be an affirmation of the identity of reason and reality as confident as Hegel's.[19]

Schelling, however, was more cautious than Hegel in his claims about the completion of the historical process, about the "end of history." The documentary record that registered the transformation of existence into essence was not yet complete and could, after all, not be logically predetermined, since it developed not as a rational emanation of existence from essence but as a freely formed shaping of existence into essence. Yet, much like Hegel, Schelling often seemed convinced that his own philosophy marked an epochal turn to the final moment of reconciliation. This eschatological dimension was evident not only in Schelling's messianic posturing, but also in his descriptions of the historical development of religious consciousness.

The history of mankind could be understood as a meaningful narrative, as something more than a litany of human vanity or a cycle of despair, in Schelling's view, only from a perspective that transcended it, that is, within the context of the evolution of being as a theogonic process. Human history was a story of freedom in the sense that temporal development was instigated by mankind's voluntary act of rebellion against the divine order of integrated being, an act that released the first potency, indeterminate desire or will, from its proper place as the ground of divine personality and set in motion a conflict-ridden relation of the three potencies in historical time.

[19] During the 1950s, there was a broad scholarly effort to rehabilitate the positive philosophy of the late Schelling as a fulfillment of the program of German idealism to fully grasp the conditions of existence in rational reflection. See Horst Fuhrmans, *Schellings Philosophie der Weltalter* (Duesseldorf: 1954); Walter Schulz, *Die Vollendung des deutschen Idealismus in der Spaetphilosophie Schellings* (Stuttgart: 1955); and Emil Fackenheim, "Schellings Begriff der positiven philosophie," *Zeitschrift fuer philosophische Forschung* 8 (1954): 321–35. The focus on existential will and radical freedom, which distanced Schelling from the Hegelian ambitions for a rational system, has attracted the attention of twentieth-century existentialist philosophers and theologians like Martin Heidegger, Paul Tillich, and Karl Jaspers.

The evolution of this conflict, however, proceeded in the same pattern of progressive integration as the original self-determination of absolute spirit before creation. The major epochs of human history were imagined as stages in the self-determination of created humanity that culminated in a reintegration of the creature into the creator. What was genuinely meaningful in history was this sacred history of mankind's fall away from and return to the godhead, articulated in the history of religious consciousness.

Schelling divided the evolution of religious consciousness into two major epochs. In the age of mythology, the conflict and integrative possibilities of the three "potencies" were represented in human consciousness as both voluntary and unconscious acts objectified as "external" gods. In the historical sequence of mythological systems, Schelling traced the relationship of the potencies as a series of conflicts in which gods of material and natural being were gradually subordinated to the power of rational form and spiritual control. This process culminated in the three "completed" mythologies of Egypt, India, and Greece.[20] The appearance of Christianity marked the movement from an unconscious to a conscious process of human and divine self-making: The program of spiritualization and integration was presented to consciousness as a divine revelation that needed to be recognized and reproduced as an internal identity.

The Christian epoch was itself divided into three epochs, the ages of the Apostles Peter (Catholicism), Paul (Protestantism), and John (the future universal community of the absolute spirit). In Schelling's view, his own philosophical activity marked the point of transition from the age of Paul to the age of John, the beginning of an era in which the division between external revelation and subjective inwardness would be overcome and the external facts of Christian revelation would be recognized and appropriated as inner, spiritual truths. What Schelling prophesied was a new post-Protestant philosophical, or "scientific," Christianity: "My standpoint is that of Christianity in the totality of its historical development; my goal is to build the church (if church is the proper word) which is genuinely universal, and to build it in spirit alone, in the complete fusion of Christianity with universal science and knowledge." Germany, as the universal historical culture containing both Catholic and Protestant versions of Christianity, would also be the culture in which the question of Christianity's full self-realization in a new culture of self-conscious spirit would be decided. The decisions and actions of contemporary Germans would determine the fate of Christianity as the truth of existence.[21]

Schelling was usually very reserved about drawing out the specific institutional and cultural implications of his positive philosophy, aside from

[20] Edward Allen Beach, *The Potencies of God(s): Schelling's Philosophy of Mythology* (Albany: 1994), examines this neglected aspect of Schelling's philosophy in illuminating detail.

[21] *Philosophie der Offenbarung*, pp. 320–21.

the identification of his philosophical mission with the historical tasks of the German nation. There is no doubt that he imagined the Johannine post-Protestant church of the Spirit as emerging from within the self-consciousness of German language and culture, even though its scope was universal. More specifically, Schelling did project the church of the future as a liberation of spiritual community from political conditions and controls, through a separation of church from state.[22] By achieving final comprehension of the structure of existence, the members of the Johannine church not only possessed the content of Christian Revelation "genuinely and in itself," but also established the conditions for an ethical life grounded in a ritual, liturgy, and poetic narrative that articulated the "historical path" of human self-creation and self-possession from its earliest articulations in primitive mythology to its final synthetic form in Schellingian self-conscious knowledge. Ethical community, the association of free individuals within a common divine life, was a reconciliation with history finally understood, a free "resignation" to the objectively differentiated structures of a divinely ordered world in which all the potencies were finally in a state of integrated rest.[23]

The priority Schelling gave to the inner reform and external liberation of the church in his vision of perfected community implied a reduction of politics to a mere external discipline that prepared human existence for church membership. Part of Schelling's critique of Hegel involved an attack on what he considered the idolatrous belief that the substance of free individuality and ethical community could be found in the "formal" or "abstract" arrangements of law and political institutions. The general categories of modern constitutional politics, in Schelling's view, did not touch the core of human existence. Hegel had divinized (*vergoettert*) the state and thus reduced the life of existing human individuals to purely abstract relations among conceptual essences. To grasp the human existence that the state presupposed as its ground was to move toward a transcendence of the state in a shared relation to the absolute ground of individual existence within the symbolic discourses of art, religion, and philosophical "science." For Schelling the disorientation within German culture after 1815 was expressed at least partly in an exaggerated belief that politics was the site where ethical community could be attained.[24]

Schelling's positive philosophy, however, did suggest certain specific views about the role of the state as "means and background" rather than "goal and

22 "Aus einem oeffentlichen Vortrag zu H. Steffen's Andenken, April 24, 1845," in *Schellings Werke*, ed. Manfred Schroeter (6 vols. and 6 supplements; Munich: 1927ff), suppl.vol. 4, p. 497.

23 *Philosophie der Offenbarung*, pp. 324–25.

24 The explicit connection of Schelling's Hegel critique to politics is contained primarily in a series of unpublished lectures of 1833–34 cited at length in Alexander Hoellerbach, *Der Rechtsgedanke bei Schelling* (Frankfurt: 1957), pp. 209–11.

substance" of ethical life.[25] The state associated human beings not as existing individuals but as "species-beings," or conceptual essences: It was the realm of the "merely" human rather than that of the existing individual. As part of the rationally comprehensible order of objectified, "natural" being, the state organized human beings according to a "natural" order of hierarchical distinctions and patriarchal authority. The rationality of politics was inherent in the historical actuality of patriarchal and monarchical institutions, and in the historically evolved customs that required the individual to subordinate himself to a necessity beyond the control of his ego, thus preparing him for the higher ethical order of voluntary subordination to the divine personality. The state's function was to discipline the rebellion of existence against divine order, to impose an external order that would eventually produce the conditions for an internalized spiritual order. The proper form of the state was modeled on that of the family, the site for the cultural discipline of the individual in preparation for entry into the spiritual world of culture. Politics was coercive discipline and tutelage – intrinsically, not just in its limited historical forms. Authentic community transcended politics. Existence grasped its place in Being through relation to its ultimate ground. This activity could only take place in the "internal" world of culture, the site where human interrelations occurred as actions in the symbolic realm of language, metaphor, and ritual.[26]

Schelling did not share the desire of many of his Prussian and German contemporaries to transform the state itself into the site of an ethical community, or to use the institutionalized church as an ideal model and pedagogical instrument for the moralization of politics. However, his radically apolitical stance obviously did embody a specific form of philosophical politics, through its "positive" affirmation and historical justification of the hidden divine purpose in those "free" actions that created positive laws and institutions on the models of personal authority and patriarchal power and that rejected as abstract and ahistorical any notions of rationally and voluntarily constructed public will. The transcendence of the "merely" political – the separation of church and state and the elevation of church above the

[25] "Philosophische Einleitung in die Philosophie der Mythologie oder Darstellung der reinrationalen Philosophie," in *Ausgewaehlte Schriften* 5: 561. Schelling's general considerations on the relations between the external order of the state and the internal sphere of spiritual existence is contained in Lectures 22–24 of this course, whose Berlin version is printed in *ibid.*, pp. 526–82.

[26] Schelling's focus on authentic community as a community of inner disposition, or *Gesinnung*, is analyzed in Martin Schraven, "Recht, Staat und Politik bei Schelling," in Hans-Joerg Sandkuehler, ed., *F. W. J. Schelling* (Stuttgart: 1998), pp. 199–204. Schelling's position is confusing because of his use of the terminology of community and society in ways precisely opposite to their later common usage in German social theory, that is, *Gemeinschaft* represents the realm of social necessity, *Gesellschaft* that of freely willed social identification. See also H. J. Sandkuehler, "F. W. J. Schelling-Philosophie als Seinsgeschichte und Anti-Politik," in H.-M. Pawlowski, S. Smid, and R. Specht, eds., *Die praktische Philosophie Schellings und die gegenwaertige Rechtsphilosophie* (Stuttgart: 1989), pp. 199–226.

state – became a means for legitimating the authoritarian containment of liberal and democratic reform within the political realm, and for opposing any attempts to give the political realm itself the positive content of a community of ethical life.

Schelling was called to Berlin to displace the power of Hegelian philosophy and provide philosophical legitimation for the cultural policies of the Historical School. In one sense the project Schelling defined for himself ended in dismal failure. After the initial excitement that greeted his appearance in Berlin, interest in his philosophical message rapidly waned. By the time he had progressed in his lectures to speculations about the future triumph of philosophical religion as the historical goal of German national development, both the enthusiasm and the size of his audience had noticeably dwindled. Yet in the spring of 1842 he still seemed confident of his messianic calling and the epochal significance of his presence in Berlin. Among members of the court, the ministry, and some academic circles, his reception remained supportive, making him feel quite at home. His daughter became engaged to the son of the government minister Johann Albert Eichhorn, increasing his sense of belonging to the insiders of a new cultural "family." When some students honored him with a traditional torchlight procession after his first semester, he interpreted their action as a sign that his philosophy had demonstrated its ability to endure the "fresh air" of life and the "full light" of day. "What is it which has drawn you to me in a personal way?" he asked rhetorically. "It can only be this: that I have helped you to recognize the highest things in their whole truth and particularity, that I have not given you stones, claiming they were bread, but the bread for which you sought, and have demonstrated to you that it is really bread."[27]

Schelling's optimism about the effectiveness of his teaching and its cultural impact of his positive philosophy continued through the summer and early fall of 1842. He revived his long-delayed plans for publication of his lectures and completed the negotiations with the Bavarian and Prussian governments that made his move to Berlin permanent, and gave it the form of a national, rather than a merely Prussian, appointment. But as the published responses to his lectures began to appear, his self-affirming optimism began to crumble.[28] Members of the Hegelian School effectively defended their positions and attacked Schelling in print, remaining unimpressed by his critique.[29] They continued to believe that reason ultimately ruled reality,

[27] Cited in Max Lenz, *Geschichte der Koeniglichen Friedrich-Wilhelm-Universitaet zu Berlin* (4 vols.; Halle: 1910–18), vol. 2, part 2, p. 48.

[28] For a broad sampling and overview of the responses, see Xavier Tillette, *Schelling im Spiegel seiner Zeitgenossen* (Turin: 1974), p. 435ff, and Horst Ulrich, "Schelling's Spaetphilosophie und die zeitgenoessische Kritik," in Steffen Dietzsch, ed., *Natur-Kunst-Mythos. Beitraege zur Philosophie Friedrich Wilhelm Joseph Schellings* (Berlin: 1978), pp. 194–216.

[29] The leader of the orthodox Hegelian center in Berlin had already joined the critique of Schelling with a critique of the radical leftist critiques (by Bruno Bauer) of Hegel's rational reconciliations of

that rational self-consciousness was the culmination of the struggle for freedom, that the constitutional postrevolutionary state was the site for the integration of individual and public will in ethical community. Publication of student copies of his lecture notes interspersed with critical commentary – especially that by an old acquaintance, the Kantian theologian H. E. G. Paulus – made him bitter.[30] When he took Paulus to court for breaking copyright laws and lost, he discovered how shallow and narrow his public support really was. By May 1844, Schelling had begun to complain that his time and his culture were not ready for his message. His treatment in the court of public opinion led to a loss of faith in the mission of his culture. His "constant feeling," he claimed, was best expressed by the words of the Swedish king Gustav Adolf: "It wounds my heart to have to deal with such a perverse nation."[31] By 1846 he had canceled all of his lecture courses at the university (his contract with the government did not require him to lecture or even participate in university affairs) and had withdrawn to his study to prepare his message for posthumous publication.

Schelling had not been defeated by his Hegelian opponents. The framework of idealist philosophy within which both Schelling and the Hegelians argued and blustered, their belief in the possibility of constructing some kind of system of speculative knowledge that could encompass finite existence in all its dimensions and return a fragmented world to unity by reconnecting it to its divine origins, simply faded into irrelevance. Schelling's decision to finally end his frustration and stop his public lecturing coincided with the decision to halt publication of the journal that had represented the voice of Hegelian philosophy since 1827, *Jahrbuecher fuer wissenschaftliche Kritik* (Annals of Scientific Criticism). However, just as Schelling retreated from

reason and reality in May 1842. See Philipp Marheinecke, *Einleitung in die oeffentlichen Vorlesungen ueber die Bedeutung der Hegelschen Philosophie in der christlichen Theologie* (Berlin: 1842), and also by the same author: *Zur Kritik der Schellingschen Offenbarungsphilosophie. Schluss der oeffentlichen Vorlesungen ueber die Bedeutung der Hegelschen Philosophie in der christlichen Theologie* (Berlin: 1843). Karl Rosenkranz, the biographer of Hegel and a loyal Hegelian, similarly attacked Schelling as a throwback to pre-Hegelian modes of romantic intuitionist philosophy in *Ueber Schelling and Hegel* (Koenigsberg: 1843) and *Schelling* (Danzig: 1843). In the philosophical faculty of the university, the lecturer Karl Ludwig Michelet used his course in the history of modern philosophy in the summer semester of 1842 to dismiss Schelling's attempt to go beyond Hegel as conservative posturing that had given up on the task of grasping the world as rational and sought a transcendent ground for meaning: C. L. Michelet, *Entwicklungsgeschichte der neuesten deutschen Philosophie mit besonderer Ruecksicht auf den gegenwaertigen Kampf Schellings mit der hegelschen Schule* (Berlin: 1843).

30 H. E. G. Paulus, *Die unendlich offenbar gewordene positive Philosophie der Offenbarung oder Enstehungsgeschichte, woertlicher Text, Beurtheilung und Berichtung der Schellingschen Entdeckungen ueber Philosophie ueberhaupt, Mythologie und Offenbarung des dogmatischen Christenthums in berliner Wintercursus von 1841–42* (Darmstadt: 1843). Schelling's bitter fight against Paulus and those who advertised and sold Paulus's book is recounted in his letters to the publisher Cotta through late summer and fall of 1843. See Horst Fuhrmans and Liselotte Lohrer, eds., *Schelling und Cotta: Briefwechsel, 1803–1849* (Stuttgart: 1965), pp. 216–31.

31 Schelling to Dorfmueller, May 5, 1844, in Plitt, *Aus Schellings Leben*, vol. 3, p. 189.

the public sphere there emerged the beginnings of a body of work that portended the resurrection of many of his principles in altered forms, disjoined from the systematic and absolute claims in which they had been framed and presented. In writings by Karl Marx, Soren Kierkegaard, Ludwig Feuerbach, and Max Stirner during the mid 1840s, the critique of Hegel's panlogism and the program of a "positive," "historical" philosophy of existence took on a whole new secular sociopsychological dimension and a new essayistic and experimental style.[32]

Schelling's fate in Berlin during the 1840s was also important as a representation of the fate of the cultural program of both the leaders of the Prussian regime and the representatives of the Historical School, or "historical party," who at various levels of commitment and for various periods of time, were willing to work under its banner. What was worked over and struggled through not only in Auditorium 6 but in the public cultural spaces of Berlin and Prussia in the 1840s was the problem of making historical consciousness the very foundation of personal and communal identity, of defining human existence as historical to its very core, historical through and through. Schelling enveloped his conviction that personal and cultural identity was inherently historical in a fog of abstract ontological analysis that eventually drove his audience to sleep or despair. Yet wrapped in that fog was the intimation of something new in the world: Schelling's philosophy was an old wineskin heavy with some new and heady wine.

[32] Developing connections between Schelling's historicist critique of Hegel and that of the antiphilosophical or at least anti-idealist critics on the cultural left became prominent during the late 1960s. Juergen Habermas had taken major steps in this direction with his 1954 doctoral dissertation at Bonn University: *Das Absolute und die Geschichte: Von der Zwiespaltigkeit in Schellings Denken*. The impact of Schelling on Habermas himself is discussed in Werner Marx, *The Philosophy of F. W. J. Schelling: History, System and Freedom*, transl. Thomas Nenon (Bloomington: 1984), pp. 1–32. Important works in this Left-wing interpretation of Schelling were Hans-Joerg Sandkuehler, *Freiheit und Wirklichkeit: Zur Dialektik von Politik und Philosophie bei Schelling* (Frankfurt: 1968) and especially Manfred Frank, *Der unendliche Mangel an Sein. Schellings Hegelkritik und die Anfaenge der Marxschen Dialektik* (Frankfurt: 1975). Frank's focus on the radical content beneath the conservative veneer is continued in Axel Wuestehube, *Das Denken aus dem Grund: Zur Bedeutung der Spaetphilosophie Schellings fuer die Ontologie Ernst Blochs* (Wuerzburg: 1989). In a recent English introduction, Andrew Bowie has tied Schelling's late philosophy to a wide array of "poststructuralist" philosophical developments. See his *Schelling and Modern European Philosophy: An Introduction* (London: 1993). See also the works of Slavoj Zizek, noted previously in footnote 18.

Part I

Historicism in Power: 1840 and the Historical Turn in Prussian Cultural Politics

1

Nation, Church, and the Politics of Historical Identity: Frederick William IV's Vision of Cultural Reformation

In his inaugural lecture at the University of Berlin in 1841, Schelling had claimed that philosophical systems should be judged by "life" on the basis of their ethical and religious implications. Philosophical understanding was one dimension of a process through which social solidarity was produced as subjective identification rather than as the imposition of external conformity. It instigated an inner transformation of the self by recognizing the self's origin and essence in the transcendent personality of absolute being, thus changing the isolated ego into an integrated person that was both culturally and cosmically "at home." Among Schelling's Berlin audience there were some who might have agreed that Schelling's philosophy should indeed be judged by life, but in a critical sense, as a tendentious metaphysical justification for the particular brand of cultural politics pursued by Frederick William IV of Prussia and his most prominent advisers and ministers. As the young Karl Marx would claim in 1843, following the lead of Friedrich Engels and other Left Hegelian critics of the Prussian regime, Schelling's philosophy could be read as "Prussian politics *sub specie philosophiae.*" From this perspective, criticism of Schelling's philosophy was "indirectly" an "assault" on the new Prussian regime.[1] This chapter and the next will examine Marx's claim by investigating the formulation and contexts of Prussian cultural policy as articulated by the two primary initiators of Schelling's appointment, the king himself and his trusted personal confidant and advisor, Christian Bunsen.

Frederick William IV came to the throne with a broadly conceived vision of how he intended to use his royal authority to initiate a cultural reformation and set Prussia on a particular historical course. Bunsen had been his longtime partner in formulating this vision, so it was not surprising that he would use Bunsen as an intermediary to induce Schelling and other cultural luminaries to join his regime. The views of the king and Bunsen did not in themselves constitute the cultural policy of the regime, which was marked by unclear patterns of authority and the constant formation and dissolution of influential cliques at the court, in the administration, in the military, and in the church, but they were of primary importance in producing the

[1] Marx to Ludwig Feuerbach, October 3, 1843, in Karl Marx, Friedrich Engels, *Werke* (41 vols.; Berlin: 1956-) vol. 27, pp. 420–21.

content and setting the tone of what came to look like an "official" cultural ideology in the early 1840s.[2]

Aside from individual programmatic statements and administrative actions emanating from the king and his personal spokespersons, the most important directives for the new course in cultural policy came from the ministry with oversight over ecclesiastical and educational affairs, the *Kultusministerium*, literally, ministry of "cults" (the public forms of religion), but perhaps more accurately translated as the Ministry of Culture.[3] As the office for state administration of religion and education, very broadly defined, the *Kultusministerium* was responsible for the discipline and mobilization of the subjective loyalties of the state's inhabitants: Its concern was not so much the imposition of behavioral conformity through physical threats or material inducements as the production of an internalized "disposition" (*Gesinnung*) of obedience and identification through manipulation of the symbolic realm.

Between 1817 and 1840, this ministry had been under the direction of two of the few remaining members of the administration that led Prussia through the era of reform and liberation between 1807 and 1815, Baron Karl von Stein zum Altenstein and his special aide for educational affairs Johannes Schulze, the latter a member, or at least sympathetic fellow traveler, of the Hegelian School. The new king and his closest advisers were convinced that under Altenstein and Schulze's leadership the official direction of the public institutions most important in the formation of public consciousness had been misguided, favoring an educational philosophy that assumed that rational identification with the laws and constitutional structures of the secular state was the highest form of ethics and the basis of all communal solidarity. When Frederick William IV assumed power in 1840, the transformation of this policy was one of his major concerns. The new minister of culture, Johann Albert Friedrich Eichhorn – and his new chief aide, Gerd Eilers – quickly made it clear that the government's cultural policy was not neutral but "partisan, totally partisan."[4] During the next five years the leadership of the *Kultusministerium* worked actively, not just to administer and regulate, but also to mobilize and produce a specific cultural *Gesinnung* within the

[2] The recent biography of the Frederick William IV: David E. Barclay, *Frederick William IV and the Prussian Monarchy, 1840–1861* (Oxford: 1995), provides an excellent overview of the various factions and personalities that jockeyed for power around the Prussian king in the 1840s and also devotes a separate section to Bunsen's specific influence as the king's "special friend" (see pp. 49–84).

[3] For a history of the ministry, see Ernst Muesebeck, *Das preussische Kultusministerium vor hundert Jahren* (Stuttgart: 1918), which covers the period 1817–1840, and Rudolf Luedicke, *Die preussische Kultusminister und ihre Beamten, 1817–1917* (Stuttgart: 1918).

[4] Eichhorn made this comment in a policy speech during the early months of the new regime at one of the strongholds of fundamentalist neo-orthodoxy, the Wittenberg seminary. Cited in Max Lenz, *Geschichte der koeniglichen Friedrich-Wilhelms-Universitaet zu Berlin* (4 vols.; Halle: 1910–18), vol. 2, part 2, 39.

Evangelical State Church, the institutions of higher learning, elementary and secondary schools, and in the print culture of journals and newspapers.

The official policy of the state was not simply to maintain order and repress subversion, but to actively nurture a Christian-German cultural consciousness grounded in the "historical" principle. Primary emphasis was placed on shaping the consciousness of the educators themselves, on producing the appropriate *Gesinnung* among the trainers of future church officials, civil servants, and teachers at the universities and the secondary schools. But attempts were also made to move beyond this education of the educators and work directly on the formation of public opinion on a broader, more popular level.[5] This study does not examine the processes by which the programmatic positions of the formulators of policy were institutionalized in educational reforms and personnel policies, censorship and propaganda initiatives, and ecclesiastical reforms, but the creation and transformation of the content of the program itself. In these first two chapters, the focus will be on three elements of this program: the emphasis on "reformation" of dispositions, rather than "revolution" of institutions and laws, as the royal road to a transformation of a fragmented and passive population into an integrated community of autonomous subjects; the definition of the intended suprapersonal identity as a combination of ethnic German identity achieved through recognition of participation in a common "immanent" fate, and religious Christian identity achieved through internalization of transcendent authority; and, finally, the claim that the appropriate foundation for cultural reformation through subjective identification was the "historical principle" that both German and Christian identifications would occur through the insertion of individual self-experience into public narratives that appropriated traces of the past as present memory. The Prussian regime that came to power in 1840 presented its goal as the generation of a Christian-German community based on recovered or discovered collective memory. The mediating material through which individuals were to accomplish their identification with each other was the inherited substance of their shared historical past.

In the period after Hegel's death in the early 1830s, Frederick William, then the crown prince, had thrown his influence behind a concerted attempt to lure Schelling to Berlin as Hegel's replacement. He had gathered support among various intellectual factions in Berlin and sent Bunsen to Munich to speak to Schelling. At that time, however, Schelling's own hesitations and suspicions about how he might be received in the home of his philosophical rival were matched by those of Altenstein and Schulze, who harbored doubts about the compatibility of Schelling's philosophy with the cultural

[5] A beginning has been made in describing the practical realization of these policies in the actions undertaken by Eichhorn and Eilers in the Kultusministerium by Lothar Dittmer, *Beamtenkonservatismus und Modernisierung: Untersuchungen zur Vorgeschichte der Konservativen Partei in Preussen 1810–1848/49* (Stuttgart: 1992).

policies of the Prussian state.[6] In the late 1830s both Frederick William and Bunsen had displayed a renewed interest in the development of Schelling's new "positive," "historical," and "Christian" philosophy. Frederick William informed himself about Schelling's late philosophy through discussions with his nephew, the Bavarian Crown Prince Maximilian, a devoted Schelling student. Bunsen made a personal pilgrimage to Munich to visit Schelling and pore over the widely circulated but unpublished notes to Schelling's lectures on the philosophy of mythology and revelation. Therefore the notion that Schelling might provide the philosophical centerpiece for a redirection of Prussian cultural policy had been evolving in the consciousness of the king and his advisor for some time before 1840. When Frederick William acceded to the throne in June 1840, one of his first acts was to empower Bunsen to negotiate Schelling's appointment. From the very beginning it was imagined as a government appointment with implications that extended beyond the walls of the university.

Although Bunsen wrote to Schelling that the king wanted him at his side as a personal philosophical adviser to "draw personally from your wisdom and to lean on your experience and strength of character,"[7] there is some evidence that Frederick William was less certain about the need for philosophical grounding for his cultural, historical, and religious positions than Bunsen, and even suspicious of a tendency among philosophers to be seduced into the ubiquitous modern errors of secular humanism, rationalism, and pantheism, all of which disavowed the radical dependence of finite human beings on their transcendent creator. Such suspicions were evident in the king's response to a memorandum from Bunsen just a few months before he approved the offer to Schelling.[8] The memorandum concerned the revision of Prussian divorce law, one of the king's pet projects, but in Bunsen's usual garrulous manner it had expanded into a long treatise with many philosophical and theological digressions that were formulated in the terminology of Schelling's late philosophy. Although Frederick William claimed that he had read the philosophical sections of the memorandum with great enjoyment, he found some of Bunsen's language objectionable. The term *divinization* (*vergoettung*), for example, seemed to him to be a misleading description of a redemptive process that was instigated in human history by the specific acts of a transcendent personal power. The historical process whereby individuals within ethnic communities were transformed into redeemed members of a spiritual community might more aptly be

[6] This attempt to get Schelling is described in the letter of Humboldt to Bunsen in 1835, which includes the memorandum in which Altenstein expressed his reasons for opposing the appointment. See *Briefe von Alexander von Humboldt an Christian Carl Josias Freiherr von Bunsen* (Leipzig: 1869), pp. 14–23.

[7] Bunsen to Schelling, August 1, 1840, in Schelling, *Philosophie der Offenbarung*, p. 409.

[8] "Schreiben des Kronprinzen vom 24. Maerz, 1840," published in Leopold von Ranke, "Aus dem Briefwechsel Friedrich Wilhelms IV mit Bunsen" (1873), *Saemmtliche Werke* (54 vols., Leipzig: 1867–90), vols. 49/50, pp. 372–92.

termed christianization (*verchristung*), he suggested, to make clear that the transformation occurred through a transcendent intervention in human history. Even after the Second Coming and Last Judgment, Frederick William insisted, the faithful segment of mankind would remain in the subordinate relationship of a "pure, sinless, and immortal human body" to the lordship of the "divine head." Along similar lines, he complained that the philosophical terminology Bunsen borrowed from Schelling seemed to imply that mankind was not the product of a free act of creation, but a necessary emanation of God's eternal essence and thus "a part of God himself." Such viewpoints he insisted were both illogical and heretical and could only lead to an arrogant denial of mankind's dependence for existence and for meaning on a power outside of itself.[9] At the same time that Frederick William expressed these caveats, however, he also insisted that he was not actually accusing Bunsen (or Schelling) of drawing such conclusions from their own ambiguous language. It was almost as if the king were protecting himself against his own interpretive tendencies.

There clearly did exist a tension between the king and Bunsen regarding the balance of immanent and transcendent dimensions in their view of cultural reformation and its historical foundations. But this tension also marked the king's own views and was part of the reason he was drawn to Bunsen in the first place. And the same tension defined the very core of Schelling's late philosophy. It was the source of a conflict between two rather different conceptions of history and culture or, more aptly, the source of the inner conflict that actually defined the complex views of history and culture among the major leaders and intellectual fellow travelers of the regime. Contrasting the views of the king and Bunsen will provide us with a preliminary and "official" expression of this tension and the kind of post-Romantic historicism that emerged from it.

Just as it would be wrong to identify the Schelling of 1840 with the Schelling of the early Romantic movement at the turn of the century, so it is misleading to see the policies of Frederick William and his advisers simply as Romantic. However, ever since David Friedrich Strauss satirized the Prussian king (through analogy with the Roman Emperor Julian, who tried to restore traditional pagan religion after Constantine) as a "Romantic on the throne,"[10] this identification has become conventional wisdom. As in Schelling's case, the views of history and culture held by Frederick William and Bunsen in 1840 had a Romantic starting point of a particular kind, which served as a reference point for revisions and transformations. The generation of government officials, intellectuals, and artists that set the tone and formulated the policies of the Prussian regime of 1840 had

[9] *Ibid.*, p. 373.

[10] David Friedrich Strauss, *Der Romantiker auf dem Throne der Caeseren, oder Julian der Abtruennige* (1847), reprinted in Strauss, *Gesammelte Schriften*, (12 vols.; Bonn: 1876–8), vol. 1, pp. 237–72.

received their ideological baptism under the impact of the second wave of north German Romanticism, in which the principles constructed out of the postrevolutionary vortex by thinkers and poets like Schelling, Hegel, Friedrich Schleiermacher, Friedrich and August Schlegel, Novalis, and Ludwig Tieck were attached to liberalizing domestic reforms and the mobilization of nationalist sentiments between 1807 and 1815. Frederick William and Bunsen, like the older Schelling, constructed their mature positions in a difficult process of moving beyond the Romantic historical hopes and cultural conceptions to which they had committed themselves in their youth. In this transcendence of the past, however, the past was not left behind but assimilated into a new framework. The tensions evident within the "Christian-German" or "German-Christian" conceptions of culture and history that marked the official cultural policy of the Prussian regime were themselves related to a developmental tension between two experiential moments in the formation of the regime's leaders.

Battles over the meaning of German and Christian historical identities were also struggles to define the meaning of the movement for reform and liberation of 1807–15 as a foundational memory and orienting framework within the present. For the leaders of the new regime in Prussia, the heroes of the earlier reform and liberation movement were "founding fathers." At times it appeared as if Frederick William hoped to recreate the Prussian leadership of the earlier period when he came to power. Baron Karl vom und zum Stein and the cadre of intellectual advisors who helped create the legislation of reform and mobilize the national awakening, men like Wilhelm von Humboldt, Barthold Georg Niebuhr, and Friedrich Schleiermacher, were imagined by the crown prince during the late 1820s and into the 1830s as a kind of leadership in exile that could be induced to return to power and also "return" inhabitants of Prussia and Germany to that moment when they had first discovered their authentic national identity as an historical identity.[11] The assertion of the historical principle as a foundation of state and national solidarity in 1840 was itself connected to a return to the original formulation of that principle in 1807–15.

By 1840 most of the leaders of the earlier cultural reformation were dead. Stein, Wilhelm von Humboldt, Niebuhr, and Schleiermacher, as well as the military leaders Clausewitz and Gneisenau, had all died in the early 1830s. Frederick William had to be content with secondary figures of the earlier period, the military reformer Hermann von Boyen, Stein's chief aide for national affairs; Johann A. F. Eichhorn; the "other" brothers, August Wilhelm Schlegel and Alexander von Humboldt; the political professor and legal scholar Friedrich Karl von Savigny; patriotic publicists and literary

[11] Ernst Lewalter, *Friedrich Wilhelm IV: Das Schicksal eines Geistes* (Berlin: 1938), pp. 269–78. This detailed biography remains an indispensable source for the plans and personal relations of Frederick William during his long career as the Prussian crown prince before 1840.

figures like Ernst Moritz Arndt, Friedrich Ludwig Jahn, Friedrich Rueckert, Friedrich de la Motte-Fouqué, and Ludwig Tieck; and a host of veterans (mostly aristocratic officers) of the military campaigns of 1813–15. Local humorists satirized the personnel policies of the new regime as "monument preservation" (*Denkmalschutz*), with special reference to aging cultural heroes like Schelling, Tieck, Arndt, and Alexander von Humboldt.[12]

The starting points from which the spokespersons of the Prussian regime of 1840 had developed their mature cultural stances were not the same, just as their personal movements beyond these starting points took different paths. But they centered on two historical "awakenings" in which Romantic principles that had been developed around 1800 were attached to broad sociocultural movements and reshaped and transformed in the process.

The first of these awakenings was the awakening of the ethno-cultural people (*Volk*) in response to the call of their leaders to assume the responsibilities of self-determination and liberate themselves from the tutelage of the oppressor. This awakening was itself composed of two interrelated processes. It involved, first of all, the domestic mobilization of popular will through legal and institutional reforms. Equality under the law and participation in institutions of local self-government provided the framework for the individuals who composed the people to assert their responsibility and express their solidarity as a people through self-conscious and voluntary recognition of their collective identity. This inner liberation and subjective identification in turn found its appropriate expression in defiance and resistance to the imposition of a foreign identity by the Napoleonic occupation forces. Domestic emancipation led to national liberation.

The second awakening that defined the version of Romantic consciousness dominant among the leaders of the regime of 1840 emerged from disillusionment with hopes for the historical reconciliation of autonomy and solidarity that had been aroused by the reformist commitments and nationalist fervor of 1807–15. By the time of Napoleon's return from Elba and his second defeat at Waterloo, the Congress of Vienna had displayed quite clearly that the national hopes of the Prusso-German patriots would not be realized in the foreseeable future. Emotions of inner, subjective identification were disjoined from "objective" historical reality, and either displaced into imaginary worlds and distant futures or recontextualized in universalistic theories in which national transformation was grounded in world-historical speculation about the necessary emergence of the Germanic cultural form as the culmination of human civilization. Response to the postwar disillusionment took a number of forms, but culturally dominant was the religious revival that presented itself as an "awakening" to the transcendent conditions of human liberation and community. Fulfillment of the desire for freedom

[12] Wilhelm Hansen, "Die Brueder Grimm in Berlin," *Brueder Grimm Gedenken 1963* (Marburg: 1963), p. 270.

and community through self-sacrificing submergence in the immanent historical solidarity of the "people," the recovery of such freedom and community (after the experience of disillusionment) as the gift of a transcendent power – broadly and schematically stated, these two experiential moments structured the perceptions and hopes of the leaders of the Prussian regime of 1840.

Born in 1795, the Prussian king was a man of the generation of 1813. Although growing up as the Hohenzollern crown prince made Frederick William a distinctive member of his generation, it would be misleading to confine his self-formation to a uniquely focused socialization into the functions and duties of Prussian kingship. Like the social companions and intellectual interlocutors with whom he surrounded himself, Frederick William was himself caught up, from very early on, in a complex process of personal and cultural identity formation. One of the reasons Frederick William appeared to others ultimately as a weak and indecisive king was his experiential immersion in the conflicting forces he was trying to reconcile, manage, and transform within the world he felt fated and called to govern.[13]

BECOMING GERMAN: ACTUALIZING THE SPIRIT OF 1813

In the official letter of invitation to Schelling, Bunsen had sketched a picture of the present as a moment "pregnant with the future." For the first time since the end of the Napoleonic wars, a cadre of leaders had attained power in Prussia who were capable of regenerating the spirit of 1813 and mobilizing the energies and hopes of a new generation. In focusing on the way in which the current Prussian regime intended to build on recovered memories of German solidarity in the wars of liberation, and in setting the German model of cultural "reformation" against the French model of political "revolution," Bunsen touched on two of the most obvious elements in the self-presentation of the new Prussian leadership. During the first years of the reign of Frederick William IV, it sometimes appeared as if the king, in agreement with some of his closest advisors and most important ministers, were ready to commit the Prussian regime to a cultural policy that publicly promoted the formation among its subjects of a historical consciousness centered on their ethnic identity as members of the German *Volk* and that he would define his own monarchical identity as a *Volkskoenig* (people's king), as what Bunsen called an "organ of the nation."[14]

[13] The interaction of personality and environment, partially constructed around an Eriksonian conception of psychological identity, informs the biography of Dirk Blasius: *Friedrich Wilhelm IV, 1795–1861, Psychopathologie und Geschichte* (Goettingen: 1992).

[14] Bunsen to Schelling, August 1, 1840, in Schelling, *Philosophie der Offenbarung*, p. 409; Blasius, *Friedrich Wilhelm IV*, pp. 88–94.

The constantly repeated claim that the historical lesson to be drawn from the consciousness of national solidarity evident in the wars of liberation was that the power and freedom of Germany were grounded in a union of princes and peoples, although emphatic in its insistence on the principle of consensual unity, was vague in its designation of the specific institutional implications of such unity, and could be appropriated in a number of ways. Most problematic was the meaning attached to the connection between liberation and integration. Was the subjective identification of the individual with the "people" premised on a liberation of the individuals who constituted the people from traditional forms of privilege and tutelage? Or was this identification an identification with inherited traditions (including hierarchical ranks and unequal rights), and simply a transformation of external, customary obedience into internal, voluntary obedience to existing authority? As a personal symbol of the essential identity shared by all Prussians (in the traditional sense of the political or civic nation), or even all Germans (in the postliberation sense of the ethno-cultural nation), the king would gain his legitimacy and power from the energies that flowed to him and through him from all who recognized the core of their communal being in his person. The king was not opposed to such interpretations in principle, though difficulties soon arose around opposing conceptions of how this union of princes and peoples should be institutionalized and connected historically to the patrimonial and state service traditions of the Prussian monarchy and to the diversity of territorial states within the German Confederation. If the prince were the conduit of the people's will, how did this will express itself to the prince? If both the prince and his subjects were subordinate to a higher identity as members of a people that existed prior to them and extended across existing state borders, how was this union to be historically articulated in laws and institutions?

If Frederick William IV had in fact been willing to place his government at the vanguard of a movement for the mobilization of a collective ethno-cultural German identity that possessed its own historical narrative, from archaic origins to future fulfillments, certainly this would have marked a startling reversal of previous policy. Since the Congress of Vienna and especially since the Carlsbad Decrees of 1819, the official leadership of the German Confederation, and the governments of its two most powerful states, Austria and Prussia, had treated the movement for German national unity as threatening and subversive.[15] The claim that an inherent solidarity among ethnic Germans should present itself through solidarity in deed and

[15] Matthew Levinger's *Enlightened Nationalism: The Transformation of Prussian Political Culture* (New York: 2000) analyzes the gradual rejection after 1815 of the discourse of nationality by proponents of forms of civic unity or consensual solidarity modeled on the paternalistic state or the conservative aristocratic estates. "From the 1820s onward," Levinger argued, "most Prussians who wrote of the nation used this term to indicate a harmonious pan-German community organized according to the principle of civil equality." (p. 159). One could say that the cultural politics of the new Prussian regime after 1840

in political institutions was dangerous to the established order after 1815 in two senses. First, it implied a form of populism in which the privileges of birth and cultural membership were equally distributed among all Germans, thus justifying democratic claims for participation of the people in their own political governance and cultural institutions. The demand for the actualization of ethno-German identity in visible, legal, and institutional forms assumed that the *Volk* would be able to express itself in a public forum and act out its autonomy in a constitutionally defined way – through some kind of representation of the people – within the government. That Frederick William III had assumed this himself when he made his call to the people to rise up and resist the French occupying forces in 1813 was suggested by his promise in May 1815, that the people's sacrifices would be rewarded by the creation of institutions permitting participation in their own governance.[16] Second, the territorial boundaries separating the recently expanded states of the German Confederation threatened to dissolve once existing states were reimagined as mere provinces within a larger German polity, whether modern nation-state or reconstituted medieval empire. From the nationalists' perspective, the pragmatic politics of territorial states assumed the taint of national betrayal.

By 1820 the movement toward national unity and liberal reform had lost its momentum, both through external repression and inner disillusionment. It was noteworthy, therefore, when one of the first official actions of the new regime in the summer of 1840 was to cease police surveillance, and lift restrictions on public speaking, publication, travel, and residence imposed on many of those targeted as "demagogues" in 1819–24. These amnesties and rehabilitations of the early days of the regime seemed to include both the leaders of domestic liberal reform and the spokespersons of national autonomy and integration. Some of the reformist civil servants who had lost their influence in the government or were forced to resign their positions in the early 1820s now were honored and given the status of political insiders. General Herman van Boyen, the last living member of the core of military reformers that had transformed the Prussian army into a "people's army," and who had resigned his post to protest the repression of the nationalist movement after 1819, was appointed minister of war. Eichhorn, who had emerged as a major proponent of national unity during the campaigns of 1812–14, was given the *Kultusministerium*. Although Eichhorn had not been arrested or disciplined in the 1820s, he had been under suspicion as a friend and fellow traveler of the nationalist "demagogues." His appointment was thus a clear sign of a reversal of policy. Even more striking was Frederick

was marked by an attempt to recuperate the discourse of nationality for the paternalistic state and the traditional social order, and thus remove its subversive and revolutionary implications.

[16] Thomas Nipperdey, *Germany from Napoleon to Bismarck, 1800–1866*, trans. Daniel Nolan (Princeton, N.J.:1983), p. 241.

William's attempt to honor and memorialize the nationalist exaltation of the campaigns of 1813 by seeking out the popular propagandists and poets of national resistance for public rehabilitation. Ernst Moritz Arndt (1769–1860), who, as a virtual propaganda minister for Baron Stein in 1812–13, had appeared to many as a personal incarnation of the nationalist exaltation of the liberation campaigns; Friedrich Ludwig Jahn (1778–1852), the founder of the patriotic gymnastics associations (*Turnvereine*) and the author of the tract that defined the cause of liberation as a recovery and self-assertion of a Germanic ethnic identity; and Friedrich Rueckert, the author of one of the most popular collections of nationalistic war poems in 1814, were all rehabilitated as honored mentors of the regime.

The cultural rehabilitation of nationalist "demagogues" like Arndt and Jahn suggested a policy that would end censorship of voices that spoke from outside the official circles of government. However, Frederick William IV did not actually abrogate the censorship laws imposed in 1819; he simply made exceptions to them, indicating his willingness to tolerate free discussion of public issues if the discussion remained within the bounds he considered to be appropriate. The relaxation of censorship regulation for about a year (December 1841 to January 1843) was meant to nurture a specific kind of expression of public consciousness. It was matched by an increased hostility by the government toward those professors and journalists who were less than enthusiastic about the ideal of a Christian-German community based on the "historical principle." Eichhorn's ministry attached clear criteria of "sound" opinions and dispositions to processes of hiring and promotion at the universities and within the ecclesiastical hierarchy, and they not only favored those journals and journalists whose stance supported the official cultural policy of the regime but also created what amounted to a propaganda bureau in order to produce and disseminate their message to the educated estate and more broadly to the literate populace. While Arndt was returned to his academic post at Bonn, his colleague Bruno Bauer lost his teaching license, as did the Hegelian lecturer at Berlin Karl Nauwerck and the poet Hoffman von Fallersleben in Breslau. Although some intellectuals and academics received government help to publish journals supportive of the regime's policies, the reapplied censorship laws sent Karl Marx and Arnold Ruge into exile.[17]

When Arndt was reinstated in his position as professor of history at Bonn University, and once again allowed to publish freely as a cultural historian and political publicist, his rehabilitation quickly became a public event in its own right. In the fall of 1840 he was elected by the faculty, in an obviously symbolic gesture, as rector of the university. In January 1842, he

[17] The strategies employed by *Kultusministerium* to "liberate," nurture, and ultimately construct the right kind of people's voice or public opinion through personnel politics and the organization of an official press are recounted in Dittmer, *Beamtenkonservatismus*, pp. 159–244.

was inducted into the Prussian Order of the Red Eagle.[18] Similarly, when Jahn was finally released from police surveillance and permitted freedom of movement, domicile, and public expression, he was honored with the Prussian Iron Cross for his services with the national volunteer brigades in the campaigns of 1813 and 1814. With the approval of the new ministers Eichhorn and Boyen, Jahn's pedagogy of ethnic and political regeneration through collective physical exercise was instituted in the Prussian school system. A patriotic activity of 1813 that had barely survived as a voluntary activity among private associations was incorporated into official state policy.[19] By 1842, Jahn, like Arndt, had been transformed from an oppositional demagogue into a spokesperson for a cultural stance that was not only allowed free expression but was officially sanctioned by government leaders.

The rehabilitations of Arndt and Jahn revived the public significance of their particular construction of the period between 1807 and 1815 as a moment of cultural self-recognition produced by the resistance of a collective German ethnic subject (the "people") to the imposition of alien customs and values on its essential, archaic identity. Certainly Arndt and Jahn viewed their return to public favor as an affirmation of their own experience of 1813 as the authentic revelation of the meaning of the national past and future. At the center of their public stance was a firm belief that the sacred, unconscious core of personal character derived from membership in a *Volk*, that individual subjectivity and communal identity were grounded in an ethnic substance. Jahn claimed that *Voelker* were the primary units of historical development: "in them history is generated and recounted, they are the carriers of memory." He coined the term *Volksthuemlichkeit* (ethno-cultural identity) to articulate that mysterious substance which made a people into a people:

> It is that which is common, shared by people, its indwelling essence, its life and movement, its reproductive power and generative capability. Through it there reigns in every member of the people a characteristic thinking and feeling, loving and hating, happiness and sadness, passivity and activity, denial and enjoyment, hoping and yearning, intuiting and believing. It brings all the individuals of a people into a beautifully bonded community; not destroying their freedom and independence but rather enhancing this freedom and independence in the manifold and totality of relations with their fellows.[20]

Drawing eclectically from ethnological and linguistic theories developed in the eighteenth century (especially those of Herder) concerning distinctive

[18] Ernst Moritz Arndt, *Briefe*, ed. Albrecht Duehr (3 vols.; Darmstadt: 1975), vol. 3, p. 66.

[19] See Dieter Dueding, *Organisierter gesellschaftlicher Nationalismus in Deutschland 1808–1847: Bedeutung und Funktion der Turner- und Saengervereine fuer die deutsche National bewegung* (Munich: 1984), pp. 213–19.

[20] Friedrich Ludwig Jahn, *Deutsches Volksthum* (Berlin and Weimar: 1991), p. 22. This is a facsimile reprint of the text originally published in 1810.

national characters articulated in self-contained worlds of thought and feeling, Arndt and Jahn presented an ideology of incommensurable ethnic peoples struggling competitively to articulate their inner being in the external communal forms of both public meaning (language, religion, art, social ritual) and the organized power relations of legal and political institutions. In the form in which Arndt and Jahn had articulated German *Volk* identity, during the period between 1807 and 1815 its self-defining differences found expression in a combination of ways whose priorities were only roughly defined: as a linguistic community, as an ecological community grounded in a common experience of topography and climate, as an amalgamation of related tribal communities (*Staemme*) or communities of biological descent, and as a community of common historical tradition and collective memory. No matter how archaic and fundamental such elements might seem to be, however, they were all expressive of some deeper, more essential core that gave itself visibility in language, shaped itself to its natural environment, experienced collective historical suffering, engaged in collective historical action, and expressed its identity through time in a collective historical narrative. Either as a "natural" life force, energy or potency, or as a "cultural" collective subject, spirit or idea, this irreducible core of sameness was the never quite graspable sacred origin from which all individual lives gained their visible, concrete meaning. Membership in this ethnic *Volk* was the irreducible, essential identity of any individual self. To lose, to be separated from, betray, hide, or deny one's *Volk* was thus also the most radical loss or denial of selfhood, the most egregious sin. On the other hand, rediscovering and recognizing membership within the collective identity of the *Volk* was an experience of salvation, a return from alienation, reconciliation with one's true being.

During the years culminating in the campaigns of 1813, Arndt and Jahn had drawn out a number of implications of a belief in the priority of *Volk* identity. First, they tended to associate the return to authentic self-identity with a purification of language down to its archaic native forms. The return to authenticity was also a return to the original forms of speech that defined each historical culture. Second, they looked toward the recovery of "natural" geographic frontiers that would conform to something like the borders of linguistic–ecological communities. In the case of the German *Volk* a return to such frontiers would have incorporated Alsace, the Rhine valley, the Swiss Alps, the North Sea territories of the Low Countries, and parts of Denmark as natural elements of the greater German "empire." Third, the ideology of German *Volk* identity produced an ideal politics of empire in which the medieval period in central European history gained particular prominence. From the division of the Frankish Empire by the Treaty of Verdun in 843 to the fragmentation of the Holy Roman Empire after the Protestant Reformation, there emerged a recoverable public narrative of a time when the unity of the German peoples was expressed and developed

through shared legal institutions and political leadership, a common sacred art (Gothic), a national mythology and epic literature, and a fraternal warrior ethos. The diversity of Germanic "tribes" and the fragmentation of princely sovereignties and social estates had, in this historical vision, been politically and culturally fashioned into a solidarity based on the core values of *Deutschtum* for more than six hundred years. This medieval, "Old German" imperial period was a guarantee of the reality of a unity that had become increasingly invisible since the sixteenth century and thus a model and inspiration for the task of once again building a world that would express national self-recognition. But the medieval imperial model as the appropriate political form for the German *Volk* was always problematic for both Arndt and Jahn because of their populist conceptions of authentic Germanic culture, and their commitment to the connection between individual liberation from social privilege and hierarchical authority and the creation of a fraternal national polity.

Confusions were especially prominent in the meaning given to the regional and social diversification embedded in the traditional form of corporate institutions, or "estates." On the one hand, a state founded on historically inherited and legally articulated ranks exemplified German respect for individual diversity as produced by the particularities of historical experience. The "state of estates" or *Staendesstaat*, was the Germanic alternative to the ahistorical "mechanical" state of atomized individuals ordered by abstract general laws, a foreign horror attributed to both the Napoleonic empire and the Jacobin republic. On the other hand, the feudal forms of communal, provincial, or county "estates" displayed a hierarchy of privileged castes and divided the "fatherland" into legal fragments that made any public sphere of national solidarity seem illusory. Could the old ranks, orders, or estates be modernized in a form that recognized the diversity of historically produced and developed individuality, socialized the isolated individual into an incorporated functional group whose participation in the organism of society was guided by historically developed rights and responsibilities, and yet affirmed the individual's freedom to choose vocation and domicile and participate in the formation of the rules which defined their incorporation? Both Arndt and Jahn were populist nationalists. Although they affirmed the self-sacrificing devotion and fidelity of populations to customary "leaders" (and thus could easily adapt themselves to the rule of princes and kings), they looked askance at the rigidity of legal and social divisions that fragmented and stratified the *Volk*.[21]

[21] Arndt's populist nationalism during the period of the Liberation Wars is described in Karl Heinz Schaefer, *Ernst Moritz Arndt als politischer Publizist* (Bonn: 1974); and Alfred Pundt, *Arndt and the National Awakening in Germany* (New York: 1935). In the 1840s, Arndt tended to reiterate his old positions and justify them by reprinting documents, including private correspondence, from the earlier period. But he does seem to have taken a turn between 1815 and 1840 toward a greater emphasis on the essence of the *Volk* as a divine creation that was hammered into perfected self-expression by the

Both Arndt and Jahn tended to see the spontaneous self-sacrifice and obedience of the warrior brotherhood, as embodied in 1813 by the volunteer brigades and given voice in popular war songs and ballads, as the purest expression of German *Volk* identity. In many ways the preservation of the memories of 1813 was merged with the recovery of national collective memory.[22] The poetry of the wars of liberation was poetry that celebrated self-sacrificial response to the call of inner duty in solidarity with one's ethnic "brothers." "Fraternities" of warriors, regardless of their actual impact on the course of the war, became the representative image of the meaning of the war, the projection of the German community that the war was intended to produce. In the crucible of battle it was the individual's recognition of his ethnic identity that provided the sacred core of meaning, turned the battle into a holy war against threatening others, and gave death the meaning of self-sacrifice in the service of the sacred.[23] And it was in the war experience of facing death together that "peoples" and "princes" overcame their differences and identified with each other as leaders and subjects within the same prior Germanic *Volk*.

The *Volk* ideology propounded by Arndt and Jahn had a significant impact on the formation of Frederick William IV's political and cultural identity. When the crown prince set off for Breslau with his father, brother, and cousins in March 1813 in order to join the Prussian forces as they prepared for the campaign that would drive Napoleon's armies out of central Europe, he was only seventeen years old, but he had been the object of a pedagogical and ideological tug-of-war at the Prussian court for more than five years. Up to the moment of Prussia's military defeat and humiliation in 1806–7, the educational formation of the crown prince had been structured by a belief in the spontaneous development and self-expression of emotional and aesthetic sensibilities within a nurturing environment, an applied

conflicts of history. The Germanic core, the character of the German "Michael," he insisted, like Schelling, was connected to a deep commitment to answering the religious–metaphysical question; Germans' divinely ordained fate was to resolve the "highest and most ideal tasks of history." "We are a god-seeking, spiritual, pious people," he wrote in *Versuch einer Vergleichender Voelkergeschichte*, 2nd ed., Leipzig: 1844), p. 418.

22 For a discussion of the forms in which this memory was sustained during the years of the repression of the national movement after 1819, see Christopher Clark, "The Wars of Liberation in Prussian Memory: Reflections on the Memorialization of War in Early Nineteenth-Century Germany," *Journal of Modern History* 68 (1996): 550–76.

23 There is an excellent discussion of this form of national consciousness in the literature of 1813 in Michael Jeismann, *Das Vaterland der Feinde: Studien zum nationalen Feindbegriff und Selbstverstaendnis in Deutschland und Frankreich, 1792–1918* (Stuttgart: 1992), pp. 27–102. See also George Mosse, *Fallen Soldiers, Reshaping the Memory of the World Wars* (New York: 1990), pp. 15–50. For an analysis of the ways in which the recovery of honorable masculinity was tied to the regeneration of German national character and fraternal bonding, see Karen Hagemann, "Of 'Manly Valor' and 'German Honor': Nation, War, and Masculinity in the Age of the Prussian Uprising Against Napoleon," *Central European History* 30 no. 2 (1997): 187–220.

and modified Rousseauism purveyed by his tutor Friedrich Delbrueck.[24] After the royal family fled to exile on the North Sea coast of the eastern Prussian provinces and government leaders focused their energies on inner reform and regeneration of the body politic, new concerns arose about the crown prince's preparation for his future tasks as leader of a transformed Prussian-German community. The crown prince's consciousness of his calling became a matter of extreme interest not only to his parents but also to conflicting groups at the court and in higher levels of state administration. In this context the young prince developed an acute sense of his own inadequacies for the tasks facing him. It was not just a matter of being trained in the competencies necessary to fulfill his duties, but of being worthy of his calling. The construction of a satisfactory self-identity became central to his educational development; the discovery and construction of himself became the object of his lessons and ruminations.[25] Two groups with differing visions and pedagogical aims jockeyed for the right to mold the emotionally undisciplined, impulsive, imaginative heir to the throne into their leadership ideal. Traditional Prussian statists in the Frederician tradition, like the king himself and J. P. A. Ancillon, the Calvinist theologian, royal historiographer and political advisor who became the crown prince's primary tutor after 1810, sought to discipline the emotional and imaginative elements in the prince's character in order to fashion a sober, pragmatic, objective sense of reality and encourage rational control over the will. Ancillon was especially disturbed by the prince's tendency to use his aesthetic talents for the construction of imaginary medieval buildings, cities, and landscapes. "As the state is not a Gothic temple and a nation has never yet been governed by means of Romantic pictures, this eternal sketching is a true waste of time," Ancillon admonished his tutee in 1811, a part of a constant barrage of admonitions the prince received concerning his need to discipline himself for the historical tasks that lay ahead.[26]

It would be misleading to claim that the second group – the patriotic reformers led by Baron Stein, supported by Queen Luise, and consisting of a coterie of energetic young intellectuals and military leaders like Humboldt, Fichte, Niebuhr, Savigny and Schleiermacher, Scharnhorst, Boyen, Clausewitz, and Gneisenau – believed that the state could be

[24] Friedrich Delbrueck, *Die Jugend des Koenigs Friedrich Wilhelm IV. von Preussen und des Kaisers und Koenigs Wilhelm I.: Tagebuchblaetter ihres Erziehers Friedrich Delbrueck (1800–1809)*, ed. Georg Schuster (3 vols.; Berlin: 1907). See especially Schuster's introduction to vol. 1, pp. xli–xlv.

[25] The young Frederick William's constant self-examination and self-questioning is evident in the published documents of his relations with his tutors Delbrueck and Ancillon from his formative years. But this pattern persisted long after the prince had outgrown his tutors and remained a mark of his correspondence with family and friends for the rest of his life. See the comment in Blasius, *Friedrich Wilhelm IV*, pp. 41–47.

[26] From a letter of Ancillon to Prince Frederick William, July 1811, published in Paul Haake, *Johann Peter Friedrich Ancillon und Kronprinz Friedrich Wilhelm IV von Preussen* (Munich: 1920), p. 33.

governed according to some emotionally charged, medievalizing blueprint. Queen Luise and Baron Stein certainly supported attempts to encourage young Frederick William to discipline his emotions and fantasies and focus on his duties and obligations, but they were more interested in integrating the crown prince's aesthetic sensibilities and emotional energies into his public role than stifling them or confining them to the private realm. Clausewitz, Frederick William's military tutor between 1810 and 1812, for example, constantly portrayed political and military leadership as the channeling of collective enthusiasm and national feeling.[27] In the political vision of the reformist circle, the mobilization of subjective loyalties through identification with personal leadership and the symbols of historical community was as critical as the pragmatic pursuit of reasons of state.

The crown prince's letters and campaign diaries from 1813 to 1815 reveal that despite the influence of his father and Ancillon, his heart and mind had been won by the viewpoints of the party of patriotic reformers. Originally he had followed the lead of his tutor and father in his suspicions about the emergence of a nationalist fervor – even among some of his private tutors like Clausewitz – which seemed to place obedience to the cause of national liberation above loyalty to historically constituted authorities.[28] But when these enthusiasms were mobilized and controlled under royal authority after the king's "call" to his people in March 1813, the young prince became as zealous a German patriot as any of his generational peers among the volunteers. By July 1813, he was convinced that the military campaign was an expression and celebration of the national will.[29] The war was quickly transformed into a holy crusade, a battle of liberation from the chains of cultural domination by an evil foreign power, not just an attempt to restore Prussian autonomy and territorial integrity and reconstitute the traditional power balance in Europe. And the crown prince viewed this crusade for freedom as the uprising of an ethnic people against cultural repression. It was the divine enthusiasm of the *Volk* that made the difference. Young Frederick William also clearly imagined this *Volk* as the same ethno-cultural subject that had expressed itself in the aesthetic, religious, and political forms of the medieval empire. On Easter 1814, the young prince wished that the festival of Christ's resurrection could also be celebrated for the resurrection of "the old Holy German Empire."[30] He connected the rising of the people to a recovery of its shared memory of unity, freedom, and power in the past.

[27] Hans Rothfels, "Ein Brief von Clausewitz an den Kronprinzen Friedrich Wilhelm aus dem Jahre 1812," *Historische Zeitschrift* 121 (1920): 282–86; Peter Paret, *Clausewitz and the State* (New York: 1976), pp. 193–201.

[28] Paret, *Clausewitz*, p. 232.

[29] Haake, *Ancillon*, p. 63, quoting from the crown prince's diary.

[30] Crown prince to Princess Charlotte, April 7, 1814, in *Hohenzollernbriefe aus den Freiheitskriegen 1813–1815*, ed. Hermann Granier (Leipzig: 1913), p. 233.

When he left Berlin in spring 1813, the crown prince's imagination was filled with the medieval campaigns and crusades of Germanic warrior knights described in the fictions of Friedrich de la Motte-Fouqué. He carried Fouqué's just published *Der Zauberring* (The Magic Ring) with him, and often imagined his own present mission within the frame of the world Fouqué had constructed in the novel – as the crusade of a brotherhood of knights that saved the "Old Empire" from the forces of darkness and anarchy, and constructed a world of aesthetic grace and moral order against the threatening powers of disintegration.[31] Like so many of his contemporaries, the crown prince depended on Fouqué's feudal romances to recreate the world of the medieval German epics that was being unearthed by contemporary scholars in the various fragments and versions of the *Nibelungenlied*.[32] He entered the campaign of 1813 as if joining a medieval crusade against the satanic hordes of an evil Empire, and as a participant in a historical mission sanctified by the spirit of his recently deceased mother, who had first asked him to commit himself to the battle for German liberation in 1807[33] and whose grave he had visited with his father the night before his departure from Berlin. He interpreted the Allies' victories as a product of the common identification of princes and peoples with their German cultural essence and authentic historical traditions. Landscapes, castle ruins, folk traditions, literary allusions from the Nibelungen saga, and other Old German epics all helped to shape his enthusiasm for a view of liberation as a regeneration of the ethos of the Old German imperial period. The year 1813 was a year of constant exaltation for the crown prince. His emotions and fantasies became attached to the collective representations of the nationalist prophets (as with so many members of his generation, the war songs of 1813 remained inscribed in his memory) as well as to the conceptions of domestic reform purveyed by the group of patriotic reformers around Baron Stein. Throughout his life he continued to use the archaic spelling of Germany as *Teutschland* to designate the German ethno-cultural essence embodied in the institutions and aesthetic expressions of the old empire.[34] In 1818, when the architect Karl Friedrich Schinkel was constructing the Kreuzberg monument to the wars of liberation, the crown prince chose to have himself

[31] Frederick William's intense and lifelong interest in the fictionalized medieval worlds of Fouque's novels is documented in Frank-Lothar Kroll, *Friedrich Wilhelm IV. und das Staatsdenken der deutschen Romantik* (Berlin: 1990), pp. 46–53.

[32] Fouque had made his literary reputation in 1810 with a trilogy that "translated" the world of Siegfried and his exploits into modern German prose: *Der Held des Nordens: Heldenspiel in drei Teilen*. Frederick William's fascination with the stories of the Nibelungen saga is described in Gerd-H. Zuchold, "Friedrich Wilhelm IV. und das deutsche Mittelalter: Die Nibelungen. Die deutsche Heldensage als Bedeutungstraeger staatshistorischen Denkens des Monarchen," in Peter Krueger and Julius H. Schoeps, eds., *Der verkannte Monarch: Friedrich Wilhelm IV. in seiner Zeit* (Potsdam: 1997), pp. 159–80.

[33] Blasius, *Friedrich Wilhelm IV*, p. 34.

[34] Ernst Lewalter, *Friedrich Wilhelm IV*, p. 117.

represented in the medieval, or Old German, costume of a member of the people's militia (*Landwehr*).[35]

In the immediate aftermath of the campaigns, Frederick William's conceptions concerning the foundations of cultural and political authority were further developed in the areas of law and history under the tutelage of academic reformers like Niebuhr and Savigny. German *Volk* identity was construed as the guarantor of authentic solidarity among the enormous visible diversity of German-speaking central European peoples. In June 1815, as Savigny was preparing the prince for instruction in law and politics he reminded him of his historical calling:

> Before you, gracious prince, lies a career of a kind that has opened itself to only few individuals in the course of history, as the leader of a noble people in whom the most vital powers are developing toward new forms: You belong to this people and this age yourself through your vital receptivity to great and free ideas and through an animated religious sensibility. . . . Oh that God will continue to sustain in the people and in you this fresh, vital heart for such blessings, which alone make life worth living, and that you will eventually succeed in bringing into reality throughout the whole beloved fatherland the ideas which have so enchanted and absorbed you.[36]

Frederick William was convinced by his family and his tutors that an important historical mission lay ahead for him, and certainly, one dimension of this mission was to make real in the world the idea of a free and unified German *Volk* that he had absorbed from his experiences in 1813.

The first major international crisis of Frederick William's reign seemed to confirm that his vision of the unity of all Germans as members of a people with an innate national character and shared historical past was not just a nostalgic construction of an ephemeral war experience, but a window into a fundamental reality of his world. Responding to perceived humiliations at the hands of the Great Powers in the divisions of territories and responsibilities in the Middle East, political leaders in the French Chamber of Deputies played the chauvinist card and instigated a popular campaign to revise the agreements of 1815 and take back the Rhine as the natural French border. Popular sentiment in the principalities of the German Confederation, as expressed in newly proliferating organs of popular print culture, responded with its own wave of chauvinistic self-assertion. The expression of this collective Germanic identity against the French threats took many of the forms of the popular enthusiasms of 1813. Bellicose nationalistic songs composed for the occasion echoed the warrior songs and national hymns of 1813, and

[35] Michael Nungesser, *Das Denkmal auf dem Kreuzberg von Karl Friedrich Schinkel* (Berlin: 1987), pp. 56, 58.

[36] Savigny to Frederick William, June 19, 1815, cited in Blasius, *Friedrich Wilhelm*, pp. 71–72.

in fact instigated a popular revival of those earlier songs and hymns. The voluntary organization of patriotic singing societies, gymnastic clubs, and reading associations experienced a new upsurge. Public interest in preserving historical monuments of the medieval German Empire and in creating memorials for cultural, political, and military heroes whose significance was recognized by all Germans (Hermann the Cheruskan, Frederick Barbarossa, Gutenberg, Schiller) not only revived, but also spread to broader strata of the population.[37] Frederick William experienced this wave of nationalist fervor as a sign of the uncorrupted spontaneous solidarity of the German people, a solidarity cutting across differences in political institutions, religious confession, class, dialect, and regional economic interest. In this context, the role of leadership was to mobilize and articulate what was authentically present within the population. In January 1841 he wrote to Prince Metternich that the Rhine crisis had aroused "his old enthusiasm for the German cause":

> An exalting and Germanic sensibility is moving through all the people of the German Confederation in a way that hasn't been seen since 1813–1814. If this holy fire is nourished, then Germany will in fact stand taller and be mightier than ever, taller and mightier even than it was under the Ottonians and Hohenstaufens. The whole purpose of... this letter is merely this: to do everything to forge and shape this warm iron and to avoid anything that would cool it down, and to plead to Austria to throw its powerful support on the scales so that this unique exaltation of the felt unity of princes and peoples be put to good use for the immediate future and thus also for the more distant future of Germany.[38]

The rehabilitations of Arndt and Jahn thus rode on a temporary surge of what appeared to be a broad public sentiment of German ethno-cultural identity. Was the exoneration of the demagogues a sign that the new regime would commit itself more generally to a cultural policy that aimed at recovering German ethnicity as the core of Prussian citizenship?

During the first two years of his reign, Frederick William presented himself to the public, at least in one of his dimensions, as a "people's king" whose personal identity and cultural role was defined both by the liberation wars of 1813 and the historical narrative of German development that that national crusade brought to light. From his first public audience with the Berlin

[37] A general overview of the nationalist public responses to the French threat in 1840 can be found in Irmeline Veit-Brause, *Die deutsch-franzoesische Krise von 1840: Studien zur deutschen Einheitsbewegung* (Cologne: 1967); and Manfred Pueschner, "Die Rheinkrise von 1840/41 und die antifeudale Oppositionsbewegung," in *Bourgeiosie und buergerliche Umwaelzung in Deutschland 1789–1871*, ed. Helmut Bleiber (Berlin: 1977) 101–34. There is an extended analysis of the revival of nationalist political poetry in Lorie A. Vanchena, "The Rhine Crisis of 1840: Rheinlieder, German Nationalism, and the Masses," in *Searching for Common Ground: Diskurse zur deutschen Identitaet, 1750–1871*, ed. Nicholas Vaszonyi (Cologne: 2000), 239–51.

[38] Frederick William IV to Metternich, January 10, 1841, cited in Blasius, *Friedrich Wilhelm*, p. 97.

magistrates to receive their condolences after his father's death, Frederick William used his public appearances to remind his subjects of the symbiotic relation between princes and peoples that had marked the years between 1807 and 1815. When he made public his father's will and testament to the Prussian Council of Ministers, he tied his own role to that of the father who had called for the assistance of his people to throw out the French invader, and he asked his subjects to respond to his own "calls" with the same self-sacrificing devotion and solidarity they had shown in 1813.[39] To the Berlin magistrates he presented himself in his military tunic, emphasizing his position as the leader of the community in arms. His first policy decisions in the face of the French threat were directed toward strengthening the institutions of German military solidarity in the constitution of the Confederation.

Even the cultural policy of drawing the heroes of Germany's national awakening and liberation to Berlin was meant not so much as an adornment of the Prussian court with cultural celebrities as the creation of a center of national cultural revival. In 1842 the king created a new Order of Merit for heroes of the arts and sciences of peace to parallel the older Military Order of Merit established by Frederick the Great. The Order was to honor not only Prussian but especially German cultural giants (Thirty Knights of the Spirit), and even included a group of foreign honorees to express the European unity of the arts and sciences. Although critics soon noted that the list of honorees included a large number of Prussians, many of these Prussians – like Schelling, Jacob Grimm, Rueckert, Tieck, Peter Cornelius, Mendelssohn, and Giacomo Meyerbeer – had only recently been recruited to come to, or return to, Prussia by the new regime.[40] The point of the cultural politics of the new regime was not to make Berlin the most prestigious cultural capital among the German states but to make it the center of German national culture.

The desire to present himself as the ideal prince who embodied the collective will of his people, both the Prussian people under his immediate jurisdiction and the German people whose essential will he hoped to represent in a broader sense, was most dramatically articulated in the ceremonies of homage that were staged first in Koenigsberg (to receive the homage of the estates of East and West Prussia that were outside the boundaries of the German Confederation and the former German Empire) and then in

[39] *Reden seine Majestaet des Koenigs Friedrich Wilhelm des Vierten seit seiner Thronbesteigung*, 4th ed., ed. J. Killisch (Berlin: 1861), p. 6.

[40] *Orden Pour le Merite fuer Wissenschaften und Kuenste; Geschichte und Gegenwart. Eine Ausstellung der Deutschen Bibliothek Frankfurt am Main (Juni/Juli, 1977)*, esp. pp. 24–39. Also noteworthy was the ecumenical and cultural notion of German-ness applied in the original selections, including not only Catholics but also three prominent scions of Jewish families – Johann Jacoby from Koenigsberg, Mendelssohn, and Meyerbeer. The converted Jews Friedrich Juluis Stahl and August Neander also were favored in the academic politics of the new regime. For this regime it was still obviously not simply racial descent that defined one's German-ness.

Berlin (to receive a similar homage from the "German" estates of Prussia's six western provinces). In both cases the homage ceremonies were performed as medieval rituals, emphasizing the organization of subjects into corporate ranks representing the organic diversity of the communal body, and presenting the relation between subject and king as a relation of mutual trust and fidelity, as a subjective identification rather than an "external" contractual arrangement based on rights, responsibilities, and interests. At the same time, Frederick William used these occasions to step out of this stage setting and extemporaneously address large crowds about identification with a common past and commitment to a common cause. To the Koenigsberg audience on September 10, he proclaimed, "With us there is unity of the head and members of the body, of the prince and the people, the total glorious unity of all estates in striving toward a beautiful end, according to the general welfare, in sacred loyalty and authentic honor."[41] A little more than a month later in Berlin, he called upon the 60,000 assembled in the rain in the Lustgarten to join him in a collective task, which he defined in the following manner:

> I want above all to aspire to secure for the Fatherland the position to which it has been elevated with divine guidance through a history without parallel, in which Prussia has become the shield for the security and for the rights of Germany . . . If you can answer me, as I hope you can, either in your own name or in the name of those you represent: Nobles !, Burghers! and Countrymen [*Landsleute*] ! and the countless others gathered here within the sound of my voice – I ask you, will you help me and stand by me with heart and spirit, with word and deed and total commitment with the sacred loyalty of Germans and the even holier love of Christians, to maintain Prussia as it is . . . and how it must remain if it is not to decline? Will you help me and stand by me in order to develop those characteristic traits with more and more splendor through which Prussia with its mere fourteen million inhabitants must take its place alongside the Great Powers of the world? Namely: Honor, loyalty, striving toward justice and truth, striding forward with both the wisdom of age and the heroic strength of youth? Will you never abandon me in this task but endure with me through good as well as evil days? Oh then answer me with the clearest, most beautiful sound in our mother tongue, answer me with a convincing Yes.

After the echoes of the crowd's response had died away, the king accepted their answer as the confirmation of an alliance that bound prince and people together "indissolubly in mutual love and loyalty," as in a marriage vow.[42]

The rhetoric of subjective identification and mutual recognition set the tone during the first two years of Frederick William IV's reign. It informed his desire to change censorship regulations away from police surveillance and control to a more juridical and self-regulating system. He imagined

[41] *Reden*, p. 11. [42] *Ibid.*, pp. 18–19.

an authentic liberation of a responsible public opinion that would display itself as the disposition of a *Volk* ready to see its collective identity mirrored in leaders like Frederick William. And it produced that disconcerting confusion that allowed populists and social radicals like Bettina von Arnim and even (briefly) Heinrich Heine to imagine that the king might step forward as a real defender of the "people" against traditional privileges,[43] or liberal nationalists to imagine that Frederick saw himself as a kind of George Washington who would lead Germans into a new world in which "subjective" membership in the national historical culture would find its appropriate forms in equal membership in a liberal civil society and equal citizenship in a modern constitutional state. The self-presentation of the king as the leader of a Prussian government that would ground its legitimacy on an identification with the people and their collective German-ness reaching its climax in the fall of 1842 at the huge national festival that marked the laying of the cornerstone for the project to complete the Cologne cathedral. In the king's eyes the project to finally complete this greatest of the Gothic Old German monuments was clearly built on "the fraternal sentiment of all Germans, of all religious confessions." As he thought of this work of solidarity, the king confessed that his "eyes filled with tears of ecstasy." The portals that were about to arise according to the original medieval plan, he claimed, would be built by a spirit which was common to all Germans, by their German-ness, and would become the portals to a great and splendid age of German unity and strength. Everything inauthentic and un-German would be refused passage through these gates to the future. In the king's tear-filled eyes, the cathedral revealed the unity within differences of region, confession, and social estate, and merged rulers with the ruled, princes with peoples. The spirit of this building was the same spirit that had liberated Germany from the chains of French occupation twenty-nine years earlier and had responded to the renewed threats of 1840: "It is the spirit of German unity and power. Let it build! Let it perfect and complete itself!"[44] The cathedral project seemed a perfect example of the symbolic politics of Germanic identification, but it also made manifest, in the diversity of the public response to the meaning of the event, what had begun to emerge as the obvious limitations of this

[43] Bettina von Arnim's hope that the new king might bind his will to the popular will and become an authentic *Volkskoenig* was most clearly expressed in her 1843 publication *Dies Buch gehoert den Koenig*. For the ongoing relationship between the king and Bettina, see *"Die Welt umwaelzen denn darauf laeufts hinaus": Der Briefwechsel zwischen Bettina von Arnim und Friedrich Wilhelm IV*, edited by Ursula Pueschel with the collaboration of Leonore Krenzlin (2 vols.; Bielefeld: 2001). Heine's shifting positions are detailed in Gerd-H. Zuchold, "'Und eine talentvoller Koenig wird vergebens deklamieren!' Friedrich Wilhelm IV in der Sicht Heines," *Jahrbuch Preussischer Kulturbesitz*, 21 (1987): 403–16. As late as 1842, Heine was the vice president of the Paris chapter of the association to rebuild the Cologne cathedral and very interested in some of the populist aspects of the king's Old German enthusiasms. Like many other liberals in the early 1840s, he believed the king himself was more liberal than he was allowed to demonstrate publicly because of the power of the conservative cliques at court.

[44] *Reden*, p. 37.

type of cultural politics. The various cultural perspectives that found their common ground in a vision of shared German-ness soon fragmented as they articulated in word and ritual their divergent interpretations of this common ground.[45]

As the public response to the cathedral festival revealed only too obviously, when the people spoke they did not necessarily speak with a single voice. Differences were evident not just in proposals for institutionalizing procedures of national identification but also in views about the content of that identity. And such differences were also evident among the king's most intimate confidants and advisors. Moreover, in the king's consciousness, German ethno-cultural identity was itself a base for a complex layering of associations that filled the space of identification with a series of other overlapping and sometimes contradictory contents. Transforming the ethnic people into an ethical community of free subjects involved a remaking of the fraternal relations among children of a common ethno-linguistic mother into the hierarchical structures of a patriarchal household, turning the motherland into a fatherland.

ETHNIC FRATERNITY AND THE PATRIARCHAL ETHOS

By 1840 the dreams of a restored medieval empire had themselves become a historical memory. The problem of discovering German historical identity was not just an matter of restoring an authentic Germanic past, but of grasping the developmental process through which that past was joined to its own past and to the present. After 1815, Frederick William, like many of his compatriots who were disappointed by the failure of their exalted national sentiments of 1813 to attain institutional reality, sought out more universal historical perspectives in which the present moment could be situated within a pattern of progressive development that stretched from mankind's archaic beginnings to its future fulfillment. History was reconstructed to provide not so much an archive of useful myths of a better past that could be refurbished and brought into public consciousness, as the recollection of an ongoing process in which the individual could find a secure identity in the transition from past to future. The medieval empire was seen increasingly as a moment in a larger history that placed the present situation of Germany at a critical

[45] For detailed analyses of how the responses to the king's call for an exalted subjective identification transcending confessional and political differences continued to reveal the intractability of such differences, see Thomas Nipperdey, "Kirche und Nationaldenkmal. Der Koelner Dom in den 40er Jahren," in Werner Poels, ed., *Staat und Gesellschaft im politischen Wandel. Beitraege zur Geschichte der modernen Welt* (Stuttgart: 1979), pp. 175–202; and Leo Haupts, "Die Koelner Dombaufeste 1842–1880, zwischen kirchlicher, buergerlich-nationaler und dynastisch-hoefischer Selbstdarstellung," in Dieder Dueding, Peter Friedemann, and Paul Muench, eds., *Oeffentliche Kultur. Politische Feste in Deutschland von der Aufklaerung bis zum Ersten Weltkrieg* (Hamburg: 1988), pp. 191–211.

juncture within a narrative that had its origins in the beginnings of human civilization in India and the Middle East. After 1815 the king's fantasy life tended to wander into the exotic realms of pre-Christian Eastern cultures and focus on the early moments of the conversion of human culture to Christianity.[46] The turning points in this larger universal story, moreover, were imagined as events in the relationship between human finitude and its absolute ground, between man and God. In 1813 this sacred history of humanity's relations to the transcendent had been subordinated to, and often conflated with, the progressive, immanent evolution of the national idea. By 1816–17 the evolution of the national idea had been subordinated to the sacred history of "vertical" interventions by a transcendent power in the "horizontal" networks of human cultural development.

Frederick William's conception of historical development in the wake of the disappointments of 1815 was publicly expressed in the political stances he formulated as he began to participate actively in internal Prussian politics after 1817. His position was clearest in its negations. His first principle was an implacable opposition to all "revolutions," by which he meant any attempts to construct political communities on the basis of the private, "egoistic" interests of individuals operating in a historical vacuum and in defiance of their dependent position as creatures of a transcendent power. Revolution entailed rejection of all historically evolved, diversified associations and the leveling of socialized, organized differences into a uniformity of individual units. Although it was popular revolution that was feared most by the conservative regimes of central Europe after 1815 and that fueled the "persecution of the demagogues," Frederick William was as much concerned, especially before 1830, with bureaucratic revolution from above, an attitude that tended to place him in tense relationships with his own father and some of his father's chief ministers.

Frederick William's first public political stance was in opposition to the centralizing, liberal reforms of the Prussian State Chancellor Baron Karl August von Hardenberg.[47] Specifically, he resisted Hardenberg's plans to impose a uniform administrative structure on all of Prussia's eight provinces. By affirming the necessity of historical continuity and defending the traditional laws of local, corporate institutions as the only solid foundation for the evolution of responsible freedom and "organic" adaptive growth, however, Frederick William soon found himself caught in a principled ambiguity. Two different political groups shared his opposition to Hardenberg's plans.

[46] In 1816–17, Frederick William composed for his sister Charlotte an eighty-page novella entitled *Queen of Borneo*, which involved a voyage in time and space to the cultural descendants of an early Indian Christian church founded by St. Thomas, and a "re-Christianizing" of the East as part of a new universal Christian empire centered in post-Napoleonic Europe. The manuscript is summarized in Lewalter, *Friedrich Wilhelm IV*, pp. 157–65.

[47] Paul Bailleu, "Kronprinz Friedrich Wilhelm im Staendekampf, 1820," *Historische Zeitschrift* 87 (1901): 67–73.

Most obviously, his stance allied him with those reactionary aristocratic corporations who were primarily interested in protecting and extending their traditional rights in relation to both the bureaucratic state and the less privileged groups in society. When Frederick William took the side of Gustav Adolf von Rochow and the Brandenburg estates against the Hardenberg ministry, he was throwing his influence behind a concerted attempt by the Prussian landed aristocracy to maintain complete control of local administration, law courts, and ecclesiastical patronage and thus assert its dominion (*Herrschaft*) in all areas outside of the urban communes. Hardenberg's projected reform was not only centralizing but also liberalizing; it was aimed not only at the diversity of historical provinces but also at the patrimonial rights and privileges of the aristocratic and patrician castes within those provinces. By defending the principle of historical individuality as the basis for a self-governing Prussian and German community, Frederick William found himself on the side of a self-interested, socially divisive, "party."

In Frederick William's view, however, his stance as a foe of revolution was connected to his equally strong commitment, as a "friend of reformations," to the reformers of the Historical School, two of whose leaders, Niebuhr and Savigny, had been his personal tutors.[48] His opposition to the Hardenberg reforms, he felt, was in keeping with the position of the patriotic reform party that had rallied around Baron Stein after 1806. Like those reformers, Frederick William aimed not so much at a restoration of inherited rights and privileges but at the adaptation of the spirit of traditional forms to new conditions. In the early 1820s he sought out Stein's advice on the reconstitution of the provincial assemblies of estates, and he remained intensely loyal to his teachers Niebuhr and Savigny. Even as he defended the particular historical rights of provincial noble estates, he was concerned about how such rights might be integrated into a more universal structure of national estates and a "United Diet," and his vision for preserving the aristocratic estate as part of a diversified society involved various plans for modernizing the aristocracy so that it might once again conform to its "idea," which, he thought, tied public obligations to land ownership, and public service to patriarchal authority.

Throughout the 1820s both the bureaucratic reformers who identified themselves with the Stein faction in the Prussian administration (and their academic allies of the Historical School) and the old-Prussian aristocratic counterrevolutionaries (and their conservative academic allies) perceived the crown prince as a potential guarantor of their future influence and power. Stein was clearly excited by the possibility that a king committed to his reform program might soon rule in Prussia, and even contemplated returning

[48] In a letter to Ancillon, dated October 25, 1820 the crown prince noted, "I have told the King that as much as I am a friend of reformations, I am equally a foe of revolutions." Cited in Lewalter, *Friedrich Wilhelm IV*, p. 233.

to Berlin in 1824 to provide support for "this young, moral, religious, intelligent and noble prince" who seemed determined "not to create new institutions but to develop and utilize the historically existing elements, to perfect and modify and add to them what the progress of civilization has developed and perfected, and in this manner to fortify social institutions and avoid the shocks and conflicts which occur between old and new elements if they are not combined wisely."[49] Niebuhr and Savigny, as well as military reformers like Boyen, Gneisenau, and Clausewitz, also continued to look with hope toward a future in which the crown prince would replace his father, and the prince reciprocated this confidence. After Niebuhr returned from his diplomatic post in Rome in 1823, Frederick William made every effort to provide him with a permanent position as a political advisor in Berlin. The crown prince's attempts to maintain contacts with the Stein reformers in their years of political "exile" could be seen as an attempt to create a "shadow ministry" in preparation for the future, a ministry that included, besides Stein, the military reformers, and his teachers Niebuhr and Savigny, well-known members of the liberal wing of the reform party, such as Wilhelm and Alexander von Humboldt, Friedrich Schleiermacher, and the provincial governors Georg Vincke of Westphalia and Theodor von Schoen of East Prussia. The deaths of Stein, Niebuhr, Schleiermacher, Gneisenau, and Wilhelm von Humboldt in the early 1830s robbed this shadow ministry of much of its leadership, but it also paralleled an internal shift and clarification in Frederick William's relation to the process of "reformation" in the wake of the renewed threat of liberal-democratic revolution raised by the revolutions in France and Belgium, scattered German uprisings in the summer of 1830, and the popular agitation for parliamentary reform in Britain that preceded the passing of the Reform Bill of 1832.

What became clearer after 1830 was the crown prince's selective appropriation of those "new elements" that might be integrated into the inherited diversity of German and Prussian historical tradition through a careful process of adaptation. For the Prussian bureaucratic reformers of 1807–15, the "new" had two primary dimensions – the liberal and the communal, or populist. From the very beginning, Frederick William had been drawn to the reformers by their emphasis on mobilizing individual freedom for communal ends. The consequence of individual freedom was imagined as voluntary commitment to the collective purpose animating inherited institutions and dynastic leaders. That the creation of a community of subjective identification presupposed the real legal, social, and political emancipation of individual persons from political tutelage and social privilege, however, was never fully absorbed into the crown prince's conception of "reformation." Although he was not ready to undo the reforms that had provided

[49] Stein to Kapidistrias, November 22, 1822, in Freiherr vom und zum Stein, *Briefe und aemtliche Schriften*, eds. Erich Botzenhart and Walther Hubatsch (10 vols.; Stuttgart: 1957–74), vol. 6, pp. 582–83.

individual Prussians with freedom of occupation and domicile, and with formal equality under a common public law, he did not see a need for the extension of such reforms, except in the realm of capitalist development and free market relations in labor and property.[50] He was especially averse to any notion that communal solidarity could be established on the agreement of emancipated individuals without the prior discipline of identification with inherited authority and historical custom, and in 1830 he was ready to support the repression of any and all democratic liberal movements without compunction. In fact, in the wake of 1830, Frederick William's identification with a counterrevolutionary view of German historical community was so strong, his criticism of all liberal movements so vehement, that even his brothers and sisters thought he was becoming too "ultra" for the good of the established powers in Prussia.[51]

Although one could say that Frederick William's political and cultural formation took place under the aegis of the idea of historically minded reform, his particular conception of the inner structures of an authentic Prussian or German community tended to bring him, especially after 1830, within the compass of the counterrevolutionary conservatives. He had begun to develop a circle of friends among this group in the mid-1820s, and there were two aspects of their position that he found especially sympathetic. The first was the motion that the state should function as the guarantor of historical customary law, rather than as a source for centralizing legislation. What bound the proliferation of historically evolved concrete differences together was not public law, public administration, or public power, but a hierarchical structure of personal authorities and dependencies and a sentiment of solidarity based on mutual recognition of ethnic and spiritual unity. The state was thus perceived as the supreme earthly authority that used its organized force to sustain the legitimacy of historically inherited forms, as a guarantor of customary private rights rather than the source of public law. In the debates of the 1830s, this was a vision of the "state of laws" (*Rechtsstaat*) that differed radically from the liberal vision of the state as the public institution that guaranteed individual rights and established general laws for all of its members. Second, Frederick William was clearly drawn to the conservatives by their patriarchal ideology. Frederick William often described the symbiosis between prince and people as analogous to the relation between a father and his children; the position of the king within his realm was likened to that of the patriarch in his extended household. During the homage ceremonies of 1840, he constantly referred to the people

[50] It is important to point out that the decade of the 1840s witnessed extensive economic reforms in Prussia, which abolished many restrictions on labor mobility and capitalist investment, and were characterized by vigorous state-supported economic development in heavy industry. See especially Wolfgang Siemann, "Wirtschafts- und Gesellschaftsordnung zwischen Modernisierungsdruck und romantischer Vision," in Krueger and Schoeps, *Der Verkannte Monarch*, pp. 145–58.

[51] Blasius, *Friedrich Wilhelm IV*, pp. 78–79, citing unpublished family letters.

as "my people" and reserved the right to define unilaterally the terms of their mutual accord. As he wrote to Theodor von Schoen in 1840:

> the genuinely German [*Teutschen*] model for the style and duties of the prince is a paternal regime [*Vaeterliches Regiment*]. Because rulership is my paternal inheritance, my Patrimony, that is why I have a heart for my people; that is why I want and can guide children who have not yet reached majority, to discipline those who have been corrupted, but also to include those who have attained a responsible maturity within the administration of my domain and there defend them from the arrogance of bureaucratic domination.[52]

Restrictions on patriarchal authority came only from inherited tradition and from the guidance of an even higher patriarchal authority – a transcendent personal god. The prince served as the site of identification for his subjects because he was an embodiment of their integration into both the history of the people and the providential guidance of divine authority. Frederick William was eager to see his subjects express their wishes and needs in organs of public opinion as long as they did not infringe on the king's divinely instituted and historically legitimated authority as the paternal guardian of the law.

The king's loyalty to the tradition of patriarchal rule produced some interesting anomalies in his attitudes toward the past. Although he was opposed to the conception of the state as a centralized public order as defined by predecessors like Frederick the Great, or even his own father, he was deeply committed to continuity in the dynastic succession and always aware of his obligations as an heir of the Hohenzollern patrimony. Thus he enthusiastically endorsed various projects to celebrate the historical centenary of the accession to power of Frederick the Great in 1740. He was the sponsor of a new edition of the collected works (in French) of his predecessor and also supported plans to create a – suitably neoclassical – monument for Frederick the Great in Berlin. Yet Frederick the Great's francophile, rationalist, bureaucratic "enlightened despotism" represented everything that the new king opposed and tried to expunge from recent Prussian and German history. Similarly, the king was often torn between filial loyalty to his father's memory and disagreement with his father's legacy of centralizing bureaucratic government.

In his patriarchal conception of the relationship between prince and people, Frederick William echoed the theories – widely disseminated during the Restoration period by the works of the counterrevolutionary Swiss political theorist Carl Albrecht von Haller (1768–1854) – that the East Elbian Prussian Junkers used to defend their traditional dominion over the populations in

[52] Friedrich Wilhelm IV to Theodor von Schoen, December 26, 1840, cited in Hans Rothfels, *Theodor von Schoen, Friedrich Wilhelm IV, und die Revolution von 1848* (Halle: 1937), p. 124.

the rural counties.[53] Much like the king, these noble landlords tried to construct the populations of the areas under their jurisdiction as members of extended households. The peasants and agricultural laborers were like children who had not yet achieved their legal majority and were thus subjected to paternal authority and deserving of paternal care. In other ways as well, the king's conceptions of the appropriate structure for a German community had a distinct bias toward the perspectives of the traditional landed aristocracy or, more accurately, toward the ideology that had been generated by this aristocracy as a counterrevolutionary defensive position. For the composition of the corporate organization of the provincial diets, and ultimately of the United Diet, he proposed a balance of power that favored the landowners over the urban and rural communes. His image of the proper relations between ruler and ruled often seemed to derive from romanticized conceptions of the feudal relations between lords and vassals. In his own conceptions of the political organization of the German community as a revived empire, moreover, Frederick William envisioned himself as a member of the imperial aristocracy who owed ultimate, personal allegiance to the Habsburg emperor. Instead of the eighteenth-century model of a centralizing king battling against aristocratic and patrician corporate interests, the model of kingship assumed by Frederick William brought the king and the aristocratic corporations into alliance in a defense of patriarchal authority against popular revolution.

Frederick William's patriarchal conception of public authority and of the appropriate relation between prince and people was strikingly presented in the speech from the throne he presented in April 1847, when the representatives of the provincial estates finally met in Berlin in the much debated United Diet. Nothing in the world, he insisted, would persuade him to destroy the "natural" relationship between prince and people through the "conventional" and "constitutional" mechanisms of a written constitution. A mere piece of paper should never be allowed to interfere in the sacred trust that existed between the patriarchal monarch and his subjects. The *Volk* was here clearly defined as "my *Volk*," as members of his household, and the assertion of the will of the people was clearly reserved for the father: "My people," Frederick William proclaimed, "does not want co-government by representatives, the weakening of authority, the division of sovereignty, the dissolving of the full power of its kings who have provided the foundation of its history, its freedom, its welfare and are alone able to protect its most precious treasures, and will protect them God willing as before." To think of

[53] An excellent summary and analysis of Haller's positions is provided in Robert M. Berdahl, *The Politics of the Prussian Nobility. The Development of a Conservative Ideology 1770–1848* (Princeton N.J.: 1988), pp. 231–46. Like so many of the counterrevolutionary ideologists of the Restoration period, Haller was not himself a landed aristocrat but an urban intellectual and civil servant who had begun his career as a reformist liberal.

the estates as representatives of public opinion was "completely un-German [*vollkommen undeutsch*]." The authentic German expression of the identity of princes and peoples was the rule of a patriarchal monarch limited only by historical law and religious conscience.[54]

Although Frederick William clearly admired reformers like Stein and Schoen, and revered academic intellectuals from the Historical School like Niebuhr and Savigny as his mentors, his emotional associations with the leadership groups among aristocratic conservatives were equally powerful. His social relationships with members of his own generation tended to take place, especially after the mid 1820s, within these groups. In 1813, of course, it had been noble army officers, members of the general staff and their adjutants, young Prussian nobles like Anton von Stolberg, Karl von Groeben, Ludwig von Thile, Leopold von Gerlach, and Carl von Roeder, with whom the prince shared the exalting experience of liberation, not the student volunteers in the Luetzow Rangers or the conscripted townsmen and peasants in the newer military units of the *Landwehr*. It was to the country houses of such nobles that Frederick William went when he was on military maneuvers or simply touring the central and eastern Prussian provinces. These men were his daily companions as military and later civil adjutants. During the late 1820s and early 1830s, it often seemed to outside observers that this coterie of conservative nobles was synonymous with the prince's party. Yet even though many did find themselves in important positions in the regime after 1840, the perception of their exclusive control of the prince's inner circle was certainly misleading. In fact, Frederick William, both as crown prince and as king, tended to keep a certain distance from the most dogmatic and vociferous of the Prussian aristocratic conservatives. Although his own support of a corporate, patriarchal state often overlapped with the interests (and ideological commitments) of these conservatives, it was the principles and not the interests that were Frederick William's primary concern, and he wanted to join these principles to his vision of the historical mission of the German *Volk* and the supra-Prussian imperial politics that were tied to this mission, both of which were anathema to many old-Prussian conservatives.

Although Frederick William respected the critical acumen and journalistic talents of ultraconservative theorists like Ludwig von Gerlach, he ultimately found Gerlach's position too dogmatic and one-sided, and to Gerlach's great disappointment, only used his services as an occasional consultant on specific matters like the revision of the censorship and divorce laws. Despite his general agreement with Gerlach and other ultras on the patriarchal family as the exemplary social unit, on the importance of maintaining the ties between private rights – including the right of property – and social obligation, and on the bond between authority and responsibility,

54 Speech of April 11, 1847 in *Reden*, pp. 53–64.

Frederick William could not have agreed with Gerlach's claim that the ethno-cultural solidarity of a people was the pure creation of patriarchal political authority, that kings made peoples out of the populations they ruled, that it was dominion instituted by God and not the immanent powers of language that actually constituted ethno-cultural communities. In an article published in 1840, Gerlach fulminated against what he saw as the ultimately secularizing and pantheistic claims of nationalist politics:

> It is totally erroneous that authority or magistracy [*Obrigkeit*] is a product of the life of the people [*Volkslebens*]. From the father, from the Judge, from the King, have family, tribe and people been generated. Authority [*Obrigkeit*] established by God is the first, it builds the state as the community that is bound together by this authority, and the state, which in its beginnings already existed and operated in the tent of the patriarch, is what has first made the people into a people. The people grows out of the tribe, the tribe out of the family; but the father is prior to the family. It only exists through him and the father is a magistrate or authority, a king.[55]

Even Gerlach's enthusiasm for a restoration of the political forms of the medieval empire was fueled by an anti-*voelkisch* belief that it was the personal power of the emperors' rule that constituted the various peoples under their authority into the German nation, not the German nation that found its political articulation in the law and institutions of the empire.[56]

From among the Prussian conservatives, Frederick William chose as his most trusted adviser not one of the Prussian landed aristocrats of distinguished family and generations of loyal service, but an outsider. Beginning in the late 1820s and early 1830s, Frederick William's most intimate interlocutor and adviser within the conservative coterie was Joseph Maria von Radowitz (1797–1860), a Hessian and Catholic military officer of Hungarian descent who had only entered the Prussian service in 1823. As a Hessian officer in 1813, Radowitz had actually fought against the German patriots (and the Prussian army) in the Battle of the Nations at Leipzig, only switching to the allied side with his prince in 1814. Despite the experiential and confessional differences between Radowitz and the core of Prussian conservatives, he became an important theorist for their cause after 1830 and was able to present in a principled, convincing manner their vision of the ideal German state as an organism of historically differentiated corporate individualities kept in place by the characteristically German structure of patriarchal, personal authority. In the early 1830s, his ability to articulate

[55] Ludwig von Gerlach, "Staat und Kirche," *Evangelische Kirchenzeitung* (Berlin: 1841), no. 91, col. 722.

[56] Hans-Christ of Kraus, *Ernst Ludwig von Gerlach. Politisches Denken und Handeln eines preussischen altkonservativen* (2 vols.; Goettingen: 1994), vol. 1, pp. 234–37. This huge work supercedes much of the earlier relatively uncritical work on Gerlach and his circle, especially that of Hans-Joachim Schoeps. It does not supercede the acute analysis of social context and ideological connections in Berdahl, *Politics of the Prussian Nobility*.

the ideals of patriarchal authority and the *Staendesstaat* in clear and accessible ways made him an important figure in the public self-representation of the Prussian ultras, especially in their journal, *Berliner Politisches Wochenblatt* (Berlin Political Weekly).

What drew Frederick William to Radowitz, however, was not just the clarity of his enunciation of the principles of the "historical" and "positive" point of view but the emphasis that Radowitz gave to the German national element as the foundational identity that sustained the proliferation of difference as a difference within unity, and the ways in which he self-consciously construed the patriarchal ideal as a modern response to the disorienting social effects of liberal laws and unrestricted market economics. Radowitz clearly spoke to the king's desire to maintain the consciousness of German *Volk* identity as a critical component of the politics of conservative "reformation." In Radowitz's writing, the emphasis on social obligation in pre-revolutionary notions of estate and definitions of property was drawn into the debate about the social question of the "homeless" and destitute in modern society. The question of the relationship between the prince and the people was directly confronted with the people as a suffering and fragmented entity. Radowitz tied the defense of paternalism and corporatism to the prior reality of the *Volk* in very concrete ways and saw the justification of these principles in their ability to speak to the social and political issues raised by the movement for national identity and by the disintegration of traditional forms of communal bonding.

In the early 1840s, Frederick William used Radowitz as a special envoy whose tasks focused on strengthening German solidarity in the institutions of the Confederation and in military defense arrangements among the German states. Like Frederick William, Radowitz was convinced that the public response to the French threats in 1840 revealed that a "desire for absolute community throbbed through the whole people," as it had in 1813.[57] For Radowitz, this subjective sentiment of community among Germans was needed to hold the inheritance of differentiated, individualized German existence together. The princes and their governments, in order to survive, would have to join the people as participants in a national identity:

> While in the People [*Volk*] itself the feeling of community has increased constantly in vitality since 1813, and the idea of an inner bond based on passion and joy, on the consciousness of the splendors and world historical significance of the German ethnic community [*des deutschen Stammes*] has set so many hearts glowing, such sentiments have found little entry in the Cabinets of government... This narrow-hearted particularism stands in incisive contradiction to the feelings and the needs of the nation, which,

[57] Joseph Maria von Radowitz, "Zur Geschichte meines Lebens," in Paul Hassel, *Joseph Maria von Radowitz. Vol. I: 1797–1848* (Berlin: 1905), p. 80.

despite confessional division and constitutional confusion has perhaps never yearned more for unity and community.[58]

Radowitz's advice to the king in 1840 was that Prussia should establish its moral legitimacy as a state by asserting itself as the leader of the movement for a "people's community." It should strengthen the institutions that gave visible structure to invisible sentiments of solidarity, like the Confederation and the Economic Union (*Zollverein*) that had been established in 1834, and it should work assiduously to create new "communal institutions of all kinds," for "even if they produce no material rewards, the feeling of community is completely inestimable." "Why should the striving for an ideal unification of Germany," he asked, "which has become such an effective weapon in the hands of the revolutionary party, not become such a weapon in the service of Justice?"[59]

Radowitz thus was at one with the king in his belief that the nurturing of German cultural identification from "above" was an essential component in producing the kind of ethical community that would carry the spirit of 1813 forward into the future. But the ways in which Radowitz and his king understood the construction of an ethical community out of an ethnic population had changed a great deal since 1813. Most obviously, this shift was displayed in their tendency to see the freedom of the people and the identity that bound a people together expressed and confirmed in relations of obedience; obedience, first of all, to constituted authorities, kings and princes, who represented the people's identity to them as the identity of a personality or collective subject, and, second, obedience to the inheritance of positive law that organized individual lives according to their appropriate station, or standing, in the sociocultural organism. But this political tilt toward obedience, hierarchy, and authority, which gained more prominence after the apparent dangers revealed by the European revolutions of 1830, was inextricably connected to another dimension, the move toward an evangelical, neo-orthodox pietism in religious consciousness and the search more generally for a transcendent foundation for historical norms and meanings. In the wake of the disillusionment and disappointments after 1815, the historical emergence of a national ethical community became inextricably connected to the relations not only between people and state, but also between state and church. In order to understand the identity politics of the Prussian regime after 1840, one cannot ignore the role of religious and ecclesiastical politics. For both Frederick William and Radowitz, understanding the "immanent" identification through voluntary mutual recognition of a common history among members of an ethnic population was impossible

58 *Ibid.*, pp. 88–89.

59 "Das Verhaeltnis Preussens zum deutschen Bunde" (1840), in Joseph von Radowitz, *Ausgewaehlte Schriften und Reden*, ed. Friedrich Meinecke (Munich: 1922), pp. 2–3.

without an historical understanding of the relation between the immanent and transcendent dimensions in human relations.

EARTHLY COMMUNITIES AND THE TRANSCENDENT FATHER: THE RELIGIOUS DIMENSION IN HISTORICIZING IDENTITY

Religious commitments and loyalties determined many of Frederick William's personal associations because they were so central to his perception of his historical role. It was not only that he was a deeply religious person. He was also convinced that religious sentiments and religious institutions were the foundation of political and cultural communities. A powerful desire to believe that his own identity as the heir to the Prussian throne was sustained by transcendent patriarchal authority, that his dynastic authority and obligations were divinely ordained, was as central to his personality as the belief that his vocation was to be an "organ" of the German people in their historical development toward cultural solidarity and political unity. The cultural policies of his regime were an expression of his personal project to seek self-identity through both integration into immanent ethno-cultural history and submission to the authority of a transcendent God. The particular fashion in which Frederick William understood the relationship between religious feeling and the subjective identification of individuals as members of earthly communities, both the ethnic communities of peoples and the ethical communities of states, emerged gradually out of his experience of both exalting fusion and disillusioning fragmentation in the years 1813–15.

At the time the crown prince experienced the national enthusiasms of the campaigns of 1813–14, he was already an intensely religious, if not a publicly pious person. The constant criticism from tutors, parents and chaplains of his inability to discipline his impulses and imagination had produced an exaggerated sense of guilt and a turn to religion as a consolation for, escape from, and a resource in the constant battle with himself. In April 1813 he replied angrily to his tutor Ancillon's suggestion that he should take religion more seriously as an ally in his struggle for self-discipline:

> I do not want to say any more about this except that perhaps in no one is religious faith both more secure and more hidden than in me. For I have felt the effect of the spirit of God in me in a powerful way: I have experienced the value of fervent prayer and I know what it means to need salvation and sanctification and also what an infinite comfort and truly, holy blessed joy faith provides.[60]

During the 1813 campaign, however, Frederick William's personal piety became intertwined with his public commitments and historical vision. He became convinced that he had experienced the working of the divine spirit

[60] Cited in Haake, *Ancillon*, pp. 30–31.

not only in his individual soul but also in the historical actions of the German people acting as instruments of divine judgment in their triumph over the "satanic" hordes of Napoleon. For the young crown prince, the 1813 campaign combined the religious and political dimensions of a crusade. Dreams of recreating the medieval German Empire in accordance with fictional fantasies were fused with apocalyptic notions of the coming of the perfected spiritual community. The Holy Roman Empire of the German Nation and the Kingdom of God merged in a vision of the immanent fulfillment of all redemptive desires. Frederick William's mature religious commitments evolved out of his struggle with the collapse of these millenarian dreams after 1815.[61]

The postwar religious development of the Prussian crown prince can be broken down into two phases. In the years immediately after 1815, he became seriously involved in the pietistic revival, or "awakening," that was so prevalent among Europe's social and political elites during the Restoration period, and was particularly influential in the formation of a conservative ideology of household and estate autonomy among the old Prussian landowning aristocracy.[62] Through some of his relatives at the court and some of his wartime aristocratic comrades, he made contacts with Bible study and prayer groups, as well as with some of the charismatic revivalist preachers whose popularity increased dramatically after 1815. A marked focus on direct emotional encounter with the atoning sacrifice of Christ characterized this religiosity. Those who had recognized the absolute sinfulness of their egocentrism and surrendered without reserve to the redemptive power of divine love revealed in the biblical "word" considered themselves a group apart, an invisible church of born-again Christians separated from the merely nominal Christians who constituted the majority of members in the visible state churches. Confessional differences as well as differences in social standing were downplayed in relation to the identity of a Christian community grounded on sincerity of belief and intense commitment to the life of discipleship. On the other hand, the community of piety also presented itself as a collective submission to a transcendent father in ways that appeared

[61] On the fusion of religious and political metaphors in 1813–14, see Thomas Nipperdey, "Kirche als Nationaldenkmal. Die Plaene von 1815," in Lucius Grisenbach and Konrad Renger, eds., *Festschrift fuer Otto von Simson zum 65. Geburtstag* (Berlin: 1977), 412–31, and Dietmar Klenke, "Nationalkriegerisches Gemeinschaftsideal als politische Religion," *Historische Zeitschrift* 260 no. 2 (1995): 395–448.

[62] There is a good summary of the symbiotic relations between pietist revival and Prussian conservatism in Christopher M. Clark, "The Politics of Revival: Pietists, Aristocrats and the State Church in Early Nineteenth-Century Prussia," in Larry Eugene Jones and James Retallack, eds., *Between Reform, Reaction, and Resistance: Studies in the History of German Conservatism from 1789 to 1945* (Providence, R.I: 1993), pp. 31–60. See also Peter Maser, *Hans Ernst von Kottwitz: Studien zur Erweckungssbewegung des fruehen Jahrhunderts in Schlesien und Berlin* (Goettingen: 1990), pp. 124–88, which describes the alliance between pious academics and pious aristocrats in various organizations and cultural campaigns in the 1820s and 1830s.

to confirm and internalize the patriarchal, household social models of the conservatives. During the early 1820s, Frederick William felt comfortable referring to the Protestant Chancellor Hardenberg as a non-Christian and at the same time experienced no difficulty in finding trusted friends, and even a marriage partner, among suitably pious Roman Catholics.[63]

The forms of religious experience and practice that shaped Frederick William in the Restoration period remained with him for the rest of his life. Bible studies and prayer meetings, emphasis on a personal inward relationship to Christ rather than conformity to correct doctrine, constant self-examination, confession of sinfulness and guilt, rituals of repentance, dedication to sanctified living – these continued as prominent dimensions of his religious identity through the 1830s and 1840s. For many observers, it was this kind of evangelical piety that seemed most striking among the new men Frederick William gathered around him to help set Prussia on a new course after 1840. Two of the patriotic aristocrats who fought for the restoration of the Holy Roman Empire in 1813 and then became staunch Christian fundamentalists in the postwar years, General Ludwig von Thile and Count Anton von Stolberg-Wernigerode, held high cabinet posts in his government and gave a tone of demonstrative piety to the court.[64]

The piety of the political insiders in the 1840s, however, had taken on a distinctive tone and was no longer synonymous with the piety of the religious awakening of the postwar period. The 1820s and 1830s had brought at least two major shifts in emphasis and focus among the new conservative cohort of the religiously "reborn." In theology, the shift was from a feeling of absolute dependence on the infinite powers of transcendent divinity and inner transformation through the powers of divine love to a concern for the objective foundations of correct belief and literal obedience to the statutes of divine revelation. In ecclesiology, the shift was from a focus on spiritual communion among the saved to an attempt to rebuild the visible church as a purified, militant, authoritative institution with the power to discipline its members and exclude deviants. The second phase of Frederick William's

[63] Lewalter, *Friedrich Wilhelm IV*, pp. 257–69. For Friedrich Wilhelm's piety, see also Joachim Mehlhausen, "Friedrich Wilhelm IV. Eine Laientheologe auf dem preussischen Koenigsthron," in Henning Schroeder and Gerhard Mueller, eds., *Vom Amt des Laien in Kirche und Theologie* (Berlin: 1982), pp. 185–214. An overview of the king's views on the church and ecclesiastical reform, from the point of view of their implications for the Christian ecumenical tradition, can be found in Kurt Schmidt-Clausen, *Vorweggenommene Einheit. Die Gruendung des Bistums Jerusalem im Jahre 1844* (Hamburg and Berlin: 1965), pp. 221–367. See also Hanns Christof Brennecke, "Eine heilige apostolische Kirche: Das Program Friedrich Wilhelms IV. von Preussen zur Reform der Kirche," *Berliner Theologische Zeitschrift* 4 (1987): 231–51; and Hans J. Hillerbrand, "'Ich und mein Haus, Wir wollen dem Herrn dienen': Friedrich Wilhelm IV zwischen Froemmigkeit und Staatsraeson," in *Der Verkannte Monarch*, pp. 23–33.

[64] There is a brief description of the "ministerial pietists" in Barclay, *Frederick William IV*, pp. 68–69. See also Otto Stolberg-Wernigerode, *Anton Graf zu Stolberg-Wernigerode: Ein Freund and Ratgeber Koenig Friedrich Wilhelms IV* (Munich: 1926).

religious evolution after 1815 was marked by his participation in these shifts. In his struggle to establish his own identity, gain the trust of his father, and fulfill what he saw as the mission given to him by his mother on her deathbed, Frederick William found an anchor not only in the *Volk*, but also in the authority of the divine truth, which he appropriated as a born-again Christian and represented as the administrative head, or prince-bishop (*Primas*), of the Protestant Church in Prussia. The most grandiose plans for architectural display that Frederick William considered during the 1840s involved the building of a massive basilica in the center of Berlin that would not so much embody the identity of a liberated German nation as the world-historical triumph of Protestant Christianity.

The plans for the Berlin cathedral went back to the king's collaborations with the architect Karl Friedrich Schinkel in the 1820s and 1830s. After 1815, like Schinkel, Frederick William moved away from the neo-Gothic enthusiasms that marked his period of Romantic nationalism and one-sided commitment to the idea of German ethno-cultural identity. The neo-Gothic remained an important, but limited element in the ideal worlds he had learned to articulate through architectural sketching since his early teenage years. The commitment to the completion of the Cologne cathedral according to its original medieval plan displayed this dimension of the king's historical perceptions. But just a few months after the Cologne ceremonies, in January 1842, Frederick William called together a commission to supervise the building of a different kind of cathedral in Berlin. This church, he insisted, was not meant simply to fulfill the function of a church for Protestant parishioners in central Berlin or at the court. He was building it "as the *Primas* of Protestantism for the Protestant church of Germany, and as I have expressed my hope to complete the Cologne cathedral, I should be given the right also to plan, if not to realize, a monumental structure for my own church."[65]

The style the king chose for this representation of the present moment in the sacred history of the relationship between the divine father and his human creatures was a late-antique, early Christian basilica in the form he imagined as authentic to the era of the first Christian emperor, Constantine, and that conformed to his idea of the original apostolic church. Throughout the 1820s and again in the mid-1830s, Frederick William engaged Schinkel as an interlocutor and adviser in architectural fantasizing about vast "apostolic" basilicas both in Berlin, as a representation of the culmination of Christian ecclesiastical history, and in Jerusalem, as an historical recreation of the original mother church at the site of Christ's death and resurrection.[66]

65 Cited in Carl-Wolfgang Schuemann, *Der Berliner Dom im 19.Jahrhundert* (Berlin: 1980), p. 62.

66 Cornelius Steckner, "Friedrich Wilhelm IV, Karl Friedrich Schinkel, Wilhelm Stier und das Projekt einer Protestantischen *Mater Ecclesiarum*," in Otto Buesch, ed., *Friedrich Wilhelm IV. in seiner Zeit* (Berlin: 1987), pp. 232–55. For the plans for a basilica in Jerusalem, see Christiane Schuetz, *Preussen in*

Frederick William was convinced that the early Christian basilica was the authentic spatial form for the apostolic church. It was a form that gave shape to the principle that transcendent paternal authority was the dominant factor in producing a redeemed, ethical community out of the ethnic substance of the *Volk*. It gave physical visibility to a conception of the church as ruled by God as father and Christ as lord. The rejection of Gothic and even Romanesque vaulted ceilings and the return to the classical architrave, as well as the tendency to remove the altar from the congregational space, which Frederick William saw as characteristic of old Christian basilica architecture, downplayed earthly yearning and striving for redemption and the principle of mediation between the divine and the human, focusing instead on dependent finitude and submission to patriarchal authority. The Byzantine mosaics and other ecclesiastical decoration so admired by the king reinforced this theological (and political) message. His ideal church elevated the bishop and the king over the assembled congregation and displayed ethical community as subordination to the power of the father. The early Christian basilica was a counterpoint, and in Frederick William's eyes an appropriate corrective, to the Gothic cathedral and its articulation of the church as an earthly organism striving toward the divine. His planned Berlin cathedral would have dominated the Lustgarten at the center of the city, overwhelming the existing architectural representations of the dynasty, the military, and aesthetic education, and providing a culmination point for the triumphal avenue Unter den Linden[67] (Figure 1).

Frederick William did not claim to be a theologian, and he rarely expressed theological opinions in public or on paper. His positions can be discerned indirectly and negatively from the manner in which he intervened in the policy initiatives of the *Kultusministerium* regarding the regulation of the theology taught at state universities or propagated in the Prussion Evangelical Church. By the late 1820s, it had become clear that the crown prince supported a group of "awakened" evangelical theologians, particularly Ernst Wilhelm Hengstenberg in Berlin and August Tholuck at Halle, who were engaged in a concerted attempt to reassert the total "otherness" of God as a free, transcendent personality, and the literal truthfulness of the Bible as divine revelation. Frederick William supported Hengstenberg's *Evangelische Kirchenzeitung*, which was published by this neo-orthodox academic coterie

Jerusalem (1800–1861): Karl Friedrich Schinkel's Entwuerf einer Grabkirche und die Jerusalemsplaene Friedrich Wilhelms IV (Berlin: 1988), especially pp. 76–88.

67 For a general overview of how the king's cultural projects evolved through his architectural sketching, see Ludwig Dehio, *Friedrich Wilhelm IV von Preussen: Ein Baukuenstler der Romantik* (Berlin: 1961). For details of the discussions of the 1840s, see Schuemann, Der Berliner *Dom*, pp. 51–83; and Karl-Heinz Klingenburg, "Der Koenig als Architekt," *Der verkannte Monarch*, pp. 219–33. The king's Byzantine tastes in architecture and architectural decoration are described in Gerd-H. Zuchold, "Friedrich Wilhelm IV. und die Byzanzrezeption in der preussischen Baukunst," in Buesch, ed., *Friedrich Wilhelm IV in seiner Zeit*, pp. 205–31.

Fig. 1. Frederick William IV's visions of a Protestant basilica in the Lustgarten at the center of Berlin. *Top:* Sketch from the mid-1820s. *Bottom:* Rendering for the king by Friedrich August Stueler in 1842. Reproduction permission: Bildarchiv Preussischer Kulturbesitz.

after 1827, and he intervened on their behalf on issues of academic appointments and promotions. He committed himself to the task of cleansing university theological faculties of rationalists, liberals and pantheists – that is, of all proponents of "immanent" interpretations of the sacred. In the 1830s he became especially interested in the struggle against Hegelian influence, which in his view combined the errors of both rationalism and pantheism. Here was the true face of the theological and cultural enemy: God reduced from a free, personal creator to the necessary structures of rational thought, transcendent revelation reduced to the illusions of human self-projection.

During the 1820s and 1830s, Frederick William also displayed his sympathy for a decentralized congregational Christianity that emerged from the religious experience of the people and resisted centralized bureaucratic control by the state church. In Prussia the official union of the two Protestant confessions (Calvinist and Lutheran) in 1817 and the attempt to impose a unified liturgy on the state church from 1821 onward had led to considerable tension between some local congregations and state authorities. The crown prince's choice in these battles was to sympathize with the resisters and to counsel conciliatory policies that would allow for greater diversity of congregational worship under the umbrella of the state church. When Frederick William came to power, one of his first accomplishments was a series of agreements that made peace among the warring Protestant factions as well as between the state authorities and the Catholic Church. The principle at work here was similar to that informing the conception of a "people's church" as it had been formulated by Schleiermacher – that church organization and liturgical practice would emerge from the individuated religious experiences of particular historical groups. The unity of the church should be a unity of feeling and faith emerging from diversity rather than a uniformity of worship and doctrine imposed from above.

Throughout his tenure as crown prince, however, Frederick William was concerned that the vitality of diversified congregations based on concrete religious experiences might develop into the divisive fragmentation of sectarian movements with distorted conceptions of the "true" nature of the Christian church. The pressing need of the moment as he saw it was not so much a new religious revival as a reform of religious institutions that would allow the church to nourish and mobilize the spontaneous religious energies in the life of the *Volk* and produce an ethical or spiritual community among ethnic Germans. But in order to take on this task, the church needed to be liberated from the heavy hand of bureaucratic state interference. Only a "free" church could recreate the connection to transcendent authority on which the creation of ethical community was dependent.

The starting point of Frederick William's ecclesiastical reform proposals was his belief that the existing system within German Protestant principalities had merged church governance into state administration, destroying the church as a "self-conscious and autonomous corporation" and reducing it to "malleable dough" in the hands of the territorial prince and his servants.[68] The result of this development was the manifest failure of the contemporary church to take the lead in transforming ethnic community into spiritual identity, its unwillingness to take the initiative in dealing with the hegemonic ambitions of rival faiths, and its inability to provide spiritual and physical care for the homeless "masses" and establish ethical standards in the areas of sexuality and marriage. Despite the demonstrated historical failures of the existing Protestant Church Constitution and the corruption of its leadership by the teachings of rationalism and pantheism, the majority of German Protestant Christians continued to support it, partly out of patriotic sentiment, but also because of the absence of viable alternatives.

Frederick William shared common misgivings in Germany about the presbyterial or episcopal alternatives to the German institutions of state-appointed councils (consistories) and provincial supervisors (superintendants). The presbyterial constitution in its current form, he felt, used the principles of liberal humanism to subvert divine authority within the church. The opinions of individual members of the congregation were elevated to the level of spiritual authority, and church government tended, as in contemporary political liberalism, toward the "dominion of the vulgar herd [*Poebelherrschaft*]." The presbyterial party within the church was numerically strong only because it was eagerly embraced by "the whole gang" of the "unbelieving, half-believing and falsely believing" that hoped to impose its humanist positions on the church as a whole. Frederick William was more sympathetic to the episcopal party, which wished to restore the dignity and authority of a church ruled internally by anointed bishops, but he criticized its unwillingness to come to terms with the historical failures of episcopalianism – its tendency to produce tyrannical and divisive church governments in earlier periods and other cultures.[69]

Frederick William's own reflection on the question of a proper ecclesiastical constitution for the Protestant Church went back to the 1820s. At first, inspired by the difficulties of instituting the Evangelical Union that was pushed so hard by his father, he had tried to construct a third form of church constitution that would reconcile the diverse traditions of the Calvinist and Lutheran churches. He threw himself into a study of church history, investigated the institutions of the English and Swedish, established Protestant churches as well as that of the Church of the Brethren, and meditated on the early history of the church as described in the New Testament. What had begun as a "play of fancy" became a "serious life's purpose." After years of discouragement, he experienced a breakthrough: "Then, like the sun

[68] "Zwei Aufsaetze Koenig Friedrich Wilhelms IV." (1845–46), appendices 7 and 8 to Ernst Ludwig von Gerlach, *Aufzeichnungen aus seinem Leben und Wirken 1795–1877*, ed. Jakob von Gerlach (2 vols.; Schwerin, 1903), vol. 2, p. 449.

[69] *Ibid.*, pp. 444–45.

it appeared to me, the only possible and genuinely necessary solution had been there for 1800 years, as the legacy of the apostles. One just had to build again as they had built then."[70] The "discovery" of the apostolic solution to the question of church reform filled the crown prince with an intense sense of his personal mission as church reformer. "I am aflame and fire up when I speak of the apostolic church," he claimed in 1845.[71] The genuine form of spiritual community, the institutional structure of the Kingdom of God as lived within the restrictions of earthly existence, was not to be found in a synthesis of existing fragments but in a return to the absolute model contained in the origin. Regeneration must be based on a return to the moment of generation, which meant reestablishing the connection to the moment of transcendent connection – the act of divine revelation. The spiritual revival of the sixteenth-century Reformation had also claimed to return to the purity of the apostolic faith. Now was the time to complete that Reformation and rebuild the church according to the apostolic model. The pure church, the church as it should be, Frederick William claimed, was not just "a matter of feeling," an invisible community of like-minded saints, but a historical "fact" (*Thatsache*), a real corporate institution founded by the apostles.[72] The implications that the king derived from his personal revelation of the absolute authority of the apostolic model were complex and presented in a number of slightly different versions between 1840 and 1847. In all of these versions, however, he focused his discussion on three general principles.

First, he insisted repeatedly that the original Christian church constitution was a "constitution of churches"; that is, it was the organization of a network of churches, each of which was "an independent whole, a unity, not subordinated to any other."[73] The integration of churches into the Christian church was not a result of bureaucratic domination but grew from a common recognition of a shared transcendent origin and head, Jesus Christ. Vitality was to be restored through the activities of self-governing units of manageable size in which all authority remained personal. To build the church by building churches implied for Frederick William a return to the missionary spirit and activism of the early church, producing a constant proliferation of new congregations until they covered the globe.

Despite decentralized differentiation among individual church units, the king clearly believed that all churches should have homologous internal structures. The churches were autonomous not only because their spiritual essence originated in a transcendent power that had priority over any worldly power, but also because, as institutionalized corporate entities, they received their constitutional form through the authority of divine revelation. A genuinely apostolic church "could never be absorbed by the state," not

70 Ranke, "Aus den Briefen," p. 375. 71 "Zwei Aufsaetze," p. 482. 72 *Ibid.*, p. 477.

73 Ranke, "Aus den Briefen," p. 375.

even in its external, visible form.[74] The independence of the church from the state thus had a twofold basis. The church was created in direct response to a command from the transcendent father. Its origins were independent of the existence of any particular historical state. The apostolic church was thus also universal. The communal consciousness that resulted from relations structured according to laws received from beyond the immanent realm of terrestrial associations could operate as a critical spirit, a higher conscience within the state.

The institutional link that tied the churches to each other and to their transcendent origin as members of one church was the office of supervisor (*Vorsteher*), or bishop. This supervisor was not a servant of the state, but a leader and representative of the church. The king's insistence on the apostolic origins of this episcopal structure was the second major principle in his reform proposals. Although the bishop was chosen from within the local church and governed in concert with its members, he also expressed the origins of the church's corporate existence in a transcendent source. Confirmation by the bishop of another church legitimated a *Vorsteher's* authority. He thus received his commission from a church imagined as a temporal totality reaching back in legitimate succession to the first bishops confirmed by Christ's original apostles. Frederick William was clearly concerned that the bishop be viewed as the holder of an office whose authority did not derive from the expressed will of the congregation alone, but from an act of divine ordination, passed on through historical succession. Unlike the proponents of the episcopal party, however, he insisted on the integration of the episcopal office into the general constitutional structure of offices and orders that defined the church. *Church*, rather than *bishop*, was the prior term, the name that defined the constitutional structure. Bishops were drawn from churches and were confirmed by churches. Bishops did not make churches.

The articulation of the ideal Christian community into a functionally differentiated system of offices, vocations, and orders was the third major theme in the king's vision of a regenerated apostolic church. The liberation of the church from state control would, he imagined, produce an explosive proliferation of voluntary organizations. Christian love, the submission of self to the divine spirit at work in the religious community, would find its appropriate shape in a world of religious orders analogous to the lay orders of the medieval church. The first order, the elders, was composed of all who had been called to the office of ministering, teaching, and preaching the Word, administering the sacraments, and supervising spiritual discipline. The bishop was called as the first among equals from this order, which in each congregation and church constituted the church council or presbytery. Although the king conceived of this presbytery as primarily a council of pastors, theologians, and other clergymen, he also tried to break down

[74] "Zwei Aufsaetze," p. 462.

the barrier between clergy and laity by insisting that the apostolic church occasionally call lay people into this order. The second order in the church was the office of the deaconate, which sanctified service for others (rejected by pagans as a form of slavery) as a vocation for "free human beings."[75] This office had atrophied in the modern Protestant church, but the king cherished great hopes for its revival. As the major lay order, the deaconate would administer the voluntary charitable activity directed toward the poor, the homeless, and the sick. Not only would the deaconate involve many congregational members, including women, in voluntary church activity, but it would also provide a moral and personal solution to the "social problem" and absolve the state bureaucracies of their obligation to guarantee the welfare of the disadvantaged under the conditions of market capitalism. Creation of voluntary Christian philanthropic orders was one of Frederick William's pet projects and revealed that the central thrust of his response to the social problems of modernization was moral and cultural "reformation."

The third order of the organic corporate structure of the apostolic church was the congregation per se (the *Gemeinde*). The king used this term not to refer to the actual totality of baptized members, but to the aggregate of male heads of families or households. The Christian church, like the ideal German society, was a patriarchal universe built up from household units. The strong patriarchal focus of the king's reform plans emerged strikingly at this point. Fathers were considered to be the spiritual heads of extended families (including servants and all kin living within the household) and the legitimate representatives of these population units within the church. Frederick William's keen interests in making divorce much more difficult was connected to his belief that regenerating communal ethics required recreating households as paternalistic societies in which the father's privileges were matched by his responsibilities in caring for the welfare of the household members.

Frederick William imagined his church as a church unified by the transformed subjectivities of its members rather than by uniformity of doctrine or external organization. It was this inner transformation, the identification of the individual with revealed truth through submission to the will of the heavenly father, that provided the transfiguring power that turned ethnic Germans into ethical Germans. This power ultimately derived from a transcendent authority outside the immanent development of the ethno-cultural community. At the same time, Frederick William imagined the church working within the ethno-cultural community as an active, transforming power in its own right. His belief in the separation of church and state was not connected to a concept of the absolute separation of sacred and secular spheres. The subjective dimension of existence was nourished in the community of the church through a relationship to the transcendent power

[75] *Ibid.*, p. 463.

that guided all immanent relationships. The church had to be autonomous for this work of ethical transformation to occur, but once that work was accomplished the church recovered its public role as the invisible conscience of the ethnic community. Frederick William placed such a high priority on religious reform because the very core of his notion of communal identity – that the identity among "brothers" grew from their common voluntary submission to the law and word of the father – was presented in its historical origins and in its earthly archetype in the Christian church. The genuine Christian church, the church as originally institutionalized by God himself, was the model for all forms of association that were formed through subjective identification. The patriarchal and corporate structure that Frederick William attributed to the apostolic church constitution clearly revealed that he did not consider submission to patriarchal rule and hierarchical organization of the social organism into functional orders as mere transitional forms, or simply as agents for the construction of ethical community as a "brotherhood." For Frederick William, the ethical community per se remained a community of submission to the father. He found it impossible to imagine this submission as one in which individuals freely submitted to the internal rule of the father without being trained in external obedience to father figures at the same time. He was convinced that in historical practice actual patriarchal institutions and paternalistic regimes were required to make inner submission efficacious and visible.

Frederick William's emphasis on the church as a community shaped in its internal structure and historical mission by submission to a transcendent will placed him very close to the conservative ultras with whom he had allied himself in the 1830s. During the early 1840s, Ernst Ludwig von Gerlach most forcefully articulated the ultras' position. However, Frederick William found Gerlach too rigid in his dismissal of human striving for autonomy and community as the futile, utopian desire of dependent creatures to deny their dependence. In Gerlach's view, the ethno-cultural definition of the people as an immanent historical community threatened to displace the idea of the church as a mediator of the transcendent will and thus as the conscience and spirit of earthly community. But the king had a more nuanced and problematic conception of the relationship between submission to the will of the transcendent father and the drive for autonomy and self-realization. His tendency to seek the council of Radowitz, who combined extremely conservative positions on the inner structures of church and state with an insistence on the reality of an immanent historical teleology moving states toward the goal of nationalized and socialized communities, was one sign of this distancing from the stances of the conservative circles at the court. Radowitz affirmed the general principle that once humanity had fallen away from its union with its creator, its relationship to the authority that defined its dependence had to be one of submission to a power outside of itself. The return to the godhead could not be achieved from within human relations alone. At the same time, Radowitz believed that the evolution of human relations expressed in the history of law did display an immanent movement within history toward self-regulated obedience to universal norms ultimately guaranteed by a transcendent power. Thus Kantian forms of moral autonomy were encompassed within the ecumenical scope of Christian culture.[76] Moreover, Frederick William vociferously defended Bunsen's attempt to define human freedom not only as obedience but also as self-determination. The notion of responsibility as self-incurred, "free" obligation seemed to require it. Frederick William was also not ready to let the church, or for that matter the broader ethical community for which the church provided universal norms, devolve completely into a construction of the father, the king, and the magistrate. The Protestant doctrine of the priesthood of all believers was central to the formation of an ethical community as a community that emerged from within the relations among human subjects and not only as the self-imposition of the father's law on them. While the Gerlachs attacked Bunsen's attempts to completely internalize relationships of authority as relations between the individual self and his internal universal conscience (produced by the divine Word proclaiming in the voice of the father), the king claimed that Bunsen's position was not beyond the bounds of orthodoxy and the expression of an important truth.[77]

Reform could not be imposed on the churches by the state without destroying the principle of reform as a self-determining transformation from within, in which individuals in the congregations asserted their autonomy and rediscovered, through mutual recognition of their common purpose, the truth about themselves that was contained in God's original revelation. During the first years of his reign, the king tried to encourage discussion of reform by appropriate church assemblies and, in 1846, a united synod was called to meet in Berlin to discuss the general reform of the Prussian state church. The synod's discussions and final resolutions had little in common with the king's proposals and dreams of the transformation of human society through the work of a regenerated apostolic church.

Frederick William's ecclesiastical reform plans may have remained paper proposals, but they did reveal the core of the cultural policy of his "new course" in the 1840s. As the place where human individuals encountered the transcendent paternal power that determined their life's meaning as finite, sinful creatures, the church was the foundation of social and political reform, the core of that subjective commitment that Frederick William viewed as the cement of earthly order. But his church reform proposals also displayed

[76] *Gespraeche aus der Gegenwart ueber Staat und Kirche*, 2nd ed. (Stuttgart: 1846). The general principle of the unity among all Christians on the principle of dependence on transcendent authority is the point of discussion in Conversations 12 and 13, pp. 299–350. See especially pp. 326–29.

[77] This exchange between Ludwig, and Leopold von Gerlach, and the king on the occasion of the publication of Bunsen's *Verfassung der Kirche der Zukunft* (1845), is recounted in Gerlach, *Aufzeichnungen*, vol, 1, p. 434.

in ideal form the inner shape of Frederick William's vision of a genuine ethical society: a patriarchal household order in which self-determination consisted of recognition that one's own freedom was tied to obedience to the will of the father, that the law of communal association was the law of the father rather than a fraternal agreement among the children of a common mother. Of course, obedience was imagined as voluntary rather than forced, as "free" obedience: The subject was to experience himself as genuinely represented by the father's will. Frederick William's insistence that the model of an ethical community was a "patriarchal regime" was easy to confuse with traditional notions of monarchical authority or aristocratic paternalism. To grasp the full dimensions of the modernity of this regime and the reasons why its public audience "read" its cultural policy in such different ways, it is useful to examine the political and intellectual activities of the king's most liberal and "bourgeois" adviser, Christian Carl Josias Bunsen. Bunsen thought he was a spokesperson for the king, just as he believed the king was an organ of the nation. And the king sincerely believed, at least until the mid-1840s, that no one understood him as well as Bunsen, whom he defended vigorously against his many critics within the inner court circle.

2

"Redeemed Nationality": Christian Bunsen and the Transformation of Ethnic Peoples into Ethical Communities Under the Guidance of the Historical Principle

In the spring of 1846, Bunsen lamented in a letter to one of his sons about the divisive inner antagonisms that continued to plague German intellectual life and popular culture. The road toward understanding and superseding these antagonisms was mapped by the historical principle. But drawing the map from past to future could only be pursued by someone who was "in the clear about religion and politics." Unlike other historical cultures whose self-definitions were articulated in the organic totality of their expressions, including myth and religion, Germanic culture had a religious form in Christianity that was not an historical expression of its ethnic existence, but a universal "religion of humanity." The historical mission of this culture was not simply to work out its distinctive idea in the fullness of historical self-expression, but to make Christianity real as a people (*Volk*) and as a state (*Staat*). The historical mission of German culture was to appropriate the revealed truth of Christianity as the principle of a universal ethical community and make that principle the motivating ideal or conscience of the ethnic community, and thus make the divinely revealed, universal essence of mankind real within the particular limitations of historical existence. "This," he claimed, "is redeemed nationality [*wiedergeborene Nationalitaet*]."[1]

[1] Friedrich Nippold, ed., *Christian Carl Josias Freiherr von Bunsen. Aus seinen Briefen und nach eigener Erinnerung geschildert von seiner Witwe* (3 vols.; Leipzig: 1868–71), vol. 2, p. 338; Frances Baroness Bunsen, *A Memoir of Baron Bunsen* (2 vols.; London: 1868) vol. 2, pp. 107–8. The English edition, selected and compiled by Bunsen's widow, preceded the German edition, but Nippold's German edition is not simply a translation of the English work. He added many materials and deleted some items. He translated letters originally written in English, but he also had access to many original German letters. The archival materials on which these collections were based, along with some additional items, have recently been rediscovered and used in the relatively detailed overview of Bunsen's life and work by Frank Foerster: *Christian Carl Josias Bunsen. Diplomat, Maezen, und Vordenker in Wissenschaft, Kirche und Politik* (Bad Arolsen: 2001). Foerster's researches have, fortunately, affirmed the reliability of the nineteenth-century editions on which much of this chapter is based. Hereafter the German edition will be designated simple as Nippold, *Bunsen*, the English edition as Bunsen, *Memoir*. I will generally cite the German edition, unless the letter was originally written in English. Aside from Foerster's biographical monograph, there has been relatively little scholarly interest in Bunsen's role in Prussian politics, and even less in his historical work. Attention has focused primarily on his diplomatic role as ambassador to England and his participation in the politics of church reform. See Wilma Hoecker, *Der Gesandte Bunsen als Vermittler zwischen Deutschland und England* (Goettingen: 1951); Erich Geldbach, *Der gelehrte Diplomat: Zum Wirken Christian Carl Josias Bunsens* (Leiden: 1980);

By April 1846, Bunsen had come to realize that his conception of cultural reformation in the service of "redeemed nationality" was not in full agreement with that of his friend the king. But Bunsen's attempts to work through the apparently antagonistic implications of the historical principle in the transformation of German ethnic culture into an ethical community revealed dimensions of the official cultural politics of the regime that were only obscurely and indirectly indicated in the utterances and actions of the king and the more conservative members of his inner circle.

The negotiations that brought Schelling to Berlin were carried out by Bunsen, who had been empowered to represent the king and the Prussian government in direct and secret talks with Schelling and other cultural luminaries on the basis of the mutual trust that existed between him and Frederick William. But Bunsen's original letter of invitation to Schelling was more an expression of his personal perception of the role the philosopher might play in the cultural policies of the new regime than evidence of a real consensus within the Prussian leadership. As Varnhagen von Ense noted in his diaries: Bunsen had been the prime mover behind Schelling's appointment and had "produced or at least nurtured the preference of the king."[2] Bunsen was successful in nurturing this preference – despite the king's suspicions about philosophy – because he and the king and Schelling shared some fundamental assumptions about the relationship between sacred and secular dimensions in the history of Germany and Prussia.

Bunsen presented the Prussian offer to Schelling not so much as an invitation from individual admirers as an opportunity to heed the call of history at a critical juncture in the development of Germany as a cultural nation.[3] In broadly schematic terms, he sketched out a description of the present as an age in which the national culture was threatened by a dissolution of all discipline in personal morals and family values, by the complete stultification of public energy in the institutions of state and church, and by the destructive influence of an arrogant, self-deluding philosophy (the "school of the empty concept" or "Hegelian pantheism and pseudo-erudition") in the sphere of education, scholarship, science, theology, and the arts. What had appeared thirty years earlier during the wars of liberation as a struggle for national survival against a foreign foe now appeared in the more dangerous form of a struggle against the forces of inner dissolution and self-doubt. Bunsen situated the present moment in the historical context of the exalted consciousness of national mission in 1813 and the disappointments following 1815. The human resources for a renewed struggle for national

Hans-Rudolf Ruppel, Frank Foerster, and Hans Becker, eds., *Universeller Geist und guter Europaeer: Christian Carl Josias von Bunsen 1791–1860* (Korbach: 1991); and Kurt Schmidt-Clausen, *Vorweggenommene Einheit: Die Gruendung des Bistums Jerusalem im Jahre 1841* (Berlin: 1965), pp. 19–118.

2 K. A. Varnhagen von Ense, *Tagebuecher*, ed. Ludmilla Assing (15 vols.; Leipzig, 1861–1905), vol. 1, p. 332.

3 The letter, written on August 1, 1840, is printed in Nippold, *Bunsen*, vol. 2, pp. 133–4.

emancipation and integration would come from the veterans of the earlier struggle, prepared for their current task by years of suffering and waiting. But they would also come from a younger generation, a youth waiting to be mobilized by decisive, visionary leadership. For the first time since the era of national awakening, Bunsen claimed, individuals capable of mobilizing collective energies for the task of "grounding" the "fundamental pillars of our common existence in the family, state, church, scholarship and the arts" had been brought together in the leadership of the Prussian government. Schelling's particular role at this moment, "pregnant with the future," was to be the "teacher of the age" in two senses; by providing a metaphysical foundation for diverse cultural practices in knowledge "of the real in its divine essence and significance," and by grasping the present as a turning point in sacred and secular history.

Bunsen's conviction of the importance of Schelling's positive philosophy for grounding the practices of cultural identity formation and grasping the historical meaning of the present moment emerged rather suddenly in his correspondence and diaries during the spring and summer of 1838. For Bunsen, the turn to Schelling seemed to indicate a return to the hopes, dreams, and projects of his youth. Poring over the notebooks from Schelling's lectures on the philosophy of mythology and revelation, Bunsen rediscovered the theoretical and practical mission he had shaped for himself in the years between 1809 and 1815. In this deeply held belief that the project to build a Christian-German state in 1840 represented a recovery and an extension of a Prussian and national project that had somehow been derailed for a quarter century, Bunsen expressed one of the founding myths of the new regime. But just as the rehabilitations of the still living cultural heroes of the period of reform and liberation clouded perceptions of the historical peculiarity of Frederick William's cultural agenda, so Bunsen's sense of return and recovery obscured the shifts and developments that had permanently altered his own historical and cultural perspective in the years after 1815.

THE ORIGINAL PROJECT: UNIVERSAL HISTORY, GERMAN IDENTITY, AND THE PRUSSIAN MISSION

In early 1816, Bunsen presented his recently chosen scholarly mentor, the historian Barthold Georg Niebuhr, with an incredibly ambitious proposal for an historical research project. The goal of this "study-plan for life" was nothing less than a definitive reconstruction of the universal history of mankind, from its origins in the archaic cultures of North Africa and the Middle East to its present efflorescence in the Germanic cultures of northern Europe.[4]

[4] "Entwurf eines Studienplanes, Niebuhr in Berlin im Jahre 1816 eingereicht," Nippold, *Bunsen*, vol. 1, pp. 86–90.

The project also made claim to recreate and display the synchronicity of all cultural elements, from the general structures of language to the particularities of religious myths and political institutions. Such a mammoth project, Bunsen admitted, could only be interdisciplinary in method, systematically coordinating philological, historical, and philosophical procedures.

When he submitted the project to Niebuhr, Bunsen had already gone through a process of rethinking and reformulating his study plan for at least three years. In a letter of August 1815, he traced the personal origins of his scholarly mission to a decisive visionary experience in the winter of 1812–13, when the idea first became "clear and alive" in his mind that "all that emanates from the spirit is a revelation of the Divine, developing in accordance with its own internal laws, and that in this divine ground was posited not only the origin but also the development and decline of every earthly appearance in language art, science, politics and religion."[5] Through analysis of the various expressions of human culture one could approach knowledge of the divine power that revealed its nature in the progressive transformation of historical forms. The religious component in Bunsen's scholarly ambitions was articulated in a diary entry of July 1816:

> What is the Good? Knowledge of God. What is Virtue? That which makes it possible for us to know God, to think God, to feel God. What is evil? Forgetting God. What is punishment? To be excluded from divine illumination by the prisonhouse of desire.... What is the secret of love? That it releases the wings of the soul and brings it to an intuition and feeling of its own life. All scholarship is nothing but the creation of love. What is produced without it is sterile and an unsatisfactory shadow of itself. God is love.[6]

The ethical and religious quest for knowledge of God, and its correlate – emancipatory self-knowledge – were thus placed at the very center of Bunsen's conception of the vocation of historical scholarship. But there was little confessional or doctrinal specificity in this perspective. The Christianity that Bunsen saw as defining the ethos of the third and final epoch of universal history emerged from classical philosophy and culture and found its culmination in post-Kantian German Idealism and Romanticism. The three ages of the world – Oriental, Classical, Christian – constituted a progressively evolving totality that fused sacred and secular history. The Christian idea of the Absolute as a self-determining subject embodying itself in the "positive" forms of historical cultures clearly held a privileged position in this evolution, as the principle of the third and final stage within world history. It provided the necessary orientation point for a meaningful reconstruction of the past. This Christian idea, however, was a point of orientation within history rather than a viewing site outside of the historical process. Bunsen understood the organizing perspective of his historical reconstruction not

[5] Bunsen to Hey, August 22, 1815, Nippold, *Bunsen*, vol. 1, p. 81.

[6] Nippold, *Bunsen*, vol. 1, p. 99 (footnote).

as a transcendent viewpoint, but as his own full, self-conscious participation in his culture's present moment. "Europe will be my focus of attention, the contemporary age my teacher and mentor and the fatherland the actual center of my work," he wrote to a friend in June 1814. His historical project expressed a vocational commitment to a mission that would culminate in the global actualization of the Christian idea as "Germanic world dominion [*germanischen Weltherrschaft*]."[7]

Bunsen's conception of world history as a structured progression of individuated cultures animated by "ideas," carried by "peoples," and most clearly revealed in the historical progression and transformation of languages was inspired and guided by his readings in Herder during his student years at Goettingen between 1809 and 1815, as well as by his study of the Idealist philosophies of history of Friedrich Schlegel and Schelling (he made personal pilgrimages to visit both in the summer of 1813), but it distinguished itself from this inheritance by its intense focus on the archaic origins of universal history in the cultures of the East, particularly Persia and India. Schlegel had already pointed out the significance of Sanskrit and Persian in the development of human language and culture, but Bunsen was determined to integrate them into the present state of German culture in such a way that "even the devil would not be able to tear it out!"[8] He was intent on demonstrating that the present moment in the history of the Germanic peoples as carriers of the Christian idea was the culminating point not only of European history but also of the history of human culture, that all previous cultures were absorbed, appropriated, and found their ultimate meaning in a single narrative that culminated in the current historical mission of German-Christian culture, that Germans in 1815 owned the human past as the inner essence of their present. Thus Bunsen assured a friend that his decision to study Sanskrit in Calcutta for three years should not be interpreted as an exile from his homeland, but rather as a fuller appropriation of its origins. The study of the Orient was actually a study of the past stages of the German present, a history of the fatherland in a world-historical sense. To go to Calcutta was to journey into one's own past in order to grasp and master one's own present.[9]

[7] Bunsen to Becker, June 12, 1814, Nippold, *Bunsen*, vol. 1, p. 50.

[8] Bunsen to Becker, March 6, 1814, Nippold, *Bunsen*, vol. 1, p. 50.

[9] *Ibid.* In thus defining philological and cultural studies of ancient India and Persia as a study of the origins of the German cultural identity that was to be constructed in the present, Bunsen was following the lead of the first Romantic generation, and especially of Friedrich and August Wilhelm Schlegel. What was unusual was the very specific way in which Bunsen imagined dedication to the study of Sanskrit as somehow equivalent to joining the volunteer brigades of 1813. Friedrich Schlegel's *Ueber die Sprache und Weisheit der Indier* was published in 1808. August Wilhelm Schlegel received the first chair in Sanskrit studies at a German University at Bonn in 1818. The crucial role that ancient Indian language and mythology played in the attempts by the early Romantics to establish an historical foundation for German cultural identity is described in Raymond Schwab, *The Oriental Renaissance: Europe's Rediscovery of India and the East*, trans. Gene Patterson-Black and Victor Reinking (New York: 1984); and Walter Leifer, *India and the Germans* (Bombay: 1971).

In the sketch that Bunsen presented to Niebuhr in 1816, he emphasized the methodological requirements of his project. A few months earlier he had noted that reconstruction of the history of mankind demanded a dual approach; first, knowledge of the "materials" of history, or the "appearances" of the underlying ideas, and second, knowledge of those ideas themselves. "Only, I felt, if both penetrated each other," he wrote, "could that perception of the divine in the terrestrial world toward which I was striving, emerge."[10] For Niebuhr, Bunsen reformulated this position more systematically in terms of the relations between philology, history, and philosophy.

Bunsen perceived the methodological problematic of his project in the context of the philological/historical investigations of classical antiquity he had undertaken during his student years. In 1809, Bunsen had left the University of Marburg, where he had been enrolled in the theological faculty, to study classical philology with the renowned Christian Gottlob Heyne (1729–1812) at Goettingen. Heyne, who had guided the luminaries of the first Romantic generation, like the Schlegel and Humboldt brothers, through their own studies of classical culture in the 1780s, was eighty years old in 1809 and had only a few years to live, but he took Bunsen into his home and under his wing – the first of a series of intense filial relations that marked Bunsen's intellectual development.[11] Under Heyne's guidance, Bunsen learned to perceive the structure of language as the "purest mirror" of the individuality of a culture and to interpret texts in the historical contexts of religious mythology and sociopolitical institutions. In Heyne's work classical, philology had become a form of historical hermeneutics whose aim was the empathetic recreation of the moral and intellectual worlds of the ancient Greeks. In pursuing this method, however, Bunsen soon found himself in unending oscillation between narrowly focused philological analysis of texts and broad contextual studies in which such textual traces were to find their systematic, historical significance.

The most striking aspect of Bunsen's methodological considerations was the central role he attributed to the philosophical perspective. Investigation of the past began with philological criticism of textual sources in order to determine and arrange historical facts. The arrangement of facts in relations of similarity and difference, however, demanded the philosophical ability to discern general forms within particular appearances. Such "logical" operations were especially necessary in cases where sources were rare or fragmentary or where facts were clearly instances of structural possibilities, as in

[10] Bunsen to Hey, August 22, 1815, Nippold, *Bunsen*, vol. 1, p. 81.

[11] On the historical and disciplinary perspectives Heyne purveyed to his Goettingen students, see: Clemens Menze, *Wilhelm von Humboldt und Christian Gottlob Heyne* (Duesseldorf: 1966); and Werner Mettler, *Der junge Friedrich Schlegel und die griechische Literatur. Ein Beitrag zur Problem der Historie* (Zurich: 1955), pp. 46–97. Bunsen's own comments on Heyne can be found in a letter to his friend Agricola from July 13, 1813, Nippold, *Bunsen*, vol. 1, pp. 36–37.

the study of languages. Once phenomena had been appropriately arranged, they required interpretation as representations of "ideas" in order to elevate the "dead" facts into "living" facts. Such resurrection implied a philosophical grasp of the "being" that constituted the "becoming" of appearances. Historical reconstruction of the "developmental series" (*Entwicklungsreihen*) within the separate spheres of myth, art, science, and politics, and the amalgamation of these series into a cultural totality with its own logic of development, entailed knowledge of both the patterns in the facts of experience and of the "ideas" that were expressed in these patterns. The "universal-historical extension" of philological and historical scholarship in the task of reconstructing the cultural history of mankind both synchronically and diachronically thus demanded philosophical understanding of the relations among facts, external forms, and intentional ideas within the dynamic context of the becoming of being.[12] Despite his criticism of the emptiness of philosophical construction and calls for a thorough grounding of historical knowledge in philologically validated facts, Bunsen made the idealist perspective, the concept of the historical world as the objectification of a mental intention or idea, the center of his own vision.

In practical terms, Bunsen's "study plan" was utopian, even if he could have somehow established himself as the head of a multidisciplinary research team. Yet he pursued his goal with systematic zeal. By 1816 he had already spent a number of years absorbed in the study of Sanskrit, Persian and early Germanic, Icelandic, and Scandinavian languages. He had made two research trips (to Holland and Denmark) to pursue these studies, and in the spring of 1816 he went to Paris for three months to work with Europe's most renowned Orientalist, Sylvester de Sacy. He seemed determined to master the details as well as the big picture and possessed an exuberant self-confidence that convinced or charmed many into believing he might actually accomplish his goals.

Bunsen was driven by a belief in the practical significance of his project – the transformation of the German people into an ethical community. His correspondence between 1813 and 1816 constantly criticizes the gap between contemplation and action, scholarship and politics. "There is an immense gap between the nation and academic scholarship," he lamented in 1814. "I feel this intensely. We forget what is near for the sake of the distant, the new for the sake of the old, what is our own for the sake of the foreign."[13] His scholarship was not meant to aggravate this gap, but to bridge it.

The conceptual frame of Bunsen's scholarly project was formulated at the same time as his involvement in the emotional turmoil and exaltation of the national awakening of 1813–14. Bunsen explicitly stated that the essential, "divine" life that he discovered hidden in the factual traces of the

[12] "Entwurf eines Studienplanes," Nippold, *Bunsen*, vol. 1, pp. 87–88.

[13] Bunsen to Becker, March 6, 1814, Nippold, *Bunsen*, vol. 1, p. 50.

past had only become visible to him because of his "vital feeling" for the "new life" in the present.[14] Bunsen's participation in this new life, however, was limited to subjective identification. Although many members of his study group at Goettingen joined the national volunteer brigades in the spring of 1813,[15] Bunsen traveled in leisurely style through southern Germany and northern Italy as the tutor of the son of the American millionaire John Jacob Astor. The young Astor had been Bunsen's major source of income since 1810. Bunsen's father's opposition to the war (he was a disillusioned professional soldier) may also have contributed to Bunsen's absence among the volunteers of 1813 and thus to the subsequent feelings of guilt he experienced when criticized for his behavior. At any rate, his physical absence from the armies of liberation certainly added intensity to his desire to "accomplish in peace what we have accomplished in war, especially those of us who did not bear arms and from whom the Fatherland demands with double authority that we use the power of the spirit for its benefit."[16] Many years later, in the 1850s, Bunsen would remember 1813 as the moment of "solemn baptism" that established his German identity and would compare the life-shaping significance of that experience in his own life to the meaning of 1813 (on the surface much more obvious) for Ernst Moritz Arndt.[17]

Bunsen's constantly reiterated plan to place his scholarship in the service of the fatherland had two dimensions. The first was pedagogical. Germans needed to be brought to consciousness of their identity as members of a cultural nation through representation of their historical mission within the context of universal history. The documentary traces of the past were to be uncovered or rediscovered as present memory – history transformed into the living foundation of present cultural identity. Second, this developed consciousness of historical nationality should be institutionalized as the legal and political framework for communal action. In 1814–15 such hopes for political actualization were focused on various movements for domestic political reform in the territorial states of the former German Empire. In the spring of 1814, Bunsen was inspired to write down his views of the future institutional forms of German freedom by a constitutional conflict between the recently reinstalled dynastic prince and the traditional estates in his home principality of Waldeck.

Bunsen's constitutional proposal was clearest in its negative dimensions: the rejection of the opposing extremes of bureaucratic absolutism (identified

[14] Bunsen to Luecke, June 16, 1815, Nippold, *Bunsen*, vol. 1, p. 78.

[15] Foerster, *Bunsen*, p. 26, provides a list of participants and nonparticipants.

[16] Bunsen to Bekker, May 13, 1814; Nippold, *Bunsen*, vol. 1, p. 52.

[17] Christian Charles Josias Bunsen, *Signs of the Times: Letters to Ernst Moritz Arndt on the Dangers to Religious Liberty in the Present State of the World*, transl. Susanna Winkworth (New York: 1856), p. 19.

with Napoleonic despotism) and rule by diets of incorporated estates (identified with the privileges of aristocratic and patrician elites). He was willing to support the resistance of traditional estates to royal and bureaucratic domination, but only as a temporary measure. The princes could not be trusted to secure the civic freedoms of their subjects, but the traditional estates were "imperfect representations" of the people because of their privileged exclusivity. The political task of the present was to build new constitutions not in conformity with foreign models but through liberalizing reform of the traditional corporations. The political stalemate in Germany was due to the identification of constitutional reforms with Napoleonic rule and of the "genuinely German" with traditional privilege. What Bunsen's sketchy comments seem to imply was a desire for constitutional arrangements that would restrict the power of the prince through a "more perfect representation" of the community of citizens. Popular participation in the recent wars demanded that the circle of citizens be extended beyond the traditionally privileged corporate groups.[18]

During the summer of 1815, Bunsen was convinced that the possibility of putting his vision into practice was tied to the fate of the Prussian reform movement. Like so many other German intellectuals who became Prussian by choice after 1813, Bunsen and many of his Goettingen friends envisioned Prussia as the current historical incarnation of the idea of German national community. "Prussia alone can become my fatherland," Bunsen wrote in the fall of 1815, "only here are there men in positions of leadership who possess the energy and knowledge to carry out great plans, and only in such a great state, in which the most advanced scholarship can also be accomplished, do I have the ability to gather the fruits of my scholarly investigations."[19] When he moved to Berlin in the fall of 1815, Bunsen was introduced to the circle of politically engaged scholars, including Wilhelm von Humboldt, Schleiermacher, Savigny, and Niebuhr, who constituted the core of the "Historical School" of cultural studies. Among this group Bunsen found a new mentor in Niebuhr, who appeared to incorporate in one person both the ideal of rigorous philological scholarship applied to historical documents and the identification of historical scholarship with political pedagogy in the service of a national mission. Like the crown prince, who was also under the tutelage of Niebuhr and Savigny at this time, Bunsen tied German cultural identity to the "historical principle." To become a German was to internalize as a personal memory the public narrative of German culture from the moment of its birth to the cusp of its fulfillment in the present.

[18] Although the brochure was never published, Bunsen summarized the contents for his friend Bekker in a number of letters written in June and July 1814. See Nippold, *Bunsen*, vol. 1, pp. 53–54.

[19] Bunsen to Christiane, November, 14, 1815, Nippold, *Bunsen*, vol. 1, p. 85.

THE PROJECT REVISED: TRANSCENDENT INTERVENTION AND THE PROTESTANT MISSION

The generational cohort that moved into positions of power in the regime of Frederick William IV was not just marked as a generation by the experience of inner reform and external liberation during the critical years in which their public identities were shaped, but also by a pattern of experiences that followed the collapse of the hopes for the immanent historical transformation of ethno-Germans into an ethical community after 1815. Disillusionment with the spontaneous self-determination of the idea of German national culture fed into the theology and ecclesiology of the postwar religious awakening. Despite the idiosyncrasies of his particular situation, Bunsen shared this pattern of experiential development and became a spokesperson for its effects.

Just at the moment when Bunsen's youthful visions appeared to have achieved an integral focus in a life's project unifying historical scholarship and political commitment, this project received an external shock whose reverberations produced fundamental revisions and transformations of its structure. After his three-month stint with de Sacy in Paris in 1816, Bunsen traveled to Italy for a rendezvous with his wealthy tutee. He was to meet the young Astor in Florence and then begin his journey to India. However, Astor's father suddenly called him back to New York, and Bunsen was left stranded, "bereft of all external supports." Rather than return home, he decided to wait in Florence for Niebuhr, who was traveling to Rome to assume the post of chief of the Prussian legation to the Vatican, and for Niebuhr's secretary, Christian Brandis, an old school friend. In his confusions, Bunsen found an anchor in Niebuhr, "the only person I can recognize as my lord and master," and decided to follow him to Rome to continue his studies there. With an irrepressible optimism that turned frustration into opportunity, Bunsen interpreted his shattered plans as a call to consolidate his scattered studies and secure the general foundations of his project: "I have laid the foundations of a great edifice, as great as anyone in the sphere of scholarship has conceived in this age. All the worse if I do not make these foundations secure and work through my building materials."

For all of his hopeful talk about consolidating and integrating his research, however, Bunsen sensed that he had lost his bearings in a major way and that he needed to reconsider the question of "where I as a person now stand."[20] What was needed was a general reorientation of his project as a whole.

During the ensuing year, Bunsen became convinced that such a reorientation involved two of the major "foundations" of the site on which he had stood so confidently in 1815. First, he had lost confidence in the ability of philosophical knowledge to provide the integrating synthesis for the

[20] Bunsen to Christiane, October 13, 1816, Nippold, *Bunsen*, vol. 1, p. 107.

fragmentary traces of the past that were uncovered and presented by his philological investigations. Second, he became disillusioned with the direction of postwar cultural reconstruction and had to deal with the recognition that the hoped-for ethical community of emancipated Germans was not an imminent historical probability. The collapse of his personal plans, however, created a space for the construction of a new perspective from which he could revive the hopes he had invested in philosophy and politics. His process of disillusionment stopped short of cynicism or despair. He quickly found surrogates for the earlier foundations of his historical mission, and in both cases the surrogates involved a new attitude toward religious experience.

A religious turn in the years after 1815 was a common dimension of the experience of Bunsen's historical generation. The particular shape of Bunsen's religious turn, however, was shaped by the specific personal and cultural factors impinging on his consciousness during his first years in Rome – the evangelical Anglican piety of Francis Waddington, the young Englishwoman he met in early 1817 and married in July; the darkening historical pessimism of his mentor Niebuhr; the sympathetic contact with the expatriate colony of Nazarene painters; and the impact of the revived energy of Restoration Catholicism emanating from the papacy. It would be an exaggeration to describe Bunsen's evolving piety as a religious conversion. In his letters it emerges more as the gradual attainment of a transcendent center for the reconstruction of personal and historical meaning and as the conclusion of his search for some immovable ground to secure the validity of both his belief in the progressive development of human history and his conviction of historical identity with the German cultural nation.

In February 1817, Bunsen wrote to his philologist friend Friedrich Luecke in Berlin that he was applying himself to the study of the Bible in order to bring "tranquility and order" to his philosophical and philological investigations.[21] After almost a year of such study and of mental ferment and confusion, he presented a revised report of his scholarly project to his older half-sister Christiane. He now insisted that the collapse of his plans to go to India had been a blessing in disguise. Journeying to the East would have been a detour to the periphery of a circle that had no center. He had come to the realization that only through a "thorough and deep study of the Bible and of Christianity and its history" could he "accomplish anything substantial in his other philosophical and historical investigations and quiet the thirst that had driven him since his youth into such inquiries."[22] His conception of mankind's cultural development was now divided into a sacred and a secular component. The sacred history revealed in the Bible provided the orienting center for an understanding of pagan cultures, and Christian history itself was only comprehensible through an act of faith in the truth of

[21] Bunsen to Luecke, February 12, 1817, Nippold, *Bunsen*, vol. 1, p. 111.

[22] Bunsen to Christiane, December 28, 1817, Nippold, *Bunsen*, vol. 1, p. 140.

biblical revelation. The Bible was the key to decoding the historical record; it provided both the dictionary and the grammar for reading the traces of the past.

What he had hoped to find in India's Sanskrit literature – the archaic origins of history and the key to the operations of the divine idea in human culture – could only be discovered, he now insisted, through a transformation of his inner self:

> Christianity and true faith is something inner, a fact of the inner man, transcending all scholarship and external knowledge. It can originate only in an inner, genuine, not shallow but authentic, humble consciousness of our fallen nature and of the impossibility of accomplishing anything good without God's help, without the grace of the Holy Spirit. From this arises inner sanctification and true illumination. The two are inseparably connected: there is no sanctification of the heart and will without illumination of the spirit, that is, without a vital knowledge of our life in God and of the nullity of everything outside of him. There exists no genuine and lasting illumination without inner sanctification.[23]

The new center of his work was not knowledge of the "ideas" informing historical appearances, but faith in the historical fact of redemption as revealed in the Bible and experienced in his inner life. Meaning was not immanent but transcendent, and infused into appearances through providential acts of grace. In 1821 Bunsen insisted that anyone who interpreted the Christian acts of incarnation and redemption as "mere symbols" of "true and essential ideas" was not a Christian. Three years earlier he had warned his friend Brandis that belief in the self-generating life of human cultural creations blurred consciousness of the fact that human existence was dependent and created, that its life and creativity originated in the actions of a transcendent power.[24]

Contemporaneous with this shift from philosophical knowledge of the divine idea to faith in the historical fact of Christian redemption was a related shift in Bunsen's perception of the locus of the community of autonomous subjects from the nation to the church. A precondition of this change was a growing pessimism regarding the possible transformation of the nationalist sentiment of 1813 into political practices and institutions. This pessimism was nurtured by his intense admiration for Niebuhr, whose secretary he became after Brandis returned to Prussia to pursue an academic career in 1818. It was Niebuhr, Bunsen commented in June 1819, who had "opened my eyes to the condition of the present historical moment, its fundamental

[23] Bunsen to Christiane, February 28, 1818, Nippold, *Bunsen*, vol. 1, p. 147.

[24] *Ibid.*; also Bunsen to Brandis, July 27, 1818, Nippold, *Bunsen*, vol. 1, pp. 152–53.

failings and their causes."[25] For a number of years, Bunsen abandoned his own scholarly project in order to sit at Niebuhr's feet and absorb his mentor's political wisdom. "When one enjoys the friendship of such a man," he claimed, "it is a duty to drop everything and work under his guidance." According to Niebuhr, the political collapse of the movement for liberal reform and national unity could be traced to the disintegration of the ethical foundations of European society. Radical revolutionaries who rejected the continuity of cultural traditions were arrayed against narrow traditionalists who refused to surrender their privileges and adapt old forms to new realities. Neither side displayed any sign of a self-sacrificing commitment to the common good that might give vital inner substance to external constitutional forms. Moreover, Niebuhr believed that European Christianity was bankrupt, completely incapable of collective regeneration, and he saw no other historical agency for the renewal of communal solidarity. Bunsen did not follow his mentor on this issue. He believed that Protestant Christianity had the potential for inner regeneration and could thus be envisioned as an agent of ethical renewal.

In agreement with Niebuhr, Bunsen defined the contemporary shape of evil as "lack of a natural healthy state of communal life and of such social arrangements that conform to the realities of human existence." Spiritually healthy individuals were nurtured by a healthy "communal being [*Gemeinwesen*]" and this *Gemeinwesen* required a "body" of arrangements and institutions in order to "develop, shape and secure its life."[26] The highest form of *Gemeinwesen* was the community of spirits or self-conscious subjects (*Gemeinschaft der Geister*), and the most perfect of such communities was the communion of believers in Christ.[27] The Christian community of spirits was an invisible church, or at least a church whose visible practices were an expression of a transformative identification of individual subjects with their spiritual source and essence. But such identification required appropriate historical forms for its sustenance and development. At a time when all other bonds of human society were in a state of dissolution, historical hope depended on the construction of "genuine Christian congregations": "The only germ of life that one can set against the evil spirit of destruction and death exists in Christianity and in free Christian associations. Through their spirit the general conditions of life, like marriage and the education of children, must again be animated and redirected."[28]

The regeneration of the national, ethno-cultural community as a community of spirits implied a reconstruction of social conscience on the basis

[25] Bunsen to Christiane, June 19, 1819, Nippold, *Bunsen*, vol. 1, 160; see also Bunsen to his mother-in-law, Bunsen, *Memoir*, vol. 1, p. 68.

[26] Diary entry of December 7, 1820, Nippold, *Bunsen*, vol. 1, p. 178.

[27] Bunsen to Christiane, September 27, 1820, Nippold, *Bunsen*, vol. 1, p. 177; Bunsen to Hey, July 11, 1818, Nippold, *Bunsen*, vol. 1, p. 152.

[28] Bunsen to Christiane, September 7, 1820, Nippold, *Bunsen*, vol. 1, p. 177.

of self-sacrificing commitment to communal being. Such ethical renewal in turn was dependent on religious awakening and the construction of communities of the converted among those who grounded their moral life on the fact of Christian redemption. The shared beliefs of the redeemed, however, needed articulation, nurturance, and organization in order to be historically effective. Bunsen believed that the seeds of a new spiritual life were present in the postwar religious revival, especially among Protestants. His new concept of his "political" mission was to mobilize this power through ecclesiastical reform.

How could the church be reformed in such a way that it could transform humankind into ethical communities of autonomous spirits? An imposed unity of doctrine was not the answer. Theological debates were only of interest to a few and always produced acrimonious conflict rather than reconciliation and consensus. The core of Christianity was the personal encounter with the fact of redemption, the experience of the transforming power of a transcendent intervention in the immanent relations of concrete historical life. Simple confessions of faith adaptable to individual interpretations were thus a completely adequate articulation of doctrinal unity. Bunsen also did not carry much hope for the creation of communities through imposed discipline. Obedience to the law only became ethical if it was a voluntary obedience. The center of church reform for Bunsen was the construction of rituals, liturgical symbols, and constitutional arrangements that displayed and nurtured the central Christian experiences of self-surrender to, and joyful reconciliation with, the ground of personal being.

At first glance it might seem that the positions Bunsen developed between 1817 and 1823 constituted a new project that simply displaced the old project of 1812–16. But this would be a misreading of his development and skew our understanding of an important aspect of the cultural politics of the early 1840s. The theoretical and practical foci of his original project remained recognizably present in the new. What had changed was primarily the conception of agency imagined as historically effective for turning a people into a commonwealth of autonomous subjects. Bunsen's scholarly goal remained the reconstruction of human history as the incarnation of the divine in the human. The path to such knowledge, however, had changed from philosophical comprehension of the progressive self-expression of the idea in cultural forms to the illuminating faith gained through a concrete existential encounter with a personal transcendent will. History was now less a self-expressive unfolding of immanent meaning than a narrative of encounters between the immanent and the transcendent, a narrative that was not predictable nor determined in an external causal sense, but meaningful in retrospect as a story of actions motivated by encounters with transcendent "facts." Moreover, the creation of an ethical community was no longer left to the workings of the collective *Volk* spirit as it was refined to historical self-consciousness by the educated elites, but viewed as the work of religious communities composed of converted or "reborn" individuals. Thus Bunsen retained his notion that self-identity in the present depended on a form of historical knowledge that situated present purposes within a totalizing historical account, and that the inherent meaning of such an account must be the transformation of humankind into a community of spirits.

Yet the radical shift under the impact of postwar disillusionment from immanent to transcendent agency as the prime mover of historical transformation and ground of ethical community obviously changed the substance of history and community as well. By 1823 Bunsen clearly saw communal identification as mediated through the relations of individuals to an authority outside of their own worldly experiences with natural and social others. In psychosocial terms, the ideal of fraternity had been transformed into, or subsumed under, an ideal of patriarchy; the fellowship of sons, or citizens, now depended on the self-effacing surrender of the sons to the person and law of the father. And historical development as a totality was no longer imagined in analogy to a fraternal creation, as humankind making itself into its own cultural work, but as a narrative recounting the failures of self-making and a redemptive return to obedience to the actual maker, the transcendent father. Integration into communal being was synonymous with obedience to the rule of the transcendent father. The story that gave universal meaning to individual lives was the story of dependence on, rebellion against, and reconciliation with, the father.

Bunsen's religious turn thus reveals some of the power and attraction of the cultural policies of the Prussian regime of 1840. Paternalism was not just an ideology of the patriarchal household, a defense of traditional aristocratic and patrician interests, but deeply embedded in the consciousness of the "modern" bourgeois civil service classes who had found their historical vocation in a national mission in 1813 and temporarily lost their bearings in the disillusionment of the postwar period. Patriarchy here was already a "Victorian" patriarchy, an emotional return to a household ruled by an invisible but all-powerful father in response to the collapse of rebellious fraternity.

THE PROJECT IN EXILE: THE SEDUCTIONS OF POWER AND THE FRAGMENTATION OF VISION

When Bunsen accompanied Niebuhr to Rome in the fall of 1816, he had no intention of pursuing a career in the diplomatic service. Even after he became entangled in the daily business of the Prussian legation as Niebuhr's secretary, he continued to perceive the purpose of his stay in Rome in educational terms, as a preparation under his mentor's tutelage for a dual career as academic scholar of the universal history of mankind and practical reformer of the ethos and institutions of German public life. A visit by Frederick William III, his personal staff, and his foreign minister to Rome in late 1822, however, encouraged Bunsen to rethink his career possibilities. Overcoming his notorious reserve, the Prussian king displayed an intense personal interest in Bunsen's liturgical and ecclesiastical ideas, which directly engaged his own plans to construct a unified church liturgy for the recently amalgamated Reformed and Lutheran congregations in the Evangelical Protestant Church of Prussia. Bunsen was flattered and exhilarated by the discussions, and after an unexpected promotion to the position of legation councilor he began to feel the seductive tug of political power.

In some ways a diplomatic career was a diversion from his life's project, draining time and energy from his scholarship and prolonging his exile from his homeland. Yet the personal favor of the king presented a possibility, however slight (considering Bunsen's humble social origins and lack of political connections in Berlin), of attaining a position of influence that would allow him to test his reformist visions in political practice. When Niebuhr decided to return to Germany in 1823, Bunsen was provisionally placed in charge of the Prussian legation. Overcoming his nagging doubts, he decided to test the moment and requested that he either be provided with paid scholarly leave to finish his historical project or be promoted to Niebuhr's post as full ambassador in residence to the Vatican. It took some time before the issue was decided, but in the summer of 1827 Bunsen finally stepped into his master's shoes. He remained at this post until he was forced to resign under humiliating circumstances in 1838.[29]

Although Bunsen pursued his promotion with aggressive acumen, he continued to perceive his diplomatic career as a temporary exile from his true calling and as a means to higher ends. A visit to Berlin in the winter of 1827–28 appeared to fulfill his most sanguine hopes for a rapid rise to policy-determining influence at the court. The king welcomed Bunsen into his inner circle, including his family, like an adopted son. The crown prince sought him out almost daily for intimate discussions, and members of the court and Berlin high society fell over themselves in the rush to recognize the new royal favorite. Although his wife reminded him continually that royal favor was ephemeral and that court life was a life of festering resentments and intriguing cabals, Bunsen interpreted royal favor as a sign of his providential calling. By the time he returned to Rome in April 1828, any thoughts of pursuing an academic career through the normal apprenticeship of teaching and publication were left behind. This did not mean that he had abandoned his career of scholarship in a more general sense or that he had given up on his "study project for life."

The seductions of power, however, changed Bunsen's relationship to his scholarly project in two important ways, reinforcing tendencies implicit in

[29] The detailed designations of Bunsen's promotions in the Prussian diplomatic service are listed in Foerster, *Bunsen*, p. 35.

his development since his student days. First, his research projects were increasingly reformulated as collaborative projects, involving the organization and support of groups of younger scholarly specialists. His position as head of the Prussian legation in Rome gave Bunsen the opportunity to encourage interrelations among scholars from different nations and to support the work of traveling German students and researchers. Bunsen's immense energy and enthusiasm, his wide-ranging interests and passable scholarly competence in many fields, his charm and gregariousness, all helped turn his Roman home, the Palazzo Caffirelli on the Capitoline Hill, into the center of something like an ongoing international scholarly conference.[30] Second, Bunsen's meteoric rise to political influence encouraged his tendency to subordinate his scholarship to his practical projects for ethical and cultural reform. It made the connection between scholarship and policy more obvious and direct.

One effect of these changes was that the project itself underwent a process of fragmentation in which its two components tended to separate from each other. Since his "religious turn" in 1816–17, Bunsen had relegated the secular, national dimension of his project – the reconstruction of the origins of human culture through critical examination of the vestiges of ancient languages and myths – to a subordinate position, and focused his energy on the development of religious communities after the advent of Christianity. This emphasis continued during his Rome years and was reinforced by his official tasks and practical interests in church reform. However, two ongoing scholarly projects sustained his interest in the original world-historical framework of his life's plan: participation in a massive topographical, archaeological, and historical *Beschreibung der Stadt Rom* (Description of the City of Rome), which was commissioned (as a new guidebook for tourists!) by the Cotta publishing house in 1818 and whose final volumes were not completed until the mid 1840s, and a growing involvement as both a scholar and project instigator, in the burgeoning field of Egyptian studies.

In the "Preliminary Considerations" for the first volume of the *Beschreibung* (written in 1827 and published in 1829), Bunsen returned to some of the methodological issues he had discussed in his 1816 project plan. He began by drawing analogies between the reconstruction of historical changes in nature, particularly in the geological formation of the earth's surface, and the reconstruction of human history. In both cases the scholarly investigator began with traces that could be explained in the first instance as effects of comprehensible forces. In the case of natural history these forces were the basic elements, like water, air, and fire, and the geological composition of the earth according to chemical and physical laws. In the case of human history, there was a single "force" or causal agent – human beings, with their passions and the divinely given conditions of mental and physical existence. In both cases, however, if the documentary record was

[30] This dimension of Bunsen's life in Rome is portrayed in Foerster, *Bunsen*, pp. 46–50.

relatively complete, so that reciprocal connections between elements could be easily traced, a "pragmatic history" of the relations between phenomena as relations of cause and effect was possible. Moreover, in both natural and human history, facts without much documented evidence of connections to other facts could be placed in conjectural cause-and-effect relations based on knowledge of similar relations in the historian's contemporary world. Yet human history did diverge from natural history radically in that the documentary traces from which facts were distilled were already historical interpretations. These documents were elements of an inherited tradition in which historical fact was mingled with fictional or mythical constructions. The historian was thus trained to be wary of constructions that were willfully deceptive. However, historical fictions also provided the historian with an avenue to approach his true object – the spiritual essence of the associational life of a people. If the fictional constructions emerged from actions of this collective historical subject, they could be described as "ideal facts" originating in the "unity of national life."[31] Historical facts recounted in myths, poetry, legends, and other forms could not be explained pragmatically, but operated as expressive signs of an invisible unity – the collective subject at a particular stage in its development: "they provide us with a picture of a vital, aesthetically understood and lovingly recreated existence in the mirror of another time and another culture." In relation to "ideal facts," the role of the historical critic was not to construct a pragmatic history of cause-and-effect relations but to unveil the elemental, unifying purposes behind appearances. Through appropriate interpretation, such "fictional facts" would appear as "the magnificent and exalting fragments of a great epic, which generations of mankind have created out of an inner impulse from the beginning until the end of world history, testifying to their common origin and their common purpose through the flight of time." The collective poetry of myth was the last testament of a cultural epoch whose origins lay in the formation of language. Both language and myth, Bunsen asserted, could be construed as the creations of individuals, but individuals as conduits of the collective, as operating "in the communal and transformative activity that subordinates the false individual to the authentic national personality and progressively produces and reproduces the given as a loving tradition."[32]

Returning to the analogy of natural history, Bunsen noted that just as physical powers functioning as agents of change presupposed some higher agency that made their efficacy possible, so the interpretation of cultural history ultimately presupposed the agency of a "higher life activity" than individual passions and will, a "higher individuality" that "reveals itself in

[31] Bunsen, "Vorerinnerungen" (1827) to Ernst Platner, Carl Bunsen, Eduard Gerhard, and Wilhelm Roestell, *Beschreibung der Stadt Rom* (4 vols.; Stuttgart: 1829–42), vol. 1, p. 11.

[32] *Ibid.*, p. 12.

common life and without which there could be no language."[33] From this perspective, human history emerged as an epic story of collective subjects expressing themselves in the individuality of languages and myths.

The *Beschreibung* did not provide Bunsen with an opportunity to put his principles into practice through an actual reconstruction of the national life of an ancient culture. But his investigation of the collections of antiquities in Roman collections described in the guidebook stimulated and renewed his interest in pursuing the earliest traces of human culture through linguistic and archaeological study. For a time his interests were drawn toward Etruscan antiquities, but he gradually focused his interest on the field of Egyptology. In 1825 he met Jean Francois Champollion (1790–1832), the decoder of the Rosetta stone (and thus of the ancient Egyptian hieroglyphic language), and over the next few years he became convinced that the primary clues for reconstructing the origins and early evolution of language and culture could be derived from Egyptian hieroglyphics and the archaeological discoveries made by European scholars since the Napoleonic expedition of 1798–1801.

As Bunsen became more and more absorbed in the attempt to situate Egyptian hieroglyphics in the history of language, to establish the chronology of ancient Egyptian history and to decipher the systematic and developmental structure of Egyptian myths, he also revived his earlier interest in philosophy as a source for general principles of historical interpretation. Philosophy was not mentioned in the methodological considerations of 1827, a noticeable change from the project outline of 1816. But in 1828 Bunsen questioned a friend in Munich about a possible publication of Schelling's philosophy of history,[34] and after 1830 Bunsen's interest both in the study of philosophy in general and in the construction of a philosophical perspective that would engage the historicist concern for anchoring knowledge of the past in the irreducible facticity of existence became more and more prominent. In 1831 he encouraged his friend Brandis to take up this task,[35] but he looked primarily to Schelling, whom he visited in 1835, for guidance.

Bunsen's conception of universal history as an internally driven progressive evolution of ethno-cultural communities structured by language and myth had originally (in 1812–16) been connected to hopes for the awakening of a unified German cultural nation in the wake of the wars of liberation. The gradual revival of his world-historical project during the late 1820s and early 1830s was also paralleled by a modest revival of his previous historical

[33] *Ibid.*

[34] Bunsen to Schnorr vo Carolsfeld, December 7, 1828, Nippold, *Bunsen*, vol. 1, p. 357; Bunsen, *Memoir*, vol. 1, p. 351.

[35] Bunsen to Brandis, January 22, 1831, Nippold, *Bunsen*, vol. 1, pp. 380–3; Bunsen, *Memoir*, vol. 1, p. 368.

optimism concerning the emergence of a viable national community among the Germanic peoples of northern Europe. The historical pessimism produced by the collapse of his own generation's political hopes in 1815, reinforced in his case by the collapse of his personal life itinerary and the influence of Niebuhr, gradually started to dissipate after Niebuhr returned to Prussia, and his own fortunes rose after 1827.

Bunsen's critical attitude toward the major cultural movements he saw as hindering the progress toward national identity remained prominent and consistent between 1823 and 1838. On the one hand, there was the patricidal fraternity of revolutionary Jacobins and all of their liberal half siblings who grounded social being in the interests and calculations of individuals, who leveled historically developed cultural individuality into "unhistorical, dead and deadening uniformity," and who imagined the rule of the cultural collective in terms of a mechanical organization of isolated individuals, thus denying the reality of national identity as an ongoing common life transcending individuals and generations.[36] On the other side stood the conservative ultras who mistook one particular historical form of national development – the corporate society of the old regime with all of its aristocratic and patrimonial privileges – as the only valid incarnation of the German cultural idea, thus worshipping the letter of the past instead of the spirit of history. Increasingly in the years after 1830, however, Bunsen gained confidence in the potential historical power of the reformist center, the party that distinguished general principles of national life from particular historical forms and pursued the reproduction of national life in new arrangements adapted to new circumstances. Bunsen appropriated "the historical principle" as the banner of this centrist "reformist" party.[37]

Two associations seemed to boost Bunsen's confidence in the ability of the principle of reform to develop the identity of national communities in the modern world: his close ties with the British Coleridgeans, especially their most liberal member – Thomas Arnold – and his faith in the reformist impulses of the crown prince, who had spent a number of weeks in Rome with Bunsen in the fall of 1828, reinforcing the intimacies that had emerged the previous winter.[38] Bunsen was convinced that the prince was ready to resist the pressures from the Prussian ultras and move in a progressive direction, preserving the essence of German cultural traditions by adapting them to the liberal and national tendencies of the present. It was to the crown prince that Bunsen articulated his general principle of reform in 1834: "The eternal secret of God in nature and history is the emergence of

[36] Bunsen to Thomas Arnold, Ides of March, 1833; Bunsen, *Memoir*, vol. 1, pp. 389–90.

[37] Bunsen to Thomas Arnold, January 21, 1834, Bunsen, *Memoir*, vol. 1, p. 394.

[38] This visit is described at length in Peter Betthausen's introduction to his edition of Frederick William's letter from Italy: *Friedrich Wilhelm IV von Preussen: Briefe aus Italien 1828*, edited and with commentary by Peter Betthausen (Munich and Berlin: 2001), pp. 35–108.

the new from the old, the same and yet completely different, one ring in the great chain of existence which is the expression of the eternal within time."[39]

Bunsen compared cultural reform to natural growth, as if the evolution of national communities proceeded according to the necessary laws of development of a collective organism. At the same time, he continued to insist that nations could only be sustained in the modern world as ethical communities in which cultural solidarity was grounded in a voluntary surrender of the human subject to the inner commands of a collective national conscience. Such an ethical community, however, was dependent on religious reform; it was not just a natural outgrowth of ethno-linguistic identity. It was at this point that Bunsen's interpretive frame for grasping the historical evolution of ethno-cultural peoples crossed with the alternative model, which perceived the historical event as produced by a novel encounter with facts that were outside of the immanent processes of historical evolution. The determination of individual actions by cultural context encountered the transcendent freedom of self-expression and self-determination that emerged from the individual's voluntary identification with divine will.

Examination of the construction of ethical communities on the foundations of a surrender of individual will to transcendent purposes was the central concern of Bunsen's scholarly investigations after 1823. These investigations took three forms: an attempt to reconstruct the historicity of Christ's life, actions, and sayings through an historical critique of the Bible; research into the earliest forms of Christian liturgy as a primary expression of redeemed humanity's communal reproduction of its relationship to the historical act of transcendent revelation; and finally, study of the historical relations of Christians with each other, within the church, and with the world of institutionalized political powers outside the church.

As in the political realm, Bunsen saw academic theology divided between orthodox ultras, like the Berlin fundamentalist Ernst W. Hengstenberg, who had "yielded his critical conscience to an unsound, untenable system" by insisting that every word in the scriptures was divinely inspired and thus true in a literal sense, and rationalist liberals like H. E. G. Paulus, who attempted valiantly to salvage the truth of the biblical accounts as pragmatic cause-and-effect relations, but were blind to the ways in which the historical facts of the gospel revealed the incarnation of the infinite in historical time, the intervention of the transcendent in the immanent.[40] In general, Bunsen supported the Idealist exegesis emanating from the school of Schleiermacher, which emphasized the subjective meanings contained in stories of external events, but he also insisted that such interpretations needed to be grounded

[39] Unpublished letter from Bunsen to the crown prince, August 6, 1834, quoted in Schmidt-Clausen, *Vorweggenommene Einheit*, p. 31.

[40] Bunsen to Arnold, July 14, 1835, Bunsen, *Memoir*, vol. 1, p. 418; Nippold, *Bunsen*, vol. 1, p. 445.

in a critically informed reconstruction of the objective historical truth of the major events of Christ's life, death, and resurrection. The biblical record should be subjected to the same kind of critical investigation applied to other historical documents. Poetic and factual truth needed to be distinguished, with direct reporting by eyewitnesses separated from later revisions and additions. Bunsen was convinced that unfettered historical criticism would uncover the authentic, irrefutable historical core of Christianity, and that this historical core would conform precisely to mankind's subjective need for redemption. The action of divine grace in human relations, the intervention of the transcendent in the immanent relations of empirical cause and effect, would itself be confirmed as an historical truth.

In his correspondence with Friedrich Luecke and Thomas Arnold during the 1830s, Bunsen began to speak once again of the need to balance philological criticism and philosophical interpretation in the study of both secular and sacred history. "The unfortunate separation of the subjective and the objective, the idea and appearance, of history and speculation," he wrote, "has brought us into great confusion."[41] But it was not so much "speculative" or metaphysical truth as ethical truth that Bunsen sought and found in the verifiable historical core of the Christian biblical narrative. As early as 1824 he noted in his diary that "all real vital truth is contained in conscience."[42] In 1835 he would assure Arnold that any historical criticism of the biblical texts that proceeded scientifically, without presuppositions, would reveal that "the records of things divine contain facts which are identical with our own wants and the voice of conscience, and have no value except when applied to these in faith."[43]

Bunsen did not publish his critical investigations of biblical history during the 1830s, but the results of his researches were important for his liturgical project and were eventually incorporated into it. By 1823 the development of Christian liturgy had become the main focus of Bunsen's historical investigations as well as of his practical interests in institutional reform. As he contemplated leaving government service in 1823, he saw himself devoting all his energy to a sweeping historical reconstruction of the liturgy of the various Christian churches, from the apostolic age to the present.[44] Bunsen's discussions with the king in the summer of 1822 and the king, the crown prince, and other Prussian political leaders in the winter of 1827–28, which were so critical in establishing his reputation at the court, were centered on the liturgical questions raised by the state-imposed union of the Calvinist and Lutheran confessions in 1817. The king had proposed a new liturgy that was experimentally instituted in number of garrison chapels, as

[41] Bunsen to Luecke, May 6, 1833, Nippold, *Bunsen*, vol. 1, p. 397.

[42] Nippold, *Bunsen*, vol. 1, p. 231.

[43] Bunsen to Arnold, July 14, 1835, Bunsen, *Memoir*, vol. 1, p. 418; Nippold, *Bunsen*, vol. 1, p. 445.

[44] Bunsen to Luecke, August 16, 1823, Nippold, *Bunsen*, vol. 1, p. 205.

well as the Berlin Court Chapel in 1816. Bunsen had also experimented with a new liturgy, heavily indebted to that of the Anglican Church, at the Protestant chapel in Rome. Although the king and Bunsen agreed on the importance of liturgical forms and shared a number of ideas about the substance of reform, Bunsen did not support the king's desire to impose a unified liturgy for general use in all Protestant churches. "Intervention from above, through governmental authority," he noted, "even with the best intentions, is always questionable and usually corrupting for the church." The role of the government was simply to recognize what had emerged spontaneously, from the "bosom of the church," as a product of congregational interactions. An authentic liturgy was built on a "free" church and emerged gradually through conversation and mutual criticism within the church.[45] Despite these differences, Bunsen and the king continued to exchange views throughout the 1820s, and during Bunsen's stay in Berlin in 1827–28 the king permitted Bunsen's Roman liturgy to be published at state expense, and even provided it with a short, but positive, introduction, indicating that it represented simply a variant of his own proposal.[46]

A number of issues were involved in Bunsen's liturgical researches and reform plans. First, they expressed his belief that the core of Christianity, preceding all doctrinal articulation and institutionalization, was the fact of redemption experienced as an encounter with a transcendent power. The traditional Protestant focus on the sermon, on teaching and preaching, was subordinated in Bunsen's liturgies to the communal rituals that expressed the "self-sacrifice" of the sinful, fallen ego to the redemptive power of divine love, and that gave thanks and praise in response to this act of grace. In 1832 Bunsen sent a copy of his hymnbook to the painter Schnorr von Carolsfeld with this accompanying note:

> May it declare to you, as clearly as it ought to do, that in divine life nothing is real or avails before God but the free sacrifice [*freie Opfer*] of thankful love – the childlike resignation of our own will to the will of God and the continuous offering up of our ego-centrism [*Selbstsucht*] to our Brethren. For that is the central issue of all Christian doctrine and the last and ultimate aim of all worship and religious devotion.[47]

Self-sacrifice and thankful praise constituted the core from which all liturgical, doctrinal, and institutional constructions had arisen. Liturgical reform entailed a return to this unifying experiential center of Christian culture, and

[45] Bunsen to Christiane, February 14, 1823, Nippold, *Bunsen*, vol. 1, p. 202.

[46] Frank Foerster has recently reconstructed in great detail the complicated history of Bunsen's various liturgical endeavors on the basis of previously unpublished materials. See Foerster, *Bunsen*, part 2, and especially pp. 60–69, 80–87.

[47] Nippold, *Bunsen*, vol. 1, p. 399; Bunsen, *Memoir*, vol. 1, p. 387.

the creation of rituals that articulated that experience within the historical language of the present age.

Prayers and hymns, much more than theological treatises or confessions of faith, were in this view the most important representations of Christian life and the primary forms in which that life was nurtured, sustained, and developed. Greatly impressed by the Anglican Book of Common Prayer, Bunsen had begun a critical historical analysis of German Protestant hymns and prayers in the early 1820s. With the help of resident chaplains in Rome, he worked through more than three hundred hymnbooks and eighty thousand hymns and published his results in 1833 as *Versuch eines allgemeinen evangelischen Gesang- und Gebetsbuches fuer Kirchen- und Hausgebrauche* (Draft for a General Evangelical Hymn and Prayer Book, for Use in Church and Home). The general principles informing Bunsen's conception of cultural development were strikingly evident in this collection.

First, Bunsen and his assistants selected their hymns and prayers on the basis of what they construed as universality of content. Regional and confessional differences were subordinated to presentation of documents that expressed the core of Christian experience and consciousness with the greatest concrete immediacy. The principles of historical criticism were applied to the extant texts in order to winnow out corrupted versions laden with secondary artifice and subjective elaboration. This universality of essential content, however, was to be distinguished from simple uniformity. Bunsen imagined the individual hymns as "pages of a single poem," as diversified expressions of the core experience, elaborating its possibilities in different settings.[48] There were, of course, limitations on Bunsen's concept of "universality." He imagined his book as both national and Protestant. He described it as a national epic of German Protestantism and as a "spiritual book of the people [*geistliches Volksbuch*]."[49]

Reconciling these apparent contradictions in Bunsen's eyes were two assumptions. First, he believed that the development of German Protestant liturgy since the Reformation was the historical culmination of Christian liturgy per se, incorporating all of the universal elements of past moments within its own textual productions. Second, Bunsen was clearly convinced that Protestantism was a more advanced stage in Christian historical evolution than Roman Catholicism, that it marked a universal stage in the development of the Christian community – not a particular dimension within an historical stage. Protestant German prayers and hymns constituted a complete expression of Christian consciousness in national form: "Thus emerges a dignified structure, emerging quietly and without clamor or commotion in the flow of time and from the fullness of the creative powers, like a great

[48] *Versuch eines allgemeinen evangelischen Gesang- und Gebetbuchs zum Kirchen und Hausgebrauche* (Hamburg: 1833), p. xvii and xcvi.

[49] *Ibid*, p. iii; see also Bunsen, *Memoir*, vol. 1, p. 388.

work of nature constructed on the eternal rock of the Gospel, a building in which every authentic and independent hymn constitutes a vital stone."[50]

Second, Bunsen's collection was ordered not only according to the principle of systematic totality organizing diversity from a common experiential center, but also in terms of historical progression. At the core of this development was a common essence: "We can sing with the Psalmists and pray with Saint Augustine: Thomas a Kempis and Arndt, Fenelon and Tersteegen, Storr and Reinhard speak equally to our hearts, because they speak the universal language of the Christian soul to God."[51] The expressions of this essence, however, evolved over time, as a progressive revelation of Christian truth: Every liturgical form was the "fruit and consequence of an earlier one and the seed and beginning of a new existence." Moreover, this process operated according to the "eternal laws of development that God had placed in things."[52] The evolution of ethical community grounded in appropriation of the fact of redemption thus appeared to proceed as an immanent necessity that paralleled the development of ethno-linguistic national cultures. Bunsen conceived his *Gesangbuch* as a contribution to the cultivation of German national self-consciousness, as if the redeemed conscience of the Christian convert was synonymous with the national conscience.

The third general principle that informed Bunsen's liturgical studies was the principle of populism, or the conviction that all significant reform in the realm of ethical consciousness had to emerge from the people, from "below," rather than imposed by governments or other regulatory bodies – from "above." He described his *Gesangbuch* as a *Versuch*, as a "sketch" or "experiment" that would have to be tested not only by historical scholars in terms of its philological claims, but also by congregations and synods to see whether its texts were representative of shared Christian consciousness.

Bunsen's liturgical collections aimed to represent a collective German Protestant consciousness, to display for purposes of mutual recognition the conscience of a national church. Yet Bunsen was only too aware that such a national church existed only implicitly or as an ideal among the Germanic ethno-cultural peoples, who were divided by Catholic and Protestant confessions and by internal schisms within Protestantism. The acceptance of a common liturgy seemed to assume the existence of a national church, which was not (or not yet) in existence. In 1828 Bunsen wrote to Arnold: "My motto is: no great church without a liturgy, just as no liturgy without a church. The latter is with us Germans unfortunately not . . . self-evident."[53]

The third major dimension of Bunsen's investigations of Christian culture and of his practical efforts to reform it (besides textual historical study and liturgical reform) encompassed the constitution of a German national church

[50] *Versuch*, p. xviii. [51] *Ibid.*, p. xcvi. [52] *Ibid*, p. xvi.

[53] Bunsen to Arnold, Easter Monday, 1828, Nippold, *Bunsen*, vol. 1, p. 323, Bunsen, *Memoir*, vol. 1, p. 317.

and the problematic state–church relations implied in such a project. This aspect of his activity was most closely tied to his duties as head of the Prussian legation to the Vatican, whose major task was the negotiation of satisfactory relations between the Prussian state and the Catholic Church. Bunsen's concept of church–state relations were expressed mainly in the various memoranda he sent to Berlin in his activities as a representative of the Prussian government.

Bunsen first formulated his general framework for the negotiations with the papacy in December 1823, during the transition from the moderate, accommodating policies of Pius VII and Cardinal Consalvi, to the aggressive, uncompromising stance of Leo XII and the party of zealous Ultramontanes with which he surrounded himself. Bunsen suggested to his government that Prussia define its stance in this new situation on the basis of a general conception of the role of the Catholic Church in post-Napoleonic European society and culture. The resurgence of papal claims to spiritual authority and institutional autonomy during the Restoration, Bunsen asserted, was grounded in a general recognition among princes and peoples that the altar was a primary support of civil order and that the dignity and influence of the church depended on its independence from political interference and control. These principles were as pertinent to Protestantism as Catholicism, but in the Catholic cultures of the Latin European nations they had taken a particularly reactionary, antiliberal and antinational form, making claims for the hegemony of the church hierarchy over both the individual conscience and the national solidarity of ethno-cultural peoples. The principles of Roman Catholicism had not changed over the centuries but, in opposition to the claims of Jacobin revolutionaries, Bunsen suggested, they had assumed a more obviously reactionary guise. Catholic cultures were fated to play out a dialectic of revolution and reaction that was destructive to the formation of a national conscience in which solidarity was a product of individual freedom and self-imposed conformity to social norms. In the Germanic cultures of northern Europe, particularly Prussia and England, the Reformation had inaugurated a process of ethical education – cultivating the internalization of divine will as moral conscience – that expressed itself in moderate reformism, in a respect for historical continuity and social harmony produced by the constant reproduction of general spiritual principles in particular historical forms. Prussia should not panic in the face of a new aggressive stance by the papacy. She had nothing to fear, because her Protestant religious culture was as immune to reactionary absolutism as it was to revolutionary anarchism.[54]

What about the status of the Catholic Church within the cultures of Protestant states? This was a particularly pressing issue in Prussia after 1815,

[54] Bunsen's memoranda on the situation in Rome after 1823 are reprinted in Nippold, *Bunsen*, vol. 1, pp. 507ff.

especially in its newly acquired Rhenish provinces. Bunsen was convinced that the Catholic Church could only assert disruptive claims if it could muster strong popular support. Such support, however, could be prevented or dissipated through a concerted policy of cultural education that would encourage the general population to value their individual autonomy and nationality, as well as through the assurance of full civil rights for members of all confessions. Education of the Catholic clergy was particularly crucial: "To further the historical and philological education and scholarship of the Catholic clergy, and thus improve, through such educated clerics and scholars, the education of the Catholic populace, is to rob religious and hierarchical fanaticism of its power, to annihilate it."[55] There was no need to surrender to the church's claims in order to stem the revolutionary tide. It was religious fanaticism and hierarchical rigidity that fueled the revolutionary consciousness. At the same time there was no point in repressing traditional religious practices, since that would hinder the eventual integration of Catholic populations into a national culture.

From 1823 to 1836 Bunsen generally followed the guidelines he had constructed for himself at the outset of his diplomatic career. The major issue in negotiations between the papacy and German bishops concerned mixed marriages. After years of complicated and inconclusive negotiations, the issue was brought to a head in 1835 when a secret agreement between the Prussian state and the German bishops regarding the interpretation of a papal brief of 1830 was brought to the attention of the self-confident Gregory XVI and rejected (after an initial informal promise to accept it) by the recently installed archbishop of Cologne. In the ensuing flurry of recriminations, Bunsen, still overly optimistic about producing a compromise that would satisfy all sides, misrepresented the pliability of the opponents to each other and brought upon himself charges of betrayal and incompetence that led to his humiliation and resignation in 1838.

The effect of this debacle on the development of Bunsen's views was twofold. First, his general critical opposition to Roman Catholic Christianity as an obsolete historical form of Christianity was transformed into a virulent hatred of the papacy and the Catholic Church as the primary hindrance to the creation of a national ethical community. In the early 1830s Bunsen had still perceived Jacobin radicalism as the most threatening subversive element in European society. The Catholic Church, at least in Latin cultures, could be defended as a support for moral community grounded in transcendent authority, even if its conception of community and faith was hierarchical, authoritarian, historically anachronistic, and denied the ethical freedom of the modern subject. After 1838 this judgment was reversed. Religious reaction was deemed more threatening than democratic revolution and the major source of a false conception of freedom and communal

[55] Nippold, *Bunsen*, vol. 1, p. 531.

identity. The intensification of Bunsen's hostility to Roman Catholicism was paralleled by a distancing from tendencies within Protestantism that aimed at the imposition of church unity through hierarchical structures of church discipline and doctrinal conformity. "Judaicizing" and "Romanizing" administrators of transcendent truth seemed as threatening as the "heathen" rationalists who rejected the reality of transcendent revelation altogether.

Balancing Bunsen's intensified hostility to hierarchical and dogmatic tendencies, however, was a reinvigorated focus on church reform. Since the early 1820s Bunsen had been convinced that the revival and perfection of Protestant Christianity implied the independence of the church as an organized corporate body of redeemed believers. The regulation of the church by civil authority, whether that authority was an autocrat or a democratically elected parliament, was fatal to its educational function and ethical mission. As the "divine conscience" of the nation, the church had to be free to operate as the critical judge and public educator of corrupt civil societies and governments. But the independence of the church from government control did not necessarily imply the independence of the clergy from the will of the people or the autonomy of the church in relation to the nation. The state in Bunsen's view did not represent the nation against the church; it simply expressed the legal and political constitution of the ethno-cultural national community, while the church expressed the same community's ethical conscience. But for the church to represent the ethno-cultural nation in its moral-religious dimension, its inner constitution would have to express this function. The hierarchical superiority of clergy over the laity was untenable. The Protestant principle of the priesthood of all believers relegated the clergy to the status of delegates of the congregation for particular functions. Those functions were not only spiritual, but also social and political. The church needed institutional organization to protect its independence from civil government and to organize its practical, educational, and service functions. Bunsen believed that the organizational structure most appropriate for maintaining the independence of the church, unifying the community of Christians at a national level, and representing one national church to another, was a "limited" episcopacy. Bishops and their administrative councils could represent the identity of the national church beyond the congregational level and protect this identity from incursions by civil authority, but they had no spiritual or disciplinary authority over the members of congregations.

What was distinctive about Bunsen's proposals for church reform during the 1830s was his attempt to ally the church with the nation, to define the church as the ethical dimension of the nation in both a systematic and a dynamic sense. The church was the sphere of social interaction where individuals encountered the voice of the national conscience. This conscience, however, was produced not by their interactions but by a shared relation to a transcendent father, by a common experience of redemption in the encounter with the divine fact of transcendent intervention in the world. As the institutionalization of the national conscience, the church in turn operated as the school of ethical education within the nation. It was through the church that individuals of an ethno-cultural people recognized their status as moral subjects and recognized each other as members of a moral community formed by self-sacrificial surrender to the transcendent will of the father. Bunsen's two projects, which had appeared to diverge in 1817, seemed to reconverge by 1838. The evolution of human beings as encultured subjects structured by the forms of language into ethno-cultural "peoples" began to overlap with the ethical progress of mankind toward a human commonwealth of the redeemed organized by love and the law of God. The ethical community was rooted in the linguistic, ethno-cultural nation, and the ethnic nation found its fulfillment through a process of moralization instigated by religion.

During the forced leave of absence from professional duties that followed Bunsen's humiliation and resignation in the spring of 1838, he found consolation and eventually personal renewal in a return to the original life's project he had formulated in his youth. His first stop after leaving Rome was Munich, where he hoped to discuss his Egyptological research with Schelling. The brief stop became a three-month stay devoted to an intense study of Schelling's philosophy. After a few personal conversations with Schelling, Bunsen obtained a copy of his lecture notebooks and was overwhelmed by the convergence between his own intellectual evolution and Schelling's reformulated "positive" and "historical" philosophy.[56] He threw himself into studies of ancient myth and language in an attempt to ascertain the "Keplerian" laws according to which the "eternal spirit draws his orbit of eternity around the terrestrial life we call time." He felt he was returning, like "a bird to her nest," to a vision of a comprehensive universal history that he had "perceived with fascination in the freshness of youth and to which I have returned in such a miraculous way." The return had a new twist – the evolution of mankind he had first envisioned now incorporated the sacred history of the relationship between man and God.[57] Schelling's new philosophy, he wrote to Arnold in August 1838, encompassed "all questions and problems, not of men, but of the work of God in men."[58]

As Bunsen extended his enforced "sabbatical" in a year-long visit with friends and family in England from the fall of 1838 to the fall of 1839, the philosophical enthusiasm stimulated in Munich was matched by an "elevating" experience of a "great national life, that England alone among

[56] Bunsen to Kestner Munich June 11, 1838, Nippold, *Bunsen*, vol. 2, p. 2; Bunsen, *Memoir*, vol. 1, p. 462.

[57] Bunsen to his wife, November 20, 1838, Bunsen, *Memoir*, vol. 1, p. 481; Nippold, *Bunsen*, vol. 2, p. 18.

[58] Bunsen to Arnold, August 1, 1838, Nippold, *Bunsen*, vol. 2, p. 4; Bunsen, *Memoir*, vol. 1, p. 464.

contemporary nations possesses." His first observation of parliamentary debates produced in him a vision of the fully realized life of a community of autonomous spirits:

> I wish you could form an idea of what I felt [he wrote to his wife]. I saw for the first time *man*, the member of a true Germanic state, in his highest, his proper place, defending the highest interests of humanity with the wonderful powers of speech – wrestling (as the entire vigorous man instinctively wishes), but with the arm of the Spirit, boldly grasping at, or tenaciously holding fast power, in the presence of fellow citizens submitting to the public conscience the judgment of his cause, and of his own uprightness.[59]

In the practice of national life, England was a school for the kind of wisdom that could be met on the streets and breathed in the air. Yet Bunsen noted that British deficiency in philosophical understanding stymied many of his friends' attempts to find the "seeds of regeneration" for their own "blessed institutions" by "distilling the eternal spirit" from the "decayed or decaying letter." While Germans suffered from an inability to construct reality according to their philosophical knowledge of the idea, the English failed to grasp the idea in their own reality and thus to engage in the task of reforming and reactivating it in new historical circumstances. To a German friend Bunsen wrote: "the thought is ours, it is possessed by Germans at this moment in world history: I mean the philosophical consciousness of life and the ground of divine and human things in thought and idea."[60] Stimulated by the tension between the poles of German philosophy and English national life, Bunsen soon regained his sense of historical purpose. His existence was "electrified" by the prospect of embodying the "vita nuova" of speculative comprehension in a truly worthy form in his fatherland.[61] In the fall of 1838 he informed his wife that he was confident that "his world [was] in the future time, for that I have lived and thought."[62] A few months later he noted: "a new period of life begins for me."[63]

When Bunsen's diplomatic leave ended with his appointment as minister plenipotentiary at Berne in the summer of 1839, he was eager to join with his royal friend the crown prince in planning an epochal ethical transformation of German cultural life, inspired by the English example and guided by Schelling's philosophical knowledge. The sense of national mission that had informed his work in 1813 had returned. In the spring of 1840 he wrote to his son: "at this historical moment the Germans are the people

[59] Bunsen to his wife January 29, 1839, Bunsen, *Memoir*, vol. 1, p. 499.

[60] Bunsen to Platner, December 24, 1838, Nippold, *Bunsen*, vol. 2, p. 32; Bunsen *Memoir*, vol. 1, p. 495.

[61] Bunsen to John Hills, December 26, 1838, *Memoir*, vol. 1, p. 494; Bunsen to his wife, December 8, 1838, *Memoir*, vol. 1, p. 488; Nippold, *Bunsen*, vol. 2, pp. 25, 31.

[62] Bunsen to his wife, November 18, 1838, *Memoir*, vol. 1, p. 479; Nippold, *Bunsen*, vol. 2, 16.

[63] Bunsen to his wife, January 29, 1839, *Memoir*, vol. 1, p. 498; Nippold, *Bunsen*, vol. 2, p. 35.

of God on earth and to be fully conscious of being German, one must be Prussian."[64]

TRIUMPH AND DISILLUSIONMENT: COLLECTIVE MEMORY AND THE CHURCH OF THE FUTURE

As it became obvious in the spring of 1840 that Frederick William III was dying, Bunsen waited expectantly for the call that would end his exile and provide an opportunity to work actively for the historical realization of his vision of a German Protestant community in Prussia. The crown prince's trust and confidence in Bunsen had not been broken by the Roman debacle of 1837–38. In the months immediately following Bunsen's resignation, the crown prince intensified his correspondence with his old friend and pressured the foreign ministry and ministry of culture to give Bunsen special assignments that would display his political indispensability and rebuild his reputation. All of the government documents related to the negotiations with the papacy and the German bishops were placed at Bunsen's disposal so that he could write a full report of the relations between Prussia and the Vatican during his period of tenure in Rome.

Bunsen expected that the Frederick William's accession to the throne would mark an epochal turning point in Prussian, German, and world history. Like many of his compatriots, he noted the parallels with the beginnings of the reigns of the Great Elector in 1640 and Frederick the Great in 1740. The year 1840, he believed, signified the beginning of a regime that would give "definitive form" to the modern Prussian monarchy and reveal its place in world history as the exemplary model and leader of a triumphant German and Protestant culture. Although Bunsen expected to play a significant role in shaping the policies of this regime, he was not clear about precisely what that role might be. "What I would like best of all," he wrote to Arnold in early June, "would be to be president of a Royal Commission for Church and Public Instruction, without having to undertake the administration itself."[65] His reformist zeal, his discomfort with bureaucratic maneuvering, and his strained relations with many officials in the upper echelons of the civil service made it difficult for him to imagine being appointed to one of the major ministries. The only one he thought about as a possibility was the Ministry of Public Instruction, and only if this portfolio could be separated from the administration of ecclesiastical affairs in a reconstituted *Kultusministerium*. At any rate Bunsen, was certain the king would call him to Berlin, so that he could be at his side during the critical years devoted to creating

[64] Bunsen to one of his sons, April 20, 1840, Nippold, *Bunsen*, vol. 2, p. 101; Bunsen, *Memoir*, vol. 1, p. 561.

[65] Bunsen to Arnold, June 3, 1840, *Memoir*, vol. 1, p. 567.

the framework of major reforms. Although Bunsen was consulted about the king's plans for reorganizing the Academy of Arts and Sciences and the creation of a Civilian Order of Merit to honor the heroes of culture, and given a leading role in negotiating the appointments of intellectual and cultural celebrities, summer dragged into fall without the expected call from Berlin. The king's attempt to smooth over the tensions with the Vatican and negotiate an agreement with the Catholic Church in his own Rhenish and Polish provinces, and the continued hostility toward Bunsen among the group of established old Prussian ministers, made his presence in Berlin a potential embarrassment for the regime. Bunsen had almost reconciled himself to a permanent exile in Switzerland and to the role of prophet and apostle of future transformations when the long awaited call finally arrived in April 1841. He was to come to Berlin immediately to consult with the king about a specific diplomatic project.

Bunsen's assignment – to negotiate with the British on a common policy for protecting Protestant Christians in the unstable Middle Eastern fragments of the collapsing Ottoman Empire, and more specifically to arrange the creation of an ecumenical Protestant bishopric in Jerusalem – was of great symbolic significance to both Bunsen and the king. For five busy, exhilarating weeks they engaged in intense daily discussions, rediscovering their common conception of the future of German Protestant culture.

Three general principles shaped the royal "instruction" that Bunsen took with him to London in mid-June.[66] First, it affirmed the Protestant solidarity between the established churches in England and Prussia. By establishing an ecumenical Protestant bishopric in the Holy Land, the world's two largest Protestant churches joined hands in unity and peace, "above the grave of the redeemer," thus "remembering" their common origin.[67] Second, this alliance affirmed irreducible, national differences in the expression and organization of Christian experience by respecting the rights of both churches to maintain their national language, liturgy, and doctrinal confession in the practice of their faith. Finally, the common mission of two national churches within the broader framework of Protestant Christianity was to be represented in the apostolic form of a church constitution in which individual congregations in a specific geographic area were organizationally unified under the administration of a bishop consecrated by the church as a whole. For Bunsen, the affirmation of these principles, and their acceptance by both churches and both governments, seemed to affirm his fondest hopes for the emergence of a Protestant Christian identity that would operate as the conscience of a new moment in world history. The agreement gave limited, but specific form to his concept of an alliance of nationally individuated Protestant cultures sharing a common religious faith and ethical

[66] Schmidt-Clausen, *Vorweggenommene Einheit*, chapter 5.

[67] Letter to his wife, April 26, 1841, Nippold, *Bunsen*, vol. 2, p. 159; Bunsen, *Memoir*, vol. 1, p. 594.

self-consciousness. This genuine Christian catholicity, which recognized the principle of subjective autonomy for both individuals and ethno-cultural communities, he felt, must eventually triumph over the false hierarchical, centralizing catholicity of the Roman Catholic Church.

As the negotiation for the creation of the Jerusalem bishopric moved toward successful conclusion in the summer of 1841, Bunsen was overwhelmed by the importance of the historical moment. He felt he had been called to work energetically for the idea articulated in the project of the Jerusalem Bishopric – the creation of a vital national Protestant church that could function as the internal moral conscience of the nation and enter into a global federation of ethical communities that represented the universality of Christianity. He was eager to return to Germany as the king's personal advisor on church reform and cultural policy, and he soon became impatient with a perceived lack of decisiveness from Berlin. Historical opportunities were being wasted. "I am afraid," he wrote to his wife in September 1841, that the king combines not yet cause and effect sufficiently in his government. Great preparations have been made. "The world waits and time flies by without any action being taken." "Never in the history of the world," he claimed, was a prince given a second chance to grasp his fate: "To what purpose are ideas, but to be realized? To what can thoughts serve, but to be brought into execution?"[68]

The king, however, was somewhat taken aback by Bunsen's enthusiasm for immediate and decisive action. While Bunsen, surrounded by his evangelical friends in England, felt the tug of a world historical mission, Frederick William was made aware of some of the enormous problems that would arise if Prussia's international politics was reoriented from the conservative empires of Russia and Austria to the modern national state of England on the basis of a commitment to a shared religious vision. Surrounded by conservative advisers suspicious of Bunsen's liberal and nationalist tendencies, he feared that Bunsen's excessive zeal would kill all chances for gradual reform. He counseled caution and patience, hoping that Bunsen would keep his more radical plans to himself. Although Bunsen could not imagine that the king would exclude him from a major leadership role in developing the seeds so propitiously planted by the triumph of his English negotiations, the king indicated that he would rather keep his old friend at a distance. He warmly congratulated Bunsen on his diplomatic successes but did not reward him with a call to Berlin. Instead he appointed him ambassador to England, a great plum for Bunsen, but not exactly the reward he had expected. Frederick William shared many of Bunsen's visions and enthusiasms, especially regarding church reform and the role of Prussia as exemplary leader of German cultural nationality and Protestant Christianity. But he was wary of Bunsen's belief in decisive action and his willingness to engage in

[68] Letter to his wife, September 30, 1841, Bunsen, *Memoir*, vol. 1, p. 619; Nippold, *Bunsen*, vol. 2, p. 182.

partisan battle, and he was obviously much less certain about the foundations of his imagined reformation in the modern, postrevolutionary principles of individual autonomy and self-governing community. As consciousness of disagreement between Frederick William and Bunsen became more obvious after 1841, Bunsen became more self-conscious about his historical role as a prophet of reform. During a visit to Prussia in 1845 he wrote to his wife: "the King's heart is like a brother toward me, but our ways diverge. The die is caste and he reads in my countenance that I deplore the throw. He too fulfills his fate, as we with him."[69]

The occasion for this comment was Bunsen's discontent with the king's hesitant position on political constitutional reform. Bunsen believed that Prussia should follow the English model, modernizing traditional historical freedoms within a parliamentary system that recognized all citizens as autonomous persons within the national community. But this specific disagreement brought to the surface a general divergence in their conceptions of Protestant culture and German cultural nationality. As Bunsen articulated his conceptions more systematically in response to specific government policies and initiatives in the 1840s, it became more obvious that his own historical project represented one version of the program for actualizing the idea of a Christian-German community within the lives of modern Prussians. Among the king's inner circle, Bunsen's general historical and political views were closest to the scientist Alexander von Humboldt. Humboldt noted that he and Bunsen were most obviously in agreement with each other, and most isolated from the king's aristocratic advisers in their "more liberal viewpoint" regarding the "inevitable development of modern bourgeois [*buergerliche*] political institutions" (that is, institutions that recognized subjects of the king as free and responsible citizens of the state), and on most philosophical and historical issues as well, as displayed in their admiration of Schelling and their concerted attempts to move him to Berlin. Where they differed, Humboldt suggested, was in the relative importance they placed on "Christian ecclesiastical affairs." In the latter area, Bunsen's interests were more in tune with the pious nobles around Frederick William. For Bunsen the creation of a fraternal community of free, responsible citizens out of an ethnic "people" could not be uncoupled from the regeneration and transformation of the Christian church.[70] And the Christian church was not for Bunsen simply the religious self-expression of the national community, but a community founded on transcendent principles that engaged the "natural" ethnic community of the people in a normative and redemptive fashion.

[69] Bunsen to his wife, August 19, 1845, Nippold, *Bunsen*, vol. 2, p. 324; Bunsen, *Memoir*, vol. 2, p. 92.

[70] Humboldt to Bunsen, December 14, 1840, in *Briefe von Alexander von Humboldt an Christian Carl Josias Freiherr von Bunsen* (Leipzig: 1869), pp. 43–47. The plan to bring Schelling to Berlin in 1835 is described on pp. 14–23.

Bunsen's major publications during the 1840s represented a continuation of the two paths of his life's project as they had developed in the 1830s. Between 1840 and 1845 he published three studies on the nature, implications, historical development, and future prospects of Christian culture, all culminating in an assessment of the present mission of German Protestantism and the most pressing issues in church reform. His *Die heilige Leidensgeschichte und die stille Woche* (The Sacred History of the Passion and the Holy Week), published in 1841, continued his project of developing an appropriate liturgy for contemporary Protestant religious experience. In *Die Basiliken des christlichen Roms* (The Basilicas of Christian Rome) of 1843, based on his earlier researches on Roman topography and archaeology, he examined the architectural structuring of worship space as a symbolic representation of Christian community. Finally, in *Die Verfassung der Kirche der Zukunft* (The Constitution of the Church of the Future), published in 1845, he brought together in a systematic manner his thoughts on the inner constitution of the church as an ethical community and its historical and structural relationships to both ethno-cultural communities, or peoples, and to legal–political organizations of power, or states. The other dimension of his original plan – to define the meaning of the present through a reconstruction of the ancient origins and evolution of human culture on the basis of a linguistic and mythological analysis – attained its first major public articulation with the publication of the first three volumes of *Aegyptens Stelle in der Weltgeschichte* (Egypt's Place in World History) in 1844 and 1845. The simultaneous publication of major works on the archaic origins and on the future of human culture, on the immanent determinations of human cultural development, and on the relations between transcendent divinity and immanent humanity expressed not so much a continuing dualism in Bunsen's thinking as an important convergence in his vision. As he consciously articulated the premises of both sides of his project in response to the events in Prussia, Bunsen revealed that they really were components of a single vision that merged the evolution of national communities defined by common language structures with the evolution of ethical communities grounded in voluntary religious obedience to the transcendent father's law.

Since the early 1820s, Bunsen had been concerned with identifying and defining the essence of Christian culture as a "practice" or "life" that proceeded from a direct historical experience, a "factual" encounter with a personal "other," rather than as a concept that evolved according to an inner teleological necessity. For Bunsen, the historical principle had very clear active and passive dimensions. Its active side was the firm belief that human cultures fulfilled their historical mission through a process of becoming in which the idea of the culture expressed in its symbolic and institutional arrangements what it was in essence. The passive dimension was constituted by his belief that the development of human communities was not simply determined by this inner self-determining teleology of the cultural idea but dependent on historical encounters between individual subjects and a power that existed outside the immanent circle of human relations. His work on the liturgy of the Passion Week was particularly focused on the passive side of this experience – the encounter with the historical fact of God's actions in the world. The reading of the narrative of divine action in history was a critical component of the week, and the powerful effect of this action on the subjective constitution of the human spirit marked all of the liturgical responses of the week as well. One of the reasons Bunsen was so intent on salvaging a core of literal truth in the historical accounts of the gospel was that he believed Christian experience was grounded in the belief that Christ's life, death, and resurrection actually occurred and were not created "by us," were not a psychological projection or cultural product.[71]

In the introductory chapter to *The Constitution of the Church of the Future*, Bunsen expressed this conviction in systematic fashion by describing Christianity as a stage in the relationship between the human self and its ground in both natural and spiritual reality. In the pre-Christian period, this relationship to the natural and spiritual "beyond" took the form of a dualistic, contradictory structure of dependence and estrangement. The individual's consciousness of dependence on a divine creator was continually regenerated by "memories" of a primal "natural" identity of creature and creator, and these memories themselves generated repeated longings for a return to that original state. The longing to reestablish the bond between creator and creature expressed itself in utterances of love and thanks, and in attempts to transcend finite human existence and merge into the creative source of all beings. The drive to overcome division in such merger, however, was stymied by the individual's inability to transcend his own selfishness, by the sin of pride or imagined self-sufficiency: "all religions whatsoever have as their inward ground that feeling of need which springs from the interruption of man's union with God through sin, and for their final object, that reunion, for which, however dimly and uncertainly, men were encouraged to hope."[72] Attempts to resolve this conflict took the form of ritual sacrifice, both propitiatory sacrifice to assuage guilt and deflect the anger of the god(s) and love offerings or sacrifices of gratitude that articulated the dependence

[71] Christian Carl Josias Bunsen, *Die heilige Leidensgeschichte und die stille Woche* (2 vols.; Hamburg: 1841). The first volume contains a proposed liturgy for the week, with Bunsen's introductory comments. The second volume is a collection of appropriate musical scores for both the choir and the congregation, edited by the composer Sigismund Neukomm. The passive dimension is expounded on pp. lii–lv. The emphasis on the reading of the historical narrative as the story of a transcendent series of events is on pp. vi ff.

[72] *The Constitution of the Church of the Future: A Practical Explanation of the Correspondence with the Right Honourable William Gladstone, on the German Church, Episcopacy and Jerusalem*. Translated from the German under Bunsen's supervision and with additions (London: 1847), p. 6. I will cite from this edition using the German edition of 1845 primarily to check Bunsen's translation of some key terms: *Die Verfassung der Kirche der Zukunft: Praktische Erlaeuterungen zu dem Briefwechsel ueber die deutsche Kirche, das Episkopat and Jerusalem* (Hamburg: 1845), p. 62.

of the finite creature on its creator. In ethical terms, pre-Christian human experience was torn apart by the conflict between a moral law demanding "perfect holiness"[73] and the imperfection of an actual existence defined by individual finitude. The conflicts between pre-Christian human beings and God, between the individual self and its ground, could not be resolved because the relationship was conceived as external, mediated by statutory law and material sacrifice rather than by a "moral disposition of the heart," and because human beings did not possess the power to consummate the inward transformation that their outward acts attempted to express.

This "unhappy discord" of religious consciousness was resolved only by a "self-sacrifice of the Deity Himself," when Christ freely sacrificed his own particular existence to the will of the divine father in order to atone for human sin and assuage human guilt once and for all. Henceforth propitiatory sacrifices were unnecessary: All that was required was belief that God had accomplished man's atonement through the sacrifice of his son. The altar was transformed from the place where sacrifices were made to the place of remembrance where the historical act of divine self-sacrifice was continually reaffirmed and the reunion of the creatures with God and, through their mutual recognition of shared dependence, with each other, was celebrated. The altar of sacrifice became a table of communion and commemoration. Moreover, once the barrier of sin and guilt separating the human and the divine had been abolished through the historical act of divine self-sacrifice, humanity could give conflict-free utterance to its consciousness of dependence through acts of self-surrendering love:

> The inward consciousness of the eternal redeeming love of God (that is, faith) imparted the capacity of feeling at one with God in spite of sin; for it gave men the power of severing sin as an evil hostile element from their real self and therefore of freeing their life from selfishness which is the root of all evil in it. A free devotion to God and our brethren in thankful love now became possible.[74]

The two external sacrifices of ancient religions became internalized realities in Christianity. The sacrifice of atonement for sin was accomplished through faith in the historical act of divine self-sacrifice; the sacrifice of thanks that emerged from recognition of dependence on the creator became the permanent incorporation of the divine in the human through self-sacrificing ethical action under the rule of the Holy Spirit. Identification with others in the fraternity of the "brethren," self-sacrifice under the guidance of internal conscience: These were the experiential realities of Christian second birth.

In Bunsen's view the social, interpersonal articulation of the Christian transformation of the relationship between God and man was the priesthood of all believers. Faith in the reality of redemption through divine love

[73] *Constitution*, p. 8. [74] *Ibid.*, p. 9.

and self-sacrifice erased the necessity for any "external" acts of mediation between God and man. The individual approached the divine father without human mediation, with complete responsibility for his or her own acts and thoughts: "every individual became a priest of the most high because responsible to Him alone" and thus "moral responsibility" became internalized as "the inseparable appendage of the awful gift of personality."[75] The inward dispositions of faith and love made actual the reconciliation between the human and the divine that had been hopelessly sought in ancient sacrifices of atonement and gratitude. But faith and love were free acts of the person, even though they were also responses to an historical act by the divine father. Man was not free to save himself, but he was free to accept or reject the salvation given by God's self-sacrifice. Within Christianity, Bunsen claimed, piety and morality were equivalent. Faith in God's self-sacrifice produced a transformation of the moral disposition of the heart. Recognition of dependence resulted in self-sacrificing acts of love, self-transcending action in the service of God and the community. Christianity as an experience found its ultimate worldly existence in the progressive actualization of a brotherhood of autonomous spirits, in the creation of an ethical world order [*sittliche Weltordnung*] as the genuine Kingdom of God [*Reich Gottes*].[76] The relation between the divine and the human became an internal self-relation between the universality of conscience and the finite particularity of natural and historical being. The self-relating subject found its home in a community in which the relationship to the other was mediated not through an external law or person but through the relationship to the universal embedded in one's own conscience. This conscience was not natural or ethno-cultural, but "divine." Individuals did not obey it out of necessity, as they obeyed the structural determinants of language, but voluntarily, as free subjects. The liberation from egoism that was required to obey the universal law of internalized conscience derived from the encounter with God's historical act of self-sacrifice and, more particularly, with the proclamation of that act through his Word. The emergence of the free subject of an ethical community was tied to that subject's surrender to the "objective" historical reality of God's acts and claims.

As Bunsen attempted to construct a description of the essential meaning of Christian experience and practice that provided the continuous core in the progressive historical transformations of Christian culture, he oscillated between different forms of discourse. In describing the "objective" side of the religious relationship, that is, the acts of the creator in relationship to his creation, he usually began with the discourse of divine revelation. He also affirmed, however, that it was a legitimate and useful human enterprise to comprehend the narrative of God's acts in the language of speculative metaphysics, to translate the language of revelation into "the general

[75] *Ibid.*, p. 12. [76] *Ibid.*, p. 35; *Kirche*, p. 94.

philosophical language of our time."[77] Philosophical comprehension could not replace the experiential encounter with God's redemptive acts in history, but it brought to self-consciousness the critical universal dimension of that unique encounter. Philosophical understanding of infinite being could easily degenerate into abstract formalism or ahistorical mysticism if it lost its grounding in the historical encounter, but a mere external assent to the facts of revelation ignored the vital, subjective element in the repeated encounters with revelation by the succession of human generations. Both theology and metaphysics were "epiphenomenal" from Bunsen's perspective. They were secondary elaborations of a direct experience, but as clarifying illuminations of experience they served an important cultural function. For Bunsen, Schelling clearly provided an important cultural service in thinking through the metaphysical core of sacred history:

> Schelling's great and fundamental idea of the Infinite and Absolute as the eternal source and foundation of the finite and conditional, as well as his doctrine of the divine unity of all life, though it appears to us in antagonistic forms, have given to the ideas of the spiritual world that independence of the merely outward and historical which Christianity presupposes and requires for the right understanding of its divine doctrines, and of which it actually assures believers by the inward experience of their hearts.[78]

The philosophical capacity to grasp and reconstruct the eternal laws embodied in the historical acts of divinity was an important component of human freedom. It expressed mankind's ability to appropriate as a critical element of its internal nature what was originally given from the outside. The historical command to submit one's creaturely status to the law and will of the creator was internalized as a subjective identification of the individual with the rules of the ethical community of mankind. Belief in the historical act of divine self-sacrifice was internalized as continuous self-giving love toward one's "brethren" under the rule of conscience. Historical criticism of the texts of tradition was justified by the continuous need to draw out this core of essential, redemptive meaning from the husks of historically circumstantial tradition.

The subjective, human side of the God–man relationship in sacred history, the component that constituted the vital "life" of Christianity, was for Bunsen most easily understood through the language of Kantian moral philosophy: "Kant's doctrine of the freedom of the moral sense in man founded on the independence of the moral law written in his conscience – as being the law of the divine government of the world and therefore higher than all natural power – did more for the resuscitation of Christian life than all the dry dogmatism of the watchmen of Zion had done for centuries."[79] For Bunsen, Christian obedience to the commands of the Holy Spirit could

[77] *Constitution*, p. 37. [78] *Ibid.*, p. 99. [79] *Ibid.*, p. 99, and also pp. 271–73.

be fully translated into Kantian obedience to the internal laws of conscience, and the tasks of building God's kingdom on earth could be translated into the mission to construct "an ethical world order" in which all men voluntarily obeyed the laws of their common human essence, thus affirming their dependence on the creator of human subjectivity and their solidarity with other human subjects at the same time.

But in Bunsen's texts, the Kantian discourse of moral autonomy and duty was inevitably supplemented by the discourse of creaturely dependence and the discourse of self-sacrificing love. It was the encounter with the transcendent other that revealed the self's dependence and thus propelled the movement toward self-sacrificing merger with the other. By hearing and accepting "the divine word of redeeming love," human beings were actually "enabled to act on the ground of free moral principle, not from the natural center of their own individuality."[80] Thus like the ultras at the court, Bunsen tended to define freedom as a form of obedience. But in Bunsen's case, the obedience was obedience to the voice of conscience installed within the self by the internalization of the father's word as one's own essential, "true" voice.

The permanent, essential core of the Christian experience – the transformative internalization of the divine–human relationship as a life in God – was articulated in the historical development of the redeemed in two primary forms: in the patterns and rituals of worship in which the new relationship to the divine was nurtured, reenacted, and reaffirmed, and in the constitutionally instituted relations among the redeemed in the historical church. In Bunsen's work on liturgy and church architecture, he sought out the cultural forms that confirmed and nurtured the progressive development of subjective autonomy and communities of mutual recognition among free spirits. Historical commemoration was central to these forms. In the forms of worship, the individual subject remembered, and thus continually made present, the historical encounter with the transcendent father, his word, and his law.

For Bunsen the architectural form of the basilica as inherited and adapted from the classical world by Christian culture was the perfect space for expressing the nature of human freedom and community. In its original form, according to Bunsen, the basilica was characterized by the combination of a people's hall where the public enacted its business, and the tribune where they gathered to hear the proclamation of laws by lawgivers and the verdicts of their judges. This dual relationship of passive reception and active interaction was perfectly suited to provide a spatial configuration for the Christian community, which fulfilled the idea embodied by the classical basilica in its division into a clergy that presented the divine message and a congregation that received it and acted on it. The basilica form found "its genuine purpose

80 *Ibid.*, p. 85.

and inner determination [*ihre eigene Bestimmung*]"[81] in the relation between nave and apse in the Christian church. However, Christianity made an important change in the basilica form. The space between the tribune and the people's hall, between apse and nave, became a zone of interaction and reconciliation through its transformation into the altar space of the crossing, or transept. In Christian communities, this crossing became the center of the process of building community: Reconciliation and unification emerged as the core of the community's values, and the hall-like structure of the basilica was increasingly reshaped into the cruciform structure of the great Christian cathedrals. This transformation of communal self-representation in space, Bunsen insisted, was produced by the combination of immanent "natural energies [*Naturkraefte*]" and the experienced power of the transcendent divinity: "The shaping power of German nature that is called to create the world anew, here goes through its apprenticeship under the aegis of the Roman mother, filled with exaltation and dedicated to the sacred battle through the passively absorbed proclamation of the incarnate God and the Kingdom of God on Earth."[82]

Medieval Gothic, which Bunsen, like most of his contemporaries, imagined as a peculiarly Germanic style, appropriated the pointed arch as the perfect idiom for describing the identity of the community in terms of a subjective freedom with a transcendent origin. What was at stake in this adaptation was an understanding of the relationship between God and man as an internal "spiritual" relation that gave human beings the power to transfigure the particularity and opacity of nature. The Christian space articulated in a Gothic cathedral represented the transformation of external necessity into spiritual freedom.[83] Bunsen, unlike Frederick William, imagined the shape of mankind's relationship to the transcendent revelation as evolving in a constant transformation and adaptation of the original basilica form. His particular focus on the transept, or crossing, rather than on the hierarchical separation of apse and nave made his religious vision easily adaptable to the proposals by his architect friend Wilhelm Stier (1799–1856) for a domed neo-Gothic cathedral at the center of German Protestant culture, a cathedral that was dominated by a large rotunda in which the people could congregate around the altar, where they commemorated the gifts of divine grace and affirmed their common dependence on the transcendent power of the father[84] (see Figure 29).

[81] *Die Basiliken des christlichen Roms nach ihrem Zusammenhange mit Idee und Geschichte der Kirchenbaukunst* (Munich: 1843), p. 57.

[82] *Ibid.*, p. 60. [83] *Ibid.*, pp. 73–74.

[84] Stier had collaborated with Bunsen in late 1827–28 in Rome on a plan for an "evangelical cathedral" that modeled itself on the early Gothic–Byzantine rotunda. See Cornelius Steckner, "Friedrich Wilhelm IV, Karl Friedrich Schinkel, Wilhelm Stier und das Projekt einer Protestantischen *Mater Ecclesiarum*," in Otto Buesch, ed. *Friedrich Wilhelm IV und seine Zeit* (Berlin: 1987), pp. 232–40.

Ecclesiastical architecture in Bunsen's conception was a representation of the ideal of Christian community. The "constitution" of the church, the arrangement of the relations between functional officers and congregation, between the leadership and the *Volk*, also developed progressively toward the point where the church articulated its reality as an ethical fraternity in a constitution that clearly affirmed the ultimate responsibility of each human subject to the internalized voice of the father. The altar as a communion table between the church of the clergy and the church of the congregation expressed the Christian claim that before God the Christian community was one brotherhood; divisions between clergy and laity were purely functional, articulating the passive and active dimensions of Christian community, the reception of the divine revelation through the presentation of the Word and the articulation of inner transformation in ethically motivated action. This reciprocal relationship between the submission to the father and the assumption of responsible autonomy defined the essence of each church member and was a sign of the unity among believers rather than of their division into two hierarchically ordered classes. Although Bunsen's church constitution shared many characteristics with that envisioned by Frederick William, he saw the offices of the clergy, including the bishops, as external functions that could be fulfilled by any church members, and as temporary offices tied to specific circumstances. The church was not constituted by the voice of God speaking through the authority of the bishops but through the inner appropriation of the word in the conscience of all members. The father had been turned into the Word that could be internalized by all, and that defined their universal membership in the ethical community of mankind. Bunsen's reformist enthusiasms and demands during the early 1840s were grounded in his conviction that the historical moment for the fulfillment of this development had arrived. The Protestant churches of northern Europe were called to bring to full realization the concept of Christian community in both their liturgy and their inner constitution. This reform of the inner church structure would bring the community of spirits to the point where it really could function as the conscience of the people. In 1845, Bunsen could still exalt in utopian hopes for a restoration of the harmony between "heaven and earth," the "visible and the invisible" and the "secular and the sacred."[85]

Three kinds of communities were entangled in complex ways in Bunsen's conception of the historical evolution and cultural role of the Christian church. First, there were "peoples" (*Voelker*) or ethno-cultural communities, whom Bunsen tended to see as linguistically defined. Shared structures of language were the "primal inscription" (*Urniederschlag*) of cultural identity within the embryonic life forces of tribal existence.[86] Ethno-cultural

[85] *Constitution*, p. 28.

[86] Bunsen to Usedom, January 8, 1844, in Nippold, *Bunsen*, vol. 2, p. 249.

peoples were the actual existing subjects of history: "*Voelker* are the real units, so to speak the higher personages in the history of the world."[87] The linguistic differences among such ethno-cultural peoples were given in a primal division of the human race and remained the natural basis of historical development. Churches evolved as the ethico-religious dimension within ethnic cultures. The church's historical purpose as a separate institution was to transform the ethnic people into a Christian nation. The church must be free from state interference in order to pursue this task. However, the separation of the church from the ethno-cultural nation made no sense in Bunsen's conception. The perfected church was the ethno-cultural nation in its perfected form as an ethical community. Thus, even if in future humankind transformed itself into a universal ethical community, the historical reality of this community would still be a federation or family of peoples: "Nations [*Voelker*] even thus constitute, in the great and complete development of the human race, the grand units and personages of the Kingdom of God; every nation forms even thus a member of the vast body of mankind in its process of restoration."[88] As the constituent members of a universal church, nations would be internally connected through homologous relations to the divine; but their earthly existence would remain individuated by ties of language and other symbolic relations of the cultural sphere. Through the church, the individuals of a *Volk* ordered their mutual life in relation to the eternal father, who was their ultimate source and ground.

States, on the other hand, organized the individuals of an ethno-cultural nation in terms of their external activity in the world. Politics and religion also could not easily be separated. The morals of subjective self-determination were a condition for responsible citizenship. The church and the state related to the people, respectively, as powers of inner transformation and of external discipline. The laws and institutions that gave external recognition to every citizen's moral autonomy required citizens who had been internally "moralized" if they were to function as more than empty forms. Similarly, the religious transformation of a peoples' inner life ultimately demanded external arrangements that encouraged practical expression of autonomy and fraternity in relations of work and power. "A free ecclesiastical constitution requires the full acknowledgment of the paramount importance of the free inward disposition above the outward act, consequently liberty of conscience, and therefore political liberty."[89] Both church and state were temporary historical arrangements whose purpose was the historical transformation of ethno-cultural peoples into a family of "communities of free spirits." The goal of their activity was a nation of free citizens internally ordering their freedom according to the rule of a universal conscience created

[87] *Constitution*, p. 42; *Kirche*, pp. 100–1. [88] *Constitution*, pp. 54–55; *Kirche*, p. 111.
[89] *Constitution*, p. 26; *Kirche*, p. 84.

through the religious encounter with the redemptive acts of a transcendent father.

In his discussion of contemporary issues of church reform, Bunsen developed what he saw as a Protestant version of the relationship between catholicity and national diversity. The organization of ethical life occurred within the framework of the ethnic existence of peoples, but the unity among these peoples, which allowed them to relate in peace as members of a common Christian family, was grounded in their shared relationship to the transcendent. All ethical communities in the modern world possessed a national conscience that was shaped by the redemptive experience of encounter with a transcendent loving father. Yet as Bunsen pushed his investigation into the archaic origins of linguistically defined peoples, he also presented the historical possibility that the implicit identity of all members of Christian nations in a "catholic" church community might be imagined as an historical "return," as a transformative restoration of an archaic ethnic identity.

Bunsen's studies of the immanent processes of human cultural development as they related to the role of ancient Egyptian culture in world history were published simultaneously with his prophetic ruminations about the "Church of the Future." What fueled Bunsen's fascination with contemporary archaeological and philological discoveries about ancient Egyptian culture was the possibility that the decoding of old Egyptian script and the reconstruction of the oldest Egyptian myths might hold the clue to the origin of human cultural development.[90] First, he saw in the hieroglyphic script decoded by Champollion an indication that previous views of an archaic duality between Indo-German and Semitic languages (and thus, in Bunsen's view, "peoples" as well) could be superseded by real evidence of a primal single language. The earliest forms of Egyptian script, he claimed, clearly were situated between the Semitic and Indo-German:

> for its forms and roots could not be illuminated out of one but pointed to both. If it is of Asiatic origin, and thus a result of an immigration which found a new home in the valley of the Nile; then we should be able to draw a valid historical conclusion concerning the oldest language of Asiatic

[90] His first title for his Egyptian studies was "A Contribution Towards the History of the Human Race in its Beginning." See his letter to Arnold, August 1, 1838. Bunsen, *Memoir*, vol. 1, p. 464: Nippold, *Bunsen*, vol. 1, p. 4. The first three volumes of Bunsen's study, published in 1845–6, were distinguished by significant collaboration younger Egyptologists such as Samuel Birch (1813–55), Moritz Schwarze (1802–48), and especially his own protégé, Richard Lepsius (1810–84), and were quite well received in the academic world. His last two volumes, published in 1856–57, which contained more of his own speculative chronologies of world history, were generally dismissed as falling short of the "scientific" standards of academic Egyptology. See Ursula Kaplony-Heckel, "Bunsen-der erste deutsche Herold der Aegyptologie," in Geldbach, ed., *Der gelehrte Diplomat*, pp. 64–83.

humanity, and thus about an historically lost period in the development of the spirit of primal Asia [*Ur-asien*].[91]

Moreover, in Bunsen's view, this primal Asiatic culture whose script and myths were preserved in one of its immigrant colonies could not be just a primal form of Asian humanity but of humanity per se, the unified, linguistically homogenous "people" of the period before the division of mankind into diverse peoples represented in the biblical account of the Tower of Babel.[92] Through chronological reconstruction of Egyptian dynasties, Bunsen tried to show that the connection between the earliest monuments of Egyptian culture and such a unified culture of origin was possible and likely. Basing his arguments on what he felt were the scholarly methods of historical and philological critique developed by his mentor Niebuhr, he claimed to provide an empirical base for the unified teleology of human cultural development articulated by Schelling. The scientific historical investigation of human origins, Bunsen thus insisted, provided empirical justification for constructing the history of mankind as a single history of the human spirit. The history of this collective spirit as a spirit that was necessarily entangled in the diversifying, communalizing power of language was always a history of peoples. But it was also a history that began with one language and one people and thus demonstrated that linguistic cultural diversity was diversity within a larger unity and that the process of historical development was moving toward a reunification of that which had been separated and fragmented. Not that Bunsen imagined the future in terms of a single state and a homogeneous people. The developed diversity of historical evolution would be maintained in a state of affairs in which unity was recognized as a unity of ethical consciousness and reflective understanding within the inevitable ethnic differences of concrete historical existence. A universal ethical community of spirits obeying one internal voice was not a transcendence of immanent cultural development, but its fulfillment. From the earliest moment of historical evolution, mankind defined itself as a subject of meaning in language and myth. From the beginning, the subjectivity of the creature was involved (as expressed in myth) in a double relationship; to its creator, and to the other creatures of this creator. Thus, Bunsen claimed that human culture displayed a unitary evolutionary narrative (*Gesammtentwicklung*) organized around an immanent teleology that defined the present task of mankind as the fulfillment of "an eternal

[91] Christian Karl Josias Bunsen, *Aegyptens Stelle in der Weltgeschichte*, (5 vols.; Hamburg [first 3 vols.] and Gotha [last 2 vols.], 1844–57), vol. 1 (1845), p. xiii.

[92] Bunsen's claim that the Land of Origin, or "Urland," of Egyptian immigrant culture and the biblical Babel – the "Urreich" – were synonymous is made near the end of the first volume: *Aegyptens Stelle*, vol. 1, 515.

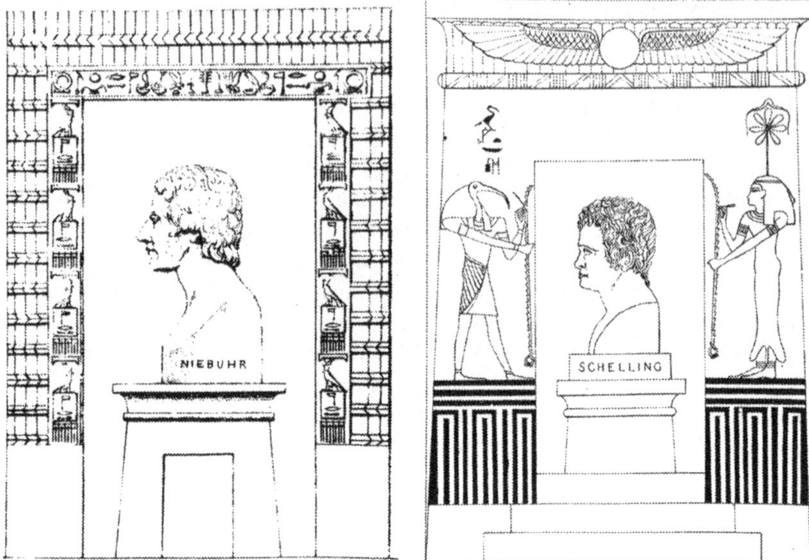

Fig. 2. Mentors for Bunsen's concept of historical identity: frontispieces for volumes 1 and 5 of his *Aegypten's Stelle in der Weltgeschichte*, 1845 and 1857.

law, and not an external law, but its own, inwardly comprehensible law."[93] This law of the immanent development of peoples was comprehensible because it was the same law that continued to work within the consciousness of the contemporary researcher: "insofar as laws of development are discernible, the laws of the subject of research and that of the researcher collapse into one."[94]

In 1845 Bunsen thus seemed to have come full circle to reaffirm the central tenets of his youthful project of 1815. The methods of scientific historical investigation – philological and textual criticism – eventually produced the same result as philosophical construction on the basis of an understanding of the nature of absolute being. In his study of Egyptian antiquity, Niebuhr's portrait provided the frontispiece for the first volume, while Schelling's portrait served the same purpose in the fifth and last volume (Figure 2). The methods of Niebuhr eventually produced a historical account that confirmed the philosophical construction of Schelling. But of course, Schelling's final "positive" philosophy was not the same as the philosophical method Bunsen had integrated into his program in 1815, and Bunsen's return to Schelling in 1838 was not just a return to the Romantic historicism of his youth. The late Schelling had incorporated the relation to the transcendent other, the submission of the intellect to the prior experience of that which made it

[93] *Ibid*, p. 7. [94] *Ibid.*, p. 16.

possible, the origins of meaning in the preconceptual "thatness" of blind being, the dependence of human fraternity on the internalized law of the father, into his own recreation of the immanent "laws" of the development of human cultures. Bunsen's texts displayed the implications of this shift for imagining the contemporary identities of people, church, and state, or at least one possible implication. But Bunsen also revealed the ways in which such entangled identities ultimately produced a focus on the notion of the human self-identity as essentially historical.

Bunsen's Egyptian investigations can be seen as an assimilation of Egyptian culture into a single history of humankind culminating in the historically self-conscious ethical communities of German Protestant Christians. Ancient Egypt was absorbed into the history of nineteenth-century Prussia. How much the leaders of the Prussian "new course" after 1840 shared this intellectual perspective was illustrated by the Egyptian expedition led by the archaeologist, historian, and decoder of ancient languages and monuments, Richard Lepsius, in 1842–45. This expedition was enthusiastically promoted by Bunsen and Alexander von Humboldt, endorsed by the monarch, and funded by the Prussian state. Its purpose was what we might call historical colonization. Lepsius himself displayed this dimension of his "scientific" study of Egyptian antiquities in the engraving he sent back to the king of his "conquest" of the pyramid of Cheops. The act of decoding the monument was represented by a ceremonial planting of the Prussian flag on its peak and by chiseling (in ancient hieroglyphic script) a commemorative verse to the Prussian monarch into the stone of the tomb itself.[95] The Lepsius expedition not only mapped and measured monuments and copied inscriptions on-site but returned with more than fifteen thousand items for the Prussian Egyptian collections, including whole tombs and major components of temple ruins. These artifacts were appropriated as part of the history of civilization to be represented in the Prussian national museums as a crucial component of the historical memory of German culture and western European Christendom.[96] Within the context of the programmatic hopes of the regime of 1840, the Lepsius expedition seems like a counterpoint to the creation of the Jerusalem bishopric. In both cases an attempt was made at "spiritual" conquest of what were considered to be the archaic original spaces of current communal identity. Historical expeditions aiming at conquest and appropriation of the "past" were imagined as expeditions for the "recovery" of cultural memory.

95 Suzanne L. Marchand, *Down from Olympus: Archaeology and Philhellenism in Germany, 1750–1970* (Princeton, N.J.: 1996), pp. 62–65.

96 The expedition and the cultural exploitation of its spoils is described in Georg Ebers, *Richard Lepsius: A Biography*, transl. Zoe Dana Underhill (New York: 1887), pp. 140–66, and in Elke Freier, "Die Expedition von Karl Richard Lepsius in den Jahren 1842–1845 nach den Akten des Zentralen Staatsarchivs, Dienststelle Merseburg," in Elke Freier and Walter F. Reineke, eds., *Karl Richard Lepsius (1810–1884)* (Berlin: 1988), pp. 97–115.

Although Bunsen's scholarly attempts to conquer the past for the present – to turn the documentary traces of past cultures into dimensions of current memory – focused on a reconstruction of the history of languages (the most general structures of the collective lives of peoples), this focus was never exclusive. As we have seen, Bunsen, like Frederick William IV, was intensely aware that the production of collective memory as a making present of a common history involved mnemonic techniques that operated in space and sound, and constructed a sense of identity in ways that went beyond a conscious appropriation and affirmation of the textual narrative of universal cultural history as one's one personal history. An important dimension of the friendship between Bunsen and Frederick William was a shared conviction about the importance of architectural and musical forms in giving shape to a community as an historical community whose continuity through time was made continuously present in the commemorative and liturgical shaping of space and sound.

Part II

Architectural and Musical Historicism: Aesthetic Education and Cultural Reformation

3

Building Historical Identities in Space and Stone: Schinkel's Search for the Shape of Ethical Community

Just a few months after Frederick William's accession to the Prussian throne, on September 9, 1840, Karl Friedrich Schinkel collapsed from a stroke after a day in which he had strolled, perhaps with premonitions of his imminent death, past the architectural monuments and through the designed public spaces that inscribed his personal signature on central Berlin.[1] During a late afternoon conversation with the Prussian State Theater Inspector Carl Gropius, his mind had been full of more sweeping, universal visions than those he had been able to construct in the reality surrounding him in Berlin, visions of a vast circular historical panorama that would display the history of civilization in its progressive development from ancient central Asia to contemporary "Germanic" Europe through representations of architectural monuments in their characteristic geographic settings. His friend and collaborator Gustav Waagen, who reconstructed Schinkel's last hours in his 1844 biography, commented that Schinkel's last project would have encompassed "the spiritual [*geistige*] culture of different times and peoples, which he had sought so often to express individually in the forms of their art, in one great unity [*ein grosses Ganzes*], that would have preserved the most interesting oppositions and analogies and displayed their connection in a pictorial fashion." By 1840, however, this vision of "one great unity" may have been grounded more on nostalgia and hope than on confident conviction. The work that Schinkel left behind as he fell into the coma that would lead to his death a year later certainly expressed a concerted attempt to construct spatial forms that would represent the unity of self and culture as above all an historical unity, but it also displayed the conflicted and problematic nature of that very project.

Schinkel was more than a brilliant artist, architect, and urban designer. For more than two decades he played a leading role in the Prussian State Building Commission (Oberbaudeputation), which planned and supervised all public construction throughout the kingdom – not only administrative and military buildings, but also churches, theaters, concert halls, museums, bridges,

Schinkel's last day is described in detail in the biographical tribute of his friend Gustav Friedrich Waagen: *Karl Friedrich Schinkel als Mensch und Kuenstler: die erste Biografie Schinkels im Berliner Kalendar von 1844* (Berlin: 1844), pp. 304–428. Reprint edited by Warren Gabler (Duesseldorf: 1980). Descriptions and citations in this paragraph are taken from p. 420.

mines, mills and factories, hospitals, and schools.[2] Moreover, since serving as interior designer for Queen Luise of Prussia in 1808–10, he had developed close personal ties to the royal family and especially to the crown prince, whose imagination found its fullest expression in architectural dreaming and sketching. From 1814 until Schinkel's death, Frederick William often appeared in Schinkel's plans and sketches as a major instigator of new projects and designs, as a supportive and knowledgeable critic of preliminary conceptions, and as a persistent conversational partner.[3] Some of this closeness was due to the fact that Schinkel was the primary designer of Frederick William's personal spaces in the royal residences in Potsdam and Berlin, but the association spilled over into the public realm as well. Schinkel's sudden collapse at the age of sixty (there had been warning signs, including some partial paralysis since 1835) and eventual death was a great blow to the new monarch, who imagined his accession to the throne as the moment when he and Schinkel together would be able to build public monuments and design public spaces in Berlin that would transform it into the representational center of a regenerated Prussian state, German national culture, and Protestant Christendom.[4]

Although Schinkel's intellectual itinerary in the twenty-five years between 1815 and 1840 had often pushed him close to the king's vision of a Christian-German state, he clearly retained much closer ties to the neoclassical, humanist versions of cultural reform and moral education represented by his original patron in government circles, Wilhelm von Humboldt, his lifelong intellectual heroes, Goethe and Fichte, and his architectural mentors and teachers, David Gilly, Friedrich Gilly, and Heinrich Gentz. Schinkel began his career convinced that the profession of architecture was not subordinate to the representational needs of church and court or to the practical need for efficiently designed functional spaces, but a cultural calling with the status of autonomous "high" art, an art in which space and stone became physical expressions of spiritual purposes, or "ideas," and that its serious pursuit entailed a duty to participate in the historical mission of public moral education that would transform an aggregate of individual egos into a community of free agents. Like all the fine arts, architecture was perceived as

[2] The scope of Schinkel's activity as a Prussian civil servant, first as an aesthetic assessor in the Oberbaudeputation and, ultimately, after 1830, as its head, is described in Mario Zadow, *Karl Friedrich Schinkel* (Berlin: 1980), pp. 41–50; and Paul Ortwin Rave, "Schinkel als Beamter. Ein Abschnitt preussischer Bauverwaltung," in *Karl Friedrich Schinkel: Architektur, Malerei, Kunstgewerbe* (Berlin: 1981), pp. 75–94.

[3] Schinkel recognized the critical importance of this relationship for his creative work in the introduction to the final version of his unpublished architectural textbook. See Geord Peschken, ed., *Karl Friedrich Schinkel: Das Architektonische Lehrbuch* (Berlin: 1979), p. 151. This volume, which includes a chronologically organized, critical edition of most of Schinkel's notes as well as extensive editorial commentary, is cited hereafter as *Lehrbuch*.

[4] Ludwig Dehio, *Friedrich Wilhelm IV. von Preussen: Ein Baukuenstler der Romantik* (Berlin: 1961), pp. 62–69, 109; Karl-Heinz Klingenburg, "Der Koenig als Architekt," in Krueger and Schoeps, eds., *Der verkannte Monarch*, pp. 219–33.

Fig. 3. Friedrich Gilly's drawing of a projected monument to Frederick the Great on the Potsdamer Platz in Berlin (1797). Reproduction permission: Bildarchiv Preussischer Kulturbesitz.

eliciting subjective, emotional experiences and cultivating or shaping them in an ethical direction. Following in the footsteps of an older generation of neoclassical humanists and philosophical idealists, and inspired by the ideals (if not necessarily the practices) of the French Revolution, Schinkel, as a youthful apprentice architect, sought to create appropriate spatial contexts for an enlightened public order, to produce a built environment for individuals who affirmed their freedom as self-legislating subjects through stringent devotion to the universal rational law defining their duties as citizens of an ethical community. The magnificent drawing of a proposed memorial to Frederick the Great imagined by his teacher Friedrich Gilly in 1797 (Fig. 3) remained one of Schinkel's most prized possessions after Gilly's death in 1800 at the age of twenty-nine. It represented his intellectual roots in a Franco-Prussian, humanist, neoclassical tradition, which combined loyalty to the modernizing reforms of enlightened monarchy with commitment to the historically imagined civic community of the classical Greek polis.[5] The family motto he chose for his home after his marriage in 1809 was genuinely Fichtean in inspiration, proclaiming the pursuit of moral virtue through self-overcoming as the royal road to the "blessed" experience of freedom.[6] Schinkel was always somewhat uncomfortable with the religious cultural politics of many of the king's more pious friends and advisors. His most powerful political supporter during the teens and early 1820s (especially

[5] On the development of an austere, monumental neoclassicism in Prussia during the 1790s, focused on elemental geometric forms and inspired by revolutionary visions of a civic order grounded in the laws of nature, see David Watkin and Tilman Mellinghoff, *German Architecture and the Classical Ideal* (Cambridge, Mass: 1987), pp. 59–83. Schinkel's relation to his neoclassical predecessors, especially Friedrich Gilly, is analyzed in some depth in Andreas Haus, *Karl Friedrich Schinkel als Kuenstler: Annaeherung und Kommentar* (Munich and Berlin: 2001), pp. 41–73.

[6] The motto is cited in Alfred Freiherr von Wolzogen, *Aus Schinkels Nachlass: Reisetagebuecher, Briefe und Aphorismen* (4 vols.; Berlin: 1862–4), vol. 1, p. 23.

after Humboldt's resignation in 1819) was the state chancellor Karl August von Hardenberg, a bureaucratic liberal with strong philosophical ties to Kant and Fichte, a man whom the crown prince and aristocratic conservatives at the court regarded with distrust. After 1830, however, a deepening historical pessimism was evident in Schinkel's work, marked by disillusionment with many of the historical hopes for the imminent creation of an ethical community on Prussian soil, which had fueled earlier phases of his development. It is difficult to envision how Schinkel would have been able to reconcile the growing tensions in his work in "one great unity," or organize the narratives describing the formation of the historical identities of the German ethnic nation, or "people"; the ethical community of autonomous agents that constituted the modern state; and the religious community of Protestant Christians into a single history.

COLLECTIVE EMANCIPATION AND SELF-RECOGNITION: THE CATHEDRAL OF NATIONAL LIBERATION AND THE GOTHIC SHAPE OF GERMAN IDENTITY

In June 1814, still basking in the glow of the recent triumph over Napoleon's armies and the reversal of the defeats and humiliations of 1806–7 through the imposed Peace of Paris, the Prussian king Frederick William III asked Schinkel to develop a plan for a monumental church to commemorate the victories of 1813 and 1814 and celebrate the liberation of the Prussian nation and German people. The king also suggested, perhaps prompted by his sons, that it would be appropriate to construct the memorial in the "Old German," or Gothic, style of the "Fatherland."[7] For Schinkel, hints of this kind were hardly required. In the wake of the Napoleonic conquest and occupation of Prussia, Schinkel was swept along by the Romantic enthusiasms that attached individual emancipation to identification with a linguistically defined national community and its distinctive historical traditions. By the time of his initial appointment in the Prussian Civil Service in 1810, as aesthetic assessor in the recently created *Oberbaudeputation*, Schinkel had clearly come to identify the emancipation of the German people from foreign domination and the regeneration of the Prussian state as an ethical community of autonomous citizens with the forms of Gothic architecture, and particularly with the monumental structures of the Gothic cathedral. Schinkel responded to the royal commission by noting that the assigned task

[7] The Prussian proposal was only one among many proposals to memorialize the wars of liberation with a Gothic cathedral. See Thomas Nipperdey, "Kirchen als Nationaldenkmal. Die Plaene von 1815," in Lucius Grisebach and Konrad Renger, eds., *Festschrift fuer Otto von Simson zum 65. Geburtstag* (Berlin: 1977), pp. 412–31.

was already a self-assigned mission that he had been "working through in my inner life for a long time."[8]

Schinkel had been engaged for a number of years in the study of medieval architecture in his search for a new architectural language for his generation. As early as 1803–5, during a study tour through Italy, he had expressed dissatisfaction with the rigid symmetries and starkly impersonal forms of late-eighteenth-century neoclassicism. He focused his attention on the ways in which public and ecclesiastical construction, especially in eastern and southern Italy, had absorbed strong influences from the Arab Orient into the inherited antique styles and produced a stunning mixed architecture, both imitative of inherited forms and adapted to the needs and consciousness of its own historical period. He was also fascinated by the ways in which the domestic architecture of the classical villa was adapted to differences in landscape and climate and to the subjective freedom of its individually variegated inhabitants and creators.[9] In both cases, Schinkel was in search of exemplary techniques and principles for creating appropriate spaces for particular historical needs and experiences, for producing forms whose individualized "character" was adapted to cultural and natural contexts. On his return to Berlin, and especially after the defeat of Prussia by the French armies, these general tendencies were focused on the need to find a way of building that would express the individual historical character of the Prussian and German peoples in their present historical situation. Like his literary and scholarly friends in Berlin, Achim von Arnim and Clemens Brentano, who collected Old German folk poetry and fragmentary texts of Old German sagas in their search for a historical tradition that might inspire a modern national literature, Schinkel attempted to recover, with his pen and sketchpad, the essential Old German cultural idea contained within the historical remains of the medieval period through systematic study of the structure of Gothic churches and cathedrals. In two of his first submissions for major state and court commissions, the design for a mausoleum for Queen Luise of Prussia in 1810 and a plan for a new church to replace the burned out Saint Peter's parish church in Berlin in 1811, he accompanied his drawings and plans with programmatic manifestos about the distinctively German and "modern" qualities of the Gothic style. The Gothic became for Schinkel, at least briefly, the appropriate architectural

[8] Karl Friedrich Schinkel, "Denkschrift vom Sommer 1814," in Paul O. Rave, *Karl Friedrich Schinkel: Lebenswerk: Berlin I: Bauten fuer die Kunst, Kirchen und Denkmalpflege*, (Berlin: 1941), p. 190. Two versions of Schinkel's memorandum concerning the projected Liberation Cathedral were originally published in Wolzogen, *Aus Schinkel's Nachlass*, vol. 3, pp. 189–197, under the mistaken date of 1819. They are reprinted with the corrected dates of summer 1814 and January 1815 in Rave, *Schinkel: Berlin*, vol. 1, pp. 187–201.

[9] See Schinkel's letters to the bookdealer Johann Friedrich Unger in July 1804, and to his teacher David Gilly in December 1804, in Hans Machowsky, ed., *Karl Friedrich Schinkel: Briefe, Tagebuecher, Gedanken* (Berlin: 1922), pp. 74, 85.

form for authentic German culture, for the culture of a "genuine primal people [*wahres Urvolk*]"[10] that had been repressed by the recent occupation after being weakened and diverted from its inherent historical destiny by centuries of French and Latin cultural domination. Thus the Gothic also became for Schinkel the language of liberation for the German people, an instrument for cultural self-recognition and self-affirmation that would make possible the assertion of historical autonomy not only vis-à-vis the oppressive weight of the classical heritage but also against French and Italian cultures in the present.

In most of his historical reconstructions and imaginary constructions of the Gothic as the architectural form of the German national spirit, Schinkel was working within a literary discourse that had been initiated during the 1770s in the writings of the Sturm und Drang (Herder and Goethe) and gained a new philosophical, metahistorical significance in the influential writings of Heinrich Wackenroder, Ludwig Tieck, and Friedrich Schlegel at the turn of the century. In the work of this founding generation of German Romanticism, the Gothic was connected to the distinctive elements of the Christian "idea" of dynamic, self-transcending, spirit-filled existence in contrast to the classical "idea" of static, nature-centered, self-contained existence.[11] Conceptions of the Gothic as the aesthetic expression of spiritual autonomy were tied to the forms of cultural organization distinctive to the German ethnic peoples by the slightly younger generation of Romantic poets and scholars born around 1780 – the Arnims, Brentano, Savigny, the Grimms – who were members of Schinkel's generational cohort and constituted his primary intellectual circle in Berlin after he established a family and a stable residence there in 1809. The connection between Gothic architecture and German nationality gained a special intensity during the years of defeat, occupation, domestic reform, and military liberation.[12]

Schinkel's plans for a *Befreiungsdom* (Cathedral of Liberation) in 1814 and 1815 also revealed the way his "patriotic" appropriation of the Gothic style was connected to his participation since 1810 in the Prussian reform movement, and his powerful attachment to its leaders. The freedom that Schinkel imagined as embodied in the Gothic style was not just national independence from Napoleonic domination and French cultural hegemony, but also the freedom of individuals to participate as autonomous subjects in the making of their own world. It was not only a freedom from the French, but also "with" the French against the restrictions of the old regime. In fact, the

[10] "Entwurf zu einer Begraebniskapelle fuer ihre Majestaet die hochselige Koenigen Luise von Preussen" (1810), in Wolzogen, *Aus Schinkel's Nachlass*, vol. 3, p. 157.

[11] W. D. Robson-Scott, *The Literary Background of the Gothic Revival in Germany. A Chapter in the History of Taste* (Oxford: 1965), pp. 55–151.

[12] See the account of the connection between nationalist and Gothic enthusiasms in Hannelore Gaertner, "Patriotismus und Gotikrezeption der deutschen Fruehromantik," in Peter Betthausen, ed., *Studien zur deutschen Kunst und Architektur um 1800* (Dresden: 1981), pp. 34–52.

development of a distinctive version of the Gothic style had been evident for a while in Schinkel's studies of the Christian-German cultural idea and its architectural expressions.[13]

Between 1805 and 1814, the conditions of war and foreign occupation virtually halted public construction in Prussia. During this decade, Schinkel developed his conception of the relationship between architectural form, public space, and communal identity in sketches, oil paintings, and popular forms of visual exhibition like dioramas and panoramas.[14] In these genres, Schinkel was able to experiment visually with the connection between his emotional identification with the German people's resistance to Napoleonic occupation,[15] his ethical commitment to the inner transformation of the Prussian state into a "free" community of autonomous subjects, and his architectural vocation.

Schinkel firmly welded Gothic forms of representation to the idea of self-transcending freedom that had been developed in Kantian and post-Kantian German philosophy, especially by Fichte.[16] Schinkel had been an assiduous reader of Fichte's popular works (like *The Vocation of Man*) since 1802–3. During the period of French occupation, he attended the famous "Speeches to the German Nation," and after Fichte was appointed the first rector of the newly created university at Berlin in 1810, Schinkel also attended a number of his lecture series on more advanced philosophical themes. What made the Gothic an architectural inscription of the liberation of the human subject from natural and customary determination, in Schinkel's view, was the restless movement of pointed-arch construction, constantly pressing upward in an infinite repetition of polar tensions that could never achieve the immanent repose of rounded resolution. Gothic cathedrals moved upward with a dynamic striving and an infinite reach that affirmed the subjective spirit's continuous struggle with the physical limitations of embodiment in space and time. In the imaginary cathedrals of Schinkel's sketches – optical showpieces and oil paintings between 1808 and 1815 – Gothic towers,

[13] For a detailed analysis of Schinkel's Gothic sketches and studies, see George Friedrich Koch, "Karl Friedrich Schinkel und die Architektur des Mittelalters," *Zeitschrift fuer Kunstgeschichte* 29 (1966): 177–222; and Koch, "Schinkels architektonische Entwuerfe im gotischen Stil, 1810–1815," *Zeitschrift fuer Kunstgeschichte* 32 (1969): 263–316.

[14] Between 1808 and 1815, Schinkel produced more than forty large "perspectival optical" drawings, many of them transparencies used in the diorama theater of his friend Wilhelm Gropius. See Birgit Verwiebe, "Schinkel's Perspective Optical Views: Art Between Painting and Theater," in John Zukowsky, ed., *Karl Friedrich Schinkel: The Drama of Architecture* (Chicago: 1994), pp. 36–53.

[15] Schinkel's enthusiasm for the national awakening of 1813 was displayed in his participation in the training exercises for a national guard in Berlin and his support for his brother-in-law's decision to join the volunteer brigades in 1813. See Schinkel's letter to his father-in-law from Berlin, January 18, 1813, in Machowsky, *Schinkel*, pp. 89–91.

[16] Fichte's influence on Schinkel was pointed out by his friend and early biographer, Franz Kugler, in *Karl Friedrich Schinkel. Eine Charakteristik seiner kuenstlerischen Wirksamkeit* (Berlin: 1842), p. 17. More evidence and commentary is provided by Goerd Peschken in *Lehrbuch*, p. 24.

Fig. 4. Schinkel's oil painting of an imaginary Gothic cathedral (1811). Reproduction permission: Stiftung Preussischer Schloesser und Gaerten, Berlin-Brandenburg; photo Joerg P. Anders.

the culmination of bristling pyramids of spires and arches, reach upward into a gossamer filigree stonework that seems weightless and virtually transparent to light (Fig. 4). Beginning with his first memorandum promoting the Gothic as a national style in 1810, Schinkel emphasized the elevating, liberating aspects of this spatial language of infinite striving for transcendence. It marked German culture's distinctiveness in relation to Greek and Roman antiquity, its rejection of static repetition of conventional forms in order to pursue individuating "characteristic" historical forms in a continuous dynamic development.

Two dimensions of Schinkel's conception of the internal bond between the Gothic and the idea of freedom expressed the particularities of his appropriation. The ability of the Gothic to use modest earthly materials of brick and stone to articulate the self-transcending qualities of the human and divine spirit revealed that the central religious building of Christian and Germanic culture was an "aesthetic work" that transformed material being into meaningful signs and freed expressive content from merely functional requirements. In the classical era, the style of construction connected the materials and spaces of construction through functional, utilitarian purposes, emphasizing the ways in which human existence was embedded in its natural conditions. The Romans, for example, had understood the functional value of arched vaulting for spanning large spaces and attaining great heights.

But only German builders who had incorporated the Christian idea of self-transcending freedom into their consciousness and daily practice were able to grasp the arched vault as a symbolic structure that articulated their own essential being, and could thus elaborate its inner logic to the fullest expressive extent. Arched architectural forms in the Gothic building were not just building techniques, but expressions of a spiritual meaning informing the minds of their creators. A Gothic cathedral was the idea of freedom built in space, made visible as art.[17]

Second, Schinkel was intent on interpreting the Gothic concept of freedom as an immanent process, as an animating purpose informing the everyday activities of human existence. What was articulated in the spaces and forms of the Gothic church was the divine nature of life as a self-transcending creativity. In this sense, liberation was not an abandonment of the material realm, but a transfiguration of the physical world through meaning. Self-transcending striving was the soul of the Gothic organism, the life force coursing through its external structure. To imagine a happier and freer existence as possible only outside of the conditions of earthly life was "a sin against the vocation of humankind." States were guilty of this sin not only if they hindered human emancipation, but also if they did not actively further its historical actualization.[18]

Schinkel's concept of Gothic freedom also involved a synthetic incorporation, rather than rejection, of past cultures. A culture that defined the classical world as its radical opposite remained unfree, bound by the limitations of a past it had disavowed or excluded from itself. Even in his first and most dogmatically Germanic and Christian manifestoes of 1810 and 1811, Schinkel imagined the fulfillment of Christian-German culture and its Gothic style as a transformative assimilation of the essence of classical culture. Once the members of Christian-German culture had recognized their own center in the idea of freedom, domination by the classical past and its current incarnations in the Latin West would cease, and the classical idea of horizontally oriented, materially grounded "natural" existence could be freely absorbed as the historical and conceptual foundation of Christian and German culture. One of the major ways in which the idea of Christian culture asserted its all-encompassing self-sufficiency was through appropriation of the foreign and the past as components of its own nature.[19]

Schinkel's insistence on the progressive and synthetic nature of a fully realized Gothic style also found expression in his claim that the Gothic

[17] "Entwurf zu einer Begraebniskapelle," Wolzogen, *Aus Schinkel's Nachlass*, vol. 3, 157.

[18] Karl Friedrich Schinkel,"Lehrbuchstudien und Architekttheoretische Skripten der Hoch romantischen Zeit, um 1810–1815," in *Lehrbuch*, p. 27.

[19] See especially, Karl Friedrich Schinkel,"Architektonischer Plan zum Wiederaufbau der eingeascherten St. Petrikirche in Berlin" (1811), in Rave, *Schinkel: Berlin I*, p. 176.

represented a specific form of "rational" unity. It produced identity as the organic totality of differences, rather than as a symmetrical system of uniformities.[20] The principle of order in the Gothic building as Schinkel conceived it was not the imposed domination of the one over the all, but the unity of a common animating principle repeating itself in, and informing the structures of, an infinite proliferation of differences. Gothic branching columns, repeated pointed-arch gables, baldachins over niches, and proliferating spires were symbolic of a culture that grasped unity as a unity of articulated differences animated by the same life principle, or "idea." In Gothic art, he wrote, "the divine idea was made visible in every single object . . . but this divinity must still as a whole be represented through the universe of these objects, and precisely as the principle of this universe."[21] The Gothic achieved full self-representation as a complete process of differentiation in which all individualized elements were recognizably informed by the same principle, that is, as a vast universe of arches and spires that were different and separate yet also transparently parts of the same organic structure. Unlike classical ornamentation, Gothic "decoration" was no more superfluous to the form of the building than leaves or flowers were superfluous to the forms of nature. Although articulated in the most symbolic and thus "artificial" of cultural styles, the Gothic architecture also translated the structuring principles of the natural world into comprehensible meaning. The imitation of nature in some Gothic decoration – the recreation of heavens between the ribs of the vaulting or in window glass; the branching, arborial stonework of fan vaulting; the stone "flowers" that marked the junctures in rib vaulting or the tips of spires – simply affirmed this deeper structural bond with the natural order of the universe. The very activity of building informed by the Christian-German idea, the imaginative and material practice of architecture as a "high art," reconstituted this divine act of creativity in a free flow of energy that moved easily from the building to the universe of which it was a part:

> True and pure imagination, having once entered the stream of the idea it expresses, has to expand forever beyond this work, and it must venture out, leading ultimately to the infinite. It must be regarded as a point where one can make an orderly entry into the unbreakable chain of the universe. Striving, budding, crystallizing, unfolding, driving, a splitting, fitting, drifting, floating, pulling, pressing, bending, bearing, placing, vibrating, connecting, holding,

[20] Schinkel, "Versuch ueber das glueckselige Leben eines Baumeisters" (ca, 1812), in *Lehrbuch*, p. 33. Schinkel's critical distancing from an "absolute order" imposed on nature through symmetrical organization of uniformities in favor of a "relative, individual order" in which unity is represented as a "characteristic" unity emerging organically from a historically unique individual goes back to his first attempt to bring together his architectural principles in book form in 1803–5. See the materials and discussion presented in *Lehrbuch*, pp. 18–20.

[21] "Skripten der hoch Romantischen Zeit," *Lehrbuch*, p. 33.

> a lying and a resting – where the latter two, which contrast with the kinetic properties, must represent an intentional and obvious repose, and therefore also a living action – these are the ways in which architecture must manifest life.[22]

In an often quoted aphorism, Schinkel described architecture as "the continuation of nature in its constructive activity," and added: "this activity operates through that natural product – the human being [*das Naturproduct Mensch*]."[23]

Schinkel's studies of the antiquities of Old German art and architecture in the decade before 1814 displayed the principle informing his representation and appropriation of the past. In sketches and showpiece optical drawings of the Strasbourg and Milan cathedrals, "representing" became a "completion" or "fulfillment" according to what Schinkel discerned as the organizing principle of the building, and of the culture of which that building was the symbolic center. Decorative elements that did not conform to the structure of proliferating differentiation in upwardly moving arches and spires were removed. Towers and façades were "completed" to express the infinite dimensions of the upward movement, baldachins were added to sculpture niches, windows and portals provided with properly arched gables, and the stone fretwork of the spires developed into transparent webs as they reached skyward. Even interior spaces and external structural relations were "revised" to conform to what Schinkel understood to be the architectural logic of the Gothic style. In the imaginary cathedrals of Schinkel's historical landscape paintings, the soaring movement toward light and lightness of being within a unified organic form that arises out of continuity with nature is especially noticeable. Schinkel's paintings of the Gothic do not have specific historical references – they articulate his conceptions of the informing idea of German-Christian culture. And even his representations of actual buildings were not empirical replications but constructions of what he considered to be the coherent structural logic of the building's "idea."[24] Schinkel was thinking with the past to grasp the present and imagine the future.

Self-transcending freedom and aestheticized organic unity were complemented by an emphasis on materially grounded stability in Schinkel's vision of the Gothic as the shape of a cultural world suitable for modern Germans. His imaginary cathedrals are set on vast pedestals so that their soaring spiritual aspirations appear as the culmination of a broadly based pyramid, firmly rooting the possibility for German-Christian transcendence in the very earthly

[22] *Ibid.*, p. 32: The translation is borrowed from Herman G. Pundt, *Schinkel's Berlin: A Study in Environmental Planning* (Cambridge, Mass., 1972), p. 195, where the quotation is used out of context, i.e., as a general statement of Schinkel's mature architectural theory.

[23] "Skripten der hoch Romantischen Zeit," Peschken, *Schinkel's Lehrbuch*, p. 35.

[24] Koch, "Karl Friedrich Schinkel und die Architektur des Mittelalters," pp. 190–98, 203–9.

Fig. 5. Frontal perspective of Schinkel's planned Cathedral of Liberation. Reproduction permission: Bildarchiv Preussischer Kulturbesitz; photo Joerg P. Anders.

achievements and "natural" foundations of ancient cultures (Fig. 4). At least this is the way Schinkel himself justified the exaggerated pedestal weight and horizontal baselines of his imagined Gothic cathedrals. He thought that actual Gothic cathedrals often produced feelings of instability, insecurity, and lack of solidity. Imperfect, one-sided Gothic expressed the false sense that meaning was to be sought in transcending the inhibiting limitations of earthly existence altogether, in separating Christian culture from the pagan cultures from which it had evolved and in which it was grounded. Despite their elaborate filigree ornamentation and absence of strongly articulated wall space and horizontal lines, Schinkel's Gothic cathedrals thus do seem anomalously classical in their tendency to structure the movement upward in pyramidal shapes. The sketches and plans for the Liberation Cathedral prominently display both perfected arch and spire dynamics in its pyramidal façade and decoration and the grounding of upward striving on a very substantial pedestal (Fig. 5). There were functional reasons for such large pedestals (to carry the weight of the crowds that Schinkel expected for memorial festivals, to provide a cover and structural sign for the crypt beneath the church), but they also symbolized his vision of a nature-affirming, historically rooted autonomy.[25]

Besides the logic of upward, liberating dynamics and the emphasis on horizontal grounding, Schinkel's plan for the Liberation Cathedral is marked by the prominence given to the domed altar space of the octagonal choir (Fig. 6). This rotunda church, another progressive absorption of a classical element into the Gothic cultural form, balances the spires of the façade and creates the most important interior space – the space for ritual reenactment of subjective transformation at the "altar." This rotunda space was for Schinkel clearly the culmination of the individual's psychological experience of the Gothic cathedral as the sacred center of German-Christian culture, the place of self-recognition and subjective identification with the "idea" of the culture. The "genuine" religious building, Schinkel insisted, should not be a building for "teaching" or for "service" (a *Lehrgebauede* or a *Dienstgebauede*), but a place where individuals were guided toward recognition of their inner essence through aesthetic experiences of the divine principle that animated both the universe and themselves.[26] The altar space under the dome was a space of self-affirmative participation in the life of the totality, not a space for self-abnegation, renunciation of the world, or longing for escape to another life and another world. The sacrifice of the individual ego on the altar of the communal essence was imagined as a joyous elevation to a new level of freedom in which the empirical self became an image of its own essential being. Schinkel could become emotionally overwhelmed

[25] Schinkel also meant the greatly expanded size of the portals to enhance the pyramidal shape of the structure. See his "Die Denkschrift von Januar 1815," in Rave, *Schinkel: Berlin I*, p. 199.

[26] "Das religioese Gebaeude," *Lehrbuch*, p. 32.

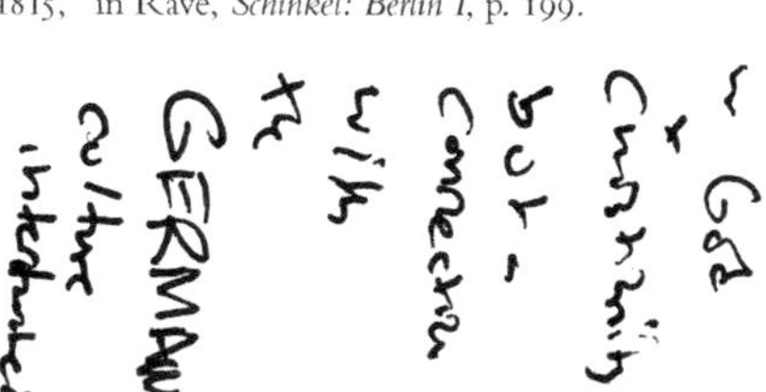

Fig. 6. Side view of Schinkel's planned Cathedral of Liberation. Reproduction permission: Bildarchiv Preussischer Kulturbesitz; photo Joerg P. Anders.

imagining the experience of identification that occurred in this space. At least the editor of his marginal jottings explains (or imagines) the erased words in the midst of a description of the sacred experience of self and communal recognition as due to the author's tears falling onto the paper.[27] For Schinkel, the Gothic church was a space of inwardness. Recognition of identity with others was not forged in the public spaces of daily business, where self-interested egos engaged in mutual exchanges, but produced through the mediation of a common principle shared by all, through inner participation in the idea of the national community. Although the "people" were "gathered" together in this space of identification, "the solemnity [*Wuerdigkeit*] of the space," Schinkel suggested, "disposed everyone to fulfill themselves quietly within themselves."[28]

The religious experience in the domed space was clearly an experience of art, of the aesthetic transformation of determination into self-determination. The cathedral was a "built work of art" (*gebautes Kunstwerk*) that confirmed that "art is itself religion."[29] Yet Schinkel also insisted that this aesthetic experience culminated in a consciousness not only of the essential idea that informed experience, but also of an ethical task that was to be realized in

[27] "Skripten der hoch Romanatischen Zeit," *Lehrbuch*, p. 33.

[28] "Versuch ueber das Gleuckselige Leben eines Baumeisters," *Lehrbuch*, p. 33.

[29] "Das Religioese Gebaeude," *Lehrbuch*, p. 32.

experience. The German-Christian idea of freedom was an idea of self-transcending struggle opening into infinity. To recognize this was also to commit oneself to the struggle to achieve the intuited identity in historical reality, to turn the aesthetic experience into social practice as a member of the cultural community. Art encompassed religious experience and created ethical purpose. The notion of ethical community as a historical project was expressed in the Gothic cathedral's characteristic incompleteness. It was a structure on which the whole community continued to work, building itself as it built its own representation of itself. Schinkel imagined his *Befreiungsdom* as a "living monument in the people [*ein lebendiges Monument in dem Volk*]," as a construction project that would give life to the aesthetic, self-affirming labor of the nation's artists and artisans for many years, returning the nation to its original culture as it projected its past into the future[30] (Fig. 7).

Schinkel's conception of the experience of cultural identification among members of a people was expressed in his spatial siting of Gothic cathedrals. His studies of existing Gothic churches often revised their sites. A striking example is his displacement of the Milan cathedral, purified of all baroque and neoclassical additions and monumentalized with the addition of a vast staircase and pedestal, onto a hill overlooking the harbor at Trieste (Fig. 8). The imaginary Gothic cathedrals of Schinkel's oil paintings also tended to be outside or above cities, rising above the everyday world of the people as objects of reverence, centers of visual self-recognition. The path to the "sanctuary" on the occasion of a national festival, Schinkel insisted, should be "a kind of pilgrimage [*eine art Wallfahrt*].[31] The symbolic, sacred center of the "people" was a place where individuals could separate themselves from their daily activities and look into themselves, where they could participate in symbolic rituals apart from the functional, utilitarian activities of the workplace. Schinkel vehemently resisted the king's expressed wish that the Liberation Cathedral be sited near the center of the old city, on the Spittelmarkt. Instead he placed it at the Potsdamer Tor and Leipziger Platz, thus immediately setting it in contrast with the imposing neoclassical Brandenburg Gate at the entry to the other great western artery into the center of the city, also situated on a great square – the Pariserplatz – renamed, like the Leipzigerplatz, in honor of recent military triumphs. The cathedral's apse broke the former plane of the city's walls, and the nave, façade, pedestal, and forecourt reached out into the countryside beyond the former city tollgates. As a shrine, a pilgrimage site, a public theater for ritual enactments of subjective identification, the Gothic religious building should be set apart on consecrated ground. The center of the community as a cultural nation was not the center of the city, the juncture of actual interactions

[30] "Denkschrift von Sommer, 1814," in Rave, *Schinkel: Berlin I*, p. 192.

[31] "Die Denkschrift von Januar 1815," in Rave, *Schinkel: Berlin I*, p. 197; Wolzogen, *Aus Schinkel's Nachlass*, vol. 3, 202.

Fig. 7. Completing the Gothic after military victory. Schinkel's oil painting *Medieval City on a River* (1815). Reproduction permission: Bildarchiv Preussischer Kulturbesitz.

Fig. 8. Schinkel's imaginary reconstruction of Milan cathedral (ca. 1805–11). Reproduction permission: Bildarchiv Preussischer Kulturbesitz; photo Joerg P. Anders.

among individuals, but the symbolic place where each individual appropriated the idea of the culture. This appropriation was an inward process, but it was represented in visible rituals so that individuals could recognize their identity with others in the sacred center of their collective being.[32]

The experience of subjective identification with the national essence, or "idea," was the starting point for an insertion of individual memory into a public memory, for a reading of individual life histories within the framing script of a narrative of the people. In the traditional and still "incomplete" Gothic monuments of the Middle Ages, this process was displayed through insertion of the story of the individual soul's secular suffering and struggle into the sacred story of human relations to the divine, into the story of the fall and the road to salvation as recounted in biblical myth and the history of the church. In 1815, an historical moment marked by recognition of the identity of the Christian idea with German cultural experience and consciousness, the experience in the altar space of the church opened up an historical narrative that merged the sacred history of redemption with the historical struggle of peoples to give full cultural actuality to the divine idea informing their existence. In Schinkel's projected Liberation Cathedral, the very structure of the building signified a historical dialectic in which preclassical and classical forms were transformed into components of the universal Christian idea. In fact, some of his sketches for a memorial to the wars of liberation articulated the historical layering of structural space as a pyramid in which Egyptian

[32] "Die Denkschrift von Sommer, 1814," in Rave, *Schinkel: Berlin I*. pp. 190–91.

Fig. 9. Schinkel's sketch for a projected war memorial (ca. 1815). Reproduction permission: Bildarchiv Preussischer Kulturbesitz; photo Joerg P. Anders.

bases and Greek temples were topped by Gothic spires, thus turning the different styles into expressions of stages in human development (Fig. 9).

More specifically, the decorative stonework and external sculptures of Schinkel's *Befreiungsdom* placed the recent events of the Wars of Liberation into three interlocking narratives. The sacred biblical narrative framed all stories with its mythic projections of a struggle against, and victory over, material determination and egoistic will – from the Archangel Michael's triumph over Lucifer represented in a colossal free-standing sculpture above the main portal to the youthful triumphant Christ figure standing with a waving banner on a winged globe at the place of the altar under the dome. This biblical story provided the context and model for the structurally similar stories of, first, the emergence of the German cultural nation from tribal solidarity in resistance to Roman hegemony to self-recognition as an ethnic and linguistic cultural community during the wars of liberation, and, second, the Prussian construction of a civic community from a primitive state of rational order externally imposed by heroic soldier kings to the emergence of a constitutionally articulated community of self-legislating citizens. Around the forecourt of the projected memorial church and in the gabled niches along its exterior walls, Schinkel imagined a sequence of heroic figures that marked progressive stages in these stories of the liberation and national self-determination of the German people under Prussian leadership, and the inward transformation that made the German nation the chosen "church" of the Christian idea of freedom. In the gable of the main portal, a frieze representing the ceremonial dedication of the iron cross in 1813 brought together the religious and national forces mobilized by Prussian political leadership in what Schinkel imagined, like his nationalist heroes Goerres and Arndt, as a populist crusade by the German people against their foreign oppressors.[33]

The external history of resistance and conquest, visualized in images of military and political leaders, was completed by an inner history of recognition of the national essence in the works of artists, poets, scientists and philosophers, who were to be memorialized in busts and plaques along the pillars of the nave inside the church. Their spiritual conquests merged into the traditional iconography of the path to salvation, marking stages on the path to the full recognition of participation in a shared historical destiny that occurred in the space of the rotunda. The historical narratives inscribed in the figurative decoration of the cathedral illuminated the recent events of inner reform and external liberation as the integrating culmination of sacred and secular history, joining individual fulfillment with national self-assertion, connecting cultural consciousness of the idea of freedom in literature, philosophy, and the arts with Prussian military power and political will.

For the Schinkel of 1814–15, the general sign of this historical conjuncture of sacred and secular narratives was the Iron Cross. Designed by Schinkel himself in 1813 as the Prussian decoration for individual valor in the Wars of Liberation, the Iron Cross connected the recent struggle against Napoleonic domination to the defense of Christian-German civilization by the medieval

[33] Schinkel describes the projected ornamentation of the cathedral in his memorandum of January 1815, in Rave, *Schinkel: Berlin I*, pp. 194–96. See also Koch, "Schinkels architektonische Entwuerfe," pp. 298–99.

order of the Teutonic Knights. In its emphatic use of iron, widely recognized as a popular and patriotic metal, it expressed the striking entry of the voluntary agency of the people into the making of their own history, an event marked by the king's "call" to his people in 1813, the vast expansion of the citizen militia component in the army through the reforms of military leaders like Scharnhorst and Gneisenau, and the formation of volunteer brigades like the Luetzow Rangers. Crowning the spire of the façade, prominently displayed in the ceremonial consecration of self-sacrifice in the frieze above the main portal, woven into a decorative themes throughout the building, the Iron Cross connected the church to the war memorials, many also designed by Schinkel, recently constructed or under construction at significant battle sites around the kingdom.[34] In 1814, when Johann Gottfried Schadow's Goddess of Peace driving a four-horsed chariot was recaptured from her French kidnappers, brought back from Paris, and festively restored to her original site atop the Brandenburg Gate, she was reconsecrated as a Goddess of Victory and given a military standard with a prominently displayed Iron Cross, making her a symbol of national liberation and a rediscovered national identity.

The entangled narratives that Schinkel tried to display in his *Befreiungsdom* project clearly included the story of the entry of the "people" into its historical adulthood. The emergence of the people as the collective agent of their own history was affirmed by their acts of self-liberation and armed resistance to external oppression, and their self-sacrifice for the cultural idea that constituted their essential identity. But this mobilization of previously fragmented and marginalized populations into a unified cultural and political nation was still an unfinished project. Schinkel imagined his Cathedral of Liberation not only with empty niches both outside and inside for the future heroes of the national history, but also as a long-term construction project in which the process of building would continually reaffirm the historical project that the building commemorated. The continuous work of the people in the actual building of their national monument expressed the more general task of building a world that would complete the narrative of the national spirit – from awakening, to self-sacrifice, to victory over the enemy, to the creation of a fully articulated, "organic" ethical community. Schinkel's other large-scale planned memorials from this period, a "Hermann" monument to the spirit of the German people and a civic memorial to the spirit of Prussia, contained narrative friezes that articulated the same pattern of development, culminating in the task of building a nation commensurate with the sacrifice and self-recognition displayed on

[34] There is an extensive description of Schinkel's role in the creation of the Iron Cross, as well as the design of various monuments to the Wars of Liberation throughout Prussia, in Paul Rave, ed., *Karl Friedrich Schinkel Lebenswerk. Berlin II: Bauten fuer Wissenschaft, Verwaltung, Heer, Wohnbau und Denkmaeler* (Berlin: 1962), pp. 259–69.

the battlefield, of transforming the act of liberation into an institutionalized culture of autonomous subjects.[35]

The Befreiungsdom at the Potsdamer Platz was never built. Its place was taken by a much more modest memorial, a single, cast-iron Gothic tower constructed on the sandy Tempelhofer hill (renamed the Kreuzberg at the time of the memorial's dedication in 1821) just outside Berlin between 1818 and 1821. Already in 1814, the Romantic painter Caspar David Friedrich had complained to Arndt that as long as Germans remained "slaves of princes," no great monument to the deeds of the people would be built: "Where the people have no voice the people are also not allowed to feel and honor their strength."[36] The Carlsbad Decrees effectively marked the end of the political significance of the populist nationalist movement in public life throughout Germany. The popular leaders of these movements were exiled or jailed, their sympathizers among academic and government reformers were silenced and stripped of significant power, their cultural supporters in literature and the fine arts (like Caspar David Friedrich) restricted to indirect modes of speech. Symbolic indicators of commitment to recreate Old German identity in modern political forms like the floppy black Old German hat or long Old German hairstyles became pale residues of dashed hopes.[37] The Kreuzberg Memorial was, among other things, a representation of this moment of repression and compromise, disillusionment and resignation.

The memorial to the liberation wars constructed on the Kreuzberg consisted of a cast-iron Gothic steeple with four tiers of spires soaring sixty feet above a huge cruciform pedestal and capped with a prominent Iron Cross[38] (Fig. 10). The steeple itself served as an architectural setting for twelve large sculpted figures set in gabled niches.[39] Like the projected Liberation Cathedral, the Kreuzberg Monument was intended as a pilgrimage site on the

[35] This "Hermann" monument design is printed and described in Karl Friedrich Schinkel, *Sammlung Architektonische Entwuerfe* (*Collection of Architectural Designs*), (New York: 1989), Plate and Commentary #6. (This edition is cited hereafter as *Collection*.) The design for the more "democratic" monument to Prussian civic consciousness was found among Schinkel's unpublished designs. It is printed in *Karl Friedrich Schinkel: Eine Ausstellung aus der Deutschen Demokratischen Republik* (Berlin: 1982), no. 4.24.

[36] Letter from Friedrich to Arndt in E. M. Arndt, *Nothgedrungenen Bericht aus meinem Leben (mit Urkunden der demagogischen und antidemagogischen Umtriebe)*, (2 vols.; Leipzig: 1847), vol. 2, p. 175.

[37] See Jost Hermand, "Dashed Hopes: On the Painting of the Wars of Liberation," trans. James D. Staekley, in Seymour Drescher, David Sabean, and Allan Sharlin, eds., *Political Symbolism in Modern Europe: Essays in Honor of George L. Mosse* (New Brunswick: 1982), pp. 217–38; and also Christopher Clark, "The Wars of Liberation in Prussian Memory: Reflection on the Memorialization of War in Early Nineteenth-Century Germany," *Journal of Modern History* 68 (1996): 550–76.

[38] A detailed account by Paul Rave of the planning and building of the Kreuzberg memorial, complete with alternative designs and preliminary sketches, is available in Rave's *Schinkel: Berlin II*, pp. 270–96.

[39] Schinkel described the Gothic spire as an "architectural mass" that served "merely as the protecting cover erected for the veneration of these figures." See the descriptive commentary for Plate 22 in *Collection*, p. 38.

Fig. 10. Schinkel's design for a war memorial on the Kreuzberg in Berlin.
Source: Schinkel, *Sammlung Architektonische Entwuerfe*, no. 22. Reproduced from facsimile in Karl Friedrich Schinkel, *Collection of Architectural Designs* (New York: Princeton Architectural Press, 1989).

outskirts of the city where the "people" could meditate on the events of the recent war and their hopes for the future. The memorial was inscribed with a statement of gratitude from the king to his people for their response to his "Call" of 1813, and the Gothic structure, self-consciously based on models from the Cologne cathedral, was meant to tie these recent memories of the unity of prince and people specifically to the historical memory of the medieval, Old German period.

The public history that was portrayed by the figures and individual inscriptions focused on twelve decisive military engagements and turning points of the campaigns of 1813, 1814, and 1815. Each sculpted figure was conceived as the "spirit" or "genius" (as indicated by prominent wings) of an historical event, and was constructed according to recognizable characteristics of a contemporary personage.[40] Aside from the field marshals Bluecher and Yorck, these representations of the "spirit" expressing itself in the wars of liberation were members of the Prussian royal family. The monument thus displayed traditional kings and military leaders as embodiments of the divine and national spirits, represented by the Gothic spire and the pattern of Iron Crosses. The twelve statues, despite the apostolic analogy, were clearly imagined as embodying secular rather than traditionally Christian "spirits" and costumed in either ancient Greek or Old German dress. The Kreuzberg monument was both more specifically a memorial to the heroic deeds and sacrifices of the wars of liberation and the embodiment of a more secular historical narrative than the unbuilt Befreiungsdom. Most strikingly, it forged a balance, through its representation of the spirits of the battles and the costuming of their exemplary figures, between classical and Old German historical narratives. It may very well be that this balance was a product of compromise and adaptation. Schinkel had originally proposed a classical column as a more appropriate form for the monument but had bowed to the wishes and visions of the crown prince for something more Germanic and Christian. Moreover, the style of the sculptures was uniformly classical, even though half of the figures (including the crown prince) were clothed in the medieval costumes of the citizen's militia. Although the final concept of the monument and the foundation-stone-laying ceremony date back to 1818, the spire was not completed until 1821, and the last sculpture was placed in its niche in 1826.

The siting of the monument, despite the conservative tones of its inauguration festivities (the Russian Tsar Alexander I participated in the groundbreaking ceremonies, and the dedication was attended by virtually the whole court, the military leadership, and the ministry) and the probable royal source of its final form, was clearly "popular." It became,

[40] A description as well as production history of the sculpted figures is provided in Peter Bloch, "Das Kreutzbergdenkmal und die patriotische Kunst," *Jahrbuch Preussischer Kulturbesitz* vol. 2 (1973): 142–59.

as Schinkel had intended, an excursion site for the families of urban artisans, tradesman, merchants, retailers, and minor civil servants. But the excursions that culminated in an afternoon at the Kreuzberg were not reverential pilgrimages in which participation in a common national spirit was recognized and nurtured. With the nearby construction of the amusement park Tivoli in 1829, the Kreuzberg was well on its way to being transformed into a recreation site (*Vergnuegungsort*) for Berliners and tourists. This function overwhelmed its intended character as a pilgrimage site where secular history might be sacralized and sacred history secularized in the making of a public memory for an historical culture. The *Volk* did come to the Kreuzberg, but not quite according to Schinkel's original expectations.[41]

Despite the continuing presence of populist elements in the Kreuzberg memorial, the failure of the Befreiungsdom project seemed to mark the beginning of a general shift in Schinkel's attitudes. This shift may have been instigated in part by a need to adapt to the Prussian king's increasing hostility to any reforms that would increase the role of formerly excluded classes in their own governance, and the reaction against the nationalist movement of 1807–15 as a dangerous demagoguery that threatened the established boundaries of sovereign power in the states that constituted the German Confederation. Schinkel's promotion to the status of councilor (*Rat*) in the State Building Commission in March 1815 may have tempered his populism and increased his identification with the governing cadres. But Schinkel's work after 1815 also indicates a powerful, if often inwardly conflicted, shift away from belief in the myth of a national essence incarnate in the archaic depths of an ethnic population, of an *Urvolk* that merely needed to be "awakened" and "liberated" in order to appropriate its past in creative fashion and produce a new political and cultural form for itself. His disillusionment was already evident in 1816, when he reported to the Prussian government both on the project of completing the construction of the Cologne cathedral as a national monument and on the possibility of purchasing the famed Boisseree collection of Old German art and antiquities for the royal collections. The preservation and purely imitative "completion" of historical monuments like the Cologne cathedral according to their original historical design, Schinkel noted, was not the same as creating a culture that fulfilled the potentials of such recovered memories through creative practice.[42] The Gothic for Schinkel was now viewed as an object of historical preservation rather than as an incomplete historical form through which the present could give

[41] The transformation of the Kreuzberg is recounted with copious illustrations in Michael Nungesser, *Das Denkmal auf dem Kreuzberg von Karl Friedrich Schinkel* (Berlin: 1987).

[42] See "Schinkel's Berichte und Briefe ueber die Erwerbung der Boisseree'schen Gemaeldesammlung fuer den preussischen Staat (1816–1817)" in Wolzogen, *Aus Schinkel's Nachlass*, vol. 2, 171–204; and "Bericht ueber den Zustand des Domes zu Koeln (March 9, 1816)," cited in Georg Friedrich Koch, "Schinkel's architektonische Entwuerfe im gotischen Stil (1810–1815)," *Zeitschrift fuer Kunstgeschichte* 32 (1969): 301–2.

shape to its own highest cultural goals. By 1816, in fact, Schinkel had begun to reverse his earlier concept of the relations between classical and Gothic in the formation of the present and the future. Beginning with his new plans for the center of Berlin in 1816–17, Schinkel developed a historical vision in which the Gothic religious building, imagined as the symbolic center of a narrative of national self-recognition, was relegated to a subordinate place in a more broadly conceived vision of the progressive development of the classical tradition and the humanist educational model for building cultural identities. With this shift, however, there also emerged a more chastened interpretation of the idea of freedom. National identity and subjective autonomy did not simply drop out of Schinkel's work in 1815–18, but his sense of historical mission did take a turn that was radical enough to make the Gothic style appear henceforth as an object of nostalgic distortion and dangerous misrecognition rather than as a path to ethical commitment and self-recognition. Along with many of his contemporaries, Schinkel eventually repudiated the nationalist dreams of his youth as sentimental and dangerous illusions. By 1825 he could refer to his Gothic enthusiasms as the sins of youth (*Jugendsuenden*).[43]

Schinkel repudiated nationalist dreams

THE TEMPLE OF AESTHETIC EDUCATION: THE TUTELARY STATE AND THE DISCIPLINE OF CIVIC CULTURE

Perverted by the Regime

In early 1823 Schinkel submitted a plan for the construction of a public museum to house the Prussian royal art collections on the open, northern side of the square and pleasure garden, or park (the Lustgarten), that marked the end of the boulevard leading into the city center from the Brandenburg Gate and was bordered on three sides by the baroque buildings of the Military Museum and Arsenal (*Zeughaus*), the City Palace of the Hohenzollern family, and the Royal Cathedral. The plan received almost immediate royal approval, construction was begun in the summer of 1823, and the monumental structure that eventually came to be known as the Altes Museum (Old Museum) was dedicated and opened to the public in the summer of 1830. The planning and building of the Altes Museum marked the culmination of an intense period of building and urban design in which Schinkel transformed the representational center of the Prussian capital in ways that are still discernible. The most obvious visible characteristic of the structures that marked this transformation – the New Guardhouse (Neue Wache) on the major arterial boulevard and "triumphal way" (Unter den Linden);

[43] In a letter to Frederic Soret of May 17, 1825, published in *Lehrbuch*, p. 72, Schinkel thought through his critique of Romanticism as subjective illusion in the company of his friend, the aesthetic philosopher Karl Wilhelm Friedrich Solger, with whom he was in constant contact between 1815 and 1819. Aesthetically, his turn was marked by a self-conscious adherence to the neoclassical views of Goethe and members of the Goethe circle during the 1820s. See Maria Erxleben, "Goethe und Schinkel," in *Karl Friedrich Schinkel und die Antike: Eine Aufsatzsammlung* (Stendal: 1985), pp. 20–32.

the Palace Bridge (Schlossbruecke), which joined Unter den Linden to the Lustgarten; the remodeled Royal Cathedral; the Royal Theater on the Gendarmenmarkt; and the Altes Museum – was their elegantly urbane neoclassical style. At the moment (1816) when Schinkel was finally given the possibility of actualizing his projects in constructed buildings, he seemed to have changed his aesthetic commitments (in terms of constructive styles) in rather drastic fashion from Old German–Gothic to neoclassical Greek. Although Schinkel only provided oblique and partial reasons for this "turn" in historical perspective in his public pronouncements and commentaries, the notes and sketches he gathered for his never completed or published architectural textbook (*Lehrbuch*) in the early 1820s give evidence of significant changes in his perception of communal identity and the role of architecture in its construction.

At the most fundamental level, Schinkel displayed increasing uneasiness about defining the idea of German-Christian culture as self-transcending freedom. His critique had psychological, social, and aesthetic dimensions. He now insisted that human striving for identification with the universal originated in the fact that "man seeks the stability of a permanent order – the divine – in the constantly changing worlds of appearances: not everything must change and go under, he wants to possess something that is permanent."[44] Insofar as restless, self-transcending striving and openness to the infinite informed Gothic architecture, this architecture reproduced feelings of anxiety and homelessness, thus reinforcing rather than healing the "nullity" (*Nichtigkeit*) of an age in which intense competition among individual interests kept people from reflecting on the purpose of their own neurotically driven activity.[45] Concerns about the instability of Gothic buildings that were not appropriately grounded on substantial pedestals were now expanded into a critique of the psychological and social meaning of Gothic forms in general. Pointed arches restlessly refusing to resolve their tensions in the closure of circles or rectangles, spires constantly attempting to deny their materiality by moving toward the transparency of light – these became less exhilarating than terrifying. They were signs of the denial of earthly limitation and reflected the anxiety of a rootless individual subjectivity.

The alleged freedom expressed in Gothic constructive principles, Schinkel now suggested, was actually a deceptive denial of material conditions and historical–cultural limitations. The miraculous ability of the Gothic to transform material objects into aesthetic expressions seemed a dangerous disavowal of the reality of the object. In its merger of decorative and structural elements, the Gothic building hid its constructive and material conditions under a layer of artifice. What Schinkel had praised earlier as a

[44] Karl Friedrich Schinkel, "Die Klassizistische Fassung des Architektonisches Lehrbuches, gegen 1825," *Lehrbuch*, p. 70.

[45] *Ibid.*

purified symbolic speech, as poetry in stone, now emerged as hypocrisy and dangerous illusion. The tension in pointed-arch construction was defined as a destructive conflict (*Widerstreit*) between fragments that refused to subordinate themselves to a higher order. The expression of such tension in the medium of inanimate material objects produced a vision of a world without anchor, verging on cosmic chaos.[46]

In contrast to the Romantic nationalist idealization of the Gothic, Schinkel now reconstructed the neoclassical humanist ideal of stable order, serenity, reconciliation of tension, and "artistic peace" (*Kunstruhe*).[47] The expression and production of this ideal in the construction of public buildings and organization of public spaces had two major dimensions. First, the relations among general spaces and material elements should articulate horizontal rest and solidity as well as vertical stability. Parts should connect in ways that confirmed the laws of gravity, pressing down at right angles or in equally distributed weight in rounded arches. The impression of dynamic tension in the relations of materials and forces should always be clearly subordinate to the framework of stable structure. A building or public space should be a home above all, a place that confirmed the substantiality and order of the world. Moreover, Schinkel now claimed that such order and peace was dependent on hierarchical relations. The Gothic vision of an organic order produced by the flow of a life energy through all individual elements was rejected in favor of the proper subordination of individual parts to their limited functions in constructing the relations of the whole. Tension among equal parts emphasized their fragmentary character and exaggerated the disruptive qualities of life's oppositions. Strife was always "destructive"; the creation of an authentic ethical consciousness from the experience of spatial and tectonic relations required structural resolution and reconciliation.[48] In psychosexual terms, Schinkel saw the classical as a masculine style that needed to assert its domination over the "indeterminate excitability" that defined the Gothic as "feminine."[49]

These claims about the cultural role of architecture in representing and producing psychological and social stability were matched by an emphasis on the honest presentation of material and constructive techniques. Schinkel now saw Gothic architecture as an architecture of deception, hiding its dependence on specific structural techniques and physical materials in order to present the image of weightless soaring to the light. Honesty to materials and transparency of the structural conditions of external form became dominant architectural values in the period of Schinkel's disillusionment with the Gothic projections of subjective freedom. The notion of limitation could of course be expressed in different ways. Schinkel tended to emphasize the limitation of natural, earthly conditions and the functional requirements produced by physical human needs. But this also meant a turning away from the alternative vision, chosen by many of his contemporaries, including the

[46] *Ibid.*, p. 71. [47] *Ibid.*, pp. 59, 69–73. [48] *Ibid.*, p. 71. [49] *Ibid.*, p. 73.

crown prince, of the transcendent limitations on human construction of meaning and value, and the dependence of human self-creation on the power of an otherworldly divinity.

Because Schinkel moved away from the Romantic feeling of identification with infinite subjectivity and stressed the limitations placed on human striving by physical conditions, historically produced social relations, and technology, his work after 1816 seemed to take a significant secular turn. Building churches, as we shall see, remained an important dimension of Schinkel's cultural task, but in terms of the architectural representation of cultural values, Schinkel's neoclassical turn produced a shift from the National Cathedral of Liberation to the Temple of Aesthetic Education as the sacred center of public memory and cultural identity. The historical role and cultural function of the Cathedral of Liberation was displaced in the 1820s, not, or at least not primarily, onto new ecclesiastical projects, but onto cultural institutions like the museum, the theater, and the concert hall – sites in which "emancipated" individuals of an emerging civil society experienced the ethical power of aesthetic experience. It was in the new temples of art that the isolated ego was to be transformed into an integrated member of an ethical community and discover the memory that tied him to that community's past.

For purposes of comparison with the plan for the Befreiungsdom, we can divide the Altes Museum into three general spaces: the façade, with its colonnade and external staircase; the rotunda; and the galleries. The museum façade contrasts dramatically with the soaring pyramid of gables, baldachins, and spires that expressed the idea of German-Christian freedom for Schinkel in 1815. An open porch, or portico, that runs the length of the front of the building and is divided into twenty segments by eighteen free-standing ionic columns and two corner antae functions as a public walkway punctuated by busts and statues between the interior of the building and the Lustgarten (Fig. 11). Raised on a prominent pedestal, it is entered via a broad stairway, spanning one-third of the façade. The Prussian eagles above the cornice that mark off the rhythmic linearity of the columns highlight the horizontal lines of the rectangular façade. The flattened rectangularity of the building is repeated in the central boxlike "attic" above the roof that hides the curves of the interior rotunda.

Aside from its exaggerated horizontal emphasis and its insistent rectangularity, the exterior of the museum has one further striking trait: The interior wall is pushed back in the center third of the façade to provide space for an exterior (open to the air, but under the roof of the building) stairway leading from the first floor to a second-floor balcony from which the museum visitor can enter the second-floor galleries and the rotunda balcony, or stop to view the Lustgarten through the spaces between the columns (Fig. 12). This staircase reinforces the duality of the porch as a boundary area and walkway linking the activity of the city and the space of the temple of art, the practical

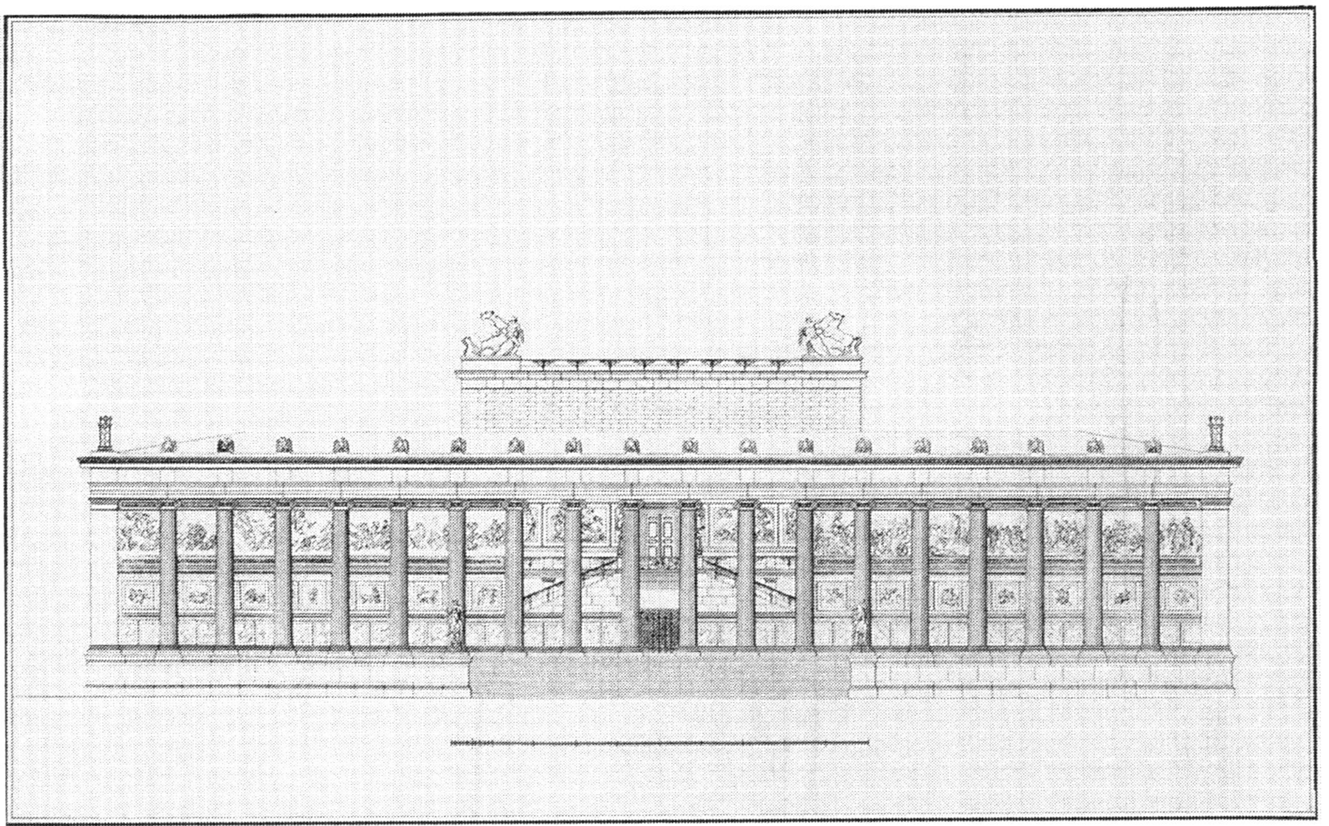

Fig. 11. Main façade of the Altes Museum.
Source: Schinkel, *Sammlung Architektonische Entwuerfe*, no. 39, reproduced from facsimile in Karl Friedrich Schinkel, *Collection of Architectural Designs* (New York: Princeton Architectural Press, 1989).

Fig. 12. Upper balcony of the main staircase of the Altes Museum with a view through the colonnade into the Lustgarten.
Source: Schinkel, *Sammlung Architektonische Entwuerfe*, no. 43, reproduced from facsimile in Karl Friedrich Schinkel, *Collection of Architectural Designs* (New York: Princeton Architectural Press, 1989).

life of public action and the interior dimensions of spiritual understanding. As in many of his buildings, Schinkel also allowed for the possibility that visitors might use the roof of his building as a viewing platform, thus expanding the horizons of their panoramic view of city and environs, as well as providing closer views of the roof statuary connecting the interior aesthetic experience to a cosmic order. The view from the stairwell balcony through the columns from a site near the top of the columns, moreover, provides an interesting perspective from inside a classical structure into a world framed by the orders of that structure. Finally, the stairway provides an interesting guide for the way in which Schinkel imagined a visit to the museum – separating the two gallery levels through movement outside into the urban present before reentry into the world of historical art objects.

The second distinctive element of the Altes Museum is the rotunda that dominates its interior space. Because the main staircase is outside, entry into the building coincides with a direct entry into the rotunda, the space that Schinkel conceived, in analogy to the domed altar space of the cathedral, as the sanctuary where the individual visitor was drawn into an aesthetic experience that offered the possibility of subjective transformation and self-recognition (Fig. 13). This experience was no longer imagined as

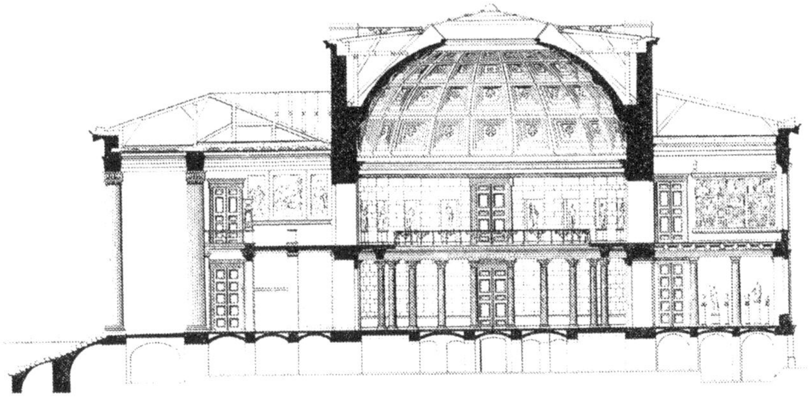

Fig. 13. Tranverse section of the Altes Museum (*detail*).
Source: Schinkel, *Sammlung Architektonische Entwuerfe*, no. 40, reproduced from facsimile in Karl Friedrich Schinkel, *Collection of Architectural Designs* (New York: Princeton Architectural Press, 1989).

identification with the spirit of self-creative freedom pulsing through the historical life of a people, but as the mastery of natural and historical limitation in the serenely balanced harmonies of aesthetic form, an experience of the secular, "natural" incarnation of the divine in the human, through contemplation of the paradigmatic cultural forms of classical Greece. Against the criticism of the aesthetic theorist and cultural historian Alois Hirt, who would rather have used the money and space consumed by the rotunda to expand the museum's collections, Schinkel defended the necessity of creating a "dignified central focus" (*wuerdiger Mittelpunkt*), a place that could function as a "sacred space" (*Heiligthum*) in which the most precious aesthetic objects were put on display. "One must first experience this space," he insisted, "when one enters from the external portico. The perception of a beautiful and exalted space creates a sensitivity and mood for the enjoyment and knowledge of that which the building preserves more generally."[50] This experience of aesthetic enjoyment was a prerequisite, Schinkel felt, for the aesthetic and historical knowledge Hirt wanted the collections to purvey. The museum as a built artwork was to take the visitors into an experience of art, accessible through the feelings without special "expert" knowledge or guidance. This experience would then open their sensibilities to the artworks that were on display in the galleries.

50 "Votum zu dem Gutachten Herren Hofrat Hirt" (Feb. 23, 1825), cited in Rave, *Schinkel: Berlin I*, p. 35.

The rotunda space was conceived on the model of the classical pantheon, with the addition of an interior balcony supported by freestanding Ionic columns in the cylindrical space of the first floor.[51] Original or restored statues of the Greek gods were placed between the columns. The central space of Schinkel's new temple was thus religious in a particular historical and aesthetic sense – it presented a model experience of the way in which a culture represented its core ideals to itself through aesthetic representation of its divinities. Modern Germans did not find the essence of their own peculiar cultural identity as they entered this space, but rather a universal model for the way in which any culture could perfect and articulate its essential being in aesthetic form. Greece was presented here as a universal norm for a unified culture, but also as a particular culture that could not be recreated or imitated in a historical sense. As they viewed their city through the Greek columns of the portico on their way to the painting galleries of the second floor, modern Prussian Germans might nourish a consciousness of their historical mission to build here, in nineteenth-century Berlin, as the Greeks had built in antiquity.

The second-floor galleries were devoted primarily to what Schinkel and the art curator Gustav Waagen considered to be the high points of modern Christian art, works of the Italian and northern European Renaissance, organized in regional schools and culminating in the works of Raphael and the German and Dutch painters of the fifteenth, sixteenth, and seventeenth centuries, like the Van Eycks and Albrecht Duerer, the heroes of Old German nationalists.[52] The content of these galleries of European Christian art did not "transcend" that of the plastic classical arts displayed in the ground-floor sculpture gallery, but were also organized around the rotunda (on the balcony level), allowing visitors to reenter the world of classical perfection for temporary refreshment or historical reflection as they wandered through the upper galleries, just as they might move out to the open platform facing onto the Lustgarten in order to situate their enjoyment of past art in relation to the present and future tasks of building their own city.

[51] The modern use of the classical rotunda as a sacred space on the model of the Roman pantheon was familiar to Schinkel from his visit to the Pio-Clementina Museum in the Vatican. In 1818 he had drawn a classical temple in the form of a rotunda in which the dome rested on a circle of freestanding Corinthian columns for the stage set of Spontini's opera *Die Vestalin*. See Erik Forssman, *Karl Friedrich Schinkel. Bauwerke und Baugedanken* (Munich: 1981), pp. 123–26.

[52] In 1816, when Schinkel first viewed the Old German art and antiquities collected by the Boisserees in Cologne, he was especially impressed by the Van Eycks' art as a concentrated epitome of the cultural world of the Christian-German idea. See his letter to the sculptor Christian Rauch, of November 14, 1816, printed in Mackowsky, *Schinkel*, pp. 92–94. Later, Schinkel produced an altar picture in honor of Duerer for the Berlin Duerer Festival of 1828. But by 1828, Duerer was seen less as a painter of the German people than as an early proponent of the Protestant German state. See Peter Klaus Schuster, "Schinkel, Friedrich und Hintze: Zur romantischen Ikonographie des deutschen Nationalgefuehls," *Zeitschrift des deutschen Vereins fuer Kunstwissenschaft: Sonderheft zum Schinkeljahr*, 35, no. 1/4 (1981): 30.

The importance of the rotunda in Schinkel's plan was reinforced for the external viewer by its centrally located rectangular housing floating above the cornice. The galleries were subordinate and constructed in a less obviously representational fashion. As Goerd Peschken has pointed out, Schinkel's gallery spaces are strikingly innovative in their completely functional, variable, design.[53] Open columned galleries on the main floor allowed sculpture to be displayed in various arrangements and also gave the individual visitor the option of bypassing certain exhibitions. No designated path guided the visitor through the galleries. Upstairs, the arrangement of galleries as partitioned halls at right angles to the external walls produced a similar arrangement, allowing individuals to select the path of their own itinerary.

The specifics of the art-historical narrative where thus left somewhat open to individual selection, even though the larger epochal shifts and their relation to the present historical moment as well as to a larger cosmic order were clearly controlled by the porch, rotunda, and staircase of the building. Schinkel and Waagen both favored a focus on exemplary works of high quality as representatives of epochs, or cultural "ideas" rather than a detailed historical narrative of the development of Western painting.[54] Again the focus was on public accessibility through aesthetic enjoyment rather than on the scholarly interests of the art historian, and on historical moments of creative originality rather than on periods of quantitative penetration and expansion of existing aesthetic principles.

The porch, staircase, and rotunda defined the museum as more a work of art than a house of art, as some of Schinkel's critics had complained from the beginning of the project.[55] The experience of the art displayed in the building was subordinated to the experience of the building itself as an aesthetic experience with ethical consequences. Schinkel defended his building as a place where the enjoyment of great works of art took precedence over the didactic tasks of teaching art history, but the experience he intended to produce with his building was also the basis for teaching a certain kind of historical narrative, much as the altar space of the Liberation Cathedral had created the conditions for an assimilation of the idea of the people that informed the narrative of national self-determination.

[53] Goerd Peschken, *Baugeschichte Politisch: Schinkel, Stadt Berlin, Preussische Schloesser* (Braunschweig: 1993), pp. 24–45.

[54] On Waagen's historical conceptions around this time, see Gabriele Bickendorf, *Der Beginn der Kunstgeschichtsschreibung und der Paradigma der "Geschichte": Gustav Friedrich Waagen's Fruehschrift "Ueber Hubert und Johann van Eyck"* (Worms: 1985).

[55] Extensive documentation of the debates within the Prussian administrative elite regarding the purpose of the museum are available in Steven Moyano, "Quality vs. History: Schinkel's Altes Museum and Prussian Arts Policy," *Art Bulletin* 72 (1990): 585–608; and Reinhard Wegner, "Die Einrichtung des Alten Museums in Berlin: Anmerkungen zu einem neu entdeckten Schinkeldokument" *Jahrbuch der berliner Museen* vol. 31 (1989): 265–87.

The historical narrative articulated in Schinkel's museum, as in his earlier cathedral, was not a linear sequence of events but a narrative of dialectical relations between epochal cultural ideas. In contrast to the cathedral, the museum was organized around the immanent self-sufficiency of the Greek individual and social body, not the dynamic transcending activity of the Christian spiritual subject. The Christian cultural epoch appeared in the individual painterly visions of artistic geniuses in the second-floor galleries not as a fully constructed world, but as a subjectively envisioned project that remained as an uncompleted historical task for the present generation. The task for the future was the creation of a cultural world like the world of the Greeks, but within the conditions of modern European existence, that is, in terms that affirmed, in a disciplined and controlled way, individual subjectivity and the constant movement of historical re-creation.

After 1816 Schinkel tended to define the cultural mission of the present in terms of discipline, refinement, and control, rather than liberation. Or, perhaps more aptly, freedom itself was reimagined primarily within the frame of discipline and order. Schinkel still believed that military liberation from foreign domination was for the Germans, as it had been for the Greeks in their Persian Wars, the condition of cultural efflorescence and the construction of an ethical order. He originally intended to flank the staircase of the museum with large equestrian statues of the king and crown prince in military poses and to decorate the porch and open staircase with memorials to the heroes of the Liberation Wars, thus emphasizing that the process of aesthetic education intended by the museum itself was made possible by the recent military triumph over the external tyrant. The internal liberation produced by aesthetic education was built on the external liberation produced by military might and self-assertion. The most prominent decorations of the museum, however, clearly gave priority to the tasks of controlling the inner barbarism of human nature in the project of constructing a cultural community of moral subjects. The most striking decorative element on the outside of the building was provided by the colossal sculptures of Castor and Pollux, the horse-taming Dioscuri, on the corners of the rectangular structure covering the rotunda. These figures presented two obvious messages: the need for disciplined energy in the production of cultural order and, especially, as articulated through the stars attached to their crowns and their placing as imaginary corners of a virtual heavenly vault – the connection between such self-dicipline and participation in a cosmic order.

These themes were spelled out in complex detail in the murals that Schinkel sketched for the upper half of the walls behind the porch pillars and the ends of the second-story viewing platform, but which were not fully executed until the 1840s, after his death. Schinkel described the general theme of the murals as the "cultural history of the human race," but the story told in these naked figures of classical mythology was less a history of culture than a history of the formation of culture out of nature as a process of emergence, defeat, discipline, reconstitution, growth, defense, and remaking. This was no story of the liberation of the national idea from external repression, or of a struggle against the limitations of material conditions in the battle for full self-expression, but a story of the laborious construction of meaning within the natural sphere of quotidian struggle and the movement of the days and seasons. The large mural on the left side of the stairway portrayed the birth of human culture through a tangled flow of naked figures in empty space, as an evolution and struggle of principles that allowed for the gradual triumph of light and the dawning of human culture. The right side mural provided a more crowded, layered representation of moments in the development of culture within the limitations present in the light of day. Schinkel was constantly revising the plan of his museum murals during the late 1820s and early 1830s. The trend in these revisions was toward a darker vision, a vision of the transformation of nature into culture that revealed the possibilities of catastrophic collapse, that emphasized the heroic self-discipline and self-sacrifice demanded for the creation of a human world out of nature's potentialities, and that ultimately accepted the limitations of all attempts to create a permanent cultural order in the face of the impersonal Dionysian powers of death and regeneration that ordered the natural cosmos. His last two sketches, designed for the walls of the stairway balcony and completed in 1834, paired an allegorical representation of "self-sacrifice in the face of natural catastrophe" on the left with "self-sacrifice in defense against human barbarism" on the right. Nowhere was it clearer that Schinkel intended his building to function as a means to create an ethical community in which individual egos would find their fulfillment through submission and devotion to a public will that was able to control the vagaries of external nature and the barbarism of human nature.[56]

The narrative of human development recounted in the iconography of the museum's decorative materials was couched in the universal language of classical myth and moral allegory. The figures in the frescoes were not historical personages from Greek and Roman history and did not wear historical costumes or operate within the limitations of particular historical systems of technology and culture. The background narrative of the museum thus placed the cultural function of art as a moralizing power into a universal, cosmic context. But Schinkel also saw the Greeks as the paradigm of an historical culture, not just as exemplars of the universal. In a painting completed in 1825, he portrayed the moment in the development of classical Greece – the moment of "blossoming" (*Bluethe*) – that he hoped to bring

[56] Except for a few small panels, the museum murals were destroyed during World War II. They are described and analyzed on the basis of photographs in two articles by Helmut Boersch-Supan: "Zur Etnstehungsgeschichte von Schinkel's Entwuerfen fuer die Museumsfresken," *Zeitschrift des deutschen Vereins fuer Kunstwissenschaft* 35, no. 1/4 (1981): 36–46; and "Die Kunst im Herzen der Stadt-Schinkel's Idee vom Museum," *Jahrbuch der kunsthistorischen Sammlungen in Wien* 88 (1992): 21–38.

into structural analogy to the present moment in the history of Prussia and Germany (Fig. 14). After defeating the Persians (echoed in contemporary history by the Greek war of independence against the Ottoman Turks), the heroes of battle returned home to build themselves into a moral community that made itself visible in the harmonious relations of classical art.[57] In Greece at least, the conquest of the external enemy produced the impetus for the creation of an ethical world. It was this moment that Schinkel was waiting for and trying to produce in the present. But he also realized that the building of his own temple of art was a preemption of the ethical task. His museum was not an expression of an accomplished community of will and feeling but an instrument to help construct such a community. In the mid 1820s, Schinkel suggested that this reversal of temporal order between the artistic "expression" and the accomplished ethical reality might be a characteristic of modern history. Art went ahead of practice, probing the possibilities of human community and intervening in history as an ethical actor in its own right. The museum was conceived as an intervention in history that might set in motion a sequence of events that could not have been predicted:

> To be historical does not mean simply to preserve or repeat the past. For in this fashion history would come to an end. Historical action is that which creates the new and thus moves history forward. But precisely the demand that history should move forward necessitates serious reflection concerning what is new and in what way this new element should be introduced into the circle of the given. Such reflection requires the highest cultivation. The fine arts that place everything into measure and repose are perhaps the testing ground. Formerly art followed great political events and was a consequence of them. It would perhaps constitute the highest product of a new form of action in the world if the fine arts went ahead, somewhat in the way in which experiment precedes discovery in science. This could be perceived as a distinctive element of the modern age.[58]

From this perspective, the Altes Museum was a self-conscious, experimental act of the educated elite whose aim was to create a community like the Greek polis within the conditions of post-Napoleonic Europe.

The historical narrative Schinkel was trying to express through the spatial relations and visual ornamentation of the Altes Museum becomes clearer from an examination of the museum's place in his general design for the center of Berlin. It was an important personal triumph for Schinkel to convince

[57] See Haus, *Schinkel*, pp. 243–53; H. C. L. Jaffe, "'Blick in Griechenlands Bluete' – ein Bildungsbild," in Hannelore Gaertner, ed., *Schinkel-Studien* (Leipzig: 1984), pp. 199–205; and especially Adolf Max Vogt, *Karl Friedrich Schinkel, Blick in Griechenlands Bluete: Ein Hoffungsbild fuer "Spree-Athen"* (Frankfurt: 1985).

[58] Schinkel, "Klassizistische Fassung," *Lehrbuch*, p. 71.

Fig. 14. Schinkel's oil painting *View of the Blossoming of Greece*, displaying the building of culture after military victory (1825). (1836 copy by Wilhelm Ahlborn) Reproduction permission: Bildarchiv Preussischer Kulturbesitz.

Fig. 15. Schinkel's 1823 drawing of the projected Altes Museum in the context of the Lustgarten ensemble as viewed from Unter den Linden. Reproduction permission: Bildarchiv Preussischer Kulturbesitz; photo Joerg P. Anders.

both the appointed state commission and the king that the building should be sited across from the Royal Palace on the far side of the Lustgarten, straddling the bed of an old canal. From the very beginning, Schinkel imagined the museum as transforming this space and turning the Lustgarten into the new civic center of the Prussian capital. Despite its modest size, the elevated and colonnaded porch of the museum provided a powerful counterweight to the royal palace and turned the space between them from a royal garden into an urban square. As Schinkel's earliest drawing of the projected museum revealed, it was meant to provide a spatial reinterpretation of the central pillars of the Prussian state, balancing the representations of dynasty, army, and church with the cultural power of aesthetic education (Fig. 15). The cornices of the three rectangular buildings, the arsenal, the palace and the museum, created a continuous horizontal line that was reinforced by the double row of trees and only broken, briefly and modestly, by the vertical lines of the cathedral's columned portal and three cupolas. The external façade and decorations of the Museum were placed into communicative relations with these other pillars of the community. The planned equestrian statues of the Hohenzollern king and crown prince, as well as the Latin inscription on the cornice designating the museum as a royal endowment for the education of the public, placed the temple of art into positive, somewhat filial, relations to the paternalism of the palace. The columns of the porch connected to both the row of trees on the north side of the square that hid the "inappropriate" buildings of the stock exchange and royal pharmacy and harmonized with the Ionic columns of the portal Schinkel had added to the cathedral in a recent renovation. The Prussian eagles, the equestrian statues, and the memorials to the recent war in the stairwell and porch were meant to connect the flourishing of cultural creativity to the human sacrifices required by the battle against external enemies and to confirm the military foundations of cultural autonomy and social peace. Unlike the Befreiungsdom of 1815, the museum of the 1820s presented itself as one element in the construction of an urban public space. All of Schinkel's drawings, including the interior views, emphasized this communicative siting of the building as its essence. This central civic space was not, however, any more than the sacred altar space of the national cathedral, or the rotunda of aesthetic illumination within the museum, a place of meeting, dialogue, and the construction of public will; it was a space for the intersection of various functional elements that together constituted the artificial organism of an ethical community. It expressed a vision of the civic order as a panoramic ensemble that could be internalized as a rational, lawful, harmoniously balanced order through contemplation and cognitive appropriation by the individual.

The spatial arrangements of the Lustgarten complex were accompanied by the construction of certain narrative patterns, or scripts, into which the individual subject could be inserted. Among these narratives, the most powerful at the time of the museum's construction was one that drew Schinkel back to a Prussian state ideology that had marked his own roots as an architectural apprentice in the late eighteenth century and whose outlines had already been inscribed in the center of Berlin by the architects of the Prussian monarchy in the seventeenth and eighteenth centuries. The buildings and public spaces that marked the path of Unter den Linden from the Brandenburg Gate to the Lustgarten told a story of the construction of Prussia as a public order, and of Berlin as its "Athens on the Spree," through military discipline and self-sacrifice on the one hand, and through the knowledge and ethical example of a cadre of cultured civil servants and educators on the other. The Brandenburg Gate, constructed as a Greek Propylaea during the early 1790s, just as Schinkel began his early training in Berlin, was laden with iconography of the translation of military victory into spiritual greatness and the arts of war into the arts of peace. It opened into an avenue that was flanked by the Royal Opera, the Royal Library, the recently created (1810) university in the former residence of a Hohenzollern prince, the Academy of Fine Arts, as well as residences of the royal family, the royal stables (which shared their building with the Academy of Fine Arts), and the Arsenal. One of Schinkel's first important responsibilities as a Prussian civil servant had been to decorate this avenue in 1814 as a triumphal way for the returning Prussian armies, and his first projects after 1815 extended and expanded the Prussian ethos of this symbolic street in the light of the recent events of liberation, consolidation, and expansion.

Schinkel's first completed project in Berlin was the New Guardhouse for the royal palace guards, which was built between 1816 and 1818 near the end of the north side of Unter den Linden, in the small park of chestnut trees that separated the Arsenal from the university. In its setting among the public buildings that created the broad opening just west of the bridge that led into the Lustgarten, this squarely set structure with massive corner piers, a strikingly sculpted Doric portico, and a classical pediment with a decorative frieze, was clearly intended to serve representational as well as functional purposes. The figures of victory along the cornice, the image of self-sacrifice on the pediment frieze, and the statues of two heroes of 1813, the generals von Buelow and Scharnhorst, that Schinkel set in front of the building, all emphasized the military ethos of the Prussian state and memorialized the recent victories as an expression of that ethos. The New Guardhouse continued the themes introduced by the Brandenburg Gate and was part of Schinkel's plan for a general redesign of the end of the avenue that would make it an appropriate conclusion to the street's narrative of the alliance of physical and spiritual strength, and external and internal discipline in the forging of the Prussian civic order.

Just a few years after the completion of the New Guardhouse, construction began on the new bridge that would join the avenue to the Lustgarten and replace the narrow wooden Hundebruecke (Bridge of the Hounds) with its obsolete reference to a time when Unter den Linden was the road joining the rear of the palace to the royal hunting grounds in the Tiergarten. Schinkel's broad span over the Kupfergraben was conceived as a monumental entry into what he now clearly imagined as the representational center of the state. From his very first drawings, Schinkel had envisioned the bridge as flanked by a series of eight colossal sculptures of allegorical figures. Each of these sculptures consisted of a nude "Greek" youth and a clothed, winged female goddess who functioned as a "genius," or "spirit," guiding the youth through the stages of recovery after defeat, preparation for renewed battle through assimilation of the lessons of history, self-sacrifice, and elevation into the realm of spiritual transcendence. In this narrative of cultural regeneration through recognition of historical identity and communal obligation, suffering was transfigured through beauty, and historical memory motivated sacrifice for the public good. The Schlossbruecke thus presented a prolegomena to the message that Schinkel attempted to display in the murals of his museum porch. Like the murals, the bridge sculptures were only completed after Schinkel's death, at a time when their meanings no longer seemed accessible to most observers and the idealized nude figures seemed less like images of universal truths than anachronistically unhistorical and undressed figures.[59]

Throughout the 1820s Schinkel also tried out various plans to complete the Prussian iconography of the avenue with a crowning monument

[59] See the useful historical monograph on the historical context, production, and reception of the Schlossbruecke: Peter Springer, *Schinkels Schlossbruecke in Berlin: Zweckbau und Monument* (Frankfurt: 1981).

connecting recent victories and future tasks to the memory of the military heroics and enlightened rational politics of Frederick the Great, thus again taking up the themes of Gilly's submission to the competition of 1797, which had inspired his original commitment to architecture as a public vocation.[60] In one of his last great oil paintings, completed in 1817, Schinkel imagined a huge triumphal arch spanning Unter den Linden that contained within its covered space colossal equestrian statues of Frederick the Great and Frederick William the Great Elector in antique costume (Fig. 16). The viewer's perspective through the triumphal arch and past the darkly foregrounded statues takes in a vast throng celebrating the return of the triumphant troops after the victory over Napoleon in a brightly lit landscape with the shimmering skyline of Berlin in the distance. A glimpse of the dome of Schinkel's unbuilt Cathedral of Liberation, just behind the celebratory parade accompanying the stolen Brandenburg Gate Quadriga back to its original home, emphasizes the merger of national and Prussian traditions. The spontaneous, inner identity of the nation is given disciplined form and protected from oppression by the iron will of the Prussian state and by military force.[61] The people are allowed to reappropriate their heritage by passing through the gate created by the military strength and discipline of the Prussian state. At the same time, this state draws its life from the surging will of the people, just as the army in 1813 drew its energies from the power of popular resistance to the foreign oppressor. The play of light and dark in the painting suggests that in 1817 Schinkel still thought that authoritarian Prussian leadership was of instrumental and temporary historical value and would ultimately give way to the populist civic community it made possible. During the 1820s the populist and national element of this vision virtually disappeared and Schinkel increasingly imagined the "spirit" of the civic and moral community as the disciplinary authority of Prussia's leaders. After 1821 Schinkel's major plan for a memorial that would articulate and distill the essential meaning of the spatially constructed narrative of Unter den Linden was not a memorial to the awakening of the people in 1813, but to the heroic will of the eighteenth-century creator of a rationally ordered secular state – Frederick the Great. The significance that Schinkel ascribed to the Frederician tradition in the formation of his ideal moral community was evident in a project for a memorial that would have dwarfed the cathedral and matched the impact of the museum in the Lustgarten ensemble[62] (Fig. 17). The public story

[60] The story of the project for a Berlin memorial to Frederick the Great is told with copious illustrations in Jutta von Simson, *Das berliner Denkmal fuer Friedrich den Grossen. Die Entwuerfe als Spiegelung des preussischen Selbstverstaendnisses* (Frankfurt: 1976).

[61] There is an interesting discussion of this painting in Haus, *Schinkel*, pp. 110–112.

[62] Schinkel's published engravings of seven different variants of a memorial for Frederick the Great in the area of the Lustgarten were published in his *Architectonische Entwuerfe*. See *Collection*, Plates 35, 163–68.

Fig. 16. Reimagining 1815 in the context of Prussian military leadership: Schinkel's oil painting *Triumphal Arch* (1817). Reproduction permission: Stiftung Preussischer Schloesser und Gaerten, Berlin-Brandenburg; photo Joerg P. Anders.

Fig. 17. Design for a memorial to Frederick the Great in the Lustgarten, between the Royal Palace and the cathedral (1829).
Source: Schinkel, *Sammlung Architektonische Entwuerfe*, no. 167, reproduced from facsimile in Karl Friedrich Schinkel, *Collection of Architectural Designs* (New York: Princeton Architectural Press, 1989).

within which Schinkel imagined his buildings and urban designs in the years after 1815 was thus quite different from the Romantic nationalist narrative he had tried to articulate in the previous decade. The nation was defined as the Prussian civic community, rather than the German ethnic community, and this civic community was presented as an historical creation of military and moral discipline inspired and sustained by an education in the history of cultural achievements. The identity of Prussia was not expressive, making visible the innate potentialities of a people, but a civic artifice historically constructed through the disciplined control of external and internal nature and guided by a trained elite of political administrators, military leaders, and cultural educators. The aesthetic experience produced by the internal spaces of the Altes Museum nourished a story of the dialectical connection between political discipline and spiritual meaning that was told in stone and public space between the Brandenburg Gate and the Lustgarten ensemble.

As Schinkel's ideal narrative of cultural education and political formation emerged in central Berlin during the 1820s, two tensions in this story of the disciplined "construction" of communal identity by the leadership cadres of the Prussian state became increasingly apparent. Both tensions were implicitly present in the form and cultural purpose of the Altes Museum. Its powerful educational animus indicated the extent to which Schinkel had come to doubt that "liberation" would be marked by the spontaneous expression of an innate identity of will among the people. The first tension might thus be defined as the tension between the people conceived as an inherent unity shaped by the evolution of their innate ethnic and linguistic potentialities, and the ideal community embodied in the educational ideals and administrative regulations of the ruling elites. Schinkel seemed increasingly convinced after 1815 that integration of the mass of individuals caught up in modern processes of labor and exchange into a community of will that could express its meaning in a public historical narrative demanded an activist educational and administrative policy by the state class of educated administrators. Two separable issues were involved in the cultural task of disciplining, refining, and "spiritualizing" individuals emancipated from traditional communal bonds and inherited systems of meaning during the era of revolution, reform, and national liberation. First, this task involved the transformation of the raw productivity of labor in the service of physical needs into an aesthetic creativity that expressed the remaking of natural force and matter into a cultural cosmos that mirrored and sustained the values of human autonomy and ethical community. Second, it entailed the integration of emancipated individual subjects, pursuing selfish interests in a market-driven civil society, into a public, ethical community based on moral consensus and voluntary mutual identification. In social terms this meant the integration of the new laboring classes (produced by the emancipation of the serfs and the dissolution of the guild system) and the middle classes operating outside of the circle of the state service class (produced by an expanded free market of goods and services) into the community of rational law and cultural meaning embodied in and propagated by the state class of historically educated, aesthetically cultivated civil servants. In both cases the solution seemed to entail a combination of administrative control, discipline imposed from above, and the socializing and moralizing education of individuals under the guidance of their cultural superiors.

The second major tension that became obvious at the height of Schinkel's neoclassical reconstruction of central Berlin was the tension between sacred and secular versions of cultural identity. The Altes Museum implied that the sacred center of a modern culture, the point of communal identification, could emerge from within the immanent development of human culture in relation to, and in harmony with, nature. At the same time, the cathedral across the square and the Christian art within the museum itself suggested that the creation of an ethical community required submission to a higher authority. This tension was played out for Schinkel in the pressure to imagine a new sacred center for Prussian culture at the center of Berlin (a new cathedral), a pressure that was partially grounded in his own questions about the sacred and secular foundations of culture, but was certainly reinforced by the plans and dreams of his royal employers, the king and the crown prince, as well as by the constant demand to construct local churches for the urban congregations composed of the newly emancipated, socially and geographically mobile, post-Napoleonic "people." In both of these areas, a process of rethinking that had begun in the early 1820s culminated in projects that were completed, or at least fully articulated, in the decade of the 1830s.

A COMMUNITY OF HISTORICAL MEANING FOR COMMERCE AND LABOR: THE BAUAKADEMIE AS A HYMN TO HISTORICAL SELF-MAKING

Since his first years in the Prussian civil service, Schinkel had developed exceptionally close ties to a generational contemporary and fellow bureaucrat – Peter Christian Wilhelm Beuth (1781–1853) – who was one of the most active and influential promoters of state support for entrepreneurial initiative, technological innovation, and modern methods of production in postreform Prussia. As the head of the technical commission for the development of trade and manufacture in the Prussian ministry of finance, Beuth was in charge of using the regulating and educational power of the state to mobilize the productive powers of individual economic activity in the market-oriented civil society that had begun to emerge after the dissolution of the feudal and guild restrictions of the old regime. Besides his official positions within the government, he also headed an association for the promotion of new technology and industrial design that included manufacturers and merchants as well as technocrats and educators from the state service elites.[63] Like Schinkel, Beuth was concerned with mobilizing and guiding the emancipated individual energies released by the Prussian reform movement toward new forms of voluntary identification with the historically evolving spiritual substance of the collective culture. Beuth shared Schinkel's early Romantic enthusiasms for a national culture grounded in the awakening of German ethnic identity and had also accompanied him in his turn toward neoclassical models of cultural community and aesthetic education after 1815. Schinkel, in turn, combined his own primary interests in the social shaping of individual subjects through aesthetic stimuli with strong inclinations toward technocratic management and rational planning. Since 1819 Schinkel had been a prominent member of Beuth's technocratic commissions and associations. Beuth, at the same time, incorporated many of Schinkel's perspectives in the creation of his School for Industrial Engineering and Design. Their careers seemed to overlap almost completely around 1830, when Beuth became head of the Prussian General School of Architecture and Schinkel presided over the State Building Commission.

Since 1821 Beuth and Schinkel had collaborated on a project that expressed their shared interests – publication of a series of engravings and commentaries intended to encourage aesthetic refinement as well as technical skill in the engineering and building trades such as machine making, metalwork, masonry, woodworking, ceramics, and textiles. The various volumes of *Vorbilder fuer Fabrikanten und Handwerker* (Models for Manufacturers and Craftsmen) placed particular emphasis on the integration of new materials, machine technology, and industrial methods into a vision of production defined by historical knowledge and cultivated aesthetic taste. As Beuth commented in his introduction to the first volume of the series, the aesthetic dimension of the product, as much as its more obvious economic and social utility, constituted the value added to the raw physical material in the process of production: "How necessary and useful it is to endow your work not only with technical excellence but also with the highest perfection of form. Only work which combines the two can bring the work of the craftsman close to the work of fine art, stamp it with a sense of refinement and give it more lasting value than the cost of its materials."[64]

A manual of models of this type, however, also expressed the belief of both Beuth and Schinkel that refining simple labor into aesthetic production and sheer technical control into beautiful form occurred through submission to the historical understanding and cultural sensibilities of the educated leaders

[63] There is an interesting chapter on Beuth's technocratic perspectives and policies in Eric Dorn Btrose, *The Politics of Technological Change in Prussia: Out of the Shadow of Antiquity, 1809–1848* (Princeton, N.J.: 1993), pp. 98–132.

[64] Cited in Barry Bergdall, *Karl Friedrich Schinkel: An Architecture for Prussia* (New York: 1994), pp. 172–4.

of the state service class. It is noteworthy that Schinkel separated the "higher" pedagogy of his detailed architectural designs and the explanations and theoretical conceptualizations of his never completed *Lehrbuch* from the popular pedagogy of the *Vorbilder*. The workers who shaped the materials according to the designs were not imagined as serious interlocutors in the creation of those designs. The historical and aesthetic self-consciousness that added meaning to matter and turned produced commodities into components of a world of human communication and meaning was an achievement of the educated elite, and legitimated its management of those individuals in civil society who pursued their self-interests without a clear understanding of the larger cultural context of their activities.

Schinkel's interest in the technical management of the movements and energies of emancipated individuals in the emerging civil society was perhaps most evident in the designs for revised street patterns and traffic flows that accompanied most of his building projects.[65] In 1817, as he worked on the design for the Neue Wache and the Schlossbruecke, he also conceived a general plan for concentrating the siting of particular social functions and types of production and exchange in particular areas of the city and joining them together with efficient arterial streets, bridges, and canals. In such plans the city seemed more like a rationally organized mechanism of functional parts than a site for the construction and representation of historical and cultural identities. However, Schinkel always sought ways to connect the everyday activities of production and exchange to forms of communal meaning and ethical consciousness.

During the summer and fall of 1826, Schinkel joined Beuth for an extended tour of France and Great Britain, and his diary responses to some of the consequences of unrestricted freedom of exchange and industrial capitalism expressed his ambivalence about the emergence of a world shaped by competitive individualism and the drive to extract private profit from human productivity. Like Beuth, Schinkel was immensely impressed by British innovation in engineering and technology, especially as it affected the construction of built environments for industrial production and exchange. At the same time he was appalled by the social consequences of a lack of historical and aesthetic consciousness in much of this new construction. The huge brick factories of the British Midlands both impressed him by their technical engineering feats and frightened him with their disregard of the ethical effects of environments determined completely by economic utility. "It gives one a frightfully sinister impression," he wrote. "Colossal masses of building substance are being constructed by builders without any regard for architectural principles, solely for utilitarian ends and rendered in red

65 Schinkel's concerns for general urban and environmental design are the subject of Pundt, *Schinkel's Berlin*.

brick."[66] And just as he was impressed by the productivity that blossomed from competitive commodity production in a market society, he was frightened by the signs of social anarchy and uncontrolled economic fluctuation that seemed to characterize this society of emancipated individuals guided only by the vagaries of self-interest and market rationality. The example of England indicated that architecture and urban design were called upon, more than ever before, to integrate the individual into self-transcending patterns of a historical and cultural meaning.

After returning from England, Schinkel conceived an ambitious plan to bring the world of the new civil society into the boundaries of the cultivated civic community through construction of a huge retail mall (*Kaufhaus*) right in the middle of the rows of monumental buildings along Unter den Linden, on the site of the old Academy of Arts and Royal Stables. This *Kaufhaus* was designed to encompass two hundred shops on its first and third floors, with space for residential apartments on the second and fourth levels for the storekeepers. The design followed the new framing principles Schinkel had admired in British commercial and industrial architecture. It used a skeleton of piers and shallow spanning vaults to create flexible, neutral interior spaces covered by an external curtain of brick and glass. However, Schinkel elevated the exterior to a classical monumentality in keeping with the surrounding buildings by designing the façades in two-story rectangular segments that transformed the pier and vault interior skeleton into large classical planes rhythmically articulated by pilasters and entablatures layered over the brick construction. An ornamental balustrade reiterated and emphasized these proportional harmonies. Behind this slightly deceptive façade, however, the building consisted of an uncentered aggregate of multiple-use spaces that allowed individuals to construct their own particular itineraries, choose their own paths in the flow of pedestrian traffic, or relax, converse, or stroll in the open courtyard fronting the avenue. The ground-floor shops took on the character of an arcade through the innovative use of canvas awnings supported by removable poles (Fig. 18).

Schinkel's attempt to invite the new world of bourgeois commerce into the sphere of the traditional Prussian aristocratic, administrative, and cultural elites, however, was rejected by his royal patron as brash and inappropriate. Despite this discouragement, he persisted in his efforts. Signs of a possible resurgence of the social and political turmoil of the revolutionary era (news of the July Revolution in Paris arrived in Berlin during the festivities marking the opening of the museum on the Lustgarten) simply increased the intensity of Schinkel's concerns about the civic and cultural consequences of economic and social modernization.

[66] Karl Friedrich Schinkel, *Reise nach England, Schottland und Paris im Jahre 1826*, ed. Gottfried Riemann (Munich: 1986), p. 244.

Fig. 18. Schinkel's drawing of a planned retail mall on Unter den Linden (1827). Reproduction permission: Bildarchiv Preussischer Kulturbesitz; photo Joerg P. Anders.

Fig. 19. Schinkel's engraving of the Packhof from the Palace Bridge with the Arsenal on the right and the Altes Museum on the left.
Source: Schinkel, *Sammlung Architektonische Entwuerfe*, no. 149, reproduced from facsimile in Karl Friedrich Schinkel, *Collection of Architectural Designs* (New York: Princeton Architectural Press, 1989).

In 1830, he began another ambitious project to extend the representational space of the Lustgarten and Unter den Linden into the world of labor and commerce. The construction of the museum at the north end of the Lustgarten had entailed a revision of river traffic through the city center as well as a rearrangement of the customs, shipping, and storage facilities that served that traffic. Just to the northwest of the museum, Schinkel designed a consolidated new Packhof (customs station) along the reconstructed banks of an enlarged Kupfergraben to replace the previously dispersed jumble of buildings that had housed these facilities. According to the plan executed in 1830–32, three connected cubelike structures were built in a line along the waterfront. The building closest to the museum and most clearly visible from the Lustgarten and the Schlossbruecke housed the residence and offices of the head of the state customs administration. Its brick structure was covered with a neoclassical grooved stucco façade, and a classical pediment with an allegorical frieze emphasized the incorporation of commercial activities into the classical proportions of the represented civic relations of the Lustgarten ensemble. The second building, housing general customs offices and meeting rooms, lacked the pediment but continued the rectangular lines and stucco exterior of the first. Connected to this intermediary structure by a waterfront colonnade and docking area loomed a massive five-story warehouse of exposed red brick that unlike the two administrative buildings, revealed its interior skeletal framing in its arched doorways and window openings. As seen from the vantage point of Schinkel's Schlossbruecke, the Packhof complex suggested how efficient utilitarian structures serving the demands of commercial society could be composed into an urban panorama that articulated the principles of classical proportion and historical memory (Fig. 19). In a sense, the Packhof was a statement in stone and space of the state-controlled market expansion and commercial development represented by the German *Zollverein* (customs union) that the Prussian Department of Finance was negotiating at precisely this time. This was a vision of commercial society organized, contained, and given historical and aesthetic meaning under the aegis of the administrative state. But the project that most fully articulated Schinkel's hopes for the transformation of emancipated individual egos into historically self-conscious, aesthetically cultivated members of an ethical community was the construction between 1832 and 1836 of his own "home," not just his private residence (Schinkel lived with his family in a third-floor apartment from 1836 until his death in 1841), but his home as a civil servant, urban designer, architect, and building supervisor – the Allgemeine Bauschule, or Bauakademie (General School of Construction and Design, or Building Academy), on the west bank of the Kupfergraben just south of the Schlossbruecke, backing onto the northeast corner of the Friedrich Werder Square and facing Unter den Linden and the Lustgarten ensemble.

The plan to build a new structure to house both Beuth's Bauakademie and Schinkel's Oberbaudeputation emerged soon after Beuth was appointed Head of the Bauakademie in 1831. The two friends justified their proposal first of all in terms of functional consolidation and rational efficiency. The cramped and dispersed quarters of the old Bauakademie made the centralized organization and oversight of various tasks virtually impossible. Moreover, the old buildings threatened the safe preservation of its heritage of books, engravings, and drawings. Since this library was also a major resource for Schinkel's Oberbaudeputation, a shared structure seemed most efficient. The Bauakademie was thus imagined on one level as an efficiently organized multiple-use space. The design needed to encompass well-lit studio spaces and classrooms, safe, fireproof, storage areas, administrative offices for both institutions, and personal residential quarters for the two chief officers. Schinkel also proposed a ground-floor level of upscale shops whose rents would help defray the cost of constructing and maintaining the building. The building housed a mix of private and state activities, of administrative, educational, retail and residential functions, of personal and public spaces.

The appropriate spatial structure for this exemplary embodiment of the relations between state, society, and culture in the postreform era was imagined and constructed by Schinkel as a simple cube with a skeletal frame composed of massive brick piers connected (with the help of iron clamps) by shallow, segmented vaulting.[67] The skeleton was constructed first, the floors and roof were added, and only then were the walls "filled in" like a shell or curtain over the structural frame. Finally, the windows and decorative

[67] Detailed descriptions of the building and the history of its construction and use are available in Paul Ortwin Rave, *Karl Friedrich Schinkel, Lebenswerk, Berlin III* (Berlin: 1962), pp. 38–60; and Jonas Geist, *Karl Friedrich Schinkel: Die Bauakademie: Eine Vergegenwaertigung* (Frankfurt: 1993).

components were set, as prefabricated components, into their appropriate spaces. The building was a symmetrical square four stories in height, with eight bays between the piers on each side and a small inner courtyard. The four façades were identical, except for the side facing north toward the Schlossbruecke and Lustgarten that was marked as the "front" by two large doors in the central bays of the ground floor. But even this apparent focal point was misleading, as the doors led not to a grand central staircase or large foyer, but to separate hallways and stairwells – one to the studios, classrooms, and library of the Bauakademie on the second floor, the other to the administrative offices of the Oberbaudeputation on the third floor. One could imagine a hierarchical order in the organization of the three main stories (the fourth was simply a storage attic with an inwardly sloping roof for efficient drainage). The commercial floor was situated at the bottom, under the floor for the educational training of productive labor in both technical competence and historical aesthetics. Finally, Schinkel's offices on the third floor embodied the elevated sphere of professional expertise and cultural self-consciousness inhabited by members of the state administration. The vertical organization of the building could be read as a narrative of civil society transmuted by the state and its cultural educators into a harmonious, rationally planned totality. But the levels were functional, not ceremonial, and the spaces of the structure were neutral and available for other purposes (Fig. 20).

Schinkel built his personal and public home almost completely out of the "common" material of *gebrannte Erde* (burnt earth), or fired clay – both the primary structure of raw and glazed brick and the terra cotta ornamentation and moldings. The earthy (natural), populist (social), and northern German (historical–cultural) connotations of exposed brick construction had been part of Schinkel's consciousness since his first memorials to the liberation wars. The idea of "burnt earth" resonated with Schinkel's almost alchemical sense of the power of architecture to transmute the simplest and most common raw materials into beautiful "humanized" form. The Bauakademie was itself an expression of the transformation of social utility and rational function into aesthetic, and thus cultural, value, of the workplace into the artwork. Presenting its material and structural substance unabashedly on its exterior exposed brick façades, the building sought to display aesthetic "serenity," not through the imposed artifice of historical imitation or decoration, but from within, as the essence of its own constructive principles. Window and door framing echoed the broad and shallow interior vaulting. The great structural piers divided the façades into evenly proportioned wall surfaces like huge classical columns, but also created a rhythm of vertical bays as in a Gothic cathedral. Glazed layers of lilac-colored brick, repeated at every fifth layer of the exposed red brick exterior, emphasized the horizontal, stratified (*lagerhaft*) character of the structure, and underscored the "architectural peace" already present in the broad rectangularity of its

Fig. 20. Main façade of the Bauakademie, showing five of the eight bays and the two entrances.
Source: Schinkel, *Sammlung Architektonische Entwuerfe*, no. 121, reproduced from facsimile in Karl Friedrich Schinkel, *Collection of Architectural Designs* (New York: Princeton Architectural Press, 1989).

four façades.[68] The combination of "medieval" arched brick vaulting and "classical" piers and entablatures appeared to evolve naturally from constructive principles of the building and the nature of its materials, not as a programmatic historical synthesis of competing historical styles.

The ornamentation of the Bauakademie echoed and expanded the messages implied in its tectonic relations, spatial proportions, and raw materials.[69] Two important series of terra cotta panels under the window sills of the second floor (repeated on each of the four sides) and around the two large north-side entry doors articulated in sequential images the narrative embodied in the building's structural and spatial relations. Schinkel exhibited the window panels independently at the Art Academy in 1832 and devoted a full

[68] *Collection*, commentary to plates 115–22.

[69] For a detailed description of the Bauakademie's decorative bas-reliefs, see Paul Ortwin Rave, *Genius der Baukunst: Eine klassisch-Romantische Bilderfolge an der Berliner Bauakademie*. (Berlin: 1944). Additional references are provided in Elke Blauert, "Ikonographie der Bauakademie: Eine Annaehrung," in *Karl Friedrich Schinkels Berliner Bauakademie. In Kunst und Architektur, In Vergangenheit und Gegenwart* (Berlin: 1996), pp. 22–36.

page in his *Sammlung Architektonischer Entwuerfe* (Collection of Architectural Designs) to them (Fig. 21). He described the panels as representations of "various moments in the developmental history of the art of building."[70] The twenty-four panels, grouped in threes in eight bays under the windows of the second floor, could thus be seen as his attempt to provide an historical framework for his home, to articulate the cultural narrative within which his own building emerged as a culminating historical action.

Moving from left to right, the nine panels in the first three bays portray the story of the decline, fall, and resurrection of the spirit, or "genius," of the art of building. As in his earlier representations of the "ideas" of the German people or the Prussian civic nation, the agent of the history that Schinkel inscribed on his Bauakademie was a dynamic, purposeful inner essence visualized as a winged (spiritual) being. Six panels are devoted to the collapse and apparent death of this spirit through the historical decline and collapse of the principles of classical architecture. Broken columns and fractured pediments form the background for scenes of mourning and death. The panels in the third bay, however, are marked by a resurrection of the spirit, who flies aloft, a burning torch in each hand, and is flanked by scenes portraying the revival of architectural competence and trained skill in the building arts during the Christian Middle Ages – the laying of foundation stones and the sculpting of the ornamental flowers of a Gothic spire. The six panels of the middle two bays (which are thus situated above the entry doors on the north façade) have a less historical, more systematic content. Each trio centers on a Greek divinity, Apollo to the left and Pallas Athena to the right. Apollo with his lyre, flanked by representations of painting and sculpture, is presented as the protector of the spirit of architecture as a fine art. Athena, set between scenes of scientific teaching and the technical mastery of construction methods, is presented as the protector of technical knowledge and skills involved in the mastery of natural forms. The laying of the foundation stone of the Bauakademie itself (marked by the date 1832 and a Prussian eagle) by two "spirits" is flanked by social scenes from building sites – morning or noon meals, with the family and the return of the laborer to the family circle at the end of the working day. The last six

[70] *Collection*, commentary to Plates 115–22.

Fig. 21. Schinkel's designs for the terra-cotta panels under the first-floor windows of the Bauakademie. The engraving shows only seven of the eight sets (the set for the fifth bay, with Pallas Athene, is missing), and they are not in the order in which they were finally placed on the building. From top to bottom, the sequence of the constructed panels is 4, 1, 2, 3, 7, 6, 8 (left to right on the four sides of the building). Moreover, the third panel in set 6 was exchanged with the first panel of set 8 in the final placement.

Source: Schinkel, *Sammlung Architektonische Entwuerfe*, no. 118, reproduced from facsimile in Karl Friedrich Schinkel, *Collection of Architectural Designs* (New York: Princeton Architectural Press, 1989).

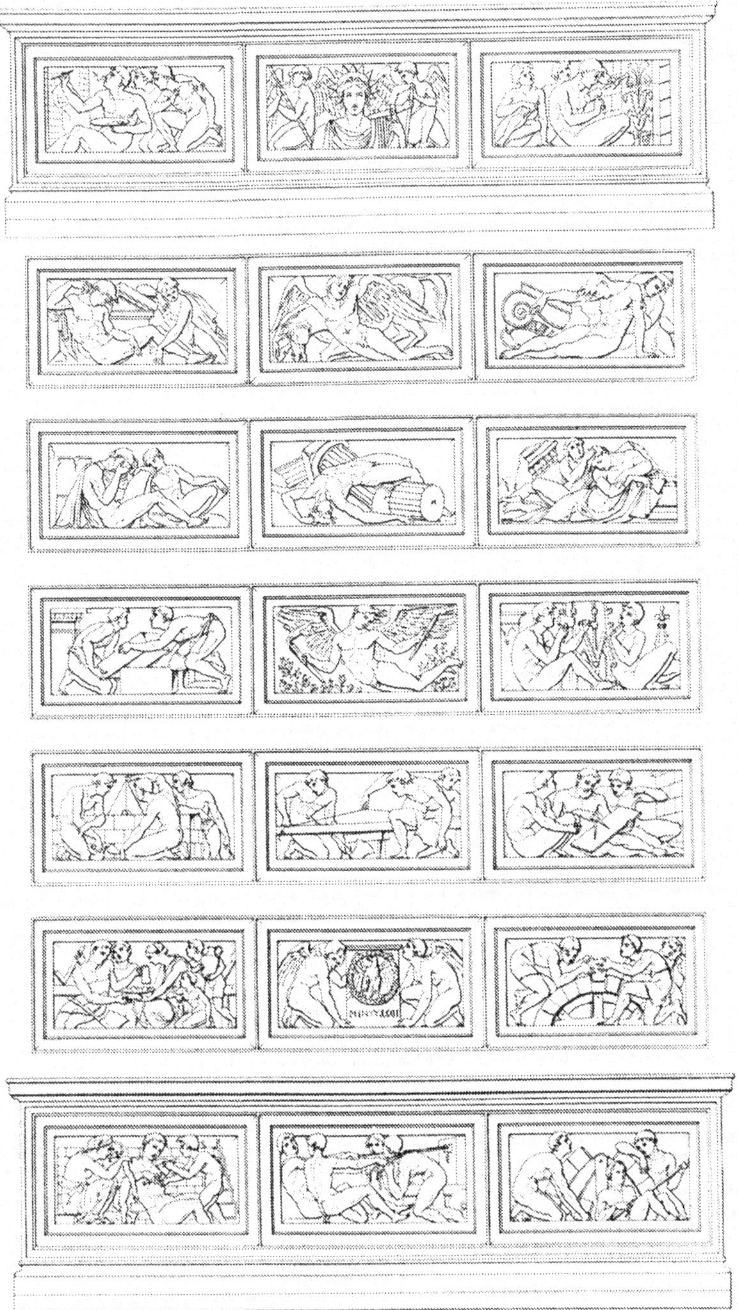

panels portray a set of scenes that express the active scientific control over matter through technical progress and the discovery of scientific principles that make possible the construction of the human environment according to rules and ideal forms that sustain the natural order. In these last panels, the figures themselves conform to the general pattern of the classical nude, but the work presented has a pointed arch form, indicating a strong continuity between postclassical building techniques and classical methods and principles.

The panels surrounding the two doors provide further clues to the historical and cultural meaning Schinkel was trying to embody in the Bauakademie (Fig. 22). Each portal arch is composed of seven panels that repeat the same figuration of the spirit of the architectural art as a winged nude youth with a torch. In these panels, the youth emerges at waist level from an acanthus leaf. This emergence of art from nature, and the repetitious, constantly reproduced transformations of nature into art throughout the evolution of aesthetic form constitute the major themes of the door panels. The side panels on the door on the left (the door to the architectural school) begin from the bottom with representations of the acanthus plant in both its blossom and seed-cone phases of development. Above this pair appear the archaic architectural forms of the Egyptian and Doric orders, followed by a pair of kneeling female nudes holding harvest baskets on their heads in the shape of Ionic and Corinthian capitols. Moving upward, the next pair features a nude male youth discovering the principles of architectural form through an intuitive revelation of the inner forms of organic natural life (the myth of Kallikrates discovering the Corinthian Order). Finally, in the upper corners, Schinkel paired two mythical figures (Orpheus and Amphion) who conjure up constructed "artificial" worlds of brick and stone through their musical harmonies.

The panels around the door on the right (leading to the offices of Schinkel's Building Commission) emphasized not so much the evolution of aesthetic form from principles of natural life, and thus the continuity between nature and culture, as progress in the technical mastery and control of nature. The bottom panels portray a dreaming youth whose imagination soars with his eagle and an active harvesting youth picking fruit from a tree – suggesting the origins of theoretical contemplation and productive labor as basic forms of human mastery over the natural world. The next panels presents a youth balancing on a boat and a maiden riding a panther while playfully balancing two balls in her hands, representations, perhaps, of the conquest of the animal kingdoms of sea and land for purposes of human play and enjoyment. At the next level, the mastery of nature takes the more abstract form of representations of writing and formal calculation by clothed female figures (perhaps muses?) carrying large torches. The portal is completed by scenes of two master builders with their measuring instruments being crowned with laurel wreaths by the "spirits" of their professional arts.

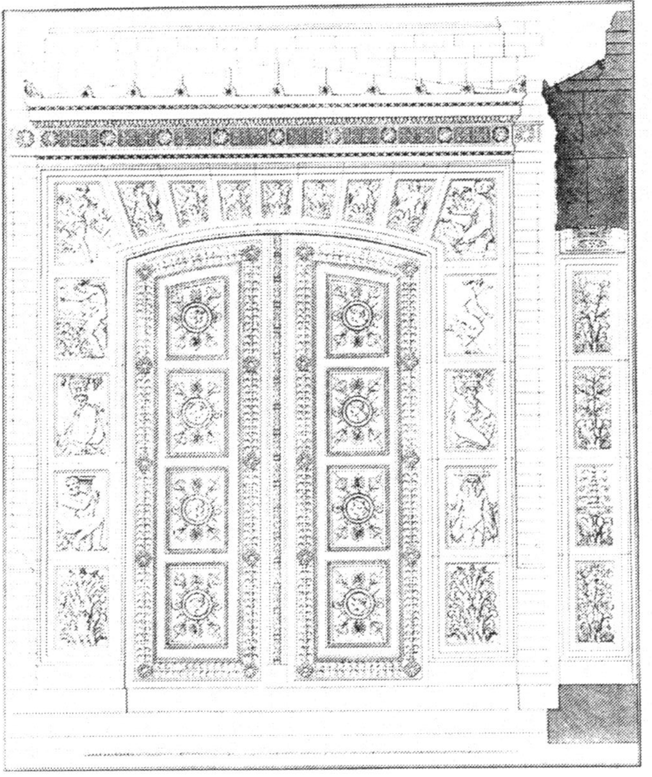

Fig. 22. Designs for the portals and doors of the Bauakademie.
Source: Schinkel, *Sammlung Architektonische Entwuerfe*, no. 120, 122, reproduced from facsimile in Karl Friedrich Schinkel, *Collection of Architectural Designs* (New York: Princeton Architectural Press, 1989).

The door panels thus present a complex developmental perspective on the relations between art and nature on the one hand, and art and science on the other. On the one hand, Schinkel represents architectural form as emerging from innate tendencies in the natural world. The genius of the arts emerges as the spirit of nature rediscovered and made actual as a self-conscious agency. Organic development and aesthetic construction are portrayed in a continuous line of development, and in a systematic relation of analogy. Architecture completes and echoes the natural materials and inherent organic principles from which it creates something new. The interior side panels around both doors emphasize this theme of culture as a repetition of nature, with their series of acanthus plants transforming themselves in various stages of organic growth and maturation.

The panels around the door to Schinkel's Oberbaudeputation, however, also tell a story of technical control for practical use, of the mastery of natural forces and materials to fulfill human needs and create human value. Whether the relationship of human spiritual activity (as art or science) to nature was imagined as harmonious continuity or technical mastery, however, Schinkel presented it as an immanent process guided by the spirit or idea inherent in the material, rather than as a transcendent imposition of order on the basis of revealed knowledge external to nature, or to man as a part of nature. The narrative of the temple of work as art, or of art as the production of a human world from the ground of nature, was a secular, immanent narrative. The metahistorical frame of this narrative was developed from a belief that meaning is inherent in nature. Even the meanings established against nature's forces, as a defense against raw and unrefined nature, emerged from within the natural order of being.

The ornamentation of the Bauakademie placed it into at least two significant communicative relations with its built urban environment. On the north side, the terra cotta panels seem to be set into a conscious conversation with the murals on the inner wall of the museum façade, whose sketches Schinkel was completing at the same time. In the message inscribed on the building where he presided as creator, resident, and patron, his perspective was oriented toward the future and exemplified the shape of the project that the history of art had set for the present generation. The strenuous discipline, harsh conflicts, and visions of potential disaster portrayed in the museum murals' version of the historical struggle to create a human world from the recalcitrant materials and energies of nature appeared in the iconography of the Bauakademie in a more optimistic light. Even the mastery over nature in the Bauakademie panels emerged as the progressive understanding of the laws and relations inherent in nature. One way of reading this relationship between the two inscriptions is that the Bauakademie took up the challenge thrown out by the museum and affirmed the possibility of turning natural man into a subjectively cultivated, voluntarily integrated member of an ethical community.

At the same time, the Bauakademie panels on the south side self-consciously engaged (they were set at the same height in relation to the street) the figures of the neoclassical frieze circling the middle of the austere classical cube of the Royal Mint on Friedrich Werder Square. This frieze, conceived by Schinkel's revered teacher Friedrich Gilly just before his death in 1800, had exploited classical references and images to tell a story of the appropriation of natural materials and natural forms for the production of human wealth and the construction of social forms that could withstand the onslaught of uncontrolled natural powers.[71] For a few years after 1800, some of the rooms in the upper story of the Royal Mint were used to house the nascent Bauakademie.

One of the peculiarities of Schinkel's panels becomes more comprehensible in this context. The mint frieze tells its story within the formal language of the classical tradition. The narrative of Schinkel's panels begins with the decline and destruction of the classical tradition. The new building emerges as a regeneration of the spirit of architecture from the husk of an obsolete historical form. Although in some ways a tribute itself to the power of classical models, the Bauakademie is also a statement of liberation from unquestioning submission to the authority of Greek forms. It asserts that the spirit of architecture that bloomed in the initial flowering of Greek building can only be regenerated by adapting the essential principles of architecture to the needs, functions, and historical mission of the present, and by adapting and fully appropriating all the developmental stages that had brought the spirit of architecture from classical Athens to nineteenth-century Berlin. Gilly had helped Schinkel imagine the past as a foreign country that could function as a model and norm for the present. But for Schinkel the past lived in the present through all of the historical forms in which its principles had been transfigured and passed on through time. To think historically was not to make an imaginative leap into a past world, but to view oneself within the flow of time in which historical forms were in a constant process of making and remaking.

The contextual relations of Schinkel's Bauakademie panels point to the larger issue of the ways in which this building, like Schinkel's other structures in central Berlin, was built not as an isolated monument but as a part of a broadly conceived urban design. The Bauakademie's ornamented portals faced north toward the Arsenal, the Schlossbruecke, and the Altes Museum – thus toward the civic ensemble in the Lustgarten rather than across the canal toward the Royal Palace or south and west toward the commercial district. The building itself was clearly visible from the staircase balcony of the museum and thus an important component of the constructed ensemble that Schinkel imagined at the center of Prussia as a civic and cultural community. Its ornamental figures engaged those on the museum and on the

[71] Alste Oncken, *Friedrich Gilly, 1772–1800* (Berlin: 1981), pp. 91–92; Haus, *Schinkel*, 60–63.

Fig. 23. Schinkel's drawing of the Bauakademie as seen from the Palace Bridge with the towers of the Friedrich Werder Church in the background.
Source: Schinkel, *Sammlung Architektonische Entwuerfe*, no. 115, reproduced from facsimile in Karl Friedrich Schinkel, *Collection of Architectural Designs* (New York: Princeton Architectural Press, 1989).

Schlossbruecke. Yet the Bauakademie, as Schinkel was the first to emphasize, also operated within the urban space as a functional component in the efficient regulation of the flow of people, goods, and services. The construction of the building opened up two new urban arteries – one along the river and one connecting the Friedrich Werder Square to the areas of Alt-Coelln and eastern Berlin across the Kupfergraben and the Spree. The Bauakademie centralized certain economic and social functions in one place and opened up links to other areas of the city, thus transforming the city from an aggregate of relatively isolated neighborhoods into a single economic and social organism. The shops on the ground level of the Bauakademie were integrated into the commercial character of Friedrich Werder Square and its surrounding streets. Along the eastern, waterfront façade, the Bauakademie opened up an opportunity to modernize the Kupfergraben embankment and create a tree-lined promenade that joined the triangular park north of the building to complete an important part of an urban landscape that now reached along the canal to the last of the warehouses in the new Packhof (Fig. 23). The representational avenue of Unter den Linden and the symbolic public space of the Lustgarten were crossed by, and integrated into, a cityscape along the artificial waterway of the Kupfergraben that portrayed the new creative forces of commerce, productive labor, and technocratic management. The individual strolling along the canal and crossing over to the Lustgarten on Schinkel's Schlossbruecke would encounter aesthetically composed, "built" views unrolling toward both the south and the north. In this panorama, as in the buildings themselves, the constructed world was related to a technically mastered natural environment, producing a world of order and freedom in which the individual subject might attain aesthetic serenity.

On the Friedrich Werder side, the Bauakademie was also set in relationship to Schinkel's Friedrich Werder Church, a building that had been in planning and construction stages since the early 1820s but was just completed in 1830. The exposed red brick and terra cotta decoration of the church, its rectangular blocklike body with its large, windowed bays, mirrored important dimensions of the new Bauakademie. At the same time, the significance of the Friedrich Werder Church as a religious building opened up the problematic issue of the role of religious meaning and transcendent authority in Schinkel's concept of constructed historical and cultural identities.

During the time between his English journey and the completion of the Bauakademie (1826–36), Schinkel's theoretical positions regarding the relations between architectural form and the historical evolution of human culture seemed to be an elaboration of the views constructed during his shift toward a fairly rigid neoclassicism after 1815. The new passages that he composed for the introductory section of his *Lehrbuch* after 1825 still strongly affirmed the foundational nature of Greek principles. "European architecture," he wrote, "is equivalent to Greek architecture in its progressive development."[72] Greek architecture had a foundational status because it was itself firmly, self-consciously based on "nature and her forms."[73] All constructed human meanings grew from these natural forms and their progressive transformations, interpretations, and applications. The fine arts of architecture, sculpture, and painting, in Schinkel's view, communicated in the language of perceptions rather than the language of concepts, and were thus closer to the language of nature than the culture of the spoken or written word, and they established a more secure basis for the construction of a human world that would maintain harmonious relations with the natural forms that were its foundation. The history that most concerned Schinkel during the decade between 1825 and 1835 was not what he defined as the "trivial," "genre" history of contingent differences in the external appearances of costume and custom, but the immanent structural history of the progressive relationship between nature and the human attempt to recreate and represent nature in the artifice of culture. Architectural honesty and wisdom were ultimately tied to the relationship between constructed forms and the objective materials that were the substance of those forms. Buildings should display the ways in which their material elements – brick, stone, wood, glass, or metal – implicitly suggested certain forms appropriate to their inherent qualities. Progress in architecture was not a series of

[72] Schinkel, "Die Technizistische Konzeption des Architektonischen Lehrbuches, Gegen 1830," *Lehrbuch*, p. 114.

[73] Schinkel, "Technizistische Konzeption," p. 114: The citations in the following paragraph are all from this passage.

leaps from one cultural idea to another, and architectural genius did not consist in transforming an internal vision into a physical embodiment, thus transcending the limitations of the material world by making objects into "words," stones into poems. What Schinkel envisioned was a continuity in the progressive struggle to recreate the inherent forms of the world as human cultural artifacts, to make natural being self-conscious and comprehensible, to transform the apparent hostility of the external world into a human being's "natural" home.

Central to Schinkel's theorizing in this period was the idea that the forms of art should emerge from the immanent progress of the subjective agent's relation to the natural object. Within human culture, objects became communicative symbols. But if art was to fulfill its mission and represent the human world as a home within nature, it should also allow the object to present itself as an object, as a historical being in its own right, as "a carrier of its own nature [*Traeger seiner eigenen Natur*]."[74] The natural world was not just the "other" of the cultural order, but also its origin. The dialectical struggle between nature and culture was an immanent progress within nature. In the artifice of architecture, nature finally spoke its own meaning.

Although Schinkel's theories might seem "progressive" in their secular emphasis and their search for the principles of cultural development within the material foundations of the natural world, they were also conservative in their deep suspicion of any human intervention into historical processes that was not itself based on a humble submission to the objective reality of nature. Freedom was now defined as submission to a higher "objective" law, but since the relationship between nature and culture was dynamic, constantly changing both poles of the relationship, Schinkel also claimed that the "higher law" was subject to historical change. Since no law remained absolutely valid in the infinite transformation of relations, a "higher" insight justified the "freedom to move beyond the currently valid law and set a new, more advanced one, in its place."[75] Yet freedom still remained obedience to this higher law, not subjective self-determination.

Schinkel's cultural hero during the 1820s was Goethe rather than Fichte,[76] a model who provided him with a critical perspective on the restrictive, parochial character of Christian-German construction of idealized pasts and utopian futures, but also helped him to justify his resignation to the "given" as a form of higher understanding of universal principles embedded in the natural order of things. For Schinkel, "man" made his own history. In architectural constructions of form and space, human beings created a cosmos they could call their own, but only as a part of nature and only in submission to nature's rules.

During the late 1820s and the early 1830s, Schinkel construed the barbarism of his age primarily as a subjective hubris that denied human finitude

[74] *Ibid.*, p. 114. [75] *Ibid.*, p. 119.

[76] See Peschken's comments in *Lehrbuch*, pp. 38–40, and the works cited in footnote no. 43.

within the natural order, that aggressively asserted the power of the subject over the object, that imagined historical communities as arbitrary constructions of human imagination and will. The barbarism of the present was not so much raw brutality or lack of civilized refinement as a cultivated barbarism of overrefinement that ignored the natural foundations of cultural creation and alienated human culture from its source and foundation. Modern culture became barbaric in its belief that the world was there simply to service the needs of the self-interested individual ego, in the "refined avoidance of all laws of society for egoistic purposes."[77] Greek art and culture represented a "revelation" of the highest order because if its ability to bring nature and culture into harmonious relationship, thus revealing the "faults and sins [*Maengel und Suenden*]" of the contemporary age as a disavowal of humanity's modest and limited place in the universe as a part of nature.[78]

Schinkel's constructivism was thus severely limited by his metaphysical faith in the dynamic and progressive order of nature as the source of form and law. Nature, to be sure, was not static. As a part and product of nature, human agency, defined as that creative productivity that constantly transformed objects into human meaning, was a part of the dynamic nature–culture relationship that itself defined the objectivity of nature in historical time. History in Schinkel's vision, so clearly presented in his buildings of the early 1830s and the inscriptions he placed on them, was defined as a dynamic process in which human beings transformed the natural world of which they were a part. This process was progressive, moving persistently toward a humanization of nature, a process of spiritualization in which nature became conscious of itself within culture. But it was never free of the conditions that made it possible. The creation of an appropriate built environment for the modern emancipated ego entailed conscious possession of the historical traditions that produced the conditions of the present, but also of the natural principles that were the permanent ground of historical cultural construction itself. Since nature itself was historical, a part of the nature–culture interaction that constituted history, obedience to natural law, which was the highest form of freedom, was obedience to history. And to obey history was to move from every given to the creation of something new, to construct the future on the foundations of the present. In this sense Schinkel's loyalty to the "natural" principles of construction and objective materiality were the very foundation of authentic historicism in architecture.

CONSTRUCTED IDENTITIES AND TRANSCENDENT AUTHORITY: BUILDING CHURCHES AND BUILDING THE NATION

The cultural meaning of the complex and diverse ecclesiastical architecture Schinkel designed during the 1820s and 1830s becomes more understandable

[77] Schinkel, "Technizistische Konzeption," p. 117. [78] *Ibid.*, p. 115.

when it is set against the background of the abandoned project of the Cathedral of National Liberation.[79] In his plans for the Befreiungsdom, Schinkel had joined a number of elements into one vision. The house of public memory and communal identity was consciously conceived as also a "religious building," since the sacred center of Germanic and Christian cultural traditions was perceived as the divine idea of self-transcending freedom. Representation of the state as a civic community, protected and led by its dynastic rulers, was merged with representation of the community as a people expressing its essence through its evolving cultural institutions. More generally, the idea of community as a constructed realm analogous to an aesthetic work that transcended the limitations of physical materials and functional purposes to communicate spiritual meaning was joined to a concept of the cultural community as an extension and clarification of the natural forms of terrestrial existence. In the period after 1815, Schinkel gradually came to see all of these mergings and identities as too easily constructed, as subjective, speculative visions that did not honestly confront the limiting conditions of material and historical existence.

In 1819–20 Schinkel reconsidered some of his assumptions from the period of national awakening and liberation in his design for a large church on the Spittelmarkt at the opposite end of the Leipzigerstrasse from the site he had imagined for the Liberation Cathedral. Although Schinkel designed this church in the Gothic style, which he described as the most "functional, simple, and original" for ecclesiastical buildings, the discontinuities between his conceptions of the Gothic in 1815 and 1820 seem more striking than the continuities. The reasons for using the constructive principle of pointed-arch vaulting were now stated in purely technical terms related to the function of the building as an auditorium for a large group of individuals listening to a sermon or congregating around an altar, and connected historically to constructive principles developed in the Arab Middle East rather than to the Western Christian idea of self-transcending spirit. The thin columns and spacious elevation of the Gothic vaulting provided good acoustics and easy visual access to the pulpit for the audience, and also made possible the construction of a rotunda space for the altar, where the gathered individuals could symbolically internalize their common essence. Brick vaulting, moreover, allowed the construction of a fireproof roof. What Schinkel now eschewed as unnecessary to the Gothic style was the spire and the repetitive elaboration of ornamentation. In the plan for St. Gertrude's on the Spittelmarkt, the tower was separated from the main church building,

[79] Schinkel's ecclesiastical architecture has generally received much less attention than both his other public buildings and the private villas and homes he designed. Brief surveys can be found in Gerlinde Wiederanders, *Die Kirchenbauten Karl Friedrich Schinkels: Kuenstlerische Idee und Funktion* (Berlin: 1979); and Eva Boersch-Supan, "Zur stilitischen Entwicklung in Schinkel's Kirchenbau," *Zeitschrift des deutschen Vereins fuer Kunstwissenschaft. Sonderheft zum Schinkel-Jahr* 35, no. 1/4 (1981): pp. 5–17.

and the expanses of the brick walls were articulated into bays and marked by large windows, not smothered in gables, baldachins, and pyramids of spires. All the symbolic elements Schinkel had earlier emphasized as a part of the language of transcendence and spiritualization were now rejected as superfluous decoration. What remained as essential to the Gothic style was a technique for the efficient exploitation of materials indigenous to northern Europe (brick) to create functional spaces and pleasing tectonic relations. The simplicity of these relations, the "truth" of the building's materials and constructive techniques, should be articulated in the relations of lines and spaces on the exterior walls and façades.[80]

By rejecting the spire as superfluous decoration, Schinkel flattened or squared off the Gothic forms. This was most obvious in his concept of the tower, which he now imagined as a bell tower in the medieval Italian style, often separated from the church building as a freestanding structure that related to a street vista or marked an urban square, and whose clock and bells were a part of the secular communal organization of time as much as a call to sacred service. The tower was not an aspiration toward heaven but a "platform" from which individuals could survey the panorama of the built environment as well as its natural setting.[81] The spireless construction and simplicity of unornamented exterior walls gave Schinkel's post-1815 Gothic designs a decidedly classical look (Fig. 24).

In his design for the church on the Spittelmarkt, Schinkel clearly presented his concept of the functional bases for church construction in the post-1815 era. What was required first of all was an amphitheater or hall-like space for the preaching of sermons and reading of texts. This element of the church was specifically connected to the Protestant tradition, as was the emphasis on simplicity and "horizontal" religiosity. The second requirement was a suitable altar space, preferably a circular or octagonal rotunda, as a setting for the experience of subjective identification with symbols representing the core content of the faith. In this space individuals recognized their common identity by internalizing an image of that identity through ritual practices. In the plans for St. Gertrude's these functions were clearly marked by separate parts of the building and, at least in the designs of 1819–1820, the relations between these parts indicated that Schinkel still saw the altar or rotunda space as primary, as the place where the experience of identification actually took place. In his later plans and constructions, the public meeting house for the reading and preaching of the word and the ceremonial stage for the

[80] Schinkel's comments on the meaning of the Gothic in his plans for St. Gertrude's on the Spittelmarkt are contained in his commentary to the publication of his drawings in *Collection*, in 1824, four years after the sketches were completed. The church was not built because of funding issues. Instead, the old building underwent a very modest renovation. See *Collection*, commentary to Plates 31–34.

[81] Schinkel provided this justification for his platform tower and its crowning statue in a memo reprinted in Rave, *Schinkel: Berlin I* (Berlin: 1941), p. 246.

Fig. 24. Side view of the projected Saint Gertrude's Church on the Spittalmarkt. *Source*: Schinkel, *Sammlung Architektonische Entwuerfe*, no. 32, reproduced from facsimile in Karl Friedrich Schinkel, *Collection of Architectural Designs* (New York: Princeton Architectural Press, 1989).

symbolic reenactment of the individual's identification with the sacred were often merged.

The first significant church after 1815 completed according to a Schinkel design was the church in the Friedrich Werder Square, just at the edge of the representational center of Berlin and clearly visible from the balcony at the top of the stairs of the Altes Museum. The Friedrich Werder congregation was composed of two congregations, one French (previously Calvinist) and one German (previously Lutheran), which were now both part of the United Evangelical Church of Prussia. Schinkel had thought about a new church for this congregation as a part of his redesign of the areas along the Kupfergraben and around Friedrich Werder Square since 1817. When plans for a new church entered into discussion at the Oberbaudeputation in 1820–21, Schinkel first submitted a plan for a large classical temple based on the Pseudoperipteros model in Vitruvius and the Roman Maison Carree at Nimes in Provence, reputedly built by the Emperor Augustus. This design featured a porch with a classical pediment and two rows of Corinthian columns. Although his original plans did not include a tower or an apse, and thus any external signs of the building's ecclesiastical purpose, Schinkel was willing to adapt his classical temple design to the wishes of the king and ecclesiastical officials. In 1824 Schinkel submitted a second classical design constructed around four domed bays formed by thick, rounded, "girdle" arches. The structural design was mirrored in the façade by a large rounded recessed portal set in a plain brick wall and crowned by a classical pediment with a biblical frieze. Schinkel's plan to create a sober neoclassical temple with a festive, well-lit, and brightly painted interior (the domed vaults were to be painted light blue and dotted with stars) and a freestanding bell tower, however, was stymied by the wishes of the king and crown prince, who believed that a church in Old German style was more appropriate for a parish in one of the medieval sections of the city. Schinkel submitted two plans for Gothic alternatives to his original classical designs, but he insisted that simplified English Chapel Gothic was more suitable for the limited space of the Werder Square, as well as for its urban bourgeois Protestant congregation, than the elaborately ornamented continental cathedral Gothic.[82] The result was to a certain extent a compromise produced by the opposing ideas of the royal patron and architect and by the limitations of the site, but still a striking example of a Schinkelian solution to the problem of religious building in the context of the identity politics of the Restoration period.

The Werder Church made only a weak attempt to conjure up a national identity or the public memory of a national history. Symbolic reminders of the era of national liberation were limited to the large terra cotta statue of the archangel Michael crushing the serpent (a favorite motif of the Wars of Liberation) above the portal. (In the 1819 St. Gertrude's plan, Schinkel had placed a similar Michael atop the bell tower.) The emphasis in Schinkel's design was on simplicity, honesty to the local materials of the "land"[83] (the burnt earth of exposed brick and terra cotta), and integration into the urban setting. The Werder Church did not attempt to reconstruct or revive a cultural idea or juxtapose one cultural form or style against another, but to construct something new on the basis of the progressive development of historical church building. The values it embodied were those of a human construction of public sacred space in which the past was continually remade according to the techniques, materials, and ideas of the present.

As in the plans for the Spittelmarkt church, the Werder Church's plain, exposed brick walls were divided into large bays (five in this case), with simple rectangular proportions framing the Gothic windows. The shallow gabled roof (covering the internal Gothic vaulting and hidden from street-level view) and pair of short flat towers on one end gave the church a distinctively square and "solid" look, despite its rather narrow rectangular base. These towers had viewing platforms rather than steeples or spires at the

[82] The various stages in Schinkel's designs for the Friedrich Werder church are described in Gottfried Riemann,"Die Friedrichwerdersche Kirche-Vorgeschichte und Planung Schinkels," in *Schinkelmuseum: Friedrichwerdersche Kirche* (Berlin: 1989), pp. 8–15; and in Rave, *Schinkel: Berlin I* (1941), pp. 254–300.

[83] *Collection*, commentary on Plates 85–90.

top – one feature in which Schinkel was able to exert his own convictions against royal wishes. The purpose of the towers, he wrote in his commentary to the published prints of the church designs, was not symbolic, but functional – to provide an "overview of the environment."[84] The Berlin artist Eduard Gaertner painted a famous 360-degree panorama of Berlin from the roof of the Werder Church in the early 1830s.

The interior was a single vaulted hall with the Gothic pillars attached to the walls, allowing the light to flood the church through the five large windows along each side of the nave. A narrow balcony was set between the pillars (which had connecting doors running through them) about one-third of the distance from the floor to the top of the vaulting. A cornice running along the line at which the pillars differentiated and bent into the arch provided a fairly even division of the height of the building into three segments marked by horizontal lines, a pattern that was repeated on the exterior, both along the sides and on the façade. This emphasized the rectangular, horizontal elements of the Gothic structure and gave the church a solid pedestal (Fig. 25).

Unlike the Spittelmarkt design, the altar space in the Friedrich Werder plan was subdued, restricted to a semicircular choir at the end of the hall behind the pulpit. This choice may have been dictated by the size of the lot and the king's unwillingness to accept a design that included a rotunda. One might also note that the Werder Church's siting in the Werder Square set it in relation not only to the administrative and commercial buildings of that quarter, but also, especially from its viewing platform, to the symbolic center of the Lustgarten, where Schinkel was just completing the rotunda of the Altes Museum. Like the cathedral in the Lustgarten, the Werder Church seemed to find its appropriate setting within a space defined by the buildings of secular culture.

The general principles expressed in the construction of the Friedrich Werder Church were also evident in the designs that Schinkel developed in 1828, and then again, on a more modest scale, in 1832, for parish churches in the new working-class suburbs north of the city.[85] In each case he developed five alternative designs for Protestant churches in new parishes. These designs were abstract in terms of their relation to any particular already-built environment, but they did assume a social world of new urban arrivals who were, at least temporarily, morally and socially anchorless.[86] The major design problem for these suburban parish churches was how to efficiently

[84] *Ibid.*

[85] The best general description of these churches and their planning process is still Rave, *Schinkel: Berlin I*, 301–42. The more recent booklet: Christiane Segers-Glocke, *Karl Friedreich Schinkel: Die einstigen Berliner Vortstadtkirchen St. Johannes, Nazareth, St. Elisabeth und St. Paul* (Munich and Berlin: 1981) adds material on the churches' fates during World War II and after.

[86] The ecclesiastical report on the need for these new parishes described the new districts as areas "where immorality [*Sittenlosigkeit*] among the population is great." Cited in Rave, *Schinkel: Berlin I*, p. 339.

Fig. 25. Cross-sectional drawings of the final design of the Friedrich Werder Church.
Source: Schinkel, *Sammlung Architektonische Entwuerfe*, no. 87, reproduced from facsimile in Karl Friedrich Schinkel, *Collection of Architectural Designs* (New York: Princeton Architectural Press, 1989).

bring large groups of people into close proximity – as audiences for the spoken word – within a relatively small space. Long hall churches, even with balconies, like the Werder Church, were inefficient for these purposes, and Schinkel moved to boxlike or circular structures with tiers of balconies surrounding a central space. His designs provided alternatives in both "classical" and in "medieval" style, but it was clear by now that this stylistic dichotomy had very little to do with the structure and even the look of the buildings. A simple amphitheater space with relatively little ornament and clearly transparent tectonic and spatial relations took on a similar appearance whether it was constructed with arched brick vaulting or as a classical box with a pillared gabled portico on one end, a small semicircular apse on the other, and pilaster or column wall divisions. Two of the five plans submitted in 1828, however, presented domed structures, one built on a circular, the other on an octagonal base. These designs combined an amphitheater for the congregation as a passive assembly absorbing the word from the pulpit with a rotunda space in which the altar for rituals of identification could be centered within the congregation rather than elevated and isolated at one end of a hall. Schinkel's domes or rotunda models, with their focus on the symbolic acts occurring at the altar, were not considered acceptable for suburban parish churches, either in 1828 or later in 1832. The churches of the "people" remained spaces in which the primary religious experience was defined as hearing and receiving the word and in which the symbolic acts of identification were placed not in the middle of the people as their common center but on a raised platform in the apse or choir at the "clerical" end of the church. Even within these imposed limitations, however, Schinkel's simple designs were able to convey a sense of a terrestrial or immanent sacred space emerging from the common materials of the earth and a desire to construct communal identity along horizontal rather than vertical lines. One telling incident during the construction of the four suburban churches in 1834 occurred when the king noted that Schinkel had chosen the youthful Christ standing triumphantly on the globe as his altar "crucifix" for all of the new churches, the same design he had sketched for the Cathedral of Liberation in 1814. The king found this iconography inappropriate and vetoed the design.[87]

Although Schinkel developed a number of designs for domed churches with a central interior rotunda and seemed to favor this design as most appropriate for modern Protestantism because of its emphasis on the mutual, fraternal identification of autonomous individuals, only one of his domed church designs was actually constructed – the St. Nicholas Church across from the city palace in Potsdam. Even this design, however, was only fully realized as a domed church in the 1840s, after Schinkel's death, by his

[87] *Ibid.*, pp. 332–33.

student Ludwig Persius. During the lifetimes of both Schinkel and Frederick William III, the Potsdam church appeared as a larger version of the brick cubes with classical porches and semicircular apses Schinkel had constructed for the new Berlin suburbs.

Although the rotunda church did not emerge as a feasible alternative for the new parish churches, it remained a central aspect of Schinkel's planning for the churches nearer to Berlin's representational center. Even before Schinkel's museum had transformed the Lustgarten into a representational square for Berlin and Prussia, discussion had begun about the construction of a new Berlin cathedral to replace the modest eighteenth-century building on the east side of the Lustgarten. The existing *Dom* seemed an inadequate expression, in the eyes of many church and state leaders, of the role of the Protestant Evangelical Church in relation to the other powers represented on the square, and thus within the historical evolution of the Prussian state and the German cultural nation. Schinkel proposed a radical rebuilding project that would have left very little of the old building intact. He imagined a large rotunda within the frame of the old walls, covered on the exterior by a classical dome and encircled in its bottom half by a line of Corinthian columns. When this plan was rejected, Schinkel developed another model, based on a huge barrel vault with a classical porch entrance and two connected bell towers. Even this plan was much too ambitious and expensive for the king, and Schinkel had to be content with a modest remodeling of the porch, the three small domelike towers, and the interior hall. This remodeled cathedral was easily integrated into the borders of the square and certainly not threatening to the Altes Museum, the Arsenal, and the Palace. One could suggest that Schinkel had built his rotunda in the museum – making a specifically Christian rotunda superfluous in the central square. However, the crown prince was certainly not content to surrender the sacred space of cultural identification at the center of Berlin to an institution of aesthetic education. He dreamed, as was noted above, of a massive basilicalike structure with a large atrium and forecourt that would occupy most of the Lustgarten and transform all other buildings into its dependencies – a vision in keeping with his personal convictions about the relations between sacred and secular culture[88] (see Fig. 1).

Although Schinkel was certainly willing to experiment with constructing churches in basilica form, he was not convinced that the basilica was culturally appropriate or technically viable for the needs of post-1815 European Christendom. He doubted whether vaulted arches and domed ceilings, for example, could be transferred easily to the basilica form, with its large central nave, clerestory, and smaller side aisles, in an aesthetically pleasing, or

[88] Karl-Heinz Klingenburg, "Die Plaene Friedrich Wilhelms IV. Fuer die Bebauung des Lustgartens," in Karl-Heinz Klingenburg, *Studien zur Berliner Kunstgeschichte* (Leipzig: 1986), pp. 143–59.

technically efficient, form.[89] Although one might think that Schinkel would appreciate the turn from Gothic to classically oriented models in this shift to "Old Christian" ecclesiastical spaces and images, he seemed to think that the basilica structure was premedieval in its lack of technical control over the vaulting methods required to span a large space with a common material like brick. The basilica style favored by the crown prince was a historical reconstruction of a past moment in the human history of building rather than a progressive resolution of current problems using the most advanced technical knowledge. Moreover, there is some evidence that Schinkel was not unaware of the implications of the basilica form for arguments about the nature of cultural identity and civic community in post-1815 Prussia. Whereas Schinkel's rotunda designs were based on a populist notion of participation in the inner spiritual substance that bound persons into communities, the basilica presented a model in which the revealed laws of a transcendent God were mediated through ecclesiastical authorities. Although both conceptions connected religious and political notions of community, and emphasized continuity between classical and christian cultural forms, the crown prince' s conception was more authoritarian and patriarchal, Schinkel's more communitarian, or "fraternal."[90]

In 1827 and 1828, under pressure from the crown prince, Schinkel did produce a design for a cathedral in the Lustgarten according to a basilica plan. The drawings were personally presented as a gift to the crown prince and seem to have functioned as an imaginary concept and historical reconstruction rather than as a proposal to the Oberbaudeputation or to the king. It is interesting that in these drawings Schinkel emphasized the classical elements of the basilica style, the porch of Corinthian columns, the classical frieze (rather than a large gable mosaic), and an interior space, filled with strolling citizens, that seemed more like a precinct for the social activities of the "people," imagined according to the political model of the Roman basilica, than a setting for a Christian congregation. Images of Christ as king and judge or elevated places for the bishop and his assistants (the tribune) were not in evidence in these drawings. In 1835 a concept of the basilica as the primal spatial form, or *Urform*, of Christianity appeared again in Schinkel's speculative designs for a Christian mother church at the site of the Holy Sepulcher in Jerusalem. Produced for the 1,500th anniversary of Constantine's dedication of the Jerusalem church, these drawings fit into the category of imaginary historical reconstructions of the inner logic of a cultural

89 Schinkel's many doubts about the basilica as an appropriate architectural form for a modern cathedral are documented in his many sketches, drawings, and marginal comments pertaining to the crown prince's plans for a cathedral on the Lustgarten. See the materials gathered under the rubric "Der Dom des Hohenzollernhauses," in *Lehrbuch*, pp. 163–72.

90 The tension between Schinkel and Frederick William about the appropriate form for a cathedral in the city center is discussed in Karl-Heinz Klingenburg, *Der berliner Dom. Bauten, Ideen und Projekte vom 15. Jahrhundert bis zur Gegenwart* (Berlin: 1986), pp. 74–95.

style and are akin to Schinkel's attempts to recreate the designs of Pliny's villas from written descriptions or to his work on the historical restoration of the medieval castles Stolzenfels on the Rhine and Marienburg in Prussian Poland. As in these other cases, Schinkel's design for the Jerusalem "mother church" (*Mater Ecclesiarum*) reconstructed the inner logic of the historical style that was implicit in many of the extant "early Christian" churches, using the verbal descriptions of Eusebius's *Ecclesiastical History* as a guide.[91]

In Christian churches individual members of specific historical communities ritually reenacted the principles of their shared identity. Such acts were entangled within the general processes through which cultural worlds were built, revised, and rebuilt on the basis of the inherited forms of historical tradition. By the 1830s Schinkel had consciously rejected the possibility of historical recreation of the past as an "unhistorical" attempt to put an end to the infinite creative processes of cultural making and remaking. Architecture could not operate outside of the historical conventions or styles that were its inherited language. Knowledge of the progressive creation and recreation of such conventions since the classical "revelation" of the fundamental principles of construction was a precondition for meaningful building. But a building itself became historical when construction became historical action, when the transformation of what already existed in the world produced a new object or statement that could intervene in the traditional reworking of stylistic conventions and redirect the processes of human building into the future. This transformation of building into a creative, historical act represented the "poetic" as well as "historical" dimensions of architecture. It emerged in part from imaginative internalizations of past forms as present possibilities, but primarily from the "higher freedom" that was a product of the "cultivation of feeling" [*Bildung des Gefuehls*] through which the human subject embodied, shaped, and disciplined its psychic energies. Building as historical activity could not be taught through presentation of rules and conventions, but only represented in exemplary architectural "acts." The historical lawfulness (*Gesetzlichkeit*) of architecture as a creative activity was not determined by any authority outside of its own creative action, but carried its authorization (*Begruendung*) within itself.[92] While Frederick William IV sought to embody his vision of the Christian community through a return to primal origins, to history as the site of revealed truth, Schinkel remained tied to the notion that historical community in the modern world was grounded

[91] Margarete Kuehn, "Schinkel's Darstellung der konstantinische Grabeskirche in Jerusalem," in *Klassizismus: Epoche und Problem. Festschrift fuer Erik Forssman zum 70. Geburtstag*, ed. Juerg Meyer zu Capellen and Gabriele Oberreuter-Kornabel (Hildesheim/New York: 1987), pp. 209–47; Christiane Schuetz, *Preussen in Jerusalem (1800–1861). Karl Friedtrich Schinkel's Entwurf der Grabeskirche und die Jerusalemplaene Friedrich Wilhelms IV* (Berlin: 1988).

[92] Schinkel, "Die Legitimistische Fassung des Architektonischen Lehrbuches," *Lehrbuch*, pp. 149–50.

in the freedom of constant self-recreation, that it found its center in human existence as a self-making activity.[93]

When Schinkel imagined the architectural forms of a built community for the present and future, a massive basilica representing human dependence on the will of a transcendent father was not at the center. Instead he imagined a contemporary acropolis. In the revisions that Schinkel made in the drafts of his *Lehrbuch* during the last half of the 1830s, he ordered his imagination around the task of designing the spaces and building the forms of civic life in the form of a residence for a ruler. The emphasis on rulership (*Herrschertum*), with its authoritarian connotations, of course, was quite different from the notions of a national community with which Schinkel had begun his own distinctive architectural projects in the first decades of the century. To some extent this focus was produced by his close relationship to the crown prince, who tried to include Schinkel within his dreams of building a cultural center conforming to his own concept of divinely authorized patriarchal rule.[94] However, there were also internal reasons for Schinkel's shift in perspective in the mid-1830s. His attempt, culminating in the construction of the Bauakademie, to ground the construction of aesthetic forms in the natural dynamics of organic form and inherited technique, had ignored the poetic and historical dimensions of architecture as creative action and intervention in history, and left him in a "huge labyrinth" manufactured by his own abstractions about the material, technical, and functional determination of cultural forms.[95] His reassertion of architecture's role as free poetic action, as an intervention in history that brought something new into the world, was thus tied to disillusionment with the progressive nature of historical evolution. Although not in full agreement with his royal patron's concepts of rulership as a conduit for the imposition of divinely ordained order on the fallen world, Schinkel's conceptions moved gradually toward a separation between the spheres of meaning and experience, value and fact, and he searched for ways to impose meaning on the world through a creative, constructive action, from the "outside," rather than to discover and recreate the meaning already present in nature and history.

[93] Schinkel expressed this sentiment most succinctly in a letter to the Crown Prince Maximilian of Bavaria just a few months before his debilitating stroke in 1840, printed in Machowsky, *Schinkel*, pp. 189–91.

[94] In the introduction to his last version of the *Lehrbuch*, Schinkel specifically mentioned his collaboration with the crown prince as a critical element in his formulations of the model of the Ruler's Residence. See *Lehrbuch*, p. 151. In an earlier rough draft of this introduction, Schinkel had complained about the narrow-mindedness of powerful clients who could only understand the historical mission of architecture in imitative, reconstructive ways, a possible critique of the crown prince's insistence on the authority of the basilica style. Both versions of the introduction are printed in *Lehrbuch*, pp. 148–52; and discussed briefly in Haus, *Schinkel*, p. 356.

[95] Schinkel, "Legitimistische Fassung," *Lehrbuch*, p. 150.

Three ambitious, visionary projects display the peculiar characteristics of this turn in Schinkel's thinking. These designs have usually been seen as imaginative utopian dreams, as a diversion from the contextual, pragmatic planning that was forced upon Schinkel by the limitations of his position as a civil servant and court architect and a turn toward the freedom of pure architectural design. All three designs were versions of a princely or royal residence that combined public and private functions and mixed private and public spaces.

The most elaborate and utopian of these designs was the plan for the "Ruler's Residence," which became the focus for the final versions of his *Lehrbuch* after 1835. Developed and sketched out within a few weeks in March 1835, this design imagined a ruler's residence as a modern acropolis set on a hill in the midst of a city of ordinary citizens engaged in the private activities of civil society. The ruler was imagined as a kind of philosopher king operating at the highest levels of knowledge and cultural refinement (*auf der Hoehe der Bildung*)[96] and surrounded by a "court" of cultural and political administrators drawn from the educated classes. The public institutions that Schinkel situated within this elevated city of cultural guardians and rulers were heavily weighted toward the cultural sphere – a memorial temple for public heroes, a theater, concert hall, various historical and art museums, and offices and working studios for artists and writers. The three functions that had been combined in earlier cathedral projects were separated. A circular church with Gothic windows and vaulting provided the ceremonial altar space for the inner appropriation of the cultural essence. The hall for the gathering of the people to hear the word of their leaders became an ornate throne and reception room at the center of the palace complex. The hall of national memory (a Valhalla for the military and cultural heroes of the nation) was separated out from both the public meeting room and the altar space in a classical temple on the edge of the acropolis, suggesting a more civic and secular conception of national memory than the king's persistent visions of a dynastic Camp Santo (Fig. 26).

Schinkel's "residence" was actually a complex of buildings representing the various functions that comprised an authentic ethical community and that sustained the leaderships groups that preserved, recreated, and purveyed the essential idea of the community in changing historical circumstances. What was striking in Schinkel's vision was the separation of the class of educators and administrators from the individuals in the society who were the object of their educational and administrative efforts. The acropolis was set off from the surrounding city by a monumental gated entryway and a ceremonial ramp that led up through a tunnel with hairpin turns (analogous to the stairwell in the Altes Museum) to the second entrance hall on top of the hill. It seems clear that the "people" were only participants in the

96 Schinkel, "Legitimistische Fassung," *Lehrbuch*, p. 148.

Fig. 26. Complete panoramic view of the plan for a ruler's residence, from Schinkel's *Lehrbuch*, 1835. Reproduction permission: Bildarchiv Preussischer Kulturbesitz.

activities of the acropolis as either the object of the educators' activity or as invited guests. Moreover, this separation also made obvious that the authority of the cultured, educating, and administering classes was derived from the authority of the king rather than the authority of the people. The center of identity was a core of cultural values preserved by, and embodied in, a specific group – not in the common historical inheritance of the nation. Or at least the meaning of this inheritance was only preserved by the activities of the cultured elites. Cultural memory was in possession of the classes who had self-consciously made that memory the object of their activity. The nation as an historical and ethical community appeared as a product or construct of this group.

From one perspective, the project of the Ruler's Residence in Schinkel's *Lehrbuch* indicated a narrowing of his social and historical vision. Modern emancipated individuals of civil society, the inhabitants of the city on the plain around the acropolis, were only passive participants in the production of their cultural identity. The real content of community was contained in the ruler. Only the educated elite was able to grasp the principle infusing the totality of relationships and to develop policies and plans that would actually produce and sustain this unity throughout the national culture. At the same time, however, Schinkel's new vision expanded and universalized the content of the idea of community. The task of constructing an identity for a particular culture within Europe, a German, Prussian Protestant culture, gave way in these projects to a pan-European vision of Western classical–Christian civilization as the fulfillment of human culture.

This development in Schinkel's historical thinking, in which western Latin and eastern Greek Christian cultures, as well as Christian culture per se and its ancient classical predecessors, were merged into a common civilization developing in a single narrative and defining itself against the forces of barbarism both within and without, was suggested as well in the designs for two actually commissioned "dream" projects prepared in 1838–39 and eventually published as *Werke der hoeheren Baukunst* (Works of Higher Architecture) in 1840–42. Both projects were designs for princely residences, and both grew out of the historical situation of the collapse of the Ottoman Empire and the reassertion of Western and Christian control over areas of the eastern Mediterranean.

The first of these designs was for a royal residence integrated into the ruins of the Athenian Acropolis.[97] This project was planned for the Bavarian Crown Prince Otto von Wittelsbach, who had been chosen by the European powers to occupy the Greek throne after the conclusion of the Greek wars of independence in 1832. Although Schinkel displayed his reverence for ancient Greek culture in his pious attempts to preserve all the remnants of

[97] Rand Carter, "Karl Friedrich Schinkel's Project for a Royal Palace on the Acropolis," *Journal of the Society of Architectural Historians* 38 (March 1979): 34–46.

the classical Acropolis (insofar as he knew about them) within the precincts of this new residence of a European Christian ruler, the design was also obviously an "appropriation" of the ancient Greek heritage by a modern European Christian. Contemporary western European culture and its principles of building were presented as the appropriate heir of Greek civilization, building on and completing what had been begun in classical Athens. Contemporary Athenians and other Greeks were left out of this process. The Islamic remnants of Ottoman rule were expunged from the Acropolis. A Christian chapel in the form of a Greek temple with a crucifixion frieze on its pediment and praying angels on its crown marked the assimilation of ancient Greek civilization into the Christian present. At the same time, a colossal recreation of Phidias' bronze statue of Pallas Athena gave shape to Schinkel's continuing belief that the real foundation of contemporary European culture lay in pagan Greece rather than Christian Rome or Byzantium (Fig. 27). As in Bunsen's attempt to present the history of ancient Egypt as an integral component of a universal history that culminated in contemporary Protestant Germany, the ancient cultural monuments of Greek civilization were presented by Schinkel as the legitimate past of contemporary German culture: They embodied the collective memory of modern northern Europeans and were integrated into their identity. Schinkel believed that his own assimilation of the idea of European civilization made him perfectly qualified to know, recreate, and appropriate, with modern techniques and constructive principles, the heritage of classicism.

The second project published in 1838 was a design for a classical seaside villa on the Black Sea coast of the Crimea for the Russian Empress Alexandra (the sister of Frederick William IV). Schinkel's rehabilitation of the idea of the Roman villa was enhanced with modern forms of public culture – such as a museum that contained the historical remains of classical civilization that had been excavated in the Crimea and the Caucuses – and was capped by a translucent pavilion in the form of a Greek temple (Fig. 28). Here again the representatives of Christian culture (including in this case the Eastern Orthodox Church) were presented as the historical heirs of the Greek civilizing mission. In a letter to the empress, Schinkel stated that his intention was to give focus to Russia's mission to establish and develop European civilization on the recently reconquered borderlands of Asia. For Russia to concentrate its vast but anarchic energies on the tasks of building a truly European state, Schinkel advised a return to the "roots of European culture" in ancient Greece.[98] By constructing a museum for the antiquities of the ancient Greek provinces in Asia Minor, civilization was

[98] "Schreiben Schinkels ... vom 1838 an Ihre K. K. Majestaet Kaiserin Alexandra Feodorowna von Russland, die Plaene zum Bau des Schlosses Orianda in der Krim betreffend," in Wolzogen, *Aus Schinkel's Nachlass*, vol. 3, pp. 336–41.

Fig. 27. Drawing of a projected palace for King Otto of Greece on the Acropolis in Athens (*detail*). Reproduction permission: Staatliche Graphische Sammlung, Munich.

Fig. 28. Drawing for a part of the projected Villa Orianda in the Crimea, with a museum of classical antiquities and a neoclassical temple. Reproduction permission: Bildarchiv Preussischer Kulturbesitz.

to be preserved and protected against the threat of barbarian invasion and corruption.

The historical narratives displayed in the projects of Schinkel's last years thus suggest the construction of a specific kind of Western identity. This identity fused pagan and Christian traditions, in effect absorbing the Christian era as a moment in a historical development toward a synthetic culture in which the foundations of Christian civilization in Greek antiquity would be acknowledged and affirmed in daily practice. At the same time, this civilization tended to take on the character of a possession of a relatively small group of cultural guardians elevated above the general population, or the "people." In a building like the Bauakademie, Schinkel could still claim that the cultural guardians expressed the meaning of a historical process in which everyone, as a "worker" in society, was a participant. The projects of his last five years however, display a tendency to see the continuous identity of a culture as the product of contingent actions of a select group of cultural guardians who were constantly challenged to renew the thread of public memory on the basis of their special knowledge of historical tradition.

SCHINKEL'S HERITAGE IN THE 1840S: FRAGMENTS OF A NEW HISTORICISM

Although Schinkel's stroke in August 1840 cut short any personal collaboration with the new king in the project to construct an ethical community of Christian-Germans in Prussia through the recovery of public memory, his legacy was certainly present during the 1840s in at least two forms. It was present, first of all, in Frederick William's personal commitment to complete Schinkel's unfinished projects according to their original plans. Both the historical restoration and "completion" of medieval, Old German monuments, like the Marienburg in East Prussia, the Stolzenfels castle on the Rhine and the Cologne Cathedral, that Schinkel had supervised and the unfinished neoclassical reshaping of the center of Berlin (the statues on the Schlossbruecke, the murals on the façade of the Altes Museum) were pushed toward completion in the 1840s. Second, the king placed Schinkel's students and former assistants in positions of authority: Building in Prussia continued in the tradition of the "Schinkel School." The general supervisory authority that Schinkel had exerted as head of the Oberbaudeputation was divided between two students to whom he had already delegated a great deal of authority before his stroke – Ludwig Persius (1803–45) and Friedrich August Stueler (1800–65), who also became architectural collaborators of the king, though neither gained the personal authority at the court that Schinkel had exerted during the 1820s and 1830s. Persius completed some Schinkel projects – like the Saint Nicholas Church – and continued Schinkel's overall plans for the Potsdam area until his death in 1845. Stueler moved ahead with the king's grandiose plan to expand Schinkel's original vision for the Berlin center with a whole new complex of museums and cultural institutes, a vast new cathedral project, and a remodeling of the Royal Palace. Art and architectural history at the university, art criticism in government newspapers, teaching at the Bauakademie – all were dominated by Schinkel's disciples. After Schinkel's death, Frederick William bought the huge Schinkel *Nachlass* of papers and drawings, in part to support Schinkel's widow and children, but also to provide the materials for a Schinkel archive and museum that was installed in Schinkel's old work space at the Bauakademie in 1844.[99]

The division of labor and administrative jurisdiction among Schinkel's professional "sons" was indicative of a more fundamental fragmentation of his vision of the cultural and historical role of public architecture as a site for the creation of historical identities. Different conceptions of the relation between past and present and between sacred and secular history, which Schinkel had absorbed into his work in succession between 1815 and 1840, tended to drift apart after 1840 and coexist as virtually autonomous positions. If there was any synthetic vision informing public building in Prussia in the 1840s, it was a vision dominated by the ecclesiastical and cultural politics of the king, one that Schinkel had never fully shared.[100]

The historical restoration of Old German monuments as a means to produce public memory of German cultural identity emerged more prominently in Prussian cultural policy after Schinkel's death. Fredrick William enthusiastically supported the restorations of the Marienburg and Stolzenfels, as well as the completion of the Cologne cathedral.[101] The appeal of his youthful fantasy of a restored or reconstructed medieval Germanic Empire never fully faded, and he remained conscious of the political value of conjuring up images of ancient solidarity to override the divisions and conflicts of the present, and to inspire projects for constructing new forms of German solidarity. By 1840, however, Frederick William's concept of historical restoration extended beyond the simple Gothic enthusiasms of his youth, subordinating the primal community of the *Volk* to the apostolic community of the Christian church. In 1843 Ferdinand von Quast (1807–77), another Schinkel student, was appointed to head a new section in the *Kultusministerium* for the restoration and preservation of historical monuments. One

99 Geist, *Karl Friedrich Schinkel*, p. 66.

100 Eva Boersch-Supan, *Berliner Baukunst nach Schinkel 1840–1870* (Munich: 1977), provides a broad survey of the work of the first thirty years of the Schinkel school after Schinkel's death.

101 Ursula Rathke, *Preussische Burgenromantik am Rhein. Studien zum Wiederaufbau von Rheinstein, Stolzenfals und Sooneck (1823–1860)*, (Munich: 1979); Hartmut Boockmann, *Die Marienburg im 19. Jahrhundert* (Berlin: 1982). Schinkel's work on Stolzenfels is described in Eva Brues, ed., *Karl Friedrich Schinkel: Lebenswerk. Die Rheinlaende* (Munich and Berlin: 1968), pp. 128–49.

Fig. 29. Wilhelm Stier's design for a national cathedral on the Lustgarten, 1842. Reproduction permission: Bildarchiv Preussischer Kulturbesitz.

of his first assignments was to supervise the reconstruction of the Roman basilica in Trier as a Protestant church.[102]

Not all of Schinkel's heirs had lost their faith in the Gothic style as a viable expression for German cultural identity for the present. Wilhelm Stier, who had engaged both Schinkel and Bunsen in discussions about the appropriate spatial form for modern German consciousness since the 1820s, produced a grandiose design for a national Gothic cathedral in Berlin's Lustgarten during the first months of the new regime (Fig. 29). Like Bunsen, he was convinced that the Gothic had not lost its connections to the essential idea of the German *Volk*. Stier's plan appropriated and exaggerated many of the elements of Schinkel's designs for a Befreiungsdom in 1814–15. Stier remained fully committed to pointed-arch construction as a symbolic representation of the German idea of self-transcending spirit. But he was particularly interested in the transformation of the cruciform structure of medieval cathedrals into a modern (circular) Protestant space. The domed rotunda in Schinkel's designs was expanded into a huge circular amphitheater, a multifunctional space for preaching the word to the masses, theatrical representation of the stages of life from birth to death, and the spiritual identification with the Holy Spirit of the community around the communion table. The nave was imagined as a forecourt to this sacred space and transformed into a hall for heroes of the national history in both politics and culture. Thus Stier once again combined the history of the people as an ethnic community with the history of the Christian religious community. Stier's plan was not just a

[102] Julius Kohte, "Ferdinand von Quast (1807–1877), Konservator der Kunstdenkmaeler des preussischen Staates: Eine Wuerdigung seines Lebenswerkes," *Deutsche Kunst und Denkmalpflege*, 35 (1977): 114–38.

revival of Schinkel's original vision of a cathedral of national liberation, but also a visual representation of Bunsen's "Church of the Future."[103]

Schinkel's projects for the production of ethical community through aesthetic education in classical forms, which dominated his construction of the spaces around the Lustgarten in the Berlin center, were also continued in both a radically expanded and transformed fashion into the 1840s. Soon after Frederick William became king, he called upon Stueler and the Director of Museums and Collections, Ignaz Olfers, to collaborate on a master plan for transforming the area behind Schinkel's museum into a "sanctuary" (*Freistaette*) for scholarship and the arts.[104] The plan, which was completed in early 1841, included a new museum to house the expanding collections that had quickly outgrown the spaces of Schinkel' s museum, and a complex of buildings, colonnades, and courtyards devoted to the aesthetic display and scholarly reproduction of the historical development of the human spirit in past cultures. Both the royal academies and the relevant university faculties were to have a new home in this "sacred" place set apart for the study and teaching of the "spirit" and its forms (Fig. 30). Aesthetic and historical education were merged in the design for a cultural acropolis in "Athens on the Spree," a design based on the belief that art objects found their primary meaning as signs representing the values of historical periods and cultures. But the contextual framework of stones and spaces for the new cultural sanctuary remained neoclassical. Dominating the campus was a classical Parthenon-like temple raised on a two-story podium. The plan referred to this building as the Aula, and the king apparently imagined it as a temple of culture in which the historical consciousness emerging from the arts and scientific scholarship would be communicated to the public. The cultural sanctuary's courtyards and buildings, moreover, were separated from the rest of the city and connected internally by colonnades that were imagined both as classical stoas and medieval cloisters. The whole complex echoed some of Schinkel's ideas of the segregated polis of governors and educators, the acropolis of the philosopher king and his cultural guardians, that he designed as the ideal residence of the ruler in his *Lehrbuch* and envisioned in his plan for a modern royal residence on the Athenian Acropolis. The plan of 1841, however, radically revised Schinkel's original conception of the role of aesthetic education in civic life and of the place of the Altes Museum within its urban setting. The cultural center envisioned by

[103] Stier's project is described in Cornelius Steckner, "Friedrich Wilhelm IV, Karl Friedrich Schinkel, Wilhelm Stier und das Projekt einer Protestantischen Mater Ecclesiarum," in Buesch, ed., *Friedrich Wilhelm Wilhelm IV in seiner Zeit*, pp. 233–55. See also Eva Boersch-Supan, *Berliner Baukunst nach Schinkel, 1840–1870*, p. 162; and Carl-Wolfgang Schuemann, *Der Berliner Dom im 19. Jahrhundert* (Berlin: 1980), pp. 111–16, 120–31.

[104] Frederick William publicly announced his intention of transforming the northern half of the Spree Island into a form of cultural acropolis in March 1841. See Renata Petras, *Die Bauten der Berliner Museums Insel* (Berlin: 1987), p. 54.

Fig. 30. Stueler and Frederick William IV's plan for a cultural acropolis in Berlin, 1841. *Top*: Side view from the Spree, showing the footbridge joining the Altes Museum and the Neues Museum. *Bottom*: Frontal view from the Lustgarten with unobstructed view of the Neues Museum on the left (Altes Museum removed). Reproduction permission: Bildarchiv Preussischer Kulturbesitz.

Frederick William and Stueler was a refuge and sanctuary turned inward on itself: It turned Schinkel's museum around as well, so that the flow of human traffic moved not out to the public squares of the city, encompassing the sites of commerce and work, but back into the halls of academe and the temples of art.

Although the plan of 1841 was a preliminary model for what eventually became the Berlin Museum Island in the late nineteenth century, it was much too ambitious for the financial resources available to Frederick William IV in the 1840s. What was built in the 1840s and 1850s was the Neues Museum (New Museum). Stueler clearly conceived this structure as a large annex to Schinkel's masterpiece. Although the Neues Museum was three stories high and larger than the Altes Museum, it was positioned at right angles to the back wall of the older building. Its exterior façades were not meant to open out onto any grand perspectives, but were partially hidden by other buildings (Schinkel's Packhof complex virtually hid the long west façade) and by the ground-floor colonnades on the south and east sides, which were designed to join the whole network of colonnades that would tie all of the buildings of the cultural acropolis together. The external façades of Stueler's museum were not elaborately decorated and were adapted to harmonize with the sides and back of the Schinkel building. A covered walking bridge over a city street at the second-floor level connected the Altes Museum to the new building. Moreover, the construction of the building's interior spaces was consciously intended to display Schinkel's principle of the adaptability of Greek tectonic and constructive principles to new materials and technology.

All of the reverence for Schinkel displayed by the building's creators, however, could not hide the different cultural message it presented. The shift toward a new kind of cultural historicism was most evident in the grand three-story hall and staircase that constituted the center of the rectangular structure and paralleled the famous staircase and rotunda in Schinkel's museum. The staircase in this instance was clearly interior and introduced visitors to the pedagogical lessons inscribed in the central hall's elaborate wall paintings and sculptural objects. Not only did the stairwell clearly pull the visitor into the building and away from the outside world, but it also redirected traffic flow to and from the Altes Museum in ways that robbed Schinkel's original staircase of much of its educational function. By cutting a new entrance (complete with staircase access to the upper galleries) into Schinkel's building at the main floor level and thus joining the sculpture galleries of both museums, Stueler allowed visitors to Schinkel's museum to avoid the movement from inside to outside, from the aesthetic ideal to the civic task, which had been such an important part of Schinkel's original conception. After the completion of the New Museum, Schinkel's staircase became increasingly decorative, a place to view the Lustgarten but not a necessary element in the museum visitor's educational itinerary.

A more striking shift was the "replacement," or partial "displacement," of Schinkel's classical pantheonlike rotunda in the Altes Museum with a heavily decorated, grandiose staircase hall in the Neues Museum. Frederick William and Stueler used this central entrance hall to overwhelm visitors with their own view of universal history. The king personally selected the Munich artist Wilhelm von Kaulbach to paint a series of historical wall paintings for the hall depicting the great turning points in human history – a human history that was conceived as a history of peoples transformed into ethical communities through their relationship to the transcendent providential will of the Christian God. Six huge paintings portrayed the division into linguistic and ethnic peoples after the collapse of the Tower of Babel, the flowering of Greek culture in the era of Homer, the destruction of Jerusalem and the end of antiquity, the triumph of Christian discipline over the barbaric pagan tribes of northern Europe, the reconquest of the holy sites of Christian history during the Crusades, and the recovery of the authentic apostolic meaning of the Christian faith during the German Reformation. Other large paintings in a secondary entrance rotunda at the southeast corner of the museum portrayed scenes like the Emperor Constantine's recognition of the Christian Church and the Emperor Justinian's dedication of the Hagia Sophia as a Christian temple.

These paintings reflected the organization and decoration of the galleries. Much more attention to chronological sequence was given to the displays in the Neues Museum than in the Altes Museum. Although classical plastic art still held a prominent place, monopolizing most of the main-(second) floor galleries, it was historicized in two obvious ways. First, the detailed representation of chronological narrative through the use of plaster-cast models to fill the historical gaps between original pieces, which had been rejected for aesthetic reasons by Schinkel and Gustav Waagen in the 1820s, was accepted for reasons of historical comprehension in the Neues Museum. Most of the pieces on the museum's main floor were plaster casts rather than original artworks. Second, the classical period was clearly placed between collections of artifacts from "prehistoric" northern European tribal cultures and ancient Egyptian culture, and the extensive collection of Christian art from late antiquity through the Middle Ages. The two most striking spaces for visitors were the Egyptian rooms, with their funerary monuments displayed in settings that mimicked the interiors of their original sites and a reconstructed early Christian chapel (with an impressively backlighted apse) in which early medieval sculpture was displayed.

The attention given to historical context and detail in display spaces like the Egyptian rooms and the medieval chapel was characteristic of all the galleries in the Neues Museum. While Schinkel had tried to create neutral and flexible spaces for the display of art objects, the Neues Museum created appropriate environments for the comprehension of their historical meaning. Wall paintings, friezes, and sculpture were used to "explain" the objects in display cases or on the walls. Rooms were constructed with scholarly historical specificity. The historicizing pedagogy embedded in the structure and interior decoration of the Neues Museum thus marked a double shift away from Schinkel's conception. The mythical, "universal" story of the transformation of nature into culture, which Schinkel had portrayed in his murals for the Altes Museum, was transformed into a linear historical narrative in which unique events marked the major turning points of a process in which the transformation of human beings into members of an ethical community was not produced through aesthetic education and the recreation of "nature and its forms," but through submission to a transcendent authority and its revealed truth. Thus artworks were robbed of their aura as exemplars of an immanent transformation that continuously recurred in the here and now, and became documents of a process that occurred, or at least was directed from, somewhere else.[105]

Although the "sanctuary" for art and scholarship that Frederick William planned for the north end of the Spree island may have seemed like a place apart in its isolation from the civic life of the city, its inner direction was constantly related, at least in Frederick William's conception, to powers that transcended its secular activities of historical self-discovery and self-expression. And in fact the king imagined this sanctuary as a part of a larger ensemble in which such dependency would be obvious: His plans for the Lustgarten space included a remodeling of parts of the baroque city palace (*Schloss*) and the construction of a massive Protestant cathedral.

The great reception room and the royal chapel in the *Schloss* were rebuilt to conform to the king's view of Prussian history as an expression of divine will working through the agency of the Hohenzollern dynasty as it transformed the disciplinary order of a patriarchal state into an ethical community built on the voluntary identification of the people with historical tradition and constituted authority. In the new palace chapel, the Hohenzollern monarchs were integrated into a lineage that mixed together figures from the history of both the Christian church and the Germanic Empire, both apostles and emperors.[106] More important to the king than the representations of historical culture and divinely sanctioned political authority that faced each other across the Lustgarten, however, was the plan to build a new cathedral in the center of the square, and thus at the end of the triumphal avenue of Unter den Linden, a cathedral that would give visible form to the ideal religious center that informed his concepts of both politics and culture.

From the king's perspective, the center of the city, state, and nation was imagined not as cultural acropolis, or a "Ruler's Residence," but as a cathedral. During the first two years of his reign, Frederick William IV solicited proposals for this ecclesiastical completion of the Berlin center. Two competing visions soon gained prominence among the competing proposals. The king continued to imagine his Mother Church as a basilica modeled on early Christian churches in the Byzantine and late Roman Empires. The basilica structure, with its elevation of the authority of the bishop and the king over

[105] Detailed descriptions of the design and the interior decoration of the Neues Museum, which was almost totally destroyed during World War II and is only now undergoing a process of restoration, can be found in Petras, *Die Bauten*, pp. 54–76; Volker Plagemann, *Das Deutsche Kunstmuseum 1790–1870* (Munich: 1967), pp. 117–26; Han Reuther, *Die Museumsinsel in Berlin* (Frankfurt: 1978); Hartmut Gogerloh, "Zu Baugeschichte und Wiederaufbau des Neuen Museums in Berlin," *Kunst-Chronik*, 44, no. 2 (1991), 112–21; and Eva Boersch-Supan and Dietrich Mueller-Stueler, *Friedrich August Stueler, 1800–1865* (Munich and Berlin: 1997), pp. 64–78.

[106] See Helmut Engel,"Friedrich Wilhelm IV. und die Baukunst," in Buesch, ed., *Friedrich Wilhelm IV. in seiner Zeit*, pp. 179–81.

the assembled people, came closest to his conception of a church organized around obedience to transcendent authority and dependent in its earthly arrangements on the divinely instituted authority of the emperor. An early Christian, "apostolic" basilica set on a raised platform (under which there would be space for a crypt) and surrounded by a forecourt and atria with colonnades (in which the Campo Santo could be located) corresponded to his ideal vision and to the design by Friedrich Stueler that he approved in 1845. Clearing and excavation for the construction of the Camp Santo and the foundations of the cathedral were begun, but prohibitive costs and then revolution put an end to the king's plans. The empty construction site between the old cathedral and the city palace remained as a reminder to Berliners for decades that Frederick William was never able to create the architectural centerpiece of his concept of Christian-German culture organized according to the historical principle.

During the 1840s, Frederick William's own favored plans were placed in competition with the belief that a Prussian and German Protestant cathedral should be a huge domed structure on the model of Rome's Saint Peter's or London's Saint Paul's.[107] The domed cathedral was imagined both as closer to a "people's church" in its expansion of the altar and preaching space into a huge circular or semicircular space for the congregation, and as a modern progressive Protestant culmination of the development from the hall basilica to the cruciform church to the domed cathedral in the centuries of the Christian history. Many of the competing plans for the new cathedral involved large domed structures either built into the cruciform structure over altar crossings, or as circular churches. Frederick William was not completely resistant to grandly conceived domed churches. Throughout the 1840s, his Potsdam architect Ludwig Persius was fulfilling Schinkel's original planes for the Saint Nicholas Church by constructing the huge dome that Frederick William III had refused to fund. At the very center of the Christian-German community, however, the new king did not want a massive rotunda where the people could gather as a "fraternity" to receive or encounter the power of the word, but a basilica in which the authority of God's patriarchal representatives, the king and the bishop, controlled the proclamation of the Word to their "children."

The historical vision embodied in Frederick William's imagined Lustgarten complex was never constructed. The official historicism of the 1840s did not produce a representative architectural ensemble, and its hopes for collective public identification with the kind of community embodied in this vision remained a utopian project. The visions of a modernized Gothic representation of national identity supported by Stier and

[107] Karl-Heinz Klingenburg, "Kuppelbau kontra Basilika: Die Berliner Dombauplaene der 1840er Jahre in der Kritik ihrer Zeit," in Karl-Heinz Klingenburg, ed., *Studien zur Berliner Kunstgeschichte* (Leipzig: 1986), pp. 244–58.

Bunsen also never proceeded beyond the design stage. Schinkel's vision of the center of Berlin as a public space dominated by the temple of aesthetic education thus triumphed by default after his death, at least for a generation.

Although the king was stymied by circumstance in his attempt to subordinate Schinkel's vision to his own concept of public identity as historical identity, his historical views did find an actualization at another level, as a personal vision, as an architectural self-expression or confession built among the hills and rivers and woods of the Potsdam countryside. It was in the architectural historicism of the king's and his siblings' domestic architecture that the personal subjective dimension of the historicism of the 1840s was most clearly displayed. In the Charlottenhof villa and its neighboring Gardener's House (*Roemische Baeder*) on the grounds of Sans Soucci, the adaptation of classical form to the natural landscape and its "organic" forms was combined with a multiaxial design that conformed to the itinerary of an individual subject wandering through particular constructions of the past that helped shape his or her own cultural narrative. The religious views of the king were also finally architecturally realized in a private royal chapel at Sans Soucci – the neo-Romanesque Friedenskirche with its Byzantine ornamentation. Schinkel's architectural historicism had aimed at constructing a public narrative in space and stone that would draw the emancipated individuals of the new society into a community of memory. But the public realm remained the site of fragmented memories and competing historical narratives. It was only in the controlled world of the private park and villa that the imaginatively reconstructed world of Christian-German cultural identity could find a consistent representation and a cultural home. Here the project of constructing self-identity as historical identity emerged as a characteristic project of the homeless individual self.

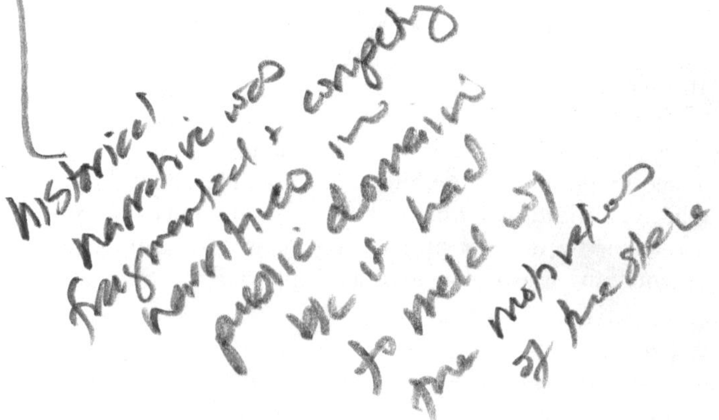

4

The Generation of Ethical Community from the Spirit of Music: Mendelssohn's Musical Constructions of Historical Identity

MENDELSSOHN'S CALL TO BERLIN AND THE CONTEXTUAL FRAME OF HIS MUSICAL MISSION

The name Felix Mendelssohn seems out of place on the roster of philosophers, scholars, and artists that Frederick William IV called to Berlin to provide historical justification, aesthetic symbolization, and public language for his vision of an ethical community of Prusso-Germans nurtured, disciplined, and bound together by its revitalized relationship to the patriarchal God of the apostolic Christian church. How was it possible that the grandson of Moses Mendelssohn and the child prodigy so carefully trained by teachers and family to become the spiritual heir of the cosmopolitan humanism of neoclassical Weimar would be asked to join the company of Schelling, Ludwig Tieck, Peter Cornelius, Friedrich Rueckert, Friedrich Julius Stahl, Leopold Ranke, Friedrich Karl von Savigny, and the Grimm brothers and participate in the project of Christian-German cultural reformation? What in Mendelssohns' achievements as composer or conductor attracted the attention of influential figures at the Prussian court? And why would Mendelssohn, apparently so securely and happily established as the director of Germany's finest orchestra in Germany's most musical city (the Gewandhaus in Leipzig) accept this invitation and, however hesitantly and tentatively, attach his reputation and talent to the dreams and projects of the Prussian king and his close advisors?

In his private correspondence Mendelssohn often suggested that his primary reason for moving to Berlin was the desire to be closer to his family, especially his recently widowed mother, but also his brother Paul and sister Fanny, his most intimate confidantes on musical, personal, and more generally political and cultural matters.[1] Some of the pressure to come to Berlin certainly originated in the wishes of family members and personal friends.[2] At the same time, Mendelssohn's critical distance from the

[1] For a comment representative of many others, see Mendelssohn's letter to Karl Klingemann of March 15, 1841, in which he stated that the main reasons for going to Berlin were "the mother, the siblings, and the parental home," in K. Klingemann ed., *Felix Mendelssohn Bartholdy's Briefwechsel mit Legationsrat Karl Klingemann* (Essen: 1909), p. 258.

[2] Mendelssohn's younger brother Paul (head of the Mendelssohn banking firm and Berlin household since the death of the father, Abraham Mendelssohn, in 1835), was particularly active in mediating between Felix and the Prussian officials, and in encouraging him to come to Berlin. See *Felix Mendelssohn*

exclusionary ethnic German nationalism that reappeared so prominently during the Rhine Crisis of 1840, and his distaste for the more dogmatic, neo-orthodox forms of evangelical Christian piety, were clear. The seductive simplicity of dichotomies between private and public spheres, and between liberal and conservative cultural politics, however, ignores the areas of substantial agreement between Mendelssohn's understanding of the historical mission and cultural function of music and the views of at least some of the influential insiders in the new regime, including the king and Bunsen, or the fact that the eventual estrangement between regime and composer was not due primarily to ideological conflict but to Mendelssohn's frustrations with bureaucratic bungling and inertia, exhausting infighting regarding jurisdictional authority over various institutions and petty intrigues at the court. Mendelssohn claimed that his loyalty to the king's ideas (or at least to some of his projects), and attraction to the king's person actually kept him from severing his ties to the regime earlier than he did. An extended personal interview with Frederick William in the fall of 1842 convinced him to extend his commitments over two more years.[3] Moreover, the family loyalties and personal friendships that drew Mendelssohn to Berlin clearly had a public dimension, involving definitions of the cultural calling he had absorbed during his childhood and youth, and historical hopes for the reformation of German national culture that he had shared with his siblings and friends during the late 1820s.

Alexander von Humboldt and Bunsen, with the enthusiastic support of the king, simultaneously initiated the administrative process that led to Mendelssohn's invitation to Berlin. Both Humboldt and Bunsen can be situated within the liberal wing of the king's circle of advisors, but

Bartholdy, Briefe aus den Jahren 1830 bis 1847, 3rd ed. (2 vols., Leipzig: 1875), vol. 2, pp. 164–74. The king, Humboldt, and Bunsen, were also strongly influenced by personal considerations. Frederick William had come out as a personal supporter of Mendelssohn's public performance of the *St. Matthew Passion* in 1829 and had visited Mendelssohn in Duesseldorf in 1833 (see Susanna Grossmann-Vendrey, *Felix Mendelssohn Bartholdy und die Musik der Vergangenheit* [Regensburg: 1969], pp. 56–57). Mendelssohn had dedicated the publication of his three concert overtures (opus 35) to the crown prince in 1835. After Humboldt returned from his world travels in 1827, he reestablished old ties to the Mendelssohn family. In 1828 he commissioned Felix to compose a secular cantata for the International Conference of Natural Scientists in Berlin. Throughout the 1830s and 1840s, the Mendelssohns continually came to his aid during his financial difficulties. One of Humboldt's protégés, the mathematician Gustav Lejeune-Dirichlet, married Felix's younger sister Rebecca (see Hanno Beck, *Alexander von Humboldt* [2 vols.; Wiesbaden: 1959–61]; and Karl Bruhns, ed., *Alexander von Humboldt. Eine wissenschaftliche Biographie* [3vols.; Leipzig: 1872]). Bunsen visited in the Mendelssohn home and discussed his concerns about liturgical music with Felix in 1827–28. Felix reciprocated the visit during his stay in Rome in 1830 (see Friedrich Nippold, ed., *Christian Carl Josias von Bunsen* [3vols.; Leipzig: 1868–71], vol. 1, pp. 309–10, 365–66).

[3] Mendelssohn described his positive perceptions of the king's intentions in letters to his friends Heinrich Schleinitz on October 17, 1842, and Igaz Moscheles, on November 18, 1842. See Felix Mendelssohn, *Briefe*, ed. Rudolf Elvers (Frankfurt: 1984), pp. 221–22; *Briefe von Felix Mendelssohn-Bartholdy an Ignaz und Charlotte Moscheles* (Leizpig: 1888), pp. 231–32.

their positions were based on different generational and intellectual perspectives. Humboldt, whose official position as royal chamberlain had not completely extinguished his youthful loyalty to the ideals of the Prussian reform movement, framed his recommendation within the ethical and pedagogical terms of the tradition of liberal bureaucratic reform.[4] He envisioned a wide-ranging educational and administrative role for the young composer as head of a new musical section of a reformed Royal Academy of Arts and as director of a state musical conservatory. These proposals echoed and recalled the negotiations during the original reform era instigated by Mendelssohn's composition teacher and musical mentor Carl Friedrich Zelter, negotiations that involved the Minister Hardenberg, Humboldt's brother Wilhelm, and the indirect interventions of Goethe and Schiller.[5] They thus also implicitly recalled and revived a conception of the cultural role of music that Mendelssohn had absorbed from his mentor during his musical apprenticeship in the 1820s and that remained an important element of his historical self-consciousness throughout the years of his maturity.

The general principles informing Zelter's conception of the role of music in culture can be gleaned from his various memoranda to Prussian officials as well as his extended correspondence on musical matters with Goethe. First, he insisted that music must be liberated as a cultural activity from its artisanal status as a mere handmaid of particular human needs, desires, and activities, and elevated to the status of an integral member of the "free" and "higher" arts, which aimed at the cultivation and expression of the universal, spiritual dimension of human experience. As one of the "free" arts, music could be described as "religious" insofar as its aim was to represent the consonant harmonies of the ethical "world being" that emerged from a mobilization of the innate divinity within all human individuals.[6] On the basis of this conviction, Zelter taught that the general laws of harmony, from the simplest rules for the construction and progression of chords to the contrapuntal complexities of canon and fugue, were the basis of all musical training and knowledge. For Zelter, Johann Sebastian Bach was above all the "greatest harmonist," and he saw himself as carrying on the northern

[4] Humboldt's political and cultural perspectives and his various attempts to influence the king to form his policies in accordance with them are described most clearly in Alfred Dove's contribution to Bruhns, *Humboldt*, vol. 2, 93–389. See also Beck, *Humboldt*, vol. 2, 233–35. Humboldt's proposal and his discussions with the king can be indirectly discerned from Bunsen's letter to him on November 1, 1840, in Nippold, *Bunsen*, vol. 2, 143–44.

[5] These negotiations are recounted, with citation of the original documents, in Cornelia Schroeder, *Carl Friedrich Zelter und die Akadamie der Kuenste* (Berlin: 1959), pp. 69–135, See also *Briefwechsel zwischen Goethe und Zelter*, ed. Max Hecker (3 vols.; Frankfurt: 1913, reprinted 1987), vol. 1, pp. 82ff.

[6] Carl Friedrich Zelter, "Erste Denkschrift an Hardenberg, Sept. 28, 1803," Schroeder, *Zelter*, p. 73; Zelter to Goethe, July 22, 1804, *Briefwechsel zwischen Goethe und Zelter*, vol. 1, p. 89.

German tradition of music as a "serious business" and "high art" as it had been passed on to him by the generation of Bach's sons and immediate students during the last decades of the eighteenth century.[7]

Zelter's second major principle was that music's central cultural function was the moral cultivation of the feelings. Music's tonal language awakened, nurtured, disciplined, and spiritualized the feelings so that humanity might achieve the "perfection and nobility" implicit in its innate divinity.[8] But the educational purposes of music, the moralization of human feelings through their integration into "the ethical world being of the human community," was often at cross-purposes with music's mimetic function as a mirror of the divine structure of the universe. As a form of public moral education, music was obligated to communicate in accessible ways; its harmonic structures and melodic lines had to be comprehensible to all human beings. In Bach's complex artistic representations of the hidden harmonies within the apparent dissonances of the sensible universe, however, the harmonies and melodies were often inaccessible to the untrained ear. They needed to be simplified and clarified in order to communicate the goal of the educational process and elicit the desired emotional responses.[9]

Zelter thus developed a two-tiered conception of music's cultural function. On the one hand, the artistic masterpieces in the complex contrapuntal style of the elder Bach should be collected, preserved, and studied, like great literary or philosophical texts, to provide insight into the complex structure of the cosmos as an organic totality. Their influence was limited to an elite of aesthetic connoisseurs among the educated classes, like his own choral society (*Singakadamie*), which had become a musical university, or "school of wisdom" under his mentorship.[10] On the other hand, the "people," or general public, could only be educated through a technically simplified and morally edifying music based on the simple melody lines and chord sequences of hymn tunes and popular songs.

7 Zelter to Goethe, June 9, 1827, *Briefwechsel zwischen Goethe und Zelter*, vol. 2, p. 578. Zelter's self-consciousness as heir of the Prussian Bach tradition is a persistent theme of his various autobiographies, written from 1793 through the 1820s. See Johann Wolfgang Schottlaender, ed., *Carl Friedrich Zelter's Darstellungen seines Lebens* (Weimar: 1931). There is an excellent and wide-ranging discussion of this tradition in Gerhard Herz, "Johann Sebastian Bach in the Age of Rationalism and Early Romanticism," in Herz, *Essays on J. S. Bach* (Ann Arbor: MI, 1985), pp. 1–124. Zelter's promotion of this tradition as the peculiarly German tradition of "serious" music is highlighted in Celia Applegate, "How German Is It? Nationalism and the Idea of Serious Music in the Early Nineteenth Century," *19th-Century Music*, 21 (1998): 288–96.

8 Zelter, "Erste Denkschrift," p. 79. See also Zelter, "Zweite Denkschrift Zelters," in Schroeder, *Zelter*, p. 82.

9 Zelter described his "adaptation" of Bach for public consumption in a letter to Goethe, April 5, 1827, *Briefwechsel zwischen Goethe und Zelter*, vol. 2, p. 566. See also Herz,"Bach," pp. 92–98; Georg Schuenemann, "Die Bach-Pflege der Berliner Singakademie," *Bach-Jahrbuch*, 1928 (Leipzig: 1929), pp. 149–50.

10 Zelter to Goethe, March 5, 1804, *Briefwechsel zwischen Goethe und Zelter*, vol. 1, p. 80.

Zelter clearly privileged vocal over instrumental music as the primary form of "high" and "serious" musical art. He did appreciate, after some hesitation, the dramatic use of contrasting tonal areas in Haydn's and Mozart's instrumental sonata forms,[11] but he did not understand how such music could fulfill a public educational function. It might be clever, witty, or even profound for trained musicians, who could grasp its compositional logic, but it did not speak as directly to the human feelings as the human voice, nor was it as accessible to the people as music whose meaning was indicated by words.

On the basis of these general principles, Zelter arrived at a number of practical conclusions about the appropriate institutional forms for music's public function. First, he made every effort to transfer the cultivation of serious musical art from scattered voluntary organizations to centralized public institutions. Although Zelter was the leader of one of the first and most prestigious choral societies in Germany, he had little faith in the ability of such organizations to transform the ethos of the culture from "below," without direct state support and centralized leadership. In 1804 he wrote to Goethe: "one cannot expect from the public that which is still to be constructed." Ethical education could only come from above and from a unified leadership that could hold the balance "against the masses."[12] In this context it is important to note that Zelter did not see the ethical organism represented in harmonic structures as the product of some original "natural" harmony implicit in popular folk song or archaic religious chant, but as an artificial, "spiritual" construct imposed "from above" as a domination and organized control of nature.[13]

Second, although Zelter did not envision moral reform emerging from traditional religious teaching, he did see the churches as the primary institutions and sacred music as the primary medium for extending the educational function of music to the people. The traditional religious disciplines, he claimed, had lost their power to moralize the people and transform them into a spiritual organism. This task had been taken over by art and scholarship (*Kunst* and *Wissenschaft*), which should use religious institutions and liturgical traditions to construct a moral public through aesthetic means.[14]

[11] Klaus Kropfinger, "Klassik-Rezeption in Berlin (1800–1830)," in Carl Dahlhaus, ed., *Studien zur Musikgeschichte Berlins im fruehen 19, Jahrhundert* (Regensburg: 1980), pp. 342–43.

[12] Zelter to Goethe, May, 1804, *Briefwechsel zwischen Goethe und Zelter*, vol. 1, p. 85; and Zelter, "Zweite Denkschrift," pp. 84–88.

[13] Zelter to Goethe, July 3, 1808, *Briefwechsel zwischen Goethe und Zelter*, vol. 1, p. 229. See also *ibid.*, vol. 3, p. 109 (Dec. 22, 1828). On the relationship between natural and cultural theories of harmony in eighteenth-century Germany, see William J. Mitchell, "Chord and Context in 18th-Century Theory," *Journal of the American Musicological Society*, 16 (1963): 221–39.

[14] Zelter, "Aus der dritten Denkschrift" (Dec. 28, 1803), in Schroeder, *Zelter*, pp. 89–92. The debate about the relationship between traditional religious institutions and traditions and the cultural function of art, as carried on in 1803–4 between Goethe, Schiller, and Zelter, is documented in *ibid.*, pp. 95ff. The focus on sacred music as the primary means of reaching the general public was evident in the

By the time Mendelssohn had completed his musical apprenticeship, he had thoroughly assimilated not only the traditional compositional techniques of the Berlin Bach tradition, but also Zelter's perspective on music's cultural function.[15] His early compositions reveal how quickly he became a master of the techniques of thorough-bass and contrapuntal writing.[16] Moreover, over the years Mendelssohn remained loyal to Zelter's vision of the ethical function of serious art music. He constantly reiterated his disdain for the immoral egoism implied in virtuosic display, and his mistrust of sensual, "materialistic" music that produced titillation of the senses rather than elevation and discipline of the feelings.[17] Finally, Mendelssohn tied his personal musical goals to his public duties as a representative of music's educational function. As the conductor of public performances and director of various musical organizations, Mendelssohn sought to mobilize musical craftsmanship and technical skill in the service of "purely spiritual purposes," to elevate musical performance and composition to the "expression of a higher idea." During the early 1840s he wrote memoranda for both the Prussian and the Saxon governments regarding the establishment of musical conservatories that revealed his continuing commitment to the cultural function of music as an instrument for public moral education, a function that could only be fulfilled if music was given the dignity and autonomy of one of the fine arts. State-supported musical education, he insisted, must "ensure that all dimensions [*Faecher*] of music be taught and learned in relation to the thought they are to express, to the higher calling to which technical perfection in art must be subordinated."[18]

When Humboldt imagined Mendelssohn in 1840 as Zelter's legitimate heir, therefore, he was not entirely wrong. However, even if Mendelssohn never rejected the perspective of his musical father, by 1840 he had revised

memorandum that Wilhelm von Humboldt sent to the king in 1809, entitled "Ueber geistliche Musik," also in *ibid.*, 120–23. See also Humboldt's letter to Caroline von Humboldt, May 19, 1809, in *Wilhelm und Caroline von Humboldt in ihren Briefen* (3 vols.; Berlin: 1909), vol. 3, p. 111.

15 The mentorship of Zelter was the major musical source of Mendelssohn's "classicism." For other sources, see Leon Botstein, "Neoclassicism, Romanticism, and Emancipation: The Origins of Mendelssohn's Aesthetic Outlook," in Douglass Seaton, ed., *The Mendelssohn Companion* (Westport, Conn.: 2001), pp. 1–23.

16 Mendelssohn's training in traditional techniques is documented in his exercise books, analyzed in R. Larry Todd, *Mendelssohn's Musical Education: A Study and Edition of his Exercises in Composition* (Cambridge and New York: 1983).

17 Contemporaries like Robert Schumann noticed the striking emphasis on moral self-discipline and public duty both in Mendelssohn's personal practice and his general aesthetic judgments: Robert Schumann, *Erinnerungen an Felix Mendelssohn* (Zwickau: 1947), p. 51. In his letters, Mendelssohn often echoes Zelter's views, but there is also a newer, "Romantic" tone in Mendelssohn's moralizing – especially in his focus on personal authenticity and resistance to the blandishments of popular taste and fashion. See his letter to his aunt Lady von Pereira, July, 1831 (*Briefe*, vol. 1, p 205).

18 "Pro Memoria wegen einer in Berlin zu errichtenden Musikschule, May 1841," in *Briefe*, vol. 2, 191–3. See also his earlier plan for an academy in Saxony presented in a letter to the Saxon official von Falkenstein on April 8, 1840, in *ibid.*, vol. 2, 150–54.

and transformed that perspective in various, sometimes far-reaching, ways – elevating the representational and educational capacities of instrumental music to at least equal status with vocal music, liberating liturgical musical traditions from the ecclesiastical ghetto and integrating them into more secular forms of concert music, and, finally, adapting the public forms of symphonic and choral music to the complex new dissonances, lyrical expressiveness, and harmonic possibilities of his own "Romantic" moment in history and its distinctive focus on the inner depths and complexities of human subjectivity.

Although Bunsen shared Humboldt's perspective on the need for a centralized musical conservatory and agreed with Mendelssohn's views on the ethical power of music, he also held to a more specifically ecclesiastical conception of the sacred foundations of music than either Zelter or Humboldt. Bunsen's concept of cultural change and sense of historical mission achieved its focus, as we have already seen, during the post-Napoleonic religious revival. The transformation of social dissonance into communal harmony, he believed, was ultimately possible only through a regeneration of religious faith in the biblically revealed "objective" foundations of all ethical norms in the will of a transcendent personal god. Throughout the 1820s and 1830s, Bunsen had been particularly interested in liturgical reform that would restore what he imagined to be the authentic forms of worship of a purified, apostolic Protestant church. He avidly supported, especially during his years in Rome, the "Palestrina" movement to revive a strict a capella style and traditional modal harmonies in church music. At the same time, Bunsen was clearly interested in expanding the impact of sacred music on the general public through festive performances of sacred concert music, and in modernizing liturgical music through a Protestant emphasis on congregational participation and individual subjectivity. The distinctive role he envisioned for Mendelssohn was as a court composer and church composer ready to accommodate the personal commissions of the king for liturgical music in an appropriately early Christian style and to organize performances of sacred concert music for the general public.[19]

Bunsen had reason to believe that Mendelssohn would be interested in the roles he had conceived for him. When Bunsen first met Mendelssohn in the winter of 1827–28, the young composer had been fascinated with "Old Italian" liturgical music and had composed a number of major choral works inspired by it.[20] During his stay in Rome, in 1830–31, Mendelssohn spent many hours with Bunsen discussing liturgical music and the relations between the Old Italian school and the German Bach tradition. Moreover, both Bunsen and the king responded enthusiastically to Mendelssohn's creative modernizations of the baroque tradition of sacred concert music in

[19] These positions are clearly stated in Bunsen's letters to the king (October 30, 1840) and Humboldt (November 1, 1840), reprinted in Nippold, *Bunsen*, vol. 2, 142–43.

[20] Rudolf Werner, *Felix Mendelssohn Bartholdy als Kirchenmusiker* (Frankfurt: 1930), pp. 38–45.

his oratorio Paulus (Saint Paul, 1836), the Lobgesang (Hymn of Praise) Symphony Cantata (1840), and his many religious cantatas based on biblical psalms or Lutheran hymns. Mendelssohn seemed to be the only living composer capable of both restoring the great traditions of Christian sacred music and bringing them into a creative relationship to "the general life of the people."[21] For Bunsen, however, in contrast to Zelter, the sacred in sacred music did not just refer to the spiritual essence of mankind, but more specifically and traditionally to mankind's dependence on a transcendent personal being. The function of sacred music was to point beyond itself; not just to elicit feelings of human brotherhood, but also to instill reverence for the authority of the transcendent father of all human harmonies.

In 1840 Mendelssohn's concept of his musical calling and of the cultural function of music more generally lay somewhere between and perhaps beyond the conception inherited from Zelter and that projected for him by Bunsen. Sometimes during the early 1840s it seemed that Mendelssohn simply shifted between these two roles, increasingly finding that he could fulfill the role defined by Humboldt more easily in Leipzig, where the government was more efficient in supporting the institutional infrastructure needed to sustain art music within public life, but returning to Berlin as the king's personal composer, with special commissions to write and perform "incidental" music for dramatic performances at the court or liturgical music for the royal cathedral. Yet neither of these roles, nor simply shuffling from one to the other, satisfactorily fulfilled the vision Mendelssohn had brought with him into the 1840s. At least Mendelssohn seemed determined to diminish his commitment to both roles by 1845–46. When he resigned from his Prussian positions in 1845, he also withdrew from most of his commitments in Leipzig, indicating that his attachment to the Prussian cultural project had been serious and sincere, and that his disillusionment effected not only his place of residence or political loyalties but also the way he conceived the cultural function and historical role of music.

It is not easy to ascertain with precision how Mendelssohn did conceive the cultural function and historical role of music at different points in his career. Unlike his more loquacious contemporaries, Robert Schumann, Franz Liszt, Maria von Weber, Hector Berlioz, and Richard Wagner, Mendelssohn did not engage in extensive public discussion of the meaning of his own or any other music. In the 1820s he tended to let his more verbal and theoretical friends speak for him. By the early 1830s his attitude began to approach that of principled silence. In 1842 he noted that if words could say what he intended, there would be no point in making music: "People usually complain that music is too polysemic, what one is to understand by it is so ambiguous, and words, of course, everyone can understand. But with me the reverse is true . . . What music expresses to me (music that I like)

[21] Nippold, *Bunsen*, vol. 2, pp. 142–43.

are not thoughts which are too indefinite but thoughts which are too definite to be put into words."[22] Hegelian claims that aesthetic experience could be made fully transparent in conceptual thinking and communicated in philosophical language tended to merge in Mendelssohn's mind with the chatter of Berlin music critics who thought their words more important than the notes they wrote about. For Mendelssohn the autonomy of music inhered in its ability to communicate through notes a consciousness of an ethical reality (described usually as "feeling") that inhabited a realm beyond words.[23] At the same time, Mendelssohn tied this communicative capacity of music to the tasks of illuminating the ethical meaning of a higher form of communication, the "word" of divine revelation hidden in both nature and the inherited musical and other nonverbal texts of historical cultures. Music was able to communicate the experience of a deeper, more universal meaning concerning the relation between the sacred and the secular than was possible in words.

The specificity of Mendelssohn's views on the relations between sacred music, ethical community, and historical consciousness as they had evolved to the moment of his call to Berlin in late 1840 must be derived from his musical works, although the explication of their meaning(s) also requires some contextual analysis. This chapter examines four musical works as critical moments in the development of Mendelssohn's views concerning the historical grounding of sacred and secular identities – the Reformation Symphony of 1830, the oratorio *Paulus* of 1836, the Lobgesang Symphony Cantata of 1840, and the oratorio Elijah of 1846 – in order to illuminate his response to the cultural politics of the regime of Frederick William IV.

REMEMBERING THE PAST AS THE ESSENCE OF THE PRESENT: THE REFORMATION SYMPHONY AS AN EXPERIMENT IN INSTRUMENTAL SACRED MUSIC

Mendelssohn's Reformation Symphony (Symphony no.5 in D Minor, opus 107) was composed during the fall and winter of 1829–30, with finishing touches and revisions extending until the summer of 1832.[24] The external stimulus for the work was the tercentenary celebration of the Augsburg Confession of Faith in the summer of 1830, and the autograph score was

[22] Letter to Marc Souchay, Oct. 15, 1842, *Briefe*, vol. 2, p. 221. For an earlier statement of his position, see his letter to the composer Wilhelm Taubert of August 27, 1831, in *Briefe*, vol. 1, pp. 253–58.

[23] Mendelssohn's views about the relations between music and language are connected to questions of Jewish identity in Leon Botstein, "Songs Without Words: Thoughts on Music, Theology, and the Role of the Jewish Question in the Work of Felix Mendelssohn," *Musical Quarterly* 77 (1993): 561–78.

[24] For a detailed reconstruction of the compositional history of the work, see Judith Silber, "Mendelssohn and his *Reformation* Symphony," *Journal of the American Musicological Society* 40 (1987): 310–33.

entitled "Symphony for the Celebration of the Ecclesiastical Revolution." However, the symphony was not a commissioned piece, and its significance in Mendelssohn's development extended far beyond the occasion of its composition. It can be seen as an exemplary work, bringing to culmination a decade of creative assimilation of two major German musical traditions, as an experimental attempt to merge the contrasting musical forms and historical perspectives of sacred music from the Protestant baroque, represented most forcefully for Mendelssohn by J. S. Bach, and the self-sufficient, secular musical universes of the classical sonata form exemplified most dramatically in the instrumental work of Beethoven.

The formal structures and programmatic content of the symphony, moreover, were clearly connected to Mendelssohn's personal struggle to define not only his distinctive compositional voice but also his religious and national identity during the years between 1825 and 1832. On February 3, 1824, Zelter had officially announced the end of Mendelssohn's apprenticeship and welcomed him as an independent master into the guild of musical composers: "in the name of Haydn, in the name of Mozart and in the name of the elder Bach."[25] A year later, in March 1825, Abraham Mendelssohn took his son to Paris for two months to face the scrutiny of Luigi Cherubini and other composers whose judgment would determine his willingness to accept Felix's choice of music as a life's vocation. By 1825 Mendelssohn had already displayed prodigious, precocious productivity in musical composition along the whole spectrum of vocal and instrumental genres. But it was only in 1825 and 1826 that some of his works began to take on a clearly individual style that distinguished them from the models he had learned to imitate with such amazing competence and self-confident ease. Whereas in the period before 1825 Mendelssohn's reverence for the achievements of the tradition had confirmed his loyalty to the world of his father and teachers, after 1825 his historicism became a means for asserting his own identity and the distinctiveness of his own generation and its historical mission. Three years of travel abroad in 1829–32, first a six-month stay in England and Scotland, and then, after a brief stopover at home, a two-year tour of the major cultural centers of southern Germany and Italy, crystallized and brought to musical fruition the process of emancipation that had begun earlier. The Reformation Symphony, in its distinctively "Romantic" merger of Bach and Beethoven, was one major expression of this process.

Mendelssohn's introduction to the music of Bach had occurred as part of his youthful initiation into the northern German Bach tradition that was nurtured in almost cultlike fashion within his own extended family and within the choral society led by Zelter. As toddlers, he and his sister Fanny

[25] *Die Familie Mendelssohn, 1729 bis 1847*, ed., Sebastian Hensel, and with a new Afterword by Konrad Feilchenfeldt (Frankfurt: 1995), p. 175.

had exercised their fingers and minds over Bach's *Well-Tempered Clavier*, under their mother's guidance. As they grew into their teenage years they participated in the instrumental and choral music making of Zelter's *Singakadamie*, where they were introduced to some of the Bach cantatas and passions. Mendelssohn received his own personal copy of the score of the *St. Matthew Passion* (a rare collector's item at the time) as a Christmas present from his maternal grandmother, Babette Salomon, in 1823. This grandmother and her sister Sarah Levy were both well-known keyboard players and Bach worshippers, who passed on their skills and viewpoints to the younger generation, including Mendelssohn's mother, Leah Salomon.[26] Under Zelter's direction, moreover, Felix started his compositional exercises with Lutheran chorale harmonizations and fugue and canon writing according to Bach models.

The Bach enthusiasm that developed among Felix, Fanny, and their friends during the mid-1820s, however, was clearly perceived both by themselves and their older mentors as something new; it focused more on the spiritual content and emotional expressiveness of Bach's sacred music, less on its learned contrapuntal complexity. When Mendelssohn and some of his friends, a group that included his classical language tutor Gustav Droysen, the music critic Adolf Bernhard Marx, and the actor and opera singer Eduard Devrient, began to rehearse parts of the *St. Matthew Passion* in 1827 and then push for its public performance in the face of Zelter's doubts about its public intelligibility and accessibility, they were driven by the conviction that their own generational perspective had found an authentic voice in this music. In Bach's music, traditional Lutheran faith in the power of divine grace to create a spirit-filled community was recreated within the forms of modern, aesthetic self-consciousness. Bach's musical structures were not seen as echoes of a past world of metaphysical security and cosmic order, but prophetic indicators of a new national and religious consciousness. From this standpoint the chorale, or congregational hymn, in the passions or in other sacred "art" works did not just function as a liturgical response to the recited biblical text, but articulated the national community's appropriation of its essential unity and collective historical mission through remembrance of its textual traditions. Although Mendelssohn left extended public commentary on the meaning of the Bach revival to friends and allies like Droysen and Marx,[27] occasional comments in his own letters,

[26] For details about the Bach tradition in the Mendelssohn family and extended kinship groups, see Grossmann-Vendrey, *Felix Mendelssohn Bartholdy und die Musik der Vergangenheit*, pp. 13–15, and Todd, *Musical Education*, pp. 3, 10–11.

[27] Marx's and Droysen's articles about the revival of the *St. Matthew Passion* are reprinted in Martin Geck, *Die Wiederentdeckung der Mathaeuspassion im 19. Jahrhundert. Die Zeitgenoessischen Dokumente und ihr ideengeschichtliche Deutung* (Regensburg: 1967), pp. 55–60, 131–43. An interesting contemporary account of the performance and its preparation can be found in Eduard Devrient, *Meine Erinnerungen an Felix Mendelssohn Bartholdy und seine Briefe an mich*, 2d ed. (Leipzig: 1872), pp. 48ff.

as well as the focus of some of his compositional projects, indicate that he shared their perspective. He also imagined the historical role of Bach's sacred masterpieces as an emancipation of the experiences of ethical rebirth and communal integration from the confines of established churches and confessional liturgies. Wherever Bach's music was performed, he claimed, it transformed the participants and audience into a religious community.[28] Although lay musicians performed the *St. Matthew Passion* in a neoclassical temple of art before a ticket-holding audience, Mendelssohn thought that the music transformed a secular concert into a sacred service.[29]

The emotional and intellectual conviction that informed Mendelssohn's belief not only in the historical significance of Bach's music as the fountainhead of the distinctively German tradition of serious art music,[30] but also in its contemporary relevance, was evident in the compositional projects that paralleled his efforts to bring Bach's masterpieces into the public concert repertoire. The attempt to appropriate Bach's "living essence" within the forms of the present can be discerned in some of his keyboard music, as in his transformation of strict fugal forms into the more subjectively expressive, "free" forms of the "characteristic" piece,[31] but it is most strikingly evident in his project to compose a whole series of sacred chorale cantatas. As he began rehearsals of the passion music in 1827–28, he also addressed the task of composing sacred cantatas based on Lutheran hymns that would be more than mere imitations of past forms. A gift of a volume of Luther's hymn texts from a friend in Vienna as he began his southern European trip in the summer of 1830 gave new impetus to this project. To the two completed cantatas of 1827–28 he now added plans for eight more. As Mendelssohn traveled through the Catholic centers of southern Europe, he persisted in this distinctively Protestant and German project. When he arrived in Paris in late 1831 he had composed cantatas for all but the final hymn on his list – the great popular anthem "*Ein' feste Burg*" ("A Mighty Fortress"). As Mendelssohn put the finishing touches to his score of the Reformation Symphony, he may very well have decided that the final cantata of his project was already

[28] Abraham Mendelssohn repeats this comment of Felix back to him in a letter of March 10, 1835, in *Briefe*, vol. 2, 52.

[29] In a letter to Franz Hauser in 1830, he described the 1829 performance: "They sang as if they were in a religious service, as if they were in a church." Cited in Grossmann-Vendrey, *Felix Mendelssohn Bartholdy und die Musik der Vergangenheit*, p. 49. Fanny described the performances similarly in a letter to Klingemann on March 22, 1829, in *Familie Mendelssohn*, p. 239.

[30] Arno Forchert, "Von Bach zu Mendelssohn," in Wagner, *Bachtage Berlin* (1985), pp. 211–33. The formation of the canonical tradition of German serious art music in relation to its historical "others" has recently been analyzed in Bernd Sponheuer, "Reconstructing Ideal Types of the 'German' in Music," in Celia Applegate and Pamela Potter, eds., *Music and German National Identity* (Chicago and London: 2002), 36–58.

[31] See, especially, Wulf Konold's analysis of no. 3 and no. 5 of Mendelssohn's opus 7 (*Sieben Charakterstuecke fuer Klavier – 1827*), in Wulf Konold, *Felix Mendelssohn Bartholdy und seine Zeit* (Laaber: 1984), pp. 141ff.

written: the symphony's finale is entitled "*Choral: Ein' feste Burg.*"[32] Within the context of Mendelssohn's critical years of self-definition between 1827–32, the Reformation Symphony emerges as an integral part of the larger project to recreate the essence of Bach's sacred music for a new age.

Two elements of Mendelssohn's chorale cantata project are especially significant for interpreting the content and form of the Reformation Symphony. The first is the imitative dimension of Mendelssohn's compositions. Even some of Mendelssohn's closest friends, who had wholeheartedly supported the revival of the *St. Matthew Passion*, were concerned that Mendelssohn might dissipate his energies in the antiquarian activity of writing baroque liturgical music. Devrient wished that Mendelssohn would focus his talents on opera composition and thus speak more directly in the idiom of his own age.[33] However, Mendelssohn insisted with some vehemence that his cantatas were not mere acts of historical piety but authentic expressions of his current feelings. If his responses to Luther's hymn texts sounded similar to the music of Bach, he insisted, it was not due to mere imitation but because he must at some level have felt the same way Bach did when he read those words or heard those tunes. The similarity in musical language was based on a similarity of inspiration and spiritual content.[34] His chorale cantatas were creative acts of cultural translation, mediating the spirit of the historical letter to a new generation. In a letter to Zelter he insisted that his apparently imitative composition was a "development" rather than "a lifeless repetition."[35] Recent analyses of some of Mendelssohn's chorale cantatas have in fact pointed out the ways in which Mendelssohn adapted and revised the traditional texts and melodies, and freely appropriated Bach's musical forms on the basis of neoclassical and Romantic usages of tonal tension, melodic continuity, and instrumental sonority in order to communicate a personal aesthetic response to the Protestant German heritage.[36]

The creative freedom with which Mendelssohn appropriated the forms of the past, however, led to criticism from the older generation. Zelter and Abraham Mendelssohn both expressed reservations about the free development of the texts and tunes of the Lutheran hymns, an integral component of the traditional Protestant liturgy. Zelter noted that the chorales belonged to the Protestant congregation and expressed the distinguishing doctrine of German Protestantism – the priesthood of all believers. If the tunes were

[32] The whole "Lutheran" project is outlined in Mendelssohn's letter to Zelter from Venice of October 16, 1830: *Briefe*, vol. 2, pp. 37–38. For a very general overview of the cantatas and their publication history, see Brian Pritchard, "Mendelssohn's Chorale Cantatas: An Appraisal," *Musical Quarterly* 42 (1976): 1–24.

[33] Devrient, *Erinnerungen*, pp. 107–9, 113–15.

[34] Letter to Devrient, July 13, 1831, printed in Devrient, *Erinnerungen*, pp. 114–15.

[35] December 18, 1830, cited in Konold, *Mendelssohn Bartholdy*, p. 140.

[36] See especially R. Larry Todd's analysis of "O Haupt voll Blut und Wunden," in "A Passion Cantata by Mendelssohn," *American Choral Review* 25 (1983): 2–17.

simply used as motifs in a composition, the composer was free to use them as he saw fit, but if they were actually cited as chorales they should be left alone.[37] Mendelssohn's father felt that "no liberties ought ever to be taken with a chorale," because it was so bound to its liturgical function.[38]

Although Mendelssohn published two of his cantatas in 1830 under the title of "Church Music" ("*Kirchliche Musik*"), it is not at all clear that he intended his series of chorale cantatas for liturgical purposes. There is little reason to doubt the sincerity of the religious feelings and convictions expressed in his sacred music. Contemporaries like Berlioz, who encountered Mendelssohn in Rome in 1830–31, found him a rather naïve, but firm, Protestant believer, who could easily be scandalized by jokes about the Bible.[39] During the late 1820s, Mendelssohn associated with a number of Schleiermacher's students, like Julius Schubring and Albert Christian Baur, who remained lifelong friends, and in November 1830 he wrote to one of them that he had become a "disciple of Schleiermacher."[40] He made this claim, however, to indicate the cultured, ecumenical, liberal character of his religiosity, and to differentiate his views from the confessional dogmatism and religious display of contemporary fundamentalists. Mendelssohn found it difficult to disassociate confessional and musical loyalties. For him the north German Protestant tradition was intrinsically connected to the moral ethos he found in Bach and his followers, and consonant with the inheritance passed down by his parents.

When Mendelssohn was born in Hamburg, in February 1809, religious or confessional identity in both of his parents' extended families was an issue of some confusion and conflict. His mother's brother, Jacob Salomon, had converted to Protestantism and changed his name to Bartholdy. Two of his father's sisters, Dorothea Veit Schlegel (who had already converted to Protestantism in 1804) and Henriette Mendelssohn, had recently converted to Catholicism. Although the 1812 Prussian Edict of Emancipation seemed to promise full civic rights to Jews, a state council order of 1816 provided a restrictive interpretation of the edict that reneged on much of that promise. Soon after this order, Abraham Mendelssohn decided to have his four children baptized into the Protestant church in Berlin. This baptism was not publicly announced and was kept a secret from certain family members – such as Felix's orthodox Jewish grandmother on his mother's side, Bella Salomon. The parents were baptized secretly during a trip to Frankfurt six

[37] In an unpublished letter from 1830, cited in Eric Werner, *Mendelssohn: Leben und Werk in neuer Sicht* (Zurich: 1980), p. 306.

[38] Letter to Felix Mendelssohn, March 10, 1835, *Briefe*, vol. 2, p. 52.

[39] See his comments in letters from 1831, May and September, in Hector Berlioz, *Correspondence Generale*, ed. Pierre Cirton (Paris: 1972), vol. 1, pp. 441, 486–87, as well as Hector Berlioz, *Memoirs*, transl. David Cairns (New York: 1969), p. 293.

[40] Letter to Julius Schubring, Nov. 18, 1830, in *Briefwechsel zwischen Felix Mendelssohn und J. Schubring* (Leipzig: 1892), p. 15.

years later, in 1822, and a public announcement together with the addition of the "Christian" name – Bartholdy – was not made until after the death of Bella Salomon in 1825. Confessional identities were thus quite confused and often secretive and hidden within Mendelssohn's family during his childhood.[41] Family loyalty (and thus to some extent Jewish "ethnic" identity) within a family clan that included Jews, Protestants, and Catholics required a downplaying of confessional differences.

In a retrospective self-justification contained in an 1829 letter to Felix, Abraham Mendelssohn tried to explain the principles that had guided the religious education of his children. What he had inherited from his illustrious father, the philosopher Moses Mendelssohn, he claimed, was the firm conviction that "truth is one and eternal while its forms are multiple and historically transient." He had thus educated his children, as long as political circumstances permitted, "free of all religious forms." The Mendelssohn children, though they were only baptized in 1816 (when Fanny was eleven and Felix seven), had never been educated in the Jewish religion, though they obviously assimilated some knowledge of Jewish traditions from the extended family and maintained a general ethnic loyalty and sensitivity to their Jewish heritage. Abraham's religious commitments were to the creed of the Savoyard Vicar in Rousseau's *Emile* – a universal, "natural" religion grounded in obligation to the voice of conscience, as it expressed itself through the feelings of the heart, especially the social sentiments of family life. His original intent had been to allow his children to choose the appropriate historical form for their religious beliefs and moral convictions when they reached the age of majority. Historical developments after the collapse of the Napoleonic empire, however, had forced his hand. Faced with the decision of deciding for his children, he chose the "Christian form." He felt no "inner calling" to educate them as Jews, since Judaism was the most "antiquated, corrupt, self-contradictory and impractical" of historical religious forms. Christianity, on the other hand, was the "purest" of natural religion's transient forms, and the most modern, "recognized by the greatest number of civilized peoples."[42]

Mendelssohn certainly retained much of his father's belief in a natural religion whose moral and cognitive content was expressed in the universal "spiritual" essence discernible within the various "letters" of the

[41] These confessional confusions and secrets were described by Fanny Mendelssohn's suitor Wilhelm Hensel in a letter to his sister Luise in December 1823 as he tried to explain why his commitment to Fanny could not take the form of a public engagement. The letter is printed in Felix Gilbert, ed., *Bankiers, Kuenstler und Gelehrte, Unveroeffentlichte Briefe der Familie Mendelssohn aus dem 19. Jahrhundert* (Tuebingen: 1975), pp. 57–61.

[42] Abraham to Felix Mendelssohn, July 8, 1829, in Werner, *Mendelssohn*, 59–61. This letter is consistent with the long letters Abraham Mendelssohn sent to Fanny at the time of her confirmation classes in 1819. See Abraham to Fanny Mendelssohn, April 5, 1819, and midsummer, 1820, in *Die Familie Mendelssohn*, pp. 117–22.

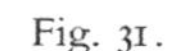
I
Andante.
Flauti.
Oboi.
Clarinetti in C.
Fagotti.
Corni in D.
Tromboni Alto e Tenore.
Trombone Basso.
Trombe in D.
Timpani in D. A.
Violino I.
Violino II.
Viola.
Violoncello.
Basso.
div.
Andante.
A
a 2.
cresc.

Fig. 31.

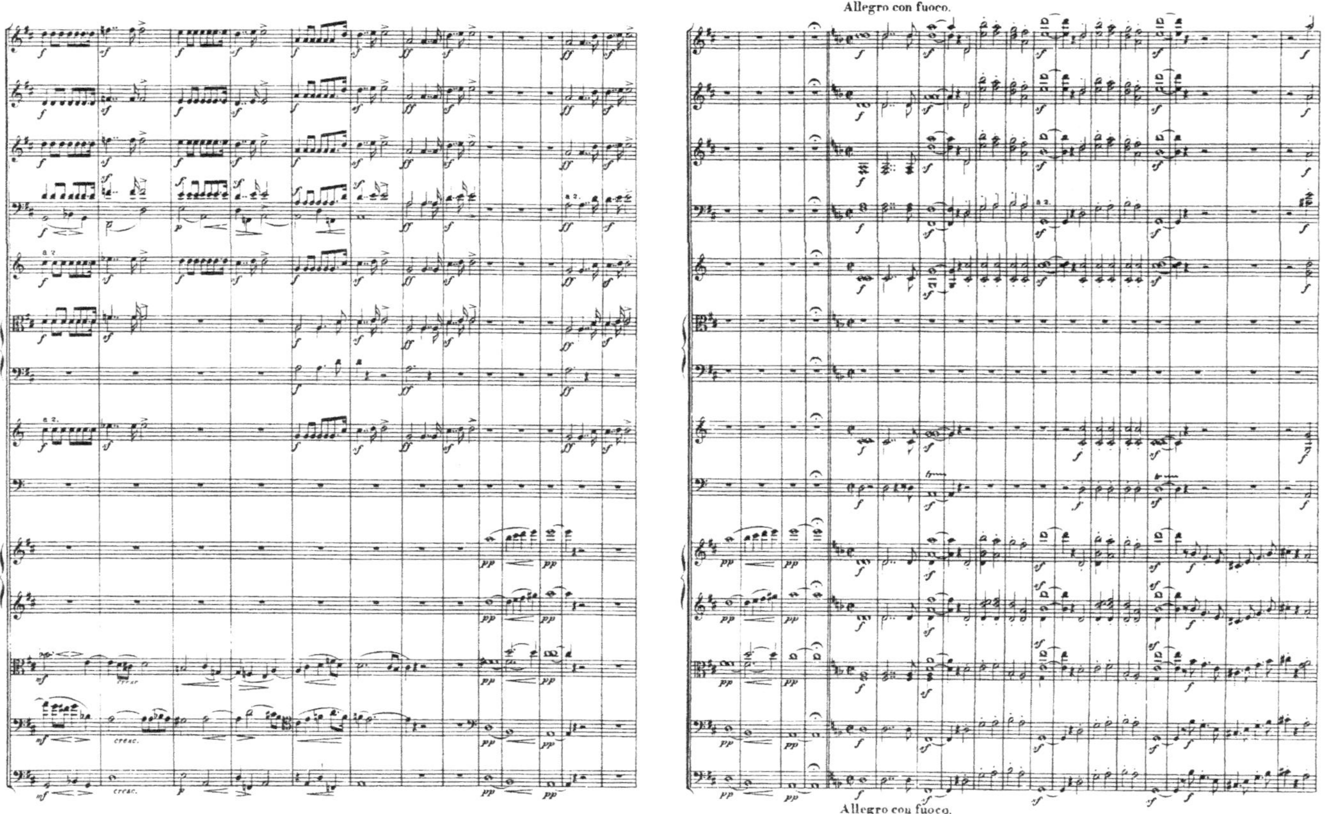

Figs. 31 and 32. The musical subject as historical citation: the opening andante and transition to the allegro of the Reformation Symphony.
Source: Reproduced from the Gregg Press facsimile edition of the *Werke* (Leipzig: Breitkopf and Haertel, 1874–77).

historical religions, but he did develop a more comfortable emotional and personal relationship to the specific historical symbols of Protestant Christianity than members of the older generation of Jewish converts. What differentiated the younger generation from their parents was not so much a withdrawal from ecumenical universalism, as a more pronounced sentimental and evangelical piety in their relation to specific historical forms, such as sacred texts and church liturgy, that suggested a transcendent ground for ethical life. What appeared especially noteworthy about Mendelssohn's piety in the years around 1830 was his interest in articulating the fulfillment of the personal religious quest within the forms of religious community, musically expressed in the chorale. The chorale became a musical symbol for the communal foundations of his religious faith and ethical principles, pointing to the hidden, essential truth within the historical forms of the traditional ecclesiastical service. In Bach's compositions Mendelssohn found a model for the elevation of such historical forms to the universality of art. In fact, he would not concede that Bach's passions and cantatas could be reduced to their liturgical function, and thus subordinated to the specific ecclesiastical needs of their time. The *St. Matthew Passion*, he insisted, was an "autonomous piece of music" designed for religious "edification" (*Erbauung*).[43]

The transformative and creative historicism evident in Mendelssohn's cantata project was also clearly present in the Reformation Symphony. The basic musical materials of the symphony, as well as its musical "resolution" in the finale, are presented through striking citations from the liturgical tradition. The forty-one-measure opening andante (an introduction to both the first-movement allegro and the symphony as a whole) functions generally as a textual citation from which the explications and interpretations of the remainder of the work evolve and from which its ultimate unity derives (Figs. 31 and 32) This introductory text is itself composed of direct thematic and formal citations from liturgical music, at least in some of its most characteristic parts.[44] The rising phrase of the opening canon, with its modal intervals and dark dissonances at the entry point of each new instrumental voice, simulates the opening phrase of the traditional chant of the *Magnificat* canticle (with its Gregorian associations) – Mary's hymn of praise. Prefiguring the general structure and message of the symphony, the elevation of the individual soul into the divine order culminates in the descending homophonic harmonies of a choralelike phrase. After a brief development in which the polyphonic

[43] In a letter to Pastor Albert Baur, January 12, 1835, *Briefe*, vol. 2, pp. 47–48.

[44] See, especially, Martin Witte, "Zur Programmgebundenheit der Sinfonien Mendelssohn," *Das Problem Mendelssohn*, ed. Carl Dahlhaus (Regensburg: 1974), pp. 120–22; Wulf Konold, "Opus 11 und Opus 107; Analytische Bemerkungen zu zwei unbekannten Sinfonien Felix Mendelssohn Bartholdys," in *Felix Mendelssohn Bartholdy*, ed. H. K. Metzger and Rainer Riehn (Munich: 1980), pp. 19–21; Mathias Thomas, *Das Instrumental werk Felix Mendelssohn-Bartholdys. Eine systematische-theoretische Untersuchung unter besonderer Beruecksichtigung der zeitgenoessischen Musiktheorie* (Goettingen: 1972), pp. 243–45.

and homophonic moments are divided into a conflict between lower strings continuing the contrapuntal phrase and the winds transforming the chorale-like phrase into a unison fanfare, Mendelssohn brings in the violins for the first time, answering a fortissimo fanfare of the winds with an eerily transcendent phrase of ascending fifths in pianissimo that imitates the concluding Amen (conventionally chanted to the words "and with thy spirit") from the doxology of the Saxon Lutheran liturgy (and thus referred to as the Dresden Amen, but more familiar perhaps to later listeners as the "Grail motif" in Wagner's *Parsifal*). Even without specific knowledge of these citations, however, it is easy enough to recognize the liturgical reference in the opening canon, the chorale of the descending chords, and the transcending spirituality of the violin phrase. In fact, these opening forty-one measures are obviously not simply a presentation of musical material, the creation of a musical field, from which a meaningful structure will be constructed; they are already loaded with meaning brought into the music from elsewhere and constitute a rich musical text that must be explicated and interpreted, like a citation from biblical revelation at the head of a sermon.

The second obvious "external" liturgical reference in the symphony is the full citation and exposition of Luther's hymn "*Ein' feste Burg*" in the finale. This citation plays a complex double role in the symphony. On the one hand it is a part of the interpretation and development of the opening citations, an unveiling of the meaning of the "spirit" theme and the relationship between string counterpoint and unison winds. But it is also a "given" text in its own right whose meaning must be interpreted and integrated into the musical structure of the symphony. One might say that the ultimate interpretation of the opening text comes through transcendent revelation, or at least external reference, and that this transcendent quality must be assimilated, made immanent, to conclude the musical piece.

Finally, it is important to note Mendelssohn's use of formal citations, his imitations of musical forms traditionally associated with sacred vocal music, not only that of the traditional liturgy, but especially of J. S. Bach. Such historical citations would include the figuration and harmonization of the chorale in the finale, the heavy uses of fugue and fugato to articulate the analytical dissection and working over (the development) of thematic and harmonic materials in the first and last movements, and especially the overall cantatalike structure of the last two movements, in which a slow movement echoing the forms of recitative and aria is followed by an elaborate figured chorale (Fig. 33).

If one continues this mode of analysis, pursuing references to, or echoes of, liturgical and historical sacred music, the Reformation Symphony, in keeping with its title, can rapidly be transformed into what might be called an historical program symphony, in which the external references needed to discern the meaning of the notes are not so much particular actions or scenes but textual citations and historical forms. Moreover, Mendelssohn's

Fig. 33. Instrumental sacred music: the transition from aria to chorale in the Reformation Symphony.
Source: Reproduced from the Gregg Press facsimile edition of the *Werke* (Leipzig: Breitkopf and Haertel, 1874–77).

musical interpretation and integration of these references could be read as an historical narrative of the religious "idea" from the time of the Lutheran reformation, a story of the historical struggles and ultimate communal triumph of the Protestant principle of spiritual freedom as the subjective assimilation of divine will.[45] From this perspective, the first-movement allegro con fuoco might represent the moment of religious conflict and war in which two interpretations of the spirit motif take on militant form, oppose each other as exclusive opposites, represented by Mendelssohn not only in terms of tonal oppositions but also by instrumental (strings versus winds) and formal (polyphony versus homophony) antiphonies. The development section of the movement culminates in a radical expression of this opposition, which is silenced only by the reentry of the motif in its original form. A reflective, composed, somewhat resigned recapitulation and coda conclude the movement. The second movement, a classical scherzo–trio, seems like an entry into a different world, with its idyllic, secular dance rhythms, ceremonial march music, and harmonic consonances. Only a few darker dissonant moments indicate that this intermezzo of popular celebration and secular optimism might be an illusion. The third movement, a short andante (fifty-four measures), however, returns to the religious theme expressed as suffering and longing through a combination of traditional aria–recitative forms with modern, "romantic" song forms. This subjective plea for salvation leads directly into the exposition of the chorale that begins the finale. The message thus seems to be that the longing of the romantic subject will be stilled, the dissonance of the separation of self from the other will be resolved, through elevation into the community of the spirit, through collective appropriation of the divine revelation in the congregation, or, in secularized form, the nation. Yet this "idea" of the communal incarnation of the spirit remains isolated, surrounded by countervailing forces, and must win its way to triumph in the world, just as the chorale in Mendelssohn's composition must go through a lengthy process of variation and development before it can assimilate the other musical forces that Mendelssohn has put into play and penetrate the whole structure of the symphony. As in his musical commentary on Bach's passions and cantatas, Mendelssohn's view in the Reformation Symphony appears to be that Bach's musical forms provide the means for a transition from the purely confessional meaning of

[45] In a long analysis of Mendelssohn's symphonic music published after this chapter was completed, Thomas Grey recognized that "Ein feste Burg" could be read as an emblem not only of the Lutheran Reformation but also of a certain form of national community during Mendelssohn's own time, thus overlaying the historical narrative of the symphony with an account of Mendelssohn's assimilation to contemporary German Protestant culture. See Thomas Grey, "The Orchestral Music," in Seaton, ed., *Mendelssohn Companion*, pp. 416–26. Judith Silber Ballan has argued that the programmatic historical narrative of the symphony was inspired in large part by the ideas of Mendelssohn's influential older friend Adolf Bernhard Marx about narrative music. See Silber Ballan, "Marxian Programmatic Music: A Stage in Mendelssohn's Musical Development," in R. Larry Todd, ed., *Mendelssohn Studies* (Cambridge and New York: 1992), pp. 154–55.

the Protestant idea to its universal, human meaning. But in the Reformation Symphony, Bach's musical forms remained a historical reference. The ultimate integration of content into form occurs through the assimilation of citations of Bach's sacred music into the structures of the classical symphony as it had developed in the works of Haydn, Mozart, and especially Beethoven. For Bach to become a living moment in the present, he had to be assimilated and transformed into a dimension of Beethoven.

Mendelssohn had been introduced to the music of Beethoven early in his development, not so much by Zelter, who found Beethoven largely incomprehensible, but by his instrumental teachers in piano (Ludwig Berger) and violin (Eduard Rietz). By 1825 he could write a birthday letter to Fanny that took on the Beethoven persona. Speaking in the voice of the older, isolated, and misunderstood Beethoven, who had moved beyond the popular music of his youth in his search for originality and truth, Mendelssohn praised his sister for her performances of Beethoven's later keyboard works and sent her a copy of the *Hammerklavier* sonata (opus 106).[46] The devotion to Beethoven's later work solidified Mendelssohn's friendship with Adolf Bernhard Marx, whose journalistic writings and polemical books elevated Beethoven's chamber and symphonic music to the status of a culminating fulfillment of the classical ideal.[47] The devotion to Beethoven produced clear tensions with Zelter and Mendelssohn's father, who tended to hear only the contrasts and dissonances on the surface of Beethoven's music and feared for the collapse of all musical structure, order, and harmony. For a few years the Beethoven debate in the Mendelssohn household clearly expressed and exacerbated generational tensions.[48] For Felix, Fanny, Marx, and the other young Beethovenites, Beethoven's instrumental music expressed the tension-filled and complex unity within difference of their historical experience. Marx declared the classical symphony the most significant instrument for the moral and philosophical education of the public.[49] In the classical symphony, music fulfilled the sacred duties of art completely within its own terms, without the aid of words, scenic representation, or the allure of egoistic virtuosity; it emerged as pure tone poetry, as the representation of the "universal idea," and thus as autonomous, "absolute" art.[50]

[46] The letter is printed in Werner, *Mendelssohn* (1980), p. 128.

[47] See especially his article "Etwas ueber die Symphonie und Beethoven's Leistungen in diesem Fache," in *Berliner Allgemeine Musikalische Zeitung* (1824), pp. 165–68, 173–76, 181–84. The same sentiments run through his discussion of the German musical tradition in Adolf Bernhard Marx, *Die Kunst des Gesanges, theoretisch-practisch* (Berlin: 1826).

[48] In a letter to his sisters written from Rome on November 22, 1830, Mendelssohn recalls this tension and even an incident in which his father sent him from the table because of irritation with his incessant advocacy for Beethoven's music. See *Briefe* (Elvers), pp. 127–28.

[49] *Berliner Allgemeine Musikalische Zeitung* (1824), p. 443.

[50] Marx, like Mendelssohn, rejected the notion that music should imitate or represent ("paint") the surface of experienced reality, Yet both clearly also believed that music represented a content – the essence, the idea, the spirit – that existed outside of the musical form itself. Thus music could also

Mendelssohn's absorption in, and creative confrontation with, the later works of Beethoven is especially obvious in the piano sonatas and fantasies (opus 6 in E Major and opus 106 in B flat, opus 28 in F *sharp* minor, opus 15 in E Major) and string quartets (opus 12 and 13) he composed in the second half of the 1820s, although the consequences of this confrontation pervade all of his work.[51] Mendelssohn was particularly fascinated by Beethoven's ability to sustain the identity of the musical idea in his compositions within a context of radical fragmentation and disjuncture. Unlike many recent commentators, Mendelssohn did not perceive this identity in terms of Beethoven's faith in the elemental power of the abstract dynamics of the tonal structure that shaped the sonata form, but in terms of a hidden spiritual subject that provided a narrative core within the kaleidoscope of expressive possibilities.[52] In focusing on, and appropriating for his own compositional use, this particular element in Beethoven's late works, Mendelssohn is sometimes seen as moving from a dramatic to a cyclic conception of musical form, but more appropriate terms for his procedures (and more revealing of their connections to developments in other cultural forms) would be "hermeneutic" or "historicist." In the works of his early maturity, the post-1825 works that bear his clear individual signature, the unity of the composition is usually defined not by structural relations of opposition and synthesis but by the unveiling of an underlying subject through a series of episodes, by the bringing to light of an essence joining together a succession of appearances. This subject is often introduced at the beginning as a citation that then undergoes musical interpretation until it returns in transformed guise at the end of the musical narrative. The well-known quartet opus 13, based on the song "The Question" (*Die Frage*), which Mendelssohn composed separately from, and prior to, the quartet, is a striking example of this technique, but his famous program overtures (most of which were composed between 1826 and 1832) clearly have a similar organizational

represent the idea present in other art forms, like poetry or painting. It could recreate the "soul" of such works as experienced by the composer. See Adolf Bernhard Marx, *Ueber Malerei in der Tonkunst: Ein Maigruss an die Kunstphilosophen* (Berlin: 1828). Marx played a major role in encouraging Mendelssohn to compose concert overtures as tone poems that recreated the "ideas" of literary masterpieces, as in the overture to "*Midsummer Night's Dream*" or "*Calm Sea and Prosperous Voyage*."

[51] For interesting analyses of Mendelssohn's struggle with Beethoven in the late 1820s, see Joscelyn Godwin, "Mendelssohn and Late Beethoven," *Music and Letters* 55 (1974): 272–85; Gerd Schoenfelder, "Zur Frage des Realismus bei Mendelssohn," in Gerhard Schuhmacher, ed., *Felix Mendelssohn Bartholdy* (Darmstadt: 1982): 354–75; and especially Friedhelm Krummacher, *Mendelssohn- Der Komponist. Studien zur Kammermusik fuer Streicher* (Munich: 1978), pp. 70–73; and Konold, *Mendelssohn Bartholdy*, pp. 111–38.

[52] Mendelssohn views on Beeteehoven's compositional strategies are most forcefully stated in his analyses of the late quartets in letters to his Swedish friend Adolf Fredrik Lindblad in the spring of 1828. See *Bref til Adolf Fredrik Lindblad*, ed. L. Dahlgren (Stockholm: 1913), pp. 18–26. For a modern interpretation of how Beethoven sustained the classical principles of the sonata form, see Charles Rosen, *The Classical Style: Haydn, Mozart, Beethoven* (New York: 1972).

structure. Mendelssohn did not abandon the frame of inherited classical sonata form. Most of his instrumental music can be analytically dissected easily enough according to the standard schema of exposition, development, recapitulation, and coda, with the appropriate thematic and tonal relations, but Mendelssohn hollowed out this form, since the exposition of oppositions and their ultimate reconciliation was no longer the driving impetus of his compositions. Instead, his works derived their energy from the purpose pursued by the musical subject through a progress of many episodes that might encompass not only single movements but also a whole multimovement work and that might end at different points. The subject was given, albeit often in undeveloped or not fully interpreted form. The musical process provided the interpretation, revealing the subject as the hidden identity tying together its various moments. From this perspective, the Reformation Symphony displays a formal similarity to Mendelssohn's other instrumental works from the period 1825–32, including the first drafts of the unpublished Italian Symphony (opus 90), composed at virtually the same time. It begins with a musical subject that is already semantically rich and present in a characteristic, particular, recognizable form. This theme becomes the unifying, "hidden" core of the ensuing musical moments (that operate more like historical episodes or scenes than structural oppositions), and goes through a process leading to a "return" in which the various moments are "remembered" as elements of the same subject. In the Reformation Symphony, the tonal intervals of the "spirit" theme function in this fashion. A number of analysts have noted that the major themes of all movements in the symphony are derived in some way from this central motif. Mendelssohn does not build an independent musical world from elemental musical parts, but unveils both the essential identity underlying the appearances of the musical surface, and the progressive enrichment of the meaning of that identity in the process of musical interpretation. Thus the classicism of the sonata form does not really provide the final frame for Mendelssohn's historical references, but itself becomes a historical structure adapted and revised from a Romantic perspective in which expressive subjectivity, rather than classically structured dramatic order, dominates. Luther, Bach and Beethoven are all absorbed as historical moments in the narrative of the Romantic subject.

The character of the direct citations and historical references in the Reformation Symphony, however, add a further problem to its analysis. The citations from the Catholic and Lutheran liturgy and from Bach's sacred music all imply reference to a transcendent religious dimension, to a revelation that precedes and preforms the musical structure of the work. The "spirit" is not just an immanent principle that reveals itself as the unity of the musical structure, but also a transcendent power that must be appropriated by the immanent processes of the musical composition. The climactic moment in this process of incarnation or appropriation is the entry of the chorale at the beginning of the finale, a moment in which a new transcendent intervention occurs through a musical element whose preexisting, highly charged meanings must also be assimilated. The last movement thus recapitulates the narrative structure of the whole symphony, as Mendelssohn attempts to absorb the musical form of the chorale within the structure of a sonata movement, or, more accurately, as he tries to reconcile the chorale and the sonata movement from a broader perspective in which both become means for the expression of the spirit. The final movement seems to become excessively complex and "intellectual" in its layering of different forms that only gradually reveal their interrelationship and finally merge in the concluding recapitulation of the final two lines of the chorale. The chorale does not simply function as a theme within the sonata structure, but as an independent musical form, fully stated and developed, that is gradually intertwined and merged with the sonata form, which also begins with the appearance of independence and autonomy. The symphony thus becomes an attempt to reconcile not only opposing forces within a common framework, but also different formal structures, immanent and transcendent perspectives, secular and sacred worlds. Finally understood and assimilated by the collective human subject, the transcendent spirit becomes the ruling immanent spirit of the historical and natural worlds.

As a complex amalgamation of different historical musical styles and as an heroic attempt to assimilate liturgical music with its transcendent references into the immanent "pantheism" of the instrumental symphony, the Reformation Symphony was also a personal and ideological statement that articulated, perhaps in a somewhat forced and artificial way, a resolution of Mendelssohn's difficult search for a satisfactory cultural identity. It seemed to affirm with conviction both his membership in German national culture and the Protestant Christian tradition. His symphony expressed not only an interpretation of the Protestant Reformation but also advocated reformation in a more general sense, as an appropriate attitude toward the historical assimilation of his cultural inheritance. The essence of the past, the idea of spiritual community hidden within the historical forms of the confessional church, was to be sustained and revived in the present as both the core contemporary German national culture and an open-ended, universal human possibility.

Mendelssohn had been sent on his European tour of 1830–32 specifically to explore the various possibilities of cultural identification and musical style that were available to him. Abraham Mendelssohn clearly was much more enthusiastic about this trip than his son, and open to the possibility that Mendelssohn might establish himself as conductor or composer in France, England, or Italy. At the end of his journey, Mendelssohn confirmed a choice from which he had never really wavered: He would make his home somewhere within the German cultural sphere, the only place where he really felt at home, musically and ethically.[53] Mendelssohn made this choice despite his discomfort with many of the postwar forms of nationalist enthusiasm – including national "folk" music – and his constant dissatisfaction, as a reformist liberal, with the state of German political life.[54] The elements of continuity in this cosmopolitan liberalism with the older generation of assimilated Jews, like his father, was unmistakable and recognized, but Mendelssohn also was clearly more attached to German culture, especially its Protestant northern German variety, than members of his father's generation, who could quite easily imagine Felix at home in Paris or London.[55]

Mendelssohn's commitment to Protestant Christianity contained the same elements of continuity and discontinuity with the older generation. For Mendelssohn's father, conversion to Christianity had been a cultural rather than a religious act. Christianity was merely the most historically progressive and culturally dominant form of natural religion.[56] Mendelssohn maintained significant elements of this outlook. He seemed as comfortable with Goethe's neoclassical humanism as his father and his father's generation had been. In fact, while he was composing the chorale cantatas he was also at work on a secular cantata (eventually published in 1843 as *Die Erste Walpurgisnacht*, opus 60), based on a Goethe poem that celebrated the universal ethical dimensions of pre-Christian pagan religion and in which Christian priests appeared as misguided, persecuting dogmatists.[57] But Mendelssohn also seemed more open to the claim that Christianity, and especially German Protestant Christianity, was not merely one of any number of possible historical expressions of natural religion, but a culminating fulfillment of religious history. Thus, in his response to the visionary prophecies of the Saint-Simonians in Paris in 1831–32, Mendelssohn completely rejected the notion that a new religion would replace Christianity. The ideas trumpeted as novel by the Saint-Simonians – universal brotherhood, the end of egoism,

[53] See his letter to Zelter, February 15, 1832, from Paris, in which he claimed that his travels had convinced him that that he was really a German who could only feel truly at home within his own culture, and to his father, February 21, 1832, in which he insists that Germany provides the only satisfactory moral atmosphere for the kind of music he wanted to write: *Briefe* (Elvers), pp. 150–1; *Briefe*, vol. 1, pp. 321–22.

[54] See his comment from a letter of August 25, 1829, to his father during his English trip, *Briefe* (Elvers), p. 85.

[55] See Mendelssohn's letter from Paris to his father, December 19, 1831, in *Briefe*, vol. 1, pp. 284–94.

[56] Abraham Mendelssohn's position is most succinctly stated in a letter to Fanny on the occasion of her confirmation, in *Die Familie Mendelssohn*, 120–22. The general problem of conversion in Abraham Mendelssohn's generation within the Mendelssohn family is analyzed in Gilbert, *Bankiers, Kuenstler und Gelehrte*, pp. xvi–xxviii.

[57] See especially Konold, *Mendelssohn Bartholdy*, pp. 93–109; and Richard Hauser, "In ruehrend feierlichen Toenen, Mendelssohn's Kantate *Die erste Walpurgisnacht*," in Metzger and Riehn, eds., *Mendelssohn Bartholdy*, pp. 75–91.

the purely "mythical" reality of hell, the devil and damnation – were all, he insisted, contained within the Christian idea and merely needed to be revived through reform and reinterpretation in each historical generation.[58]

Similarly, Mendelssohn, unlike his father, felt that he could retain his Jewish identity within the larger frame of Christianity. In the late 1820s he and his siblings had a number of confrontations with their father about the use of the Christian name of Bartholdy as a replacement for Mendelssohn. His father insisted that "a Christian Mendelssohn is an impossibility," but Felix had no difficulty in perceiving himself as a "Christian Mendelssohn."[59] By clearly identifying himself as Felix Mendelssohn Bartholdy throughout his adult life, Mendelssohn did distance himself somewhat from his father's teleological conception of history, in which obsolete Jewish confessional forms were rejected in favor of more "advanced" Christian forms, although it was only in the 1840s that he moved more self-consciously toward a position of simultaneous rather than historically sequential cultural identities.

During the late 1820s in Berlin, Mendelssohn felt that his emerging vision of cultural transformation as a progressive historicism in which the spiritual essence of the cultural community was continually renewed and assimilated through processes of interpretation and reform was shared by his generational cohort. He lived and worked within the exhilarating and sustaining context of a circle of musicians, artists, students, scholars, and writers who seemed to share and mutually reinforce a common sense of historical purpose and cultural identity. His experiences with German exiles (like

[58] In a letter to his family, January 14, 1832, printed in Ralph P. Locke, "Mendelssohn's Collision with the Saint-Simonians," in Jon W. Finson and R. Larry Todd, eds., *Mendelssohn and Schumann: Essays on Their Music and Its Context* (Durham, N.C.: 1984), p. 120.

[59] Abraham Mendelssohn's comment is from a letter to Felix in London, July 8, 1829, after he had heard that Felix had allowed his concerts to be advertised under the name Mendelssohn. The letter is reprinted in Eric Werner, "Felix Mendelssohn – Gustav Mahler: Two Borderline Cases of German–Jewish Assimilation," *Yuval* 4 (1982): 252–53. A recent article by Jeffrey Sposato instigated a debate in the pages of *Musical Quarterly* about Werner's tendency to exaggerate these disagreements (with the help of some "creative" interpretation as well as "creative" transcription of documents) to make a case for Felix's strong self-identification as a Jew. Michael Steinberg and Leon Botstein, although recognizing Werner's distortions of the record, continue to insist that the issue of Jewish identity played an important role in Mendelssohn's historical self-consciousness. See Jeffrey Sposato, "Creative Writing: The [Self-] Identification of Mendelssohn as Jew," *Musical Quarterly* 82 (1998): 190–209; Leon Botstein, "Mendelssohn and the Jews," *Musical Quarterly* 82 (1998): 210–19; Michael Steinberg, "Mendelssohn's Music and German–Jewish Culture," *Musical Quarterly* 83 (1999): 31–44; Leon Botstein, "Mendelssohn, Werner, and the Jews: A Final Word," *The Musical Quarterly* 83 (1999): 45–50. For the general context of these debates in the history of Prussian, and especially Berlin Jews in the period from the late Enlightenment to the 1830s, see Albert A. Bruer, *Geschichte der Juden in Preussen (1750–1820)* (Frankfurt: 1991); Deborah Hertz, *Jewish High Society in Old Regime Berlin* (New Haven: 1988); and Steven M. Lowenstein, *The Berlin Jewish Community: Enlightenment, Family and Crisis, 1770–1830* (New York: 1994).

Heine, Boerne, and Meyerbeer)[60] and the Saint-Simonians in Paris after the revolutions of 1830, however, began to raise doubts in his mind about the progressive historical character of the younger generation or the broader public to which they appealed. The fate of the symphonic statement that articulated his notion of cultural transformation through historical reform – the Reformation Symphony – appeared to confirm his doubts. After rehearsing the symphony, the orchestra of the Paris Conservatory refused to perform it in public. The players judged it "much too learned, too much fugato, too little melody"[61] and also, as Mendelssohn insinuated in one letter, perhaps too German.[62] After conducting the symphony himself in a benefit concert in Berlin (its only public performance during his lifetime) in the fall of 1832, Mendelssohn was defeated by a 2 to 1 margin in his reluctant bid (encouraged by his parents) to succeed Zelter as director of the Singakademie. His victorious opponent was a long-term assistant director of the Singakademie, and the election was marred by anti-Semitic innuendo. Both factors clearly deepened Mendelssohn's growing sense of being suddenly out of step with his age and his culture.[63]

By the time of this defeat, in January 1833, Mendelssohn's sense of cultural isolation had deepened into a serious psychological depression, marked by self-questioning and doubts about the viability of his compositions and their relation to the "spirit" of his age. The series of deaths in 1832 that robbed him of two of his primary cultural mentors (Goethe and Zelter), as well as a number of personal friends, reinforced the feeling of abandonment he felt as he returned to Berlin in summer 1832 and found that most of his friends from the late 1820s had moved elsewhere or changed so much that he felt uncomfortable in their company. A few months after returning to Berlin, he wrote to Klingemann in London: "For several weeks now I have been feeling so unspeakably low and so deeply depressed that I can't even express my mood to you."[64] As he began to come out of this depression a few weeks after the disastrous election, he looked back on the previous half year as a time of illness: "finally it really is an illness, and an illness of the worst kind, this uncertainty, these doubts and this insecurity."[65]

In the context of these disillusioning and humiliating experiences, Mendelssohn came to regard his Reformation Symphony as a "total

[60] Mendelssohn's critique of the German exiles in Paris is most fully state in a letter to Carl Immermann on January 11, 1832, in *Briefe*, vol. 1, pp. 301–07.

[61] Ferdinand Hiller, *Mendelssohn. Letters and Recollections* (New York: 1972), p. 21.

[62] From January 7, 1832, cited in Werner, *Mendelssohn* (1980), p. 219.

[63] The election is described in some detail in Werner, *Mendelssohn*, pp. 254–57, who may have exaggerated the role that anti-Semitism played in Mendelssohn's defeat. For a critical reconsideration see Wm. A. Little, "Mendelssohn and the Berliner Singakademie: The Composer at the Crossroads," in R. Larry Todd, ed., *Mendelssohn and his World* (Princeton, N.J.: 1991), 65–85.

[64] September 5, 1832, in Klingemann, ed, *Briefwechsel*, p. 100. See also *ibid.*, p. 105.

[65] Letter to Pastor Bauer, March 4, 1833, *Briefe*, vol. 2, p. 1.

failure"[66] and never published it or allowed it to be played again during his lifetime. Less than a decade after its inception, he seemed to have come around to the viewpoint of his Parisian critics: It was too learned and unmelodic, its informing ideas were not sensuous enough to be immediately comprehensible at an emotional level, and their significance was connected too much to their external connotations.[67] In light of subsequent events, the symphony's resolutions appeared abstract and artificial, externally forced. But Mendelssohn did not give up on the general project – the creative assimilation of the form and content of traditional sacred music into the idiom of contemporary musical language and cultural consciousness – that had instigated the experiments of the Reformation Symphony and his other compositional projects between 1826 and 1832. The revolutionary hopes and utopian projects of 1830 reinforced his conviction that an authentic ethical community would emerge through creative assimilation of the spiritual essence of the past rather than historical construction of totally new forms and contents. Yet Mendelssohn was no longer convinced that such a reformation would somehow spontaneously arise from the historical triumph of his generation or the self-generating transformation of established institutions. His own generation appeared to have moved away from the liberal reformist center to positions on the right and left that either ossified or denied the legacy of the past.[68] Only his family seemed to remain stable. In fact, after 1832, Mendelssohn found himself rediscovering and cementing his bonds with his father, whose liberal, reformist positions had been reinforced by the events of 1830. What Mendelssohn sought after 1832 was a clearer definition of the foundation and appropriate musical form for his concept of cultural reformation and the most effective means for educating his contemporaries about its historical viability and cultural necessity. As he came out of his winter of depression in the spring of 1833, he began to focus his energies with increasing intensity on a project that was less an expressive celebration of the movement of his times than an attempt to educate his contemporaries about their historical situation and historical tasks. In the spring and early summer of 1833, Mendelssohn accepted two positions, director of the Music Festival of the Lower Rhine and, more permanently, music director for the city of Duesseldorf, which placed him at the center of the development of a new type of civic musical culture among the small town and urban middle classes.[69] His compositional activities in turn became focused on the type of monumental public music that had the greatest appeal and educational effect in such circles – the concert oratorio.

66 Letter to Julius Rietz, June 20, 1838, cited in Thomas, *Instrumentalwerk*, p. 243.

67 Letter to Julius Rietz, April 23, 1841, *Briefe* vol. 2, pp. 186–87.

68 See his lament to Bauer on April 6, 1833, *Briefe*, vol. 2, pp. 3.

69 Cecelia Hopkins Porter,"The New Public and the Reordering of the Musical Establishment: The Lower Rhine Musical Festivals, 1818–1867," *19th-Century Music* 3 (1980): 211–24.

THE SPIRIT IN THE WORLD AND AGAINST THE WORLD: *PAULUS* AND THE HISTORICAL ACTUALIZATION OF THE IDEA

As Mendelssohn returned to Berlin from his European tour in the summer of 1832, there was little indication that the compositional project that would absorb his energies for the next four years would be a sacred concert oratorio. Although the idea of writing an oratorio surfaced briefly during his stay in Italy and was revived by a possible commission from the Frankfurt Caecilian Society on his journey northward in 1831, Mendelssohn's correspondence from these years suggests that he was much more likely to imagine his first public musical project after his return as an opera. On August 27, 1831, he wrote to Devrient that his various musical intentions could best be united in an opera: "For I assure you, I have had, for more than six months, such an unbelievable desire to write an opera, that I can't even think about instrumental music at this moment, because I hear voices and choruses and other demons buzzing in my head, and I won't really have any peace until I have given them form."[70]

Comic opera had been one of the first musical genres to which Mendelssohn had addressed his precocious musical talents in the early 1820s. Between 1820 and 1824 he composed five *Singspiele*, comic operas with spoken dialogue, of increasing length and complexity, culminating in a full-scale two-act opera, *The Wedding of Camacho* (Die Hochzeit des Camacho). These works, which parallel Mendelssohn's twelve youthful string symphonies in many ways, were modeled on the German *Singspiel* tradition of the late eighteenth century, on Carl Maria von Weber's romantic operas, and, especially, in the dramatic musical structures of their ensemble numbers, on the operas of Mozart.[71] Four were chamber pieces written for and performed by family friends and habitués of the Mendelssohn cultural soirees. Submitting to pressure from his parents, however, Mendelssohn agreed in 1827 to submit *The Wedding of Camacho* for public performance in the Royal Playhouse. Although the opera was respectfully received by a friendly audience amazed by the composer's precocious technical talent, Mendelssohn fled before the final curtain, humiliated and embarrassed by a piece he judged as immature and an artistic failure. This experience certainly made Mendelssohn more cautious than he otherwise might have been about composing and publishing in the operatic genre after 1827. As Mendelssohn began to establish a European reputation in 1829–30, his fame was connected to instrumental composition in the genres of chamber and symphonic music, as well as to compositions in the intimate Romantic genre of vocal and piano song, or *Lied*, but he also sought a broader public forum for his musical message

[70] Devrient, *Erinnerungen*, pp. 123–24.

[71] There is an extensive description of Mendelssohn's youthful operatic production in Douglass Seaton, "Mendelssohn's Dramatic Music," in Seaton, ed., *Mendelssohn Companion*, pp. 145–77.

and continued to explore the possibility of composing an opera. Much of Mendelssohn's correspondence, especially with Devrient and Klingemann, was taken up with discussion of possible librettos. But the libretto that would set his compositional genius on fire and allow him to compose from his heart could never be conjured up, until the theme of the inadequate libretto began to sound like a litany of avoidance in his letters.

Mendelssohn's extreme caution about the choice of libretto was connected to his negative stance toward the emergence of grand opera in France. When his father suggested that he seek out a suitable librettist in Paris in 1831, Mendelssohn railed against the immorality (*Unsittlichkeit*) that had corrupted the enormously popular recent operas of Rossini (Guillaume Tell), Auber (La Muette de Portici, Fra Diavolo), and Meyerbeer (Robert le Diable). Not only were their librettos immoral in their appeal to lascivious and voyeuristic instincts, and to the political and national passions of their audiences, but the music itself was also immoral in its insincerity, in its calculated striving for commercial success through exaggerated effects, massive spectacles, and emotional extremes. For Mendelssohn this new opera was clearly outer-directed music, pandering to the worst instincts of its audience, the polar opposite of musical theater as moral education, or *Bildung*. "If this is what the age demands and considers necessary," he complained, "then I will compose ecclesiastical music."[72]

It would be misleading to claim that after 1832 Mendelssohn concentrated on the composition of an oratorio as a simple alternative to opera. He continued to discuss possible opera libretti with his friends after 1832 and never completely gave up on his hopes of writing an opera that would conform in both its words and its music to his moral and cultural vision. But the oratorio Mendelssohn composed did have some of the characteristics of a counteropera: It was a sacred, vocal–instrumental composition, of monumental, evening-filling dimensions with a spiritual text and "pure" music uncorrupted by external spectacles for theatrical effect. When Mendelssohn first conceived the idea for his oratorio, he chose the life and mission of Saint Paul, a clearly nonliturgical theme, and he envisioned it as a three-act drama with didactic moral content. He informed Klingemann in late 1831 that the oratorio would "contain a sermon."[73] Mendelssohn eschewed a modern poetic libretto, using a combination of texts from the Bible. The narrative and dramatic dialogues were extracted from New Testament descriptions of the activities of the apostles and experiences of the early church, and the chorus texts were taken mainly from Old Testament psalms or Protestant

[72] Letter to his father, December 19, 1831, *Briefe*, vol. 1, 285–86. A more sympathetic interpretation of the populist, audience-oriented forms of French grand opera during the 1830s and 1840s can be found in Jane F. Fulcher, *The Nation's Image: French Grand Opera as Politics and Politicized Art* (Cambridge and New York: 1987), especially chapters 1 and 2. Mendelssohn's critique of grand opera was related to his general distrust of the cultural and ethical implications of populist ethnic nationalism.

[73] Letter to Klingemann, December 20, 1831, Klingemann, ed., *Briefwechsel*, p. 90.

chorales. Although Mendelssohn exploited the special knowledge of his friends, especially the theologians among them, for appropriate biblical and hymn passages, he had a very clear concept of the general structure of his dramatic story and pieced their recommendations together according to his own vision. He began with a general sketch of three acts subdivided into scenes along the lines of a theatrical or operatic work.[74] Without the staging and costumes of an opera, however, these scenes become more obviously spiritual or mental "moments" (Mendelssohn's own term)[75] in the development of the musical idea.

Two aspects of Mendelssohn's libretto for *Paulus* were especially striking to his contemporaries. The first was his almost exclusive use of texts from Luther's German Bible. This choice was tied to Mendelssohn's admiration for the dramatic stories and dialogues of the biblical texts, and his dissatisfaction with the sentimental poetic "translations" of the original Christian texts so prevalent in early-nineteenth-century oratorios.[76] Mendelssohn's texts did include framing dogmatic or theological choruses and lyrical reflections on the events of the story, but he greatly extended the use of recitative and dialogue, marking what seemed to many contemporaries a historicist return to the oratorio styles of Bach and Handel. Mendelssohn's libretto also gave his oratorio more of the character of a musical explication of the biblical text, of a radical return to the original sources in order to recover their meaning for the present.

Mendelssohn's use of chorale tunes and texts in Paulus also aroused surprise and controversy among his contemporaries. First, since the Oratorio was clearly not related to a liturgical theme, it was unclear how the chorales were to be interpreted. Within a work so obviously intended as a concert work for a nonecclesiastical audience, the chorale seemed to function either in a purely historical fashion as a representation of the responses of the early apostolic church, or in a symbolic fashion, as in the Reformation Symphony. Mendelssohn claimed that he conceived the chorales in the sense in which they were used in the Bach passions, but in this case the participating, present "congregation" was simply a representative segment of the *Volk* rather than a confessionally defined church membership.[77] Moreover, Mendelssohn took great liberties with both the texts and tunes of the chorales in *Paulus*. One

[74] The process of libretto construction is described in some detail in Arntrud Kurzhals-Reuter, *Die Oratorien Felix Mendelssohn Bartholdys. Untersuchungen zur Quellenlage, Entstehung, Gestaltung und Ueberlieferung* (Tutzing: 1978), pp. 45–68; 97–114.

[75] Letter to Albert Baur, January 12, 1835, *Briefe*, vol. 2, p. 47.

[76] For an interesting discussion of the most popular of these post-Napoleonic "Romantic" oratorios, Friedrich Schneider's *Weltgericht*, see Martin Geck, "Friedrich Schneider's "Weltgericht": Zum Verstaendnis des Trivialen in der Musik," in Carl Dahlhaus, ed., *Studien zur Trivialmusik des 19. Jahrhunderts* (Regensburg: 1967), pp. 97–109.

[77] Letter to Schubring, September 6, 1833, *Briefwechsel zwischen Felix Mendelssohn Bartholdy und Julius Schubring, zugleich ein Beitrag zur Theorie des Oratoriums*, ed. Jul. Schubring (Leipzig: 1892), p. 42.

particular chorale – "Wachet Auf, ruft uns die Stimme" ("Sleepers awake, a voice is calling") – functioned as a unifying text for the whole piece. Other chorales were adapted and transformed to indicate important shifts in the status of the redeemed community as the drama progressed. Here again, Mendelssohn appeared to be returning to Bach, but with a more obviously secular, nonliturgical perspective. Mendelssohn was aware of the disturbing historical associations that would be aroused by his citation and "translation" of musical forms with liturgical associations in his work. The chorale became a musical means for producing consciousness of both historical difference and potential historical connection between the past and the present, of situating the creation of ethical community in historical context.[78]

Mendelssohn's first sketch of the overall structure of the oratorio divided the work into three main parts: the persecution and martyrdom of Saint Stephen, the conversion and baptism of Paul, and the preaching of the gospel by Paul up to the moment of his farewell from the church and return to Jerusalem. In the final version, the first two acts were combined in part 1 of a two-part work, which produced a more obvious distinction between the moment of spiritual enlightenment and moral conversion on the one hand, and the duties and tasks of religious practice and educational dissemination on the other.

Two intertwining themes formed the backbone of Mendelssohn's dramatic narrative. The first was conversion, or spiritual enlightenment. This process was defined as openness to a transcendent truth, as an awakening to the message coming from above, from the father who sustained the metaphysical and moral order in the universe. Stephen emerges in the first scenes as a spiritual hero who sustains his awakened consciousness in the face of persecution and preaches the truth revealed to him regardless of consequences. His actions are affirmed and assimilated as a communal tradition of spiritual enlightenment by the chorales of the redeemed. Paul's conversion, the dramatic center of the work, reveals the transformation of the blind, persecuting rebel into a faithful, exemplary son through recognition and appropriation of the divine message. The second part moves from the experience of personal illumination to the tasks of public enlightenment, preaching, and cultural education, and thus in a sense also toward a return to the tensions of the first scenes in which Stephen was presented preaching the word in a hostile world. This circular pattern emphasizes what gradually emerges as the second major theme of the piece: the hostility or opacity of the world to the words of the enlightened and to the transcendent, revealed truth that is expressed through those words. Unlike the Reformation Symphony, *Paulus* does not move toward a triumphant incarnation of the

[78] Mendelssohn's self-conscious, reflexive treatment of chorales in *Paulus*' is noted in Peter Mercer-Taylor, "Rethinking Mendelssohn's Historicism: A Lesson from 'St. Paul,'" *Journal of Musicology* 15, no. 2 (1997): 208–30.

spirit in the historical community. The spiritual order of a universe sustained by a transcendent and loving God is affirmed, as is the possibility that every individual can participate in this order through self-overcoming and acceptance of divine revelation. But the second half of *Paulus* seems to express these affirmations as consolations in the face of the hostility of the "people" (both pagans and Jews), and more in an attitude of resignation than triumph. What had seemed a historical reality in the Reformation Symphony now is clearly presented as a historical hope and a practical task.

Despite this apparent shift in Mendelssohn's perception of the relationship between the divine spirit and the historical ethical community, the music of the oratorio reveals less a radical break than a process of continuity and intensification in relation to Mendelssohn compositions from 1827–32. Continuity between the Reformation Symphony and *Paulus* is most obvious in the oratorio's overture. It begins with a homophonic, cantional exposition in the tonic (A major) of the opening lines of "Wachet Auf, ruft uns die Stimme," the subject of one of Bach's most famous and beloved cantatas (no. 140). A repetition of the chorale lines an octave higher and with greater figuration, however, leads to a dissolution of the traditional anthem into thematic fragments and a series of key modulations that culminate in a symphonic transition passage to a second theme (in the parallel minor), which opens in the form of a strict fugue that echoes the harmonic intervals of the chorale theme. This fugue, like the opening chorale, is gradually transformed into a freely composed passage that makes possible a new relationship to the tentative but then increasingly insistent reentry of the chorale theme. As the chorale intensifies and moves toward the tonic key, it is eventually able to sustain itself against and then merge with the fugue theme on its own terms in the concluding coda, in which the chorale lines are effectively reinforced by the entry of the organ, used not as a traditional baroque continuo instrument but as a powerful means of sonorous intensification. The similarity of musical structure and apparent musical intention between the *Paulus* overture and the finale of the Reformation Symphony is striking, but in the overture, Mendelssohn's transformation of baroque liturgical forms into dynamic moments of classical symphonic structure is less strident and more accessible. Chorale and fugue are very clearly contrasted and eventually reconciled as moments of an immanent musical structure. And, if we can continue to read the chorale as a sign of spirit-filled community and the fugue as a symbol of the divinely ordered universe, the utopian qualities of the Reformation Symphony finale, the assimilation of the ordering principles of the created universe into the ethical consciousness of the human community, seem to be more confidently and effortlessly confirmed than in 1830.

The overture to *Paulus* presents a program for the oratorio on a number of levels. First, the central chorale functions as a sermon text for the oratorio, a call to religious awakening and enlightenment. The full, choral, cantional exposition of "Wachet Auf" occurs at the climactic moment of the narrative to represent the Christian community's appropriation of Paul's dramatic confrontation with the divine light and his radical conversion from blindness to enlightenment. Mendelssohn conceived the oratorio as a musical intervention in the conflicts of his contemporary culture, as a "sermon" meant to instigate an ethical reformation through return to the spiritual core of the religious tradition. The extended sermon by Saint Stephen in the first scene, calling on his "brothers and fathers" to stop resisting the power of the Holy Spirit and to recognize the authority of the God who had rescued them from oppression and provided them with a moral law for their earthly existence, presents a succinct summary of the oratorio's general message. Mendelssohn's text and musical discourse indicates quite clearly that he interpreted the process of moral reform as dependent on a change in the relations between finite individuals and the transcendent being who created and sustained them, as the reconstruction and renewal of a moralized patriarchal family, rather than the victory of a patricidal brotherhood. The majestic fugal choruses that introduce and conclude both halves of the oratorio clearly place the narrative of the relations between the individual and community firmly in the context of the relations between God and man, the transcendent and the immanent spirit, between the objective reality of the divinely created moral and cosmic order and the human subjects, individual and collective, who are free to deny or appropriate this substance. Paul's dramatic conversion from persecutor to propagator of the spirit is instigated by a transcendent intervention. It is a response to a voice calling from above, not from within the circuit of earthly relations. This voice of Jesus is musically represented, not in the conventional bass, but in the high-pitched chords of a soprano ensemble, with an ethereal effect that recalls the representation of the divine spirit by the violins in the Reformation Symphony (Fig. 34).

The overture is also a program for the oratorio in a more structural sense, as an exemplary statement of the transformation of the letter of the past into the vital, dynamic musical forms of the present. The pattern of citation, working through, and transformation of chorale and fugue into moments of a classical, sonatalike symphonic movement occurs throughout the oratorio, in all of the recitatives, arias, ensemble pieces, and choruses. Although composed in the genre of sacred music in which voices carry the divine message and are accompanied by instrumental music, *Paulus* has the artistic character of an extended symphonic work in which instruments and voices are joined together in a work that is itself "religious" as a work of art, in which the sacred message is spoken through the music itself.[79] This process

[79] Friedhelm Krummacher has succinctly summarized the issue in Mendelssohn's modernizing translation of traditional religious music as "Where all art is religious, religious art becomes a tautology." See Krummacher, "Art–History–Religion: On Mendelssohn's Oratorios *St. Paul* and *Elijah*," in Seaton, *Mendelssohn Companion*, p. 309.

Fig. 34. Paul's call to conversion by the transcendent divinity in *Paulus*.
Source: Reproduced from the Gregg Press facsimile edition of the *Werke* (Leipzig: Breitkopf and Haertel, 1874–77).

is especially striking in the recitatives, in which the objective declamation of the biblical text is transformed into the lyrical, emotional expressiveness and linear melodic continuity of the singing subject, often with a greatly expanded and intensified instrumental component. This "Romantic" transformation of traditional solo and small ensemble forms gave Mendelssohn's oratorio a modern and sentimental aspect that certainly helped produce and sustain its enormous popularity in the nineteenth century. Sometimes, as in the aria "Jerusalem" or the chorus "Wir preisen selig," the subjective internalization of the text and traditional form appeared to produce a new text altogether in which the original words hardly mattered and the notes did all the talking.

In the context of this Romantic subjectivity in Mendelssohn's work, the overture can also be understood as a critical, future-oriented (as well as a nostalgic backward-looking) commentary on the music that shapes the dramatic scenes and narrative history of Paul's life in the main body of the oratorio. At least the relationship between the overture and the work as a whole indicates a disjunction, or conflict, between Mendelssohn's theoretical and musical conception of the revelation and assimilation of the divine spirit, and the imperfect or incomplete evolution of this process in historical reality. Like the finale of the Reformation Symphony, the *Paulus* overture concludes with a majestic triumphant chorale, but this apparently successful appropriation of the musical cosmos by the communitarian ethos only corresponds to the first half of the oratorio, up to the response to Paul's conversion and enlightenment. Mendelssohn had no great difficulty imagining his audience as an exemplary, ideal community assimilating and affirming the dramatic conversion of the apostle, or the martyrdom of his precursor. The second half of the oratorio, however, tells a story of resistance to the word, of persecution, misunderstanding, and isolation, not a story of the triumphant transformation of pagans and Jews into members of the kingdom of the spirit on earth. Chorales thus play a much more limited and subdued role in part 2. In contrast to the three chorale numbers of part 1, part 2 has only two, and the full choir sings neither. The first is a prayerful plea by a small ensemble of the soloists (the righteous remnant?) that God might change the hardened hearts of their tormentors, and the second is a *cantus firmus* overlaying a chorus, sung by a boys' or children's' choir, affirming the traditional creed in the face of isolation and persecution and on the basis of a childlike faith in the goodwill of a transcendent God. The concluding chorus praises the divine father for making the possibility of living a life in the spirit, as exemplified by Paul, available to everyone, but there is no concluding chorale to indicate the historical assimilation of this possibility by the Christian community. The spiritual enlightenment demanded by the opening "Wachet Auf" is presented as a historical reality only among a restricted group of converted apostles, of enlightened prophets sustaining the message of the word against a hostile world of both hardened traditional elites and an irrational rabble. The transformation of the world, the educational reformation of the people into an ethical community, remains as an ongoing task. And the fulfillment of this task, Mendelssohn strongly implied, involved a revitalizing translation of the spiritual inheritance; not a "revolution," but a "reformation" that recognized the essential, "eternal" content hidden in the letter of the past and recreated this essence in modern idiom.[80]

REVELATION AND ENLIGHTENMENT: IDENTIFYING WITH THE FATHER'S VOICE

The compositional process that culminated in the musical form and historical content of Saint Paul in 1836 was inextricably entangled with important shifts in Mendelssohn's personal relations, his professional status and vocational choices, and his affirmation of a particular compositional, artistic direction, or musical "voice." These changes did not mark radical breaks with the past, but confirmed tendencies in Mendelssohn's earlier career, resolved or transcended the tensions of the early 1830s, and inaugurated a period of self-confident compositional maturity, cultural acceptance, and relative contentment. The Lobgesang Symphony Cantata in B major, opus 52, first performed in June 1840 as part of the celebration of the four-hundredth anniversary of Gutenberg's invention of the printing press, can be interpreted as the musical epitome and culminating public expression of the reconciliations of this phase in Mendelssohn's career.

A number of changes in Mendelssohn's personal and professional circumstances contributed to the shift in his cultural perspective during the mid-1830s. In November 1835 his father died unexpectedly of a cerebral hemorrhage. The death came at a time when Mendelssohn had already made significant moves toward reconciliation with his father after the conflicts over musical reform and religious identity that had marked their relationship in the 1820s. The psychological impact of the event was to seal and confirm this process. It marked, he wrote to Klingemann, the decisive end of his youth and thus also of his identification with the fraternal world of rebellious sons, and produced a conscious identification with the father's role and perspective. As he finished *Paulus*, he felt himself driven by the wish to "become like his father" and to fulfill all his father's expectations.[81] One sign of this change in Mendelssohn was a tendency to take on his father's role vis-à-vis Fanny's professional musical ambitions,

[80] Mendelssohn discussed his conception of movement and change through reformation in opposition to the French conception of revolution in a number of letters to his sisters Fanny and Rebecca in the fall of 1834, during his composition of *Paulus*. See *Briefe*, vol. 2, pp. 38–47.

[81] Letter to Klingemann, December 14, 1835, Klingemann, ed., *Briefwechsel*, 195.

asserting a severe patriarchal position regarding her attempts to break out of the confines of culturally defined domestic roles.[82] It was also at this time that he broke off relations with the "brother" who had supported his earlier muted rebellion against his father's rule in the 1820s – Adolf Bernhard Marx – and renewed his interest in the heritage of his famous grandfather, Moses Mendelssohn.[83]

Mendelssohn's self-conscious internalization of his father's "spirit" was connected to an equally self-conscious desire to end his bachelor days and establish a family of his own, thus fulfilling his father's longstanding wish that he might emancipate himself from romantic fantasy and attain the solid ground of ethical responsibility.[84] During a visit to Frankfurt in the summer of 1836, after the triumphant premiere of *Paulus* at the Lower Rhine Music Festival in Duesseldorf, Mendelssohn found a socially appropriate marriage partner in an elegant, somewhat conventional, and pious young woman from a well-known patrician Huguenot clan. The Calvinist traditions, ecclesiastical professions, and pious tastes of this family might have seemed radically different from the Jewish heritage, financial professions, and aesthetic tastes of the Mendelssohns, but the bourgeois, "Victorian" moralism and strong familial loyalties of the combined Jeanrenaud–Souchay families made their Frankfurt world seem quite familiar and homelike to Mendelssohn. The first child (a son) arrived less than a year after the marriage, and Mendelssohn soon found himself the patriarchal center of his own domestic world. In letters to his old friends during the late 1830s, Mendelssohn often alluded in a gently ironical and joking manner to the "philistine" happiness of his domestic relations, but he also sincerely believed he had reached a state of inner equilibrium and peace, and insisted that he felt more at home, more "comfortable" in his own skin, than he had since first leaving his protective parental "nest" in Berlin in the late 1820s.[85]

Mendelssohn's feelings of domestic tranquility were clearly protected and reinforced by two important changes in his professional life. In early 1835, in conformity with the expressed wishes of his father, he decided to leave the conflict-ridden post of city musical director in Dusseldorf and accept the directorship of the Leipzig Gewandhaus Orchestra. Although Mendelssohn was not as sure as his father that he should take on the responsibilities of this post, it proved a very comfortable fit for his proclivities and talents. In the Gewandhaus he found one of Europe's most competent orchestral

[82] Mendelssohn to his mother, June 2, 1837, where he claims it would be entirely inappropriate for Fanny to publish her compositions and even give the appearance that her domestic duties were not her first priority. This echoes Abraham Mendelssohn's position about Fanny's possible musical career during the 1820s. See John E. Toews, "Memory and Gender in the Remaking of Fanny Mendelssohn's Musical Identity: The Chorale in Das Jahr," *Musical Quarterly*, 77, no. 4 (1993): 739–41.

[83] Werner, *Mendelssohn* (1980), pp. 300–3.

[84] *Ibid.*, p. 321.

[85] *Briefe*, vol. 2, pp. 100, 116, 122.

ensembles, which he was able to develop rapidly into an efficient instrument for his ambitious program of public education through historically organized concerts of "serious" music in the German tradition.[86] Moreover, the local choral society and the musical institutions and traditions of the famous St. Thomas Church (where Bach had been cantor) provided excellent opportunities for the modernizing revision and performance of works in the liturgical tradition. Finally, in Leipzig he found a middle-class, Protestant evangelical culture that affirmed his beliefs in the moralizing function of serious art music and looked with concern on the tendencies toward the egoistic virtuosity, shock value, and surface brilliance that seemed to dominate the new music emanating from Paris. Here was a "genuine German" society of solid bourgeois citizens equally removed from the sycophancy and theatricality of court society and the illiberal, conformist pressures of metropolitan, "mass" society. It was a context in which ethical education toward spirit-filled community could proceed through inner reform and as a positive remaking of the essence of tradition, and not fall into the schematic political confrontations of revolution and reaction.

The comfortable world, the "home" Mendelssohn found in Leipzig, however much he may have liked to set it against the disintegrative tendencies he perceived in larger urban centers, also extended far beyond the small-town world of the Leipzig *Buergertum*. The tremendous popular response to *Paulus* not only among the professional and commercial Protestant middle classes in the Rhineland and Westphalia, but also within similar social contexts throughout northern continental Europe, the English midlands and even New England, was the second decisive event in Mendelssohn's public career during the mid and late 1830s. Mendelssohn modestly played down his new celebrity status and interpreted his fame as a public recognition of his general program of musical historicism and moral reform.[87] In an important sense he was correct in perceiving his fame in the 1830s (in contrast to his celebrity as a child prodigy in the 1820s) as connected more to his cause or message than to his personal genius. The response to Paulus revealed a powerful affinity between his personal musical vision and the moral and historical perspective of a significant segment of middle-class society in Protestant Europe.

Mendelssohn's bolstered self-assurance about the cultural relevance of his moral and aesthetic conceptions was expressed in his musical compositions between 1836 and 1840 as a progressive maturation and formal mastery of his distinctive musical voice. In 1838 he wrote to a friend that he had never felt more comfortable within the recognized limitations of the German musical

[86] The innovative elements in Mendelssohn's self definition of the role of conductor and performer as a moral educator and interpreter of texts are pointed out in Donald Mintz, "Mendelssohn as Performer and Teacher," in Seaton, *Mendelssohn Companion*, pp. 87–134.

[87] Letter to Paul Mendelssohn, October, 1837, *Briefe*, vol. 2, pp. 98–99.

tradition and had reached a new level of self-confidence in his ability to find the appropriate musical forms for his feelings and intentions.[88] Although Mendelssohn's creative accomplishments within his continuing project of reinterpreting baroque sacred music within a modern classical–romantic idiom were considerable between 1836 and 1840 (as in the Preludes and Fugues for Organ, opus 37, and the psalm cantatas, opus 42, 46, and 51), the most striking examples of his compositional maturation and self-confidence were in the genres of instrumental chamber music, and especially in the epitome of classical sonata form – the string quartet.

Mendelssohn's set of three string quartets, Opus 44 (1838) achieved a full articulation of the transformative revisions of classical sonata form adumbrated in his confrontation with Beethoven's late works in the 1820s. The dramatic contrasts, conflicts, and discontinuities that impelled the classical sonata through the analytical work of the "development" and the mediating resolutions of the "recapitulation," were subdued to the point of vanishing altogether. They were replaced as an organizing and unifying principle by the evolution of a relatively simple subject toward full self-disclosure through a process of contextual enrichment and variation. The striving for organic unity and continuity through a succession of musical episodes tended to displace the dramatic unification of opposites as the principle of aesthetic unity, or closure. Mendelssohn's self-conscious, elaborate application of complex musical techniques to sustain the identity of the musical subject through a narrative sequence of transformative variations and enriching episodes produced for many later listeners (as well as some contemporary critics, like Richard Wagner) an impression of bland homogeneity, effortless simplicity, and "smoothness." Mendelssohn, however, worked laboriously to achieve this sense of a unity not immanently constructed within the work or yearned for as a future ideal, but discovered, revealed, and illuminated in an exegetical process. Two elements marked the distinctive character of Mendelssohn's musical narratives of the spiritual subject, or idea as stories of recognition and acceptance of a pregiven, revealed integration into absolute order. First was the belief that the subject entered into the world already formed as the child of a father or creation of a transcendent power. Even though Mendelssohn's musical subjects were relatively simple so as to allow for flexibility in variation, adaptation, connection, and merger, they did have a figural identity that placed limitations on self-determination. Second, Mendelssohn conceived the evolution of these subjects within strictly defined boundaries established not only transcendentally but also historically. The external frame of his instrumental compositions remained the classical sonata form, and however much he may have hollowed out its impelling internal dynamics, the ideal of working within an inherited set of rules that guaranteed

[88] Letter to Ferdinand David, July 30, 1838, *Briefe*, vol. 2, pp. 110.

closed structure and organic unity remained central to his aesthetic conceptions.[89]

During the late 1830s, Mendelssohn also worked on the application of his compositional principles to the monumental public forms of the classical symphony. His drafts and constant revisions of the Symphony in A Major (the "Italian" Symphony, opus 90), and his Symphony in A Minor (the "Scottish" Symphony, opus 56), however, did not attain a form that satisfied his own requirements for publication. As conductor of the Gewandhaus Orchestra, Mendelssohn acted as the authoritative performer and interpreter of the classical symphonic tradition from Haydn to Beethoven. The task of assimilating this tradition, especially the gigantic Beethoven corpus, proved intimidating. This was especially true of the Ninth Symphony, which Mendelssohn had studied, puzzled over, and performed as both player and conductor on many occasions since its northern German premiere in 1826. He conducted the Ninth in each of his first two seasons at the Gewandhaus, as well as at the Lower Rhenish Music Festival in the summer of 1836, but in December 1837 he still expressed his bafflement with the musical meaning of the final movement. Although he considered the instrumental movements among the greatest achievements in the history of art, the final choral movement remained a puzzle for him.[90] As a true believer in Beethoven's genius, he was not willing to follow his sister Fanny in judging the Ninth a colossal "monstrosity" that degenerated into a burlesque in its final choral movement. But he did find the ways in which Beethoven tried to express transcendence of the immanent structures of classical form in the last movement difficult to comprehend and virtually impossible to perform.[91]

It would be misleading and unfair to judge the Lobgesang as a self-conscious attempt to "outdo" Beethoven or to "remake" the Ninth Symphony in a manner that resolved its problematic relations between vocal and instrumental forms, and between immanent structures and transcendent yearnings.[92] Although Mendelssohn's contemporaries immediately drew comparisons between the two works, Mendelssohn saw his work as

89 A detailed formal analysis of Mendelssohn's revisions of the sonata form in his chamber music is provided in Krummacher, *Mendelssohn*. A summary of the conclusions drawn from this study can be found in Friedhelm Krummacher, "Zur Kompositionart Mendelssohns: Thesen am Beispiel der Streichquarttete," in Dahlhaus, ed., *Das Problem Mendelssohn*, pp. 169–84.

90 Alfred Doerffel: *Geschichte der Gewandhausconcerte zu Leipzig vom 25. November, 1781 bis 25. November, 1881* (Leipzig: 1980; reprint of 1884 edition); Mendelssohn to Droysen, December 14, 1838, in Rudolf Huebner, ed., *Johann Gustav Droysen's Briefwechsel. Vol. I: 1829–1851* (Osnabrueck: 1967: reprint of 1929 edition).

91 Fanny's comment after the performance at the Lower Rhine Music Festival in 1836 is cited in Werner, *Mendelssohn* (1980), p. 314.

92 After the Lobgesang was completed, Mendelssohn suggested to Klingemann that he had lacked the courage to compose a choral symphony on the Beethoven model because the task appeared too daunting. See his letter of November 18, 1840, Klingemann ed., *Briefe*, p. 251.

addressing similar issues from a different perspective. In fact, the Lobgesang emerges from Mendelssohn's own development as an interesting attempt to merge his parallel reforms of sacred music (with Bach as model and mentor) and classical sonata form (with Beethoven as model and mentor) into a single musical concept of the relations between the sacred and the secular, and to address the question of the integration of the individual subject into an ethical community in terms of the historical and structural relations between these two dimensions. And, all invidious comparisons aside, the Lobgesang does reveal how differently Mendelssohn conceived these sets of relations from the Beethoven of the Ninth Symphony.

The general organization of the Lobgesang does parallel the Ninth Symphony in a number of ways, and it is difficult to imagine that the Beethoven model was not in Mendelssohn's mind during the process of composition.[93] Three instrumental movements – an opening sonata allegro, a scherzo–trio, and an adagio – are completed with a choral finale. However, the balance of these movements within Mendelssohn's work diverges from Beethoven's in that the three symphonic movements are only half as long as the choral finale, and thus almost give the impression of a three-part symphonic overture. The narrative of dramatic conflict, struggle, suffering, and yearning leading up to the vision of transcendent resolution is less intense and troubled in Mendelssohn's work, and the resolution is much more self-assured, affirmative, and extended. But Mendelssohn did conceive the instrumental movements as more than an introduction to a sacred cantata celebrating divine order, and he defined his genre as Symphony with Chorus and Orchestra (the final title, Symphony Cantata, was later suggested by his friend Klingemann).

Like Beethoven, Mendelssohn composed his choral symphony in relation to a specific written text. However, Mendelssohn's text was not a secular poem about human relations but an arrangement of sacred poetry (the psalms) concerning the relations between God and Man, centered on a textual theme: "*Alles was Odom hat preise den Herrn*"("All That Has Life and Breath, Praise the Lord"). Both instrumental and vocal movements, he informed Klingemann, were composed on this text, as an intensifying, elevating pattern of praise, progressing from instruments to human voices.[94] On the title page of the published score, Mendelssohn added another text, from Martin Luther: "I would like to see all of the arts, and music in particular, in the service of Him who created them and gave them to us." The

[93] My comparative analysis has been most influenced on the Beethoven side by the interpretations in Maynard Solomon, *Beethoven Essays* (Cambridge, Mass.: 1988); and Leo Treitler, *Music and the Historical Imagination* (Cambridge, Mass.: 1989). As far as I know, there exists no systematic musical analysis of the Lobgesang. I have found brief commentaries in the following studies helpful: Thomas Ehrle, *Die Instrumentation in den Symphonien und Overtueren Felix Mendelssohn- Bartholdy* (Wiesbaden: 1983); Thomas, *Instrumentalwerk*.

[94] July 21, 1840, Klingemann, ed., *Briefe*, p. 200.

joys celebrated in Mendelssohn's symphonic ode were not so much the joys of Schiller's and Beethoven's odes to human freedom and brotherhood, as the joys of filial piety, reverence for tradition, and enlightened reconciliation through subordination to the revealed will of the divine father. The historical memories aroused and transcended in Mendelssohn's musical narrative were not the memories of the revolutionary dawn of the late eighteenth century, but those of Luther's religious reformation in the sixteenth century and his own hopes for moral reformation in the late 1820s. Mendelssohn's themes were spiritual enlightenment through receptivity to divine revelation and filial reconciliation through understanding of the essential meaning of the father's word. As a celebration of Gutenberg's achievement in making the word available to the people and thus breaking the spell of the dark night of ignorance, the Lobgesang was also an ode to enlightenment in a more general sense, to the awakening that comes from grasping the word as it is presented through tradition and assimilated into the consciousness of the present.

The first movement of the Lobgesang opens with a stately introduction of twenty-two measures (*maestoso con moto*) in which the hymnic motif of the whole piece is intoned by the deep brass (trombones) playing in unison (Fig. 35). Both the ascending and descending phrases of the motif are repeated in antiphonal fashion in homophonic chords by the rest of the orchestra, and then combined in a concluding phrase merging the brass into the full orchestra. Although this simple, memorable, opening "hymn" is not a direct citation from the liturgical tradition, Mendelssohn constructed its intervals according to the requirements of a premodern modal scale connected to liturgical music (the eighth psalm mode), thus highlighting its sacred, and ancient, character. The fluttering open fifths of ambiguous tonality through which sound gradually emerges from silence in Beethoven's Ninth are replaced in Mendelssohn's work by a fully developed, authoritative declaration, resonant with the authority of divine revelation and historical tradition. Beethoven's own striking use of archaic modal tonality in one of the choral variations of the "Ode to Joy" (the *andante maestoso*) produces the effect of an ecstatic mystical yearning for spiritual transcendence. In contrast, Mendelssohn affirms the revelation of the divine creator's authoritative word as the starting point of the human spiritual quest.

After this introductory statement, Mendelssohn's first movement switches quickly into the rapid tempo of what appears to be the opening allegro movement in standard sonata form. The first theme, a lively, driving phrase with the violins taking the leading voice and echoing a theme from Beethoven's first Leonore Overture, seems to leave the solemn "ancient" tones of the sacred hymn far behind. But after forty measures, in what might schematically be defined as a transition, or bridge, passage to the second theme, the hymn reenters. It is now caught in the driving, rapid "secular" tempo of the allegro, and engages in a brief dialogue with the first "Beethoven" theme before fading into the tentative opening measures

Fig. 35. The initial proclamation of the hymnic motif (the "idea") in the Lobgesang Symphony Cantata.
Source: Reproduced from the Gregg Press facsimile edition of the *Werke* (Leipzig: Breitkopf and Haertel, 1874–77).

of the second theme, a pastoral, songlike phrase that seems more like a lyrical intermezzo than a fully developed second theme in classical style, announcing the claims of human subjectivity for self-expression and recognition. These claims are almost immediately silenced and displaced by what appears (again in contrast to conventional sonata form) as a third theme, whose rhythms and intervals are more easily integrated into the dominant relational web between the hymnic motif and the first theme.

Mendelssohn obviously recognized Beethoven's creative use of reminiscences and premonitions as a unifying thread in the Ninth Symphony, but the balance of reminiscence and premonition is entirely different in the

Lobgesang. His emphasis is on the continuous underlying presence of the opening hymnic revelation, which constantly reappears as the essence within the appearance, whereas the "Ode to Joy" melody in Beethoven is gradually and laboriously pieced together and then finally articulated in a construction of unity from previously isolated fragments. If the Ninth could be imagined in Mendelssohnian form, the "Ode to Joy" theme would have appeared in its lapidary instrumental totality as the introduction to the first movement. It would have been the given "idea," or spiritual subject, which would then be subjected to interpretive exegesis through contextualization and combination.

The "development" section of Mendelssohn's first movement, the moment of analytical dissection in standard classical sonata form, is transformed into a narrative of musical episodes, in which the themes, tonalities, and rhythmic structures of the exposition are set in relation to each other and subjected to variations. The development moves through four distinct episodes culminating in a "return" (the fifth episode) to the first theme (the "Beethoven" theme) on the dominant (F). The evolving pattern of these episodes is a gradual movement away from the dominance of the hymnic theme (which controls the first three episodes) toward a restatement of the lyrical intermezzo (the second theme, which dominates the fourth episode). This songlike theme is strikingly framed by changes in tempo and dynamics, emerging from virtual silence and calm and then suddenly breaking off in a sudden return to the allegro tempo. Again, the impression is one of emergence of the individual subject that is not integrated into the sacral–secular relations between the hymn and the main "Beethoven" theme.

This procedure is emphatic and striking and may suggest the problem of the whole first movement as the integration of individual subjectivity into the collective historical process of struggle, transformation, and "reformation" whereby the transcendent, sacred revelation achieves historical incarnation, or secularization, through incorporation into the immanent structures of sonata form. At least such an interpretation helps make sense of the conclusion of the first movement, in which the apparent progress toward merger of the hymnic and "Beethoven" themes suddenly falters and stalls. A unison restatement of the opening hymn by the brass is greeted by a hesitant and tentative response that unexpectedly shifts into a lyrical recitative by the solo clarinet ushering in the transition (without pause) to the dance rhythms of the scherzo.

The thematic subject of the scherzo is a simple Romantic song with strong suggestions of a folklike, rustic melody and dance rhythm. This scherzo is much less animated and driven than its Beethoven correlate. The second movement in Mendelssohn's symphony begins with the problem raised in the first movement – the status of the individual "natural" subject, still defined in idyllic pastoral tones, in relation to both divine will and human community. The central trio section of the second movement breaks the blithe naiveté of the scherzo by juxtaposing it with the phrases of an artificially constructed religious chorale. The first and last lines of the chorale echo well-known Lutheran hymn tunes. The hymnic motif from the first movement appears almost unnoticeably integrated into the chords of the chorale in the middle voice of the oboes (Fig. 36), perhaps a reminder that the liturgical community confronting the natural subject is a spiritual community incorporating the revealed will of the divine father. Each line of the chorale is interrupted by a lyrical intermezzo from the rustic dance theme of the scherzo, creating a musical dialogue between natural, individual subjectivity and the united voice of the religious community. Throughout the trio the two voices appear to simply alternate and talk past each other, but when the scherzo returns in the third part of the movement, Mendelssohn's score suggests that the dialogue has marked a change in the natural subject. The repetition of the scherzo is not developed in full *da capo* form, but is short, truncated, and troubled; the serene repetition of the full melody is cut off. It is as if the natural subject has been forced to recognize its finite limitations, its lack of self-sufficiency, and been pushed to a boundary at which it can begin to experience a longing for integration into the spiritual world of the community and for reconciliation with the transcendent power of the father's will. The hidden integration of the ancient proclamation (the hymnic motif) into the communal chorale may suggest that for Mendelssohn the relationship between the natural human subject and its moral or spiritual essence (a relation defined by the demand for ethical integration into the community) assumed a fusion of patriarchal will and communal tradition. The achievement of the first movement might be represented as precisely this merger, (that is, of the hymn and the Beethoven theme), although the identification of human moral essence and divine will still left the integration of the natural subject into the universal (in both senses) unresolved. The second movement breaks the naive self-sufficiency of the natural subject, instigating an ethical claim and a religious need, or at least a feeling of spiritual discontent and desire.

Mendelssohn's scherzo–trio clearly has functional analogies to Beethoven's second movement, in that its intention appears to be a critical examination of the idyllic illusion of self-sufficient natural subjectivity. But where Beethoven places an ironic frame around his idyll (in his case placed in the middle trio section) with the hectic rhythms and driving power of the scherzo, Mendelssohn uses the scherzo to represent the idyll and then places it into a self-questioning dialogue with the forces of communal ethos and divine will. The illusion of the natural idyll does not decompose under the driving energies of modern life in Mendelssohn's musical narrative, but comes to recognize its own limitations in the face of the higher authority of the community and its divine creator. The disquietudes of Mendelssohn's symphony are backward oriented, pointing toward the need for an awakening and comprehension of the hidden, essential meaning contained within historical tradition.

Fig. 36. The Father's proclamation (the oboes) integrated into the communal chorale and confronted by the romantic subject (strings). From the Lobgesang scherzo.
Source: Reproduced from the Gregg Press facsimile edition of the *Werke* (Leipzig: Breitkopf and Haertel, 1874–77).

The third movement – *adagio religioso* – explores the new depths and complexities of a subjectivity that has been confronted with its own limitations and the hopelessness of its longings for a return to arcadia. It does so in a series of variations of a sweeping expressive melody orchestrated with emphasis on the darker tones of the middle instrumental voices. Mendelssohn's conception of subjective religious yearning was not dramatically anguished. Tonal leaps, chromatic complexities, and dissonances are avoided. Only the surging upward arc and soft fading of the melodic phrases and the broken triads of the accompaniment indicate the pain and suffering of unrequited longing within what appears overwhelmingly to be a song of resignation and contemplative expectancy – of "waiting for the Lord." The longing for transcendence is not pushed to the emotional extremes evident in Beethoven's adagio. Again, an echo of Beethoven marks the difference. In the middle of the adagio, Mendelssohn, like Beethoven, used a fully orchestrated crescendo (including brass) to mark a climax. Whereas Beethoven's crescendo brings the aching to an anguished breaking point, Mendelssohn's issues in a fanfarelike phrase that points ahead to the introductory phrases that immediately precede the choral affirmation of the finale. Mendelssohn's climax is a consoling look backward and forward, to the original revelation and its ultimate recognition and appropriation. The intensifying beat that introduces the "awakening" of the dreaming soul by a choral version of the hymnic motif at the beginning of the finale is thus also much more subdued than the "terror fanfare" that introduces the finale of Beethoven's Ninth. For Mendelssohn, the awakening from the dreamlike state of subjective longing and expectancy was more like a response to a long-familiar voice, finally recognized.

The musical narrative of the instrumental movements of the Lobgesang thus culminates in the expression of a Romantic subjective longing ready to grasp the meaning of revelation in tradition once it is presented in the self-conscious articulation of the "word." Mendelssohn's choral finale is the end point of a quest inaugurated by the trombones' first declarations. The opening chorus of the cantata movement, a majestic Handel-like chorus that provides the verbal text for the hymnic theme, could thus be seen as the climax of the work, bringing to full self-conscious clarity the opening revelation. Unlike Beethoven, Mendelssohn conceived this resolution as a "discovery," as a human appropriation of revealed truth. But like Beethoven, Mendelssohn treats the first full articulation of the resolution as the beginning of a new process of subjective appropriation and contextual enrichment that duplicates or repeats the evolutionary progress of the symphony as a whole.

The cantata of the Lobgesang is structured on the pattern of a journey of moral and spiritual education. The extended opening choral declaration of praise is followed by a tenor recitative that demands that individual human subjects bear witness to their redemption, or awakening, from the powers of darkness. The next four numbers expand this process of confession and self-conscious examination with increasing intensity. The popular soprano duet "*Ich harrete des Herrn*" ("I waited for the Lord") duplicates with verbal specificity the instrumental adagio in its lyrical sweep, as well as in its emotional indulgence in the blissful surrender to the embrace of an "inclining" heavenly father. The culmination of this section of the cantata, however, clearly arrives with the dramatic anguish of the tenor solo: "*Stricke des Todes hatten uns umfangen*" ("The bonds of death had closed around us").

With rising urgency, the tenor voice repeats its cry: "Watchman, will this night soon pass?" The cautious stepwise modulations and extremely subdued use of dissonance and chromaticism throughout the work are temporarily abandoned as startling leaps in tonality and strikingly dissonant chords emphasize the crisislike turning point of this yearning for redemption as a plea for light (Fig. 37). Finally, after the fourth repetition, a high soprano voice responds, "The Night is departed, the day has dawned," an announcement that is immediately followed and reinforced by a majestic full chorus greeting the dawn of enlightenment and raising a battle cry for a concerted assault on the powers of darkness.

This conversion, or transformation, scene, which has striking parallels to the conversion of Saul into Paul in *Paulus*, expressed Mendelssohn's particular conception of cultural reformation. Reform came in the form of internal illumination, and this enlightenment occurred as an intellectual recognition of, and moral surrender to, the spiritual power of a transcendent father speaking through the revelation of historical tradition. Mendelssohn's own piety, as he himself noted, was defined not as a desire to escape the conditions of finitude, to attain salvation from the "sin" of being a mere human creature, but as a desire to live in enlightened recognition and conformity with his created nature, his divinely given spiritual essence as a human being.[95] Unlike Beethoven, Mendelssohn seemed to harbor no doubt that the process of enlightenment was sustained by a divinely created cosmic and moral order, or that this order was embodied and represented in the man-made order of the cultural tradition, which functioned as the letter of the divine spirit. Whereas Beethoven's Ninth can be seen as a search for the fundamental principles of its own order, the musical foundations of Mendelssohn's symphony are never in doubt. The symphony organizes itself firmly in a journey grounded on a definite key, and its final chorus concludes with a repetition of the opening hymnic phrase unmistakably on the tonic chord.

The second half (postawakening) of the cantata movement, however, also addresses the issue of the relationship between individual enlightenment (as reconciliation with the understood will of the father) and communal identity. The choral celebration of enlightenment is immediately followed

[95] Letter to Schirmer, November 21, 1838, *Briefe*, vol. 2, pp. 115–16.

Fig. 37. The musical narrative of crisis and conversion in the Lobgesang.
Source: Reproduced from the Gregg Press facsimile edition of the *Werke* (Leipzig: Breitkopf and Haertel, 1874–77).

by a well-known Lutheran chorale (*Nun danket alle Gott*), whose first stanza is given a full traditional exposition in the a capella, cantional style of the liturgy before the orchestra enters with an independent theme configured with an elaborated version of the third stanza. This typically Mendelssohnian modernization of a liturgical form is followed by a tenor–soprano duet in the style of a romantic *Lied*, assimilating the experience of spiritual enlightenment into the processes of individual subjectivity. The concluding chorus then appears to move outward into the sphere of communal ethics and politics again, suggesting a desire to transform the specifically confessional, liturgical expression of congregational solidarity into the more inclusive secular relations between princes and peoples. Unlike the ending of *Paulus*, therefore, the Lobgesang does, at least briefly and tentatively, suggest a collective "redemption," or "awakening," as the culmination of the musical narrative.

This suggestion of a collective appropriation of revelation in a secular ethical community, however, is not only tentative, but also presented as a demand on the future and firmly embedded in traditional patriarchal forms. The cultural unity of nations or peoples is not portrayed as a self-constructed human fraternity but as a union of children who share a common identification with the father's revealed will. Mendelssohn's decision to complete his choral symphony with a religious cantata was thus in keeping with his historical belief that the resolution of the human process of moral education, both individual and collective, would occur as the attainment of a regenerated, "reformed" version of the universal truth contained in traditional religious forms. The immanent relations of the symphonic structure itself, the rules of its order, were ultimately given and guaranteed from the outside, derived from and dependent on the revealed truths of the historical tradition, the spirit in the letter of the father's voice.

PUBLIC MEMORY, PERSONAL MEMORY, AND THE AUTONOMY OF ART: MENDELSSOHN AFTER 1840

The structure and content of the Lobgesang symphony suggests why it was not surprising that Mendelssohn might feel a strong attraction toward the cultural program of the regime of Frederick William IV. Nor is it surprising that Frederick William, Bunsen, and other regime insiders would see their historical and cultural perspectives mirrored in the musical universes of works like the Lobgesang or *Paulus*. Mendelssohn shared their conviction that individual redemption and ethical community were ultimately grounded in a transcendent power, that this power had a personal, patriarchal form, that its voice was embodied in historical tradition, and that this tradition had been articulated most transparently in the history of German-Protestant religious and aesthetic culture.

After Mendelssohn moved back to Berlin in the summer of 1841 and tried to define his positions within the framework of the Prussian regime's cultural policies, it soon became evident, as he had suspected all along, that the affinities between his own conceptions of a German–Christian cultural community and those of the official representatives of the government veiled important, sometimes decisive, differences. These differences were evident in three general areas.

First, it had become obvious in the summer of 1840, a year before his return to Berlin, that, for Mendelssohn, German national identity had a nonethnic character. He was appalled by the chauvinist response to the Rhine crisis and certainly did not share Frederick William, Radowitz, or Bunsen's hopes for a revival of the populist national "awakening" of 1813. Despite numerous requests, he refused to compose music for the patriotic nationalist hymns that had become a popular focus for Germanic ethnic self-consciousness in the summer of 1840. He recalled, in a letter to his mother, how angry his father had become whenever patriotic enthusiasm for the German "Michael" instigated a new wave of ethnic self-consciousness (and anti-Semitism) in German choral societies. The German fatherland, he claimed, was a "boring thing" and not capable of arousing genuine musical creativity. He found it disgusting when national identity was viewed as an exclusive privilege rather than as a simple affirmation of one's own cultural traditions.[96] As a friend who had been forced to listen to many such complaints noted: Mendelssohn had little empathy for the experience of ethnic identity because he remained at heart a cosmopolitan, or "citizen of the world" (*Weltbuerger*).[97]

At the same time, Mendelssohn had been able to translate the religious forms of a Lutheran chorale into a festive secular cantata for male choir and brass band honoring Gutenberg as German hero, which was performed at an open-air celebration in Leipzig in June 1840.[98] In 1843 he was willing to compose a similar festival cantata, merging secular history and religious identities, which the Prussian king had commissioned for the Berlin cathedral to commemorate the thousandth anniversary of the founding of the Holy Roman Empire. These two assignments did not arouse Mendelssohn's particular enthusiasm and did not result in memorable works, but they did display his insistence on distinguishing a broadly defined cultural nationalism from a more exclusive ethnic chauvinism.

The increased visibility of populist forms of German ethnic self-consciousness in the 1840s was of course not peculiar to Prussian or its

[96] Mendelssohn to his mother, October 27, 1840, *Briefe* vol. 2, p. 159. Similar sentiments are expressed in letters to Fanny and Paul Mendelssohn, and Klingemann, during the same period.

[97] Juluis Schubring to Mendelssohn, March 11, 1841, in *Briefwechsel zwischen Felix Mendelssohn Bartholdy und Julius Schubring*. p. 184.

[98] Werner, *Mendelssohn*, p. 338.

cultural leaders, but created a disturbance between Mendelssohn and his audience throughout Germany. In Prussia he was most annoyed by the attempts to control cultural life by either royal fiat or bureaucratic regulation. Mendelssohn had risen to international fame in the late 1830s because of the resonance of his music within the civic and religious culture of the urban middle classes. What he missed most of all in Berlin was the kind of civic culture that could sustain the musical institutions he needed to pursue his mission of making music an integral part of the moral reformation that would bring about a community of subjective identification. In Berlin he felt himself divided between an isolated domestic existence with his extended family and a few friends and a frustrating public activity in which he was constantly forced to battle for administrative jurisdiction and authority with the leaders of government agencies and official cultural institutions, and to vie for personal favor at the court. In Leipzig the plans for a conservatory went forward under the stimulus of a large private endowment and the support of a government administrator who was also a participating member in the civic culture that recognized itself in Mendelssohn's music.[99] In Berlin, Mendelssohn felt he was always jockeying for individual power and influence with competing agencies and individuals. As early as July 1841, after he had made his decision but before he actually moved to Berlin, Mendelssohn wrote to Klingemann that it was false to imagine the choice between Berlin and Leipzig as one between the challenge of a national pulpit in a metropolitan center and the security of a comfortable private existence in a provincial backwater. In Berlin all his musical efforts were reduced to struggles for private favor and personal influence, "without an echo in the country"; in Leipzig, on the other hand, his work resonated in the public arena.[100]

Finally, the peculiarly "enlightened" and ecumenical nature of Mendelssohn's Christian piety was a potential source of tension with his Berlin patrons. The composition of spiritual music based on biblical texts and using the forms of the liturgical tradition had been a dimension of Mendelssohn's musical identity since the 1820s. But his methods of translating confessional traditions into modern musical forms and integrating church music into civic culture were not in perfect harmony with some of the ecclesiastical and religious viewpoints of his Berlin patrons. This issue came to a head when Mendelssohn was appointed general director of ecclesiastical and spiritual music in Prussia by Frederick William in the fall of 1842. By 1840, Mendelssohn had developed a highly refined technique

[99] Klaus Haefner, "Felix Mendelssohn Bartholdy in seinen Beziehungen zu Friedrich August II von Sachsen: Ein Beitrag zur Biographie Mendelssohns," *Mendelssohn-Studien* 7 (1990): 219–68; Herman F. Weiss,"Neue Zeugnisse zu Felix Mendelssohn Bartholdy und Johann Paul von Falkenstein," *Mendelssohn-Studien* 9 (1995): 53–88.

[100] Mendelssohn to Klingemann, July 15, 1841, Klingemann, ed., *Briefe*, p. 265.

for translating the traditional musical language of the "Old Italian" or "Palestrina" style, the "Old German" congregational hymns of the Lutheran church, and the sacred concert music of Bach and Handel into the sonata structures of German classicism and the lyrically expressive narratives of the Romantic movement.[101] The king, however, wanted something closer to a literal recreation of the liturgical musical forms of his idealized apostolic church when he put Mendelssohn in charge of composing music for the services in the Berlin cathedral. Mendelssohn soon found himself chafing under these demands to maintain the letter of the tradition as well as its essential spirit – or to find that spirit exclusively within one historical musical form. He did produce some remarkable modern translations of traditional liturgical music, especially in his psalm settings. He could even work his magic within the restrictions of an a capella style that emphasized unison and antiphonal response rather than the polyphony of the fugue or the Lutheran chorales. Fanny marveled at his ability to compose original works in a manner that sounded "very Gregorian and Sistine."[102] But Mendelssohn maintained his right to modernize tradition and was not interested in engaging exclusively or repeatedly in this kind of translation. After a few experiments he found his obligations a burden, which drew him away from his musical calling and tended to stifle his own musical voice.[103]

Mendelssohn was certainly aware of such areas of tension and potential conflict as he moved to Berlin in 1841. The disastrous experience of the election for Zelter's successor at the Berlin Singakadamie in 1832–33 and his subsequent decision to leave Berlin had engraved them in his mind. Yet the mere fact that he had been called back seemed a vindication of his positions (and perhaps a revenge on his former enemies?), and raised hopes that he could work productively toward a reform of Berlin's musical culture. Certainly the hopes and dreams for a reformation of German ethical life through the translation and modernization of the spirit in the letter of tradition, which had animated Mendelssohn and his youthful cohort of intellectual friends and collaborators between 1826 and 1829, were continually at the forefront of his consciousness during the 1840s, right up to the moment when the sudden death of his sister Fanny in May 1847 instigated the depressive tailspin that ended with his own death from a series of strokes in early November of the same year. The intensity of Mendelssohn's focus

[101] For a defense of Mendelssohn's alleged "imitation" of ancient forms as a genuinely creative "translation" see James Garratt, "Mendelssohn's Babel: Romanticism and the Poetics of Translation," *Music & Letters* 80 (1999): 1–23.

[102] Fanny to Rebecca Dirichlet, December 26, 1843, *Familie Mendelssohn*. p. 746.

[103] For a reconstruction of Mendelssohn's relations with the Berlin Cathedral chapter and an analysis of his liturgical compositions in Berlin 1842–44, see Wolfgang Dinglinger, "Ein neues Lied: der preussische Generalmusikdirektor und eine Koenigliche Auftragskomposition," *Mendelssohn-Studien* 5 (1982): 99–111: and David Brodbeck, "A Winter of Discontent: Mendelssohn and the *Berliner Domchor*," in Larry Todd, ed., *Mendelssohn Studies*, 1–32.

on the personal memory of this earlier defining moment in his life, and his repeated attempts to integrate that memory into the consciousness of the present, complicated the general tasks of collective memory work pursued in his music during the 1840s.

Mendelssohn's experience in the early 1840s appeared to repeat his experience of the early 1830s. In 1832–33 he had returned after a period of travel and self-imposed exile to a home that seemed utterly changed. Mentors and friends had died, his sister and other close collaborators had established personal and intellectual lives apart from the earlier circle, and many had left the city. In 1841, Mendelssohn felt the same sense of loss of an earlier collective generational mission that he had felt and lamented in 1832–33. In March 1842, Mendelssohn wrote to Droysen, who had left Berlin for a position at the University of Kiel in 1840: "You have no idea how terribly much I cling to, and wistfully recall the whole time of our youth and how shattered I am when I am forced to see on all sides such passive broken companions from those years, and how glorious it is when among all of them there is one who remains a friend like before."[104]

The effort to sustain in the present the memory of youthful collaboration in a project of cultural reformation runs like a red thread through the last six years of Mendelssohn's life. In one of his last letters to Droysen, on April 5, 1847, he indicated that although the specific circumstances of that youthful moment could not be recreated, its spiritual essence remained:

> How everything in Berlin, both internally and externally, has changed! And how almost everything that seemed fresh and youthful in our earlier time together has now disappeared, dried up, aged and become worse! But only almost everything, thank God, not everything. It is still true, thank God, that the best does not disappear, but rather renews itself eternally, even in death. And there is also that pathetic misunderstanding, which one always believes in the happy time of youth, that every springtime brings the possession of something that is the best, and which then peels off leaf by leaf. But precisely the best does no peel off. God only knows how that is possible, but it does not peel off.[105]

The 1840s thus seems to have been a period in which Mendelssohn found himself testing, clarifying, and reaffirming the general cultural and musical identity that had been forged in the optimistic "springtime" of the 1820s and that he had consolidated within the context of his new public roles in the second half of the 1830s. A number of compositions published in the early 1840s testified to his desire to assimilate his personal memories into the present cultural moment: the revision and completion of the Goethean

[104] Mendelssohn to Droysen, March 11, 1842, *Droysen Briefwechsel*, vol. 1, p. 212.

[105] Mendelssohn to Droysen, April 5, 1847, *Droysen Briefwechsel*, vol. 1, p. 351.

cantata *Die Erste Walpurgisnacht*, which was originally written during his Italian trip in 1830–32; the extension of his *Midsummer Nights Dream* overture (1826) into the incidental music for the whole play; and the working through of the idea for the Scottish Symphony that he had first articulated in 1829. Even an apparently new work like the Violin Concerto in D Minor was packed with reminiscences of work written in that youthful springtime of his creativity.[106]

There are some indications that Mendelssohn's conviction about the redemptive and generative power of identification with historical tradition changed during the mid 1840s. His disappointment with the public role envisioned for him in Berlin did not lead simply to an enthusiastic return to his old haunts and Leipzig obligations, or to a compositional "repetition" of earlier work like the Lobgesang. When he reestablished his permanent residence in Leipzig in the summer of 1845, he had begun to pull back from his public commitments there as well. In December 1846 he wrote to Klingemann that "every official, public appearance" had become "repugnant" to him: "I believe that the time is coming, or perhaps has already come, when I will resign from every aspect of this kind of public, regularly scheduled music-making in order to make music at home, compose notes and let everything outside in the public realm go its own way."[107] In a conversation recorded after his return to Leipzig, Mendelssohn vehemently rejected any historical inspiration or public mission for music. Like any fine art, he insisted, music dealt with universal feelings and resisted any input from the particular social, cultural, "subjective" viewpoints of the composer. By devoting his art completely to the illumination of the objective universals contained within the particulars of individual experience, by sacrificing his subjectivity to the object, the composer was able to transcend the conditions of his mere historical existence and enter "the loftier, purer, kingdom of art." Only in the musical means available to pursue his aesthetic purposes was the composer dependent on historical traditions. Music, however, was separate from other domains of society and culture, concerned only with articulating essential relationships within the particular means available to it.[108] In a letter to Ignaz Moscheles in March 1845, Mendelssohn insisted that the public role of the musician and composer faded in importance before the importance of art as the means for shaping the "inner life." Public life was ultimately only important as it entered into the inner life, where it found its significance. The inner life did not find its meaning in the

106 See Reinhard Gerlach, "Mendelssohn's schoepferische Erinnerung der 'Jugendzeit': Die Beziehungen zwischen dem Violinkonzert,op. 64, und dem Oktett fuer Streicher, op. 20." in Schuhmacher, ed., *Felix Mendlessohn Bartholdy*, pp. 248–62.

107 Mendelssohn to Klingemann, December 1846, Klingemann, ed., *Briefe*, p. 316.

108 J. C. Lobe, "Gespraeche mit Felix Mendelssohn" in Lobe, *Consonanzen und Dissonanzen: Gesammelte Schriften aus aelterer und neuerer Zeit* (Leipzig: 1869), pp. 376–81. Quotation from p. 379.

public realm.[109] Music, it seemed, was less an instrument of cultural reformation than a refuge from history, a private avenue to the consolations of the universal.

The questions raised by such pessimistic outbursts during Mendelssohn's last years are complex. Mendelssohn did not abandon the notion that music could translate the essence of tradition into the language of present feeling and thus illuminate personal identity as a profoundly historical identity, but he seemed to privatize this process. The aesthetic representations from the past in which individuals had assimilated divine meaning as the essence of social being – like the Lutheran chorale or the Bach fugue – were important not as models for the future but as spiritual refuges. What the traditional Lutheran congregational chorale "represented" could not be transferred from the church congregation to the national community, but could only be absorbed by the individual as a symbolic expression of the kind of home that might be attained in and through art.[110] Music was the end rather than the means, the site of historical identity and universal meaning for the individual, not an instrument for their realization in the intersubjective world of human culture. Perhaps it is significant that the last celebratory public cantata Mendelssohn composed and conducted, for a festival in Cologne in 1846, was "Celebration for Artists"("*Festgesang an die Kuenstler*"). And yet, the most important work composed by Mendelssohn after 1845 was a massive public choral work in the genre of spiritual concert music – the oratorio *Elijah* – whose premiere in Birmingham in the spring of 1846 was the most stunning public triumph of his career. Mendelssohn's unexpected death at the age of 38 in November 1847 also transformed this work into his final statement regarding the historical meaning and purpose of music. Did *Elijah* mark a return to past affirmations and thus avoid the troubling questions that had arisen in Mendelssohn's consciousness of his personal and cultural identity during the 1840s? Had Mendelssohn fallen into a mode of imitating himself, as some of his contemporaries, including Schumann, suggested? Or did *Elijah* integrate the historical pessimism of the 1840s into a new synthesis of personal and historical memory? The tangled, troubled development of Mendelssohn's historical consciousness through his compositions of the 1840s may hold a possible answer to these questions.

During Mendelssohn's first few months in Berlin he worked with intense concentration on two major works that articulated the relationship between music and memory in different ways – the incidental music for Sophocles' *Antigone*, first performed at a private performance for the court at Potsdam

[109] Mendelssohn to Ignaz Moscheles, March 7, 1845, *Briefe von Felix Mendelssohn-Bartholdy an Ignaz und Charlotte Moscheles*, p. 239.

[110] This seems to be the function that the chorales seem to serve, for example, in Mendelssohn's Cello Sonata, opus 58 (1843), the Piano Trio, opus 66 (1845), or the Six Organ Sonatas, opus 65 (1844–45). See Gerd Zacher, "Die riskanten Beziehungen zwischen Sonate und Kirchenlied," in Metzger and Riehn, eds, *Felix Mendelssohn Bartholdy*, 34–45.

in late October 1841 and repeated as a public performance in Berlin the following March, and the Scottish Symphony, completed in January 1842 and first performed in Leipzig on March 3.

The *Antigone* music was a product of Mendelssohn's first royal commission in his new position. Inspired by the readings and interpretations of Ludwig Tieck, the king requested a performance of the play and asked Mendelssohn to compose music for the choruses. After a brief hesitation, Mendelssohn enthusiastically adopted the king's wishes as his own desire, transforming a royal commission into a personal project. As he read through the whole Sophocles trilogy, Mendelssohn found himself deeply moved, enchanted, and inspired: "I did not let myself be drawn into the project until this *Antigone* with its exaggerated beauty and magnificence drove everything else out of my head, and left me only with the wish to see it performed as soon as possible," he wrote to his old friend Ferdinand David in Leipzig.[111] After the first performance, he informed Droysen that he had originally been amazed and delighted by "the life that still inhabits it today."[112] As Mendelssohn studied the choruses he found them full of feelings, or moods (*Stimmungen*), that transcended the temporal and cultural divide between classical Greece and the present and presented themselves as "genuinely musical" materials for contemporary composition.[113]

By participating in this modern production of *Antigone*, a play that had come to epitomize the cultural values of classical Greece for German intellectuals during the earlier part of the century, Mendelssohn placed himself at the center of historicist controversies of the early 1840s. Was *Antigone* a cultural text whose historical "otherness" was central to its ethical value as an alternative critical perspective on the present? Should a modern production emphasize the radical difference between past and present, and present the work in its original, and thus alien, archaic forms? Or could the text be translated, assimilated, and modernized? The text used for the production was in fact a modern German translation (Johann Christian Donner's of 1839), but this translation had tried to maintain, somewhat awkwardly in Mendelssohn's opinion, the original Greek meter. The staging, directed by Tieck with the help of the classical scholar August Boeckh, tried to recreate at least some aspects of what was known of classical productions. Some critics at the court and the university believed that the choruses should be set in ways that replicated as closely as possible original Greek performance practices and recommended chantlike recitatives and musical accompaniment restricted to period instruments. Mendelssohn could only attach himself to the project, however, once he was able to experience the living spirit

111 Mendelssohn to Ferdinand David, September 23, 1841, *Felix Mendelssohn Bartholdy: Briefe aus Leipziger Archiven*, ed. Hans-Joachim Rother and Richard Szeskas (Leipzig: 1971), p. 166.

112 December 2, 1841, *Briefe*, vol. 2, p. 203.

113 Mendelssohn to Ferdinand David, October 21, 1841, *Briefe aus Leipziger Archiven*, p. 169.

in the ancient texts, the *Stimmungen* that could be translated into modern forms.[114]

Although Mendelssohn was asked to comment in print on the principles of his musical translation, he refused to do so.[115] As in his 1829 revival of the *St. Matthew Passion*, he let others analyze in words what he felt he had clearly stated through his tones. Both his friend and former classical tutor Droysen, and Droysen's mentor, Boeckh, despite some original misgivings, rallied to Mendelssohn's defense.[116] Droysen and Boeckh were historicists who rejected presentist constructions of the meaning of ancient documents and sought to interpret historical artifacts within their social and cultural contexts, but they were not purists ready to accept a radical disjuncture between past and present. Both believed that the ancient Greeks could still speak to modern Germans, that a spiritual thread connected ancient Greece and modern Prussia, and that Greek artists and thinkers should be assimilated into contemporary German consciousness through creative translations that allowed a dialogical encounter with the past and eventual recognition of the spiritual bond between past and present. Both felt that Mendelssohn's music constituted an appropriate form of mediation between the historical letter and the spirit of the past. But within such discussions of historical method, the actual content of the living essence that could still be expected to produce authentic subjective responses and genuine musical ideas in the present was left somewhat obscure.

The context of a specific tradition of *Antigone* interpretation in early-nineteenth-century Germany operated as an assumed background of the debate. Since the modern revival of Sophocles by the early German Romantics, critical interest was focused on the ethical and social meaning of the conflict between Antigone's absolute loyalty to her subjective feelings for her brother and family, feelings that she experienced as grounded in traditional religious beliefs, and the claims, represented by King Creon, of the rationally ordered life of the city as a public community of strangers. Ancient customs versus rational law, subjective convictions versus public order – these were the tragic, apparently irresolvable conflicts in *Antigone* that absorbed the attention of early-nineteenth-century Europeans, and probably were at the root of Mendelssohn's personal absorption as well. As Michael Steinberg has argued, it is difficult to conclude, simply from Mendelssohn's music, exactly where he stood in this debate.[117] What is clear is that he didn't fully support in anything like a one-sided fashion, either a pro-Creon or pro-Antigone interpretation. Perhaps more significantly, there is no real

[114] Mendelssohn's friend Devrient, who played Creon's son Haemon in the production, has described this debate in his memoirs: Devrient, *Errinerungen*, p. 220.

[115] Letter to Professor Dehn, October 28, 1841, *Briefe*, vol. 2, pp. 204–5.

[116] Konold, *Mendelssohn*, pp. 215–16.

[117] Michael P. Steinberg, "The Incidental Politics to Mendelssohn's *Antigone*," R. Larry Todd, *Mendelssohn and His World* (Princeton: 1991), pp. 137–57.

musical indication that Mendelssohn held to the kind of historical hopes expressed in his youth by Hegel and still held to some degree by Droysen and Boeckh – that the conflicts displayed in the play were open to future historical resolution in the ethical community of the modern state. And although Mendelssohn's choruses may have sounded much like the spiritual concert music he wrote for Christian texts, there is no reason to believe that he accepted the interpretation apparently suggested by Tieck (and shared by the king) that Antigone's martyrdom prefigured a Christian sacrificial death and led to a moral transformation of those who had sinned against her. Instead, Mendelssohn's music seemed to accept the rhetorical modesty counseled in the play's concluding lines, which rejected the presumptuous claims of overweaning words and fanatical hubris of any kind and found consolation only in a self-reflective wisdom based on resignation to transcendent authority. Yet one could also say that Mendelssohn's own ambition in supplementing the text with his music was to frame its conflicts with a contextual meaning that gave voice to precisely this often ignored "universal" message. There is no triumphant choral finale in Mendelssohn's score, but the final chorus does look back to the orchestral introduction in a typically Mendelssohnian cyclical fashion in order to produce an aesthetic unity where political and ethical conflicts persist. Art cannot resolve the conflicts of earthly existence, but by transcending them it also submits to divine will, to the transcendent authority of the father.

The Scottish Symphony, whose composition paralleled that of the Antigone music, dealt with similar conflicts between past and present in a slightly different way.[118] In this case the historical moment that Mendelssohn was trying to translate into the musical present was most obviously a personal one. The haunting theme around which the symphony is built was written out in July 1829, during Mendelssohn's youthful tour of Scotland with his friend Karl Klingemann, soon after his initial leave-taking from the parental nest. Specifically, it refers to a moment in which a *Stimmung* of the haunting of the present by the past was evoked by a series of historical associations. He "discovered" his theme in the deep twilight hours of July 29, 1829, as he walked through the rooms of Holyrood palace, observed its ruined chapel, and thought about the tragic fate of Queen Mary Stuart. His general mood had already been set by his associations of Scotland with the historical novels of Walter Scott (whom he visited the next day) and perhaps Schiller's famous play, as well as his observations of Highland clan members who had come to Edinburgh in traditional folk dress for a festival. "It seems that time moves very rapidly when I have so much of the past right next to

[118] The dating of the composition of all but the opening theme of the Scottish Symphony in the summer and fall of 1841 was established by Stuart Douglas Seaton from a study of manuscript drafts in his Columbia University doctoral dissertation, *A Study of the Collection of Mendelssohn's Sketches and Other Autograph Material* (New York, 1977), pp. 211ff.

the present before me," he had written on July 28.[119] Just after accepting the call from Berlin, Mendelssohn began developing and working through this youthful memory of historical loss, ruin, passing, and melancholy contemplation, which he had scribbled down as a pensive balladlike theme in 1829, into what would become his most famous symphonic work.

The four movements of the symphony are structured as a continuous narrative of episodes, or scenes, in which the introductory memory evolves through a series of complex variations and conflicts.[120] The accomplished maturity of the musical historicism achieved in the Scottish Symphony is exceptional, but the pattern it reveals is largely familiar and in many ways echoes the pattern of the rejected Reformation Symphony of 1830–32. The first two movements evoke historical tableaux of ancient times, in both chivalric and folk dimensions, conjuring up a lost world that gradually collapses under the pressures and demands of the modern individual subject. The third movement, adagio, explicates the contrast between a theme of subjective longing and the apparent opacity of a martial order that excludes or denies it. The major part of the final movement – designated *allegro guerrioro*, or "warlike allegro," in Mendelssohn's premiere program – sets opposing public principles into conflict that remains unresolved. Instead, the conflicts fade into quiet resignation, only to be displaced by a surprising second finale, a *finale maestoso*, that begins afresh and intones a triumphant hymn of unity and victory in a manner that Mendelssohn himself compared to a powerful male chorus. A recent analysis of this structurally eccentric second finale has revealed that it actually brings another "memory" into play to resolve the apparently irresolvable musical tensions of the symphony and provide a conclusion to its inconclusive narrative, by incorporating reminiscences of the triumphant hymn to the German cultural idea that Mendelssohn had composed for the Gutenberg festival in 1840.[121] The melancholic theme of the introduction is thus assimilated into a communal chorus of affirmative jubilation and thanksgiving, but this affirmation itself remains the memory of a hope Mendelssohn was trying to reaffirm in a period when his confidence in a cultural resolution of dissonance and the continuous regeneration of the spirit from the letter of tradition had become troubled and uncertain.

Both the *Antigone* music and the Scottish Symphony were attempts to revitalize not only the idea in the letter of tradition, but also the hopes of Mendelssohn's youth. After the completion of these projects, Mendelssohn's

[119] Mendelssohn to his mother, July 28, 1829, *Die Familie Mendelssohn*, p. 268. The moment of inspiration is described in a letter to his mother of July 30 (*ibid.*, p. 270).

[120] There is a wonderful analysis of the connection between Mendelssohn's technique of creating a narrative from evocative historical tableaux and the popular visual entertainments of dioramas, panoramas, and *tableaux vivants* in Thomas S. Grey, "Tableaux Vivants: Landscape, History Painting and the Visual Imagination of Mendelssohn's Orchestral Music," *19th-Century Music* 21 (1997): 38–77.

[121] Peter Mercer-Taylor, "Mendelssohn's 'Scottish Symphony' and the Music of German Memory," *19th-Century Music* 19, no. 1 (1995): 68–83.

attempts to sustain and work through his own memories of historical possibility became even more pronounced. The two most important works he completed and performed publicly in 1842–43 were directly related to earlier compositions. The revised *Die Erste Walpurgisnacht* expressed a conscious reaffirmation of his fidelity to what he saw as the universalism embedded in Goethe's aesthetic and historical stance, and his loyalty to a type of religious truth that was accessible through enlightened feeling and that outlived the particular historical rituals and dogmas in which it first appeared in space and time. By representing the ancient pagans as enlightened universalists, and the historically emerging Christians as narrow-minded persecutors, the cantata also clarified some of the ambiguities about Mendelssohn's relationship to contemporary Christianity and reasserted his commitment to the tradition of enlightened Judaism represented by his father and grandfather. The truth that spoke through the voice of religious tradition was a transcendent truth, the word of the father, rather than the self-made truth of mere finite humans, but this truth was universally accessible and not restricted to any particular confessional revelation. In this context, the liturgical music that Mendelssohn composed during the same period for the Evangelical Church in Prussia, the Anglican Church in England, the Reformed synagogue in Hamburg, and a Catholic cathedral in Liege were clearly revealed as aesthetic "translations" in which exclusive liturgical forms were saved from historical obsolescence by translating their living spirit into modern idiom. Mendelssohn's difficulties in remaining within the restrictive boundaries of liturgical requirements, his tendency to transform every piece of church music into a fully composed piece of modern autonomous music, displayed his view of translation as a creative act of aestheticization. Mendelssohn seemed to have an increasing need after 1841 to make clear that his historicism was not restorationist and his piety not confessionally exclusive.[122]

The incidental music that Mendelssohn added to his already famous concert overture for a production of Shakespeare's *Midsummer Night's Dream* in the summer and fall of 1843 displayed an even more obvious "return" to the memories of youth than *Die Erste Walpurgisnacht*. For the siblings and friends who were invited to the first private performance at the New Palace in Potsdam, the *Midsummer Night's Dream* music seemed an intensely personal attempt to revive memories of the family and intellectual circle in which that play had been a constant favorite during the 1820s. The fact that Mendelssohn was able to compose almost an hour of new music that appeared seamlessly connected to a concert overture he had composed seventeen years earlier has often been viewed as an indication that he was

[122] Charles Rosen has recently repeated the longstanding judgment of Mendelssohn's religious music as religious kitsch because of its focus on evoking religious piety as a subjective feeling without substantial content. See Charles Rosen, *The Romantic Generation* (Cambridge, Mass.: 1995), 590–8. Lawrence Kramer provides a spirited defense of the cosmopolitan, enlightened religiosity evident in works like *Die Erste Walpurgisnacht*, in "Felix Culpa: Goethe and the Image of Mendelssohn," in Todd, *Mendelssohn Studies*, 64–79.

simply repeating himself in his last years, that he could not move beyond the compositional achievements of his youth. But the music composed in 1843 was also a remarkable achievement: the explication and assimilation of an earlier historical moment into a more mature, clarified affirmation in the present. Here the overture itself functioned as the thematic prologue that was explicated, worked through, and recreated into a more convincing aesthetic totality by the incidental music. Mendelssohn's music was also a striking interpretation of the Shakespearean play as an expression of the ability of art to provide a perspective from which the confusions and conflicts of mundane existence could be resolved into harmony and organic meaning.[123]

Mendelssohn composed the first (English) version of *Elijah* during the year after he returned to Leipzig as his primary residence and home, and finished and revised it during the last year of his life. Although hardly a last testament or a final synthetic culmination of his development of the principles of musical historicism, it did constitute a reflection on his commitments in the wake of the Berlin experience.

Consideration of the Old Testament story of the prophet Elijah as the subject for an oratorio first appeared in Mendelssohn's correspondence a few months after the successful premiere of *Paulus*. For three years, from the fall of 1836 to the fall of 1839, Mendelssohn tried intermittently, first with Klingemann and then with Schubring, to sketch out an appropriate libretto from the biblical texts. A number of elements in the Old Testament accounts attracted Mendelssohn's imagination: the scene where God passed over Elijah like a breath of air, the final ascent into heaven. But it was the personality of Elijah himself that drew Mendelssohn most persistently to these texts. "I had actually imagined Elijah," he wrote to Schubring in 1838, "as a proper dyed-in-the-wool prophet, of the kind we could use again in our own day – strong, zealous, somewhat malicious, angry and dark, in opposition to the popular rabble as well as the rabble at the court, and pretty much in contradiction with the whole world, and yet carried along as if on the wings of angels."[124]

This first attempt to compose *Elijah* seems to have foundered on Mendelssohn's inability to get his librettists – either Klingemann or Schubring – to grasp his conception of the piece. Mendelssohn insisted that he wanted his new oratorio to be set in a "dramatic" rather than an "epic" mode. What he meant by "dramatic," however, was not always obvious. He did not mean that the movement of the music should be driven forward by the visible actions of the characters on the stage. He did, however, want to regain the immediacy of the original texts by eliminating the third-person narrator and recitative passages as much as possible. The singers, both

[123] Friedhelm Krummacher, "'. . . fein und geistreich genug': Versuch ueber Mendelssohns Musik zum Sommernachtstraum," in Dahlhaus, *Das Problem Mendelssohn*, 89–117.

[124] Mendelssohn to Schubring, November 2, 1838, *Briefwechsel zwischen Felix Mendelssohn Bartholdy und Julius Schubring*, p. 135.

individuals and choral groups, were to present themselves as living and acting speakers, creating a sense of immediate connection to the "genuinely vivid, concrete world [*recht anschauliche Welt*]" of the Old Testament. The meaning of the text should be conveyed to the audience not so much in the form of a commentary on the action but through the voices and the emotional tone (*Stimmung*) of the acting persons themselves.[125]

Schubring interpreted Mendelssohn's wishes as a desire to construct an historical "tone picture," as an attempt to recreate a scene from the past without drawing out its meaning for the present. He insisted that Mendelssohn would have to make a choice between conjuring up scenes from the historical past or integrating the Old Testament story into a teleological construction that culminated in Christ's resurrection and the descent of the Holy Spirit into the Christian community. Only the latter choice, Schubring felt, could make the text emotionally gripping and edifying for a present audience.[126] Mendelssohn, however, resisted a Christian interpretation of Elijah's life and sought to make an "objective" historical reconstruction convey its own meanings.

After Mendelssohn received the commission to compose an oratorio from Birmingham in the summer of 1845, he renewed his conversation with Schubring about an appropriate libretto. This time he was more insistent, confident, and clear about his own conceptions and ignored Schubring's doubts and misunderstandings as he pushed forward with the composition. Elijah was to be the central, and only, dramatic figure in the oratorio. The other persons and groups entered the action only at points where they might reveal the internal struggles of the major character. The public sphere became the arena in which the central character came to understand the contradictions of his inner life and his ultimate dependence on a transcendent power. The style was to be that of a succession of dramatic scenes with a minimum of recitative narrative to provide transitional material. Those choruses that were not themselves part of the dramatic action were to comment on the meaning of Elijah's actions and his fate. Assimilation of the Old Testament story into New Testament meaning through the use of chorales and a culminating apotheosis in which Elijah would appear as Christ's forerunner was rejected as "too historical."[127]

[125] Mendelssohn to Schubring, December 6, 1838, *ibid.*, p. 147.

[126] Schubring to Mendelssohn, November 1, 1838, *ibid.*, p. 139.

[127] Mendelssohn to Schubring, May 23, 1846, and Schubring's response, June 15, 1846, *ibid.*, pp. 221–3. In this sense, Mendelssohn shifted more drastically away from the progressive historical notions still evident in his composition of the incidental music for Racine's seventeenth-century play about an Old Testament story – *Athalie* – a year before, In the *Athalie* music, however, Mendelssohn was dealing with a text that already drew the analogy between the Old Testament and the problematic of Christian monarchy. In his incidental music, Mendelssohn had celebrated the king's return to his calling in relation to his people and culture with a reworked version of the festive Christmas chorale "Vom Himmel Hoch." See Douglass Seaton, "Mendelssohn's Dramatic Music," in Seaton, ed., *Mendelssohn Companion*, pp. 210–33.

It was difficult for Mendelssohn to find the appropriate musical language for his conception of the historical meaning of Elijah. His composition did not fit into existing conventions of either a symbolic oratorio that used its historical materials to develop certain ethical or theological conceptions without serious regard for their historical settings, or the epic form, in which historical moments were absorbed into a story told by a narrator. His view of history did not conform easily to either the model of a "tone picture" that provided a window into a foreign and distant world, or of a progressive historical narrative in which all pasts became mere moments in the inclusive totality of the present. Popular audiences responded enthusiastically to Mendelssohn's musical message; musical critics and commentators, however, were puzzled by what seemed to be a contradictory or confused compositional conception. What critics saw as weakness or confusion in Mendelssohn's composition, however, was often the result of his conscious intentions and integral to the relationships among personal identity, ethical community, and transcendent authority, which he wished his music to convey.

Although Mendelssohn preferred the numbers of the oratorio to be performed without pause, *Elijah* is not an unbroken narrative account of the prophet's development toward divine illumination and self-recognition, but a series of scenes or episodes, joined by connective or bridge passages, that display specific moments of dramatic interaction in which a movement toward self-knowledge can be discerned. The oratorio opens not with an overture or chorus but, unconventionally,[128] with a short (12-measure) expressive recitative in which Elijah, confidently identifying himself with the voice of God, announces a curse of drought and famine as a punishment upon the people of Israel. Two striking elements of this opening provide an initial characterization of the prophet, his stance, and his fate. Four solemn minor chords, followed by an ascending D-minor triad, resonant with tragic implications and premonitions of death, announce Elijah's entry and the pronouncement of the curse. In the statement of the curse itself, the strikingly dissonant falling intervals of the tritone (diminished fifths, or intervals of three full tones, C to F-sharp, G to C-sharp, and then, in the instruments alone, D to G-sharp) suggest the existence of a disharmonious relationship between God and his people, but also perhaps a dissonant note in Elijah's own stance and a problem in his self-confident identification with the divine voice[129] (Fig. 38).

[128] Unconventional, but not unique. Mendelssohn may have had Handel's opening to *Israel in Egypt* in mind as a model. He had recently studied and conducted this work.

[129] The "tritone" was a very well-known, traditional "sign" of some kind of emotional or spiritual dissonance. Mozart's *Don Giovanni* and Weber's *Der Freischuetz* used it prominently as a motif for the devil's presence. More generally it was a common marker of unease, misery, and alienation. See *New Grove's Dictionary of Music and Musicians*, ed. Stanley Sadie (20 vols.; Washington, 1980), vol. 15, pp. 485–7.

Fig. 38. Speaking in God's voice? Elijah's curse on his people.
Source: Reproduced from the Gregg Press facsimile edition of the *Werke* (Leipzig: Breitkopf and Haertel, 1874–77).

In their repeated use throughout the oratorio, both motifs would become prominent, suggestive signs for "reading" the musical text.[130] Their first function, however, was to introduce a group of musical numbers – the overture and numbers 1 to 5 – that provide the setting for the scenes that follow. The curse leads immediately into a short instrumental overture, which presents a gradual crescendo of instrumental voices that enter separately in a fugal manner but never resolve themselves into a true fugue. Instead they build toward a massive climax of despair and confusion, as the effect of the curse is felt in the world, and merge without pause into the opening measures of the first choral number, in which the growing sense of calamity and desperation culminates in the anguished cries of the people for help. Choral expressions of unjust suffering and pleas for relief turn into a multivoiced fugal lament that expresses bitter resentment at God's apparent betrayal and abandonment of his people, before it turns into a homophonic choral recitative of deep despair that leads into a prayerful plea into which Mendelssohn melded elements of a traditional Jewish song of lamentation. The prophet Obadiah then appears (numbers 4 and 5) as an interpreter of Elijah's curse, asking the people to seek the cause of their suffering in their own hearts and to trust that God will answer a sincerely felt and properly formulated request. The scene closes with a large two-part chorus. The first part, in C minor, is an agitated *allegro vivace* in which the people return to an accusatory mode and lament the unjust severity of a jealous God rather than their own sins. The tritone again makes its appearance here (more pervasively, perhaps a sign of its dissemination throughout the "people") as an indicator of the exaggerated disharmony produced by the people's attempt to reject their complicity in their own suffering. The chorus modulates into a C-major coda that emphasizes God's mercy toward those who sincerely love and obey Him. The introductory section of the oratorio thus opens up the scene of a world cursed by self-imposed suffering and of people entangled in futile attempts to place the blame for this suffering on others. It is this self-righteousness that Elijah must address without falling into self-righteousness himself. Although the music briefly suggests some hope for self-recognition and reconciliation, it is not clear that Elijah represents or knows how to fully articulate the path toward such a resolution. There is a dissonance between his message and his character, and the possibility of a tragic fate informs his own voice.

The remainder of the first half of *Elijah* consists of three episodes set as dramatic dialogues between Elijah and the victims of his curse. The first

[130] *Elijah* does not contain nearly as many historical citations – either melodic or formal – as *Paulus* or *Lobgesang*. Friedhelm Krummacher has argued that the unity and expressiveness of the musical narrative in *Elijah* is much more dependent on internal harmonic and structural techniques that are internally referential than Mendelssohn's earlier sacred music. See Krummacher, "Art–History–Religion," in Seaton, *Mendelssohn Companion*, pp. 323–83.

episode finds Elijah in a personal encounter with a widow and her orphaned son, who are both victims of his curse and instruments of divine compassion, since God has chosen them to sustain Elijah with food and drink. In response to the widow's accusation that the divine curse is destroying her child (in number 8, where the tritone makes a clear appearance in measures 10 and 11), Elijah pleads for God to reveal his compassion and mercy by saving the son's life. The prayer is answered, and Elijah and the widow join the chorus in celebrating the enlightenment that makes it possible for the pious to recognize God as compassionate, just, and merciful. The choral conclusion of the scene is set in the confident unclouded harmonies and sweeping lyrical lines of a G-major fugue.

The familiar minor chords and dissonant tritone intervals in Elijah's voice immediately shatter this idyllic moment, as we are displaced into a new scene in which the prophet confronts the infidel King Ahab, the misguided people, and the priests of the false god Baal. Returning to his public role, Elijah once again takes on an accusatory stance, mocking his enemies and calling down God's wrath on the unrighteous. God sends a miraculous fire from heaven, apparently justifying Elijah's self-confidence, cowing the people and scattering his enemies. In what appears to be a misreading of the message of a quartet of angels who advise him in a choralelike hymn to place his burden upon the Lord, Elijah aggressively calls down the fire and the hammer of vengeance on his enemies. The relationship between music and text presents a complex message in this scene. The priests of Baal are represented at first (in F major) as a confident chorus of believers, more misguided than malicious, and seem to fall into a genuine disillusionment (in F-sharp minor) when their misguided faith is exposed as ignorance. Elijah, on the other hand, sings in a voice of self-righteousness and brutal vengeance as he encourages the people to slaughter his enemies. How his identification with a God whose word is like a fire or a hammer and who constantly threatens his creatures with destruction is connected to the angel's representation of God's voice as one of justice and harmony is not clear. The scene ends not with a chorus of triumph or reconciliation but with a meditative alto aria about the woeful fate of those who hide from the enlightening power of the divine word in the deceptive web of their own lies.

The final scene in part 1 places Elijah in a different situation. He must now show the people that God is a God of compassion and mercy who can end the drought and alleviate their suffering. With the help of his own disciple, Obadiah, and a young boy who scans the skies for the promised rain, Elijah pleads for his people as deserving of divine mercy. The rain comes, and the people vanquish their deceivers and regain their faith on the basis of an enlightening miracle. The community returns to its spiritual center, finds its genuine leader and intones a rousing chorus of jubilation and thanks. Thus ends part 1. But like so many of Mendelssohn's resolutions, this one is only temporary, and in some sense illusory. As the tenors enter in D flat over a sustained C in the basses, in the final chorus of part 1, a strikingly dissonant transition introduces a line – "But the Lord is above them and almighty" ("*Doch der Herr ist noch groesser in der Hoehe*") – which suggests that the apparent reconciliation between the transcendent father and his earthly children is not yet accomplished, or perhaps that the people's exultant confidence that a transcendent purpose is embodied in their national history is a subjective illusion. In the second half of the oratorio, Mendelssohn made quite clear that an earthly triumph of the righteous with God's help was not the moral message he meant to convey to his contemporaries.

Mendelssohn introduced part 2 with a soprano recitative and aria, which convey that, despite the miracles of part 1, the people have not heeded the divine commands. Thus Elijah must begin his task of preaching moral conversion once again and must come to recognize the limits of his powers. What follows is again a series of scenes, or episodes, but now the drama moves increasingly toward Elijah's inner life, the relationship between the self and its transcendent ground and between the earthly son and the divine father. The people are removed from the narrative and the choruses become meditative commentaries on Elijah's inner states. The first scene brings us back to the court to reveal an Elijah still hoping that a wave of destruction will prove his righteousness, an unrepentant king and queen presiding in a public sphere ruled by self-interest, and a people easily persuaded by their leaders to fall back into deception and direct their resentments against the prophet who asks them to look into themselves for the source of their woes. Driven to despair by the people's refusal to see the light and transform their inner selves, Elijah removes himself once again to the desert. Here Mendelssohn, in one of his most popular and moving arias – "It is enough" – portrays a prophet who is in despair not only because his people would not heed his warnings but also because he sees himself as "not better than my fathers." The key here (F-sharp minor) is the same as that of the chorus of the Baal priests who had lost faith in their god. As Elijah struggles with the failure of his moral mission and despairs about his own identity as a mouthpiece for the divine voice, his inner battle is accompanied by an angelic choir and then a consoling chorus that try to focus his attention on his relationship to the transcendent father, rather than on his earthly trials and failures. The lyrical, sentimental beauty of these hymns to paternal love (the a capella trio "Lift thine eyes" and the chorus, "He, watching over Israel") drove nineteenth-century audiences to tearful ecstasy. They introduce the climactic scene in which God deigns to reveal himself to Elijah on Mount Horeb. Elijah approaches this moment still hoping that God will reveal himself in miracles, and especially in acts of vengeance on his enemies. An angel counsels him to let go of his anger and his resentments against the world. But it is the music that displays that God does not reveal his true self in stormy anger and fiery vengeance but in an almost imperceptible "whisper" or "murmur" (*saeuseln*) that can only be heard once the storms and quakes and fires have passed by.

The final dramatic scene centers on Elijah's return from the mountaintop in order to bring the vision that he has received to the faithful remnant among the people. But Elijah's return seems to have left him unchanged. He spits angry fire at his enemies, encouraging the people to overthrow their deceitful, tyrannical rulers. He brings from Mt. Horeb a loud message of vengeance rather than the quiet murmur of trust and resignation. In the whirlwind of his own manic activity, he is snatched away by God in a fiery chariot and taken up into the heavens.

The last four numbers comment on the meaning of the Old Testament story. It was at this point, Schubring had argued, that Mendelssohn should bring in a Christian resolution. Certainly there is a suggestion of this in the final numbers, which hint at a time when fathers will be reconciled to their children by a light-bringing messianic figure. But the texts here are from the Old Testament, not the New, and the salvation that is imagined is, in typical Mendelssohnian fashion, a salvation of enlightenment. The emphasis in the penultimate chorus falls obviously on the phrase that the dawn will come, if it does come, through the power of the "spirit of wisdom and the spirit of understanding." But even this projection of a future in which gains in enlightenment will be matched by gains in the improvement of the human condition is imagined by Mendelssohn not as a newly discovered fraternal mutuality, but as a new relationship between human beings and their transcendent father. The vision of reconciliation is vertical rather than horizontal, a vision of reconciliation between father and children.

Elijah thus projected in its texts and in its music a conception of history that is consistent with the views Mendelssohn had developed through the 1830s and consolidated and reaffirmed during the 1840s. The music presents a narrative, not of the assimilation of tradition in the formation of a new cultural identity, but of an individual subjectivity that could never be fully actualized in any fixed communal identity, and needed to return to the source of all identities in the transcendent power that made them possible. To achieve enlightenment was to see this truth, to hear in tradition not the voice of the people but the voice of the father from which all peoples arose. *Elijah* could be interpreted as an attempt to validate Jewish culture as a moment in this process that was equal in value to classical and Christian cultures. Mendelssohn was not willing to reduce any of these moments to an assimilated component of one of the others. The meaning of *Elijah* was not unveiled for him by the "higher" illumination of the New Testament. All past and present historical cultures were "absolute" or immediate to God – the dilemmas of human finitude were equally present in all – but absolute precisely in their common historical limitations. Remaining conscious of the relationship to the transcendent father protected the individual subject against the tyranny of homogenized fraternity, against surrender to idols that claimed to represent fulfillment as a specific historical achievement.

This historical message, this conception of personal identity as an internalization of an essential humanity defined through its dependence on an absolute ground – humanity imagined as the son, the absolute as the father – was best articulated, Mendelssohn believed, ever more insistently in his last years, through commitment to the autonomy of art. It was in the realm of aesthetic production and consumption that the meaning within the historical evolution of cultural ideas was revealed. Personal identity as historical identity was defined through the vertical relationship of individual subjectivity to the transcendent ground of subjectivity, through recognition of the self's contingency as an historical being and of its foundations in the divine Being from which all historical beings were produced. It was in the production of art, and especially in the making of music, that this relationship was most fully articulated. The artist grasped and expressed the meaning of history most profoundly. Curiously, it was a tribute to Mendelssohn penned by Prince Albert of England after the London performances in April 1847 that focused on this dimension in *Elijah*:

> To the Noble Artist who, surrounded by the Baal-worship of debased art, has been able, by his genius and science, to preserve faithfully, like another Elijah, the worship of true art, and once more to accustom our ear amid the whirl of empty, frivolous sounds, to the pure tones of sympathetic feeling and legitimate harmony: to the Great Master, who makes us conscious of the unity of his conception, through the whole maze of his creation, from the soft whispering to the mighty raging of the elements.

Mendelssohn reportedly responded to this royal tribute with "rapturous exclamations of delight, as over and over again he read each word of the description."[131]

[131] The tribute and Mendelssohn's response (as recorded in the report of the London Sacred Harmonic Society) are cited in Werner, *Mendelssohn's "Elijah,"* p. 31.

Part III

Law, Language, and History: Cultural Identity and the Self-Constituting Subject in the Historical School

5

The Tension Between Immanent and Transcendent Subjectivity in the Historical School of Law: From Savigny to Stahl

Friedrich Karl von Savigny, Jacob Grimm, and Leopold von Ranke have all been recognized as founding fathers of the "Historical School," as preeminent scholar–intellectuals who transformed the historical perspective that emerged among members of the first Romantic generation during the period of domestic reform and national liberation into the foundational principles of the nineteenth-century academic disciplines of jurisprudence, Germanic philology, and historiography.[1] At the University of Berlin, the line defining the boundaries between "historical" and "philosophical" schools was constructed in a series of academic controversies and appointment battles during the 1820s and early 1830s.[2] Within this academic context, the Prussian "new course" of 1840 represented a triumph for the Historical School and public recognition of its founders. But the historical perspective that triumphed with the Historical School in 1840 was no longer equivalent to the perspective propounded in the decade following the defeat of Napoleon in 1814–15. In the following three chapters I will examine the ways in which the early "Romantic" historicism of Savigny, Grimm, and Ranke was transformed in response to the changing historical context between 1825 and 1840 in similar, parallel, ways, producing an inwardly conflicted perspective on the nature of historical identity and the experience of becoming historical.

As the founder of the Historical School of Law (*Historische Rechtsschule*), Savigny has often been described as a representative figure of that peculiarly early-nineteenth-century Romantic version of faith in incarnate divinity – belief in the self-determination and self-validation of truth and value within the immanent historical sphere of human cultural relations. However, it is significant that during the 1830s and 1840s Savigny increasingly identified himself with Prussian intellectuals and officials who were critical of this "pantheistic" perspective of Romantic historicism and sought to ground ethical norms and political authority on obedience to the revealed will of a patriarchal, transcendent God. The intellectual and personal foundations

[1] See, for example, Erich Rothaker, "Savigny, Grimm, Ranke: Ein Beitrag zur Frage nach dem Zusammenhang der Historischen Schule," *Historische Zeitschrift* 128 (1923): 415–45, an influential essay summarizing the "crisis of historicism" debates in Germany in the early twentieth century.

[2] As Ranke vividly remembered in the 1860s: See "Beim fuenfzigjaehrigen Doktorjubilaeum," Leopold Von Ranke, *Saemmtliche Werke* (54 vols.; Leipzig: 1867–90), vols. 51/52, p. 588.

for this accommodation between Savigny and political and religious ultras on the Right were gradually forged during the 1830s and put to the test by Frederick William IV's accession to the Prussian throne in 1840. Savigny had been the crown prince's tutor immediately after the Napoleonic wars and remained in close personal contact with him through the ensuing years, emerging as a key figure in Frederick William's coterie in the 1830s. In 1842 he was appointed to the post of Minister of Justice for Legislation and Legal Revision and found himself faced with the task of giving legislative shape to the new king's desire to reconstruct civil law and social ethics on transcendent foundations and to mold the historical identities of his subjects as Germans and Prussians according to Christian principles. At this point tensions between contrasting ethnical and ethical conceptions of what it meant to possess a historical identity merged into dilemmas in practice, leading to what has often been seen as a failure of political will on Savigny's part.[3]

In this chapter I will examine the tension between Savigny's original model of the immanent historical genesis and evolution of law, and the alternative model, in which the rules of social bonding were grounded in transcendent authority, through a three-step contextual analysis. Focusing on an internal analysis of the most familiar and representative of Savigny's published writings, the first step will delineate the changes that emerged in his conception of the historical foundation of legal institutions between his programmatic essays of 1814–16 and his great synthetic work of the 1840s, the *System des heutigen roemischen Rechts* (The System of Contemporary Roman Law), paying particular attention to the tensions between immanent and transcendent models of the genesis and development of law. The second part of the chapter will interpret the shifts in Savigny's theories as responses to his experiences of a changing configuration of cultural and political forces, especially in Prussia, during the 1830s. Finally, the immanent–transcendent tension in Savigny will be examined in comparative context, by contrasting it, in somewhat schematic fashion, to the stance of Friedrich Julius Stahl (1802–61), a legal philosopher of a younger generation who aggressively developed into closed dogmatic positions what had been tendencies in Savigny and who, soon after being called to Berlin with Savigny's enthusiastic backing in 1840, began to overshadow his older mentor as a public spokesperson for the legal and political policies of the new regime and its conception of the identities of communities and individuals as historically determined identities.

[3] The connection between Savigny's historicist theories and his administrative actions in the 1840s was already noted by contemporaries like Karl Varnhagen von Ense and Ernst Ludwig von Gerlach, and assumed in historical accounts of Savigny's political activity published later in the century: Heinrich von Treitschke, *Deutsche Geschichte im neunzehnten Jahrhundert* (5 vols.; Leipzig, 1895–97), vol. 5, pp. 250–4; and Adolf F. Stoelzel, *Brandenburg-Preussens Rechtsverwaltung und Rechtsverfassung*, (2 vols.; Berlin: 1888), vol. 2, pp. 535–620. See also Mathias Freiherr von Rosenberg, *Friedrich Carl von Savigny (1779–1861) im Urteil seiner Zeit* (Frankfurt: 2000), pp. 147–51.

FROM *VOLKSGEMEINSCHAFT* TO STATE AND RELIGION: TRANSFORMATIONS OF SAVIGNY'S LEGAL HISTORICISM, 1815–1840

The first volume of *System des heutigen roemischen Rechts*, conceived and written during the late 1830s and published in the spring of 1840, summarizes Savigny's historical and methodological positions at the moment of transition to the new Prussian regime. It thus serves as a convenient reference point for examining elements of continuity and discontinuity in Savigny's conception of the genesis, evolution, and foundation of law as both the ordering shape and the ordering process for the integration of individual subjects into ethnic and ethical communities.

The starting point of Savigny's analysis of the origins of law in the *System*, and the claim for which he is most widely known, was that every system of positive or actual law that appeared in recorded history originated as a particular dimension of the objectification or external self-shaping of the "powers and activities" (*Kraefte und Taetigkeiten*) of a collective human subject – the "people" (*Volk*). At the moment of its documented historical appearance, Savigny insisted, law already possessed "real existence" as "positive law" in the shared feelings, thoughts, and convictions of this collective subject. "If we seek the subject in which and for which positive law has its existence," Savigny wrote, "we find the people. Positive law lives in the common consciousness of the people and we must therefore call it people's law [*Volksrecht*]."[4] Although Savigny occasionally referred to the people as a "natural unity" or "natural totality," he refused to speculate about the possible prehistorical evolution of natural tribes into cultural peoples (whose boundaries were linguistic rather than biological) and claimed that the genesis of positive law in the consciousness of a people was ultimately inaccessible to the historian who depended on extant written documents for his reconstructions.[5] Savigny's theory of origins was thus restricted to the moment of transition from an internal, invisible reality to a visible, external reality, from oral to written culture. What was crucial, however, was his insistence that although the historical scholar had documentary access only to the external law, this law was not self-explanatory but should be interpreted as a manifestation of something deeper, of a "reality" that made possible the documentary "appearance." The assumption that positive law existed in the consciousness of a collective subject prior to its external appearance was justified, he claimed, by the general recognition among historical peoples of the external manifestation once it actually became manifest, by the feelings of necessity or timeless "given-ness" of the law that accompanied such recognition, and by the universal cultural production of myths that ascribed

[4] *System des heutigen roemischen Rechts* (8 vols.; Berlin, 1840–49), vol. 1, p. 14.

[5] *Ibid.*, vol. 1, pp. 19, 20.

divine origins to the laws that articulated the social bond among any given people.[6]

Savigny's description in 1840 of the generation of historical law as the objectification of positive law already existing in the collective consciousness of a communal ethnic subject was consistent with a position he had zealously defended since the publication of his polemical historicist manifesto *Vom Beruf unsrer Zeit fuer Gesetzgebung und Rechtswissenschaft* (On the Vocation of Our Time for Legislation and Jurisprudence) in 1814. Some elaboration and terminological modification – most notably the adoption of the term *Volksgeist* to designate the invisible common consciousness of the people – did not detract from this substantial continuity. Similarly, Savigny appeared to remain generally consistent in some of the propositions he derived from or justified by his theory of the genesis of law. First, it grounded his claim – directed against theories of universal natural or rational law – that all systems of historical law were, and necessarily had to be, culturally individuated and particular. Although individuated national legal systems shared common elements that could be called universal and might be derived from a common human essence, such universal elements did not possess a historically actual, positive existence in and for themselves. They attained reality only within the culturally differentiated forms of national law. The creation of law, Savigny insisted, was a "communal deed" that could occur only among those "for whom community of acting and thinking is not merely possible but actual." Since "such a community is present only within the boundaries of an individual people, it is only through a people that real law can be created, even though in this act of creation the externalization of a universal drive toward cultural self-determination and self-expression can be discerned."[7] In 1815, after stating that any attempt to discover a universal law valid for all peoples was as hopeless as trying to replace actual individual languages with a universal language, Savigny had recognized that "universally human, uniform tendencies [*Richtungen*], which could be defined as the philosophical element in all positive law, can be discerned in everything individual and differentiated."[8]

Between 1815 and 1840, however, Savigny's interest and intellectual focus had shifted markedly toward the universal elements incarnate in individual law, toward "the universal spirit that reveals itself in the people in an individual way,"[9] toward the philosophy implicit in history. In general conformity with the post-Kantian Idealist and Romantic traditions, Savigny defined human essence as the freedom of a subject capable of determination by self-imposed commands or rules. Human beings were differentiated from

[6] *Ibid.*, vol. 1, pp. 15–16. [7] *Ibid.*, vol. 1, p. 21.

[8] Savigny, review of Goenner, *Zeitschrift fuer Geschichtliche Rechtswissenschaft* 1 (1815), p. 396. Reprinted in Savigny, *Vermischte Schriften* (5 vols.; Berlin: 1850), vol. 5, pp. 115–72.

[9] *System*, vol. 1, p. 21.

animals primarily by their ability to master and control the natural determination of the self by instinctual drives and to act according to self-imposed rules of duty, to conform their aims and behavior to the inner promptings of their spiritual essence rather than the external necessities of their natural existence. The uniform elements in all historical legal systems thus emerged in Savigny's analysis as the general lawful relations of the free subject to itself, to the world of nature or material objects outside of itself, and to other free subjects in the world of social and political relations. In the *System*, Savigny treated the particular, historical, documentary materials of Roman law as signs of the general or "philosophical" element that was incarnate in them. Legal institutions, or institutes (*Rechtsinstitute*), that regulated property, marriage, paternal authority, and inheritance were presented as types of fundamental relations between a free being and its natural and human environment: They articulated the formal element in these concrete relations and protected the exercise of the individual human subject's essential freedom in these relations. "If free beings are to maintain themselves in mutual contact," Savigny wrote, "not restricting each other but aiding and nurturing each other in their development, this is possible only through recognition of an invisible boundary within which the existence and activity of each individual attains a secure and free space. The rule by which this boundary, and through it this free space, is established, is the law."[10] However, Savigny still maintained that the actual positive law regulating essential human freedom, as well as the ethical self-determination made possible by legal relations, remained historically individual; the actual shape of universal human freedom was always historical and national. In fact, the universality of the spatial and temporal limitations that defined all human existence in history ensured that in any particular national culture legal forms of dependence, reciprocity, and communal obligation would always complement the legal forms of individual autonomy.

The second principle that Savigny derived from his conception of the historical genesis of law was the principle of "organicism," or "totality." Over the years, Savigny remained consistent in his conviction that every individual rule, every lawful relation, and every legal institution could be successfully and fully comprehended only as a component of a system of relationships – economic, ethical, religious, political, or aesthetic – that constituted the ordered world of an historical subject in one of its major dimensions. Even if particular elements within these systems of relationships were not visibly articulated, they could be constructed or filled in by an interpreter who had grasped the guiding principles (*leitenden Grundsaetze*)[11] that informed the totality of relational networks. The tasks of exegesis and interpretation were contextual, moving in the hermeneutic circle from parts

[10] *Ibid.*, vol. 1, pp. 331–32. See also *ibid.*, vol. 1, pp. 347, 371; and *ibid*, vol. 1, p. 2.

[11] *Vom Beruf unserer Zeit fuer Gesetzgebung und Rechtswissenschaft*, 3d ed. (Heidelberg: 1840), p. 22.

to the whole and back again, but always gravitating toward that original, unifying, and unified subject that expressed its powers in visible systems of structured relations with nature, itself, and other subjects.

By 1840, however, Savigny's conception of both the totality of law and its place in the totality of national culture had become more complex and multilayered than in its original formulation in 1814. First, in his conceptual distinction between legal relations and legal "institutes" in the *System*, Savigny presented three clear layers within the relational system of civil law: the totality of the human subject's actual historical life relations, the formal structures implicit in these "material" life relations, and the systematic totality of legal "institutes" of an historical people that transformed these implicit forms into both abstract "types" and ordering rules. Although the organism of legal institutions was clearly derived from the actual totality of lived subjective relations, it was also characterized by an impersonality and "objectivity" that could be set against any specific existing life relation as its ideal or norm.[12] Second, in his early writing, Savigny had grouped the totality of the institutes of civil law with the systematic totalities of linguistic relations, ethical relations, and public or constitutional law relations as one dimension of the cultural expression of a unified collective subject.[13] In the *System*, Savigny retained this concept of the multiple dimensions of related totalities in an historical culture but also placed a new emphasis on the hierarchical ordering of these cultural layers, an ordering that positioned the public, constitutional law of the state and the religiously grounded commands of ethics as higher totalities enveloping and subordinating the system of civil law.

Finally, Savigny consistently claimed that positive law was not only a component of cross-sectional or synchronic cultural totalities, but also integrated into the temporal, successive, or diachronic totality of historical evolution.[14] The identity of individual cultures, and thus also of systems of law, over time was provided by the "inner necessity" of the "cultural drive" (*Bildungstrieb*) that impelled the collective national subject toward full self-determination and self-expression.[15] Each moment or stage in this development was a moment in a "fate" regulated by the potential innate activities and powers of the national spirit and its ability to actualize those potentialities (through adaptation, assimilation, and domination) in the face of opposition and adverse circumstance. The individual's consciousness of belonging to a particular national culture was thus connected not only to a recognition of the shared essence present in the *Volksgeist*, but also to an appropriation of the historical development that had given the *Volksgeist* its particular shape up to and including the historical present. It was not enough

[12] *System*, vol. 1, pp. 6–11, 332–33, 386–87, and *ibid.*, vol. 2, pp. 1–2.

[13] *Beruf*, pp. 8, 30; *Zeitschrift* 1 (1815): 3–6, 416.

[14] *Beruf*, p. 11, *Zeitschrift* 1 (1815): 2–3; *System*, vol. 1, p. 17.

[15] *System*, vol. 1, p. 17.

for Germans to recognize their roots in the pre-Roman and pre-Christian customary laws of the ancient Germanic tribes; they also needed to recognize themselves as part of a larger European cultural community that had become integral to German identity through the assimilation of Roman law and Christian ethical values since the fall of the Roman Empire. Historical identity did not consist merely in a recovery of the "memory" of birth or primal origin, but also in the reconstruction of the narrative of development that led from that origin to the present.[16]

The overall structural pattern that Savigny discerned in the development of individual cultures remained fairly uniform between 1814 and 1840, deriving as it did from the dialectical Romantic and Idealist paradigms inherited from his mentors and predecessors. In these historical models, development began with an original, unmediated, "natural" unity, followed by a fall into individuation, fragmentation, and alienation that culminated in a "return" to a higher, fully mediated, self-conscious identity within a systematic relational structure of recognized differences. The historical contents that Savigny inserted into these formally structured moments, and especially into the culminating moment of "return," however, shifted significantly in the years after 1830.

Savigny's description of the original stage of historical evolution changed least over the years. The historical moment of a culture's youth was characterized first of all by an almost total overlap of individual and collective consciousness. The individual members of an original ethnic people experienced and perceived the particular linguistic, legal, and ethical forms that gave shape to their common culture as the living forms of their own individual lives and thus possessed a full and clear, though unself-conscious, knowledge of the "relations" and "conditions" of their existence. Second, Savigny claimed that in this original historical consciousness, the world of legal relations and institutions through which the individual gave form to his mutual relations with other subjects was experienced not as an aggregate of separate individual parts, as rules and norms that were functionally bound to different activities, but as an integrated totality within an integrated culture. Law lived in the consciousness of the people not as an "abstract rule" but as a "living perception of law institutes in their organic connection" and within a "total perception" of all cultural forms. Finally, Savigny consistently stated that consciousness of law in the earliest stage of cultural evolution was fixed in inheritable structures in a concrete, sensuous fashion through symbolic actions, rituals, and ceremonies (the original "grammar of law") rather than in abstract rules, external statutes, or conceptual formulations.[17] Law was embedded in the evolving structure of social action before

[16] Tracing this development was the theme of Savigny's first great multivolume historical study, begun in 1815: *Geschichte des Roemischen Rechts im Mittelalter* (6 vols.; Heidelberg: 1815–31).

[17] *Beruf*, pp. 9–10; *System*, vol. 1, pp. 16–17.

it was articulated and thus separated out as a distinct reality in words and sentences.

In both 1814 and 1840, Savigny also described the historical progression beyond original cultural unity as a necessary evolution instigated not by external circumstance or arbitrary individual actions, but by the silently working, invisible drive of the national subject for full cultural expression of its innate powers. This progression took the form of a social division of labor and a differentiation of sociocultural functions. The professional specialization of individuated cultural vocations was socially articulated in the formation of specific function groups, or "estates," that in turn promoted differences of individual life experiences among members of a common culture and thus introduced complexities and difficulties into the maintenance of cultural integrity and continuity. Experience of membership in a single cultural totality became more and more diluted and abstract for individual members, and the activity of reproducing and adapting the forms of this totality in the process of continuous development and change was gradually surrendered to specialized functions and the social strata that embodied them. It was at this point, where the role of representing the cultural totality in a particular dimension was given over to a particular function and group, that Savigny's analysis in 1840 began to diverge sharply from his earlier historical vision.[18]

In the *Beruf* of 1814, Savigny constructed a theory in which the functions of the unified people as the collective creator, interpreter, and reviser of law was gradually transferred to the specialized estate of legal scholars and jurists, and the shared consciousness of law as an organic totality was reconstituted as a systematic comprehension and conceptual organization of the law in jurisprudence. "Law now articulates itself," he wrote, "in language and takes a scientific direction. As it formerly lived in the consciousness of the whole people, so it now finds a home in the consciousness of the jurists, through whom the people is henceforth represented in this function."[19] The potential and not infrequently actualized danger in this shift was that jurisprudence might forget the representative nature of its function within the totality of cultural relations and pursue the technical elaboration and revision of the letter of the law without constantly drawing on the life-giving and meaning-giving source of that law in the popular consciousness, or *Volksgeist*. This is what had happened to the tradition of Roman law in Germany in the later Middle Ages.[20] The collective consciousness of the people, however hidden and inarticulate it may have become, remained the final judge of whether or not the interpretations, elaborations, systematizations, and revisions of the jurists remained in harmony with the national will. Yet without the professional interpretative and systematizing skills of

[18] *Beruf*, pp. 1–12; *System*, vol. 1, pp. 17–18, 38–50. [19] *Beruf*, p. 12.

[20] This is the theme of the last two volumes of the *Geschichte*, published in 1829 and 1831.

the jurists, Savigny claimed, it would be impossible for a modern complex culture to assimilate and master the inherited materials that documented the collective memory of the people and constituted its continuity through the past, present, and future. For a modern culture to master its past and thus attain consciousness of its own identity, it required an estate or corporate body of jurists, trained in national institutions (universities), with access to the documentary record and in possession of an historical method that could sustain the life-giving contact between the collective consciousness of the people and the letter of the law. The purpose of the *Beruf* was to encourage such a development, oppose dangerous initiatives for the creation of artificial, ahistorical systems of national law, and thus close the circle of an inwardly "necessary" historical evolution. The original "natural" consciousness of cultural identity, in which historical memory was continuously present in the rituals of customs and repetitive social action, could be reconstituted in the conceptually elaborated, systematically organized world of self-conscious historical knowledge. There was a definite utopian element in Savigny's vision of historical "return" in 1814:

> Once jurisprudence as here described [i.e., as an historical science] has become the common possession of jurists, we will have attained once again, in the estate of jurists, a subject for living customary law and thus for true progress. . . . The historical material of the law, which now restricts us on every side, will be assimilated, mastered and enriched. We will then possess our own national law and a powerful, effective language for it will not be lacking. Then we can surrender Roman law to history. We will not possess merely a weak imitation of Roman culture, but our own completely individual and new culture. We will have gained something greater than a more rapid and effective judicial practice. The condition of clear, perceptual self-possession which is characteristic of the law of youthful peoples, will be united with the heights of scientific culture.[21]

The inner reform of legal scholarship and scholarly institutions according to historicist principles, Savigny projected, would produce an authentic representation of the collective cultural subject and provide the basis for a legal–political unification generated from within and "below," rather than imposed from without and from "above." Under the modern historical

[21] *Beruf*, p. 133. As a specialist in Roman law, Savigny tried to convince his compatriots that (1) Roman law was exemplary for them as a legal system in which the fragmentation of the national spirit had been overcome by a rediscovery of the formal elements that articulated unity within difference, and (2) that the actual assimilation of Roman law into German customary law since the late Middle Ages exemplified a similar quest for unity within difference among the fragmented German tribes and estates. Once this process was completed, Roman law as the "other" of German fragmentation would disappear. For a good discussion of the Roman law tradition in Germany and Savigny's particular place within it, see James Q. Whitman, *The Legacy of Roman Law in the German Romantic Era: Historical Vision and Legal Change* (Princeton, N.J.: 1990).

conditions of functional differentiation and cultural complexity, this implied the creation of a class of "organic" intellectuals (to borrow Gramsci's famous phrase), whose internal relations would prefigure the social relations of a community of free subjects and whose collective intellectual production would speak for the historically revealed, consciously recognized and mastered, will of the *Volk*.

By 1840 this vision had been revised at a number of critical points. In 1814, Savigny had conceded only a derivative and largely negative function to legislation, statutory law, and the state in the process of legal evolution. In the *System*, however, legislation was presented equal to jurisprudence as an "organ" of collective cultural consciousness. In fact, as the incorporation of people's law in the form of explicit written statutes enforced by the sovereign power of the state, legislation often appeared, in 1840, to have attained the status of a representative of the collective will that was superior to jurisprudence. The public law that defined the relations of authority in any cultural community, Savigny now claimed, was the highest phase in the self-expressive determination of a people's law. In the institutions of the state, the implicit, invisible identity of the people attained the visibility and corporeal organization that provided the community with a personality and thus also the capability for collective action. The state not only gave explicit form to the totality implicit in reciprocal relations among individual subjects, but it also enforced the dominion of this totality over the merely individual consciousness that was prone to "error," and over the individual will, prone to self-interested perversion of the collective will, or "evil."[22] As a member of a state, the individual encountered his communal being within the common life and consciousness of a people in an external, objective, and normative structure that controlled potentialities for error and perversion in his subjective freedom, and directed his will toward conformity with its deeper, essentially communal, nature. The first duty of the state was "to give dominion to the idea of law in the visible world."[23] Savigny continued to insist that the state was not the creator of cultural community; its power remained external, within the sphere of the visible world, and it originated "in the people, through the people and for the people."[24] At the same time, however, the state was essential for actualizing the invisible community of will as a visible power in the world, and for preventing the disintegration of that community into an aggregate of selfish wills. What was new in 1840 was Savigny's emphasis on self-conscious organization and coercive discipline as a necessary means to sustain the communal organism and thus also individual identity as membership in historical community.

Savigny also viewed the legislative power of the state as playing a critical role in guiding the historical evolution of the communal organism. In 1840 the legislative power was described not as a threat to the spontaneous,

[22] *System*, vol. 1, pp. 38, 39. [23] *Ibid.*, p. 25. [24] *Ibid.*, p. 29.

silently working power of the communal spirit, but as the authentic representative of that spirit. The adaptation of the collective cultural subject to new historical circumstances and challenges demanded conscious acts of legislative leadership that could separate legitimate from obsolete tradition and resolve contradictions between inherited structures and new experiences. The creation and adaptation of law through legislation, Savigny now claimed, possessed an "autonomy" and "dignity" equal to that of the gradual and spontaneous operations of the *Volksgeist*.[25] Moreover, while in 1814 jurisprudence was portrayed as the ally of the *Volksgeist* in opposition to the codifying and legislating activism of the state, in 1840 jurisprudence was presented as virtually a handmaid of legislation. As the conceptually, systematically articulated tradition of national law, jurisprudence provided the material for the form-giving authority of the legislator. On the more practical side, jurisprudence was given the function of mediating between the relatively abstract, statutory forms of legislation and the actual life relations this legislation was meant to guide and regulate. The jurists were thus conceived as performing a mediating function between the positive law that still existed within the evolving consciousness of the people (however buried or hidden by error and perversion it might have become) and the disciplining, organizing representation of that positive law by the state.

Savigny's newfound confidence in the ability of the state to represent the original and essential unity of a national culture against the expressed will of the individuals who comprised the substance of that culture but had forgotten or rejected their collective historical identity should also be placed in the context of a further revision of his earlier theory – the new emphasis given to religiously grounded ethical principles. In the *System*, Savigny discussed the universal element in the laws of particular cultural communities not simply in terms of their origin in man's essential nature as a free subject, but also in terms of the goal toward which this freedom should be directed. "The general task of the law," he wrote, "can be reduced simply to the ethical determination of human nature as the latter is presented in the Christian view of life."[26] The relationship between the universal and historically individualized dimensions of law as presented to legislators and legal scholars, therefore, was not just a problem within the sphere of law but pertained to the relationship between law as the historically immanent regulator and form of historical life relations among free subjects and the higher sphere of ethical demands that were directed toward a transformation of the motivational structures of the will. Positive law could not in itself produce the ethical determination of the will that was the ultimate goal of the historical education of free subjects. But it received its meaning from this higher task and served as one of the conditions of its fulfillment. The reciprocal relations and possible tensions between the legal and ethical spheres

[25] *Ibid.*, pp. 43, 48. [26] *Ibid.*, p. 53.

opened up a "new and higher vocation" for legislation as it attempted to guide the development of an historical nation – the "struggle to recognize with assurance the universal goal, and to approach it, without weakening the fresh powers of individual life."[27]

Savigny's discussions about the ultimate subordination of culturally individuated national law to a universal, ethical task were cryptic, hedged in with qualifications and more than a little ambiguous. He stated, for example, that the Christian view of life was not only a rule for life based on the transcendent will of God, but also an immanent historical power within Christian culture that had "transformed the world so that our thoughts, as alien and hostile to Christianity as they may sometimes seem, are still dominated and penetrated by it."[28] In this sense, the disciplining of the life of the people in obedience to transcendent command entered into this immanent life of the people as an element in the further progress of its self-determination and self-expression. There was clearly a parallel between Savigny's concept of Roman civil law as the perfected incarnation of the universal elements of law in a particular form and his view of Christianity as the perfected historical representation of the universal ethical principles that constituted the ultimate normative claims on the human will. In both cases as well, Savigny imagined the German ethno-linguistic *Volk* as assimilating and becoming a particular historical actualization of these models in a progressive development of the Christian–German state. In paradoxical fashion, the immanently determined fate of ethnic Germans as a national people was to assume voluntarily the calling of making certain universal principles real in the world. The significance of the shifts in Savigny's viewpoint by 1840 was that he now felt that voluntary obedience to a higher will could only be achieved within the framework of religious faith in a transcendent power, that religious belief was the foundation of social ethics and national identity. By 1840 it had become clear to Savigny that the spontaneous working of the collective ethnic consciousness was not an adequate ground for the fulfillment of mankind's social and moral purposes. State and religion entered into his schema as necessary additional educators, with disciplining power and transcendent authority, transforming historically particular, immanent ethno-cultural communities into ethical realms with universal dimensions.

THEORY AND PRACTICE: HISTORICAL CONTEXTS OF SAVIGNY'S TRANSFORMATIONS OF HISTORICISM

Savigny's writings were already subjected to ideological critique during his own lifetime, most persistently from the liberal and socialist Left, particularly in its Hegelian, "statist" varieties, but also, though less publicly, intensely or

[27] *Ibid.*, p. 56. [28] *Ibid.*, p. 54.

relentlessly from the conservative ultras on the Right.[29] In 1840, Savigny lamented that he hardly expected or dared to hope any more that his works would be read as objective contributions to historical scholarship, rather than as expressions of party opinion.[30] To a large degree, Savigny had drawn this type of criticism upon himself. The *Beruf* of 1814 was written as a polemic against the public proposal of A. D. F. Thibaut, that the construction of post-Napoleonic German unity should proceed through national codification of customary Germanic law uncorrupted by Roman additions and revisions.[31] In 1815, in the introductory manifesto of a new historicist journal, Savigny had described the historicist perspective as a partisan position in the contemporary debate over goals and methods for the reconstruction of German politics after the defeat of Napoleon.[32] In a letter to Wilhelm Grimm from the same period, he noted his inability to separate scholarly principle from political stance, either in himself or in his opponents.[33] In the years between 1813 and 1819, between the national "awakening" of the liberation wars and the repression of the nationalist movement by the Carlsbad Decrees, Savigny's concept of the unity of theory and practice had an activist and self-consciously partisan tinge that was often hidden in later years. This partisanship, however, should not be construed as an admission on Savigny's part that the principles of the Historical School represented the one-sided position of a limited interest group within German culture. Savigny clearly believed that the general principles and aims informing his thinking and acting expressed a modified universalist, historically objective, perspective. That is, they were limited by time and national culture but still represented the common consciousness of the German people at a particular moment in its historical evolution. Opponents were seen as misreading the national spirit and alienated from it by their narrow, self-interested, perspectives. Their positions remained "merely" subjective because their personal interests prevented them from recognizing and living within the historically evolving national consciousness.[34]

When Savigny accepted Wilhelm von Humboldt's invitation to join the original faculty of the University of Berlin in 1810, he was making a political

[29] The Hegelian critiques of the Historical School are described in John Toews, *Hegelianism: The Path Toward Dialectical Humanism, 1805–1841* (Cambridge and New York 1981), PP. 60–63, 109–11, 121ff, 244, 247. See also the older work: Ernst Simon, *Ranke und Hegel* (Munich and Berlin: 1928), pp. 16–54, 79–87.

[30] *System*, vol. 1, pp. xii–xiii.

[31] See H. Hattenbauer, ed., *Thibaut und Savigny* (Munich, 1973); Whitman, *Legacy of Roman Law*, pp. 105–10.

[32] "Ueber den Zweck dieser Zeitschrift," *Zeitschrift fuer geschichtliche Rechtswissenschaft* 1 (1815), pp. 2–3.

[33] Savigny to W. Grimm, November 25, 1815, in Adolf Stoll, *Friedrich Karl von Savigny* (3 vols., Berlin: 1927–39), vol. 2, p. 147.

[34] An analysis of Savigny's claims to objectivity and neutrality in the context of his commitment to this particular post-Kantian idealist perspective is a major theme of Joachim Rueckert, *Idealismus, Jurisprudenz und Politik bei Friedrich Carl von Savigny* (Ebelsbach: 1984).

and cultural statement as well as a career move. Savigny began his association with the Prussian state as an active, enthusiastic member of the party of bureaucratic and academic reformers, formed under the leader of Baron von Stein after the military debacle of 1806–7, who were committed to the creation of a framework of political and cultural institutions that would mobilize previously passive Prussian subjects and transform them into an ethical community of free and loyal citizens capable of resisting the blandishments of a foreign culture and breaking the chains of foreign political domination. For Savigny, as for so many of the non-Prussian intellectuals drawn to Prussia by the Stein reforms, Prussia had become the vanguard of a general German awakening and liberation, the disciplining and organizing instrument of an ethno-linguistic collectivity. Three general assumptions that had informed Savigny's scholarship before 1810 made possible this alliance with patriotic reformers like Stein, Humboldt, Schleiermacher, and Niebuhr.

First, Savigny shared the reformers' general conviction that the dignity and essential worth of human beings was grounded in subjective freedom, in the right to obey only those laws that could be recognized as expressions of one's own essential will. This Kantian assumption had been modified, for Savigny as well as for his fellow reformers, through participation in the first phase of post-Kantian Romantic idealism at the turn of the century, in which Kantian universality had been redefined in terms of the evolving, differentiated will of particular peoples, as both historical and national. To obey oneself became synonymous with obeying one's own essential will as member of a historically particular, cultural community. Conscience and duty lost their abstract quality and gained a national and historical content. During the first decade of the nineteenth century, as Savigny began his academic career in the Hessian university at Marburg and the Bavarian university at Landshut, he affiliated himself with a second-generation Romantic circle that included the poets Clemens Brentano and Achim von Arnim, as well as the Grimm brothers (who were among his first students at Marburg). The members of this group devoted themselves to the recovery and historical reconstruction of the original, essential spirit, or "idea," of German culture as it was documented in the texts of medieval literature and popular folk culture.[35]

Recognition of the Kantian and post-Kantian Romantic–Idealist elements in Savigny's perspective is crucial if one is to attain an adequate

[35] On Savigny's Kantian assumptions, see Friedrich Wieacker, "Friedrich Carl voin Savigny," *Zeitschrift der Savigny Stiftung fuer Rechtsgeschichte* (Roem. Abt.), 72 (1955): 12–13; H. Kiefner, "Der Einfluss Kants auf Theorie und Praxis des Zivilrechts im 19. Jahrhundert," in *Philosophie und Rechtswissenschaft*, ed. Bluehdorn and Ritter (1969): 3–25, and Stephan Meder, *Urteilen: Elemente von Kant's reflektierender Urteilskraft in Savigny's Lehre von der juristischen Entscheidungs- und Regelfindung* (Frankfurt: 1999). Savigny's reception of various forms of post-Kantian idealism (Fichte, Fries, Schelling, Schlegel, Hoelderlin) at the turn of the century is systematically documented in Rueckert, *Idealismus*, 232–300, and in Dieter Noerr, *Savigny's philosophische Lehrjahre: Ein Versuch* (Franfurt: 1994).

definition of the historical and political implications of his alleged conservatism. Savigny did express significant reservations about particular aspects of the emancipation edicts of the reform era, but he never denied their general historical necessity, and he rejected the possibility of any simple return to pre-reform political and cultural institutions. His first major work, a study of the right of property, attempted to grasp property rights as part of the gradual evolution of Roman law within Germanic customary law in the transition from feudal to more modern, individualistic forms. The focus of his work was on the continuity of law within the gradually self-transforming identity of a historical culture.[36] He clearly rejected the French revolutionaries' claim for a radical disjunction between the old regime and modern social relations. The desired continuity represented by the preservation of traditional legal, political and cultural forms, however, could be maintained only if these forms were revitalized through recognition of the essential human autonomy expressed in their continuous evolution and self-transformation.

Second, Savigny shared the Prussian reformers' neohumanist classicism, their belief that the literatures and cultures of classical Greece and Rome represented models of ethical communities that could be remembered and appropriated by the present generation through the philological recovery and contextual, historical interpretation of ancient texts and artifacts. As a student of the Roman legal tradition, Savigny was especially drawn to the Roman historian Barthold G. Niebuhr, whose critical reconstruction of early Roman history was guided by questions pertaining to the contemporary German transformation of feudal agrarian relations and laws.[37] Savigny's own concept of the normative, universal qualities of Roman law, he admitted as late as 1840, was part of the broader belief among members of his generation that classical culture represented both a model for the tasks of bringing a distinctive German national culture to full self-expression and a particularly significant historical moment in the formation and historical memory of that culture.[38]

Finally, Savigny agreed with the Prussian reformers' claim that political reform and the progressive development of German national culture would be achieved through a reform of the educated elite and its institutions, especially the universities. Along with Humboldt and Schleiermacher, Savigny was convinced that an ethical community of free citizens would emerge from a process of historical cultural education, nurtured and guided by an

[36] Savigny, *Die Rechts des Besitzes: Eine civilistische Abhandlung* (Giessen: 1803). Savigny's early emphasis on historical hermeneutics as the royal road to grasping the essential meaning of legal forms in a continuous process of change is evident in Jacob Grimm's lecture notes from Savigny's methods course at Marburg, published as *Juristische Methodenlehre, nach der Ausarbeitung des Jakob Grimm*, ed. G. Wesenberg (Stuttgart: 1951).

[37] See Savigny, "Niebuhrs Wesen und Wirken," *Vermischte Schriften*, vol. 4, pp. 220–24.

[38] *System*, vol. 1, p. xxxi; F. Schaffstein, "Friedrich Carl von Savigny und Wilhelm von Humboldt," *Zeitschrift der Savigny Stiftung* (Ger. Abt.), 72 (1955): 154–76.

inwardly reformed educational vanguard. Scholars and artists were to take on the cultural mission of recovering the national memory and giving voice to the collective national consciousness.[39] At the same time, Savigny experienced the fraternity of professors and students at the university as an image of what the larger national culture would be like as it reached full expression. As the community of scholars devoted itself to the historical mission of recovering national memory, it became an exemplar of the goals it pursued.[40]

These general assumptions, inherited and assimilated from an earlier generation of neohumanist, Idealist and Romantic German thinkers, were modified and synthesized into a distinctive generational perspective by the experiences of defeat, occupation, and liberation in 1806–13. Savigny was rector of the new university at Berlin (after Fichte's brief term in office) in the critical year of 1813 and was awarded the Iron Cross, Civilian class, for his efforts in mobilizing students and faculty into civil militias for the defense of the city and for the cause of liberation.[41] Savigny treasured the experiences of this year as a "sacred memory" and an "unforgettable excursion into practical life," which affirmed the reality of a collective national consciousness, at least among the educated classes.[42] Although aware of the many self-serving and pragmatic aspects of the campaign against Napoleon, Savigny was convinced that he had participated in an authentic national awakening, a solidarity of feeling and purpose in which the Idealist model of self-legislating citizenship had found expression in voluntary obedience to the voice of a shared national conscience. In the debates that accompanied the political reconstruction of the liberated German states after 1815, however, it soon became evident that Savigny had developed a distinctive perspective on the common experience of his intellectual generation.

This distinctiveness was expressed on a number of different levels. First, Savigny opposed any direct translation of the consciousness or feeling of national solidarity into the laws and institutions of external political unity. The awakening of national consciousness in 1813, he believed, was not an adequate basis for permanent political structures, but merely the starting point for a process of cultural education that would eventually provide a fuller comprehension of the guiding principles of national life and an extension of this consciousness among both the governing elites and the general populations

39 Savigny, "Rezension von F. Schleiermacher, Gelegentliche Gedanken ueber Universitaeten in deutschem Sinn" (1808), *Vermischte Schriften*, vol. 1, pp. 255–69.

40 See, especially, a short essay on the need for reform of the German universities (1803), published in H. Marquardt, "Ein Unbekannter Aufsatz F. C. von Savignys," in *Die Sammlung: Zeitschrift fuer Kultur und Erziehung* 6 (1951): 321–36.

41 Stoll, *Savigny*, vol. 2, pp. 24–25.

42 "Vorrede zuir zweiten Aufgabe" (1828), *Beruf*, p. iii; Savigny to J. A. S. Eichhorn, December 3, 1813, in Stoll, *Savigny*, vol. 2, p. 94. For Savigny's participation in the patriotic movement of 1813, see also Iris Denneler, *Friedrich Karl von Savigny* (Berlin: 1985), pp. 65–68.

of the various German states. Savigny thus focused his efforts on the tasks of sustaining and extending the inner reform and expansion of educational institutions and scholarly organizations.[43] Second, the focus on educational gradualism and the transformation of consciousness through the recovery of collective memory was connected to Savigny's perception that his own perspective on the appropriate political forms for a German national culture, however much he may have been convinced of its essentially collective and thus "objective" grounding, was not shared by many of his contemporaries. He disagreed with his non-Prussian friends and fellow German patriots, like the Grimms in Hesse or the Creuzers in Baden, about the appropriate focal point of national leadership. By 1815, Savigny had become a Prussian patriot who rejected Austria's traditional leadership role in Germany (a position reinforced by Metternich's leading role in the repression of nationalist movements among the educated elites after 1819) and opposed any attempts to reconstitute the institutions of the pre-Napoleonic empire. The German national identity that some imagined still haunted the moribund institutions of the old empire that had been dissolved by Napoleon in 1806, he told his more nostalgic friends, the Grimm brothers, was nothing more than a "veiled grave" (*vertuenchtes Grab*).[44] A new unity would emerge only when one prince and one people became the focal point of the national mission. He affirmed Prussian territorial expansion within Germany after 1815 as a confirmation of Prussian national leadership during the wars of liberation and rejected the expansionist plans of other states as a form of divisive self-aggrandizement.[45] Finally, and most significantly, Savigny found himself in growing disagreement with segments of the Prussian governing elites regarding the creation of appropriate constitutional structures for a distinctively German national community.

Under the postwar leadership of Chancellor Karl August von Hardenberg, the Prussian government appeared to be moving, in Savigny's view, in a direction that threatened to reproduce the destructive policies of the enlightened absolutism of the eighteenth century. In the actions of the Hardenberg administration, Savigny discerned a tendency to define freedom in terms of the individual pursuit of economic self-interest unrestricted by customary communal bonds, and community as the imposition of uniform rational laws by centralized government. As a member of two important administrative bodies, the State Council (*Staatsrat*), an assembly of notables that advised the chancellor and his ministers on matters of legislation, and the commission for the revision and abrogation of laws in the newly acquired

43 Sees especially *Beruf*, 151ff; R. Kawakami, "Die Begruendung des 'neuen' gelehrten Rechts durch Savigny," *Zeitschrift der Savigny-Stiftung* (Roem. Abt.), 98 (1981): 303–37.

44 Savigny to W. Grimm, April 29, 1814, in Stoll, *Savigny*, vol. 2, p. 104.

45 Savigny to the Grimms, April 29, June 18, and October 12, 1814, in Stoll, *Savigny*, vol. 2, pp. 104, 109, 119.

Rhenish provinces, Savigny worked quietly but diligently to restrict the administrative activism of the state and to modify its policies. In the State Council he concentrated his energies on modifying the procedures whereby the emancipation process was carried out in rural areas so that traditional patrimonial and communal restrictions on economic individualism could be sustained.[46] In the commission on Rhenish legal changes, he supported the abrogation of the Napoleonic Code and opposed the extension of the Prussian General Legal Code (which Savigny saw as a typical codification of eighteenth-century natural law assumptions) over the distinctive historical legal traditions of the Rhenish provinces.[47] Such opposition to both the emancipatory and centralizing policies of the government gave Savigny's reformism an ambivalent appearance during the 1820s. His conservatism was most apparent in his attempts to modify and even reverse the process of Jewish emancipation, which he perceived as a threat to the development of an authentic communal consciousness, both in its implied secular individualism and in its potential for creating an "alien" cultural community within the broader German national culture.[48] At the same time, Savigny appeared to many of his contemporaries as a liberal in his persistent defense of the independence of the universities, including the freedoms of teaching and learning within them, against government intrusion and domination, and in his support for the creation of political institutions – diets at the provincial and state levels – that would provide at least some form of organized corporate representation of the popular will.[49] In both areas, however, Savigny saw himself acting in conformity with his original vision of national reform, opposing state authoritarianism and tutelage from above and encouraging the emergence of a shared national consciousness from below, in continuity with historically individuated local traditions.

In the decade after 1819, Savigny achieved only very limited success in his attempts to shape Prussian policy according to his vision of national reform and self-development. By 1820 he was severely disillusioned:

> "I do not understand it," he wrote to his friend Jacob Grimm, "I had expected a magnificent spiritual fructification, much richer and more revitalizing than that which followed the Seven Year's War, from the miracles that God bestowed upon us in 1812–1815. What has ensued, however, is sterility [*Duerre*], distorted growth, and hard times."[50]

[46] W. von Hall, "Friedrich Carl von Savigny als Praktiker: Die Staatsrat Gutachten (1817–1842)," *Zeitschrift der Savigny-Stiftung* (Ger. Abt.), 99 (1982): 285–97; Stoll, *Savigny*, vol. 2, pp. 164–65.

[47] W. Schubert, "Savigny und die rheinisch-franzoesische Gerichtsverfassung," *Zeitschrift der Savigny Stiftung* (Ger. Abt.), 93 (1978): 158–69.

[48] Van Hall, "Savigny als Praktiker," pp. 293–94.

[49] Van Hall, "Savigny als Praktiker," pp. 294–95; Savigny, "Stimmen fuer und wider neue Gesetzbuecher (1816)," reprinted in *Beruf*, pp. 179, 186, 188–89; Stoll, *Savigny*, vol. 2, pp. 261–62.

[50] Savigny to J. Grimm, November 18, 1820, in Stoll, *Savigny*, vol. 2, p. 271.

This pessimism was reinforced by Savigny's personal experiences in the institution on which he had concentrated so much of his hope for progressive national self-determination – the university. The Prussian and German universities were under continuous pressure from the state during the 1820s, but even within the universities Savigny noted a disturbing trend toward personal accommodation to state interference in educational affairs. For Savigny this trend was exemplified by the growing influence of Hegel and his disciples, especially at the University of Berlin. In 1828, after the minister for educational and religious affairs ignored Savigny's protests and promoted his most virulent Hegelian critic, Eduard Gans, to a full professorship in the law faculty, Savigny resigned from all his nonteaching obligations at the university. The debilitating migraine headaches that restricted Savigny's scholarly productivity during the 1820s appeared to give physical expression to his general depression and sense of historical disillusionment during these years.

The liberal political revolutions of 1830 in France, Belgium, and some of the smaller German states (including Hesse-Kassel, Savigny's "homeland") reanimated Savigny's political interests and commitments and also provided a starting point for a revision of his political and historical perspectives. His response to the wave of political unrest that once again seemed to be sweeping across Western Europe was ambivalent. On the one hand he conceded that much of the political discontent was justified by the inept administrative policies and unacceptable abuse of power by despotic regimes; there was an inherent historical "necessity" in the revolts.[51] Prussia had remained relatively immune to political unrest because it had adapted to historical necessity through successful institutional realization of major portions of the Stein reform program, particularly in the creation of decentralized self-administration in the urban communes and rural counties, and through a financial and economic policy that preserved, at least partially, customary communal restrictions on the socially fragmenting, competitive pursuit of self-interest in the marketplace. On the other hand, Savigny now viewed in a positive light the fact that the principle of citizen participation in governance had not been extended, as originally promised, to the state level through the creation of a unified diet, an aspect of the reform program that Savigny had supported in 1815. "Do not expect too much from Diets in contemporary Germany," Savigny warned Jacob Grimm in late 1830.[52] Without prior education in the politically responsible use of individual freedom, assemblies tended to degenerate into partisan squabbles between the hapless and pathetic simplicities of liberalism and reactionary conservatism, or "ultraism." In 1832, Savigny wrote that the democratic participation that provided the necessary subjective element in a healthy

[51] Savigny to Grimm, December 18, 1830, in Stoll, *Savigny*, vol. 2, p. 420.

[52] *Ibid.*, p. 421.

political community was adequately provided for in Prussia through local and regional institutions of self-administration.[53] In this context, Savigny reiterated his belief in the importance of maintaining the universities as centers of an ongoing national education, especially an education of the educators. However, he now warned against any encouragement of passionate political enthusiasms and commitments. Training in political responsibility was defined in terms of self-denying commitment to the duties of function and vocation. Participation in the collective solidarity of the national community was transformed into obedience to the rules imposed by one's "office" within the functional differentiation of an organized cultural system.[54]

Savigny insisted that the events of 1830–31 had merely confirmed, with slight modifications, the political commitments he had formed in the era of reform and national liberation.[55] These modifications, however, clearly involved a limitation of the populist element in his previous stance and a concomitant accommodation to state authority. During the 1830s, Savigny's identification with the Prussian government remained tenuous and partial. He established an informal alliance in the *Staatsrat* with moderate conservatives, led by the foreign minister Count Bernstorff and his chief aide for German affairs, Johann Albert Eichhorn (a close friend and former student of Savigny). During the early 1830s, Savigny was an avid contributor to the semiofficial *Historisch-Politische Zeitschrift*, edited by Leopold Ranke, which was strongly supported by, and supportive of, the Bernstorff group in the government and tried to defend the moderate conservative concept of Prussia as the exemplary German state against both the authoritarian paternalism and neofeudalism of the restorationist Right and the anti-Prussian constitutionalism of the southern German liberals.[56] Savigny's tendency toward political accommodation was revealed most directly to many of his contemporaries, especially former allies like Varnhagen von Ense and Bettina von Arnim, in his failure to join in the expression of public support for the seven Goettingen professors, including his old friends the Grimm brothers, who lost their positions and were forced into exile when they refused to accept the legitimacy of the abrogation of the Hanoverian constitution by a new monarch in 1837. Although Savigny deplored the actions of the Hanoverian king and was willing to acknowledge the moral purity of the professors' motives, he refused to sanction what he saw as support

[53] Savigny, "Die preussische Staedteordnung" (1832), *Vermischte Schriften*, vol. 5, pp. 208–9.

[54] Savigny, "Wesen und Werth der deutschen Universitaeten" (1832), *Vermischte Schriften*, vol. 4, p. 302. See also Stoll, *Savigny*, vol. 2, pp. 353–54.

[55] Savigny to L. Creuzer, August 19, 1831, in Stoll, *Savigny*, vol. 2, p. 435.

[56] On the political context and implications of Ranke's *Zeitschrift*, see Theodor von Laue, *Leopold Ranke: The Formative Years* (Princeton: 1950), pp. 55–71. In 1831–32, Savigny's participation in the formation of this journal brought back memories of the feelings of solidarity and collective activism of 1813. See Stoll, *Savigny*, vol. 2, pp. 442, 458.

for the principles of constitutional liberalism, and thus criticism of Prussian policy, implied by their actions.[57]

Savigny's commitment to a slightly modified conception of Stein's reformed Prussia and his accommodation to established state power represented only one aspect of his response to the events of 1830–31. In a more negative vein, he expressed dismay at the abyss of moral decay and social disintegration revealed by the statements and actions of members, and especially leaders, of the propertied middle and upper classes that formed the core of the "people" that had played such a prominent role in his earlier political conceptions. What was most frightening in the widespread political unrest that followed the July revolution of 1830, he wrote was "the total moral disintegration, the destruction of all feelings of discipline and law." One might perhaps expect passions undisciplined by principle and shameless acts of selfish greed from the rabble, but when such moral corruption penetrated into "the essential elements of the nation," he was driven to despair. The age seemed to have lost its "bearings" altogether.[58] Such assessments of the dissolution of the people into a mass of self-serving egotists were not easily assimilated into Savigny's conceptions of historical evolution and cultural community. Rather than succumb to his friend Niebuhr's vision of a coming age of barbarism, however, Savigny hoped for the intervention of "a new type of prophecy, that would try to reform the general condition of the world from the inside, through admonition and threats of punishment aimed at an internal transformation." "Perhaps such a divinely inspired voice," he suggested, "will not be ignored even in an age adept at turning a deaf ear."[59] As the immanent historical foundations of Savigny's hopes for the development of the ethno-linguistic *Volk* of the fragmented German states into an ethical national community began to waver, he started to consider the possibilities of intervention based on transcendent principles.

Religion had played a prominent, although largely implicit, role in Savigny's historical vision of national revival before 1830. The ethos of a particular people was defined and sustained by a common religious consciousness, and Savigny experienced the national awakening of 1813 in intimate association with the religious revival that swept through the German educated classes at the same time, a revival in which he was also an avid participant. In 1816 he wrote to a friend that his confidence about Germany's political future was sustained "first of all and primarily" by the emergence of a "new authentic life" in the churches.[60] Savigny, however, did not see this new piety necessarily taking on dogmatic, confessional, or ecclesiastical

[57] Theo Schuler, "Jakob Grimm und Savigny," *Zeitschrift der Savigny-Stiftung* (Ger. Abt.), 80 (1965), 279–305. See also Denneler, *Savigny*, pp. 99–108.

[58] Savigny to L. Creuzer, February 24, and August 19, 1831, Stoll, *Savigny*, vol. 3, pp. 428–34.

[59] Savigny to L. Creuzer, August 19, 1831, in Stoll, *Savigny*, vol. 2, p. 433.

[60] Savigny to L. Creuzer, May 9, 1816, in Stoll, *Savigny*, vol. 2, p. 201, See also *ibid.*, pp. 239–40, 248.

forms. What he imagined instead was the creation of an invisible community of religious faith articulated in the ethical practice of self-sacrifice and submission of the individual will to the national conscience. While this pious consciousness was most likely to be articulated in the traditional forms of Christian faith and thus adequately channeled through the established German churches, it was also present in "noble and high-minded pagans."[61] After 1830, however, Savigny expressed increased concern that the kind of piety that might ground the solidarity of an ethical community could no longer be found in the German churches, which seemed as racked by divisive conflict between dogmatic ultras and impious liberals as German political assemblies.[62] Ethical education grounded in a pious subordination to a collective striving of the *Volksgeist* could no longer provide adequate foundation for his political hopes. In this context, Savigny began to define religious belief less as the spontaneous merger of the individual will with its universal essence, than as the disciplining imposition of the divine will on the recalcitrant aggregate of individual wills. His projected future prophets were described, like Mendelssohn's *Elijah*, as Old Testament prophets admonishing an errant and hostile people.[63] Savigny continued to insist that the revelations of the new prophets would need to be subjectively appropriated by the people as their own will if an authentic ethical community was to emerge, but he now envisioned this ethical determination of the will as coming *to* the people, rather than as emerging *from* within the people, as an intervention into history rather than a product of a developmental process within history, as an act of "grace" according to the "secret timetable of God," rather than as the expression of an immanent necessity.[64]

It would be a mistake, however, to overemphasize the shift in Savigny's religious stance after 1830. The gap between his religious views and those of the neo-orthodox Protestant ultras remained wide. In the spring of 1840, just before the publication of the first volumes of the *System*, Savigny constructed a personal "Confession of Faith" for a close friend in the form of an extended metaphor in which God was represented as a creative schoolmaster drawing students toward ethical determination of the will through a variety of educational strategies.[65] In a letter to the Grimms in 1845, he reiterated his faith that German national solidarity would be grounded on membership in an invisible church, and that if a national visible church ever emerged it would take the form of a unity of all existing Christian confessions in a higher form, rather than in the victory of one religious position over its rivals.[66] Although Savigny insisted that he was a "supernaturalist"

[61] Savigny to J. Grimm, Feb. 17, 1821, in Stoll, *Savigny*, vol. 2, p. 274.

[62] Savigny to J. Grimm, December 18, 1830, in Stoll, *Savigny*, vol. 2, p. 421.

[63] Savigny to F. Perthes, August 20, 1832, in Stoll, *Savigny*, vol. 2, p. 456.

[64] *Ibid.*, vol. 2, pp. 456, 513.

[65] Savigny to Bang, March 7, 1840, in Stoll, *Savigny*, vol. 2, pp. 523–25.

[66] Savigny to Grimms, December 8, 1845, in Stoll, *Savigny*, vol. 3, p. 70.

who believed in God's personal transcendent reality, he remained a theological liberal impatient of dogmatic argument and confessional division. Although conceding that the human will was too weak to achieve ethical determination on its own, he refused to accept the orthodox Christian belief in original sin. The individual, according to Savigny, did participate actively in his own salvation, even if he could not achieve perfect self-transcendence on his own. In 1840, as in 1815, Savigny's favorite theological reading tended toward nondogmatic edifying sermons that emphasized the kind of experiential faith that affirmed itself in ethical practice.[67]

It was not so much the content as the context of Savigny's religious piety that changed after 1830. He had lost his earlier confident belief that his personal religious experience marked his participation in the collective consciousness of his culture. By 1840 he was convinced that the kind of piety that sustained self-denying commitment and obedience to the higher self of the national community needed to be instilled into the majority of the culture's members and could not simply be distilled from the concrete variety of their individual faiths. Becoming historical took on new dimensions in this context: It moved beyond the recognition of one's essential grounding in the evolving ethno-linguistic culture of the *Volk* and encompassed recognition of the contingency of historical communities as creations of religiously motivated ethical deeds. Being German was not just a fate that needed to be recognized, but also a project that required responsible action and faith in the possible.

The tensions and ambivalences that had developed in Savigny's political and religious perceptions during the 1830s came to a head with the dynastic change of 1840. Frederick William IV's accession to the throne transformed the horizons of Savigny's immediate historical world in a number of ways. The new king was a former tutee and great admirer of Savigny and his work. He had supported Savigny against his own father's officials during Savigny's battles with the Hegelian School and had often consulted closely with him in the deliberations of the Staatsrat. The king and Savigny were united in their opposition to both bureaucratic centralization and constitutional liberalism. The circle of moderate conservative civil servants and academics with whom Savigny had allied around the *Historisch-Politische Zeitschrift* in the 1830s flourished under the new king's patronage and became political insiders after 1840. Many of Savigny's personal friends and former students played significant roles in formulating and administering the policies of the new regime. Savigny must also have been gratified by the series of symbolic acts through which Frederick William tried to identify his administration with the memory of the Stein reforms and the national awakening of 1813. When Savigny's friend and student J. A. Eichhorn was appointed to head the *Kultusministerium*, the Hegelians lost their favored position in the educational

[67] *Ibid.*; also Savigny to W. Grimm, December 23, 1817, in Stoll, *Savigny*, vol. 2, pp. 239–40.

system and Savigny could once again feel at home at the university. If the Hegelian School had experienced its moment of academic and political hegemony in the 1820s and 1830s, 1840 seemed to mark the triumphant return of the Historical School and the intellectual ethos of 1813. As one of the founders of the Historical School, Savigny might have expected to play the part of an elder statesman in the new regime, but when he was appointed to the ministry in the spring of 1842, it was clear that a more active role was expected of him.

As Savigny assumed the tasks of revising the Prussian General Legal Code according to the guiding principles of the evolving national tradition, it soon became obvious that the triumph of the Historical School was tenuous and severely limited. The elevation of Savigny and his friends to positions of power was matched by the simultaneous elevation of the king's friends on the political and religious Right, men whose dogmatic extremism had been the object of Savigny's criticism since the early 1820s. Despite the king's wish to identify his regime with the spirit of 1813 and the traditions of the Stein reforms, he continued to surround himself with advisors and ministers who looked for a return to the authoritarian paternalism of the patriarchal state and the stringent orthodoxy of the pre-Enlightenment Lutheran church as the only secure bases for reconstructing an ethical community within Prussia. The conflict between the "German" and the "Christian" components of the new regime were revealed as Savigny's ministry addressed the first task placed before it – the revision of the Prussian divorce laws.

Savigny had argued consistently since 1815 that the dignity and sanctity of the institution of marriage was one of the indispensable foundations of ethical life in an integrated national culture.[68] This was an issue in which legal and ethical issues were inextricably intertwined. The question Savigny faced in 1842 was whether legislation should simply articulate the guiding principles informing the consciousness of the historical nation and thus act as an "organ" of the *Volksgeist*, or rather construct normative standards for marriage obligations based on transcendent principles and impose these standards on a recalcitrant population through the power of the state. The extent to which Savigny had drifted toward the latter position during the 1830s was evident when he bowed to royal pressure and assigned Ernst Ludwig von Gerlach, the most committed conservative ultra among his aides, to draft the proposal for the divorce law and to defend it before the council of ministers and the Staatsrat.

Gerlach's draft rejected all the tendencies toward liberalization of the procedures of divorce cases that had evolved since the seventeenth century and restricted legitimate grounds for divorce to those allowed within

[68] Savigny, "Stimmen" (1816), p. 176; *Beruf*, pp. 46–47; *System*, vol. 1, pp. 345ff.

sixteenth-century Lutheran theology – adultery and malicious desertion.[69] Moreover, Gerlach clearly believed these restrictive standards should be enforced, against the expressed popular will if necessary, by the power of the state. Deeply disturbed by what he perceived as a growing disintegration of self-discipline and moral responsibility, especially among the lower classes, Savigny supported Gerlach's position, although with some reluctance and hesitation. Savigny's historical disillusionment and his loss of confidence in the spontaneous operations of the evolving national consciousness had gradually led him an accommodation with the principles of the new prophets. They were no longer a party of extremist others but the intimately familiar other within himself.

Savigny did not possess the dogmatic conviction required to transform his old self into a new prophetic persona. Instead, he tried to reconcile the old and the new, the historical and the transcendent perspectives in ways that convinced no one. What had begun in 1840 as the apparent triumph of the Historical School seemed by the mid-1840s more like a revelation of its historical failure. In the struggle between Savigny and Gerlach at the Ministry of Justice, this failure appeared as a failure of will and self-confidence, as reluctant submission to the more decisive, energetic will of the pious ultras on the Right. Savigny had recognized and consistently opposed Gerlach's position for over two decades. Gerlach, although he had been Savigny's student in 1810, had clearly separated himself from his original mentor by the time of the publication of Savigny's *Beruf* in 1814. "This teaching," he wrote after reading Savigny's historicist manifesto, "which, in pantheistic fashion essentially constructs a system from the individuality and historical evolution of nations without regard for their eternal origins or for universally human, divinely created and therefore permanent institutions (personality, patriarchy), cannot provide adequate defenses against the revolutionary essence of our century."[70] In 1844, Gerlach still attributed Savigny's failure of will and lack of practical effectiveness to the fact that he understood law as "the manifestation of the people's spirit" rather than as "the word of the living God."[71] That there was an inner experiential logic to Savigny's transformations and not just a failure to resist the political influence of the younger neoconservatives, however, was made evident in the relationship between his positions and the stance of another young ultra who rose to public prominence in Prussia during the early 1840s, Friedrich Julius Stahl (1802–61).

[69] These drafts are reprinted and discussed in Savigny, "Darstellung der in der preussischen Gesetzen ueber die Ehescheidung unternommenen Reform" (1844), *Vermischte Schriften*, vol. 5, pp. 222–414.

[70] Ernst von Gerlach, *Aufzeichnungen aus seinem Leben und Wirken* (2 vols.; 1903), vol. 1, p. 102.

[71] Gerlach to Bethmann-Hollweg, August 9, 1844, cited in Kantzenbach, "Ernst Ludwig von Gerlach und August von Bethmann-Hollweg," *Zeitschrift fuer Religion und Geistesgeschichte* 9 (1957): 258.

THE TURN TO TRANSCENDENT AUTHORITY: STAHL'S SUBORDINATION OF JURISPRUDENCE TO THEOLOGY

When Stahl accepted the invitation to replace the deceased Hegelian Eduard Gans on the law faculty at the University of Berlin in 1840, he was perceived by most of his contemporaries, including Bunsen, Savigny, and the other Prussian academics who supported his appointment, as an innovative, energetic, slightly revisionist, but still essentially loyal member of the younger generation of the Historical School of Law. In the first volume of his *Philosophie des rechts nach geschichtlicher Ansicht* (Philolsophy of Law in Historical Perspective), published in 1830, Stahl described the informing principle of his scholarship as the historical viewpoint first formulated in philosophical form by Schelling and applied to the sphere of politics and law by Niebuhr and Savigny. By taking the philosophy of law, the "idea" of law, as the object of his research, interpretation, and writing, Stahl saw himself as supplementing Savigny by moving into areas that Savigny had dealt with only implicitly or in passing. Savigny had been able to exempt himself from detailed consideration of the ultimate metaphysical grounds of historical law and historical cultural identities in general, Stahl noted, because his self-assurance, aesthetic sensibility, and "magical" talent for narrative description allowed him to paint a picture of the evolution of law in which a theory of such foundations was implicit. His less talented, less self-assured disciples, however, could not avoid the disturbing metaphysical questions implied in the historical viewpoint if they hoped to develop it further and apply it successfully to current historical events and practices. Without explicit philosophical clarification of the foundations of historicism, its scope was not obvious, its contemporary relevance not convincing. A consequence of this vagueness, in Stahl's view, was a withdrawal into antiquarian scholarship and an eclectic assimilation of essentially alien philosophical ideas that were increasingly evident among younger members of the Historical School.[72]

Stahl's search for more secure metaphysical foundations for personal and cultural identity than the historicism of Savigny could provide emerged from his own background and historical experience, which diverged sharply from that of the self-assured aristocratic scholar who had never strayed far from the circles of the social and political elites. Born in 1802 as Julius Jolson, the son of a Jewish retailer in Wuerzburg and raised in the household of his paternal grandfather, a well-known rabbi and leader of the Jewish community in Munich, Stahl's formative years were marked by the radical transformation of traditional identities created by both Jewish emancipation and the national and religious enthusiasms of 1813–19. In 1819, at

[72] Friedrich Julius. Stahl, *Die Philosophie des Rechts nach geschichtlicher Ansicht* (2 vols. in 3 parts; Heidelberg, 1830–37), vol. 1, pp. vi–ix.

the age of seventeen, he had converted to the Lutheran faith and became one of the leaders of the Christian–German wing of the student fraternity (*Burschenschaft*) movement. His commitments to these new identities were reinforced during his studies at the Protestant Bavarian university at Erlangen and by his contacts with both the preachers and the theorists of the postreform and postliberation conception of a national mission based on Protestant Christian revival. During the late 1820s, it was Schelling's "positive" philosophy in particular that seemed to mirror back to him his own sense of radical existential freedom and the grounding and framing of that freedom in a metaphysics of existence based in Christian theology and a Christian philosophy of history. The events of 1830 intensified his adherence to his new identities, now conceived as a radical choice in a world divided by the opposing forces of revolutionary human hubris, which denied the grounds of individual responsibility and social order in its surrender to the rational necessity of immanent historical progress toward human self-determination and self-sufficiency, and the Christian worldview, which promised a renewal of individual freedom and social harmony through surrender to the free acts and revealed meanings of a transcendent father. In the 1833 preface to the second volume of his *Philosophie des Rechts*, Stahl wrote:

> Between the principles that confront one another in hostile fashion there is no reconciliation and no middle ground. Either all order and authority is posited by man and exists for human purposes or it is posited by God in order to fulfill his will. There is no connection between legitimacy and popular sovereignty, between faith and infidelity, between truth and error.[73]

Within this battle of radically opposed positions, Stahl required absolute assurance for his choices.

At the center of Stahl's scholarly work was the problematic relationship between the historical and normative dimensions of law, and especially the question of the possible foundations of law's normative dimension. If the historical perspective was to function as a general cultural perspective with relevance beyond academe, it could not confine itself to empirical analysis of the ways in which law was produced in history, but would have to deal with the ethical and metaphysical questions of how law should be produced and what content it should have. The human desire to attain satisfactory knowledge regarding the grounds for obedience to law as a universal ethical norm was undeniable. A firm sense of being grounded in a social and cultural identity depended on it. If the thinkers and scholars of the Historical School could not provide such knowledge, their potential audience would justifiably look elsewhere, to Hegelian rationalism, perhaps, or to the natural law theories of the seventeenth and eighteenth centuries. Stahl

[73] *Philosophie des Rechts*, vol. 2, part 1 (1833), p. vi.

thus projected his own historical calling and task as the explication of a philosophy of law that would reveal the metaphysical foundations of the normative dimension of law and still remain consistent with the historical viewpoint. "That which is right," he wrote, "must possess its existence and its virtue independently of its recognition among men and knowledge of the right must thus be something other than the knowledge of the existing laws that are to be measured and tested by it."[74] But he also insisted that the historical point of view, especially as exemplified in Schelling's positive philosophy, had prepared a space within human thought for a new recognition of the transcendent power of the Christian God over the affairs of the human world.[75]

As Stahl developed his position in three large volumes between 1830 and 1837, it soon became clear that his alleged elaboration of Savigny's position implicitly entailed a particular interpretation and significant criticism of that position. In later editions, beginning with the second edition, published in 1845–47, these distinctions were made explicit. Stahl thought he discerned a belief in "the living divine government of history" in Savigny's description of the genesis of law as the self-determination of a collective national subject. It was this conviction about the divine purposes at work in the evolution of individuated cultural peoples that produced the Historical School's characteristic piety and self-abnegating reverence before the historically given – its submission to the creations of a power that transcended the individual will. The love of historical detail, the concern for the dignity of the positive, the irreducible particular, the pure fact, Stahl believed, implied a belief that history was not moved by an inner logic in schematic predictable patterns, but by the free will of a transcendent personal being.[76] At the same time, Stahl judged the Historical School's one-sided focus on the *Volk* as the primary source of law as a willful disregard of the evidence of intrusions of a higher ethical power in the events and processes of historical development. This power transcended the people and its consciousness, made normative claims on the values immanently produced within historical cultures, and provided the criteria for the present historian to judge the values that different cultures brought into play in historical evolution. Legislation and jurisprudence, Stahl suggested, were not merely organs of national consciousness, pure or impure conduits of the people's will, but also organs of "the law as such, this independent, higher power."[77] It was one-sided and prejudicial to view only the spontaneous evolution of customary law and not also "calculated energetic regulation" as an authentic expression of the workings of the divine power in history.[78] Even in the limited task of determining how historical

[74] *Philosophie des Rechts*, vol. 1 (1830), p. 1. [75] *Ibid.*, p. 56.

[76] *Philosophie des Rechts*, 6th ed. (Hildesheim: 1963), vol. 1, pp. 586–87. See also the briefer and less specific statement in the first edition, vol. 2, part 1 (1833), pp. 12–14.

[77] *Philosophie des Rechts* (1963), vol. 1, p. 587. [78] *Ibid.*, p. 584.

law emerged and developed in history, the position of the Historical School required modifications that admitted the legitimacy of legislative imposition of a higher law upon the individual people's customary laws and the national consciousness incorporated in them. More significant, however, was Stahl's conviction that Savigny's position provided no criteria, implicit or explicit, for judging the actual content of any specific laws or legal systems. He associated this failure with the fact that while the Historical School had obviously developed a certain political attitude or stance through its emphasis on the continuity of tradition and the organic integrity of a healthy national culture, it did not provide a substantive political theory.[79] The only ground for dismissing or affirming particular political theories and practices was conformity to the national spirit as documented in historical tradition.

These criticisms – the inadequacy of an exclusive focus on the cultural nation as the subject of law and the consequent need to recognize legislation as a source of law, the perceived need for a transcendent ground to sustain the ethical principles that gave law its normative dimension – were also, as we have noted, self-critical tendencies present in Savigny's own development after 1830, and were evident in the tensions informing his views in the 1840s. It is thus understandable that Savigny would approve the general direction of Stahl's revisions and recognize them as a philosophical complement to his own work. After reading the third volume of Stahl's *Philosophie des Rechts* in 1838, Savigny expressed his favorable impression of the work, especially of its religious tendencies. "I find this intervention (of the religious element)," he wrote, "not too great or extreme, but too crude. I expect a great deal from him."[80] What Savigny originally discerned as crudeness in Stahl's formulations, however, constituted a drastic, critical modification of Savigny's positions. What had begun as a slight shift in emphasis had developed by 1840 into a standpoint that was essentially new.

Stahl's construction of a philosophy of law that would complement and complete the historical viewpoint took form as a systematic attempt to integrate the positive historical realities of cultural nationality, civil law, and the state into a theological, Christian, and specifically Lutheran perspective. At the center of this self-styled "Christian philosophy" was a conception of the relationship between essence and existence, between the universal ground of being and the particularized individuated beings in the world, as a historical relation between personal wills, between absolute and contingent "personalities," between God and man, which was clearly dependent on Schelling's critique of Hegel and the construction of his positive philosophy during the years that Stahl was his student and colleague in Munich. "Personality" was Stahl's preferred term for designating the

79 *Ibid.*, p. 588. See also the first edition, vol. 2, part 1, pp. 13–14.

80 Savigny to Bluntschli, April 19, 1838, in Stoll, *Savigny*, vol. 2, p. 358.

ultimate ground for all existence, or "primal being" (*Ursein*)[81]: It was a term that conjured up a vision of the essence of existence as creative subjective activity and of the world as a product of free acts of will. "Personality" as applied to the absolute was the primal origin and cause of all being; as applied to existence it described the universal form, or "type," of created being. "Personality" pointed to the irreducible "thisness" of the unique concrete individuality of the subject, of the "I" that was the permanent center of the continuous historical transformation of empirical existence. As a personality, the absolute remained transcendent to the world it had freely created and that it continued to control and sustain as a free determination of its will. As created and thus contingent "personalities," human beings were not necessary emanations of an impersonal divine essence, but independent subjects capable of freely determining the direction of their wills.[82]

The proper relationship between God and man in Stahl's version of Christian philosophy was one in which created personalities recognized the will of their creator as the source and core of their own subjective personality and voluntarily conformed their wishes and actions to this higher determination. Such a relationship, in which the unity among human beings emerged from the voluntary obedience of the totality of created subjects to the higher authority that had created them, constituted Stahl's vision of the "ethical kingdom" (*sittliches Reich*).[83] The ultimate goal of human relations in history was not derived from the inherent logic of the immanent, horizontal relations among human beings, but from the vertical relation of each to their common transcendent source.

Although Stahl's "ethical kingdom" was the absolute norm for human ethical relationships and the final goal of history, he did not conceive of the fulfillment of this norm or attainment of this goal as an immanent historical possibility. Mankind's earthly existence was lived out under the shadow of

81 *Philosophie des Rechts* (1963), vol. 2, part 1, p. 14. See also *Philosophie des Rechts*, vol. 2, part 1 (1833), pp. 18–29, where the absolute being of personality is described as a will with "infinite choice," or absolute creative freedom.

82 *Philosophie des Rechts*, vol. 2, part 1 (1833), pp. 57–61. Warren Breckman has recently argued that Stahl's assimilation of Schelling's conception of the individual as a free subject, or personality, was the basis for his justification for freedom of private property ownership in civil society, an emphasis in his theory that distinguished him from traditional conservatives, and even from Savigny, who had a more moderate and evolutionary view about the development of private property under common law and judicial interpretation. See Warren Breckman, *Marx, the Young Hegelians and the Origins of Radical Social Theory: Dethroning the Self* (Cambridge and New York: 1999), pp. 80–89; and Whitman, *Legacy of Roman Law*, pp. 180–98.

83 *Philosophie des Rechts* (1963) vol. 2, part 1, pp. 70–190. The specific term was only developed in contrast to Romantic notions of organic community in later editions, but the idea of the ethical kingdom as a community defined by the freedom of "personality" is already implicitly present in the first edition, vol. 2, part 1 (1833), pp. 96–105, and vol. 2, part 2 (1837), pp. 1–20. See also Dieter Grosser, *Grundlagen und Struktur der Staatslehre Friedrich Julius Stahl* (Cologne: 1963), pp. 54–62.

the fall, the perversion of innate freedom, the denial of creaturely status, and estrangement from its divine origin.[84] Consequently, Stahl described the genesis and evolution of both civil law and the public law of the state under a dual aspect. On the one hand, they represented divinely ordained institutions for the righteous punishment, discipline, and correction of human perversity and corruption. Law was not the articulated letter of the communal spirit, the conscious structuring of spontaneous life relationships, but a command, backed by punishing, coercive power, that regulated human relations according to absolute norms. As the enforcer of such norms, the state and its public institutions dominated the sphere of civil society and civil law. The innate drive of personalities created in the image of the absolute personality toward the creation of a world that would express their common identity in an ethical kingdom, which Stahl described as a universal historical "pull toward personality" (*Zug nach Persoenlichkeit*), was made essentially inoperative by human corruption, and only command enforced by punishment kept human relations from deteriorating into a destructive chaos of competing selfish wills.[85] On the other hand, Stahl also perceived legal and political institutions as sustaining, in a purely external, formal way, the normative conception of the ethical kingdom. He portrayed the ideal Christian state not only as an instrument of divine wrath and punishment, but also as the culmination of an historical progression toward an organic structure of legal and constitutional forms that protected and affirmed mankind's essence as free personality and created structures of political authority and voluntary obedience and identification that prefigured the actualization of ethical community beyond history.[86]

In Stahl's theory the ideal state qua ethical community was organized according to the "monarchical principle." It did not take the form of old regime feudal monarchies in which the public realm was reduced to a set of historically negotiated, customary relations between privileged private individuals and corporations, but was clearly postrevolutionary in its emphasis on the state as a public community encompassing all of its members and ruling them according to a single indivisible legal system and under a single authority. It was, however, also not a constitutional monarchy in the liberal parliamentary sense in which the aggregated wills of the people ruled the public realm and reduced the monarch to a symbolic figure of unity. Instead Stahl envisioned, very much in conformity with the ideas of Frederick William IV, a community bound together through identification with the legitimate monarch and obedience to his personal power. It was the power

[84] *Philosophie des Rechts*, vol. 2, part 1, 1(1833), pp. 61–68. The strong focus on the fall as defining the state of human existence was somewhat attenuated in later editions.

[85] *Philosophie des Rechts* (1963), vol. 2, part 1, 22ff.

[86] *Philosophie des Rechts* vol. 2, part 2 (1837), pp. 1–20; and *Philosophie des Rechts* (1963), vol. 2, part 2, pp. 130–61, 176–85.

of the king that bound individuals, corporations, and voluntary associations together into one kingdom. The fraternal unity among the members of a state ultimately depended on the patriarchal authority of a king through whom these members experienced the source and goal of their common public life. Although representation of the "people" in its various forms was a critical component of a public political order, such representation was geared simply toward guarding and sustaining the legal structure as a whole and had merely consultative functions on particular issues. The king embodied a communal unity that stood outside of its individual members, that reached to the transcendent source of ethical life and was thus the decisive element in the common, public life of the state.[87]

In contrast to Savigny, especially the Savigny of 1814–16, therefore, Stahl envisioned the genesis of legally and politically structured historical communities not as the self-articulation of national cultural subjects, but as the imposition of an organized unity on the corrupted individual wills of the people. To be sure, Stahl continued to conceive of the public community of citizens in a state as an external, formal organization. The freely willed obedience that could transform legally organized individuals into an ethical community, into a community of subjective identification with a common will and purpose, could not be coerced; the state in itself could not transform the motivational structure of its members, although it could, and in Stahl's view should, provide the external conditions for such a transformation.

Stahl did not ignore the subjective element in the construction of an ethical kingdom in historical time. However, he insisted that the redemptive transformation of individual wills was not the function of the state or national cultural institutions like schools and universities, but of the Christian church. Stahl's church was not Savigny's invisible church, which found visible self-expression in a variety of ritual and behavior, but the church as a visible, confessionally unified, hierarchically structured, and disciplinary institution. The creation of a Christian state that was more than an external legal form and was securely grounded in the ethical commitments of its members required both a reformation of the existing churches according to standards of legitimate transcendent authority and voluntary obedience and a reconstruction of the relationship between state and church that would allow the church to pursue its specific spiritual functions without state influence or interference. In the early 1830s, in a period in which he was very much under the influence of Schelling's vision of history, Stahl occasionally expressed the hope that modern Germany would become the cultural site for a unification of Protestant and Catholic churches in a new and

[87] *Das Monarchische Prinzip: Eine Staatsrechtlich-politische Abhandlung* (Heidelberg: 1845). See also *Philosophie des Rechts*, vol. 2, part 2 (1837), pp. 73–88.

perfected Christian ecclesiastical unity. In an unpublished note from 1834 he wrote:

> Our age has experienced amazing catastrophic crises over the past half century. But the greatest of these, and the one most lasting in influence, is still in the future, the reunification of the church. With the fulfillment of the yearning of the church toward reunification the modern history of our age must find its fulfillment, just as it began with the expression of this yearning in the division of the church.[88]

By 1840, however, Stahl had transformed this hope into a strong commitment to a new reformation of a Protestant church that would triumph over its rivals. A return to contemporary German Protestantism's origin in the Reformation, and especially in the original apostolic church, would provide the ecclesiastical and confessional base for a church that could sustain the battle for the creation of an ethical kingdom in modern Germany.[89]

Like the king, Bunsen, and other leaders in the Prussian government, Stahl favored the separation of church and state. The secular control over inner church affairs needed to be replaced by a hierarchical ecclesiastical constitution that once again made bishops and pastors, the ordained Christian clerisy (*Lehrstand*), into the dominant power determining both confessional guidelines and church discipline and organization. Kingship in a Christian state remained a divine office that possessed ultimate authority over the general direction of the church as a whole, but no actual governmental jurisdiction within the church. The role of cultural education that Savigny had ascribed to the universities, Stahl conferred on the church. The task of interpreting the guiding principles of national consciousness was displaced by the task of interpreting the guiding principles of divine revelation. Jurisprudence was subordinated to interpretation by the clerisy of divine revelation in the history of the church. The education and discipline directed at the transformation of the subjective will, carried forward by church institutions, provided the ethical foundations of political order, turned external coercion into voluntary obedience and submission to authority into the free ethical determination of the will. In striking contrast to Savigny and the favorite theologian of the founding members of the Historical School, Friedrich Schleiermacher, Stahl rejected the notion that confessional and ecclesiastical forms were a visible expression of an already existing invisible community of the redeemed. Instead he insisted that the

[88] Cited in Gerhard Masur, *Friedrich Julius Stahl, Geschichte seines Lebens: Aufstieg und Entfaltung 1802–1840* (Berlin: 1930), p. 309.

[89] This was the message of Stahl's, *Die Kirchenverfassung und Lehre und Recht der Protestanten* (Erlangen: 1840), a short programmatic work that greatly influenced Frederick William IV, Bunsen, and others in their desire to draw Stahl to join them in Berlin.

invisible communality of the saved did not create the church, but that individuals were called and accepted into a church that already existed as a divinely ordained "institution" (*Anstalt*), as a "power that stands above human beings."[90] Apostles, teachers, and pastors were not the elected representatives of already existing Christian communities or congregations; rather, the congregations "were their work," that is, produced by divinely ordained leadership.[91]

By the time Stahl joined Savigny on the law faculty in Berlin in the fall of 1840, therefore, he appeared to have left the original vision of the Historical School, the starting point of his intellectual itinerary, far behind. His writings indicated only a minor interest in the spontaneous structuring of social relations into the meaningful totalities of historically evolving national cultures as expressed in the forms of private or civil law. Instead, the order of civil society was seen as controlled by and subordinated to the coercive power of the state and the transcendent will of the Christian God. He continued to insist on describing his position as "historical," but his historicism was no longer the Romantic historicism that had defined the original positions of the Historical School. It had moved toward a new and almost exclusive focus on the free acts of unique "personalities." To grasp and affirm one's own identity within history was to understand the specific acts that produced the reality in which one lived, the acts of human individuals framed by their relationship to transcendent authority. To be historical meant to grasp the freedom to act in history in relation to a will that remained outside of, or autonomous in relation to, the immanently produced patterns of historical development among fallen creatures.

Just as Stahl's focus shifted from the historical reconstruction of the evolving structures of national cultures to the historical acts that brought the power of transcendent norms into relation with the circumstances of fallen earthly existence, so his sense of calling appeared to shift from Savigny's ideal of the academic scholar and teacher to the more active and interventionist roles of ecclesiastical reformer and political ideologue. His published work after 1840 was largely devoted to reworking the positions of his earlier work in response to political and ecclesiastical developments and for broader public

[90] See Stahl, *Kirchenverfassung*, pp. 48–49, 54–55. On the critical importance of theology and ecclesiology in Stahl's political theories and the close parallels between his views and those of Frederick William IV in the 1840s, see Reiner Strunk, *Politische Ekklesiologie im Zeitalter der Revolution* (Munich: 1971), pp. 154–229. The most systematic and extensive study of Stahl's theory of church and state and his ecclesiastical politics is Arie Nabrings, *Friedrich Julius Stahl-Rechtsphilosophie und Kirchenpolitik* (Bielefeld: 1983). Nabring's attempts to derive Stahls' specific theory and practice after 1840 from a project of historical reconciliation that emerged more from a disappointed Hegelianism than a committed attachment to Schelling's late philosophy or the perspectives of the Historical School, but in doing so ignores many of the distinctive aspects of Stahl's view of an authentically "historical" existence.

[91] Stahl, *Kirchenverfassung*, p. 220.

impact.[92] Along with Ernst Ludwig von Gerlach, Stahl eventually became one of the intellectual founding fathers of the Prussian Conservative Party.[93]

There were personal and particular reasons for Stahl's divergence from the original principles of Romantic historicism, but we have seen that a similar pattern of development, in more subdued and qualified form, was also present in the internal shift in Savigny's perspective after 1830, as it was in the perspectives of Jacob Grimm and Leopold Ranke. It is also noteworthy that Frederick William IV and his advisor, Christian Bunsen, who were so drawn to Stahl's Christian philosophy of the state and historical development in the late 1830s, had also begun their intellectual developments as students of Niebuhr and Savigny. The alleged triumph of the Historical School in 1840 could perhaps be better described as a transformative crisis in Romantic historicism.

Whether we should call it a crisis or not, the internal modifications of Savigny's theory and Stahl's critical development beyond it revealed a complex of problems inherent in the original historicist model of the immanent generation of cultural forms, including law, as the silently operating, inwardly compelled, self-determination and self-expression of a collective national subject. This original model, as applied to the genesis and evolution of law by Savigny in 1814, assumed the identity of fact – the "positive," and value – the normative. For the early Savigny, the normative was historically present as the informing, animating essence of the positive in two senses. It was present within the legal and ethical dimension of human relations as the unconscious, essential will of the national subject whose directives were experienced by the individual as the sheer "given-ness" of custom and the inherent obligations of national conscience. But it was also present at the level of absolute, universal human morality insofar as essential, species-defining obligations were present in the individuated forms of national will

[92] The most obvious example of this was his *Fundamente einer christlichen Philosophie* (Heidelberg: 1846), which provided a much shortened and more dogmatic version of the central sections of the first volume of his *Philosophie des Rechts*. *Das monarchische Prinzip* could also be read as a simplified version of his previously developed political philosophy applied to the specific issues raised by the constitutional question in Prussia during the mid and late 1840s.

[93] Stahl's role as a political professor on the Right whose theoretical work was directed toward political practice and public engagement is examined in detail in Wilhelm Fuessl, *Professor in der Politik: Friedrich Julius Stahl (1802–1861), Das Monarchische Prinzip und seine Umsetzung in die parlementarische Praxis* (Goettingen: 1988). Stahl's political theory is analyzed as the ideology that allowed Prussian conservatives, especially those from the traditional nobility, to preserve their principles while accommodating themselves to the modern realities of public law and the constitutional state in Robert M. Berdahl, *The Politics of the Prussian Nobility: The Development of a Conservative Ideology 1770–1848* (Princeton, N.J: 1988). In contrast, the recent work by Myoung-Jae Kim analyzes Stahl's theoretical positions exclusively in terms of their internal logic and concludes that his attempt to develop a theory of suprahistorical personal authority that would justify the separation of state and society and provide a foundation for the authority of the state over society continues to be relevant to contemporary political debates. See Kim, *Staat und Gesellschaft bei Friedrich Julius Stahl. Eine Innenansicht seiner Staatsphilosophie* (Hanover: 1993).

and consciousness. The ethical subordination of the individual will to the national conscience was imagined as one variation of the generally human obligation to obey the revealed directives of the divine will pulsing through all the transformations of cultural life. By the 1840s, however, the assumed validity of this double identity had clearly begun to dissolve under the pressures of historical experiences that placed in question the belief that a spontaneous evolution of the national subject would necessarily progress toward an intensification and broadening of the ethical determination of individual wills. Savigny and Stahl responded to this disillusionment with the progressive evolution of history and its subjective agent – the people – by searching for extrahistorical, transcendent foundations for ethical norms, for principles that could be set against, and critically applied to, the actually existing life relations of contemporary culture. At the most general level, these developments implied a breakdown in the Romantic–Idealist philosophy of identity, in which the unity and meaningful transparency of the world of historical appearances was guaranteed by its status as the self-determination of a collective subject for whom all objects, events, and relations were objectifications of its own innate powers. By 1840 both Savigny and Stahl were convinced that the meaning and goal of human relations could not be construed or interpreted simply from the evidence of the internal relations of historical human cultures, but only through the relationship between the human and a transcendent other. The sphere of horizontal relations regulated by civil law attained its meaning and its ground only within the context of vertical relations to a personal power beyond history and beyond "man."

The breakdown of the Historical School's assumptions about the identity of fact and value, of historical genesis and normative validity, of submission to that which was, and ethical self-determination, clearly parallels the collapse of the identity between "Reason" and "Reality" in the Hegelian School. But this comparison also suggests that the theological version of the turn to historical transcendence was not the only response available to Savigny or Stahl. In the *System*, Savigny first noted and then rejected the suggestion that the institutions of civil law might attain their broader historical purpose and meaning in relation to the demands of economic self-gratification based in natural need, rather than to the demands of ego-transcending ethical self-determination based on religious faith. Man's limitations and determination through relations with an "other" that was not part of the self-produced world of cultural meanings could also be seen in terms of the free human personality's relations to nature, in productive labor, in sexual relations, and in the experience of the sheer "thatness" of the individual's contingent sensuous existence. Savigny, like Stahl, however, could only imagine man's relationship to nature as a form of "domination" (*Herrschaft*) in which nature became a mere "means through which the ethical purposes of human nature are achieved." "A new goal," he insisted, "is not contained within these means."[94] The choice to seek a reconstitution of the terms of historical identity through relation to a transcendent other was matched by a clear shift to a politics of patriarchy in the family, in the state, and in the church. For Savigny, and even more radically for Stahl, progressive development toward ethical community from the ethnic bonding among sons of a common maternal nationality could be achieved only through submission to the law of a transcendent father.

[94] Savigny, *System*, vol. 1, p. 54.

6

The Past as a Foreign Home: Jacob Grimm and the Relation Between Language and Historical Identity

PAST AND PRESENT: JACOB GRIMM IN BERLIN 1841

On April 30, 1841, a month after moving to Berlin in order to assume a research position at the Royal Prussian Academy of Sciences, Jacob Grimm presented a public lecture entitled "Legal Antiquities in Germanic Law."[1] Although the lecture introduced a course at the university on the history of Germanic law, Grimm did not have an appointment in one of the university faculties. As in Schelling's case, the appointment of the Grimm brothers was a special public appointment authorized directly by Frederick William IV without consultation of the university faculties. The Grimms were not sure that Prussia would be able to provide a satisfactory home for their cultural projects and historical aspirations: For more than twenty years they had viewed all Prussian claims to represent German national identity with great suspicion and had resisted a number of earlier attempts to draw them into the sphere of Prussian academic life.[2]

Jacob Grimm's inaugural lecture was less a statement of commitment to the policies of the new Prussian administration than a clarification of his own consciousness of cultural and historical mission as it had developed outside of the Prussian context since the first decade of the century. By working through the implications of the historical principle as it applied to the task of reconstructing the foundations of German cultural identity in myth, legend, epic narrative, folk tales, popular adages, customs, rituals, laws, and, most generally, the history of the German language and the Germanic language family, Jacob Grimm had certainly earned the right to a significant place in the post-Romantic historicism that rose to public prominence as the officially sanctioned ideology of the Prussian regime in the 1840s. Yet his own doubts about whether or not Prussia, the model of an "artificially" constructed, bureaucratic state, could function as an adequate incarnation of the "idea" of the larger, diverse "fatherland" hinted at unresolved tensions between the native and the foreign within his concept of German

[1] "Ueber die Alterthuemer des deutschen Rechts," in Jacob Grimm, *Kleinere Schriften*, 8 vols., 1864–90 (facsimile reprint; Hildesheim: 1965–66), vol. 8, pp. 545–51.

[2] As recently as 1838, Jacob Grimm had expressed his dismay at Prussia's inability to subordinate its selfish interests to the cause of the German nation. See J. Grimm to Bettine von Arnim, August 11, 1838, *Der Briefwechsel Bettine von Arnims mit den Bruedern Grimm*, ed. Hartwig Schulze (Frankfurt: 1985), pp. 42–43.

community.[3] The intense homesickness that motivated Grimm's obsessive devotion to recovery of the archaic foundations of German cultural identity was not completely stilled with his arrival in Berlin. But over time he found more and more reasons to imagine his home in Berlin as the ideal site from which to build bridges that might recreate the object of his longing – that original home forever receding into the otherness of the past – within the structures of the historical present.

By offering his first public lectures in Berlin on the theme of German legal history, Grimm made a gesture toward a return to his academic origins as a student of law under the mentorship of Savigny at the Hessian university at Marburg in 1802–5. It was Savigny, now his colleague in Berlin, who had introduced both Grimm brothers to the vocation of historical scholarship and, more specifically, to the academic science of jurisprudence as an historical discipline. In Savigny's early lectures on juristic method, which were informed by the Romantic philosophy of the young Schelling, he had taught the Grimms to grasp individual legal phenomena contextually, as expressions of a collective legislative will constantly defined and redefined by its reciprocal relations with other dimensions of "spiritual activity" in evolving political and cultural systems.[4] The meaning of laws and legal judgments were defined by their historical and cultural relations, rather than by universal principles of nature or reason. Savigny also initiated the Grimms into the sacred aura of the directly encountered past that enveloped forgotten manuscripts in musty archives and inculcated a reverence for the historically given as a revelation of the divine idea in history.

But in 1841 Jacob Grimm chose to describe the relations between his beginnings in Savigny's classroom and his present positions in terms of radical discontinuity and historical displacement. What had shaped his own sense of cultural calling, he claimed, was not so much the early Romantic notion of culture developing in progressive stages toward an ever more adequate

[3] The most intelligent and provocative general interpretation of Jacob Grimm's work is still Ulrich Wyss, *Die wilde Philologie: Jacob Grimm und der Historismus* (Munich: 1979). Reading Grimm's work as an antihistoricist archaeology of the archaic, Wyss revealed tensions that had hardly been noticed previously. My own reading tends to see practices and attitudes that Wyss judged to be antihistoricist more as indications of a specific dimension within historicism – the creation of historical consciousness through the wonder of radical historical difference. It also emphasizes the tension between two ways of conceiving the historical meaning of language and the origins of this tension in Grimm's intellectual development. See also Werner Neumann, "Geschichte der Sprache und Historiolinguistik bei Jacob Grimm. Kontinuitaet und Wandel einer Fragestellung," *Sitzungsberichte der Akademie der Wissenschaften der Deutsche Demokratische Republik* (1985), pp. 86–102.

[4] J. Grimm to Savigny, October 17, 1805, *Briefe der Brueder Grimm an Savigny*, ed. Ingeborg Schnaak and Wilhelm Schoof (Berlin: 1953), p. 16. See also the discussion in Theo Schuler, "Jacob Grimm und Savigny," *Zeitschrift der Savigny-Stiftung fuer Rechtsgeschichte* 80 (1963): 200–3. Savigny's historical conception of law is formulated in his notes for "Lectures on Methodology" (1802), published in Friedrich Carl von Savigny, *Vorlesungen ueber juristische Methodologie, 1802–1842*, ed. Aldo Mazzacine (Frankfurt: 1993), pp. 86–89.

incarnation of its essence in historical phenomena, but the experience of "shame and humiliation" produced by his homeland's occupation by a foreign power. In response to this fundamental threat to his native identity, the historical principle was put to use not so much to grasp the present as a culmination of the past as to construct a past that could function as an "invisible defensive umbrella against the enemy's arrogance."[5] The experience of national humiliation and withdrawal justified a turn away from the study of a legal tradition tainted by the alien values of Roman antiquity and modern France, and a devotion to investigation of the vestigial signs of a native German cultural community in literature, language, and popular culture. The study of German law as Savigny had envisaged it – as an examination of the progressive incorporation of Roman law into the individualized forms of tribal culture – seemed like surrender to the foreign rather than a commitment to the native. Both Grimm brothers repeatedly presented their turn to Germanic antiquity as an attempt to defend and revitalize their native sense of self, as a search for the ground of their existence as historical, cultural beings. To be able to speak in one's own tongue and assert one's own identity with assurance, one had to recreate the world in which that tongue had shaped its first meanings and that identity was originally forged. The tradition of Roman law expressed the power of the universal claims of empire and church against the resistance of "home-grown" (*einheimische*) local traditions. The remaining historical traces of "primitive and undisciplined" pre-Roman and pre-Christian Germanic ethnic life, however, could function as the foundation for an identification with an indigenous "spirit of freedom" that could be felt in "flesh and blood" and serve as a source of resistance and self-assertion within the present.[6]

By 1841, Jacob Grimm's story of the historical origins of his own life's project in an experience of radical cultural displacement had become relatively fixed in the narratives that he and his brother Wilhelm constructed about the meaning of their scholarly work. In the dedication to Savigny in his *Deutsche Grammatik* (German Grammar) of 1819, Grimm merged the encounter with Savigny and Romantic historicism in Marburg with the traumatic turning point in his own family history, the death of his father in 1796. Six children (five brothers and a sister) and a frail widow (who died in 1808) were left to make a life for themselves in a world that no longer provided them with the paternal protection they had come to expect. They had been literally expelled from their ancestral home by this catastrophe. Savigny had sustained the brothers by taking them into a new world of friendships and familial connections. He introduced them to the poets and enthusiastic collectors of Germanic literary antiquities and folk poetry – Achim von Arnim and Clemens Brentano and their families. It was, Jacob Grimm claimed, as if "heaven, after we had been orphaned and left standing

[5] "Ueber die Alterthuemer," p. 546. [6] *Ibid.*, pp. 549–50.

alone, had decided to provide us with other human beings and produced inclinations and attachments that our parents would not have been able to imagine."[7] Since both Arnim and Savigny married Brentanos, the circle became like an enlarged kinship group. But the Grimms place in this group was always anomalous, somewhat like adopted country cousins in a circle of orphaned aristocratic siblings.

Jacob and Wilhelm Grimm had originally matriculated in the law faculty and pursued a career in administration out of deference to their deceased father's profession and their mother's wishes. By abandoning jurisprudence as a professional career at the completion of their studies, they broke this filial connection as well as the mentor relationship to Savigny. But as a generational "brother" and leading advocate of the historical principle in cultural studies, Savigny continued to play an important role in their consciousness. For the Grimm brothers, the relationship to Savigny, the Arnims, and the Brentanos was a difficult combination of identification and distancing. Some of this distance was certainly based on class. The aristocratic consciousness of entitlement possessed by Savigny, the Arnims, and the Brentanos contrasted with the lower-middle-class poverty and class resentments of the Grimm brothers. Sensitivity about preference given to aristocratic students at Marburg still rankled in Jacob Grimm's mind in 1831.[8] And even in old age the Grimms could surprise their political allies with their commitment to the abolition of privileged orders and ranks as a necessary condition for the transformation of the German people into an ethical community.[9]

An important part of the story the Grimms constructed about themselves was tied to their identification with the struggle for recognition among members of the "natural," "pure," unprivileged, and untutored *Volk*. The relationship to Savigny always retained a sense of his distance from this possibility. In an 1850 speech celebrating the fiftieth anniversary of Savigny's doctoral promotion, Grimm related in embarrassing detail his own discomforts in the world of refined social artificiality that reigned at the parties held at the Savignys' Berlin residence after Savigny was appointed government minister in 1842.[10] During Jacob Grimm's years in Berlin, he never completely surrendered the belief that the paths taken by Savigny and other Prussian cultural leaders was in some sense a betrayal of their historical mission as they had originally experienced and conceived it, that their appropriation of the ethnic identity of the people was more an assertion of power over the people than a mobilization of the people's power.

7 "An Herren Geheimnen Justizrath und Professor von Savigny zu Berlin," dedication to volume 1 of *Deutsche Grammatik* (1819), reprinted in *Kleinere Shriften*, vol. 8, p. 26.

8 "Selbstbiographie" (1831), *Kleinere Schriften*, vol. 1, p. 5.

9 Jacob Grimm shocked a number of his friends at the national parliament in Frankfurt in 1848 with his speeches favoring the abolition of legal ranks and status privileges. See Roland Feldmann, *Jacob Grimm und die Politik* (Frankfurt: 1969), pp. 241–43.

10 "Das Wort des Besitzes: eine linguistische Abhandlung," *Kleinere Schriften*, vol. 1, pp. 117–18.

Jacob Grimm's discovery of his own vocation occurred as a displacement into an enigmatic, buried world of the past, a world only mysteriously indicated by textual fragments and oral traditions that had lived on into the present. To come "home" was thus to live in an exotic and foreign world, to plant one's feet in native reality was to live imaginatively in a world that had to be recreated from historical ruins and traces. Moreover, to come home in this sense was also to rebel against the world of the fathers of the present and recent past, to displace the present fathers with the recreated fathers from the ancient past. Grimm remembered his experience of entering Savigny's study as a naive and impressionable student and being mesmerized by Bodmer's eighteenth-century edition of medieval troubadour songs, a book, he suggested, that Savigny probably had never read or pulled off his shelves.[11] What he found in the book was different from the world created in Savigny's lectures. Here the language was strange, only partially comprehensible, and the world that it suggested was exotic and mysterious.[12] The evidence of native identity appeared first as a virtually incomprehensible message at the margins of the present. Thus when Grimm told the story of how Savigny introduced him to historical scholarship, his words metamorphosed into a story of a self-discovery that needed to be defended against the threat of Savigny's influence. Although Grimm claimed merely to be establishing his own autonomous scholarly space beside his teacher in choosing Old German cultural studies as his area of specialization, his actual words in his initial assertion of independence in 1807 and in later comments expressed a definite critique of Savigny's choices. The study of Roman law was less relevant to the needs of contemporary Germans than reconstruction of the ancient worlds of an indigenous Germanic culture.[13]

In the Berlin inaugural lecture, Grimm expressed his critique of both Savigny and Savigny's "world" in indirect ways. First of all, he suggested that law, language, and imaginative literature were so entangled with each other in Germanic culture that they should be understood together as dimensions of the same cultural process. His point was that the historical evolution of law was only comprehensible if it was integrated into a history of culture more generally. For this task, an understanding of the evolution of language and the symbolic self-expressions of the people in stories they told themselves about themselves was central. In fact, it was precisely in the mutual entanglement of law and language as forms of self-expressive utterance emerging from the shared core of a cultural essence that the central tenets of the historical perspective became obvious.[14] Law and language were "both ancient and youthful," he claimed, in the sense that each emerged as an individualized historical voice from an impenetrable (*undurchdringlichen*),

[11] See, especially, the description in "Wort des Besitzes," p. 116. [12] *Ibid.*

[13] "Ueber die Alterthuemer," p. 550; "Das Wort des Besitzes." 120–21.

[14] For the following, see "Ueber die Alterthuemer," p. 547–48.

mysterious ground of being and were fueled in their development by the drive to constantly renew the connection to this ground and fashion it into new historical shapes. The emergence of language as an individuated articulation of a prelinguistic cultural essence illuminated the emergence of law as a historical specification of human relations out of the world of inarticulate customary practices that had not yet been framed and recognized as law and that did not distinguish between natural acts and norms. In both cases, all succeeding transformations were dependent on this original archaic state and were recognizably tied to each other through their common ground. The ancient forms could not persist in their original shapes, just as contemporary identities could not be fashioned from within themselves without the power that originally produced the tradition of fashioning and refashioning. Language and law were both essentially historical, because they fused together the "necessity" of the inherited forms of a cultural individuality with the infinite "freedom" that empowered the continuous tasks of reshaping these forms to fit present circumstances and needs. Thus Grimm affirmed his loyalty to the principle of "reformation" that the Prussian historicists claimed for themselves, but in ways that implied a critique of their appropriation. The past should never simply become an object of present consciousness, a world of completed actions and dead elements that could be manipulated at will and fully comprehended from within the present. The vitality and power of the past was tied to its "otherness," its ability to speak out of the mysterious ground of experience as the voice of a prediscursive energy that would never be fully understood.

The unfathomable could only be encountered through intuition, through perception of a message that came from the outside, like a revelation. Yet Grimm also insisted that this otherness of the past was a recognizable dimension of present consciousness. By letting the past speak in its native tongues, his contemporaries would come to recognize forgotten dimensions of their present selves. It was precisely by recognizing the radical otherness in the past, by encountering a mode of experience that was irrecoverably lost, that the individuals of the present came in contact with the buried substance of their own existence, the origin and creative core of their particular individuality. And once the voice of the past was recognized and allowed to speak, once the "sleeping text"[15] was reawakened, an authentic dialogue and process of mediation with the present could be undertaken.

The two dimensions of Grimm's conception of historical consciousness seemed to merge in his notion of scholarly reconstruction of the past as revitalization of indigenous identity in the present. By reanimating the pastness of the past, historical documents were transformed from lifeless, homogenized and appropriated texts into messages informed with "our own life and

[15] This is the phrase Grimm used to introduce one of his collections of ancient text fragments: *Altdeutsche Waelder herausgegeben durch die Brueder Grimm*, vol. 1. (1813), (facsimile reprint: Darmstadt: 1966), p. iii.

blood, which we can feel."[16] By recognizing the difference of the past, by refusing to simply absorb it into modern categories and to see it as a world organized completely differently, the historical scholar could illuminate the meaning of the present from a point outside the present.

The uneasiness that Jacob Grimm felt about making Prussia his home in 1840 was not just due to the difficulty of synchronizing his own personal form of historicism with the forms of historicism he thought he discerned among his new hosts. The political dimension of the Grimms' move to Berlin was impossible to ignore. What had made the appointment of the Grimms in Prussia an object of contention was their participation in the protest of seven professors at the University in Goettingen – the "Goettingen Seven" – against the abrogation of the Hanoverian constitution by King Ernst August, a brother-in-law of Frederick William III of Prussia, in 1837. The Hanoverian constitution had been created through discussions among the king, administrative officials, and representatives of the Hanoverian estates in 1832–33. The Grimms, who had come to Goettingen from Kassel in 1830, during the time of the political turmoil following the July revolution in France, had, like other Hanoverian civil servants, sworn an oath of allegiance to that constitution. When the new king unilaterally abrogated the constitution, released his subjects from their oaths, and called the estates together to accept his version of an appropriate legal expression of the "monarchical principle," the Grimms, along with five other professors at the university, refused to betray their earlier oath. The protest of the professors immediately became a national public event. They were praised for their defense of liberal constitutional principles against monarchical reaction or excoriated for rebellious disregard of their duty to obey constituted royal authority.

The Grimms interpreted their decision not as one of taking a stand with a political party, but as an act of conscience. Their act, they claimed, had no political intentions; it should not be construed as an attempt to further the interests of any party or interest group. Instead they saw themselves giving public confession to an internal submission to the collective will of a cultural community that transcended all parties in the political battle.[17] In their view, the constitution of 1833 was a product of the inclusive community of the Hanoverian people, emerging from an uncoerced consensus among the dynastic prince, the government leaders, and the representatives of the people. The constitution was not a "contract" in which individuals had agreed to establish an authority over themselves that they could then dismiss at their own whim, nor was it a "gift" from the monarch. It was an expression, however imperfect, of the identity of king and people within the larger context of a historically shaped ethical community. The internal

[16] "Ueber die Alterthuemer," p. 550.

[17] Jacob Grimm "Ueber Meine Entlassung" (1838), *Kleinere Schriften*, vol. 1, p. 28.

conscience to which the Grimms claimed to owe allegiance spoke with the voice of the community of which all parties were members. No single party could abrogate authentic expressions of this communal being, and no single party could absolve individuals of their allegiance to it.[18] Although Jacob Grimm insisted that his refusal to deny his previous oath had nothing to do with his readiness to fulfill his duties as a loyal subject of his king, the Hanoverian monarch dismissed the seven professors from their positions and forced three of them – including Jacob Grimm – to leave the country within three days or face arrest and involuntary confinement. Jacob Grimm made his way back to his younger brother's home in Kassel and Wilhelm, and his family followed him there about a year later.

Public opinion was mobilized by the liberal press and by various constitutionalist groups throughout Germany to support the professors' protest, aid their reinstatement or appointment elsewhere, and sustain them financially during their temporary unemployment. It was during this time that a Leipzig publisher developed the idea of selling subscriptions for a German dictionary project as a way of sustaining the Grimms as independent national scholars. In Prussia the pressure to hire the Grimms came especially from Bettina von Arnim, the maverick writer and widow of Achim von Arnim, who succeeded in arousing the enthusiasm of the crown prince, who had been an enthusiastic fellow traveler on the Grimms' voyages of Old German cultural discovery for more than twenty years, and who threw himself into the campaign to bring the brothers to Prussia. The king and government officials resisted these pressures, in part because the king himself took his brother-in-law's side and refused to accept explanations of the Grimms' rebellion against monarchical authority based on their political naiveté and moral innocence. The growing public identification of the professorial protest with the cause of liberal constitutionalism also made it difficult for the Prussian government to appoint the brothers to university positions and accept them as servants of the state.

After the dynastic change in 1840, however, a way was found out of this dilemma. The Grimms came to Prussia as members of the Royal Prussian Academy of Sciences, to which they had been appointed as "external" corresponding members in the early 1830s. They were not appointed as civil service employees at the university but given a generous annual income as scholars working on the project of the *Deutsches Woerterbuch* (German Dictionary). They were thus given a scholarly home but not confirmed in the principles that had produced their homelessness. Although Savigny and the Germanic philologist Karl Lachmann were happy to have the Grimms nearby in Berlin, neither was willing to take a principled stand to defend

[18] The Grimms' concept of the civic community as a *Lebensgemeinschaft* (life community) and the public sphere as a *Bekenntnisgemeinschaft* (community of commitment or voluntary identification) is trenchantly analyzed in Feldman, *Jacob Grimm und die Politik*, pp. 280–83.

the Grimms' protest. It was this reluctance that so irritated Bettina and motivated her to spread the rumor that Savigny and Lachmann had betrayed their lifelong friendship because of fear of government reprisal. Although many misunderstandings fueled these suspicions and rankling resentments, the problematic status of the Grimms in Berlin in 1841 was clearly connected to their particular conception of historicism and its relation to contemporary issues of cultural identification. Along with her sisterly enthusiasm and overbearing personal concern for the Grimm brothers, Bettina did share with them a faith in the integrating power of popular culture and popular will, a faith not fully shared by Savigny, Lachmann, the king, and other Prussian leaders within the new regime.[19]

RECOVERING THE ARCHAIC ORIGINS OF NATIVE CULTURE: READING THE *POESIE* OF THE PEOPLE

Jacob and Wilhelm Grimm began to publish the results of their investigations of ancient Germanic culture in 1807. By that time their collaborative efforts in editing ancient texts and collecting the traces of ancient folk culture in oral traditions were well under way. As a research assistant for Savigny in Paris in 1805, Jacob had been encouraged by his brother to seek out medieval literary sources while he helped Savigny uncover some of the earliest texts related to the northern European assimilation of Roman law. The brothers were also eager collaborators in efforts by Arnim and Brentano to collect traditional German folk songs in order to inspire the creation of a popular national lyrical poetry in the present.

At the outset of their historical investigations, the Grimm brothers developed a number of organizing distinctions. These were drawn from the tradition of Romantic philosophy, cultural anthropology, and literary criticism, from Herder, Schelling, and Friedrich Schlegel, and clarified in relation to similar projects that engaged members of their own generation like Joseph Goerres, Friedrich Creuzer, Arnim, and Brentano.[20] Their starting point was the assumption that the written texts or oral reports that were the objects of their investigation could and should be read as fragments of an expressive "poetry" (*Poesie*) created unconsciously by an ethnic people (*Volk*). *Poesie*, the term used by the Romantic generation to designate works of the

[19] As was evident in her own concerted attempts to hold Frederick William to a notion of conscience as obedience to a communal identity that encompassed the "common people" within the larger totality of "the people," a conception of conscience that the king could never fully share. See, especially, her *Dies Buch Gehoert dem Koenig* (Berlin: 1843).

[20] The most comprehensive critical examination of this early phase of Jacob Grimm's career is Gunhild Ginschel, *Der junge Jacob Grimm, 1805–1819*, 2nd ed. (Stuttgart: 1989) Ginschel's interpretive frame, however, is narrowly focused on demonstrating the "scientific" elements in Grimm's comparative historical method before his turn to systematic linguistic analysis after 1816.

expressive imagination – "literature" in a broad cultural sense – indicated the general category in which the Grimms placed the texts they were examining. *Poesie* was symbolic utterance in the sense that it was speech that contained within its particular descriptions and representations the aura of the unfathomable, "divine" ground from which individual events and objects emerged. *Poesie* was particular speech that revealed its origin in a prior identity of language and the world: "*Poesie* is that which emerges in the form of words directly from the core of feeling [*Gemueth*], and is thus the continuous natural drive and innate ability to grasp this feeling."[21] In the preface to his first book, Jacob Grimm described *Poesie* as "nothing else than life itself, grasped in its purity and contained in the magic of speech."[22] In archaic *Poesie*, the subject of the feeling that found expression in words was the collectivity, or the "whole"; in modern poetry it was the individual person in a problematic relation to the whole.[23]

What the Grimms were looking for was the distinctive linguistic form that defined the indigenous German mode of being. Written texts and oral reports were construed as messages that gave meaningful shape to the experiences of a subject, either individual or collective. Jacob Grimm sometimes spoke of their interpretive method in later years as an interest in "words" for the sake of "things" (*Sachen*), but the things that interested him were those realities of lived experience that connected individual beings to the ground of their existence in the unfathomable realm of pure being. The words he examined to attain approximation to these realities, however, were themselves realities, or *Sachen*, in the world, not transparent signs but living agents in their own right.[24]

Following a practice first established in the modern German tradition by Herder, Grimm made a radical distinction between "natural" *Poesie* (*Naturpoesie*) and artificial or artful *Poesie* (*Kunstpoesie*), between the anonymous, spontaneously produced expressions of primitive, nonindividualized cultures and the self-consciously produced imaginative worlds of symbolic meaning created by individual authors in modern cultures.[25] Natural *Poesie* captured life as "pure act [*reine Handlung*]" in a "living book" full of "an authentic history that one could begin to read and understand on every page" but whose meaning was ultimately inexhaustible. Artful *Poesie*, on the other hand, was a reflective "work of life" that could only relate to this authentic history as a recreated historical memory, and only enter into the depths

[21] J. Grimm to Achim von Arnim, May 20, 1811, *Achim von Arnim und Jacob und Wilhelm Grimm*, ed. Reinhold Steig (Stuttgart and Berlin: 1904), p. 116.

[22] *Ueber den deutschen Meistergesang* (Goettingen: 1811), p. 5.

[23] J. Grimm to Achim von Arnim, May 20, 1811, *Achim von Arnim und Jacob und Wilhelm Grimm*, p. 116.

[24] "Rede auf Lachmann" (1851), *Kleinere Schriften*, vol. 1, p. 150.

[25] There is an early clear statement of this distinction in Jacob Grimm: "Gedanken wie sich die Sagen zur Poesie und Geschichte verhalten" (1808), *Kleinere Schriften*, vol. 1, pp. 400–4.

of the historical unconscious through sympathetic identification.[26] Grimm sometimes described these two types of relation between creative energy and articulated form as incommensurable. They could follow one another in historical succession or exist simultaneously among cultural strata that operated in different dimensions and thus possessed different experiences of historical time. *Naturpoesie* for Grimm was connected to what he tended to call the *Vorzeit*, a vaguely defined period that predated the modern experience of temporality. Yet Grimm clearly thought that some kinds of participation in unconscious communal life did persist in fragmentary fashion in a modern world that appeared to be dominated by individualized subjects attempting to communicate their unique perspectives to an unreceptive array of alien others. This persistence of the speech of natural *Poesie*, and therefore of the world of experience it expressed, was evident in the culture of the marginalized, repressed, and subordinate – the "common" people who had maintained a continuous connection to the period when *people* was a term encompassing the totality of the community rather than merely one of its fragments. The Grimm brothers' research procedures, in all of their collections between 1807 and 1819, assumed that the oral traditions of popular culture spoke to them from a different temporal world, a *Vorzeit*.[27]

The Grimms also certainly implied that the poetry of the unconscious communal psyche resonated in the depths of modern individual subjects, in mysterious areas that could never become fully transparent to their consciousness. Their whole enterprise was premised on a belief that recovered memory of the historical moment when *Naturpoesie* captured the reality of a life lived in the whole could function in a powerful, creative, integrative fashion within the individualized psyches of the present. Feelings of participation in the unconscious core of German folk culture, however diluted or repressed, existed on some level of psychic reality for all Germans.

In their first writings, however, the Grimms were not concerned so much with mediating between these two realms as in separating them out so that the world revealed through *Naturpoesie* might become present to the modern individual psyche as something radically different from its everyday consciousness. In an implicit critique of contemporary Romantic poets, and even of their friends Arnim and Brentano, the Grimms rejected the notion that modern subjects could recreate *Naturpoesie*. For the modern poet, the idiom of natural folk poetry could never be a spontaneous utterance, but would always remain an artificial construct and thus a contradiction in terms. The poetic self-expression of primitive folk cultures produced itself in an involuntary fashion. The individual was the instrument, the collective

[26] *Ueber den deutschen Meistergesang*, pp. 6–7.

[27] See, for example, the preface to the first volume of *Deutsche Sagen* (1816), republished as "Vorrede der Brueder Grimm zum ersten band" in Brueder Grimm, *Deutsche Sagen*, ed. Hans-Joerg Uther (Munich: 1993).

cultural subject embodied in the language was the agent. Modernized folk poetry could not shed its artificial quality as a self-conscious imitation of a form that had been lost. The Grimms did not want to speak for the folk subject. Their aim was to present it as a living presence in its own right, to let it speak as a voice that might hold surprises and enigmatic, unreachable depths. Their methodological strictures about the disciplining of subjective tendencies in the reproduction of the past were all directed against the intrusion of the modern subject into a material created under totally different conditions. Historical "objectivity" was approximated by allowing the voice of the past to speak as purely and clearly as possible within the terms of its own world.[28]

As the Grimms pursued their cultural archaeology in relation to similar contemporary projects in the years after 1807, the distinctive contours of their own project gradually became more apparent. They seemed most in conformity with the general patterns of early-nineteenth-century German Romantic scholarship and literature in their obsessive drive to recover the unity that preceded the cultural fragmentation and subjective individualism of contemporary life. One of the things the Grimms sought in ancient Germanic texts and the tradition of popular folklore were elements and patterns of relationship that could be systematically compared with those of other cultural traditions. The point of such comparative mythology, as practiced especially by the Heidelberg Romantics Friedrich Creuzer and Joseph Goerres, was to move closer to a primal cultural text from which individual cultures had branched off as variations. Human cultures as a series of variants emerging from a primal identity maintained a religious aura; comparative mythology emerged as a study of different inscriptions of a single divine revelation. The search for unity was an archaeological dig to uncover the layer of human culture that was closest to the moment when nature first transformed itself into cultural meaning. Certainly the Grimms imagined their own historical investigation as a religious quest in this sense. Jacob Grimm wrote to Arnim: "I believe, perceive and trust that there is something divine in us that has emanated from God and leads us back to God: this remains and lives forever in mankind and grows huge like a fire of itself, but grasped historically, that is, within our temporal concepts it reveals itself in various ways in relation to the terrestrial, the human."[29]

The Grimms seemed to accept the general theory that cultural mythologies had universal dimensions related to a common origin and that

[28] Jacob Grimm's critique of Arnim's and Brentano's positions on the reworking of historical documents is presented in letters to Brentano and his brother Wilhelm in 1809. See Reinhold Steig, ed., *Clemens Brentano und die Brueder Grimm* (Stuttgart and Berlin, 1914), pp. 38–39; *Briefwechsel zwischen Jacob und Wilhelm Grimm aus der Jugendzeit*, 2d ed., ed. Wilhelm Schoof (Weimar: 1963), p. 101. For a general discussion of the principles informing the Grimms' rejection of modernizations of ancient texts, see Ginschel, *Der junge Jacob Grimm*, pp. 72–153.

[29] Jacob Grimm to Arnim, May 20, 1811, *Achim von Arnim und Jacob und Wilhelm Grimm*, p. 117.

approximation to this origin brought the historical researcher closer to the divine meaning in all things. To move closer to the primal moment before language and the world divided was to approach the presence of divinity. Within this larger frame, the focus on Germanic texts and traditions was primarily an elevation of the nativist variant to equal status with other traditions, particularly the biblical and the classical. The point of scholarly activity was ultimately religious, an illumination of the mysterious ground from which the forms in space and time emerged, and thus the achievement of a position from which the natural and cultural work of the world would be illuminated from within as if it were a text of one's own authorship. Yet the Grimms rarely indulged themselves in such fantasies of attaining the point of origin. And though Jacob noted in 1809 that he had encountered many interesting insights in reading around in the first volume of Schelling's recently published collected works, he found the speculative metaphysics enigmatic and ultimately impenetrable.[30] For the Grimms it was not so much the theological quest as the quest for a homeland, or as they tended to say, a "fatherland," that drove their scholarly explorations. What they hoped to encounter in all of its pristine originality and distinctiveness was the communal being of Germanic culture. What they desired was to build their households in its presence. Jacob Grimm expressed this position in his critique of myth investigators like Goerres or Arnold Kanne as too obsessed with the original universal revelation that was fragmented into various historical traditions. The divine origin, Grimm suggested, was always and only to be found within the life of the world. The existential truth of myths derived from their constant infusion of meaning into the temporality of human existence. The content of primal myth was not some abstract essence that existed prior to the creation of the world, but the continual process of creation of particular beings in the world.[31]

In the decade after 1807, Jacob and Wilhelm Grimm focused their efforts not so much on the recovery of a singular undifferentiated identity of absolute origin, but on the recovery of origins at a particular level of identity within the world of historical cultures, a moment that they described as the age of narrative self-articulation, or the "epic" period. As they focused their search for the oldest manuscripts in the tradition of Germanic *Poesie*, they were guided by the view that all the legends, stories, and tales that emerged from the heart and soul (*Gemueth*) of a culture were part of an epic cycle of collectively produced narratives, a syncretistic, overarching story with many substories within it. For Germany this metanarrative that framed all actual existing stories was most fully approximated in the surviving texts of the Nibelungen saga. Individual legends and stories tied to particular tribes and

30 J. Grimm to Savigny, December 19, 1809, *Briefe der Brueder Grimm an Savigny*, p. 80.

31 See the comment in a letter to Goerres, December 5, 1811, published in Josef von Goerres, *Freundesbriefe*, ed. Franz Binder (2 vols.; Munich, 1874), vol. 2, p. 261.

regions, ballads and songs passed on in fragmented texts, individual tales elaborated in stories preserved in popular chapbooks or the oral tradition – all these found their ground in an "objective" all-encompassing story and could be read as elaborations, variants, or localizations of components of this epic narrative.[32]

The Grimms' fascination with epic narrative had a number of sources. First, they were concerned with the ways in which universal mythical patterns became embedded in the meanings that communities gave to their experience as actual historical communities. Myths were outside of history, like abstract forms that only bound individuals into communities of meaning once they had enveloped the specific relations that defined a community in space and time. By presenting concrete events and relations against a background of mythical meaning, cultural epics like the *Nibelungenlied* and the countless legends (*Sagen*) connected to particular places and times expressed the integration of the individual into the temporal experience of the community and the particular nature of the local landscape. Everyone imagined the defining moments of their lives within the same framing stories and patterns of images. The individual did not precede community, Grimm suggested, but was born with, or as a member of, community: "The beginning of the individual person is simultaneous with the origin of the people."[33] Lives were actually lived this way, as parts of the narrative cycle that gave time meaning, and it would thus be false to call these epics "fictions," as if they were aesthetic creations distinct from life. The *Nibelungenlied*, though not a "history" in the modern "critical" sense (which differentiated fact and meaning), was a true history in the sense that it provided a representation of the way life was lived at the moment of its articulation. In some sense the Grimms clearly believed that the truth embodied in the *Poesie* of a folk epic was not "also true," but "more true" than modern critical history. The apparent transparency of modern historical accounts was due to the fact that they recounted existence in time from the standpoint of the self-conscious individual separated from nature and community. Collective meanings were experienced as imposed constructs and fictions. The knowledge given through epics and legends, however, was knowledge of life experienced in time as a member of community, closer to nature and to God.[34]

The contrast between the worlds given speech in *Naturpeosie* and *Kunstpoesie* articulated a pattern of historical decline from an original state of bliss, integration, and perfection. Grimm was quite willing to claim that "ancient

[32] Jacob Grimm, "Ueber das Nibelungen Liet" (1807), *Kleinere Schriften*, vol. 4, pp. 1–7; Jacob Grimm, "Von Uebereinstimmung der alten Sagen" (1807), *Kleinere Schriften*, vol. 4, pp. 9–12.

[33] J. Grimm to Arnim, October 29, 1812, in *Achim von Arnim und Jacob und Wilhelm Grimm*, p. 236.

[34] Jacob Grimm,"Gedanken wie sich die Sagen zur Poesie und Geschichte Verhalten (1808), *Kleinere Schriften*, vol. 1, pp. 400–4; Jacob Grimm, "Gedanken ueber Mythos, Epos und Geschichte mit altdeutschen Beispielen" (1813), *Kleinere Schriften*, vol. 4, pp. 74–85.

persons were greater, purer and more holy than we; the light of their divine origin still shone in and through them, much as when bright pure bodies continue to shine, or glitter for a while when one transfers them directly from the bright rays of the sun into dense darkness."[35] The paradise of this lost world could not be reentered, although it could operate as an object of longing in the individual's heart.[36] The memory of complete integration with the "whole" provided a perspective on the present that broke apart the blinders of the isolated individual ego, allowing the construction of a new experience of community mediated through shared origins in the worlds of the past.

Jacob Grimm's convictions about the place that early medieval epic literature had in the historical development of German culture help to explain his views on a number of particular issues connected to the editing and translating of ancient Germanic texts. Since Grimm saw the Nibelungen saga as an objective (collective, unconscious) cultural production, he was not concerned with the philological construction of a correct or definitive text, a text that could function authoritatively as an aesthetic monument within the history of literature.[37] All of the variant texts of a particular legend were of interest to him as collective expressions produced at different historical moments or in different cultural locations.

Jacob Grimm was suspicious of all attempts to modernize and translate ancient texts for contemporary consumption. Translations were always deceptive and even "evil" because they ripped the original text from all of the threads connecting it to the world of its creation and set up new and artificial relations connecting it to the world of the present. To make an ancient work familiar was by definition to rob it of some of its ability to produce culture shock, to transpose the reader into a world that really was different and foreign. Grimm hated the condescension of modern scholars and artists toward more "barbaric" ages, their confident appropriation of the past, their improvements of the crudities and enigmas of old texts through the scholarly instruments of linguistic homogenization. Grimm was quite willing to say that those individuals through whom a community lived its identity and spoke its collective truths were more fully human then the atomized subjects of the contemporary world. Not that it made any sense to claim that that ancient world should be brought back, or that contemporaries should try to live in the past. Just as the biblical paradise was "lost," Grimm wrote to Arnim, so "is also the Garden of ancient *Poesie* locked to us, even though everyone still carries a small paradise in his heart."[38] The encounter with

[35] J. Grimm to Arnim, May 20, 1811, *Achim von Arnim und Jacob und Wilhelm Grimm*, p. 117.

[36] J. Grimm to Achim von Arnim, October 29, 1812, *Achim von Arnim und Jacob und Wilhelm Grimm*, p. 235.

[37] "Ueber das Nibelungen Liet," pp. 6–7.

[38] J. Grimm to Arnim, October 29, 1812, *Achim von Arnim und Jacob und Wilhelm Grimm*, p. 235.

the past in its radical difference, however, could produce changes in the present, encouraging a kind of reflection that might reform the foundations on which current patterns of community identification were based. In January 1811, Grimm wrote to Brentano that recovery of the historical existence of Germanic ancestors as a public memory had helped to create an "eye for the true nature of contemporary German events, because as we have learned to love them, we have developed a more faithful reciprocal love among ourselves."[39]

The conviction that no one could leap out of the cultural world that fate had provided for them was an essential component of Grimm's historicism. One was fully alive only as a member of one's cultural community in time and place. To make the past "live," to recreate it as a life that individuals in the present might encounter as something transcendent to themselves, as a real world that pushed back at them and was not merely a pattern of dead letters to furnish their present individual subjectivities, was to respect its difference. Modernizing translations of ancient texts destroyed their most important meaning for the present.[40] But of course Grimm was also aware that without modern editions that remade ancient *Naturpoesie* into understandable modern poetry and translated the forgotten tongues of Gothic, Old Icelandic, Old High German, and Middle High German into something recognizable to the speakers and readers of Modern High German, no contact would take place at all. Without modern translations, the past would remain a foreign country, but not one to which the modern individual could travel to experience an encounter with a world in which things were different. The world of the ancient cultural epic was a world of unself-conscious naiveté, or "innocence," in Grimm's view, because individual action and responsibility dissolved into the self-expressive action of the community operating through individual persons. He liked to say that the great epic cycles of ancient cultures, whether Germanic, Nordic, or Homeric, were not made (by individuals) but "made themselves" (*sichvonselbstmachen*),[41] that they simply emerged as the appropriate expression of a form of life.[42]

As the Grimms became more deeply involved in the conflicts and dilemmas of their project of preserving the strangeness of the past, the general contours of their complex project became increasingly visible. The Grimms' attention was focused on narrative meaning – the realm of the epic poem, the heroic saga, the folk legend, folktale, and fairy tale became their particular

39 J. Grimm to Clemens Brentano, Jan 22, 1811, *Clemens Brentano und die Brueder Grimm*, ed. Reinhold Steig (Stuttgart and Berlin: 1904), p. 164.

40 Grimm's most extensive presentation of his ambivalent attitude toward the modern translation of ancient texts is contained in a long letter to Savigny of May 20, 1811, *Briefe der Brueder Grimm an Savigny*, pp. 101–7.

41 J. Grimm to Arnim, May 20, 1811, *Achim von Arnim und Jacob und Wilhelm Grimm*, p. 118.

42 *Ibid.*, p. 116.

specialization. They were trying to recreate the stories that an original, integrated culture told about itself to itself. The core of this narrative meaning could be found in relations among certain figures, motifs, and plot sequences. Such narrative content could be passed on with the insertion of different names, events, and places at various sites in the narrative as it was fragmented into folk dialects, local and regional stories, and it could ultimately be recovered from this fragmentation and self-transformation in the still living traditions of popular culture. The echoes of the world of the *Nibelungenlied* continued on in legends, proverbs, and fairy tales passed on through the oral tradition in areas of contemporary culture not fully assimilated by the homogenizing processes of religious conversion and state building in the postmedieval era. The Grimms' original scholarly project culminated between 1812 and 1818 in two enormously influential collections of folklore, the *Kinder- und Hausmaerchen* (Fairy Tales for Household and Children), published in 1812 and 1815 (followed by a volume of notes and commentaries prepared by Wilhelm Grimm in 1822), and the *Deutsche Sagen* (German Legends) published in 1816 and 1818.

The Grimm brothers had been gathering the materials for these collections since they left the university in 1805. Working as ethnographers of the cultures of the Germanic past, they focused on the tales and moral fables that dominated the inherited fund of collective meanings still present in popular culture. All of this narrative material, from oral tales recorded in the present to textual remnants of epic cycles dating back to the sixth and seventh centuries, was classified in general under the term *Sage*, which could be translated as "legend" or "fable" but in their minds encompassed more broadly the whole tradition of narrative *Poesie* that transformed the arbitrary contingencies of discrete events and individual existences into components of a meaningful story. *Sage* was the narrative *Poesie* of a community in which the individual lived his or her essence unreflectively, spontaneously, as a member of the whole. In the present these fragments of meaningful cultural narratives were marginalized; hidden in isolated regions, historical backwaters, or private homes; and preserved, often in forms only accessible to trained literary archaeologists and philological excavators, in crumbling books on dusty shelves. Yet all of these fragments were signs pointing to the previous existence of a different kind of world. And this world, the Grimms insisted, was the true home of their contemporaries, their point of origin, and the source of the unconscious memory that bound them together into communities of language and tradition. But the signs themselves were also things – objective artifacts from that earlier world. In that world, human beings had been nearer to their sacred essence as children of a common ethnic "mother." Their language described this connection not through abstract relations but in terms of concrete realities. Stories about individual people and particular events carried in their telling the aura of proximity to sacred origins. The plot patterns, the recurring motifs, the archetypal characters, the heroes with many names that marked these stories were indicators of this communal reality out of which they had first emerged as "self-creations." In the evolution of tradition, translation and modernization occurred constantly. Yet the Grimms were convinced that a core of essential content persisted through the myriad surface changes. The stories of the past thus were not just stories from the "beyond," but stories that exemplified how this core of "sameness" was constantly renewed and retold in living variants. The life of the community did not only exist in the pastness of the past, but in its constant transformations. The *Maerchen* and *Sagen* pointed toward a process of "living" incorporation in which the substance of the past was not dissolved in renewed appropriations but evolved through a constant encounter with a living text that could be reanimated as the core of identity in the present. The recovery of ancient memory was not only material for an elegy of decline, but also a promise of future possibility and a goad to action.

The Grimms' reconstructive historical scholarship, their vast accumulation of the mnemonic materials that were meant to conjure up the world of Old German community between 1807 and 1818, paralleled the transformation of the German cultural and political landscape by the French occupation, the campaign of national mobilization and liberation, and the postwar restorations emerging from the Congress of Vienna. Jacob Grimm's life and activity was intimately entangled in these events. After the humiliating defeats of first the Austrian and then the Prussian armies in 1805–7, he experienced the collapse of the Holy Roman Empire that had provided the "German" frame for German particularism. At the same time, he suffered through the dissolution of his Hessian homeland when it was incorporated into the Napoleonic empire as part of the Kingdom of Westphalia. His hometown, Kassel, became the capitol of this puppet realm ruled by Jerome Bonaparte, and he was forced to speak French in his official duties and wear the occupiers' uniform as the librarian of his new king. In the years between 1807 and 1813, he lived a public life as a loyal servant of French authority, working as the auditor of Jerome's council of state as well as his librarian. At the same time, he devoted all his free time to archival research in the literary remains of a forgotten native culture. During these years, Jacob Grimm explained and justified his own split existence as a radical division between the external obedience demanded by established political authority and inner identification with a community based on self-surrendering love. In the introduction to his first book, a study of the transition from folk poetry to professional art music in the urban guilds of the medieval *Meistersinger,* he defined these two realms as "state" and "fatherland." His loyalty to the inner fatherland was not a treasonous loyalty to a state other than that of the constituted French authorities, but to a different *kind* of community. He could exist in psychological harmony by dividing his identities cleanly between two spheres. At the same time, he claimed that ultimately no state could provide a satisfactory environment for justice and security if it was not connected to some version of a community of love or subjective identification. State and fatherland were two different dimensions of experience, but Grimm implied that the fatherland would finally be the only viable basis for a just and lasting state, a state in which external obedience was mobilized and motivated by an inner love.[43]

When the moment of what he imagined as the liberation of the fatherland finally arrived, Jacob Grimm threw himself into the campaigns for freedom with total commitment. He and Wilhelm supported the voluntary service of two younger brothers in the allied militia. They dedicated the proceeds of one of their editions of a Middle High German poem, Hartmut von Aue's *Armer Heinrich* (Poor Henry), to the funding of the Hessian volunteers. The subscriptions raised in this fashion were almost double the amount of Wilhelm's annual salary. Jacob became a chief aide of the Hessian representative on the Allied General Staff that followed the victorious armies on their long trek to Paris in the spring of 1814. Throughout these busy days as secretary and correspondent, he continued to pursue his scholarly collecting and investigation. The two activities now seemed in complete agreement. The Old German studies were no longer an escape from a world gone awry and a consolation for a world lost, but a basis for constructing a new kind of future.

A series of occasional political writings in one of the most widely read public organs of the national awakening, Joseph Goerres's *Rheinischer Merkur* (Rhenish Mercury), between December and 1814 and May 1815, testify to Jacob Grimm's historical hope that a German cultural reformation would follow external liberation from the foreign power and that political arrangements would become an appropriate language for the inner experience of national community. In the current situation, he claimed, the conformity of outward behavior and appearance to inward sentiment and belief had become a matter of importance. The campaign for "external" liberation from the French yoke was just such a collective practice aiming at making the world of external behavior correspond to the emerging consciousness of community in a shared form of life. The many contemporary experiments that tried to represent German communal consciousness in outward behavior, however crude some of them might seem (as in the costumes and rituals of the student fraternities, or the campaigns to revive old speech patterns or boycott foreign goods), should not be treated as trivial, Grimm claimed, but as parts of a wide-ranging cultural project to transform the idea of German identity into collective practice.[44] Such practice encompassed the purification of language from recent French importations and the choice of German styles of dress and social comportment, but above all the reconstruction and reform of institutions and laws regulating relations

43 J. Grimm *Ueber den altdeutschen Meistergesang*, p. 9.

44 "Spielerei und Schwierigkeit" (*Rheinischer Merkur*, April 3, 1815), *Kleinere Schriften*, vol. 8, pp. 412–13.

of power and social exchange. The task of creating visible images and rituals for German national consciousness and legal and political institutions that joined individual freedoms to collective self-determination were at the forefront of Jacob Grimm's consciousness during his two years as a an aide in the Hessian delegation during the liberation wars and then at the Congress of Vienna.

From the fall of 1813 to the summer of 1814, both Grimm brothers tied their inner commitments to the cause of the "patriot" party led by Baron Stein and the national publicists Arndt and Goerres. For a brief moment in early 1814, the Grimm brothers themselves had hoped to buy up a Hessian paper and turn it into an organ of national mobilization. Their aim was to ensure that the voice of the people would be heard in the sites of high politics where decisions about postwar arrangements would be decided. Their foe was the pragmatic balance-of-power politics of territorial sovereign states. Populations were not to be treated as the property of governments that could be traded for pragmatic reasons, but as cultural subjects whose desire to live in a world conforming to their historical ethnic identities should be recognized. Existing princes might retain their places as legitimate rulers if they recognized their appropriate role as directors or supervisors (*Vorsteher*) of cultural communities rather than commanders and owners of populations.[45]

Grimm was incensed by the trading of land and populations by the German princes at the Congress of Vienna and especially disillusioned by the Prussians, who had so recently presented themselves as the leaders of national regeneration. The political arrangement that Grimm saw as most expressive of the reality of a German cultural community shaped by language, folk narrative, art, social customs, and manners was some version of the old imperial constitution. The institutions of the medieval empire came closest to a visible articulation of a German ethno-linguistic identity that transcended the territorial claims and sovereign pretensions of the German states. Ideally, Grimm would have liked to see the old dialects and tribal traditions – Swabian, Franconian, Bavarian, Thuringian, and others – become the foundations of the "provinces" of the empire. This empire, Grimm claimed (like Arndt and Goerres), should encompass all ethnically or linguistically related Germans (like those in Alsace or Denmark), and all German populations should have a voice in the executive and legislative processes that defined the unity within diversity of German culture. Existing princes and governments were imagined as representatives of diverse components of the national organism but remained subordinate to the general cultural consciousness of the people as a whole. The subordination of Prussia and Austria to the claims of the German people, the surrender of their status as sovereign states

[45] "Verhandlungen ueber die Bundesverfassung" (*Rheinisicher Merkur*, Jan. 2, 1815), *Kleinere Schriften*, vol. 8, p. 404.

in the European system, was a premise of this position. Although Grimm had admired the Prussian reformers and the leadership role Prussia had played in the liberation wars, he was not enamored by Prussia's postwar attempts to increase its power as a European state at the expense of German solidarity.[46]

The postwar settlement produced by the Congress of Vienna was clearly a disappointment to Grimm. It did not create a set of external arrangements for German cultural diversity and identity that corresponded to what Grimm saw as the core patterns of German cultural existence. Hopes for constitutional reform at the local and regional level also foundered in the years after 1815. In the Grimms' home state of Hesse, the returning electoral prince called the traditional estates together (with the addition of a newly created peasant curia) to discuss the creation of a postwar constitutional order, but squabbles among different groups with different conceptions of tradition and of emancipation made it easy to dissolve the diet and continue a form of petty absolutist, bureaucratic rule.

It was during these years of hope and disillusionment that Jacob Grimm began to focus his interests on the relations between *Poesie* and the law, as well as on the structures of language that shaped the narratives of the poetic imagination and the customs, rituals, sayings, and images of law within a distinctive culture at a particular historical moment. As Jacob Grimm was leaving for France with the Hessian delegation, he wrote to Savigny of his recent interest in collecting traditional adages, legal judgments, and descriptions of customary usages and rituals of prohibition and punishment.[47] The premise of this project was that ancient folk custom (*Sitte*) related to written law and jurisprudence as *Naturpoesie* related to *Kunstpoesie*. Like the history of *Poesie*, therefore, the history of law began from a state of "nature," a "prehistorical" period, or *Vorzeit*, of direct, simple, unreflective, unmediated relations between nature and culture. The state of nature was not a universal order whose laws could be reconstructed by reason as natural laws for the present, but an historical moment accessible only to historical investigation and imaginative intuition.

When Savigny sent him the *Beruf* in 1814, Grimm was astonished and pleased to see how much his own conviction about the origins of law in the unconscious collective life of the *Volk* paralleled the position of his former mentor. But Grimm's lengthy commentary on Savigny's essay continued to reveal important differences in their views. While Savigny began his narrative of the historical genesis of law with the customary practices and rituals preceding written law and refused to speculate about the ultimate source of the shaping power of these practices among a distinctive people (his casual presentation of the theory that the prehistorical state

[46] "Sachsen" (*Rheinischer Merkur*, February 21, 1815), *Kleinere Schriften*, vol 8, p. 410.

[47] J. Grimm to Savigny, December 24, 1813, *Briefe der Brueder Grimm an Savigny*, p. 149.

might be a period of animal, prehuman existence [*tierischer Urzustand*] irritated Jacob Grimm) as they had been inherited from some very distant past, Grimm focused on this problem and saw the primal origins of the people as the source that provided the ancient symbols and rituals of law with their divine aura. Like ancient epic narrative, ancient popular legal relations possessed an ambivalent quality, participating in the timeless universal qualities of myth while speaking in the concrete sensuous language of spatially and temporally bound particulars. In origin, Grimm would claim in 1815, literature and law were one; they "arose from the same bed [*aus einem Bett aufgestanden*]" with the aura of their common mother still clinging to them.[48]

The common maternal "bed" from which law and literature arose and that remained incorporated in their mutual relations and analogous structures was inscribed in the language through which they articulated these relationships and revealed these analogies. Grimm tried to demonstrate the analogy, for example, between the judge in the legal tradition and the poet in the literary tradition through an etymological series that traced both terms to one root in an everyday concrete term, revealing the origins of poetic creation and legal judgment in the act of finding the appropriate statement and thus defining meaning from within the possibilities of speech.[49]

Etymological analysis was Grimm's most prominent method for demonstrating cross-disciplinary and cross-cultural analogies in the period up to 1818.[50] It provided him with a method for drawing associations between the elements and motifs of myths, legends, and epical narratives, for discerning analogies among folktales in different dialects within a language and different linguistic traditions within a family of languages, and for tracing genealogies from the more recent into the ancient past. The associations among the roots of the words pointed toward a shared origin. Already in 1812, Jacob Grimm had noted that proper use of the etymological method required a better understanding of the history of language terms and structures, of the systematic transformations that defined the differentiation of languages and their inner shifts from one cultural stage to another.[51] Jacob Grimm's etymologies sometimes seemed to be based on free association within his incredibly vast multilingual storehouse of lexical memory. In 1813–15 Jacob Grimm's etymological associations became increasingly speculative and he was subjected to severe criticism for the unfounded character

48 "Von der Poesie im Recht" (1815), *Kleinere Schriften*, vol. 6, p. 153. Grimm's response to Savigny's *Beruf* is contained in a long letter to Savigny from October 29, 1814, *Briefe der Brueder Grimm an Savigny*, pp. 171–78.

49 "Von der Poesie im Recht," p. 155.

50 There are good discussions of Grimm's etymological method in both Wyss, *Die wilde Philologie*, chapters 6 and 8, and Ginschel, *Der junge Jacob Grimm*, pp. 326–74.

51 In a review of Rasmus Kristian Rask's comparative study of Old Icelandic and Old Nordic grammars, in *Kleinere Schriften*, vol. 4, pp. 65–73.

of his claims about analogies and associations between cultures and between different dimensions within a culture on the basis of similarities he discerned in phonetic relations and patterns of word formation.[52] What Grimm saw everywhere were the hidden roots of a pervasive popular culture that had been suppressed and expelled to the margins of modern culture, but that contained memories of the foundations of ethnic association and the divine seeds of ethical community. Hidden in the similarities between words and word patterns were clues to an ancient way of experiencing and constructing the world.

A number of factors, besides the criticism of academic linguists and comparative philologists, came together in the period after 1816 to direct Grimm's attention to the internal structure of languages, and especially the grammar of the German language in its historical evolution. The central factor in Grimm's reorientation was the disillusionment that followed the failure of the postwar settlements to produce viable connections between external arrangements and recovered historical memory of essential cultural identity. What appeared to be a common consciousness still fairly near the surface and available in the culture of the "common folk" was more deeply buried or more resistant to recovery than previously imagined. The will to translate this common consciousness into cultural and political institutions could not withstand the resistant power of the drive toward self-aggrandizement by petty rulers and their bureaucracies or the aggressive defense of privileges by social, political, and cultural elites. With the hopes for a sudden liberation of authentic German identity from layers of imposed foreign forms dashed by the events of 1815, Grimm clearly felt an increased need for a theory of cultural development and cultural difference that would provide some insight into the processes of mediation between the past and the present and into the systems that provided the contextual frame for the meanings of individual terms that had been excavated as signs of an authentic Germanic past. In other words, he needed a theory not only to explain the historical difference that separated an authentic native past from a self-alienated present, but also a historical theory of transformation and change within and between cultural systems. The archaic identity of the German ethnic community was not about to burst into the consciousness of the present as an inspiration to rebuild the national culture. Some understanding of long-term processes of structural change beneath the surface of contingent events was required. The encounter with oneself as radically other needed to be modulated into a process whereby that other could be reintegrated into a present renovated and enriched through its encounters with the past.

[52] August Schlegel, in a review of *Altdeutsche Waelder* in the *Heidelbergische Jahrbuecher*, described the Grimms' method as a "Babylonian linguistic chaos" and Grimm himself as an "etymological Heraclitus." See Wyss, *Die wilde Philologie*, 229–30; Ginschel, *Der junge Jacob Grimm*, pp. 53–57, 331.

EXCAVATING THE STRUCTURES OF MEDIATION: LANGUAGE AND LAW IN THE BUILDING OF HISTORICAL COMMUNITY

When Jacob Grimm returned in 1816 to his native Kassel after his brief foray into the realm of high politics, he joined his brother Wilhelm as a poorly paid assistant librarian in the collections of the restored royal library. The years between 1816 and 1829, the period of the German "Restoration" have become the exemplary years for descriptions of the Grimms' personal style and cultural role. Their lives seemed devoted to their scholarly projects. Although these projects may have been dedicated to grandiose notions about nurturing the collective memory of the fatherland, the brothers lived their daily lives happily separated in their Hessian backwater from the hurly-burly of the emerging modern society of post-Napoleonic Europe and far removed from the major theaters of political conflict. It was during this period, the decade of their thirties, that the distinctive characters of the two brothers became more obvious. Wilhelm's sociable nature found expression in marriage to an old family friend, Dortchen Wild, and the creation of his own family. Jacob continued to reside within this expanded family in his role as head of the Grimm sibling clan and became a somewhat irascible figure who cherished his own scholarly isolation while he engaged with polemical vigor in journalistic combat with scholars in his field. After the collaborations of the period between 1812 and 1816, the brothers now also defined the divergences in their scholarly styles and interests more clearly. Wilhelm continued the focus on medieval literature and folklore and tended to work in a relatively relaxed and patient fashion. Jacob, on the other hand, threw himself more systematically and monomaniacally into problems that emerged from his work and pursued questions in almost obsessive detail. Jacob's intellectual and scholarly preeminence, his greater focus, his tendency to pursue the most pressing and difficult issues, his readiness to engage the world of scholarship to achieve his goals, all became more prominent in the 1820s. The overwhelming center of his attention after 1816 was the writing of his historical *Deutsche Grammatik* (German Grammar), a path-breaking, monumental, multivolume work. The first volume was published in 1819 and republished in an expanded version three years later. It contained Grimm's core theories regarding the inner transformations of language through phonetic shifts. A second volume, devoted to the generation of words from phonetic units, appeared in 1826. A large volume on ancient Germanic law followed almost immediately. In the decade after 1815, therefore, Jacob Grimm devoted himself to the two issues that seemed most relevant to explaining the disappointments of 1815, the fate of German culture as a linguistic community and the distinctiveness and viability of an indigenous set of national norms governing social and political relations.

In some ways Jacob Grimm's experience during the Restoration mirrored his earlier years as a divided servant of two authorities – the external authority of the legally constituted state and the internal authority of his spiritual fatherland. But the return of this split existence was a return with a difference marked by the experiences of 1813–15. Grimm's new master was a traditional German prince who liked to imagine his territories as a patrimony that could be ruled like a personal household. Jacob Grimm could occasionally develop feelings of personal warmth toward the principle of this kind of paternalistic politics. Personal rule, however, only worked successfully when there was a moral consensus within which both prince and people operated. During most of the Restoration, Jacob Grimm felt that this shared moral culture, a community of subjective identification, or "love," simply did not exist. The old prince, despite his nostalgia for traditional paternalistic relations with his subjects, was quite willing to use modern methods to enhance his control over his subjects. Jacob Grimm was especially distressed by the politics of surveillance and censorship after the Carlsbad Decrees of 1819. Appointed to the Censorship Commission in Kassel, Grimm found himself in continual opposition to the policies of his superiors. Not that Grimm was a liberal on censorship, but he was adamant in his opposition to censorship in the realm of cultural education and public ethics. Controlling attacks on specific political policies and persons might require some government censorship, but the world that concerned Grimm most, the public sphere in which historical and communal consciousness was developed, should remain free from political interference.[53] In 1819, Grimm wrote to Savigny:

> Things have really not taken a favorable turn and one is thrown into dismay, when one must admit the possibility that our government so soon after such magnificent and exalting events as we have experienced in Germany, could descend into a system of terror and fear, mistrust, accusations and all the petty and scandalous activities of the police that prevailed during the period of French and Westphalian rule.[54]

Disappointment at the turn history had taken after 1815 pushed Jacob Grimm to think more seriously about the long-range tendencies that might determine the pace and extent of the construction of a German public community grounded on subjective identification with indigenous values embedded in ethnic origins. The analogies and associations of speculative etymologies that provided enticing glimpses into an archaic past were inadequate to the task of grasping the evolution of the linguistic foundations of community as a systematic, "organic" process. On the other hand, the belief that a community of language could find an appropriate social and political form in a native Germanic tradition of law also needed to be demonstrated.

Grimm was aware by 1815 that "language" was a cultural form emerging from some preexisting core of ethnic (*Volkisch*) being that could not simply

[53] Frederick Ohles, *Germany's Rude Awakening: Censorship in the Land of the Brothers Grimm* (Kent, Ohio: 1992), esp. pp. 51–53, 72–73.

[54] J. Grimm to Savigny, November 3, 1819, *Briefe der Bruder Grimm an Savigny*, pp. 284–85.

be listed alongside other forms like literature, epic poetry, folktales, custom, myth, and religious ritual. The associations and analogies between the other cultural forms emerged from the common structure of the language in which they were shaped. Tales, epic poems, customs, rituals, and laws were acts within language. Language was both a historical reality in the world and a system for representing the world. But for Grimm this meant that language was also in the world it purported to represent. Words had direct empirical historical connections to things. In 1815 he noted: "Everything that is originally and inwardly connected, will through closer investigation reveal its justified basis in the structure [*Bau*] and nature [*Wesen*] of language itself, in which in any case, the liveliest most convincing connection to the things which it purports to express is strikingly presented."[55] The historical development of the terms and forms of language thus presented an account of the deep structures of cultural identities, prior to their differentiation into separate cultural spheres. Language was the expressive form that was closest to the experience of being a member of the collective subject.

Grimm's *Deutsche Grammatik* began with the general principle that the family of Germanic languages had an historical and structural identity, that the variations that characterized the different Germanic stem languages (German, English, Dutch, Scandinavian) and the dialects within them could be presented as parts of an evolving language organism. Grimm was not particularly concerned with the place of this language family in the larger group of Indo-European languages. His comparative anatomy of language as an evolving system was focused on the particular history that tied the culture of pre-Roman and pre-Christian Germanic tribes (the Goths) to all of the variants of Germanic language in the contemporary world. The grammatical structure of modern High German, he claimed, could not be represented convincingly by universal grammatical rules based on reason or nature; it was an historical product. Language contained its memory within itself: It presented itself as the identity of a subject continuous through time. A "language spirit" (*Sprachgeist*) animated the linguistic organism of words and grammatical forms.[56] Grimm's *Grammatik* was an excavation of the structures of all the Germanic languages in their historical sequence, an explanation of their transitions from one stage to another, and an interpretation of the ways in which the past continuously transformed itself into the present. The rules of language change, the laws of the internal motion of the linguistic organism, could not be logically deduced from current grammatical practices but were to be reconstructed on documentary foundations. Empirical examination and reconstruction of the actual historical record of language

[55] "Von der Poesie im Recht," *Kleinere Schriften*, vol. 6, p. 155.

[56] "Vorrede" (September 1818) to *Deutsche Grammatik* vol. 1, (Goettingen: 1819), reprinted in *Vorreden zur Deustchen Grammatik von 1819 und 1822*, ed. Hugo Steger (Darmstadt: 1968), p. 7. See also *Deustche Grammatik* (Goettingen: 1819), vol. 1, pp. 546–47.

use over time was the only secure path toward understanding the "laws" of language structure. The task of the grammarian was not to construct a set of rules for language use but to recreate the rules that were displayed in the self-development of language as a form of life. For Grimm, language was a "magnificent institution of nature" that human beings absorbed into their being like mother's milk. It worked within individuals as an "unconscious secret" shaping their most intimate selves, emerging as indistinguishable from what they were. When natives heard their own tongue in a foreign land, Grimm suggested, they were filled with a profound longing for their original home.[57]

"Native," however, was not a homogeneous category. In his foreword to the first volume of the *Grammatik*, Grimm asserted the importance of dialects in preserving the close contact between language and concrete forms of life. The real German folk language was individualized into dialects and it was in the regional and local dialects that many earlier forms of the language organism – and thus its memories – were documented and preserved.[58] In the development of modern High German since the Middle Ages, moreover, Grimm also discerned a class differentiation with ambivalent implications. On the one hand, the German of the Lutheran Bible gave educated Protestant Germans a "free breathing" national dialect that became the core of written modern High German and "overwhelmed the poets and writers of Catholic faith." The emergence of this nonregional pan-German dialect separated the local oral dialects of the people from the written language of the educated and thus lay at the root of the split between the educated experts claiming to speak for the culture as a whole, and the "common people," who were relegated to the status of being spoken for. Grimm's personal view of these processes of differentiation and unification was ambivalent. He lamented the attenuation of the bonds between language and concrete activities through the homogenization of oral dialects, yet he noted that the creation of a national "dialect" (in principle accessible to everyone) in which Germans as Germans could experience the "bond of their inheritance and community" was worth a high price.[59] In 1819 he described the diverse dialects of the common people as possessing "the warmth of life" (*Lebenswaerme*), but the national dialect of the educated was not described as "cold," but rather as possessing the "warmth of cultivation" (*Bildungswaerme*).[60]

At the beginning of the first volume of his *Grammatik*, Grimm inserted a short summary of the preliminary results of his investigations entitled "Several Major Propositions I Have Learned from the History of the German Language." We might instead view these propositions as the principles

[57] *Vorreden*, p. 1. [58] *Ibid.*, pp. 9–10, 16.

[59] *Deutsche Grammatik*, 2d ed. (Goettingen: 1822), vol. 1, pp. xi–xii, xiii. [60] *Ibid.*, p. xiii.

according to which Grimm constructed the German language as an historical organism.

Grimm's general view of the historical trajectory of the Germanic language family from pre-Christian Gothic to modern High German was focused on a process of decline:

> Since the High German language of the thirteenth century reveals nobler (*edlere*) and purer [*reinere*] forms than contemporary German, the eighth or ninth century in turn purer than the thirteenth, and finally the Gothic of the fourth or fifth even more perfect forms, it follows that the language which the Germanic people would have spoken in the first century would have been superior even to the Gothic.[61]

What Grimm meant when he claimed that the earliest forms of language were "purer" and "nobler" was that they possessed a plenitude of root terms and inflections that allowed speech to describe and express the world in its concrete sensuality and pulsing energy. The enormous numbers of terms, declinations, and conjugations that were available to describe individual acts and things produced a world in which there was virtually no gap between words and things, words and acts. The sensuous immediacy of an existence close to natural being was lived through a language in which there were words or forms of words for each thing, event, and experience. The Asian languages preceding Gothic and reaching back into the "sacred language" of Sanskrit moved closer and closer to this ideal of a totally concrete language but could never fully attain it. The hypothetically "perfect" language which Grimm (and other nineteenth-century philologists) projected as prior to Sanskrit was not just undiscovered but in a sense undiscoverable. What Grimm projected as linguistic perfection, as the essence of language itself, was a merger of language with the world, a primal identity in which the word and the deed were one, and therefore no language or world existed as such.[62]

The development of language was in inverse relation to the development of human culture. As civilization produced greater distance between human beings and their natural origin, language evolved as an instrument for controlling the tensions of this division. Terms and forms became fewer and more abstract. The sensuous concreteness of experience was controlled by terms that could be used to organize the world according to abstract and flexible categories. The ancient language was corporeal (*leiblich*) and sensuous (*sinnlich*). It was naive or innocent in the directness of its relations to nature. Modern languages, on the other hand, were sophisticated and, Grimm implied, guilty of dominating the world through processes

[61] "Einige Hauptsaetze Die Ich aus der Geschichte der deutschen Sprache gelernet habe," from the Vorrede to the *Deutsche Grammatik*, vol. 1 (1819), reprinted in *Kleinere Schriften*, vol. 8, p. 45.

[62] *Ibid.*, pp. 45–46.

hostile to the natural forms of life. Grimm claimed that the progress of civilization moved toward the dissolution of language, or rather that the "cultivation of language worked gradually toward a dissolution of its own nature."[63]

The opposition between *Naturpoesie* and *Kunstpoesie* that had guided Grimm's first investigations into the world of old German poetry and folktale was reconstructed in the *Grammatik* as a tension between the origin and the conclusion of the life history of a linguistic organism. Grimm did present archaic and modern languages as ideal types. Neither type of language was actually ever encountered in history in its pure form. Both were dissolutions or negations of language that erased the distinctions between language and the world. But the historical movement from languages that approximated the natural perfection of sensuous immediacy to those that constructed a delusional world of desiccated "spiritual" abstractions was real for Grimm. It articulated what he saw as an actual transformation of human existence.

There was a major tension in Grimm's description of the general pattern of language history. The historical evolution from nature to spirit, from unmediated concreteness to completely mediated conceptualization, from a natural harmony between words and deeds to the alienation of words from deeds, was itself portrayed as a natural and organic process. The slow development of language toward artifice and self-consciousness, toward more abstract categories and mechanical inflections, seemed inexorable. There was no point in lamenting the decline of the perfect language that had articulated the undivided natural existence of human prehistory. But could the content embodied in the original unmediated unity of nature and meaning be recreated at the highest level of cultural development and self-consciousness? The message in the *Deutsche Grammatik* was not clear. Its main thrust seemed to be toward an acceptance of the present configuration of language as an historical product whose content could only be grasped through its history. Grimm focused on explanations of the technical processes through which patterned shifts in phonetics (sound shifts) produced structural changes from one language state to the next. His "laws" of transformation, however, seemed to be hermeneutic laws, that is, interpretive conceptions that read the evolution from nature to spirit into changes in sounds produced by consonant and vowel modulations. Grimm's conceptions of language evolution were not woodenly schematic. The "warm" center of language structure, its controlling *Sprachgeist*, was able to evolve from its starting point in ways that allowed for focused developments in some areas and atrophied usages in others. Some foreign terms and forms could be assimilated, but two language identities could not be melded together. Grimm was not a language purist in the sense that any intrusion of foreign words was judged as a debilitating corruption.

[63] *Ibid.*, p. 46.

What was crucial for a language's continuing growth and adaptation to new circumstances was the survival of the fundamental organizing dynamic that had emerged during its first emergence as a distinctive language form. The stronger this core, the more foreign elements the language would be able to assimilate without losing its identity.[64]

Grimm's theory of the historical evolution of the Germanic language family as a grammatical organism began with a focus on verbs and vowel modulations. From the enigmatic beginnings of undifferentiated natural being there emerged phonetic representations of action and suffering. Language began not as a relational and communicative system of signs set against nature but as a subjective articulation of nature as dynamic (and maternal) energy. Grimm's laws of language development were thus concentrated on the way conjugation and declension followed the modulation of vowel sounds at the "heart," or root, of the word, and how this heart, even of words that had become nouns, was built on the basis of verbs, the representations of action and suffering. Language as subject articulated itself first as a verb. These verbs were then combined and objectified in the construction of nouns. The primary vowel sounds (the trinity of *a*, *i*, and *u*) were ordered and structured by "masculine" consonants whose development, as language moved toward greater mastery of its primal energies, could be traced in specific laws of transformation. The organism of language thus mirrored not the exchange system of a market economy, but a spiritual organism whose empirical externality was an objectification of its internal subjective dynamics, in which the cohering "soul" of the organism was imagined as a subjective agent embodying itself in external forms. Grimm seemed to think that the Germanic language organism had produced a particularly dynamic history because it had retained its connection to the maternal energies of nature by evolving primarily through the modulation of its roots, through vowel modulation (*ablaut* and *umlaut*) at the heart of words, and not through the mechanical addition of suffixes and prefixes.[65] This phenomenon was tied to Grimm's discovery that ancient speech found its poetic rhythms more in alliteration than in rhyme. Alliteration was connected to the inner hearts of

[64] *Ibid.*, p. 50–51. Grimm had already expressed this position in his 1813 essay "Grammatische Ansichten," reprinted from *Altdeutsche Waelder*, in *Kleinere Schriften*, vol. 1, pp. 179–87.

[65] Grimm's theories of conjugation and declension and the separation of strong verbs (in which inflection takes place as vowel modulation) and weak verbs (where it occurs through suffixes and prefixes) was introduced in the 1819 volume (pp. 542ff) and then more fully developed in the long revised first chapter of the 1822 revision (pp. 571–80), and especially in the chapter devoted to the construction of words out of sounds in volume 2 (1826), pp. 5–89. In his interesting discussion of Grimm's grammatical theories in *Die Wilde Philologie*, Ulrich Wyss claims that for Grimm vowels were self-subsistent realities, while consonants operated as grammatical functions shaping these realities in historical development. Thus, although Grimm gave primacy to vowel sounds, his theory of the transformation of language from one stage to another was tied to shifts in the sounds of consonants, that is, to the masculine shaping of primal maternal energy.

words and their sound shifts, not to the production of similar endings as a means to position words in social space or time.[66]

Grimm's descriptions of the phonetic basis of language and the structure of sound shifts in the production and use of words in the first two volumes of the *Grammatik* were organized around gendered categories. The origin of language in vowel sounds and verbs was imagined as maternal, the shaping of sounds into words through consonants, and the structural forms of grammar was imagined as masculine. In volume 3 of the *Grammatik*, published in 1831, Grimm moved on to attempt to describe the categorization of nouns according to gendered categories. Grimm assumed that the beginning of gender dichotomies in grammar emerged from a natural division of sexes in reality. At the most "natural" and archaic level of language, linguistic gender and natural sexual difference were bound together by real sensual associations; grammatical gender differentiation expanded in culture on the ground of this natural connection. The words *man* and *woman* (*Mann* and *Frau*) were conceived by Grimm as the ultimate source for the development of masculine and feminine grammatical categories.[67] This masculine–feminine division was formulated in Grimm's theory through conventional stereotypical divisions opposing the masculine as dominant and controlling to the feminine as passive and controlled.[68] Yet Grimm also understood the dynamism of the original verbal forms as maternal, and thus his feminine principle had two dimensions. On the one hand, it was tied to verbs and vowel sounds as the creative energy that objectified itself in cultural forms. Consonants and grammatical forms were masculine. They gave specific shape to feminine energy, but they were also dependent on the power of maternal energy. This theory contained the implicit justification for Grimm's constant use of *fatherland* (*Vaterland*) as the term for the cultural organization of the unity uncovered in the archaic beginnings of the mother tongue (*Muttersprache*).

If the original beginning of language, the plenitude of its primal immediacy, was maternal–feminine, how should one imagine the fatherland in linguistic terms? During the 1820s, Jacob Grimm did not seem prepared to project a present or future state of linguistic forms in which the primal state of the natural linguistic community would be reproduced in a more self-conscious fashion, that is, within the grammatical frame of modern High German. Although he had taken a decisive turn toward the problems of mediation, the realm of the unmediated still seemed to dominate his imagination. A similar pattern was evident in his work on the history of legal symbols and legal relations.

Law was the external form of community, the institutionalized system of norms that shaped social relations into organic identity. It articulated the

[66] "Einige Hauptsaetze," pp. 53–55. Grimm wrote a short essay on this theme in 1817 entitled "Zur geschichte des deutschen reims," *Kleinere Schriften*, vol. 6, pp. 276–77.

[67] J. Grimm, *Deutsche Grammatik* (4 vols.; Goettingen: 1819–37), vol. 3 (1831), pp. 323–40.

[68] *Ibid.*, pp. 311, 359.

inner individuations and external boundaries of membership and the continuity of the community over time. Law structured the relations between individuals as grammar structured the relations between sounds and words. Law was the grammar of community. The intimate association between language and community, and between grammar and law, had fascinated Jacob Grimm from the time of his first studies with Savigny. His goal was to develop a history of Germanic law that, like the history of Germanic language, would demonstrate the inherent organic identity and thus historical autonomy of the Germanic ethnic community, its temporal and spatial boundaries, and its priority in time to the imposed identities of Roman imperialism and Latin Christianity. Germanic forms of community traced their origins to a period that preceded the conquests and conversions of the Germanic tribes. Roman law and Christianity had not been able to erase Germanic tribal identity, but were built into the continuous development of a communal form that preceded them. It was in these archaic legal practices that contemporary Germans could find the roots of their current identity not only as German speakers but also as members of a social order regulated by German values and German norms. Law, more than language, provided the patriarchal dimension of Germanic identity, the defining moment in making a "fatherland" from a "mother tongue."

Immediately after publishing the second volume of the *Grammatik* in 1826, Grimm threw himself, in what he described as a kind of scholarly diversion, into the categorization and interpretation of legal antiquities he had been collecting for over a decade. In 1828 he published the result in a thousand-page volume entitled *Deutsche Rechtsaltertuemer* (German Legal Antiquities). This volume had more in common with his earlier collaborative collections of folklore and fairy tales than his systematic construction of Germanic language structures in the *Grammatik*. Grimm's general thesis was familiar – the written structures of any culture's constitutional, civil, and criminal law emerged from patterns of social interaction in preliterate folk culture. These patterns were articulated in rituals, sayings and adages, and customary usages that could be gleaned from literary descriptions, legal judgments, or historical descriptions in medieval texts, but also from the more recent evidence of an oral tradition of juristic folklore and customary practices among the common people. The normative structures of the social relations of a primitive Germanic community could be distilled from distorted or mixed forms passed down into the present through written and oral tradition.

Grimm's separation of the genuinely archaic Germanic forms from historical layers of text and tradition that carried them into the present was based on confidence in his ability to detect the original within the artful, but it was also sustained by his theory of linguistic development. The actual dates of the sources from which Grimm gleaned his materials were thus not crucial to the structure of his book, and the materials were not organized according to chronological or developmental stages. What Grimm did was collect the signs of ancient Germanic community under the categories of political authority and social estate, household structures, marriage customs, property regulations, forms of mutual obligation and exchange, criminal acts and punishments, and tests for the determination and judgment of guilt and innocence. In each category he collected evidence of a "prehistorical" period in which relations of power, social functions, mutual exchange, and so forth were articulated in the unmediated directness of concrete speech. What Grimm imagined was a community in which the legislative and executive subject was the community itself. Legal forms emerged from the innocent, "natural" heart of this community. Law was a construction from "below" rather than an imposition from "above." (In fact, many of the alleged archaic materials which Grimm gleaned from collections of customary law turned out not to be the collective production of a peasant folk culture but the assimilated legislation of ruling elites.)[69]

Grimm's polemical animus in *Deutsche Rechtsaltertuemer* was focused in two directions. On the one hand, he wanted to prove that the period prior to the imposition of Roman law was not an era of barbaric lawlessness but a time when an indigenous Germanic form of community was formed. Contemporary Germans were to be provided with a legal tradition on which to build a communal being they could experience as a genuine home. Second, Grimm directed a pointed criticism against those sophisticated and elitist professional scholars who could not grasp the wonder of an "uncivilized" community life and imposed their own fears, cautions, and self-consciousness on the worlds of the past, who could not see the "joyful purity, tenderness and virtue" of primitive communities.[70] In a characteristic passage, he used the ancient community as a criterion for criticizing current arrangements of social life:

> the dependencies and servitude of the past were much less onerous and more loving than the oppressed existence of our present peasants and factory laborers. The contemporary difficulties in the way of marriage for the poor and for salaried employees borders on serfdom, and our disgraceful prisons produce a greater torment than the mutilating corporal punishments of the pre-historical era. . . . Instead of its personal penalties we have merciless punishments, instead of colorful symbols we have bundles of files, instead of a court in the open air we have smoky offices, instead of chickens paid as rent or Shrovetide eggs, the bailiff comes in all seasons to extort nameless taxes from us. . . . Individual personality and the powerful paternalistic authority of the ancient law have given way to monotonous lassitude.[71]

Grimm did not want to return to prehistoric Germanic customary regulation of social relations, but he imagined that the core of indigenous values,

[69] Ludwig Denecke, *Jacob Grimm und sein Bruder Wilhelm* (Stuttgart: 1971), pp. 108–9.

[70] *Deutsche Rechtsalterthuemer* (Goettingen: 1828), p. xv. [71] *Ibid.*, p. xv–xvi (footnote).

especially the communal responsibility exercised by a fraternity of free men in councils and courts, would have served the Germans better than the imported institutions of Latin political culture. Roman law provided no illuminating continuity with the native tradition; it broke the bonds of memory and collective identity. As a result, the common people were left without a living connection to the community as a whole; they become "dumb peasants" rather than articulate free men. Grimm was quite clear about what he hoped might be the political consequences of a recovered "memory" of Germanic law. Providing the "home-grown" with the same dignity accorded to the foreign would allow a gradual "reformation of our legal constitution."[72]

The historical theory of his *Grammatik* allowed Grimm to identify with confidence the contours of a past world from vestiges hidden within textual and oral traditions. Just as the epic cycles emerged from a collective process of community story making and storytelling, so the rules of social interaction and mutual recognition emerged from the customary usages of a preliterate communal life. The tradition of a people making the rules for its own social behavior was alive in the archaic forms. But it was not obvious from Grimm's 1828 volume that he had any idea how the "natural" group identity of ancient Germanic tribal communities might have evolved toward modern forms in ways that could sustain those original values. Grimm provided no rules of legal inflection and transformation of forms in *Deutsche Rechtsaltertuemer.*

Grimm's conception of archaic Germanic culture encompassed both verbal meanings and rules for social action. The relations between language and law, culture and politics, however, seemed to go separate ways in the present, even in scholarship. In this sense Jacob Grimm's two great works of the 1820s represented the split in his existence between the retrospective cultural anthropologist of Germanic community and the citizen of a petty absolutist state.

ETHICAL COMMUNITY AND TRANSCENDENT MEANING: IN SEARCH OF GERMANIC RELIGION IN THE 1830S

The public recognition and scholarly reputation of the Grimm brothers grew steadily during the 1820s, both nationally and internationally. Jacob Grimm particularly made a significant impact on the academic study of Germanic linguistics and Germanic law, while Wilhelm's work on the medieval epics sustained the Grimms' reputation as preeminent scholars of Old German literature and culture. Honorary memberships in learned societies and honorary doctoral degrees from prestigious universities accumulated

[72] *Ibid.*, xvii–xviii.

from year to year in the bookcases and storage chests of the assistant librarians at the electoral prince's library in Kassel. Recognition at home, however, was more difficult to achieve and was entangled with the Grimms' disapproval of the character and policies of the electoral prince. Matters came to a head in 1829, when the death of the head librarian raised expectations for long overdue promotions and salary increases. The prince was not prepared to forgive the Grimms for their opposition to his rule and passed over their claims in making the new appointment. In frustration, the brothers made the decision to finally turn their backs on their ungrateful homeland and accept positions (as both librarians and professors) at the nearby University of Goettingen in Hanover.

The July Revolution in France and the political and social discontent it mobilized in the central German states (Hesse, Brunswick, Saxony, Hanover) provided an additional political dimension to the Grimms' move to Goettingen. Between late 1830 and mid 1833, both Hesse and Hanover were transformed into moderately liberal constitutional states that placed significant checks on princely authority and diluted the privileges of the aristocratic and patrician estates. In this context Jacob Grimm's political positions became more clearly defined. In Hanover he was drawn into a close friendship with Friedrich Dahlmann, the historian who represented the university in the state diet and who was a major player in drawing up the new constitution in 1831–33. At the same time he found himself increasingly estranged from Wilhelm's brother-in-law Ludwig Hassenpflug, the conservative Hessian state minister who was intent on undermining the restrictions on princely power instituted by the Hessian constitution. Both Jacob and Wilhelm Grimm supported the claims of the liberal opposition in 1830–32. Discontent with princely rule was justified by the princes' unwillingness to fulfill their patriarchal obligations. The "people" had no choice but to take things into their own hands. Despite his own personal fear of political turmoil, Grimm stated that he would have joined the French rebels of July 1830 on the barricades just as he supported the Hessian and Hanoverian opposition to arbitrary and irresponsible use of princely power. Grimm dismissed the fears of Savigny and Niebuhr, who saw the revolution as a rising of the rabble against the principles of hierarchical order. Discontent with the existing regimes was shared by the majority of honest *Buerger*, he claimed, and expressed the authentic will of a people who had been betrayed by their leaders. Although Grimm described himself as traditional monarchist who believed that paternalistic regimes tended to provide both security and room for diversity, he was also convinced that since 1815 most of the German princes had failed to fulfill their proper role as representatives of the popular will. The liberal ideal of a community of interests distilled from the individual interests represented in an elected legislature was dismissed as a prosaic vision that promised a world of leveling uniformity grounded in purely material criteria of the social good. But the authentic community of individuals bound together by identification with their historical substance, and with the paternalistic leaders who represented that historical substance to them in symbolic form, had itself been betrayed by corrupt, self-aggrandizing rulers only too happy to use social atomization to further their personal ends. The legitimacy of the constitutional movement lay not so much in its stated goals of a liberal market society and democratic government as in the need to check the powers of irresponsible princes and reconstitute the alliance of princes and peoples within the larger context of the nation as an ethical community.[73]

Within the context of constitutional government, it was possible to imagine the gradual emergence of a shared commitment to the ideal of a community of moral agents. Dahlmann and Grimm shared this view of the priority of ethical community over political arrangements. Dahlmann, however, tended to see the "nation" as limited to citizens of the state, while Jacob Grimm continued to imagine the "people" as an ethno-linguistic community for whom the constitution of the German Confederation was ultimately of greater importance than the particular constitutions in the individual states.[74]

Grimm believed that his own political and cultural perspectives had not been changed by the events of French Revolution of 1830 and its aftermath in the German states. Although he might appear more liberal to his Prussian friends because of his position on the new constitutions, he insisted: "I am not losing my earlier direction and still cling to everything that seduced and stirred me long ago."[75] But the move to Goettingen, and the political events that accompanied that move, did crystallize Grimm's earlier commitments in a particular way. As a university lecturer he was forced to organize his materials in a systematic fashion and think about the implications of his positions more reflectively. At Goettingen he taught courses in what we might call the historical anthropology of ancient Germanic culture. His theory of the historical development of the Germanic languages through systematic transformations expressed in phonetic shifts and grounded in an increasingly instrumental use of language vis-à-vis the world of things, his great accomplishment of the 1820s, remained the assumed base of all his analyses. His constant excavation of deeper historical layers from complex multilayered texts could not have proceeded in an orderly fashion without the rules of linguistic transformation. The interpretation of legal antiquities in order to

[73] Jacob Grimm's views of the 1830 revolution are most clearly expressed in his letters to Savigny from August 12 and September 29, 1830, in *Briefe der Brueder Grimm an Savigny*, pp. 357–61. Wilhelm Grimm's parallel opinions can be found in his letters from spring 1831 to his brother-in-law Hassenpflug, published in Robert Friderici, "Harmonie und Dissonanz. Ludwig Hassenpflug und seine Schwaeger Jacob, Wilhelm und Ludwig Emil Grimm," *Brueder Grimm Gedenken*, vol. 1 (1963), pp. 159–80. See also the discussion in Feldmann, *Jacob Grimm und die Politik*, pp. 150–64.

[74] There is a good comparison of Grimm's and Dahlmann's views in Feldmann, 164–75.

[75] J. Grimm to Savigny, January 2, 1836, *Briefe an Savigny*, p. 381.

demonstrate that the pre-Christian Germanic tribes constituted an authentic rule-governed community also continued to claim an important part of his teaching time and critical importance in his view of the relationship between past and present.[76] During the 1830s, however, Grimm focused most intensely on the relationship between the communally integrated beings of early Germanic communities and that sphere that was "other" to human society but also defined the limits of human society. How did Germanic culture define its relations to nature and to the "gods"? Jacob Grimm's two major publications of the 1830s were a study of the animal fable *Reinhart Fuchs* (Reynard the Fox), which focused on folktales that explored the boundaries between the natural and the human worlds, and the *Deutsche Mythologie* (Germanic Mythology), which reconstructed the pre-Christian religious beliefs (*Goetterglauben*) of the ancient Teutonic tribes.

Grimm's work on the animal fable emphasized some familiar themes. His aim was to show that narrative accounts examining difference and similarity between animal and human worlds were native to all linguistically defined human cultures. The Germanic tribes did not borrow from the Greeks or other previous cultures but evolved their own forms of self-expression as they moved away from the primitive cultural moment in which nature and culture were indistinguishable. Animal fables and epics exuded an attitude toward nature that was much fresher and sensual than the modern, while they explored the growing alienation of humans from the animal world in stories of marginal, ambivalent creatures like foxes and wolves.[77] But Grimm's interest in how the development of human cultures involved a differentiation from the animal world and an instrumentalization of nature remained relatively undeveloped. His attention was diverted to the ways in which early Germanic communities defined themselves in relation to another form of "otherness" – the supernatural world of the gods.

Why did Jacob Grimm turn to this theme of the relationship between immanent community and transcendent reality in the 1830s? In the increasingly polemical contemporary battles between opposing ideologies, did he also feel the need to present the native Old German culture as a community founded on belief in transcendent powers? It should be remembered that 1835, the year of the publication of Grimm's *Germanic Mythology*, was also the year in which David Friedrich Strauss published the first volume of his *Life of Jesus*, which interpreted the stories of the New Testament as

[76] Jacob Grimm's Goettingen lectures notes for courses have been edited by Else Ebel and published as *Jacob Grimm's Deutsche Altertumskunde* (Goettingen: 1974). Other materials on the Grimm brothers' academic experience in Goettingen can be found in *Die Brueder Grimm in Goettingen 1829–1837*, ed. Rolf Wilhelm Brednich (Goettingen: 1986).

[77] Jacob Grimm, *Reinhart Fuchs* (Berlin: 1834). The aim of this work was to meld the extant fragments of the tale of Reynard the Fox into the primal story from which they had originated, and, in so doing, to travel back in time to that moment when the imagination of the Germanic "forefathers" first attached the threads of language to the problems of human difference from the animal world.

expressions of the myth-making collective unconscious of the Jewish people. While Strauss demystified Christian revelation as a projection of primitive, "oriental" cultural communities, Grimm rehabilitated Germanic pagan myths as an indigenous tradition of cultural encounter with that which lay beyond human finitude and transcended the particular relations of historical communities.

In 1835, however, Grimm did not present his study within this context, but as the logical outcome of a scholarly progression toward completion of a preexisting program. "Through comparison of ancient and reliable modern sources," he noted, "I have attempted in other books to show that our forefathers, stretching back into the pagan era, did not speak a raw and unregulated, but rather a free, adaptable, well-structured language which was already in the earliest ages suitable for poetry; that they did not live in confused, anarchic hordes, but practiced an ancient, inherited law within the context of a free association and powerful flourishing customs."[78] Using the "same methods," he now wanted to demonstrate "that their hearts were filled with faith in god and gods," that "serene [*heitere*] and magnificent representations, even if imperfect, of higher beings, of triumph in victory over, and disdain for, death animated and elevated their lives, that their nature and predisposition were far removed from a dull, brooding submission before idols and lumps of clay." That ancient Germans were not primitive "fetishists" but informed by faith and capable of a symbolic grasp of the infinite as a condition of the finite followed as an "inner necessity" from their existence as a linguistic and ethical community. A people with "healthy" language and customs "could not have been without religion."[79] The description of Old German mythology was thus conceived by Grimm as the description of the religious dimension of culture, commensurable with an account of the religious dimension in any culture.

In the 1835 introduction to the *Germanic Mythology*, he returned to the problem of distinguishing myth, legend (*Sage*), epic, and history, a task that had absorbed his energies in 1813–15. He began with the old distinction between legends and histories. The stories embedded in a culture's ancient literature and folklore had their distinctive basis in the symbolic structures of myth, which articulated the relations of finite man to the infinite ground of his existence. The stories of literature and folklore, however much they might refer to historical human actions, always inserted interactions between men and between nature and men into the context of relations between the created and the creator, the human and the divine. Such implied deeper meanings hovered over the actual accounts like an "aroma" (*Duft*).[80] Histories, on the other hand, found their independent foundation and

[78] From the preface to the 1835 edition of the *Deutsche Mythologie*, reprinted in *Kleinere Schriften*, vol. 8, p. 149.

[79] *Ibid.* [80] *Ibid.*, p. 148.

justification as descriptions of human acts and events. History described what man had made; legend told the story of man's encounter with that which was other to his own making. While the stories of history were unique, the stories of legend and literature were continually reborn in new guise. Only in the miraculous marriage of epic literature did universal meaning and specific event, transcendent encounter and immanent human action, come together in a story about the primal origin from which all the dichotomies of existence derived.

Collecting, reconstructing, and interpreting the materials of pagan mythology native to the Germanic tribes was thus for Grimm an act of recovering the authentic religious expressions of a Germanic culture that predated Christianity. At this level, Germanic culture was connected to the mythical world of other cultures: Stories of human relations to the gods were both repeated in various cultures and given the peculiar mark of every culture's concrete values and experiences. In *Germanic Mythology*, Grimm was especially concerned with patterns of analogy and association between the myths of the ancient Germanic tribes of central Europe and the much later evidence of Nordic mythology preserved in the Scandinavian sagas. His claim was that analogous patterns – grounded in the linguistic community from which these two branches of Germanic culture arose – gave evidence of the ancient provenance of the myths preserved at a later date in the Scandinavian countries, but also, and more significantly, of the richness and completeness of a teaching about the gods that the earlier non-Nordic evidence presented only in severely curtailed, fragmentary form. The fullness of the Nordic myths could be used to reconstruct the missing elements in the Old German myths. The ancient, pre-Christian origins of the myths preserved in relatively modern Nordic texts, moreover, could be demonstrated on the basis of analogies with the Old German fragments. The relationships between different elements in the Germanic cultural family were thus critical to Grimm's method. He was less interested in the relationship between Germanic myths and the myths contained in Sanskrit writings, the site of primal origin for all Germanic cultures. In fact, Grimm's interest in constructing relations between the vestiges of Germanic myths and Nordic or ancient Eastern myths was determined by his larger purpose of comparing and contrasting Germanic and Christian religions. Connecting the fragmentary remains of pagan mythology from ancient German texts and expanding them into a full-blown system of religious beliefs and practices bolstered Grimm's claims that an indigenous Germanic religion with its own myths, and its own literature and folklore constructed on the basis of those myths, was in existence at the moment when Christian beliefs and practices invaded Europe.[81]

[81] *Ibid.*, pp. 150–64.

As one might easily imagine, Grimm's conception of the confrontation between Germanic paganism and Latin Christianity, and of the historical triumph of the latter, was severely ambivalent. The most striking and daring dimension of the *Germanic Mythology* was undoubtedly its defense of the inherent life-enhancing values of the defeated pagan mythology. Grimm followed two different tracks in this apologia for native Germanic religion. On the one hand, he used his well-developed theory of the historical transition from the sensuous immediacy of "natural" cultural community to the reflective, instrumental abstractions of an "artificial" culture to contrast the values of Latin Christianity and Germanic Paganism. Despite all his disclaimers and qualifications, Grimm's attachment to the natural, free, naive, "fresh" relations portrayed in Germanic mythology was constantly on display. The Christian tendency to demonize pagan representations of natural existence and to intensify both the dualism of spirit and nature and the power of spirit over nature was most often described as a great impoverishment of European culture. Germanic Paganism was both more joyfully life-affirming and less inclined to the cruelty of ethical dualism than Christianity.[82] At the same time, however, Grimm used his integration of Germanic myth fragments into a general religious system to construct analogies between Christianity and paganism that suggested that major Christian (and especially Protestant) "truths" were revivals of religious positions already present in the old pagan mythology. The processes of cultural transition, in which Christians appropriated pagan myths and practices into their own religious system, and pagan believers accommodated themselves to Christianity by reading their inherited myths and customary practices into Christian stories and rituals, was thus based on a real overlap in the content of religious belief and practice.

In order to produce this conception of continuity between paganism and Christianity, Grimm subjected the Germanic myths to some interesting interpretations. As recent studies have indicated,[83] Grimm's claim that he had simply collected and described the vestiges of ancient Germanic myth hidden in the texts of the Christian persecutors, and then reconstructed missing elements and connections through analogy to other related pagan mythologies, hid a polemical construction of Germanic mythology as the foundation of an indigenous national religion. Grimm assumed that this religion would be analogous to some form of Protestant or post-Protestant Christianity. In the *Germanic Mythology*, there are definite hints of an historical concept that imagines the original myths finding their fullest expression in a reformed version of Christianity. The Protestant Reformation, Grimm suggested, while continuing the Christian project of spiritualizing and universalizing pagan sensuous diversity by ridding Christianity of the vestiges

[82] *Ibid.*, pp. 167–68.

[83] Beate Kellner, *Grimms Mythen. Studien zum Mythosbegriff und seiner Anwendung in Jacob Grimm's* Deutsche Mythologie (Frankfurt: 1994).

of religious polytheism and visual imagery, also returned to the freedom of the Old German cultural associations in which the gods were worshipped in the open air of "forest cathedrals," and the realities of natural existence were experienced as adequate symbolizations of the relationship between finite existence and its infinite ground.[84]

Grimm's representation of Wotan (Odin) as the supreme pagan deity provides a striking example of his construction of a Germanic mythology that would fit his own religious and cultural purposes. Grimm interpreted pagan polytheism not as the opposite of Judeo-Christian monotheism but as a more concrete, sensuous, and tolerant way of articulating similar conceptions of the relationship between an omnipotent divinity and the various forms in which that divinity appears in the world. "Monotheism," he wrote, "is a thing so natural and necessary, that almost all pagans have, unconsciously or consciously recognized amidst their colorful throng of gods a superior God who contains the properties of all the rest within him, so that these are to be regarded as emanations, rejuvenations, or renovations of him."[85] Grimm also imagined Wotan as a member of a trinity and as an absolute father connected in a paternalistic fashion to his many variants among the lesser gods and goddesses. Furthermore, Grimm denied that the old Germanic religion was pantheistic in any strict sense, since it clearly distinguished between gods and men and understood the distinction between the transcendent source of existence and the finite limitations of creaturely existence. At the same time, Grimm sympathized with what we might call the pantheistic "tilt" in paganism.[86] Because a cultural community closer to nature tended to see the presence of the infinite flowing throwing the finite more sensuously and concretely than a culture that constructed its world according to abstract categories, Germanic pagans tended toward intense life affirmation, were less afraid of death, and had a more joyous view of the tragic fate of individual existence than did Christians. Christianity broke the connections between a people and its divinities; it robbed their everyday existence of its direct and immediate relations to the gods. Christianity produced the disease it claimed to cure:

> Christianity was not in harmony with the life of the people [*Volksmaessig*]. It came from abroad and aimed at displacing time-honored native gods whom the country revered and loved. These gods and their worship were inextricably

[84] The attempts to imagine paganism as a populist pre-Christianity are especially noticeable in Grimm's speculations about religious worship in chapter 3 of the *Deutsche Mythologie*. The connection between archaic native religion and modern Protestantism is made more explicit in the preface to the 1844 edition, where Protestantism is described as a return to the indestructible archaic essence of Germanic religious belief (pp. xliii–xliv).

[85] Jacob Grimm, *Deutsche Mythologie*, (1844 ed.), vol. 1, p. 150.

[86] Vorrede to *Deutsche Mythologie* (1835), *Kleinere Schriften*, vol. 8, pp. 167–68. This argument is more full stated in the 1844 preface, pp. xlvii–xlviii.

> connected to popular cultural traditions, customs and legal constitutions. Their names had their roots in the people's language and were hallowed by antiquity, kings and princes traced their lineage back to individual gods, forests, mountains and lakes had enjoyed a living consecration from their presence. All this the people was now to renounce, and what was elsewhere praised as truth and loyalty was denounced and persecuted by the heralds of the new faith as a sin and a crime. The source and seat of all sacred lore was shifted away to far-off regions forever, and only a fainter borrowed glory could from now on be shed over the places in one's native land.[87]

In his discussions of prayer and sacrifice in pagan Germanic religion, moreover, Grimm, on the basis of virtually no evidence, imagined the ancient Teutons praying like modern Protestants and interpreting sacrifice as a symbolic ritual of thanks and atonement. In some passages it almost seemed as if Grimm thought of the recovery of the traditions of ancient Germanic religion as a source for the renewal of Protestant Christianity. From the beginning of its period of growth, he suggested, Christianity had found the moral energy and exaltation it demanded among the Germanic peoples, and the Germanic peoples in turn found a unity across their divisions in the homogenizing piety of Christian belief. Christianity made the Germanic spirit historically effective, and Germanic culture purified Christianity of extraneous elements produced by the special interests of an international Latin priesthood.[88]

Already in 1813 Jacob Grimm had noted that although human beings might be the authors of their history, they were not the authors of that authorship. Human creativity took place against the background of the ultimate source of creativity in the never fully transparent ground of being. It was this relationship between finite man and "god and the gods" that was the content of myth. But in the *Germanic Mythology*, Jacob Grimm extended his investigations beyond myth per se to include the whole panoply of rituals and practices connected with human relations to the transcendent. Mythological investigations became a way of talking about the religious dimension in culture. Earlier Jacob and Wilhelm seemed to have been content to imagine a culture unified through its language, its customs, and the stories that enveloped human events with an aura of deeper meaning, thus rescuing them from the abyss of pure contingency. The unique events and acts of human history were integrated into stories that repeated themselves, though always with different names and places. During the 1830s, Jacob Grimm's central concerns indicated a desire to ground the repetitious cycles, the "universal meanings" in the integrating stories of Germanic culture, on a religious consciousness and a peculiarly Germanic way of relating

87 *Deutsche Mythologie* (1835), p. 3.

88 See especially the shortened version of Grimm's theory in his 1835 course of lectures at the University of Goettingen in Grimm, *Deutsche Altertumskunde*, pp. 132–74, esp. pp. 135–36.

finite terrestrial existence to the power that made it possible. Although he continued to emphasize that the Germanic form of religious consciousness highlighted a joyful affirmation of existence in the face of death and a love of the sensuous immediacy of contingent being, and thus could hardly be allied with the religious conservatives who constantly tried to recruit him for their projects and journals, he did admit the limitations of an immanent explanation of human hope and suffering. Human historical action always took place in relation to something else, something outside of the immanent relations of culture – the grand historical narrative of the transformation of natural into "spiritual" relations did not collapse the tension between the immanent and the transcendent but simply recreated it in different terms. Considered in this light, however, it was possible to imagine a recovery of the forms of the ancient Germanic "natural" community and its "natural" relations to the gods in a modern German national community pervaded by a reformed version of the Christian myth, a version that affirmed, rather than denied, the fundamental values of the ancient Germanic mythology.

As historical events once again rearranged the Grimms' external existence in the fall of 1837, it was in fact not politics that was uppermost among Jacob Grimm's concerns. As was the case with Ranke and Savigny, his work had become centered on the relations between religious consciousness and national community. Unlike Savigny and Ranke, however, Grimm's work continued to assign to the state a merely instrumental role in the formation of ethical communities out of ethno-linguistic communities. The ethical content of the communal substance that demanded equal commitment from both princes and peoples was shaped not only by the immanent historical relations among the individuals of a linguistic and ethnic people, but also by the relations (i.e., religious relations) between those people and the transcendent power that made their communal substance possible. But defining the people's substance, their cultural essence, in terms of a relationship to an ultimately incomprehensible ground from which it arose also opened the horizon to a new view of historical freedom and contingency. The fate of the Germanic peoples was not fully contained in their past, because the structure of historical tradition was always incommensurable with the possibilities that lay in its beginnings.

An inner identification thus drew Jacob Grimm toward at least some dimensions of the Prussian regime of 1840. His own cultural homeland, his imagined and yearned-for fatherland, had, during the 1830s, begun to take on the dimensions of not only a Germanic but also a Christian–Germanic community. Moreover, the path to that homeland was not fully contained within the forces at work in inherited tradition. The past could illuminate the present and the future but could not predict the paths that would be taken in relation to that illumination. Rather, knowledge of the past opened up the future as a realm of possibility and freedom. The historical viewpoint not only affirmed the given as a sacred trust, but also emancipated the present from submission to the given, which was, after all, a historically contingent, and thus limited, expression of a "potency" (as Schelling might say) not yet fully explored or revealed.

HISTORICISM AS LINGUISTIC ARCHAEOLOGY: LANGUAGE AS THE SITE OF HISTORICAL IDENTITY

Jacob Grimm's long-standing doubts that he would ever feel properly at home in Prussia were grounded in his perception of Prussia as a German territorial state whose leaders' particularist ambitions persistently took priority over the participation of its citizens within the larger ethno-linguistic community of the German people. This was still his view in 1838, when he described his commitment to the German historical dictionary project as a patriotic activity that would enhance his free, "warm," and natural relation to the fatherland. He insinuated that a civil service position at a Prussian university would make his relationship to the German people much more ambivalent.[89]

The actual development of Jacob and Wilhelm Grimm's relation to their Prussian environment allayed most such doubts, and they gradually came to feel quite at home in Berlin. There were two major dimensions to this process of accommodation: First, their fears of being drawn away from their pan-German calling by bureaucratic service to the Prussian state proved unfounded, and second, they found the insertion of their household into the ruling circles of government leadership and official Prussian culture more congenial than they had imagined.[90]

The specific nature of the Grimms' Prussian appointment allowed them to continue in their chosen mission as servants of the fatherland without much difficulty. Although they were allowed to offer lectures at the university, they were not obligated to the university faculties or the university library as they had been in Goettingen. Jacob's tendency to define his relations to the community primarily through publication for a national audience and written correspondence with a wide network of students and scholars became even more pronounced in the 1840s. The dictionary project involved the organization of a contributor network that produced a huge correspondence with scholars across the German cultural landscape. New, expanded editions of the first volume of the *Deutsche Grammatik* (1840) and

[89] Jacob Grimm to Friedrich Blume, November 4, 1838, in *Briefe der Brueder Grimm*, ed. Hans Guertler and Albert Leitzmann (Jena: 1923), p. 25.

[90] The Grimms' social associations in Berlin are chronicled in Wilhelm Hansen, "Die Brueder Grimm in Berlin," *Brueder Grimm Gedenken*, vol. 1 (1963), pp. 227–307; Hartmut Schmidt, "Die berliner Jahre der Brueder Grimm, in *Die Brueder Grimm. Beitraege zu ihrem Schaffen* (Magdeburg: 1988), pp. 58–70; and Gerhard Ziegengeist, "Varnhagen von Ense ueber die Brueder Grimm und ihrem Umgangskreis in Berlin," *Brueder Grimm Gedenken* 12 (1997): 78–117.

the *Deutsche Mythologie* (1844), and a series of volumes of *Deutsche Weisthuemer* (German Legal Precedents), whose publication began in 1840, kept Jacob at the center of the three major areas of Germanic studies. When the first national meeting of "Germanists" (scholars of German law, language and literature, and history) met in Frankfurt in 1846, Jacob Grimm was the obvious choice for president. On this occasion, as on his reelection to this post the following year in Luebeck, Grimm took the opportunity to present emotionally charged accounts of his belief that historical linguistics would bring Germans back to their essential identity as a people and guide them in the task of defining their future as a fatherland. A "people," he proclaimed at the Frankfurt meeting, could be defined most simply as "the substantial embodiment of human beings speaking the same language."[91]

By 1846 there was certainly no indication that Jacob Grimm believed that his full commitment to the service of the German fatherland was in any way a betrayal of his obligations to the Prussian government. For the first time in their careers, the Grimms were integrated into the circles of government power and official culture. Frederick William invited them to the court for evenings with the royal family and for important cultural functions. In 1842, Jacob was among the original thirty German "Cultural Knights" (*Geistliche Ritter*) appointed by the king to the Order of Merit, Civilian Class. In this elite group he could encounter his closest Berlin acquaintances, like Savigny, Ranke, Schelling, Rueckert, August Schlegel, Eichhorn, and Alexander von Humboldt. Visitors to the Grimms in Berlin could not help being impressed by the ways in which the Grimm family, with its simply country ways and the brothers with their tendencies to scholarly withdrawal and social awkwardness, were drawn into the sphere of official society. The Grimms had definitely "arrived" by the mid 1840s. Their journeys into the popular culture of the past had placed them at the very center of the official culture of the present. And they seemed to welcome this position. Insistence on the contemporary relevance of their work, not as a therapeutic escape from the present but as a contribution toward building a better future, became a standard element in their public statements. In 1844, Wilhelm addressed a group of students who had come to celebrate his birthday with a torchlight parade and serenade: "We do not investigate German antiquity in order to lead us back into age which has long passed away into the stream of history; we investigate it in order to truly understand ourselves and through this understanding to contribute to the present, to which we owe our capabilities, our love and our concern."[92] Jacob also found it increasingly easy to note in his speeches and publications that his research into the past

[91] "Ueber die wechselseitigen Beziehung und die verbindung der drei in der Versammlung vertretenen Wissenschaften," *Kleinere Schriften*, vol. 7, 557; Feldmann, *Jacob Grimm und die Politik*, p. ii.

[92] Cited from a report in the *Koelnische Zeitung* of March 1, 1844, in Wilhelm Schoof, *Die Brueder Grimm in Berlin* (Berlin: 1964), p. 41.

was directly relevant to the creation of a national public culture in the present. Devotion to the mission of recovering a public memory in which all Germans participated as speakers of a common language seemed to have lost its oppositional edge under the regime of a king who saw himself as moving Prussia into the role of midwife of a national culture. The Grimms had always insisted that the paternalistic household was an appropriate model for the ethical community of princes and peoples. In the 1844 preface to the second edition of the *Deutsche Mythologie*, Jacob Grimm added a passage that gave special emphasis to the patriarchal household arrangements of the ancient German gods and the patriarchal form of ancient Germanic law.[93] The identity articulated through the mother tongue found its natural shape in the structures of a fatherland. The regime of Frederick William IV, in the Grimms' view, was not out of keeping with this Germanic tradition. The past was not quite such a foreign country anymore, but a memory that informed the life of the present.

A public controversy in which the Grimms became involved in the spring of 1844 gave some indication of the accommodation of their cultural and political views to the actualities of their adopted Prussian homeland. Hoffmann von Fallersleben, a popular poet and a scholar of Old German literature, had come to Berlin to visit the Grimm brothers after he had been dismissed from his university post in Breslau because of the political content of his most recent book of poetry. The Grimms had known him since 1818 and were quite willing to extend their personal hospitality. It was the evening of Wilhelm's birthday, and the students who came to congratulate him recognized Hoffmann and added a political toast to their celebration. The police detained a number of students, and Hoffmann was forced to leave the city. The Grimms were embarrassed by the incident. They were convinced that Hoffmann and Bettina Von Arnim had known of the student's intentions to stage a political rally and had used the Grimms for their own political purposes in order to embarrass the king. In contrast to 1837, the Grimms in 1844 stood with their personal obligations and loyalty to their monarch and publicly denied any support for the political demands of their friend, or the students, or even for the rights of either to assert their political discontents with the Prussian regime. In this case the constitutional issue was seen as a mere question of external arrangements. The substance of moral community was sustained by the subjective relationship between the king and his subjects. The populist, egalitarian, "fraternal" element in the Grimms' conception of cultural community thus appeared to have been attenuated in their accommodation to their new Prussian home in the 1840s.

The national project that brought the Grimms to Berlin was built on the optimistic version of their conception of the relationship between past and present, but it proceeded very slowly in the decade of the 1840s. In the 1838

[93] *Deutsche Mythologie*, vol. 1, preface to the 1844 edition, p. xxxvi.

advertisement, in which they had first announced their intent to compile a historical dictionary of the German language, the Grimms had projected an alphabetical dictionary of Modern High German that would encompass the "infinite wealth" of the "fatherland's language," which no one had previously "surveyed or measured."[94] Each word was to be treated like an historical agent in its own right, changing its external form but retaining its original essence as it progressed through the multiple contexts of changing historical usage. All the words that made up the cultural life of the present would be investigated in archaeological digs that would display their origins in the concrete reality of archaic folk experience. Using the dictionary would be an act of remembering the cultural tradition. In looking up an individual word, the user would engage the past in the present, rediscover the original status of words as both things and signs, and thus reconnect himself not only to the history of the language community but also to the natural world out of which that language community developed. In the preface to the first volume, finally published in 1853, Jacob Grimm imagined a father taking out the dictionary at night in front of the fire and reading an entry or two to his family, much in the style of the popular reading of folktales, as if the dictionary would become a universally used compendium of linguistic memory. Families would find a daily orientation for their present consciousness by inserting their speech into the millennial development of a shared tradition. The aim of the dictionary was "to create a sanctuary [*Heiligthum*] for the language, preserving the fullness of its treasures, and to keep access to this treasure open to all." The deposited treasures, this collective property of the people, would "grow like a honeycomb" and become a "majestic monument to the people whose past and present are joined together in it."[95]

In 1847, Jacob Grimm took a few months from his labors on the dictionary to write *Geschichte der deutschen Sprache* (History of the German Language), a thousand-page work that brought together the fruits of his scholarship on linguistic structures and ancient German legal and mythological antiquities into a developmental narrative that was both a history of the German language as a thing in the world and a history of the Germanic peoples that this language signified. The book was in press just as the March revolution broke out in Berlin. Grimm did not see the work as overtaken by these events and did not stop its process of publication. Instead, he thought it had become even more obviously relevant than it had been before the March revolution. The book, he insisted, was "political through and through [*durch*

[94] The prospectus is reprinted in Jacob Grimm, *Kleinere Schriften*, vol. 8, pp. 542–43, and again with extensive contextual materials and commentary in Alan Kirkness, *Geschichte des deutschen Woerterbuchs. 1838–1863* (Stuttgart: 1980), pp. 53–81. See also Jacob's letter to Bettina von Arnim from August 11, 1838, in *Briefwechsel Bettine von Arnims und den Bruedern Grimm*, p. 43.

[95] *Deutsches Woerterbuch* (introduction to vol. 1) in *Kleinere Schriften*, vol. 8, p. 315.

und durch politisch]", since one could, on the basis of its content, "measure the tasks and the dangers facing the Fatherland."[96] Although the *Geschichte* did not receive critical or popular acclaim, Jacob Grimm considered it his best book, and his brother Wilhelm saw it as the book that most clearly expressed his brother's distinctive positions.[97] Although hardly an accomplished synthesis of the various strands of Grimm's intellectual labors, it gave the fullest account of the salient tensions and ambiguities in Jacob Grimm's conception of history as a process of cultural identity formation and of historical knowledge as an archaeology of language.

In the introduction to the *Geschichte*, Grimm noted that he had never been satisfied with the study of language for its own sake but was always eager "to move on from words to things." He continued somewhat enigmatically: "I didn't want merely to build houses, but also to live in them." Perhaps what he meant was that his historical scholarship aimed not simply at a reconstruction of the past but sought a meaning that he could live by in the present. At any rate, the conventional histories of peoples were to be shaken out of their comfortable "beds" through linguistic knowledge, undone and remade from "the innocent standpoint of language."[98] Historical knowledge gained through linguistic archaeology was "innocent" because language was an anonymous, collective representation of past reality. Recreating the past through the history of language avoided the subjective fictions and distortions of individual viewpoints. It produced a history of the people from the viewpoint of the people.

What Grimm had in mind when he imagined the need for an alternative history of cultural formation was not so much conventional histories of the relatively modern period of documented events, but prehistories of tribal cultures and migrations that had been extracted from the evidence of mythology through symbolic interpretation and, more recently and "scientifically," through the archaeological recovery of artifacts found in prehistoric grave sites. But, Grimm insisted, "there exists a more animated, living testimony to the history of peoples than bones, weapons and graves – their languages": "Speech issues from the full breath of the human soul, where it sounds; or in buried, hidden monuments [*Denkmaeler*], where all indecisiveness or insecurity about the relations of a people who spoke it to their neighbors disappears." Where there was no other extant evidence, Grimm suggested, the comparative study of ancient languages could provide a foundation for historical and cultural studies that could demonstrate extremely fine and subtle differences.[99]

The first eleven chapters of the *Geschichte* reconstructed the prehistory of the Germanic tribes on the basis of a comparative linguistic archaeology of

[96] *Geschichte der deutschen Sprache* (Leipzig: 1848), p. iv.

[97] Jacob Grimm, "Ein Lebensabrisz," *Kleinere Schriften*, vol. 8, p. 461.

[98] *Geschichte der deutschen Sprache*, p. xiii. [99] *Ibid.*, p. 5.

the major known languages that had evolved within the Indo-Germanic or Indo-European language family. In Grimm's analysis, elements of similarity among these languages pointed back to the historical moment before their differentiation as distinct languages. Thus the roots of words for the basic metals in all these languages could be traced back to a common source, indicating a shared history in the Bronze, Iron, and Silver Ages. Similarly, a primal commonality in experiences of communal existence, nature, and transcendent reality in the early ages of transition from hunting and gathering to sedentary agriculture, was embedded in the comparative history of words. The comparative study of languages left no doubt in Grimm's view that the Germanic tribes emerged in differentiation from other Indo-European groups somewhere in the second half of the first century and that their connections to their Asiatic ancestors were mediated by definable Middle Eastern tribes – Scythians, Sarmations, and especially the Getae, mentioned in early Greek accounts. Through the mediation of these migratory groups, the Goths emerged as the original Germanic tribe. The Gothic as a distinctive language variation formed the basis of High and Low German and the Scandinavian, or Nordic, languages. The differentiation of a Germanic cultural identity from the larger Indo-European complex, and subsequently of the High Germans from the Goths, and finally the development from early to middle to modern High German culture could all be traced through the transformations of language. Language did not describe these developments, but constituted a type of privileged exemplification of them, an "innocent" and thus objective documentation of the formation of a people.

Two systemic "sound shifts" (*lautverschiebungen*) internal to the organic structure of Indo-European languages marked Grimm's account: the shift that created the original Germanic "Gothic" from the central Asian languages of the Scythians, Thracians, Getae, and others, and the shift that produced High German from the Gothic. In both cases Grimm treated language first of all as an organism, or "thing," rather than as a system of signs. Like any other historical organism or cultural totality, language evolved according to systematic laws of inner development. Linguistic changes were not arbitrary occurrences produced by events outside language, but took place within a context of rules governing the production and combination of sounds. When Grimm came to the historical formation of the Gothic or original Germanic culture in his account, he suddenly shifted to an internal analysis of language and phonological rules. Between chapters on the original relations among the languages of the Asiatic cultures from which the Goths' development proceeded and the chapter on the formation of the Goths, he inserted six theoretical chapters about fundamental rules governing the gradation and shifting of vowel sounds through changes in certain groups of consonants (the obstruents). His description of the systematic character of the consonant shifts and the general sound shifts they implied or made possible has come to be known as Grimm's law. Most of this analysis was derived from positions developed in the 1822 edition of the *Deutsche Grammatik*, but by 1848 his original theory of general language decline had become much attenuated. Grimm still clearly imagined languages moving away from nature in a process of spiritualization that transformed them into instruments for the manipulation of the natural world rather than expressions of participation in that world. But the energy that produced these transformations now became the object of Grimm's reverence and praise. His nostalgia for a language close to nature was balanced by an enthusiasm for the spiritual discipline and control characteristic of languages that exerted their hegemony over nature. Language was no longer a revelation of origins, a found object radiating the aura of its maternal home, but a massive human work, binding individuals together as a people in the shared tasks of cultural production. The revolution accomplished by the energy of the *Sprachgeist* in the two sound shift transformations did not occur completely without "detriment," and might be seen in part as a degeneration from the formal "perfection" of ancient Sanskrit or early Gothic. But it was "barbaric" energy, the irrepressible drive toward freedom, that motivated those tribes that moved toward High German to create the Christian culture of the Middle Ages, "from which Europe's transformation would proceed." The movement from a language of "bodily perfection [*leiblicher vollendung*]" to one of "spiritual progress [*geistiger Fortschritt*]" was a movement of both self-determination and hegemony over others. "Not without cause," claimed Grimm, "do we see triumphant ruling peoples take possession of that dialect within the language that distances them the most from their earlier standpoint."[100] The movement away from the origin was at the same time a movement toward a more self-conscious, controlled construction of identities, toward self-determination. Modern High German language and culture emerged as the culmination of a development fueled both by alienation from nature and by an enormous capacity to discipline and overpower nature. The language spoken by contemporary Germans thus bound them together in this project, just as it sustained a connection to that earlier period of integration before the process of emancipation and control turned the world into opposing spheres.

If the emergence of first Gothic and then High German was marked by transformative structural differentiations within the Indo-European language inheritance, the question still remained: Why did these changes take place? What motivated the shift? The events of the sound shift revolutions, Grimm claimed, were historically specific, occurring in the second half of the first century and then in the fourth or fifth century. They could not simply be deduced from an inner law within the language itself, since only certain groups participated in the first shift to Gothic and, despite the

[100] *Geschichte der deutschen Sprache*, vol. 1, pp. 417–18.

momentum within the language produced by that shift, only specific groups made the further shift into High German:

> When language had undergone the first step and emancipated itself from its organic phonological stage [*lautstufe*], that is, entered into the second phonological stage, it was almost impossible to avoid the next step and proceed to the third stage, through which this development came to completion. Both steps, however, did not have to occur contemporaneously or with the same scope. Just as none of the original primal related languages were effected by this powerful shock except the Germanic – thus a small component of that great primal community suddenly decided to undertake it – so only one branch of the German language family, the High German, accomplished what was left to accomplish, and only at a later date. All other German dialects remained unaffected by the second shift, just as the unrelated (non-Germanic) languages had remained unaffected by the first.[101]

Although the change was systemic, it was also specific to parts of the original organism. The *Sprachgeist* could not in itself explain this differentiated development. Language was also an expression of an existential reality outside of it, a reality that it expressed and communicated as a system of signs. Grimm perceived the differentiating cause to be an energetic drive toward self-assertion, a collective, almost instinctual, resistance to subjugation among some of the Germanic tribes. As the Roman Empire declined, "the feeling of unstoppable progressive advance throughout all parts of Europe was awakened in the undefeatable, irrepressible Germans." Migratory movement gave a disorienting shock to linguistic convention and produced pressure to shift toward conventions more in keeping with the new restlessness and ambition. It required self-assertiveness and pride, Grimm contended, to complete the consonant transfers that produced the revolutionary sound shifts. The tribes in the vanguard of the migrations, like the Franks and Allemanni, were also the tribes that made the complete (double) shift to High German.[102] High German triumphed as the triumph of a more focused, more intense life energy, just as it continued in later periods to assert its authority over other dialects through its inherent power to absorb, assimilate, and simply exclude other dialects.[103]

Despite these critical differentiations among the Germanic languages, Grimm was intent on maintaining the close family relationship among all of the dialects that emerged from the Gothic as a part of a Germanic language community. He insisted that a consciousness of ethnic identity existed among these tribes from the very beginning and attacked those writers who dismissed the notion of a "love of the fatherland" and "feeling of commonality" (*Gefuehl ihres Zusammenhanges*) among the Germanic tribes

[101] *Ibid.* [102] *Ibid.*, pp. 437–38. [103] *Ibid.*, p. 510.

from the first to the eighth or ninth centuries. It was foolish to imagine that Charlemagne had simply created the historical self-consciousness of the German people: "it would have been against all nature, for them to have waited that long in order to recognize how they were bound together through common speech, customs and power. What they had already produced in the world before that time was almost greater than what followed, and was at least its foundation."[104] Long before Charlemagne, the Germans had spread throughout Europe and their religious conversion had made possible the European triumph of Christianity.

One hundred fifty pages of linguistic theory followed this apparent coda. In this second theoretical section, Grimm focused on the factors that defined the peculiar identity of the Germanic language and thus of German identity. His task here was once again boundary definition: His aim was to demonstrate that the modern Germanic languages, including English, Dutch, Scandinavian, and modern High German, had a close family relationship that distinguished their speakers as a cultural group from speakers in the Romance, Slavic, Lithuanian, Latin, and Greek language families that had also evolved in the Europeanization of the Indo-European language core. Second, he wanted to prove that the distinctiveness of German also lay in its capacity for prolific dialectic differentiation. It remained dynamic because of its ability to shift vowel sounds in such a way that it could maintain contact with its material and maternal roots and yet adapt to constantly new circumstances. The German *ablaut* or vowel gradation, he claimed, was "a dynamic application of the law of vowels on to the roots of the oldest verbs in order to highlight the differences between past and present in all of their sensual fullness." The penetration of this capacity throughout the language gave it its distinctive timbre and power.[105] German differentiated itself from its ancestral and neighboring languages by focusing on the vowel distinctions that represented the dynamic temporal element in human existence. At the core of its being, German was a sensual intuition of life as a process of dynamic movement from past to present in which the essence of existence was continually remembered and preserved as it was transformed. For Germans the history of their language was not only the remembering of an origin in which words and things were identical, but a story of constant self-transcendence in which the very forms of the language itself, its grammatical structures, exemplified cultural existence as historical existence. Again and again Grimm found himself in the situation of claiming that what bound Germans together was a language that constantly drove them to differentiate and articulate their individuality and difference; what gave a boundary to German culture was the constant energy and desire to transcend boundaries or at least control their determination. But it was also

[104] *Geschichte der deutschen Sprache*, vol. 2, pp. 792–93. [105] *Ibid.*, p. 846.

clearly important to Grimm to insist that all of this differentiating energy emerged from a common source, and the *Geschichte* concluded with a claim for the unity of all Germanic languages and peoples:

> All Germanic languages however far their twigs and branches have grown apart from each other, visibly belong to the same trunk and confess a maternal *diota* (*piuda*) [Gothic ancestor of the term *deutsche* that contained, in Grimm's view, the meaning of belonging to a *Volk*] which gives them their name. The further one moves into the past the more the similarity among Goths, High Germans, Low Germans and Scandinavians becomes evident, and all have the same origin.[106]

During the 1840s, therefore, Jacob Grimm's historicism took on a complex dual figuration. On the one hand, he never denied, and continued in many ways to reiterate, the historical viewpoint as the recovery of a foreign "home" whose contours had been smothered and lost in the process of temporal transformation through which human communities had left their beginnings behind them. History was seen here as a progressive fall from a state of natural unity. To attain historical consciousness was to recognize that the present was not "natural" but an historical product of this "fall" and to live in the memory of loss. But beginning with the internal analysis of the linguistic organism in his *Deutsche Grammatik*, Jacob Grimm moved more and more to a view of history that placed the patterns of transformative development from past to present at its center. Language was not just an archaeological window revealing the caesura between the cultural worlds of past and present, but a medium for understanding how pasts were continually remade as presents. Language contained not only vestiges of the archaic origins of contemporary German identities, but also embodied those present identities as historical identities. As Grimm would succinctly formulate his principle in an 1851 speech: "Our language is also our history."[107] In both of Grimm's conceptions of language, the power of history in the formation of cultural identity was preeminent. The first perspective imagined the recovery of the primal age of German cultural beginnings as the production of a public memory through which Germans could create new bonds of identification. The second view looked to historical consciousness as a path toward constituting a German identity defined as an ongoing activity of discipline, control, and adaptation on the basis of a common heritage. The past was not just a mnemonic substance from which identities could be forged, but also a source from which to grasp the ways in which the process of self-making was itself central to the formation of community. Yet the *Geschichte* could hardly be described as an historical narrative of the

[106] *Ibid.*, p. 1035.

[107] Jacob Karl Ludwig Grimm, *On the Origin of Language*. trans. Raymond A. Wiley (Leiden: 1984), p. 20.

formation of modern German culture, mediating ancient Germanic roots with present possibilities. The modern period hardly appeared in Grimm's account.

Although Grimm increasingly looked to language to provide the capacity to create a civic community of ethical subjects within the present and to mediate the memory of origin with the political tasks of organizing the appropriate external arrangements for such a national community, his focus remained on the production of the general conditions for German identity as a subjective phenomenon, as a shared consciousness of membership in a "people." Politics remained for Grimm an expressive form, the external representation of an identity produced in language and culture, not a house of power in which historical identities were adapted, manipulated, revised, and recreated by active relations among free agents. In September 1848, Grimm expressed his disappointment after reading the third volume of Ranke's recently published history of Prussia. He saw it as an "unfortunate book" that once again reinforced the Prussian tendency to give the constructed community of the state more significance than the "natural" community of the linguistic nation.[108] In Ranke's view, however, it was precisely the political narrative of Prussian power that opened up possibilities for appropriating the past in a way that could provide a viable cultural identity for the future and provided a model for "becoming historical."

[108] Jacob to Wilhelm Grimm, September 6, 1848, *Unbekannte Briefe der Brueder Grimm*, ed. Wilhelm Schoof (Bonn: 1960), p. 348.

7

Ranke and the Christian-German State: Contested Historical Identities and the Transcendent Foundations of the Historical Subject

One can hardly claim originality any longer for a reading of Ranke's works that emphasizes their ideological content, philosophical presuppositions, and purposeful narrative construction. Revisionist criticism of the late-nineteenth-century image of Ranke as the founder of an autonomous professional discipline of scientific, objective historiography can be traced back to the beginning of the twentieth century and might well be described as the prevailing interpretation.[1] However much Ranke may have insisted on

[1] There are some remarkable parallels between the rediscovery of the philosophical Ranke behind the objective scientific historian during the 1920s (primarily by Friedrich Meinecke and his students) and the contemporaneous reinterpretation of Marx (primarily by Georg Lukacs). In both cases the recovery of the philosophy of the subject within historical science took the form of a reconstruction of connections to the Idealist and Romantic heritage and focused on the interpretation of early essays ignored by previous scholars. In both cases the revisionist interpretations were motivated by strong positive associations with the ideological content of the recovered philosophy (historicism as the essential philosophy of German national culture, Marxism as the self-consciousness of the world proletariat) and produced the scholarly discovery and publication of previously ignored juvenilia. In the post–World War II period this revisionism was reconstituted in a much more critical fashion in the context of National Socialist and Stalinist actualizations and distortions of the respective traditions. See, especially, Friedrich Meinecke, *Weltbuergertum und Nationalstaat* (1907) and *Die Enstehung des Historismus* (1936); Ernst Simon, *Ranke und Hegel* (Munich/Berlin: 1928); Theodore von Laue, *Leopold von Ranke: The Formative Years* (Princeton: 1950); Georg G. Iggers, *The German Conception of History: The National Tradition of History* (Middletown, CT: 1968). Two major assumptions in this revisionist orthodoxy require critical reconsideration. First, the philosophical dimension in Ranke's historiography cannot be adequately grasped in terms of continuity with the Idealist–Romantic tradition from which it emerged. It represents a distinctive development and revision of that tradition. Second, the tendency to see Ranke's work as providing ideological justification for a distinctively German form of political self-expression by conflating national power and moral self-realization ignores the complex dualism of the natural and moral models of subjectivity that emerged from his critical reconsideration of his philosophical inheritance. Leonard Krieger's brilliant *Ranke: The Meaning of History* (Chicago: 1977) marked a distinct emancipation from the assumptions of the revisionist school, but it approached the problematic nature of Ranke's dualisms from the perspective of his attempts to resolve them in the construction of a coherent universal history in his later writings. This chapter labors in the wake of Krieger's analysis, but it returns to revisionist questions about the ideological and philosophical content of Ranke's histories in the particular context of the cultural program of the Prussian regime during the 1840s, and the questions concerning historical agency and discursive contexts raised by the postmodern "new historicism" of the 1980s and 1990s.

the historian's obligation to conform to professional, critical methods that would unveil the "naked," or "unvarnished," truth of the particular historical facts contained in distorted, deceptive forms within the documentary record that mediated the past to the present, his narrative representation of these facts in his historical works now appear as forms of constructive storytelling informed by the desires and purposes emerging from his time, culture, and personal situation. Much like Jacob Grimm, Ranke entered the field of historical studies with a powerful sense of the differences between historical epochs and national cultures.[2] Unlike Grimm, however, Ranke soon turned his primary efforts toward constructing the patterns of narrative mediation that displayed the connections among ethno-linguistic cultures and the continuities between past and present. Cultural difference and conflict were transformed into conditions for a progressive political and ethical struggle for unity and reconciliation. Narrative representation of politically and religiously motivated actions transformed the sheer otherness of the past into the subjectively meaningful, communally integrating reality of an historical identity.

The revisionist critique of Ranke's "objectivity" should thus be revised further in the direction of greater historical specificity if it is to illuminate the convergence of the historical perspective developed in Ranke's early works and the identity politics of the Prussian regime of Frederick William IV. By 1840 the political and religious dilemmas that motivated and informed Ranke's historical work, and were expressed in his dualistic conceptualizations of political and religious experience, had been temporarily resolved in the historically discovered "reality" of the evolving Christian-German state through the narrative integration of the ethno-linguistic and ethical versions of historical identification. This resolution, moreover, was accompanied by a usually implicit but occasionally explicit revision of the philosophical assumptions that informed the individual and collective conceptions of historical subjectivity that Ranke had inherited from the Romantic and Idealist thinkers of an earlier generation. In both instances Ranke found his own position in general conformity with the perspectives of the public spokesmen of the new Prussian regime, a conformity that nurtured and sustained his own personal sense of having finally found a genuine political and cultural home.

[2] The focus on the connection between power and ethics in the relations between states and on the construction of narrative continuities in much of the critical literature on German historicism (and Ranke in particular) has tended to downplay the extent to which Ranke's views were grounded in notions of ethno-cultural and temporal difference, especially in the first half of his career. For an attempt to reset the balance between state and national culture (*Volk*) in Ranke's work, see Ernst Schulin, "Universalgeschichte und Nationalgeschichte bei Leopold von Ranke," in *Leopold von Ranke und die moderne Geschichtswissenschaft*, ed. Wolfgang J. Mommsen (Stuttgart: 1988), pp. 37–71. There is a shorter English version of this essay in *Leopold von Ranke and the Shaping of the Historical Discipline*, ed. Georg. G. Iggers and James M. Powell (Syracuse: 1990), pp. 70–81.

THE PERSONAL DIMENSION: MOTHERLAND AND FATHERLAND

In the summer of 1841, Ranke was appointed official historiographer of the Prussian state. The post was a minor and largely honorific one, with few specified duties or privileges, and Ranke's appointment went virtually unnoticed among the flood of major appointments, promotions, and rehabilitations that marked the first years of the new regime. Although Ranke himself had not sought the position and considered himself "virtually a stranger" on the "patriotic ground" of Prussian history, he accepted it with alacrity because the idea for the appointment had originated in the expressed wishes of the new monarch, and because it confirmed his own feelings of identification with the new regime.[3] Just a few months earlier he had informed his brother Heinrich that it was both his "vital need" and his "good fortune" to "belong to a state with whose intentions I in general agree."[4] This agreement had been a long time in the making. Although Ranke became a Prussian subject in 1815, he considered himself "virtually a stranger" in his "fatherland" during most of the ensuing years. The appointment as his fatherland's official historiographer brought to a close a long history of tension, expedient accommodation, and conditional loyalty.

Ranke's relationship to Prussia had begun on a false note. As a university student in Leipzig in 1815, he had been dismayed by the incorporation of his Thuringian Saxon homeland into the expanded postwar Prussian state and joined the protest against it. Whatever sympathies he might have developed for the state that had been the leader of German national liberation during the Napoleonic era were easily dissipated by this act of naked state power directed against a fraternal German state.[5] Moreover, when Ranke associated himself with the postwar nationalist movement spawned by the wars of liberation, he encountered the Prussian state primarily as a repressive and conservative force that persecuted his heroes Friedrich Ludwig Jahn and Ernst Moritz Arndt, some of his university friends, and even his brother Heinrich. In August 1819, after the Carlsbad Decrees, he composed a letter to a local Prussian official that vigorously defended Jahn, Arndt, and other victims of persecution and bitterly attacked their official persecutors.[6] A Prussian edict of 1822 that restricted the academic freedom of Gymnasium teachers like himself led him to describe Prussian civil servants as "public

[3] Ranke to Gustav Adolf Menzel, August 3, 1841, in Leopold von Ranke, *Das Briefwerk*, ed. Walther Peter Fuchs (Hamburg: 1949), p. 310.

[4] Ranke to Heinrich Ranke, May 5, 1841, *Briefwerk*, p. 308.

[5] Guenter Johannes Henz, *Leopold von Ranke; Leben, Denken und Wort, 1795–1814* (Cologne: 1968), pp. 176–7; Leopold von Ranke, "Tagebuecher" (1815), in Leopold von Ranke, *Aus Werk und Nachlass*, eds. Walther Peter Fuchs and Theodor Schieder (4 vols.; Munich: 1964–75), vol. 1, pp. 259–62.

[6] Ranke to "a President," August 4, 1819, *Briefwerk*, pp. 5–9. It is not clear to whom this letter was addressed or if it was ever actually sent. See also Friedrich Heinrich Ranke, *Jugenderrinerungen mit Blicken auf das spaetere Leben* (Stuttgart: 1877), pp. 99–104, 144–49.

slaves" and to seek a job in Bavaria. "The repression of teaching and teachers in the Prussian lands," he wrote to the Bavarian educator Friedrich Thiersch, "has reached such an extreme level that a man of conscience can only seek exile." It had become "intolerable" to remain "in a state which sweeps away from under its own feet the moral ground on which it rests." He added: "Prussia is not essentially my fatherland; I have no obligation to it." His only homeland was the "Mother Thuringia" that had borne and nurtured him, or perhaps the ideal "Mother Germany" that had captured his heart during the era of liberation. It was only with his ancestral "tribe" (*Stamm*) or his "people" (*Volk*) that he could feel an identity, not with any state.[7]

The hostility which Ranke felt for his political fatherland was somewhat mitigated by his appointment to an associate professorship at the University of Berlin in 1825 and the award of a generous search grant in 1827 that allowed him to leave Prussia for Vienna and Italy for three-and-a-half years. But Ranke's loyalty to Prussia during the 1820s remained narrowly expedient and dependent on continued support of his academic career and scholarly research. He continued to pursue actively the possibility of more attractive positions elsewhere, especially in Bavaria.

Ranke's social and academic associations in Berlin also expressed his distant, cool attitude toward the state. On his arrival in Berlin, he had first associated with the writer–diplomat Karl Varnhagen von Ense, who had been forced into early retirement in 1824 because of alleged sympathies for liberal and national movements, and who had written a favorable review of Ranke's first book. In the home of Varnhagen and his wife Rahel, Ranke met Bettina von Arnim and eventually became a regular guest at her soirees as well. In both homes Ranke was drawn into a lively intellectual circle grouped around a maternal figure and more or less alienated from the current political regime. His associations at the university had a similar character. Here he identified himself with the academic Romantics of the Historical School, like Schleiermacher and Savigny, who resented the government's support of their Hegelian opponents and were generally unhappy with the collapse of the liberal and nationalist reform movement and the accommodation of the educated middle classes to the political authoritarianism and cultural conservativism of the "Restoration" after 1819. Ranke's closest friend at the university, the young philosopher Heinrich Ritter, a disciple of Schleiermacher, felt that his career was blocked at every turn by the power of the Hegelian party, and Ranke himself came under attack by the Hegelian historian Heinrich Leo soon after his arrival in Berlin. Ranke perceived himself and his friends as members of a threatened minority whose

[7] Ranke to Friedrich Thiersch, April 28, 1822, *Briefwerk*, pp. 28–29; Ranke to Ferdinand Ranke, April 12, 1822, in Leopold von Ranke, *Neue Briefe*, ed. Bernhard Hoeft and Hans Herzfeld (Hamburg: 1949), p. 27.

opponents had the advantage of state patronage and support. His sense of identification with the ethno-linguistic "motherland," or *Volk*, and its historical mission remained in tension with his political obligations and state identity.[8]

Ranke's lengthy research trip to southern European archives, and the European revolutions of 1830, which occurred near the end of it, produced a significant shift in his relationship to the Prussian state. His scholarly drive to gain access to, excerpt, and understand the documents that embodied the political perspective of the diplomats and political movers and doers of the past also brought him into contact with the "men of affairs" of the present. In Vienna he spent long evenings in political discussion with the conservative social theorist Friedrich Gentz and through him met not only other conservative thinkers, like Friedrich Schlegel and Adam Mueller, but also the Austrian Chancellor Count Metternich. In Venice he developed a relationship of mutual admiration with the traveling Prussian crown prince (the future Frederick William IV) and certain members of his entourage, especially the diplomat and future foreign minister, Friedrich Ancillon. That such acquaintances and associations had produced an increasing identification with the political perspective of the conservative ruling elites became evident in Ranke's response to the events of 1830. In the fall of 1830, Ranke wrote to Ritter that he found himself in "decisive opposition" to prevailing public opinion in his conviction that the popular liberal and democratic movements should be repressed by the police and then controlled through more efficient supervision by governmental authorities. It was "intolerable," he claimed, "that apprentices and street gangs want to govern us."[9]

When Ranke returned to Berlin in the fall of 1831, it soon became evident that his new political perspective implied significant revisions in the patterns of social and political association he had formed in the 1820s. His recently formed connections with "men of affairs" continued and was solidified when the moderate conservative party in the Foreign Office, led by the Foreign Minister Count Bernstorff and his chief aide for German affairs Johann Albert Eichhorn, asked him to edit a semiofficial political journal (*Historisch-Politische Zeitschrift*) that would defend their national and international policies against both the liberal and democratic constitutionalists of the Left and the aristocratic ultras of the Right. Although Bernstorff soon fell from power, Ranke's associations with high-ranking officials in the Foreign Office continued under his more conservative successor, Friedrich Ancillon, until 1836, when Ancillon died and the journal ceased publication.[10] Such

[8] Ernst Simon, *Ranke und Hegel*, pp. 16–54, 79–87; Krieger, *Ranke*, pp. 82–89.

[9] Ranke to Heinrich Ritter, October 4, 1830, *Briefwerk*, p. 224. Ranke's gratitude to Gentz for introducing him to the world of men of affairs was expressed in a letter to Gentz on October 17, 1828, in *Briefwerk*, p. 169.

[10] Theodor von Laue, *Leopold Ranke: The Formative Years* (Princeton: 1950), pp. 55–71.

ties to the governing elite, however, had their counterpart in the loosening of Ranke's associations with the liberal cultural circles he had frequented in the 1820s. The deaths of Achim von Arnim in 1831 and Rahel Varnhagen in 1833 may have contributed to Ranke's growing distance from his former friends, but the central issue in this estrangement was clearly political. Both Varnhagen and Bettina came to view Ranke as an uncritical supporter of established authority.[11] Ranke's increasing accommodation with Prussia's governing elite during the 1830s, however, was both limited and partisan. Bernstorff, Eichhorn, Ancillon, and Bunsen in the Foreign Office and the crown prince and his unofficial cabinet of political advisors were influential components within the ruling elite, but they did not determine the general policies of the state during the 1830s. Ranke had committed himself to a particular partisan vision of the Prussian state and in the process cut himself off from the proponents and representatives of alternative positions.

A similar process of transformation was evident in Ranke's relations with his academic colleagues during the 1830s. In 1834, Ranke was promoted to a full professorship, but the promotion was instigated by his friends at the Foreign Office and pushed through without consultation of his faculty and against the wishes of the university senate. His salary was paid from a secret government fund for two years.[12] After the departure of Ritter for Kiel in 1833 and the death of Schleiermacher in 1834, Ranke's only close friend at the university was Savigny. But Savigny himself had largely withdrawn from university affairs because of the influence of his Hegelian critic Eduard Gans in the law faculty, and had made his scholarly home in the Royal Prussian Academy of Sciences, where Hegelians had been successfully excluded, where royal patronage rather than collegial solidarity ruled, and to which Ranke had been admitted in 1832. Since Savigny was a member of an older generation and was closely connected to governmental circles as a member of the Prussian State Council (*Staatsrat*), his relationship to Ranke tended to conform to the paternalistic-filial pattern that characterized Ranke's relationships with "men of affairs" in general. Moreover, Ranke's only other significant scholarly association in the 1830s – his relationship to the aspiring historians who gathered in the historical seminars he held in his home – was also clearly personal and paternalistic in character. Although Ranke directed his students toward the task of recovering the formative historical moments in the national life of mother Germany, their research and writing developed under strict patriarchal guidance.[13]

[11] The decisive break occurred when Ranke did not support the protests against dismissal of the "Goettingen Seven" in 1837–38. See Bettina von Arnim, *Andacht zum Menschenbild*, ed. W. Schellberg and F. Fuchs (Jena: 1842), pp. 320ff; and Hans F. Helmolt, *Leopold Ranke's Leben und Wirken* (Leipzig: 1921), pp. 82–83, 170–71.

[12] Gunter Berg, *Leopold von Ranke als akademischer Lehrer* (Goettingen: 1968), pp. 26–27.

[13] *Ibid.*, pp. 51–56; Ranke, "Die alten Schueler," in Leopold von Ranke, *Saemmtliche Werke* (54 vols.; Leipzig: 1867–90), vols. 53/54, pp. 649–50.

In a retrospective autobiographical account, Ranke claimed that with Frederick William IV's accession to the Prussian throne in June 1840, the horizon in Berlin was "totally transformed." This transformation was produced when the political and academic party to which Ranke had tied his loyalties during the 1830s became the ruling patriarchal "family." The crown prince, his patron, admirer, and personal acquaintance since the late 1820s, was now king. Eichhorn, his closest associate within the governmental elites, headed the *Kultusministerium*, thus providing Ranke with direct, personal access to a government minister whose decisions most immediately influenced his scholarly and professional life. Savigny, his academic mentor and closest personal friend, moved even closer to the centers of power as head of the new Ministry of Justice for Legislation. In later years Ranke was willing to describe this regime as partisan. Although the new king was "a man of his age" who "lived and breathed in its great contradictions," he claimed, "He at the same time made a partisan commitment [*hatte zugleich Partei genommen*] to the positive and the historical."[14] In the early 1840s, however, Ranke considered a commitment to the positive and the historical not so much a partisan position as a recognition of the essential underpinnings of modern culture and a generally valid resolution of the quest for individual and collective identity. Ranke also preferred to describe the state that emerged in 1840 not as a partisan state, but as a family. On June 21, 1840, he wrote to his brother Ferdinand: "We are entering a new epoch here. From the King, whom we all love and respect, nothing but good can be expected. In these days I have genuinely felt that this state is a family."[15]

Despite the transformation of the political horizon in 1840, certain aspects of Ranke's relationship to his social and political environment remained unchanged. During the first two years of the regime, there were some slight indications that Ranke had begun to perceive the possibility of incorporating a fraternal element into his persistently maternal and paternal conceptions of communal identity. In August 1841, he developed a proposal for a history of Prussia in which provincial histories would be integrated into a general history by a group of historians operating within a collegial historical "society."[16] At the same time he successfully lobbied with Eichhorn for the transfer of the national collective historical project of collecting, editing, and publishing the major documents of early German history (*Monumenta Germaniae Historica*) from Hanover to Prussia by attracting its editor, Friedrich Pertz, to Berlin.[17] During the early 1840s, it also seemed

[14] Ranke, "Zur eigenen Lebensgeschichte," *Werke*, vols. 53/54, p. 52.

[15] Ranke to Ferdinand Ranke, June 21, 1840, *Neue Briefe*, p. 273.

[16] Ranke to Gustav Adolf Stenzel, August 4, 1841, *Briefwerk*, pp. 310–11.

[17] Harry Bresslau, *Geschichte der Monumenta Germaniae Historica* (Hannover: 1921), pp. 245–54; Ranke, "Tagebuecher" (1876–77), *Aus Werk und Nachlass*, vol. 1, 426–29.

that Ranke might become more involved in the academic collegiality of the university. Attendance in his lecture courses rose dramatically during the first years of the regime, and in 1841–42 he served as dean of the philosophical faculty, the only time he ever participated in university governance.[18] But all of these tentative steps in a new direction were soon abandoned. The collective history of Prussia fell victim to the pressing demands of more individual projects. Ranke supported, but never participated actively in, the collective work of the *Monumenta*, and he soon withdrew again from university affairs. By late 1845 he had become thoroughly disenchanted with the "negative" political and religious attitudes of his students and some of his colleagues.[19]

During the early 1840s, however, there was also a subtle but significant change in Ranke's attitude toward, and experience of, the relationship between his recently established loyalty to the patriarchal discipline and moral authority of the fatherland and his prior identification with the nurturing maternal life of his *Stamm* and his *Volk*. Ranke perceived the Prussia of Frederick William IV as a "family" in a larger sense because it promised a reconciliation of these previously divided loyalties. In the new king's constitutional policy he discerned a concept of a decentralized Prussia composed of relatively autonomous provinces, in which the *Staemme* would be able to develop their own life under the protective umbrella of monarchical authority and within the moral and legal context of a historically constructed civic identity carefully managed by the educated classes and pervaded by its historical consciousness. Throughout the 1840s, Ranke consistently supported Frederick William's opposition to both bureaucratic centralization and representative constitutional government.[20] At the same time Ranke was encouraged by Frederick William's clearly expressed desire to join the expansion of Prussian power to the project of German national regeneration. The cultural policy that brought the *Monumenta*, as well as the Grimms, Schelling, Tieck, Cornelius, Rueckert, and Mendelssohn to Berlin, which rehabilitated nationalist heroes like Jahn and Arndt and supported national projects like the rebuilding of the Cologne cathedral, the German Customs Union, and strengthened military cooperation in the German Confederation seemed, to Ranke, to aim at mobilizing, protecting, and actualizing, rather than repressing and distorting, the creative energies of mother Germany. As his divided loyalties appeared to achieve reconciliation in the public family of the Prussian state, Ranke himself was finally ready and able to end his long period of bachelorhood and celibacy. In 1843 he married Clarissa Graves-Perceval, a member of a prominent Irish Protestant family

18 Berg, *Ranke*, pp. 28, 56–57.

19 Ranke to Heinrich Ranke, November 27, 1845, *Neue Briefe*, p. 316.

20 Ranke, "Tagebuecher" (1847), *Aus Werk und Nachlass*, vol. 1, pp. 334–51.

whom he had met during a research trip to Paris, and quickly, if somewhat belatedly, established a family of his own.[21] This was not an act of domestic withdrawal from the public world, but an expression of achieved reconciliation with that world.

Finally, Ranke felt at home in the Prussia of the early 1840s not only because it was perceived as a world of harmonious reconciliation between motherland and fatherland, but also because this reconciliation was achieved on the basis of a partisan commitment to the "positive and historical," that is, to the principles which informed Ranke's professional identity and historical work. The reconciliation between subjective individual freedom and collectively affirmed cultural meaning that Ranke hoped to achieve through historical knowledge now appeared to be realizing itself in historical life. The history he was writing and the history he was living seemed, for the moment at least, to be in harmony.

THE POLITICAL DIMENSION: *VOLK* AND STATE

At the moment when Ranke's political horizons were transformed into the boundaries of a home, his conceptualization of the political dimension of human existence was framed within the general relationship between the ethno-cultural *Volk* and the ethico-political state, and particularly focused on the problem of the formation of the German state as a "modification" of the German *Volk*. In the summer of 1840 he had just completed the third volume of his *Deutsche Geschichte im Zeitalter der Reformation* (German History in the Age of the Reformation), and during the first three, still hopeful, years of the new regime his energies were totally absorbed by the task of finishing the final volumes of the work he had described at its inception as "the most important that could be undertaken at this time."[22] In the critical investigation and narrative reconstruction of the actual historical processes through which the German cultural nation had organized the political forms appropriate to its own peculiar, innate "genius," Ranke felt he was making his own distinctive contribution to the fulfillment of the expressed political goals of the new regime. Not the revolutionary actualization of rationally constructed or imaginatively fabricated ideals was required to build the "true" or "genuine" German state in the present, but the cautious, conservative development of the potentialities inherent in the historical foundations of German political life that had been established in the sixteenth century.

Ranke's attempt to articulate his political perspective through historical study of the conflicts of the Reformation era can be traced back to his

[21] Gisbert Baecker-Ranke, *Rankes Ehefrau, Clarissa geb. Graves-Perceval, Historisch-Politische Hefte der Ranke-Gesellschaft*, no. 21 (Goettingen: 1957).

[22] Ranke to Heinrich Ranke, April 10, 1838, *Briefwerk*, 297.

last student years at Leipzig University in 1816–18. Similarly, the political dilemmas that he attempted to resolve in his historical research had their origin in his experience of the political and ideological ferment of the post-Napoleonic years. The decisive factor in this experience was Ranke's emotional attachment to the nationalist student movement in which his younger brother Heinrich was actively involved and that was embodied for both of them in the program for ethical renewal and national political unification proclaimed by Jahn.[23] In an essay published in 1832, Ranke could still claim that the starting point for any analysis of the problem of German political unification was the "truth" and "necessity" of the "feeling of an essential unity of Germany" that was discernable from the very beginnings of the histories of the Germanic tribes but that had experienced a noteworthy revival and become a "universal conviction" during the liberation wars. Through this feeling every German became aware of the "creative genius" animating "everything that calls itself German."[24] Just before leaving the university in 1818, Ranke reflected on the political implications of his own feeling of national identity and his yearning for a genuine "public existence" in a short literary essay that revealed that he grasped the political realm in a dualistic fashion.

The most obvious organizing theme running through Ranke's reflections was that the reconstruction of European politics after 1815 should be based on the principle of the emancipation of the long-repressed vitality of the cultural nation, of the "people," or *Volk*. In Germany, an "essential" and "vital" public life would emerge only if all Germans would act out of the conviction: "We are one people!" The "inner life of the people," Ranke claimed, would necessarily "appear in time" as a state in which every individual would experience the freedom of being bound to the community "with the nerves of his heart." Once Germans would regain possession of their common life and express it in institutional arrangements, a new foundation for European politics would be created:

> If the German spirit can build a world from the chaos of struggling forces . . . a world which represents its unified inwardness in external form and expresses the true state as closely as possible, then Europe will return to its natural condition and recognize Germany as its mother, which it is, and then Germany will rule. How? Through the freedom of all.

The emancipation and political formation of the German people thus entailed the reorganization of Europe as a family of peoples. Germany would

[23] Ranke described his brief personal contact with Jahn in 1819 as a "sacred" moment (Letter to Heinrich Ranke, September 30, 1819, *Werke*, 53/54, p. 84). In 1820 he acquired Jahn's writing desk, which he used until the end of his life (*Briefwerk*, p. 21). Although Ranke's enthusiasm for Jahn is still clearly evident in his addresses at the *Gymnasium* in Frankfurt an der Oder, where he taught from 1818 to 1825, he rarely mentioned this youthful infatuation after his move to Berlin and academic life in 1825.

[24] Ranke, "Ueber die Trennung und die Einheit von Deutschland," *Werke*, 49/50, p. 134.

rule this family not by imposing its own particular forms on other peoples but as the maternal source and exemplary embodiment of the general principle of cultural self-determination. In order to fulfill this European function, however, Germany itself would need to take political form as a maternal, familial state that allowed free development of the cultural individuality of each of its tribes (*Staemme*). The existing German state that was obviously suited to take upon itself the role of the German-European motherland was not Prussia or any of the other states that had shown themselves to be the enemies of tribal autonomy, but Austria, the multinational empire that allowed the free development of its Germanic, Latin, and Slavic peoples under the benign maternal rule of the Germanic element.[25]

Ranke's vision of the European and German political order of the future as the objectification of a natural, spontaneously evolving tribally and nationally differentiated common life, however, was balanced and opposed by a concept of the political realm as a moral order in which human beings expressed their distance and separation from nature in the creation of spiritual communities of self-legislators. From this second perspective, politics was not so much the place in which inchoate life forces expressed their essences in organized forms, but the sphere in which human autonomy expressed itself through the creation of its own distinctive ethical and spiritual world. At the present moment, Ranke claimed, the German ethical community existed only in the invisible, inner form of a shared "public conscience." Such invisible citizenship, however, soon degenerated into "hot air" (*Kannegieserei*) if it was not affirmed and expressed through actual participation in administration and legislation. The inner unity of common conscience grounded in a shared religious faith was a necessary presupposition of genuine, ethical community, but, Ranke insisted, the time had come to create a "real state" and "not just the appearance of such." "The destructive gap between will and deed must cease," he claimed; "Finally we hope to be able to do what duty prescribes." Although Ranke thought it would be foolish to describe in advance the specific constitutional forms that a community of free moral beings might impose upon itself, he did insist that the forms of political unity would have to express "the freedom of all" and that representation of the popular will in diets would have to be "complete." "The nation demands not only diets as such, or a constitution as such," he wrote, "but the right diets, the right constitution."[26]

As Ranke's hopes for an imminent transformation of German and European politics collapsed during the suppression of the nationalist movement after 1819, he also repressed his own desire for direct, active involvement in a "vital public life" and transferred his political hopes and political

[25] Ranke, "Aus den Papieren eines Landpfarrers" (1818), *Aus Werk und Nachlass*, vol. 3, pp. 474, 479–80, 481–82.

[26] *Ibid.*, pp. 474, 479.

questions to the tasks of historical scholarship. In his major historical works of the 1820s, however, it was Ranke's first model of politics – as the external form of a general human life individualized in tribes and peoples, rather than as a moral order of self-legislating spiritual subjects – that predominated in his conceptualization of the historical process. In his *Geschichten der romanischen und germanischen Voelker von 1494–1514* (*Histories of the Latin and Germanic Peoples Between 1494 and 1514*) (1824), he stated that his aim had been to illuminate the ethno-cultural foundations of modern Western history by attempting "to comprehend in their unity" the apparently fragmented developments of "the tribally-related peoples of either purely Germanic or Latin-Germanic origin, whose history is the core of all modern history." Rejecting both religious (Latin Christendom) and geographic (European) categories as inadequate for conceptualizing the major progressive trends or movements of modern history, he insisted that the particular sequences of events between 1494 and 1514 that marked the collapse of traditional imperial and papal power, the destruction of the freedom of the Italian city-states, the consolidation and conflict of the French and Spanish monarchies, the emergence of religious schism and the discovery and conquest of America, could be grasped as manifestations of the common, evolving life of the "great union of peoples" constituted by the Scandinavian, English, German, French, Spanish, and Italian peoples. In a brief introduction he described the way in which this "incomparable union" had originated in an ethnic-linguistic natural base produced by the tribal migrations after the collapse of the Roman Empire and developed into a more conscious identity in the medieval period through participation in great common endeavors of defense and aggression vis-à-vis the world beyond its borders. But when Ranke moved into the narration of the particular histories that constituted the body of his work, the promised integration rapidly collapsed, and he admitted that genuine penetration into the common, unifying life manifested in the particularity of the events and the individuality of the isolated developments that he described had ultimately eluded him. The projected history remained a collection of histories.[27]

In his other major work of the 1820s, a study of the Ottoman and Spanish Empires between 1540 and 1620, Ranke approached the problem of the ethno-cultural foundations of political forms from a different perspective. He focused on the resistance of the diverse tribes and peoples of the Latin-Germanic "union" to any attempt to impose centralized uniformity from above, whether in the form of military despotism or bureaucratic monarchy. Although the book was organized as a comparative analysis of the internal development and structure of contrasting Islamic and Christian states in the transition from the medieval to the modern period, its

27 *Geschichten der romanischen und germanischen Voelker von 1494 bis 1514*, in Ranke, *Werke*, vol. 39, pp. i–vi, xiv, xxx.

underlying theme remained the intractable reality and vitality of individualized national life, which could not ultimately be destroyed by, or absorbed into, the state. What defined the Christian West against the Islamic East was the ability of Western societies to develop reciprocity between the spontaneous forms of cultural life and the legal and political structures of authority. The West moved toward the creation of participatory national cultures because of a symbiotic relation between princes and peoples made possible by Christian religious ideas and by the vitality of ethnic life among the Germanic and Latin peoples. Government could "only facilitate, not create;" it could "restrict but never by itself destroy," Ranke insisted. This emphasis on the resilience of national and local autonomy among the Germanic and Latin peoples of the Christian West in relation to the hegemonial ambitions of centralizing, bureaucratic states had obvious contemporary relevance, not only to the recent collapse of the Napoleonic empire, but also to the Greek and Serbian wars of independence against Ottoman (and thus Islamic) rule, and even closer to home, to the opposition of Ranke's friends and associates to Prussian bureaucratic absolutism. At the same time, however, Ranke indicated that he was quite aware that the decline of decentralized feudal monarchies and the emergence of the centralized "organic" structure of the modern state could not simply be written off as an ephemeral, futile attempt to deny the concrete, living reality of tribal and ethno-cultural existence. Within his work, however, Ranke did not reveal any positive connections between the growth of "central power" and the innate drive for national self-expression. The general message of his histories during the 1820s was that such self-expression was restricted and distorted by the development of centralized state power. The state appeared as the exemplar of a false, artificially constructed, abstract unity in contrast to the immanent, vital unity embodied in the homologous development and reciprocal relationships among tribes and peoples.[28]

The political perspective implicit in Ranke's historical scholarship in the 1820s was exemplified in succinct form in the analysis of Machiavelli that concluded his *Zur Kritik neuerer Geschichtsschreiber* (Critique of Recent Historians), the critical, historiographical study published simultaneously with the *Geshichten* in 1824. In an attempt to grasp the meaning of Machiavelli's action and theory as the expression of the political life of his time and place, Ranke divided Machiavelli's career into two stages. The dispatches and reports that Machiavelli produced during the first part of his

[28] Ranke, *Die Osmanen und die Spanische Monarchie im 16. Und 17. Jahrhundert*, in *Werke*, vols. 35/36, pp. 176–77, 299. Ranke's monograph on the Serbian revolution, based largely on interviews with participants in Vienna and Venice in 1827–28 developed these themes further, with much greater emphasis on the power of religious ideas to guide the different directions taken in the relations between princes and peoples in East and West. *Die serbische Revolution: Aus serbischen Papieren und Mittheilungen* was published in 1829. It was revised and brought up to date in the second edition of 1844 and published as "Geschichte Serbiens bis 1842," in the *Werke*, vols. 43/44.

career, when he was still deeply involved in the political life of his Florentine homeland, were praised as invaluable historical sources because of their unmediated, concrete expression of the vital forces in Florentine and Italian political life. The theoretical works produced after Machiavelli's fall from power and isolation from the "original" or spontaneous life of his city and people, however, were reduced to the status of particular individual responses to a specific situation. Ranke found the amoral opportunism and abstract rationalism of *The Prince* abhorrent, but he claimed that they arose from Machiavelli's sincere belief that only extreme measures could save Italy from foreign occupation and dismemberment. It was wrong to read Machiavelli's unhistorical axioms as a general theory of politics; they were "instructions for a particular situation" and certainly not relevant to the concerns of legitimate monarchs in the "peaceful and regulated" principalities of a later era. Although Machiavelli was motivated by a commendable national feeling, his views on history and political morals were not intrinsic to this nationalism and not excusable as a manifestation of the emancipation of modern politics and political reason from "the eternal laws of the moral world-order."[29]

The political and ideological significance of Ranke's Machiavelli interpretation was highlighted in a critique published by Heinrich Leo, Ranke's Hegelian rival at Berlin, in 1826. Leo insisted that Machiavelli's amoral, impersonal conception of political power relationships was not a particular response to a specific situation but an expression of the epochal shift in the structure of communal relations that defined the emergence of the modern sovereign state out of medieval feudalism.[30] Leo clearly rejected Ranke's assumption of the primacy of national identity and self-expression in modern politics. In 1827 he claimed that "previous differences according to nations are gradually but increasingly losing their sharp contours and significance" and had been replaced by "inward, spiritual oppositions within the individual nations."[31] In Leo's view, Machiavelli's unhistorical rationalism and amoral politics was not a specific response to a particular situation motivated by national feeling driven to desperate means, but the world-historical emergence to self-conscious expression of a new political–moral order, a new stage in the evolution of the human spirit.

This debate over Machiavelli's historical significance revealed two critical gaps in the national–political conceptualization around which Ranke organized his historical writing in the 1820s. First, although Ranke was aware of the importance of the development of the centralized sovereign state in modern history, he did not integrate this awareness into his general theory of politics as the manifest expression of primal and spontaneous

[29] Ranke, *Zur Kritik neuerer Geschichtsschreiber*, in Ranke, *Werke*, vol. 34, pp. 152, 157, 172–74.

[30] Kurt Mautz, "Leo und Ranke," *Deutsche Vierteljahresschrift fuer Literaturwissenschaft und Geistesgeschichte* 27 (1953): 214–19.

[31] Heinrich Leo, review of Ranke in *Jahrbuecher fuer wissenschaftliche Kritik* (1827), col. 365.

life forces operating in the ethico-cultural sphere. Second, related to this failure in complex ways was his inability to integrate his alternative model of politics as the realm of ethical identification into his historical writing. The "eternal laws of the moral world-order" and their foundation in religious beliefs only entered his narratives obliquely, either as the basis for critical judgments by the narrator or as the occasional, inexplicable, providential interventions of a transcendent God. Despite Ranke's reiterated claims that the historian's task was to describe rather than judge, his works were replete with confident moral judgments of individual actions, characters, systems of government, and religious beliefs.[32] Such external interventions in Ranke's historical narrative indicated the limitations of the model of ethno-cultural national identity, self-expression, and reciprocal relation for comprehending the political dimension in modern history.[33]

Near the end of the decade, however, Ranke gave some indication of the direction in which a solution to his dilemma might be pursued. In his study of the Serbian Revolution, published in 1829, he wrote:

> Ever since powers [*Maechte*] have appeared on earth endeavoring to actualize, represent and advance those general ideas, which carry the life of the human race within themselves, it seems that no nation [*Volk*] has been allowed to develop by itself through the unrestrained movement of its innate powers [*Kraefte*] and natural aptitudes. Instead the process of self-formation depends much more on the relationship into which an emerging people enters with the already formed nations.[34]

From the context of this passage (contrasting the Christian Serbs with their Islamic rulers), it was clear that the "general ideas" that were significantly contrasted to the innate telos of peoples or nations were religious ideas and beliefs, and that they provided the foundation for the moral energies that helped transform the innate potentialities of a people into an historically effective, "formed" nation and "power," which could then develop these innate capacities further within the power conflicts of world history. Here it appeared that Ranke had begun to develop an historical conception in which the organized power of the modern state and the transcendent ground of moral conviction could be integrated with the realization of innate ethno-cultural potencies, or ideas, into a unified conception of political community as an autonomous "power" in reciprocal relations with other powers. It was

[32] See the examples cited in Ernst Schulin, "Ranke's Erstes Buch," *Historische Zeitschrift* 203 (1966): 581–609.

[33] The recent work by Johannes Suessman has analyzed in detail the ways in which Ranke's plan to write his first book as a narrative in which the acting subjects were cultures or peoples constantly breaks down because of his conflicted perceptions of historical agency. See Suessman, *Geschichtsschreibung oder Roman? Zur Konstitutionslogik von Geschichtserzaehlungen zwischen Schiller und Ranke (1780–1824)* (Stuttgart, 2000), pp. 215–56.

[34] "Geschichte Serbiens," p. 3. This passage is from the 1829 edition.

only after the shock of the revolutions of 1830, however, in which Ranke perceived an imminent threat to German national self-development both from the hegemonial ambitions of a foreign power and from the eruption of immoral and irreligious elements within Germany itself that he focused his attention and scholarly research on the issue of organized power in the state and the integration of ethical–religious ideas into the individuality of national, political development.

Despite their new concentration on internal state structures and international power relations, and their polemical edge, educational zeal, and activist bent, Ranke's essays in the *Historisch-Politische Zeitschrift* remained generally consistent with the ethno-cultural, self-expressive model of political life. He continued to deny that the centralized sovereign state was a universal political formation that superceded the differentiation of humanity among cultural peoples. In fact, insofar as Ranke's writings were specifically directed against the relevance of French constitutional forms and political ideologies for German political life, this aspect of his perspective was intensified during the early 1830s. What was new in Ranke's analysis was a self-conscious attempt to integrate a theory of the centrally organized state into the broader conception of ethno-cultural development. "Our theory is," he wrote, "that every people must have its own peculiar politics."[35] The task of the present German generation was to resist imitation of foreign models and "build and develop the genuinely-German [*echtdeutschen*] state, in a way which conforms to the genius of the people."[36] Just as the idea of humanity was a concrete reality only in the variety of tribes, peoples, and nations, so the idea of the true state was only real in the variety of historical states. The task of discovering the true state was not a theoretical, but an historical, task of investigating the facts of national political development, uncovering the "fundamental characteristics [*Grundzuege*]" of the historically established, and developing them further.[37]

For Ranke the state had now become the vehicle that made national self-expression possible through an organized discipline that transformed the innate, unconscious drive of ethno-cultural "genius" into the focused will of conscious power. The foundations of the modern state's strength, autonomy, and integrity remained the "god-given nature," the original "essence" of national genius. In 1836, Ranke described cultural nationality as the essential living substance of the modern state:

> Germany lives in us. We represent it, whether we want to or not, in every country in which we travel, in every climate. We are embedded in it from the beginning and we can never emancipate ourselves from it. This mysterious

[35] Ranke, "Frankreich und Deutschland" (1832), in Ranke, *Werke*, vols. 49/50, p. 72.

[36] *Ibid.*, p. 71.

[37] Ranke to Heinrich Ranke, November 21, 1821 and Karl F. Roth, February 16, 1832, in Ranke, *Werke*, vols. 53/54, pp. 258, 259.

> something that animates the humble as well as the great, this spiritual atmosphere in which we breathe, precedes every constitution. It invigorates and gives real content to all its forms.[38]

The divinely ordained task of every people was to develop and bring to full historical expression that peculiarly individual essence that constituted its modification of universal humanity. The state made the fulfillment of this task possible first by organizing the material resources of the people in order to preserve and protect cultural autonomy, the premise of all self-development. Second, the state's institutions instigated a moralization of the natural unity of the people by transforming unconsciously determined identity into "voluntary obedience" to common law and legitimate political authority, thus mobilizing national energies for the fulfillment of cooperative tasks. As the medium in which the living substance of the people became a community of law informed by a common consciousness, the state itself appeared in history as an individualized "spiritual substance," an embodied divine "idea," an "individual, unique self."[39] In the 1830s, Ranke no longer wrote of the identity of Western humanity in terms of a specific community of ethnic peoples, but in terms of the reciprocal relations of the "Great Powers."

The transformation of a people into a power, of a cultural nation into a state, was not a natural or a necessary development, although it was animated by the drive of national genius for full self-expression. Historically, peoples and states did not overlap perfectly. The modification that transformed ethnic identity into organized power, Ranke noted, involved "the nature of things and opportunity, genius and good fortune," but most of all the mobilization of "moral energies" needed in the struggle for self-expression in the context of competing powers. In 1833, Ranke wrote that the two critical elements in a state's organization of the potencies of ethnic life were law and religion. Law provided external general forms that structured the unity of a shared life, but religion produced the "moral cement" of voluntary obedience. "In most epochs of world history," Ranke claimed, "it has been religious bonds that have held peoples together."[40]

In his political essays of the early 1830s, Ranke suggested in a general fashion what the historical search for the real German state would discover. He approached this issue from two perspectives – the possible unification of the German people in a single sovereign state and the appropriate constitutional structure for this German state. The project of a single German state with one parliament, president, or king was rejected as an unhistorical fantasy. The historically developed autonomy of the individual German states could never be erased. Still, Ranke did believe that there existed

[38] "Politisches Gespraech" (1836), in Ranke, *Werke*, vols. 49/50, p. 326. [39] *Ibid.*, pp. 323, 328, 329.
[40] "Die grossen Maechte" (1833), in Ranke, *Werke*, vol. 24, pp. 38–39.

an essential German identity that framed the relations among these states as relations within a specific ethno-cultural historical community and that this identity was not adequately represented by the loose federation created by the Congress of Vienna. An "essential" and "historical" unification of Germany demanded a cautious development of existing unifying tendencies and institutions, primarily those relating to defense, the regulation of public opinion, and economic integration.[41] In stark contrast to his earlier views, Ranke now presented Prussia, rather than Austria, as the exemplary German state. Although both Austria and Prussia were recognized as legitimate German states and Great Powers that effectively brought the German "idea" into the flow of world history, Prussia was obviously targeted as the leader of German political life in the present and for the future, and it was to Prussian history that Ranke looked for those peculiar forms that differentiated the distinctively German state from its French or English counterparts. During the Napoleonic era, Prussia had sustained the continuity of German politics and eventually led the liberation of the nation from foreign domination, accomplishments made possible by its ability to draw on the natural and spiritual resources of the German cultural tradition.

What Ranke discovered as characteristically German in the Prussian state can be compressed into three general factors. First, Prussian political history, especially in the recent period of crisis and reconstruction, revealed the "ancient, ancestral, indissoluble bond" between prince and people. In contrast to developments in France, German princes had remained benevolent patriarchal rulers who never betrayed their subjects or their commitment to the general welfare. The tradition of mutual fidelity between the *Landesvater* and his children was sustained into the present political reality in the patriarchal, familial model of ruler–ruled relationships. Second, Ranke claimed that "the spirit of our monarchies" was resistant to the formal participation of citizens in the legislative process. Instead, government was conceived within the general framework of the specialization and professionalization of functions that "put the right man in the right place." The genuinely German mode for producing the merger of duty and liberty was through nonrepresentative institutions like the citizens' army, the educational system, and the civil service. These methods of mobilizing voluntary obedience were more effective than liberal or democratic methods that falsely identified citizen participation in the state with participation of untrained representatives in the professional tasks of government. Finally, Ranke portrayed German political development, as epitomized by Prussia, as a nonrevolutionary, progressive conservatism. By following the guidance of historically conscious, professional governors and patriarchal monarchs with ancestral legitimacy and authority, the German nation adapted its external

[41] "Ueber die Trennung," pp. 156–72.

forms without breaking its internal continuity or destroying the achievements of earlier generations. The secret of the success of the great reforms of the Napoleonic era, he claimed, was that they had taken place under the authority of a legitimate monarch, with the guidance of educated professional administrators and in the interest of the general welfare. Although Ranke admitted that the perfected German state was not synonymous with contemporary Prussia, the fit was remarkably close. With a few slight adjustments in internal balance, a little less bureaucratic centralization, and a little more autonomy for the provinces, Prussia would come as close as was historically possible to actualizing the telos implicit in its actual historical evolution.[42]

It is easy to see why Ranke and Frederick William IV viewed each other with mutual respect and why Ranke might have felt at home in the Prussian regime of 1840. Like Ranke, Frederick William emphasized the national context and national mission of Prussian power. Rejecting the bureaucratic absolutism of his father's regime, he envisioned his state as a patriarchal divine-right monarchy in which the relations between king and subjects would regain the personal quality of familial bonds. Legal and constitutional restrictions on royal power that gave citizens direct power over legislative and administrative decisions were seen as unnecessary for the creation of a moral community of voluntary obedience in which duty and freedom would coincide. Government by like-minded, patriotic, paternalistic administrators was perceived as more critical for the general welfare than constitutional forms. The historically guided reformism of the Stein era was presented as the ideal mode for Prussia's continuing adaptation to changing circumstances. What was strikingly absent from Ranke's political essays, however, was any obvious support for Frederick William's conviction that this whole concept of Prussia's national role was dependent on a revival of a Protestant Christian faith in a radically transcendent God, and on the reconstruction of the ecclesiastical institutions of the apostolic church. Unlike Frederick William IV, Ranke did not appear in the early 1830s to define Prussia as the exemplary *Christian*-German state.

However, this contrast is misleading. Ranke did not share the king's neo-orthodox, evangelical piety, but he did believe that religious experience connected the individual not only to the immanent spirit operating as the essence of natural and historical phenomena, but also to a transcendent power that grounded the eternal laws of the moral order. Ranke also never relinquished his conviction that this transcendent power was actively involved in history, either directly or indirectly through the power of religious faith and the moral energies that such faith released. The problems

[42] "Frankreich und Deutschland," pp. 65–66; "Politisches Gespraech," pp. 334–45; "Tagebuecher" (mid-1830s), *Aus Werk und Nachlass*, vol. 1, pp. 245–47; Ranke, "Reflexionen" (1832), in Ranke, *Werke*, vols., 49/50, pp. 245–46.

that this conviction presented to his political perspective were displayed in the concluding passage of the *Politisches Gespraech* (Political Dialogue, 1836). Here Ranke claimed that although states were "real-spiritual" communities of divine origin with a "spiritual substance," they were ineradicably individual and thus distinct from the universal, "highest and supreme community" of religious faith. He insisted, moreover, that the eternal moral laws that ordered this religious community had no direct "positive" influence on the temporal–spiritual order of peoples and states.[43] But Ranke could not sustain such a stringent separation either in his personal stance or in his histories, where the transformation of ethno-cultural life into state power was inextricably connected to the energizing power of religious beliefs.

At the time Ranke wrote the *Politisches Gesprach*, he was also completing the final volume of his *Die roemischen Paepste in den letzten vier Jahrhunderten* (*The Roman Popes during the last Four Centuries*), in which the relationship between the universal religious community and the particular political communities of peoples and states was much more problematic than his strict theoretical separation might suggest. The *Paepste* did not simply narrate the futile attempt to impose a universal spiritual dominion on a culturally individualized temporal world, but also explored the beginnings of a process whereby this universal element and its transcendent ground were absorbed into and adapted to the individuality of temporal development, becoming the universal moment in the state's particularity, the transcendent ground of its immanent development. Thus, Ranke could claim that Germany was able to assert its national individuality against the papal attempt to impose a universal dominion because it was "armed" with a commitment to a rediscovered "true religion."[44] It was not so much that the universal religious community under a transcendent god was irrelevant to the development of a humanity individualized into tribes and peoples, but that the universality of religion could never completely submerge the individualities of temporal life and form a single temporal–spiritual state. But the moral forces that derived from the conviction of participation in the universal religious community were a decisive element in Ranke's analysis of the individual developments in which states emerged from tribes and peoples. It was the transcendent sphere of religious truth that provided the objective ground for the transformation of the ethno-cultural subject of the people into the unique moral self of the state. The history that described the emergence of modern political forms could not just be a history of the secular sphere, but inevitably became a history of the reciprocal relationships between religious universality and national individuality, between church and state, between the transcendent and immanent spirit.

43 "Politisches Gespraech," p. 338.

44 *Die roemischen Paepste in den letzten vier Jahrhunderten*, in Ranke, *Werke*, vol. 37, p. 83.

The complexity of these relationships converged in Ranke's historical scholarship, as he began, in 1836, to investigate in detail the formation of the German state during the Reformation. When Ranke began his research, it seemed that the organizing theme of his project would be the inherent unity within the fragmented forms of German national politics. In an early sketch of his research, he claimed that a history of the imperial diets in the fifteenth and sixteenth centuries was "history of the government of Germany, of our unity and divisions":

> In them speaks . . . an Idea in which Germany lives, which, as long as there is a Germany will never disappear, an Idea of a higher community which moves above the activities of the smaller states, gives direction to their activity, gives them their significance . . . the Idea of fatherland and of law. Just this is the difference between the German Empire and all other states and empires: in the others the Idea of law has been connected to the content of power . . . in Germany however there always existed something over and above the individual state powers which was not itself another power . . . but grounded on imperial law, on the past, and on historical scholarship.[45]

In the context of current concerns for greater German unity, Ranke contended, it was important to appropriate historically this idea of a common German law that transcended the customary and statutory law of the individual territorial states. By the time the first volume of the *Deutsche Geschichte* appeared in 1839, however, the central theme of Ranke's work had shifted to the relationship between cultural nationality and religion. He now claimed that Germany's peculiarity was based not so much in its unique historical legal structure as in the depth of its involvement in religious and ecclesiastical matters. Right up to the present moment, he stated, German history was dominated by the theme of religious conflict and driven by a "religious-political life-activity."[46]

Ranke introduced the *Deutsche Geschichte* with the statement that in "living existence [*lebendiges Dasein*]," politics and religion were "indissolubly connected and fused" in every historical moment. There was no "human activity of genuine spiritual significance" that did not originate in a "more or less conscious relation to God and divine things." "It is impossible to conceive of any great nation worthy of the name whose political life was not stimulated and elevated by religious ideas," he wrote, "and that has not constantly concerned itself with developing and cultivating these ideas in order to give them a universally valid expression and external embodiment." The religious component in the development of nationality, however, produced

[45] Ranke, "Ueber einige noch unbenutzte Sammlungen deutsche Reichtagsakten" (1838), in Ranke, *Deutsche Geschichte im Zeitalter der Reformation*, ed. Paul Joachimsen (6 vols; Munich: 1925–26), vol. 6, p. 479.

[46] Ranke, *Deutsche Geschichte*, vol. 1, p. 3.

conflict within the nation between the universal claims of its religious idea and the innate individual genius, the "originally implanted spirit" that gave it its unique character. From the relations between these two forms of the divine spirit, Ranke now claimed, developed the "progressively freer, more inclusive, more profound movement of the spirit" that characterized western European culture. The political development of peoples was driven by the need to actualize their individual essences in the context of transcendent goals; religion progressed under the pressure to embody its universal truth in the "living representation" of individual life in ethno-cultural nations. In the context of this perspective, Ranke redefined his search for the genuine German state in terms of a complex double purpose. On the one hand, he wanted to show how the particular German political formation emerged through the instigation and appropriation of religious ideas. On the other hand, he wanted to describe the way in which the Christian "idea" was progressively transformed in this process of appropriation.[47]

In pursuing his first task, Ranke found himself moving closer to the positions of the king, Stahl, Radowitz, and the other more conservative and pious spokesmen of the new regime, who also insisted on the transcendent religious foundations of political community. Insofar as Ranke drew these transcendent foundations into the progressive movement of the historical process, however, he found himself more in agreement with the liberal and "philosophical" ideologues of the Christian state, such as Bunsen and Schelling. Ranke's claim that the transformation of the ethno-cultural nation into a state was instigated and mediated by religious convictions made him one voice in the new Berlin sacred chorale; his particular concept of these religious foundations, however, allowed him to emerge as an individual soloist with a few arias of his own.

THE RELIGIOUS DIMENSION: PANTHEISM, PERSONALISM, AND HISTORICAL FREEDOM

The conceptualization of religious experience that informed Ranke's private and public writing in the later 1830s and early 1840s was characterized by the same dichotomous perspective that was evident in his political views. As in the development of his political viewpoint, moreover, this dualism originated and achieved its first articulation during the formative, postwar university years in which Ranke became emotionally involved in the nationalist student movement and was intellectually absorbed by the tasks of appropriating the language and viewpoint of his neohumanist, Romantic, and Idealist inheritance. Although Ranke had, from childhood on, been set on an educational path that, in keeping with family tradition, would have

[47] *Ibid.*, pp. 1–3.

led to a career in the Lutheran ministry, he was not raised in a particularly pious or orthodox environment. In fact, it seems that it was only after Ranke abandoned both his theological career and most of whatever elements of orthodox piety he may have absorbed during his childhood that religious convictions and questions became a focal point of his personal reflections and public perspectives.[48]

In a diary entry dated with unusual specificity at 11:00 P.M., December 20, 1816, Ranke described an intense, visionary experience, which has often been interpreted as a religious conversion:

> The spirits stir within me. This is life, and vital life [*lebendiges Leben*]. Let them stir. Thus forms are in a constant process of external transformation. Is not the form simply an expression of inner life? How could the former remain stable while the latter changes? Everything good must have space. I hear you speak within me, marvelous, with many voices. You seek the light of day. How joyously you respond as you are touched by a related voice . . . The seed has fallen; you are like roots pushing out from it. And if the soil is good, then the green twig will not be long in coming, and only a warm sun will nourish it. But this sun already shines: I call you my sun; you united spirits of past and present ages. You stood far off, scattered and isolated, but now you are a single choir . . . witnesses of the gods among men. Now your rays, those bright, shining rays, are gathered into a single burning point. . . . Oh you one unified sun, shine down on this little green twig. Will you wait for it, maternal mother [*mutterliche Mutter*]?

Continuing with his arboreal metaphor, Ranke went on to describe how his sprouting twiglike existence attached itself to the trunk of the great tree of life and expressed its freedom and unique potentialities through "confidential dialogue" with the other branches.[49] In a short fragment composed at the same time, Ranke gave succinct expression to the vision achieved in his experience of identity with the great tree of life nourished by the "maternal mother" of the collective human spirit: "This infinite power which flows through everything outside us and within us, this inexhaustible, indestructible, self-sustaining spring which creates and maintains all things – what a superior and magnificent concept it provides for that which we name God and of that which we and all things are. All is one and one is all."[50]

Both the life forces circulating through his veins and the voices in the texts he was reading seemed to draw Ranke to this pantheistic conception of the relationship between the divine and the human, the spiritual and

[48] Henz, *Ranke*, pp. 108–13. Henz's study provides a needed corrective to conventional conceptions of the serene and "organic" evolution of Ranke's convictions, a view that characterized not only older biographies, like that of Helmolt, but also post–World War II studies like Rudolf Vierhaus's *Ranke und die soziale Welt* (Muenster: 1957).

[49] "Tagebuecher" (1816), *Aus Werk und Nachlass*, vol. 1, p. 141.

[50] "Tagebeuecher" (1816–17), *Aus Werk und Nachlass*, vol. 1, p. 142.

the natural. It provided the primary paradigm for his reflections on religion until the 1830s.

In his youthful diaries the pantheistic vision was omnipresent. That which appeared within the appearances of nature and history revealed itself to the wisdom of the heart as the infinite power of an ultimately unitary life. This is what philosophers tried to grasp with their theories of the absolute; it was the god whom poets mimicked in their art. The infinite dynamic power of "being" made all existence possible, organized the twigs, roots and branches into a single tree, focused the various lights of culture into a single sun, harmonized the apparently dissonant sounds of humanity into a world chorale. Moreover, this identity within difference, essence within appearance, could be approached and intuitively known by man, because it was his own "being and life."[51] Man was free because he was standing on "his own ground" when he experienced his individual life as immersed in the totality of being: "When the thousand voices of nature gently whisper and speak to you, when your spirit has serenely elevated itself in the marvelous harmony of joyous creation, and has perceived and made everything its own.... Oh, then you feel who you are and where you are."[52]

From the perspective of this achieved pantheistic vision, Ranke engaged in a critical reevaluation of his Christian inheritance. He rejected the traditional Protestant belief in the transcendent authority of biblical revelation. The Bible could be read like any other ancient text, as one manifestation of the infinite power of divine life. The truth of Christianity, expressed in various forms by the original apostles and evangelists, the church fathers, the Protestant reformers and other Christian writers, was simply that belief in Christ was the premise of salvation. Christ, however, was the objective representation of infinite divine life within man. To believe in Christ was to believe in one's own essential "life and being," to affirm the divinity of man. True Christian faith was not directed toward the historical appearance, but to the "idea": "The idea of Christ of which the Old Testament sings and speaks, whose story is narrated in the New Testament, which shines forth from the writings and deeds of the most pious men, to this let us hold and remain firm."[53]

Throughout Ranke's discussion of Christianity in both its apostolic and Lutheran forms, however, it is evident that another framework for grasping religious experience was also at work. In the draft of a sermon from 1816, Ranke indicated that man required faith in a transcendent power in order to control his own animality and properly fulfill his divinely ordained ethical duty – to reconstruct the divine exemplar of spiritual being within

51 "Tagebuecher" (1817), *Aus Werk und Nachlass*, vol. 1, p. 155.

52 "Tagebuecher" (1816–17), *Aus Werk und Nachlass*, vol. 1, p. 117.

53 "Tagebuecher" (1814–18), *Aus Werk und Nachlass*, vol. 1, pp. 112–13.

the "sensuous element." Such an ethical spiritualization of the natural did not develop spontaneously through the dynamic powers of an immanent life principle. It required a being outside of nature to control and transform nature.[54] In a diary entry of the same period, Ranke noted that although knowledge was subjective, human action required objective norms and convictions – "so the Godhead came to man's aid with faith." Faith also was subjective, but unlike the internal self-reflection of speculative transcendental knowledge, it was a relationship to an "other"; like empirical observation, faith was a form of seeing directed toward an objective ground "to which it can hold fast so that it does not err."[55] In his discussions of Luther, Ranke was constantly faced with the problems of the "ethico-transcendent" model of religious experience. Luther had grounded his ethical convictions on a firm belief in the objective truth of the biblical revelation. Yet Ranke himself could not accept such a view of the Bible, which as a human text was open to varying subjective interpretations and could only produce a plurality of "revelations."[56] Although Ranke occasionally lamented his inability to believe in the literal truth of the Christian revelation and expressed longing for a return to a simple, objective faith of the kind apparently achieved by his brother Heinrich, he generally tried to avoid direct confrontation with the dilemmas in which he threatened to become entangled by his ethical dualism, a dualism in which moral life somehow appeared as both the emancipation and full self-expression of innate natural human drives, and as a control over these drives through the mediation of a transcendent power. Most often Ranke tried to encompass conflict within the boundaries of the pantheistic model, as the competitive struggle for self-expression among equally justified individualizations of the infinite life principle, or as the dynamic evolutionary struggle of life against deadening fixation in forms continually becoming obsolete, rigid, and restrictive.

The predominance of the pantheistic framework in Ranke's perspective on religion and the focus on its benign aspects (which allowed it to appear self-sufficient) continued as he transferred his personal religious quest into his search for historical knowledge in the 1820s. Historical research and writing became the means for unveiling and recreating the movement of infinite divine life in the plethora of individualized living beings. In 1820 he wrote to Heinrich Ranke (before whose orthodox piety he always felt the need to justify his own): "In all of history god dwells, lives and can be recognized. Every deed witnesses to him, every moment proclaims his name, but most of all, I think, the general coherence of history as a whole." God was present in history like a "sacred hieroglyph" preserved in his "externality" so that he could be unveiled by future, "more perceptive" centuries. As

[54] "Entwurf einer Predigt" (1816), *Aus Werk und Nachlass*, vol. 3, pp. 246–49.

[55] "Tagebuecher" (1816–17), *Aus Werk und Nachlass*, vol. 1, p. 109.

[56] Ranke, "Das Luther-Fragment von 1817," in Ranke, *Deutsche Geschichte*, vol. 6, pp. 331–36.

the unveilers of the sacred hieroglyph, historians were also servants of God, "teachers and priests."[57] Two years later he wrote about his dream to write a book, a bible for his own age, which would "encompass into one powerful word" the "core of that eternal revelation which is present in nature, daily life, and in the development of the centuries, everywhere." Such a work of history would "elevate man to the full experience of his life, undivided, convincing, ideal; that life which we are called upon to live in God and in the world, as teachers and students, children and adults, as nothing and something, together in each moment."[58]

During the 1820s the pantheistic vision was expressed in Ranke's works in his attempts to grasp the coherence of historical phenomena in terms of the infinite life that appeared in particular appearances, in terms of the general ground of being manifest in the common life of all existing beings. Whenever Ranke experienced particular difficulty in discerning the unity of life in all of its fullness and immediacy, however, his alternate theology of a transcendent personal God showed its face. In his *Geschichten*, as Ernst Schulin has shown in a study of the first edition, the "hand of God" appeared primarily in the context of moral judgment and punishment of crimes against the eternal laws of the moral world order. As Ranke found himself unable to encompass the conflicts between the natural and the moral in his pantheistic vision, the patriarchal god of his ethico-transcendent theology tended to intervene in the historical process. In a passage excised from later additions, Ranke noted that the rise and fall of historical states could not be explained simply as a natural process of growth, maturation, and decay. If historical decline was derived from the web of external circumstances, he noted, life would have no meaning, and "we are like the flowers killed by an early night frost." The only alternative appeared to be the belief that god entered history not only as creator but also as the god of "doom and destruction" expressing his "pleasure and displeasure" at human actions.[59]

During the 1830s and early 1840s, Ranke's conceptualization of the religious sphere continued to be characterized by both perspectives that had emerged from his postwar experience. However, as his personal and political concerns turned more insistently to the problem of the control and moralization of the elemental forces that animated historical development in the wake of the revolutionary threat of 1830, the balance between his two perspectives shifted radically in favor of his ethico-transcendent theology. The pantheistic perspective continued to find expression in three areas. First, it appeared in his occasional personal confessions regarding the mystical joys of historical research. "One lives more in the whole than in one's own person," he wrote in 1832, defending the unsociability of his professional absorptions

[57] Ranke to Heinrich Ranke, March 1820, *Briefwerk*, p. 18.

[58] Ranke to Heinrich Ranke, November 22, 1822, in Ranke, *Werke*, vols. 53/54, p. 103.

[59] Cited in Schulin, "Ranke's Erstes Buch," p. 597.

to his brother. "Often one can hardly tell whether one still has a personality. The ego disappears. The eternal father of all things, that animates them all, draws us to himself without any resistance."[60] Second, the same conceptions informed Ranke's theoretical defense of the historian's commitment to the concrete individuality of existing finite being against the generalizing and abstracting methods of philosophers. "History recognizes something infinite in every existence, in every condition, in every being," he claimed, "something eternal, emanating from the divine, and this is its vital principle." "We believe," he continued, "that there is nothing without God and that nothing lives except through god. By freeing ourselves from the claims of a narrow theology, we do nevertheless profess that all our efforts stem from a higher, religious source."[61] Finally, Ranke occasionally interrupted the narrative of his historical works, as in the opening passage of Book 7 of the *Paepste*, to marvel at the mysterious power of the "living spirit" that revealed itself in the continuous production, development, dissolution, and recreation of historical forms.[62] In both Ranke's personal reflections and his historical writing after 1830, however, the pantheistic vision was subordinated to or even displaced by a conception of "true" or "pure" religion as faith in a supernatural personality whose power was the foundation of the moral convictions expressed in the historical conflicts of ideas and powers.

Ranke's diaries from the 1830s and 1840s display an interest in the particular content of Christian theology and its ethical implications that had not been evident earlier. His theological reflections persistently returned to the issue of the "personality" of the divinity. "The question is," he wrote, "how the personal originates in the universal and whether this is more than simply a condition of earthly existence." The Christian answer to this question, and the "secret" of both its universality and its distinctiveness, was that "the universal, the divine, is analogous to mankind in its possession of personality." To live "continually in the consciousness of God" did not imply dissolution of personality, but its perfected "essential" manifestation. In striking contrast to his earlier position, Ranke now interpreted the Christian incarnation as the historical manifestation of God's personal character, rather than as an emblem of the divinity of human life. He vehemently criticized David Friedrich Strauss's claim that Christ represented the idea of humanity mythically projected on to an historical personality by the primitive Christian community. "The most magnificent appearance that mankind had ever seen," Ranke insisted, must have had a real divine origin. Belief was always directed at and sustained by a person, not an idea or a theory, and thus the assurance of living in the consciousness of God could have originated only in a real historical encounter that provided "historical certainty." The

60 Ranke to Heinrich Ranke, November 30, 1832, *Briefwerk*, p. 253.

61 "Idee der Universalhistorie"(1831–32), *Aus Werk und Nachlass*, vol. 4, p. 77.

62 *Die roemische Paepste*, in Ranke, *Werke*, vol. 38, p. 239.

upshot of Ranke's reflections was that the distinctiveness of Christianity lay in its conception of the absolute as a personal transcendent being, with the freedom and responsibility of an ethical subject. The "living spirit" at work in human history originated in the divine breath that animated God's original creations, thus making them capable of the freedom, love, and fidelity of genuine persons.[63]

Ranke's movement toward a theology of a personal, transcendent God was explicitly connected to his political concerns of the 1830s. In one of his diary entries, he noted that the universal religious community bound together by the vertical relations of individual persons to the "eternal king" was a model of the "ideal state."[64] In another note he claimed that the principle of personal monarchy was of "divine origin" and connected to the "world dominion of the spirit, of the son."[65] The heavenly and earthly states were related to each other not only by analogy, but also through the mediation of the eternal laws of morality. The breath of the divine spirit implanted in man at the moment of creation, Ranke claimed, constituted the internal rule of moral conscience whereby man was to order his external, temporal actions. The Christian concept of sin referred to the denial of this source of moral life and the enclosure of the self within itself, as if it was not a creature dependent on a higher authority. Violation of the eternal rules of the moral order internalized in conscience cut man off from the sources of his spiritual vitality and was inevitably punished. Redemption required purification and restoration of the living "essence" of personality, a recognition that individuation was not synonymous with individualism, that true freedom was expressed in conformity to moral law rather than in egoistic self-expression.[66] In religious belief, moral order was revealed not as the full, spontaneous expression of the vitality of being, but as the control of life forces on the basis of the "ideal." Thus, Ranke suggested that the distinctiveness of Christianity might lie in its ethical demand for a moralization of the real, for "dominion" of the "higher existence" of the divine spirit. The difficulty with this claim was that "the earthly element, which also has its legitimacy" reacted against the project of spiritual domination. It was clear that the dominion of the spirit could not be actualized as a temporal "hierarchically fixed" dominion. "Ultimately, however," he concluded, "the divine will reveal itself as dominant."[67]

The problematic relationship between the universal religious community and the absolute truth of the Christian idea on the one hand, and the immanent power of individualized life and the relativities of development

[63] "Tagebuecher" (1830s), *Aus Werk und Nachlass*, vol. 1, pp. 120, 127–28, 126, 131, 128, 155, 119.
[64] "Tagebuecher" (after 1835), *Aus Werk und Nachlass*, vol. 1, p. 160.
[65] "Tagebuecher" (late 1830s), *Aus Werk und Nachlass*, vol. 1, p. 163.
[66] "Tagebuecher" (1830s), *Aus Werk und Nachlass*, vol. 1, pp. 119–20, 129–30.
[67] "Tagebuecher" (late 1830s), *Aus Werk und Nachlass*, vol. 1, p. 163.

in time and space on the other, constituted the major theme in Ranke's great historical narratives of the 1830s and 1840s. In both the *Paepste* and the *Deutsche Geschichte*, the integrating, universal element in the historical process was identified with the idea of Christianity, rather than the innate unity of a common life expressed in the analogous developments and reciprocal relations of ethno-cultural individualities. In the *Paepste*, Ranke examined the development of the Christian idea in history from the perspective of its failure to achieve actualization as a hierarchically institutionalized universal dominion against the resistance of individualized ethnic life. In the *Deutsche Geschichte*, he investigated the possibility of the historical incorporation of the Christian idea into the temporal dominion of peoples and states. Although Ranke narrated his stories in terms of the relationships between religion and politics, church and state, spiritual and temporal power, they were also, from the standpoint of his own dualistic religious perspective, stories of the war between immanent and transcendent deities, neither of whom Ranke was willing to renounce completely and whose ultimate fusion into a single absolute divinity remained his historical hope.

In the introductory chapter of the *Paepste*, Ranke provided his most explicit description of the Christian idea. By means of a few broad contrasts, he defined Christianity as above all a universal and a spiritual religion. In contrast to the particularized national religions that preceded the Roman conquests and the artificial syncretism of the consolidated empire, Christianity proclaimed the religion of "the universal father" under whose rule all men became brothers in a single "human family." "If the earlier forms of belief had ever contained an element of true religion," Ranke wrote, "this was now entirely obscured; they could no longer pretend to the slightest significance. In Him who united the nature of man with that of God there shone forth, in contrast with these shadows, the universal and eternal relation of God to the world and of man to God." Moreover, in contrast to the theocratic and idolatrous aspects of all previous religions, Christianity emancipated the human spirit from political servitude and restrictive materiality. Christianity was a religion of the "perfection of the spirit" and of "supernatural truth." It was from Christianity that "man derived the spiritual element with which he once again became self-sustaining, free and personally invincible." Christianity produced "a new vitality in the bosom of the freshened earth," thus preparing it for "the development of new production." As the universal, spiritually purified belief in the identity of all individuals in "the consciousness of a community under one true God," Christianity marked mankind's acquisition of "the knowledge of its own true nature."[68]

Once Ranke had defined the Christian idea in such sweeping terms, it was difficult to imagine how it might be capable of historical development.

[68] *Die roemische Paepste, in Ranke, Werke*, vol. 37, pp. 4–6, 8.

In fact, Ranke's narrative did not describe the internal development of the Christian idea, which never became the active subject of his histories, but the human, historical process of its diffusion, institutionalization, appropriation, articulation, distortion, and purification. The *Paepste* chronicled the final phases in what Ranke perceived as the first major stage in this process of actualization and appropriation – the papal attempt to institutionalize universal spiritual community as a temporal dominion. The failure of this attempt could be traced to an inability to recognize and act upon the Christian principle of the separation and equal legitimacy of the transcendent and immanent dimensions of human existence. The papal drive for universal dominion was inevitably opposed "by energies all too powerful, rooted in, and bound up with the deepest sympathies and sentiments of human life."[69] Moreover, by refusing to recognize the legitimacy of individualized concrete being, the church inevitably absorbed temporal motivations, drives, perspectives, and strategies into the spiritual sphere, thus corrupting and obscuring the Christian idea. By entangling universal transcendent truth in the hegemonial ambitions of temporal power, the papacy aided and abetted the emergence of a negative spirit of revolution that identified the emancipation of the temporal realm with a denial of the transcendent.

Ranke concluded the final volume of the *Paepste* in 1836 with the hopeful assertion that contemporary Christianity was moving toward a restoration of a spiritually purified apostolic faith:

> Nor do we fear to deceive ourselves by the belief that men of more profound views are returning... to the true and eternal principles of pure and spiritual religion, with a more profound consciousness of truth, and increased freedom from the bondage of restricting ecclesiastical forms. The more perfect apprehension of the spiritually immutable, which lies at the basis of all forms but which in its whole import could be expressed by none, must at length appease and reconcile all enmities. High above all conflict – this hope we can never relinquish – there will yet arise from the ocean of error the unity of conviction, untroubled in its steadfast security, the pure and simple consciousness of the ever-enduring, all-pervasive presence of God.[70]

But could such a purification of the Christian idea, which allowed the reconciliation of all men in a universal spiritual community under their common father, also make possible a genuine reconciliation between the individualized energies of life and spiritual universality? This was the religious question that informed Ranke's study of the German Reformation.

Ranke interpreted the Protestant revolt against papal authority as a "maturation" of the Christian spirit toward "a consciousness of its essential being

[69] Ranke, *History of the Popes*, transl. E. Fowler, (3 vols; New York: 1901), vol. 3, p. 173. This passage was excised after the first edition and does not appear in the *Werke*.

[70] *Ibid.*, p. 174.

independent of all arbitrary forms" through a recovery of its "origins" in the "documents that directly proclaimed the eternal covenant of the godhead with the human race."[71] Motivated by his own personal religious need for redemption and justification before the transcendent father, Luther had rediscovered the Christian idea in its pristine purity. The Lutheran belief in the transcendent reality and universality of the spiritual realm and the strict, principled separation of this realm from the sphere of individualized temporal power, moreover, became the basis for a religious movement that was able to sustain itself against both the threat of the hierarchically inclusive, spiritual-temporal domination of the Catholic Church and the particularistic, exclusive "republican" forms of spiritual-temporal fusion in the utopian radicalism of the religious sectarians. However, Ranke also placed this recovery of the true and pure religion into a complex context of positive relationships with the living spirit immanent in the individual life of the Latin-Germanic peoples.

The Reformation was, of course, not only an important movement in the history of the universal Christian idea, but also a significant national–political event. In Ranke's view, Luther's personal and universal religious quest resonated with the historical demands of the German national genius for self-determination and self-expression. The universal religious idea organized and energized the diverse impulses of the cultural nation and provided them with a transcendent foundation. Germany made its bid to become an organized political self, a "power," under the guidance of universal moral values internalized in the Protestant religious conscience. However, Ranke also connected the Reformation to "the totality of a great spiritual movement" from which it originated and to which it gave new impetus and an epochally significant historical form.[72] The Reformation was not only a theological or a national–political event, although it certainly was both of these, not only for Germany but also for Europe in general. By recovering the original Christian idea, it redirected all of Europe back to its common moral foundations in a universal spiritual community, and by emancipating the political realm from ecclesiastical dominion it served as a stimulus for the general political emancipation of the European nations. But Ranke also saw the Reformation as a critical turning point in the development of a secular, "humanist" European culture, the manifestation of an immanent spiritual unity that corresponded to the unity under a transcendent father provided by the Christian idea. By liberating the transcendent religious community from its particularized temporal forms, the Reformation also liberated the secular world from the chains of a hierarchically imposed spirituality. Restoration of a "masculine piety," which rejected material images and earthly mediations in its direct encounter with the transcendent father, also released the spontaneous self-expression of a maternal impulse that animated the productive

[71] Ranke, *Deutsche Geschichte*, vol. 2, p. 112. [72] *Ibid.*, p. 69.

powers of natural life. In this double emancipation, the Reformation also projected the possibility of a new and genuine reconciliation of the paternal and maternal forms of divine self-expression in a "deeper life" from "which they both emanated."[73]

Ranke concluded the final volume of the *Deutsche Geschichte* in 1843 with a chapter that surveyed developments in philosophy, jurisprudence, medicine, natural science, historiography, philosophy, music, and literature during the sixteenth century. In each of these areas he saw the Reformation stimulating a recovery of the humanistic wisdom of the ancient classics and the independent, "scientific" investigation of the world of immanent living spirit in all its forms. By freeing, focusing, and stimulating this great spiritual development in European culture, Ranke claimed, the German and Protestant spirit played an essential role "in the universal historical progress that unites the centuries and the nations with each other."[74] The tendencies released in the era of the Reformation had not yet been completely worked out. The creation of a unified "positive and historical" European culture, stimulated and nurtured by a German national spirit that had been awakened to world-historical activity under the aegis of a deep commitment to the moral law of a transcendent father, remained a present and future task.

The implication of this concept of the uncompleted Reformation was that the implicit harmony and possible ultimate identity of the transcendent and immanent divinities was also more of an historical hope than an experienced historical reality. But the positive relationship between the two poles of the religious dualism constructed in the *Deutsche Geschichte* indicated the optimism of Ranke's cultural standpoint in the early 1840s. It was this optimism in relation to the possible historical reconciliation of immanent life and transcendent authority that defined Ranke's place among the other theoreticians of the Christian state in the 1840s. Unlike the king, Radowitz, Stahl, and other neo-orthodox pietists, Ranke did not define the objective, transcendent grounds of human existence in terms of a Protestant confession of faith or the literal truth of biblical revelation. His transcendent father remained simply the absolute authority required to sustain the universal validity of the laws of morality and ground the spiritual freedom that defined man as a moral subject. Ranke was never willing to subordinate this conception to a completely immanent religious viewpoint in which obedience to conscience would progressively emerge as the highest form of natural self-determination. He did consider the possibility that "true" religion existed beyond the Protestant form of Christianity in a more universal, "philosophical," or "scientific" form akin to Schelling's conception of the third Johannine stage of the Christian idea.[75] He also clearly gave indication of a tendency to bring together German genius and religious conscience in

[73] Ranke, *Deutsche Geschichte*, vol. 1, p. 3. [74] Ranke, *Deutsche Geschichte*, vol. 5, p. 397.

[75] "Tagebuecher" (1840s), *Aus Werk und Nachlass*, vol. 1, p. 132.

a manner akin to Bunsen's national church of the future. However, although Ranke was sympathetic toward both Bunsen's and Schelling's positions, he remained suspicious of what he saw as their tendency to merge the transcendent into either the immanent development of national life or the immanent development of European scientific culture.[76] For Ranke the evolution of man from a naturally existing being into a free moral subject ultimately required the intervention of a transcendent power, although this intervention did not destroy, but released and shaped, the innate powers received from the other "objective" ground of subjectivity – the maternal womb of being embodied in the ethnic reality of the *Volk*.

HISTORY AS THE UNVEILING OF EXISTENCE: HISTORICAL SUBJECTIVITY AND TRANSCENDENT AUTHORITY

It may seem artificial or eccentric to tie Ranke and Schelling together as philosophical thinkers responding to the same dilemmas and questions. The problematic nature of the association goes beyond their personal relationship, which was congenial and mutually supportive from the mid-1820s through the 1840s.[77] The real issue is Ranke's clearly ambivalent attitude toward the whole project of post-Kantian German Idealist philosophy. During his student years, Ranke displayed an intense interest in the questions raised by the major Romantic and Idealist philosophers and attempted to reformulate and resolve them.[78] When he committed himself to history as a vocation in the 1820s it was, at least in part, because he had become convinced that historical knowledge could provide a resolution of the problems that philosophers posed but could not resolve on their own terms, and that the

[76] "Tagebuecher" (late 1840s), *Aus Werk und Nachlass*, vol. 1, pp. 130–31, 163.

[77] Schelling had been one of the instigators of the attempt to lure Ranke to Munich in the 1820s, and Ranke had lobbied for Schelling's appointment to Hegel's chair in the 1830s. It seems that Ranke followed Schelling's shift to his second "positive" philosophy with approval. Contrary to Krieger's claim (*Ranke*, p. 363, n.21), Ranke was not sympathetic to the early Romantic Schelling and was only mildly critical of the late Schelling during the 1840s. Schelling in turn considered Ranke the most congenial of his new Berlin colleagues. *Aus Schellings Leben in Briefen*, 3 vols., Leipzig: 1869–70, vol. 3, p. 174.

[78] Ranke's intense, personal encounter with the writings of Kant and the post-Kantians Schelling and Fichte (but not Hegel) during his student years is recounted in detail in Silvia Backs, *Dialektisches Denken in Ranke's Geschichtsschreibung bis 1854* (Cologne: 1985), pp. 10–77. Backs's attempts to derive Ranke's positions from specific texts of Fichte and Schelling remains mainly conjectural, and she does not contextualize Ranke's appropriations of the idealist inheritance in terms of the historically situated problems he was attempting to articulate and resolve. The monograph by Siegfried Baur, *Versuch ueber die Historik des jungen Ranke* (Berlin: 1998), which emphasizes the origins of Ranke's views of history in problems arising from philological interpretation, also ignores broader contextual issues. Michael-Joachim Zemlin, *Geschichte zwischen Theorie und Theoria: Untersuchungen zur Geschichtsphilosophie Rankes* (Wuerzburg: 1988), ignores developmental and contextual issues altogether but tends to focus its systematizing efforts on Ranke's later (post-1848) conceptions of universal history.

core philosophical questions of the age concerned the historical nature of existence. It was his religious and philosophical interests, "and these alone," he claimed in 1830, that had "driven him to history."[79] The consequence was a divided attitude toward philosophy and philosophers. On the one hand Ranke insisted on the autonomy of historical knowledge of the real in both its individuality and totality. History required no aid from philosophy in its quest for knowledge. On the other hand, he claimed that "if history were perfectly clear and complete and philosophy were what it ought to be, then they would fully coincide with each other" and that "history is not the antithesis, but the fulfillment of philosophy."[80] In 1835 he asserted that all forms of systematic knowledge converged in historical knowledge and that its "results" belonged to all, but especially to philosophy.[81] In this sense there is a clear parallel between Ranke's conception of the nature of historical knowledge and the positions of the contemporary Left Hegelians who projected both the "end" and the "actualization" of philosophy in the empirical knowledge of the new humanistic disciplines of anthropology, psychology, and history.

In order to grasp the philosophical claims implicit in Ranke's historical perspective, it is useful to return to his original formulation of the philosophical problem during his last two years at Leipzig, between 1816 and 1818. One essay from this period, on the general relations between human beings and nature, stands out in its systematic character. It clearly marked an attempt by Ranke to bring together his wide reading in German neohumanism (Goethe and Herder), the romantic philosophy of nature and art (Schelling, Henrik Steffens, and Friedrich Schlegel), and the Idealist philosophy of the transcendental ego (Kant, Fichte, and Jacobi) into a general concept of human beings as both natural and moral subjects.

Ranke began his essay with a general description of the dualism evident in contemporary concepts of nature. Nature was perceived as either creator or creation, as a productive, nourishing, maternal subject or as the constituted, objective, external world of lawfully ordered things. These contrasting concepts arose from the divergent modes in which man related to the world beyond consciousness. The maternal concept of nature arose from a stance of feeling and sensibility that recognized its own life in the life perceived, its own inexhaustible power in the dynamic changing forms of the other. This attitude, Ranke claimed, following Herder, was characteristic of young, still "natural" peoples and was the foundation of the aesthetic perspective. All great artists, from Homer to Goethe, had related to nature as a productive maternal principle. In contrast, Ranke attributed the objective concept of nature to the "cold, dissecting intellect [*Verstand*]"

[79] Ranke to Heinrich Ritter, August 6, 1830, *Briefwerk*, p. 216.

[80] "Idee der Universalhistorie," pp. 83, 86.

[81] Ranke to Heinrich Ranke, February 26, 1835, *Briefwerk*, p. 273.

characteristic of the physicist, for whom nature was mere mechanism or a laboratory for manipulative operations. Significantly, Ranke also described and rejected a third stance toward nature – the imaginative "constructive" view of Schelling and Romantic nature-philosophy. Schelling's recreations of nature, he claimed, mistook "subjective knowledge for objective truth," producing not a real encounter with the "holy" but merely a self-mirroring illusion that prevented an encounter with the world beyond the ego.

Having dismissed the views of Kant, Fichte, and Schelling as a rejection of the independent, creative otherness of nature, and as its reduction to a product of human consciousness, Ranke proceeded to describe the development of the human subject as a creation of the maternal natural principle, as a "product and part of universal nature." Nature provided man with the original identity of being that allowed him to develop in reciprocal relations with the external world. It was the source not only of the drives and feelings that moved him to action, but also of the categories of the understanding, which Ranke saw as evolving from sense experience. Nature thus gave man the powers that allowed him to become conscious of himself and of the general life from which he had emerged. Consciousness was merely "the most highly developed natural power [*Naturkraft*]." Ranke was thus quite willing to push the concept of man as part and product of nature to the point where not only man's "vegetative" and "animal" functions, but also his "spirit," were grasped as a product of his "pure natural being."[82]

There was one point, however, at which the theory of man as a natural being proved inadequate; it could not encompass the reality of voluntary action, of moral freedom. The human capacity for self-determination was naturally innate as a potentiality but not as an actuality. When man actualized his potentiality for self-determination and became a creature capable of giving himself laws and becoming the creator of his own fate, he appeared no longer as a product of nature, but as an "independent power" separate from and opposed to nature: "Nature receives a new meaning for him; it becomes the material of his action. The great vision of the all-creative power dissolves. He recognizes something higher above it; he restricts it with sacred moral freedom."

Natural man was not without morality. Ranke derived the morality of love from natural sources, and there was certainly a moral value in living in harmony with nature and developing and expressing this relationship in art and science. But the moral ideal of "free self-creation" constituted a higher sphere, a "realm of ethical beauty, a heavenly realm." At this point in his discussion, Ranke was willing to praise Fichte – whose comprehension of the practical sphere of ethical life was described as a model for the ages. Even Kant experienced a slight rehabilitation when his objectified view of nature was restricted to the perspective of the moral rather than the theoretical

[82] "Mensch und Natur" (1816–1818), *Aus Werk und Nachlass*, vol. 3, pp. 225–30.

self. The source and objective ground of moral experience, of man as free ethical subject, was clearly religious. The moral self was "not of this world." Unlike the natural self, which emerged as a finite expression of the infinite, "objective" ground of being, the moral self was immortal, the mysterious gift of a transcendent power.[83]

In the philosophical fragments and journal notes from the same period as this essay, Ranke tried to develop a unified concept of the philosophical task beginning first from the moral and then from the natural grounds of human existence. Inspired by Fichte, Ranke toyed with the possibility that "the highest, only possible object of philosophical knowledge is the ego (*Ich*), since through the ego the possibility of all other knowledge is conditioned."[84] By grasping the a priori forms of moral experience and judgment, it should be possible to achieve knowledge of the transcendental ego, and such knowledge could then provide the basis for a unified theory or science of all being. The attempts to deduce the world from the a priori forms of the transcendental ego, however, were soon abandoned, and viewed as a strange aberration that could only have gained attention in "the momentary excesses" of the current age.[85] On serious reflection, Ranke claimed, it became obvious that self-consciousness could only emerge from and through the consciousness of another active, subjective being. The self-identity that necessarily preceded separation and mutual recognition was not an identity of the ego of consciousness but a self-identity of existing being (*Sein*). Knowledge of this being was a "knowledge of the heart" that unveiled "the life of God in us." "Just the fact that we live and are," Ranke insisted, "that is primary and original." In a discussion of the post-Kantian philosopher F. H. Jacobi, Ranke concluded that the best definition of the task of philosophy was "to unveil existence [*Dasein enthuellen*]."[86]

As the "unveiling of existence" emerging from a wisdom of the heart and directed toward a comprehension of "being" and "life," philosophy was associated with the conceptualization of man as a part and product of mother nature and closely associated with the representation of life in art. In a number of notes Ranke paired philosophy and poetry as "insight" and "representation." Philosophy grasped the idea underlying the manifold appearances of a particular, individual existence, and poetry turned this insight into the "gold" of art. As "clear, fully experienced insight," he wrote, philosophy allowed the "marrow of being [*Mark des Seins*]" to become "transparent." In the work of the true philosopher, "life thought and thought lived and God was omnipresent." But Ranke was not ready to accept that such insight could be represented in rational, discursive prose. Only the poet was capable of representing the marrow of being in communicable forms. During this phase of Ranke's development, Goethe was his model of the

83 *Ibid.*, pp. 230–32. 84 "Tagebuecher" (1816–17), *Aus Werk und Nachlass*, vol. 1, 142.
85 "Tagebuecher" (1816–17), *Aus Werk und Nachlass*, vol. 1, 145. 86 *Ibid.*, pp. 145, 153.

ideal poet–philosopher, and he called on Goethe's spirit to help him grasp the individual as a manifestation of the absolute so that "from the secure base of the historical the idea would arise in genuine, convincing fashion, that out of the given forms would spring forth that which is not given."[87]

As Ranke entered into his historical vocation in the 1820s, it was the version of philosophy as an "unveiling of existence" that predominated in his historical work and thinking. This focus was made explicit both in the methodological comments he inserted in his writings and in the general considerations regarding the universal context of particular histories that prefaced his lectures at the university. The negative, polemical animus in his methodological statements was directed against the a priori construction of existence by philosophical theorists and the imaginative fabrication of existence by historical novelists. In both instances the palpable, unmediated reality of historical appearances had been obscured or distorted. The historian's first task was to dig down through the layers of mediated reality to the "homely" and "contingent" facts, to the "naked truth" of appearances.[88] Ranke clearly believed that this recovery of the unmediated appearances of vital existence had value in its own right. Individual existence was both unique and mortal; by recovering the lost and obscured manifestations of past existence, the historian worked to diminish the amount of death in the world.[89] At the same time, however, Ranke conceived the historical task as moving beyond such antiquarian memorializing of past life toward a comprehension of individual existence "at once in the essence of its being and the fullness of its phenomenal particularity."[90] Particular historical phenomena were to be grasped not only in their meaningful associations within "wholes" of varying extent, but also in relation to the source of such coherent connections in the "general life" that produced them.

The source of those connections that joined particular phenomena into coherent totalities, Ranke claimed, was to be sought in the "inner ground" of appearances, not in general ideas produced through inner reflection or abstract categories imposed on the material. To group and classify phenomena according to external chronological or geographical classifications was artificial and misleading. Historical epochs as well as spatial configurations were produced by the inner life that appeared in phenomena. Thus the stages of "organic" growth – birth, youth, maturity, decline, and so forth – and the "natural" grouping of phenomena as manifestations of the existence of "races, peoples, and individuals" were the starting points for Ranke's conceptualizations of universal history.[91] Ranke also rejected the derivation of

[87] "Tagebuecher" (1817), *Aus Werk und Nachlass*, vol. 1, 173–74.

[88] *Geschichten*, p. vii; *Zur Kritik*, p. 24.

[89] Ranke, "Allgemeine Weltgeschichte" (1825); in Ranke, *Aus Werk und Nachlass*, vol. 4, p. 35.

[90] *Die Osmanen*, p. 89.

[91] "Allgemeine Weltgeschichte," pp. 35–39; "Grundzuege der allgemeinen Weltgeschichte" (1826–27), *Aus Werk und Nachlass*, vol. 4, 51–61.

one appearance or group of appearances from another. The literature of a people was not to be construed as a reflection or product of a people's political or religious life. Politics, religion, and literature were connected to each other through the common source that produced them:

> For us as well, literature appears in association with the rest of life, and thus as a part of this general life itself. The ground of general life [*Grund des allgemeinen Lebens*] must be distinguished from its expressions (although we call both "life"). The ground is the spirit and its movement; the expression is the appearance. This however is thousand fold, present in every moment, ephemeral, never fully comprehensible; one part of it is constituted by literature.[92]

As this passage reveals, Ranke despaired of ever fully comprehending individual existence in both the "essence of its being and the fullness of its phenomenal particularity." Historical knowledge achieved a partial approximation at best of the full knowledge of phenomena that existed as "an aspect of God's existence."[93] Moreover, Ranke remained extremely vague in his descriptions of the ground of being that was the object of his knowledge, interchangeably using "life," "spirit," and phrases like "the true genius that lives in the depths."[94]

What was missing in Ranke's reflections about the philosophical dimension in historical knowledge was any discussion of the possibility of comprehending the a priori, universal forms of moral life. Knowledge of this type did not appear to disclose itself in historical phenomena, which seemed to manifest only the power and reality of "being," not the freedom of the transcendental self. As was noted above, the eternal laws of the moral world order appeared in Ranke's works of the 1820s almost exclusively as the assumptions of the narrator, allowing him to judge actions and characters from the perspective of the universal.

As in the political and religious dimensions of his historical thinking, the crisis of 1830 produced a significant shift in Ranke's perspective on the philosophical dimension of historical knowledge. This shift involved three closely related developments. First, it was marked by an explicit defense of the historical mode of grasping reality against alleged attempts by the philosophical "school," or "party" (i.e., Hegelians), to construct reality as a necessary emanation of the a priori structure of absolute reason or the absolute idea. Second, this defense was characterized by a gradual broadening and transformation of Ranke's concept of the general meaning inherent in individual existence so as to include the integrating historical

92 "Ueber die Entwicklung der Literatur seit den Anfaengen des 18. Jahrhunderts," *Aus Werk und Nachlass*, vol. 4, p. 63.

93 "Allgemeine Weltgeschichte," p. 35.

94 "Ueber die Entwicklung der Literatur" (1827), *Aus Werk und Nachlass*, vol. 4, p. 63.

power of transcendent religious and moral ideas consciously appropriated and acted upon by historical individuals and groups. Finally, by the end of the 1830s, Ranke was tentatively but noticeably moving toward an association of both the immanent and transcendent grounds of historical coherence in a vision of the empirically discernable progressive moralization of human existence through voluntary submission to transcendent spiritual authority, in a concept of historical totalization mediated through and manifest in the consequences of the free activity of individual moral subjects.

In his most extended defense of the autonomy of historical knowledge against the hegemonial pretensions of philosophy (a lecture introduction from 1831–32), Ranke described history and philosophy as radically opposed methods for comprehending the totality and essence of existence. The philosophical project originated through speculative, internal reflection on the a priori structure of the rational subject. From this starting point, Ranke claimed, speculative philosophers like Hegel and Fichte constructed a world of historical reality for themselves without regard for any experience, simply as the necessary exfoliation of the idea, according to "how it must have taken place" in conformity with their "idea of mankind." The truth of history was recognized "only insofar as it subordinates itself to the idea."[95] From such a perspective history had no independent value, nothing new could be learned from it; it was simply the material in which truth became manifest, in which the idea demonstrated its internal structure in temporal sequence. Paralleling his contemporaneous description of universal spiritual dominion in the *Paepste*, Ranke caricatured philosophy as a spiritual despotism riding roughshod over empirical existence, denying the reality of being in order to assert the reality of the idea. The discipline of history, like the principle of individual and national vitality within the historical narrative, appeared as the resistant power, defending the autonomy of existence against philosophy's arrogant, negative, revolutionary fanaticism. Such descriptions of both history and philosophy were stylized, one-sided caricatures. If philosophy pursued its "proper" role as scientific penetration of the "appearances of life," focused on the discovery of causal connections and on conceptualizing "the core of existence," its opposition to history would cease. History did begin with a commitment to the absolute value of existence in itself, and thus provided the world of particular phenomena with a sacred aura, but Ranke insisted that the historian ultimately vindicated his love for the finite by recognizing and representing the infinite that it contained and expressed. Through acts of "divination" or "spiritual apperception," the historian approached "the productive principle that formed and created nature" and that "confronts itself in the individual who recognizes it and through him becomes clear to itself and attains self-understanding." In order to attain

95 "Idee der Universalhistorie," pp. 74–75.

this kind of fusion of subject and object, the historian required a universal interest for all phenomenal forms, an impartiality that avoided the one-sided constructions of egoistic and partisan interests, an ability to penetrate beyond external sequence to the internal "causal nexus" uniting ground and appearance, and finally, a genuine commitment to the task of grasping existence as a complex relational totality. Ranke concluded that by describing the historical project he had arrived at a "definition of philosophy's task." History and philosophy were not really autonomous disciplines with different "objects," that is, the particular and the universal, but different approaches to the same object – the totality of existence. Moreover, Ranke rejected the validity of the philosophical approach as long as it was defined as a movement from the ideal to the real, from thought to being, as long as it did not conform to the historical movement from the individuality of existence to the unity and progressive totality of being. Genuine philosophy was thus identified with the historical approach to knowledge.[96]

Ranke's tendency in the 1830s to absorb philosophy's claims to absolute knowledge into the totalizing project of historical knowledge was connected to his growing confidence that the historian could empirically discern an actual spiritual unity in the sequence of historical events. The issue of historical progress had been a major point of contestation in Ranke's defense of the autonomy of history against the speculative idealist deduction of necessary, progressive historical stages from a priori principles. But Ranke's persistent critiques of such philosophies of history during the 1830s were always matched by articulations of his own concept of historical progress. In 1831, Ranke noted that the historian assigned special significance to the manner in which individual existences embodied "modifications" of a general spiritual life, because he could discern in the succession of such "spiritual configurations" an "immeasurable progress, in whose midst we still stand." The spiritual contents developed and modified in historical individualities were not merely emblems in the divine hieroglyph, but possessed an "indestructible influence" in "the stream of spiritual life."[97] A few years later Ranke defined this progress as a movement toward the self-conscious unity of the human race. The possibility of writing universal history, he claimed, was a result of the actual process whereby "the human spirit made itself into its own object and recognized itself," thus coming "to possess itself in its totality."[98] Although every age was not more advanced than its predecessor and each had its own tasks and perfections, he noted in 1836 that "a progress does become obvious from the unconscious to the conscious, from premonition to knowledge, from presumptive faith to knowledge, from nature to organized force."[99] By the end of the decade, he was ready to claim that

[96] *Ibid.*, pp. 76–83. [97] *Ibid.*, p. 85.

[98] "Geschichte des Mittelalters" (1836), *Aus Werk und Nachlass*, vol. 4, p. 119.

[99] "Deutsche Geschichte" (1836), *Aus Werk und Nachlass*, vol. 4, p. 132.

the unity of history as "a realm of spiritual existence engaged in constant self-progression" was "objective" and discernable through the "sober" and "simple" procedures of empirical research.[100]

Ranke's newfound confidence in the ability of historical knowledge to grasp human existence in its progressive totality was based on the incorporation of the transcendent dimension of the philosophical task – the comprehension of the ground of human freedom in an eternal moral order ruled by a transcendent divine father – into the project of historical knowledge. This incorporation had two aspects. It was expressed in the expansion of his theory of ideas to include not only the divine essence immanent in the particulars of historical appearance, but also the explicit transcendent ideas that entered the historical process as the empirically observable religious convictions, ethical ideals, and sociopolitical ideologies of concrete individuals and groups. In tracing the fate of the Christian idea in the *Paepste*, Ranke noted:

> Our European commonwealth has, however, at no time been subjected to the dominion of pure force; in all periods it has been imbued with ideas. No enterprise of importance can succeed, no power rise to universal influence, without immediately suggesting to the minds of men the ideal of a universal order that had to be implemented. From this point proceed theories. These reproduce the moral import and significance of the facts, which are then presented in the light of a universal and effectual truth as deduced from reason or religion, and, as a result, arrived at by reflection. They thus anticipate, as it were, the completion of the event, which at the same time they most effectually promote.[101]

By tracing the emergence, diffusion, conflict, and transformation of religious and moral ideas and ideals, the historian could empirically discover how human words and deeds not only revealed a hidden unity grounded in a divinely implanted, innate essence, but also actually created a progressive self-conscious unity of their own.

However, Ranke was not willing to assert that mankind's ideas concerning its vertical relationship to a transcendent order found direct expression in a pattern of historical necessity. The transcendent ideas and the transcendent divine subject were not themselves actors in history. History was neither a revelation of the "becoming God" nor the necessary self-expression of the idea of an eternal moral order. The transcendent entered history through the medium of individual human choice and conviction, as the historical expression of human freedom. In the late 1840s, Ranke explicitly rejected Hegel's philosophy of history not only because it obliterated the reality of concrete appearances, but also because it denied the efficacy of "individual

[100] "Neueste Geschichte" (1839–40), *Aus Werk und Nachlass*, vol. 4, p. 133.

[101] *Die roemischen Paepste*, in *Werke*, vol. 38, p. 120.

human consciousness" as the real subject in the historical process.[102] Already in 1837 he had criticized his friend Heinrich Ritter for identifying "life" and "freedom." "Life," Ranke claimed, was the "infinite all-connecting agency" that associated cause and effect in "unbroken continuity." In contrast, freedom remained "individual, moral, self-determined, although only in rare moments also self-originating and self-creating."[103] In most eras, human freedom took the form of voluntary obedience and conformity to the inherited religious and moral ideas of a culture. But in those rare moments in which significant, progressive, spiritual change occurred, the power of human freedom would break into the historical conjuncture of the causal nexus of life and the inherited world of moral values and appear as "self-originating and self-creating" as it provided a new direction for mankind's spiritual progress.

The narrative of Ranke's *Deutsche Geschichte* was organized around just such conjunctures, or "moments." Most of these moments remained moments of unfulfilled possibility because of the failure of a decisive moral will to grasp the conjuncture of political life and religious conviction and act upon it. At the center of the work, however, was the epochal moment in which Luther's religious and moral conviction combined with the development of the national genius and the inherited Christian idea to produce a significant progressive movement in the spiritual evolution of humanity. In the fourth volume of the *Deutsche Geschichte*, published in 1843, Ranke reflected on the historical conceptualization that informed his narrative:

> From the distance of the centuries we can perceive the great combinations that are inherent in things; the individual action in every individual present, however, cannot depend on them. Here it is a matter of the correct handling of what is immediately given, on the good cause that one represents, on the moral force one can exert. The moments that condition the progress of world history are, I would like to say, a divine secret. The value of man is grounded in his self-determination and activity.[104]

These words had obvious contemporary relevance. For Ranke, 1840 was a moment of epochal historical possibility. But the actualization of this possibility required a decisive intervention by a morally committed autonomous will, which would give a progressive impetus to both national life and the Christian idea. In a sense Ranke affirmed that the moral human subject was the creator of his own history, but acts of self-creation could only occur if

[102] "Neuere Geschichte" (1847), *Aus Werk und Nachlass*, vol. 4, pp. 187–88.

[103] Ranke to Heinrich Ritter, April 1837, *Briefwerk*, p. 285.

[104] Ranke, *Deutsche Geschichte*, vol. 4, p. 64. This is the content that found representation in the dramatic style that Peter Gay has described as characteristic of Ranke's mature historical prose in his *Style in History* (New York: 1974), pp. 59–67.

they conformed to the objective foundations of human freedom in both the irrational, maternal ground of natural being and the transcendent, spiritual ground of divine paternal authority. The human subject could exert its will as a free creator, as a maker of history, only by conforming to the restrictions imposed by its status as a creation produced in history.

After the completion of the *Deutsche Geschichte* in 1843, Ranke turned his attention, after brief consideration of the possibility of writing a history of the French Revolution, to what appeared to be the more restricted field of Prussian history. His choice of project expressed, in part, his felt obligation to fulfill the expectations of his new position as the official historiographer of the Prussian state and devote himself to patriotic (*vaterlaendischen*) history.[105] But he also insisted that the history of the formation of the Prussian state and its rise to Great Power status in the eighteenth century was a continuation of his *Deutsche Geschichte*, and even that the *Deutsche Geschichte* could be read as the first part of a history of Prussia, since the foundations of the system that was later developed and defended by the Hohenzollern dynasty were established during the German Reformation.[106] Ranke's contemporaries, like Grimm, and even his patron Frederick William IV, were not able to discern these continuities as clearly as Ranke himself. Ranke's *Neun Buecher Preussischer Geschichte* (*Nine Books of Prussian History*) did not portray the Prussian state in any clear and obvious way as the instrument of the German–Protestant idea or as the historical vanguard and embodiment of the idea of German ethno-linguistic culture. Instead, Ranke seemed to justify a relentlessly narrow focus on political self-aggrandizement that instrumentalised both cultural nationality and religion in the pursuit of territorial autonomy and dynastic power. Ranke's paradoxical claim, however, was that it was precisely the single-minded, self-interested pursuit of political power and state autonomy, and thus the emancipation from Old German imperial and Protestant confessional restrictions, that made possible the full participation of the German Protestant idea within the self-regulating system of Great Powers that defined the identity of Europe and Western Christendom in the modern age.

The spontaneous development of the inherent powers of the ethnic "people" in the formation of a national state virtually disappeared in Ranke's *Prussian History*. The people were relegated to the role of a kind of natural material, an exploitable resource for the mobilizing, disciplining, organizing activity of the state. It was obvious, Ranke insisted, that Prussia was not a "commonwealth [*Gemeinwesen*], in which human faculties could unfold themselves as nature and inclination prompted. Everything emanated from the supreme power, which had first determined the end, and then prescribed

[105] Ranke to Sayn-Wittgenstein, Stolberg-Wernigerode, and Buelow, February 23, 1843, *Neue Briefe*, p. 308.

[106] Ranke to Frederick Wilhelm IV, April 23, 1843, *Neue Briefe*, p. 296.

the means, according to its own judgment and will."[107] But since this activity aimed at the independence of the political community, and since such autonomy was the condition for the full development of the national idea implicit in the ethnic "natural" powers and material, it made possible the autonomy of a people subjected to the power of the state. "The strict discipline and subjection in which the people was held," he asserted, "cannot be considered as oppressive, for all were fully aware of its purpose. We cannot call a man a slave [*Unfreien*] who loves the power which he renders possible only by yielding the strictest obedience and which affords him a position independent of foreign influences [*Weltkraefte*]."[108] The authoritarian mobilization of populations into a sovereign power that could assert its independence as an equal player in the system of Great Powers was not a subjection of one group of individuals to another, but the formation of a public subject in whose struggle for autonomy all could participate. The priority Ranke gave to this public power of the state was also evident in his affirmation of the devolution of the old imperial constitution into a dualism between the two German states of Austria and Prussia, which represented the German idea as public power in different ways. In fact Ranke described the conflict between Frederick the Great of Prussia and Maria Theresa of Austria in the 1740s as emerging from two cultural worlds that had "nothing in common," that originated in "different perceptions, different views, sprang from totally different soil."[109] The Austrian state carried the older German imperial idea and the ancient supremacy of Catholic Christianity into the modern system of Great Powers, while Prussia was driven by the mission of establishing the German Protestant idea within the form of state autonomy, and in this sense represented for Ranke a progressive, activist, "aspiring" component of German consciousness and power. In both cases political identifications seem to subsume ethno-linguistic identifications, although Ranke clearly also suggested that this conflicting and complementary dualism of Great Powers within the German cultural sphere was the appropriate path for the German cultural idea (that encompassed this dualism) to find its entry into world politics and world history.

The relationship between religion and politics was also somewhat problematic in Ranke's *Prussian History*. Although one of the historical justifications for Prussia's pursuit of Great Power status was the entry of the Protestant idea into the system of world politics, this Protestant idea had

[107] Leopold Ranke, *Memoirs of the House of Brandenburg, and History of Prussia During the Seventeenth and Eighteenth Centuries*, trans. Alexander and Lady Duff Gordon (reprint of the 1849 edition, 3 vols.; New York: 1969). vol. 1, p. 466. This is a translation of the first (1847) edition of *Neun Buecher preussischer Geschichte*. Ranke later expanded this work but retained most of his original prose within the expanded editions. I will cite corresponding passages from Leopold Von Ranke, *Preussische Geschichte*, ed. Willy Andreas (2 vols.; Wiesbaden/Berlin: 1957), vol. 1, p. 520.

[108] Ranke, *Memoir*, vol. 2, p. 75; *Preussische Geschichte*, vol. 2, 40.

[109] *Memoir*, vol. 2, pp. 186–87; *Preussische Geschichte*, vol. 2, p. 92.

to be transformed for Prussia to attain Great Power status. First, achievement of political autonomy demanded that the confessional divisions be diluted and mitigated. A Great Power, Ranke insisted, could not "depend exclusively upon a single confession of faith"; confessional tolerance and Christian ecumenicism were conditions for mobilizing peoples into large political communities.[110] But transcendence of confessional difference was also a condition for the progressive perfection of the Christian idea: "The Christian religion is eternally striving to become universal . . . the clear and simple views of life inherent in it must always in the end destroy all artificial systems."[111] The rulers of Prussia in the eighteenth century found the foundations of the moral will needed to discipline their country into a unified, autonomous state through their connection to the universalization of Christian values in the northern German Protestant Enlightenment. Thus, Frederick the Great was able to sustain his mission to make Prussia a Great Power because he attached himself to the progressive ideas of public rationality and autonomy associated with the Enlightenment.[112] It was only by transcending its connections to a "positive creed," Ranke insisted, that the "Protestant world" was able to "assert its rights" in the realm of modern politics and operate as the ecumenical ethos of the autonomous state.[113] In Ranke's account, therefore, Frederick the Great virtually took on the role of a religious reformer à la Luther in Prussian history. As an historical actor, he found the resources to achieve his mission in a transformation of Lutheran Protestantism into a more universalistic, purified form of Christian belief. Ranke himself seemed a bit taken aback by his attempts to justify the anticlericalism and rational deism of the Enlightenment as the appropriate religious form for the Protestant principle in the eighteenth century. The complete negation of the "positive" doctrinal and symbolic elements in Christianity, he noted, could not ultimately be sustained and led to the religious revivals of the nineteenth century. But he expressed dismay at the reemergence of "sectarian hostilities" within this revival of positive religiosity. He called for new forms of an ecumenical Christianity appropriate to the modern age: "That which is imperatively called for by the actual state of things is the development of the positive forms and doctrines into a system which should include all parties – and in the meantime a mutual recognition, on the part of all, of the truth contained in each."[114]

The emergence of the institutions of the modern state and the transformations of the Protestant idea were certainly thematic elements in the *Prussian History*, but they did not constitute its narrative core. They

[110] *Memoir*, vol. 1, p. 222; *Preussische Geschichte*, vol. 1, p. 442.

[111] *Memoir*, vol. 2, p. 11; *Preussische Geschichte*, vol. 2, p. 13.

[112] *Memoir*, vol. 3, pp. 453–54; *Preussische Geschichte*, vol. 2, pp. 406–7.

[113] *Memoir*, vol. 3, pp. 465–66; *Preussische Geschichte*, vol. 2, p. 412.

[114] *Memoir*, vol. 2, p. 12; *Preussische Geschichte*, vol. 2, p. 14.

remained conditions that framed the personal decisions and actions of the Hohenzollern monarchs, especially Frederick the Great. The story Ranke wanted to tell was a story of the insertion of a resolute, decisive will into a clearly perceived frame of circumstantial limitations. Again and again, Ranke paused at the moments at which Frederick the Great had to focus and gather his moral energies, objectively analyze the information available to him without distraction by the pressures around him, discern the possibilities and probabilities in any situation, and then act. These contingent decisions and actions, emerging from a personal resolve that asserted itself as an autonomous force within the historically given, ultimately determined the course of events.[115] Frederick the Great and the other Hohenzollern rulers were not free to direct the course of history in any way they chose. Ranke's skill at reconstructing past historical "worlds" were on display in his attempts to recreate the conditions and limitations in which decisions were made. Frederick succeeded in achieving Great Power status for Prussia because he grasped the significance of the state-building institutions created by his predecessors and because he shaped his own political ethos according to the Enlightened Protestant ideas of his age. What made Frederick the Great historical, however, was not his role as representative, symbol, or spokesperson of these larger tendencies and ideas, but his ability to grasp his own historicity and act within it. In order to take on the heroic role of an historical creator, Frederick needed to both break with his father and assume the obligations and conditions his father bequeathed to him. In order to maintain and preserve the traditions of the past, he needed to build upon them, adapt and transform them in new situations.[116] In Ranke's narrative, to define one's own identity as an historical identity was both to recognize the framing conditions of personal actions in the birthright passed on from mother and father and to break away from maternal and paternal dependencies through the insertion of personal will into the historical conjuncture that was one's given fate. Historical consciousness did not simply unveil a narrative into which one could insert oneself, but opened up a field of possibility in which one was asked to produce one's own story. Perhaps it was this dimension of becoming historical that made Frederick William IV uncomfortable in his first reading of his official historiographer's history of his forefathers. Not only did Ranke provide an historical account of the cultural conditions of historical action that were far more political and secular than the king wanted to imagine, but he also insisted that the king himself could fully take on his proper role, not by mimicking roles presented to him by historically imagined pasts, but by acting decisively and with a full sense of his own responsibility in the present. As many of Ranke's contemporary and later critics have pointed out, Ranke's alleged

[115] *Memoir*, vol. 3, pp. 451–67; *Preussische Geschichte*, vol. 2, pp. 406–13.

[116] Memoir, vol. 3, p. 462; *Preussische Geschichte*, vol. 2, 410–11.

"objective" reconstruction of the "given" historical conditions that framed human action at any moment was tendentiously, conservatively framed to justify some actions and not others. In his reconstruction of the past, Ranke often seemed simply to affirm that what occurred was what should have occurred, that successful actions were rational actions, that power-enhancing achievements were ethical achievements. For the readers of Ranke's own present, however, his narrative presented a lesson of obligation and choice. Historical knowledge of how the self was constituted as an historical subject, a knowledge of itself as "object," was a necessary condition for becoming truly historical. But one needed to risk oneself, on the basis of personal belief in a transcendent reality, in order to become a constituting historical subject, and thus actualize the father's will in the world.

Antiphilosophical Epilogue: Historicizing Identity in Kierkegaard and Marx, 1841–1846

THE QUESTION OF HISTORICAL EXISTENCE IN EARLY MARX AND KIERKEGAARD

The individual intellectual itineraries of Soren Kierkegaard and Karl Marx, from their university education during the 1830s through to their monumental articulations of distinctive forms of historical selfhood in *Concluding Unscientific Postscript* and *The German Ideology* in 1846, have usually been conceptualized in terms of an increasingly radical critique of Hegelian philosophy. Both had undergone personal crises during their university years (Kierkegaard in 1835, Marx in 1837) in which they had become severely disillusioned with self-conceptions shaped by late-Romantic forms of irony that had left them without a clear orientation for integrating their subjective consciousness of the infinite freedom of self-making with the real conditions of individual experience in the world, conditions that included the need to choose a consistent self-orientation and cultural vocation that could be accommodated to existing historical possibilities.[1] For both, these "identity crises" of the 1830s led to a tentative, reluctant acceptance of culturally dominant forms of Hegelian philosophy as viable self-understandings and guides for living meaningful lives. Becoming Hegelian was conceived as a coming to terms with reality, as a decision to frame one's personal identity in accommodation to the historically given cultural world.

Already in doctoral dissertations completed within a few months of each other in the spring and summer of 1841, however, Kierkegaard and Marx expressed serious doubts about Hegel's ability to provide a persuasive

[1] Marx's crisis is extensively described in the lengthy letter from Berlin to his father in Trier of November 10–11, 1837: Karl Marx and Frederick Engels, *Collected Works* (47 vols. thus far; New York,1975–), vol. 1, pp. 10–21. The beginnings of Kierkegaard's personal crisis and its relationship to Hegelianism is presented in a letter to a friend Peter Lund and diary entries from the summer of 1835. In later years he judged his own position until the time of the completion of his dissertation as that of a "Hegelian fool." See Soren Kierkegaard, *The Concept of Irony with Continual Reference to Socrates, Together with Notes on Schelling's Berlin Lectures*, trans. Howard V. Hong and Edna H. Hong, with introduction and notes (Princeton, N.J.: 1989), p. 453. See also Soren Kierkegaard, *Letters and Documents* (Princeton, N.J.: 1978), pp. 41ff; Neils Thustrup, *Kierkegaard's Relationship to Hegel*, trans. George L. Stengren (Princeton, N.J.: 1980); Henning Fenger, *Kierkegaard: The Myths and Their Origins*, transl. George C. Schoolfield (New Haven: 1980).

meaning for their own life experiences. The Hegelian claim to infuse the historically actual with subjective meaning had itself become "abstract," requiring "actualization."[2] By 1845 this critique, which was shared by many of their contemporaries, had evolved into a principled opposition grounded in what had remained invisible within the Hegelian system of conceptual abstraction – the reality of individual existence. The preconscious, prelinguistic, and thus prerational dimension of existence, the sheer "that" of existence, which always preceded the meaning of existence articulated in discursive relations, was presented as the ground and origin of all that could be said and known.

On the rare occasions when Kierkegaard and Marx have been analyzed comparatively, emphasis has been placed on the contrasting dimensions in their analytic of existence; the individual inwardness of ethical self-choice in Kierkegaard and the external objectification of self-activity in the social practice of material production (labor) in Marx.[3] The focus of this concluding epilogue, however, is on common elements in the distinctively historical conceptions of selfhood, or subjectivity, that emerged in the works of Kierkegaard and Marx in the mid-1840s. From this thematic perspective the late Romantic historicism of the Prussian Historical School and its philosophical mentor Schelling emerges as a significant historical context for their theoretical innovations. Both Marx and Kierkegaard objected strenuously to the speculative metaphysical form of Schelling's critique of Hegel and expressed dismay at the cultural implications and functions of Schelling's method of affirming the priority of existence over self-consciousness in the definition of historical selfhood. But they also followed Schelling's lead, and the lead of the Historical School more generally, in defining the organizing problematic of their own historical and theoretical task. This task, I suggest, was to construct a convincing theory of self-identity as historical to its very core.

There were three general dimensions to this project of producing a self-conscious historical identity. First, both Marx and Kierkegaard assumed, as a self-evident premise of their analysis of historical selfhood, certain specific grounds of self-identity in the preconscious, prehistorical, unmediated reality of human existence. Second, they struggled to describe the ways in which meaningful historical self-identities emerged from this ground of existing being and attained the status of an objective reality in which individual human beings lived out their historical existences. Marx and Kierkegaard were especially concerned with how the contingent, historically specific

[2] Kierkegaard, *Concept of Irony*, pp. 328–29; Marx, "Difference Between the Democritean and the Epicurean Philosophy of Nature" (1841), *Collected Works*, vol. 1, pp. 84–86 (MEGA, vol. 1, part 1, 67–69).

[3] Karl Loewith's *Von Hegel zu Nietzsche: Der revolutionaere Bruch im Denken des neunzehnten Jahrhunderts* (Zurich: 1941) set the paradigm for summary comments along these lines.

identity of the autonomous individual self in bourgeois society had come to be experienced as the necessary, "natural" fate of human beings in the present. Finally, both were concerned with how consciousness of the historical constitution of self-identity could become the foundation for a new relationship to the prehistorical conditions of all identifications and an affirmation of the self as self-determining or self-constituting. By analyzing the historically constituted selfhood of their own time in relation to the existential ground that was its ultimate condition, Marx and Kierkegaard hoped to infuse the constituted subjects of history with a consciousness of how they had been constituted, thus opening the historical horizon for the emergence of a self that affirmed itself as a self-constituting subject not in thought alone, but in existence, and not in denial of the conditions of its freedom but in constant self-conscious awareness of those conditions. In this sense, Marx and Kierkegaard not only manifested the tensions within what Foucault called the empirico-transcendental doublet[4] that framed the meaning of self-identity in the modern historical concept of self, but also conceived a potential solution to those tensions that would continue to haunt the inheritors of their intellectual legacy, Foucault included, up to the present.

THE ORIGINS OF HISTORICAL SELFHOOD: HUMAN EXISTENCE AS DESIRE AND LABOR

Marx and Kierkegaard both rejected the Romantic-Idealist concept of historical development as a necessary unfolding of some prior metaphysical essence. History began with an act that transformed unconscious life forces into an object of consciousness and will, and thus instigated the splitting and striving that defined human existence as historical. But both also imagined the prehistorical as implicitly possessing the potentialities of historical existence. The life forces that became the object of will and consciousness in the first historical act also contained within themselves the agent of historical self-determination.

In 1843 (*Either/Or*) and in 1844 (*The Concept of Anxiety*), Kierkegaard provided extended descriptions of the prehistorical moment of human existence in terms of the dynamics of desire. Desire was defined as the psychic dimension in the psychical – physical synthesis that constituted the "sheer immediacy" of unconscious life.[5] Kierkegaard was especially concerned with how desire came to define itself as desire in relation to the physical – both as physical desire and as desire for the physical object. Such specificity emerged from a state of "dreaming desire," in which desire existed

[4] Michel Foucault, *The Order of Things: An Archaeology of the Human Sciences* (New York: 1970), part 2, chapter 9.

[5] *Either/Or* (2 vols.; Garden City, N.Y.: 1959), vol. 1, p. 73.

only as an unclarified "presentiment of itself," a neutral, androgynous state in which subject and object were without gender designation or clear boundaries.[6] In a famous passage in *Either/Or*, Kierkegaard used Mozart's Don Giovanni as the archetypal aesthetic exemplar of the emergence of desire as an amoral unconscious life force that defines itself as desire for sensuous gratification, as male sexual desire for the feminine object, but does not recognize this definition as a choice of itself.[7] Don Giovanni remains a representation of unconscious, prehistorical existence in the sense that his definition of the unity of the psychic and the physical as a unity of physical desire excludes the element of responsible, conscious choice, or "spirit."

In *The Concept of Anxiety*, Kierkegaard reexamined the immediacy of unconscious desire from the perspective of the excluded spiritual subject. In this context the state of unconscious desire was defined as a state of anxiety in which the potentiality for choosing one's own self and thus taking on the burden of guilt and the responsibility of freedom is contained in the vague, dreaming desire for a nothing beyond oneself, a nothing of boundless possibility that is a premonition of the exhilaration and terror present in the freedom of self-choice.[8] What is articulated in the dreaming self of unconscious desire is thus desire as spirit, or desire directed toward the self's potentiality to choose itself as a free subject. Acting perversely by choosing to define itself as physical desire determined by its object, the unconscious self expresses its freedom in the act of denying its own freedom. History begins with an act (the Fall) that changes innocence into guilt and ignorance into knowledge. Kierkegaard claimed that this beginning was synonymous with the act that defined the human self as sexually differentiated. Gender was a choice of self, not an expression of a preexisting, natural sexual difference, and its result was a sexual definition of the relationship between the psychical and the physical. Henceforth, sexual identity set the parameters of self-actualization.[9] Through "propagation," the original choice became the context of all subsequent individual choices. Human beings were heirs of the original sinful act of self-choice even though each individual had to repeat that original act of choosing himself as a sexually defined being in order to become a member of the human race. The choice that inaugurated history remained a choice that every individual made in order to enter history, or to become historical. Historical cultural communities were defined for Kierkegaard by the ways in which they related desire to human identity and organized ethnic communities around the task of disciplining the sexual individual to ensure the propagation of the race. The problem facing historical cultures was to find a way to transform ethnic, or "racial," communities into ethical communities in which individuals freely chose

[6] *Ibid.*, pp. 74–77. [7] *Ibid.*, pp. 83–102. [8] *Concept of Anxiety*, pp. 41–42. [9] *Ibid.*, p. 49.

themselves as members of an association of individuals possessing the same freedom and responsibility as themselves.[10]

One might expect that Marx would approach the question of the prereflective beginnings of history very differently than Kierkegaard, considering their radically different views of the social and religious dimensions in human experience and the different kinds of texts (art and theology on the one hand, political economy and social philosophy on the other) that they used to ground their interpretations. Like Kierkegaard, however, Marx was concerned with describing the prehistorical state of sensuous human existence in such a way that the potentialities of historical selfhood were contained within it, yet not determined by it. In both cases a contingent historical act made actual the possibility of historical selfhood. Marx's analyses, articulated in a series of dense, mostly unpublished manuscripts between 1844 and 1846, were constructed around two commitments. First, he strongly affirmed Feuerbach's claim that human existence in history could be grasped only once it was recognized that human beings were not contingently but essentially sensuous corporeal beings, that only a "consistent naturalism" was "capable of comprehending the action of world history." Human history was to be understood as a reflexive process within nature in which human beings produced their own objective "natures" through a self-transcending activity that changed natural being into a "being for itself." History was the "true natural history of man."[11] Second, Marx became convinced that the defining characteristic of human existence as lived in the present was not, as Feuerbach had suggested, the reciprocal relation of erotic desire but the social process of production. The life process that defined existence as human existence was manifested in the activity whereby the vital powers of sensuous being actualized themselves in the production of objects, thus making possible the self-reflexivity that gave human beings the opportunity to make their nature an object of their own historical activity. Again and again in 1845–46, Marx insisted that it was only when the life process of human beings was recognized as the production of objects that shaped nature outside of man into the forms of the creative energies existing within man that the transformation of man as a part of nature into man as that distinctive part of nature that possessed the ability to turn itself into its own historical creation could be understood. In the act of production, existing human beings differentiated themselves from the rest of nature by transforming their merely "physical life process" into an "historical life process"[12]

Marx summarized the historical dynamics implicit in the original act of production in the concept of the division of labor. The "natural" division

[10] *Ibid.*, pp. 28–29.

[11] "Economic and Philosophic Manuscripts of 1844," *Collected Works*, vol. 3, pp. 336, 337 (MEGA vol. 1, part 2, pp. 408, 409).

[12] "The German Ideology," *Collected Works*, vol. 5, p. 36 (*Werke*, vol. 3, p. 26).

of labor in the physical act of reproduction and in the differentiation of tasks based on differences in physical attributes became a historically objective and conscious division of labor with the division between mental and material labor. Prior to this division, language and consciousness were merely expressive of actual states of being. Even social consciousness presented itself as the immediate identification of individual existence with the existences of others in a "herd consciousness" hardly distinguishable from the instinctually determined groupings of animals. The division of the production of words and thoughts from the production of other material objects made possible a common consciousness of the relations of mutual interdependence among producers as a whole, while it simultaneously created a potential split between thoughts and reality, between the consciousness of human existence as historical social existence and the individual material practices of this historical existence within the division of productive labor. This split, however, could only arise from contradictions within productive existence itself. It was the division of labor in production that marked the fall from natural unity into an historical existence in which human beings' potential existence as free and mutually interdependent producers of their own nature was transformed into the ignorance and suffering of a divided, passive subordination to historical necessity. The liberation from physical nature was transformed into enslavement to the self-created second nature of historical existence.

For both Kierkegaard and Marx, descriptions of the structure of prehistorical human existence provided a foundation for examining the present historical moment as a repression and denial of the potentialities contained in the "reality" of human existence as historical existence. The freedom of self-constitution implicit in human existence had not been fully actualized; it had not been recognized and transformed into the self-conscious object of human activity. The free organization and direction of human life activity as desire or labor was stifled by the "alienation" of this freedom and the subordination of human existence to "necessary" determinations by the forces created through its original acts of self-production. Empirical individuals in the historical past and in the present lived the alien lives of human identities that were already given to them as historically constituted and "naturally" determined. If history's origins contained the promise of self-constitution, history's development up to the present manifested only constituted selves.

THE REFLECTIVE EGO AS A CONSTITUTED SELF AND A DENIAL OF HISTORICAL SELFHOOD

Both Marx and Kierkegaard presented their visions of authentic historical selfhood in the context of a sweeping critique of how selfhood was actually lived in postrevolutionary Western European culture. At the very center of the reflective ego they described as the dominant form of contemporary historical existence was the denial of the historical nature of selfhood. The contemporary self of bourgeois society was "estranged" from its potential actuality as an historical self, or in a state of "despair" because of a failure to recognize and actualize what it could be. Contemporary selfhood was lived as a necessity imposed by the inexorable forces of nature and history. The task of the cultural critic was to reveal that the ahistorical self was itself a historically constituted form of existence. Such self-recognition, however, could not come from outside history; its conditions would have to emerge from the practices of the reflective ego itself. The human practices that produced and reproduced this ego were entangled in contradictions that would eventually lead to a crisis of estrangement or despair in which the self would be confronted with the choice of itself as self-constituting and historical.

Kierkegaard presented his analysis of contemporary existence through an empathetic "internal" reconstruction of a complex variety of individual lifestyles within the broad category of what he called the "aesthetic" mode of existence.[13] Central to this mode of self-definition was the identification of the individual ego through its relations to particular others. Such self-defining relations to others centered on sensual gratification and the production of increasingly refined psychic states of "enjoyment." Kierkegaard focused his descriptions on the developed form of this stance in the discriminating consciousness and instrumental strategies of the ego, or "reflection."[14] In the aesthetic "stage," the self was not grounded within itself, but derived its reality from objects in the world toward which its strategies of gratification were directed. The potential objects of gratification were continually in flux, and no single object could provide more than temporary enjoyment. As a result, the reflective ego oscillated restlessly among different interests without a sustained, consistent project grounded in its own values.[15]

[13] Aside from the first volume of *Either/Or*, which presents the aesthetic through the mind of the poet "A" as well as "A's" projection of the inner logic of his own life existence lived as a kind of ideal type in "*The Diary of Johannes the Seducer*," the main representatives of the aesthetic in the pseudonymous writings are Constantine Constantius, the experimental psychologist of *Repetition* (1843), and William Afham, the expert in strategies for distancing experience as recollection in *Stages on Life's Way* (1845).

[14] In *Either/Or* the extreme, ultimate form of the aesthetic is represented by the book-length diary of Johannes the Seducer, for whom the enjoyment in controlling others through the management of his own personae transcends any desire for merely sensual gratification, and who devotes himself completely to the refinement of complex strategies for increasing his own enjoyment by manipulating others to surrender themselves to his power, and thus place the highest possible value on his ego.

[15] See especially A's essay on the "Rotation Method" as a means of defending the self against boredom, a constant threat to the aesthetic self because of its inherent connection to the "nothingness which pervades reality": *Either/Or*, vol. 1, pp. 280–96.

Although the self of reflective aestheticism was oriented outwardly, Kierkegaard described it as essentially narcissistic. The point of the strategic manipulations of the reflective ego was always to transform the other into an object for itself, into an occasion for self-gratification. The reflective ego was epitomized by the self-absorbed, obsessively manipulative seducer who ordered his whole life around elaborately planned performances that affirmed his power to always treat the "other" as an "other" for himself, and protected his own self from becoming an "other" for someone else. Although the reflective ego could operate with incredibly refined skill to discriminate the various objects in the world and the possible types of gratification they might provide, it was ultimately indifferent to real difference. Objects could replace each other "arbitrarily"[16] according to their quantifiable cash value for producing interesting and enjoyable psychic states. Underneath the constant, restless quest for novelty there remained a fundamental boredom, passivity, and indifference grounded in the pervasive meaninglessness of all such activity.[17]

In the world of the reflective ego, linguistic representation and conceptual thinking gained paramount significance because of their ability to transform the other into an object for the ego's manipulation and enjoyment. Conceptual thinking transformed the actualities of existence into abstract possibilities of existence. Language manipulated these possibilities in shaping interpretations of reality aimed at producing states of psychic well-being. The reflective ego of Kierkegaard's aesthetic stage was an artist, transforming everything outside of the ego into material for the creation of imaginary forms of life.[18] In Kierkegaard's descriptions, the reflective aesthete gained more psychic satisfaction from the mental recollection of events than from the events themselves, more delight from the castles of words that allowed him to shape the world into his own, controlled forms than from the actuality that the words denoted or expressed.

The strategies deployed by the reflective ego to attain psychic equilibrium were, in Kierkegaard's view, strategies for repressing the abyss of nothingness that characterized the essentially empty self, and the vertigo that emerged as soon as the self began to sense that it was free to choose not only among various strategies and objects of gratification but also to choose itself as a self-constituting agent. Despite the noncommittal "lightness" it displayed in its relation to the world, the reflective ego suffered from the psychic "heaviness" of melancholy.[19] The immanent trajectory of the reflective ego's strategies created a malaise and ultimate despair that placed the self in a position where it could finally recognize its own existence not as a given

[16] *Either/Or*, vol. 1, p. 295. [17] *Ibid.*, pp. 28, 35.

[18] Both "A" and Johannes are described as poets who extend their literary goals to the aesthetic construction of their own personae. *Either/Or*, vol. 1, pp. 19, 300–1.

[19] *Either/Or*, vol. 1, p. 28.

necessity, but as a specifically chosen way of living its natural and historical conditions.

In Kierkegaard's major writings of the early and mid-1840s, the aesthetic mode of existence was constantly connected to "the age," or historical culture, that made it possible. In a lengthy review essay published in 1846 ("Two Ages"), Kierkegaard attempted to give systematic form to his assessment of the culture of a "spiritless" age in which human existence as reflective egoism was so persistently reproduced. He framed his analysis within a contrast of the contemporary age of reflection to the revolutionary period of the turn of the century. In this earlier, but relatively recent, age, individuals shaped their lives according to passionately held, absolute commitments to values like freedom, equality, and solidarity. Consistent identities, or "characters," emerged from such value choices as they were engraved on individual existences through "repetitive" action in the world.[20] Tensions arose among individuals representing opposing value choices, just as solidarity arose through parallel individual commitments to the same values. In the current age of reflection, such character-forming values had been transformed into representations of value produced in exchange. Individuals related to each other not as selves inwardly determined by the values they had chosen, but through forms of "self-advertisement" that had been constructed to raise the individual's value in the perceptions of others. Such representations did not shape character but objectified a certain shape of life for public consumption. The individual remained a spectator of his "advertised" public self, whose determinations were always open to negotiation in response to the social value placed on them. Social relations became a competition among commodified identities. The assignment of relative monetary value to representations of self in a market society expressed the clear dissolution of difference between subjective agents into the sameness of exchangeable commodities.[21]

The dominating motive determining the reciprocal movement among individuals in a reflective culture was envy. Differentiated evaluations of self-representations produced both jealous emulation and the desire to undermine the validity of competing representations. Although individuals imagined themselves as strategic manipulators of their self-representations, they soon found themselves imprisoned within the system of reflection. Any act that tried to break out of the circle would immediately be assessed by others as a strategic move for individual advantage and subjected to an undermining cynicism. In this sense reflective egoism was not just a phenomenon that characterized individual persons, but also a system in which individuals were caught. "Reflection's envy holds the will and energy of the individual in a kind of captivity," Kierkegaard claimed. "The individual

[20] Soren Kierkegaard, *Two Ages: The Age of Revolution and the Present Age: A Literary Review*, eds. and trans. Howard V. Hong and Edna H. Hong (Princeton, N.J.: 1978), pp. 61–68.

[21] *Ibid.*, pp. 74–75.

must first of all break out of the prison in which his own reflection holds him, and if he succeeds, he still does not stand in the open but in the vast penitentiary built by the reflection of his associates, and to this he is again related through the reflection-relation to himself."[22] The individual was constructed in the reflection of others with the same power that in former ages individuals had been defined by the customary and legal constructions of estates.[23]

The proper name for the historical process that produced the age of reflective egoism in Kierkegaard's view was "leveling."[24] All individual worth was transformed into an abstract quantity, not through the political actions of defined rulers or leaders, but through the dispersed and anonymous power of social relations. As the "negative unity of the negative mutual reciprocity of individuals," leveling operated like an engulfing, irresistible natural force, transforming all distinction of character into exchangeable quantifiable values: "A demon that no individual can control is conjured up," Kierkegaard claimed, "and although the individual selfishly enjoys the abstraction during the brief moment of pleasure in the leveling, he is also underwriting his own downfall."[25]This process found its appropriately anonymous voice in the "public," in the discursive evaluation of individual worth through networks of social chatter epitomized by mass circulation newspapers. The constant linguistic interchange of the public sphere was the forum for leveling distinctions, eliminating dissent and stifling difference. The discourse of public opinion silenced the voices of any alternative life choices to reflective egoism and of the very possibility that the self could be chosen.

Did the collective process of leveling that imprisoned the individual in the self-reproducing patterns of reflective egoism contain contradictions that portended its own self-destruction? In 1846, Kierkegaard suggested that it might. First, the age of reflection opened up the scope of individual self-choice through its constantly expanding production of representations of possible lifestyles and shapes of existence. "But this extensity in turn may become the condition for a higher form." Kierkegaard suggested, "if a corresponding intensity takes over what is extensively at its disposal."[26] Moreover, the liberation of the self from the fixed natural and historical identities of the prerevolutionary period produced a consciousness of the individual as an abstract individual, an "empty" activity capable of giving itself a myriad of identities. Leveling abolished given distinctions and placed everyone as an equal and equally abstract human being into the flux of historical change. The historical constitution of selfhood as reflective egoism might lead to a boundary where a self-conscious choice of self was possible, but it could not actualize that choice. Any collective movement to change

[22] *Ibid.*, p. 81. [23] *Ibid.*, p. 85. [24] *Ibid.*, pp. 84–90. [25] *Ibid.*, p. 86. [26] *Ibid.*, p. 97.

the way in which individuals constructed their identities, however, was pointless: It merely reinforced the process of abstraction in which individuals surrendered their choice of self to the anonymous power of the group. The "principle of association" furthered the leveling process and merely prepared in a "negative" sense the possibility of genuine acts of self-constitution.[27]

Kierkegaard's dismissal of the "principle of association" as a merely negative factor in the crisis of his age would seem to place him in direct opposition to Marx. It is undeniable that Marx's consistent claim that concrete individual existence was at the same time social existence differentiated his position from Kierkegaard's, but his views can not simply be equated with the belief that the transcendence of the bourgeois ego could be achieved through the association of such egos in a collective movement. Moreover, Kierkegaard's concept of emancipation from the circle of reflective egoism, however inward and psychological its form, also involved recognition of how freedom was affirmed in the "positive" reciprocity among individuals who shared the affirmation of self-choice as the foundation of individual existence. There were, in fact, significant parallels in the development of Kierkegaard's and Marx's critique of the present as an era in which the self had been historically constituted as reflective egoism.

In 1842–43, Marx devoted much of his intellectual energy to an analysis of the way in which the emancipatory promise of the revolutionary era had been appropriated and institutionalized as the political legitimization of the atomized individualism of reflective egoism. The freedom of the liberal catechism was the freedom of the individual conceived as "an isolated monad, withdrawn into himself." The principles of equality and fraternity also never extended beyond the "egoistic man." The politics of the postrevolutionary liberal states simply assumed egoistic individuals as the "*passive* result of the dissolved society [of the old regime], a result that is simply *found in existence*, an object of *immediate certainty*, therefore a *natural* object."[28] In 1844–45, Marx sought to denaturalize this object, to reveal the way in which it emerged as the product of the relations among concrete individuals within a specific historical organization of the process of production.

Two distinctive aspects of Marx's concept of the historical constitution of selfhood in 1844–45 deserve emphasis. Although he highlighted the ways in which the division of labor and the separation of producers from their products created a fundamental class division, and thus produced radically different experiences of selfhood under capitalism, he did maintain that the general framework in which self-identity was defined was common to all individuals within this social formation. Both wage laborers and capitalists

[27] *Ibid.*, p. 106.

[28] Karl Marx, "On the Jewish Question," *Collected Works*, vol. 3, pp. 163, 166–67 (MEGA, vol. 1, part 2, pp. 158,161–62).

found their existence as individuals defined by the alienated objectifications of self-activity, and the value of their existence determined by the exchange relations among such objects. The worker as much as the capitalist was defined by the given social formation as an isolated ego, and forced to represent himself as an object for others in the relationship of "free" market exchange. The capitalist's self-worth was based on the accumulation of objectifications of human self-activity that constituted his wealth and power. All participants in the capitalist organization of production presented their identities as human beings to each other through the medium of objectified representations of self-worth, and all were dependent for the determination of their value as individuals on the system of market exchange that produced these values and expressed them through the quantitative criterion of money. The recognition of human existence as the historical activity of self-creation was universally absent. Individual egos were "spectators," to use Kierkegaard's terminology, of their social relations as relations among self-representations experienced as commodities.[29]

Second, Marx, like Kierkegaard, envisioned the production of historical identities as a process of expansion and intensification of market relations in which representations of self became completely disjoined from the historical specificity of the selves represented. As the objectifications of self-activity became less historically specific and more abstract, the self in turn became more abstract and "empty." The expansion of industrial capitalism and the market to global dimensions transformed the division of labor. All remnants of natural and cultural determination of roles and functions were dissolved by the corrosive powers of the market. The emancipation of the human life process as a universal productive capacity, as abstract labor, made the determination of specific identities dependent on shifts in market evaluations. Although the self was constantly forced to take on new shapes in order to conform to market demands, the self as producer was robbed of specific content. The ego became both empty and determined by forces outside of itself. Like Kierkegaard, Marx saw this as a potential expansion of the possibilities of freedom of self-choice and a condition for the recognition of the self as historical. But this potential could not be actualized within the capitalist system, where it existed merely as an abstract possibility. The ego could strategically manage its self-representation only within the terms of market exchange, an opaque, seemingly natural order that determined the fate of all choices. Individuals struggled with each other with envious competitiveness to make their representations of self-activity increase in relative value. In one passage in his unpublished 1844 manuscripts, Marx

[29] In a number of passages in the "Manuscripts," Marx promised an analysis of how the alienation of labor in the product of labor would effect the "nonworker" in the relations of production, but he never got beyond a few cryptic comments; cf. *Collected Works*, vol. 3, p. 282 (MEGA, vol. 1, part 2, p. 375).

echoed Kierkegaard in stating that this development ultimately "leveled" all differences as merely quantitative distinctions and produced social relations best described under the general category of "envy."[30]

The reflective ego of bourgeois society could not emancipate itself from the prison of its historically constituted identity simply through an inward act of self-reflection and self-recognition. This was the central message Marx presented in *The German Ideology*. Almost two-thirds of this six-hundred-page text was devoted to a demolition of a single book, Max Stirner's *Der Einzige und sein Eigentum* (The Single One and His Property), which had argued that the historical self-constituting subject could emerge through a reflexive recognition and affirmation of the ego's own activity as a contingent, corporeal, unique "myself." Both Marx and Engels were profoundly effected by the publication of Stirner's book in the late fall of 1844.[31] Stirner had engaged in his own demystifying critique of German ideology by analyzing all descriptions of the determination of self-identity by powers transcending the individual ego, such as God, state, and society, or love, reason, and labor, as self-deceiving illusions that the ego had constructed to avoid recognition of its own self-creating power. Marx analyzed and criticized the statements of *Der Einzige* with such exasperating thoroughness because he felt compelled to demonstrate that Stirner's stance was precisely the opposite of what it purported to be. Stirner's presentation of the life forms of the individual ego, the fluid unnamable "nothing" that was free to give itself whatever content it desired by interpreting the world as a field of its own enjoyment, was not, in Marx's view, a description of concrete human existence liberated from the historical necessities of constituted selfhoods, but an "artificial category" abstracted from the material conditions and social relations that defined the life form of actual historical individuals. Stirner had personified this abstraction as a transcendent being and presented it as a moral ideal. While Stirner battled against the linguistic fetishes to which the individual had subordinated his creative power and rebelled against the power of self-created "ghosts" in order to make a world of his own for his own self-enjoyment, in actuality he remained imprisoned and defined by the world of material determinations whose power he had claimed to dissolve. Stirner's self-sufficient "single one" was an illusory escape from an existence of impotence, servility, poverty, and insecurity. "Against his will and without knowing it," Stirner had constructed an appropriate therapeutic myth for the frustrations, resentments, and fears of the German *petty-bourgeoisie*, whose representations of self-sufficiency were being undermined by the development of industrial capitalism. In Stirner, Marx concluded, "the most trivial sentiments of the petty-bourgeois" were

30 *Collected Works*, vol. 3, p. 295 (MEGA, vol. 1, part 2, pp. 387–88).

31 See especially the long letter from Engels to Marx from November 19, 1844, in Marx/Engels, *Werke*, vol. 27, pp. 11–12.

dressed up in the "ideologically high-sounding expressions" of idealist philosophy.[32]

The point that Marx incessantly emphasized in his critique of Stirner's inflation of the reflective ego into a self-constituting agent was that Stirner ignored the constituted, historical nature of individual existence. All historical action did proceed from unique individuals, but these individuals were also produced by the actions of the generations that preceded them. The historically constituted nature of individual selfhood at any particular time was tied to the inherently social nature of individual existence. Sociability was not a product of the ego's subordination to universal ideals, but of the "egoistic" pursuit of its interests. Individuals' needs and the methods of satisfying those needs, and "consequently their nature," connected them with one another through "relations between the sexes, exchange, division of labor." Individuals entered into such intercourse with one another not as "pure egos" but "as individuals at a definite stage of development of their productive forces and requirements, and since this intercourse, in its turn, determined production and needs, it was precisely the personal, individual behavior of individuals, their behavior to one another as individuals, that created existing relations and daily reproduces them anew."[33] Like Kierkegaard, Marx thus insisted that the emergence of the self-constituting individual could only proceed from a full, disabused recognition that the self poised to make the leap into historical selfhood was itself historically given as a constituted historical form of human existence: "the history of a single individual cannot possibly be separated from the history of preceding or contemporary individuals, but is determined by this history."[34]

BECOMING HISTORICAL: THE "LEAP" AND "REVOLUTION" AS TRANSITIONS FROM CONSTITUTED TO CONSTITUTING SELFHOOD

For both Marx and Kierkegaard, the transformation of constituted self-identity into a self-constituting historical selfhood took the form of an historical act. This act was not conceived as a purely arbitrary act, as an act without conditions. At the same time, it was not simply a product of its natural and historical conditions. The emergence of the historical self was marked by a qualitative change in the way human existence was lived, a change that brought something new into the world. Both Marx and Kierkegaard expended a great deal of intellectual effort describing the historical conditions that prepared this act of self-constitution. At this juncture, however, a significant difference in their perspectives emerged. After 1844, Marx continued

[32] "German Ideology," pp. 240, 255 (*Werke*, vol. 3, pp. 223, 236).

[33] "German Ideology," p. 437 (*Werke*, vol. 3, p. 423).

[34] "German Ideology," p. 438 (*Werke*, vol. 3, p. 423).

to focus his analyses on a critical diagnosis of the historical conditions for the act of self-constitution and asserted with increasing conviction that the transformation of human existence would never come about through actions based on individual ethical commitments. Kierkegaard's writings, however, turned to an almost exclusive concern with the moment of actualization itself, a moment in which individual ethical choice and commitment played a central role. While Marx developed in increasingly rigorous detail his analysis of the capitalist mode of production and the forms of social intercourse that arose from it, Kierkegaard remained vague and cryptic in his analysis of the "external" historical conditions that might drive the reflective ego and its "aesthetic" mode of existence to the turning point of absolute despair. While Marx remained vague and cryptic concerning the structure of the revolutionary act that would bring about the actualization of historical selfhood and refused to elaborate on the precise nature of the state of collective self-making that would emerge from this act, or how it could be sustained as a way of life, Kierkegaard became increasingly specific and prolix in his description of the structure of the act of becoming historical and of the ways in which historical self-identity might be grounded and sustained.

Kierkegaard presented the moment of actualization in the first instance as a transition from the aesthetic to the ethical mode of existence through a radically personal and inward act of self-choice. In the second volume of *Either/Or*, the reflective egoism of "A" was confronted with the confident assertion of historical selfhood by "Magistrate William." The central category of William's mode of existence was "choice," not just the choosing between different representations of self in relation to the other, but the radical ethical choice of oneself as defined by the act of choosing. William referred to this as an "absolute choice," a choosing of oneself "in one's eternal validity."[35] The aesthetic mode of existence culminated in general despair due to the impossibility of finding oneself in the other; the first act in transcending this state was to choose oneself as this despair, to transform one's inner state from a product of relations to others, to a choice of oneself: "for despair itself is a choice... When a man despairs he chooses again, and what is he choosing? He chooses himself, not in his immediacy, not as this fortuitous individual, but he chooses himself in his eternal validity."[36]

To choose oneself as freedom was also to choose the self that one was, the "myself," as freely chosen. Even though the choice of self was made in an infinite and absolute sense, it remained a choice of this particular, finite, conditioned self. By choosing one's historical, concrete self in an act of freedom, something new came into existence, but at the same time what was "new" was the self that one already was. The choice did not create the self, but transformed the actual historical content of the old self into a

[35] *Either/Or*, vol. 2, p. 181. [36] *Ibid.*, p. 215.

new integrated form. Choosing oneself meant recognizing one's concrete existence in its "endless multiplicity" as a self with a specific history:

> The history is of various sorts; for in this history he stands in relation to other individuals of the race and to the race as a whole, and this history contains something painful, and yet he is the man he is only in consequences of this history. Therefore it takes courage for man to choose himself, for at the very time when it seems he isolates himself most thoroughly he is most thoroughly absorbed in the root by which he is connected to the whole.[37]

The act of self-choice was thus an act that accepted all actions that defined the self as a product of history within the new context that placed freedom at the center of self-identity. The categories of good and evil, innocence and guilt entered into the determination of the self as a self that was responsible for its historical identity. Choosing oneself was to assume a stance of "repentance" that made possible the acquisition of the self that was previously perceived as purely external, or repressed as incompatible with the representations of the reflective ego. To choose oneself absolutely was to recover one's past as one's own memory, to transform the succession of psychic states and arbitrary external relations into a continuous integral unity:

> For man's eternal dignity consists in the fact that he can have a history, the divine element in him consists in the fact that he himself, if he will, can impart to this history continuity, for this it acquires when it is not only the sum of all that has happened to me or befallen me, but is my work, in such a way that even what has befallen me is by me transformed and translated from necessity to freedom.[38]

In choosing oneself, one chose oneself with "these talents, these dispositions, these instincts, these passions, influenced by definite surroundings as this definite product of a definite environment." But by choosing oneself as a product, a person could "just as well be said to produce himself." As a product, the self was "pressed into the forms of reality," but in the act of choice it became "elastic, transforming all the outwardness into inwardness."[39]

The consequences of taking responsibility in this way for the meaning through which one's specific existence was actually lived had momentous consequences. The empty, decentered self became a centered self, its oscillation among possibilities was transformed into the focused pursuit of tasks; its isolation was changed to a consciousness of living in the universal (freedom) that encompassed all human beings within a positive reciprocity. The masks or represented identities that hid the self both from itself and others were stripped away and the self became transparent to itself and to others. Erotic and emotional instrumentalism gave way to mutuality and positive reciprocity. Work became a "calling," an actualization of one's

[37] *Ibid.*, p. 220. [38] *Ibid.*, pp. 254–55. [39] *Ibid.*, pp. 255–56.

relation as a free being to nature and to other human beings. The historical self, ethically understood, was presented by William as a "social, civic self," living out its particularity not as envy and mutual manipulation but under the self-imposed rule of the "universal," which recognized the common, essential structure of all selves as freedom.

Magistrate William's self-confident and optimistic claims about the way in which the act of self-choice could therapeutically resolve the contradictions and despair of reflective egoism and produce an integral, continuous, self-transparent historical selfhood were obviously less a resolution than a problem for Kierkegaard himself. In book after book, he continued to examine in painstaking detail how the act of self-choice that created an ethical existence could be transformed from a represented possibility into an historical actuality. The choice of oneself as responsible for one's own particular existence continually suffered shipwreck in the face of the impotence of the will to actualize the possibility of choosing itself "in absolute validity" and the inability of the given structure of social relations and cultural values to sustain the responsible, self-choosing self. Ultimately historical selfhood could be actualized only through a passionate act of faith in the transcendent power that made human freedom possible in the first place and that could sustain the choice of freedom in tension with existing cultural forms.

In *Philosophical Fragments* and *Concluding Unscientific Postscript*, Kierkegaard argued with dogged insistence that the conceptual tools of the philosophical intellectual could never grasp the actuality of "coming into existence" that characterized the nature of history. Results of previous choices might be conceptually formulated as possibilities, but "recollection" of this kind never penetrated into the acts of freedom, the moments when the eternal entered into time to bring something into existence as an historical event. It was true that the past had come into existence and thus had produced evidence that could be known externally and appropriated in conceptual form. But conceptual knowledge could never go beyond the construction of possibility: recollection was not reexperiencing and could not in itself produce "repetition."

The existence of past events was not necessary; they did not emanate from each other through a necessary progression of cause and effect.[40] As acts of freedom they always evaded historical understanding. The only appropriate way for a philosopher or historian to relate to the historical event was to "wonder" at its "coming into existence" and to attain a passionate faith that the event really did occur as an act of freedom and not as a historical necessity.[41] To appropriate inwardly the freedom that defined

[40] *Philosophical Fragments by Johannes Climacus*, eds. and trans. Howard V. Hong and Edna H. Hong (Princeton, N.J.: 1985), p. 74.

[41] *Ibid.*, p. 80.

historical selfhood required a "leap," a volitional break in the chain of external cause and effect. To apprehend the actuality of freedom in history was of passionate interest for all human beings, since it concerned the validity of their own attempts to live the truth of freedom in the acts that shaped their particular lives. Ultimately the resolve through which the self chose itself and forged its particular individuality into a work of freedom was grounded in faith that this possibility was an actuality and in a constantly renewed, passionate commitment that proved this actuality from moment to moment.

For Kierkegaard this was the question posed by religion, not just as a cultural form sustaining existing patterns of meaning, but as a personal relation of the unique existing individual to the absolute source of all such meanings. The truth of Christianity considered from this perspective was centered on the historical act through which transcendent, infinite freedom entered the world of immanent finite existence and transformed it into something new, into the historical task of making freedom actual. Kierkegaard thus imagined the leap into Christian faith as sustaining the paradox of historical selfhood, as grounding the self in its attempt to shape its individual existence as an historical existence. Kierkegaard turned to religion not in order to avoid the tasks of historical selfhood but to make those tasks the inescapable center of what it meant to exist as a particular human being, not to legitimize a particular cultural form of self-constitution but to confront the grounds of the very act of self-constitution. In his attempts to maintain the tension of human existence as both a constituted self-identity and a constituting self-identity, and to resist any and all attempts to grasp self-constituting historical selfhood as just another historically constituted identity, Kierkegaard turned to the religious dimension of self-experience as the final guarantor of the qualitative transformation of human existence that marked the transition from reflective egoism to ethical life.

Like Kierkegaard, Marx envisioned the transition to the actualization of freedom in the specific life activity of individual human beings as a qualitative transformation in the mode of human existence. In the 1844 manuscripts, Marx described the meaning of communist revolution (the abolition of private property through an appropriation of the object of production as a collective human product) as the attainment of a genuinely historical mode of existence. Under communism the "entire movement of history" was internally appropriated as communism's own "*actual* act of genesis – the birth act of its empirical existence." It was thus "the *comprehended* and *known* process of its *becoming*." "Communism is the riddle of history solved," he insisted, "and knows itself to be this solution."[42] The human substance objectified in the existing material forces of production and modes of social

[42] "Economic and Philosophic Manuscripts of 1844," *Collected Works*, vol. 3, pp. 296–97 (MEGA, vol. 1, part 1, p. 389).

intercourse was robbed of its alien form and possessed as the actual historical identity of the producing self:

> It is only when the objective world becomes everywhere for man in society the world of man's essential powers – human reality, and for that reason the reality of his essential powers – that all objects become for him the objectification of himself, become objects which confirm and realize his individuality, become his objects: that is, man himself becomes the object.

For "socialist man" the "entire so-called history of the world" was "nothing but the creation of man through human labor, nothing but the emergence of nature for man; so he has irrefutable proof of his own *birth* through himself, of his *genesis*."[43] The dilemma Marx confronted was how to conceive of an act in history – the communist revolution – as an act that so radically changed the practice and consciousness of historical existence.

In the 1844 manuscripts, the actualization of communism as "the real appropriation of human essence by and for man" emerged somewhat mysteriously through a series of transitions from the initial historical act in which the class of wage labor abolished private property and placed the forces of production under the control of the organized collective strength of individual egos.[44] In *The German Ideology*, Marx was much more specific in his descriptions of the ways in which the actual material practices of individual human beings created the historical conditions that made an act of self-appropriation possible. The essential, or common, humanity that Marx had presupposed in 1844 was presented in 1845–46 as a product of historical practices. Under capitalism the productive life activity of labor was objectively universalized as the global power of capital. Individual human laborers, in turn, as they were robbed of their particular life content (their gender, national, social-functional identities) by market forces were turned into "abstract individuals" who by this very fact "were put into a position to enter into relations with one another *as individuals*."[45] Moreover, the contradictions within the system of production tended toward a crisis in which individuals would have to join together to overthrow the existing relations of production simply in order to safeguard their physical existence as individuals. The universalizing powers of global capitalism made the revolutionary appropriation of the means of production an act of humanity that transformed not only individual histories but also human history in general, an act that changed the conditions of production for all and opened the universal potentialities of self-objectification to every individual. Marx was certain that the abolition of private property under the conditions of a fully developed global capitalism made possible the transformation of human

[43] "Economic and Philosophic Manuscripts," pp. 301, 305 (MEGA, vol. 1, part 2, pp. 393–94).
[44] "Economic and Philosophic Manuscripts," p. 294–96 (MEGA, vol. 1, part 1, pp. 386–89).
[45] "German Ideology," p. 87 (*Werke*, vol. 3, p. 67).

existence as a historical product into human existence as free historical productivity. In the revolutionary act of taking practical possession of "all naturally evolved premises as the creation of hitherto exiting men," the world of objects was stripped of its natural character and "subjugated to the power of the united individuals."[46] The self that was historically produced by forces outside of its control could now become the producer of its own history. Marx admitted, however, that for the production of such self-conscious historical identity "the alteration of men on a mass scale" was "necessary." This alteration could only take place in the "practical movement" of the revolution itself. The act of revolution was thus necessary for two reasons: "not only because the ruling class cannot be overthrown in any other way, but also because the class overthrowing it can only by revolution succeed in ridding itself of all the muck of ages and become fitted to found society anew."[47]

For both Kierkegaard and Marx, therefore, the historicization of the self appeared to involve two distinct, but closely related activities. Becoming historical involved a historical reconstruction of the current forms of self-identification – in this case, the reflective egoism of postrevolutionary bourgeois society – as a specific product of human practices in time. The goal was to experience the self that was simply given as a self that was historically particular and contingent. Implicit in this reconstructive activity was a conception of the self as not only product but also producer. Experiencing one's own individual identity as a historical product implied an act, or series of acts, that brought this existing self into being. The ontological freedom implied in historical selfhood, however, could not be known as a thing in the world. As past events, human actions appeared in their results and consequences as simply that which was something and not something else, as necessarily so. Possibility was cut off or concluded in each moment of actualization. To be an historical self, however, meant precisely to experience the given situation of one's own particularity as an actualized possibility and the ground for a new actualization. For both Marx and Kierkegaard, the crucial moment came when this process became a self-conscious practice, when the contingent production of historical identities became a consciously guided practice of self-identification. This moment, however, was itself an act that broke the power of accumulated past action, an event that ultimately was not a product but a decisive action based on faith in the actualization of one possibility rather than another. For Kierkegaard the contingency of self making was finally stabilized by recourse to the source of human freedom in a power that transcended the particular determinations of self, in the religious dimension generally for all cultures and in the paradoxical claims of Christianity for the distinctively universal historical self-consciousness of

[46] "German Ideology," p. 81 (*Werke*, vol. 3, p. 70).

[47] "German Ideology," pp. 52–53. See also p. 214 (*Werke*, vol. 3, pp. 70, 195).

his own age.[48] Marx adamantly refused to take this leap, but one can see his own view of the revolutionary act as a self-conversion experience moving in similar directions. Both the leap and the revolutionary act were presented as historical actions that emerged from the specifically situated site of a constructed self. The self that acted was a product; in its act it proved itself a producer. It was the relationship between these two dimensions that defined individual human existence as historical.

Thirty-five years ago, Michel Foucault attempted to account for the peculiar historicity that defined the nature of experience in modern, postrevolutionary European culture by displaying it as a discursive product, as the contingent emergence of "man" in time, as an historical artifice that would disappear as human knowledge and practice produced awareness of both its contingency and the possibility of a shape of existence that might transcend its peculiar contradictions and limitations and become qualitatively otherwise. The archaeological reconstruction of the historically constructed self, by creating self-consciousness of the parameters of who we are as products, also opened up the self to its ethical task of free self-creation. In the pattern of his own works, Foucault thus affirmed the historical power of the actuality of human existence in modern times as an experience of historical selfhood.[49] From the early nineteenth century to the present, the reciprocal tensions within a self experienced as both product and producer, however wide the oscillations from one pole to the other, have continued to define what it means to be a historical self. This stereoscopic vision is not necessarily a contradiction that demands resolution from some monocular perspective, but simply the way we live and understand our lives as historical selves. From this perspective, the project of historicizing identity in Prussia during the early 1840s marks an important, clarifying moment in the stories we tell ourselves about ourselves as we engage in our own projects of becoming historical.

[48] It is important to note, however, that Kierkegaard agreed with Marx in his critique of the cultural form of Christendom as an ideological legitimization of the reflective egoism of bourgeois society. The close connection between Marx's critique of the conservative religious ideology of the "Christian state" and his analysis of the atomized egoism of liberal market society has recently been analyzed in Warren Breckman, *Marx, the Young Hegelians, and the Origins of Radical Social Theory: Dethroning the Self* (Cambridge and New York: 1999), pp. 258–97.

[49] I have discussed the tension in Foucault between historically constituted and historically constituting selfhood in some detail in John E. Toews, "Foucault and the Freudian Subject: Archaeology, Genealogy, and the Historicization of Psychoanalysis," in Jan Goldstein, ed. *Foucault and the Writing of History* (Oxford and Cambridge, Mass.: 1994), pp. 116–34.

Index